Impediments to Exercising Jurisdiction over International Crimes

For my parents, Ikram and Jane Naqvi

Impediments to Exercising Jurisdiction over International Crimes

by

Yasmin Q. Naqvi

T·M·C·Asser press

ISBN 978-90-6704-320-5

PRINTED IN THE NETHERLANDS

FOREWORD

Amnesties, Pardons, Statutes of Limitation, Immunities, the principle of *Non Bis In Idem*, and Abuse of Process are well known in most legal systems. Together, they are evaluated afresh in this challenging and timely work, as presenting the most significant impediments today to the exercise of international criminal jurisdiction.

These impediments manifest themselves differently in a variety of international and national courts. The policy issues which arise have been the subject of widely varying appreciations by scholars, judges and governments. There are marked divergences of approach.

Incisively, and at times controversially, the author examines each of these impediments and their justifications. Both national and international decisions, as well as learned commentaries, are reviewed. Attention is often drawn to issues and consequences which may have become familiar and are thereby unnoticed, in national jurisdictional contexts but which take on a significance in an international setting which demands renewed evaluation. The result is both extremely informative and deeply challenging.

This book will be of immediate value in many national legal systems. Its primary focus, however, is in the developing perspective of international criminal jurisdiction. Here it offers an innovative and valuable resource. The work will commend itself to learned scholars, judges, diplomats, students and the many other persons and organisations for whom this subject is of increasing significance.

The depth and scope of research, the clarity of expression, and the quality of analysis to be found in this volume are commendable. Work in this area of law will be enriched, and its further development significantly assisted, by the author's most welcome contribution.

The Hague, 31 August 2009

H.E. the Hon. Kevin Parker AC RFD QC
Judge, UNICTY

ACKNOWLEDGEMENTS

This book is the expanded and updated version of the work I conducted while researching my Ph.D. at the Graduate Institute of International and Development Studies, Geneva. I would therefore like to foremost thank Professor Andrew Clapham for his inspiration, support, and theoretical and practical help in the development of this book. I would also like to convey my gratitude for the helpful comments and suggestions of Professor Andrea Bianchi and Professor Paola Gaeta.

The final drafting and research phase for this book was made possible through the generous funding of the Swiss National Science Foundation, and I therefore extend my gratitude to them. Special thanks also to Professor John Dugard who allowed me to join the Leiden University Law Faculty as a research fellow in 2006-2007.

This book also benefited enormously from discussions with my fellow researchers Théo Boutruche, Biatriz Garcia, Divvya Rajagopalan-Vorburger, Deborah Ruiz-Verduzco and Els Debuf. In addition, I would like to thank Judge Christine Van den Wyngaert for reading an early version of the book, and Judge Mohamed Shahabuddeen for professional encouragement

The research for this book was conducted primarily at the Graduate Institute of International Studies Library, Geneva, the United Nations Library in Geneva, the Library of the International Committee of the Red Cross, Geneva, Leiden University Law Faculty Library, Leiden, and the Peace Palace Library in The Hague. I would like to warmly thank the staff of all these libraries for their extensive and friendly help in finding books, articles and resources.

I am grateful to the T.M.C. Asser Press for their help and support throughout the publication process, and to the anonymous reviewers for providing useful comments and suggestions.

A huge thanks must go to my family for their forbearance, love and support throughout many years of completing this project. In particular, a heartfelt thank you to my husband, Joel Rache, whose unconditional love, support and remarkable resilience to stress I will always treasure.

The Hague, September 2009 Yasmin Q. Naqvi

The views expressed herein are those of the author alone and do not necessarily reflect the views of the International Tribunal or the United Nations in general.

TABLE OF CONTENTS

Foreword by Kevin PARKER V

Acknowledgements VII

Abbreviations XIII

Part One
Exercising Jurisdiction over International Crimes

Chapter 1
INTRODUCTION 3

1.1 Impediments to exercising jurisdiction over international crimes 9
1.2 Impediments 11
1.3 Jurisdiction 13
1.4 International crimes 21
1.4.1 War crimes 32
1.4.1.1 Grave breaches 32
1.4.1.2 Serious violations of the laws and customs of war 34
1.4.2 Crimes against humanity 37
1.4.3 Genocide 49
1.4.4 Torture 59

Part Two
Impediments

Chapter 2
AMNESTIES 75

2.1 Definition and historical context 75
2.2 Amnesties and international and hybrid criminal courts and tribunals 85
2.3 Contextual and policy considerations 93
2.3.1 The need to secure the peace and maintain the peace 95
2.3.2 The need for a public accounting of the truth 98
2.3.3 The need to strengthen the rule of law and uphold the principle of legality 102
2.3.4 The question of deterrence 103
2.3.5 The need for reconciliation 106
2.4 Legal rationales with regard to the exercise of jurisdiction in the face of amnesties 110

2.4.1 The scope of the obligation to prosecute international crimes 110
2.4.2 Whether victims' fundamental rights vitiate the validity of amnesty laws 124
2.4.3 Whether States are constrained not to amnesty international crimes due to the peremptory character of international crimes 138
2.5 Preliminary conclusions 144

Chapter 3
PARDONS 149

3.1 Definition and historical background 150
3.2 Pardons and international and hybrid criminal courts and tribunals 154
3.3 Contextual and policy considerations 155
3.4 Legal rationales with regard to the use of pardons covering international crimes 161
3.4.1 The scope of the obligation to punish those convicted of international crimes 163
3.4.2 The possibility of pardons or commutation of sentence by international criminal courts 171
3.4.3 Clemency by way of the guilty plea 175
3.4.4 The possible *ne bis in idem* effect of pardon 177
3.5 Preliminary conclusions 181

Chapter 4
STATUTES OF LIMITATION 183

4.1 Definition and historical background 184
4.2 Statutes of limitation and international and hybrid criminal courts and tribunals 188
4.3 Contextual and policy considerations 190
4.4 Legal rationales with regard to statutes of limitation covering international crimes 192
4.4.1 International customary law precludes the use of statutes of limitation over international crimes 192
4.4.2 Obligations to prosecute international crimes or to ensure fundamental human rights are incompatible with statutes of limitation 209
4.4.3 The purposes and principles underlying the use of statutes of limitation do not account for the specificities of cases dealing with international crimes 211
4.4.4 Time may be tolled in many cases where international crimes have been committed 214
4.5 Preliminary conclusions 217

Chapter 5
IMMUNITIES 221

5.1 Definition and historical background 222
5.1.1 Functional immunity 223

5.1.2 Act of State doctrine 226
5.1.3 Personal immunity 228
5.1.3.1 Diplomatic immunity 229
5.1.3.2 Head of State Immunity 230
5.1.3.3 Head of government and foreign minister immunity 233
5.1.4 State immunity 236
5.1.5 National immunity 240
5.2 Immunities and international and hybrid criminal courts and tribunals 243
5.3 Contextual and policy considerations 246
5.3.1 Functional immunity 246
5.3.2 Act of State doctrine 248
5.3.3 Personal immunity 249
5.3.3.1 Diplomatic immunity 249
5.3.3.2 Head of State immunity 249
5.3.3.3 Head of Government and Foreign Minister immunity 250
5.3.4 State immunity 251
5.3.5 National immunity 253
5.4 Legal rationales with regard to functional and personal immunities for international crimes 253
5.4.1 Treaty obligations to prosecute or extradite persons accused of international crimes are incompatible with immunities 254
5.4.2 States have impliedly waived immunity of their officials by signing treaties criminalising certain international offences 258
5.4.3 Customary international law lifts functional (and personal) immunity in case of international crimes 262
5.4.4 The *jus cogens* nature of international crimes overrides immunity 268
5.4.5 International crimes fall outside of the notion of 'acts performed in a sovereign capacity' 277
5.4.6 The fundamental rights of victims are incompatible with fundamental human rights 281
5.5 Preliminary conclusions 284

Chapter 6
THE PRINCIPLE OF *NE BIS IN IDEM* 287

6.1 Definition and historical background 288
6.1.1 Historical background 288
6.1.2 *Ne bis in idem* and international and hybrid criminal courts and tribunals 290
6.1.3 Definition 292
6.1.3.1 What constitutes an '*idem*' 295
6.1.3.2 Types of procedures to which *ne bis in idem* may attach 300
6.2 Contextual and policy considerations 306
6.3 Legal rationales with regard to the principle of *ne bis in idem* and international crimes 310
6.3.1 Legal arguments countering a transnational *ne bis in idem* principle 310
6.3.2 Fundamental defects in the trial/Sham trial 315

6.3.3 Retrial in the case of newly discovered evidence or facts 318
6.3.4 The State claim to exercise jurisdiction over offences committed on its territory 322
6.3.5 Exception for certain offences 323
6.3.6 Additional serious offences 323
6.4 Preliminary conclusions 325

Chapter 7
ABUSE OF PROCESS 329

7.1 Definition and historical background 330
7.2 Contextual and policy considerations 332
7.2.1 The need to ensure a fair trial 332
7.2.2 The need to preserve the integrity of the judicial system 333
7.3 Legal rationales with regard to the doctrine of abuse of process and international crimes 336
7.3.1 Abduction/Disguised extradition 336
7.3.1.1 National level 336
7.3.1.2 International level 341
7.3.2 Procedural rights 347
7.3.2.1 National level 348
7.3.2.2 International level 348
7.3.3 Delay 352
7.3.3.1 National level 352
7.3.3.2 International level 353
7.3.4 Withholding of exculpatory evidence 355
7.3.5 Double jeopardy 357
7.3.6 Breach of promises of non-prosecution (amnesty) 357
7.3.6.1 National level 357
7.3.6.2 International level 358
7.3.7 Misuse of the criminal process 361
7.4 Preliminary conclusions 362

Part Three
General Conclusion

Chapter 8
GENERAL CONCLUSION 367

Bibliography 381

Table of Cases 395

Index 413

ABBREVIATIONS

A.D.	Anno Domini
A.L.J.R.	Australian Law Journal Reports
AC	Appeal Cases (England and Wales)
ACHPR	African Charter on Human and Peoples' Rights
ACHR	American Convention on Human Rights
AFJS	Area of Freedom, Security and Justice
AIDI	Annuaire de L'Institut de Droit International
AILC	American International Law Cases
AJIL	American Journal of International Law
All ER	All England Law Reports
Ann Dig	Annual Digest
AP I	First Additional Protocol to the 1949 Geneva Conventions of 1977
AP II	Second Additional Protocol to the 1949 Geneva Conventions of 1977
App. Ch.	Appeals Chamber
Art.	Article
ASAP	Action in Solidarity in the Pacific
ATCA	Alien Tort Claims Act (United States of America)
Austl.	Australia
AZAPO	Azanian Peoples' Organisation
B. & C.	Barnewell & Cresswells Reports
B.C.	Before Christ
B.O.E.	Boletin Oficial del Estado
BCLR	Butterworths Constitutional Law Reports
BGH	Bundesgerichtshof (German Supreme Court)
BILC	British International Law Cases
Bull. crim.	Bulletin criminal (Judgments of the French Supreme Court)
BVerfGE	Entscheidungen des Bundesverfassungsgerichts (Judgments of the German Federal Constitutional Court)
BYIL	British Year Book of International Law
CA	Court of Appeal (England and Wales)
CAT	Convention against Torture and Other Cruel, Inhuman or Degrading Treatment or Punishment
CB	Common Bench Reports
CCAIL	Code of Crimes against International Law (Germany)
CD	Collection of Decisions
Chinese JIL	Chinese Journal of International Law
CHR	Commission on Human Rights (United Nations)
Cir.	Circuit
CLP	Current Legal Problems
CLR	Commonwealth Law Reports
Cmd.	Command Paper
CMR	Court-Martial Reports (United States)

CODICES	Case-law collection of constitutional courts (at: http://codices.coe.int)
Columbia JTL	Columbia Journal of Transnational Law
Columbia LR	Columbia Law Review
Cornell ILJ	Cornell International Law Journal
CP	Code pénal
CPM	Code pénal militaire
Cr App R	Criminal Appeal Reports
CRA	Community Reconciliation Process
CRC	Convention on the Rights of the Child of 1989
CrimLR	Criminal Law Review
CSJN	Corte Suprema de Justicia (Argentina)
CUP	Cambridge University Press
D&R	Decisions and Reports
D.D.C.	District Court for the District of Columbia (US)
DEA	U.S. Drug Enforcement Agency
Dep't St. Bull	US-Federal, Department of State Bulletin
Dist. Ct.	District Court
Doc.	Document
DPP	Director of Public Prosecutions
DR	Deutsches Recht
Draft Code 1996	Draft Code of Crimes Against the Peace and Security of Mankind 1996 (ILC)
Duke J of Comp. & Int. L	Duke Journal of Comparative & International Law
E.A.S.	Executive Agreement Series
E.R.	English Reports
EC	European Community
ECCC	Extraordinary Chambers in Courts of Cambodia
ECHR	European Convention on Human Rights
ECJ	European Court of Justice
ECommHR	European Commission of Human Rights
ECOSOC	UN Economic and Social Council
ECR	European Court Reports
ECtHR	European Court of Human Rights
EDNY	Eastern District of New York
EHRR	European Human Rights Report
EJIL	European Journal of International Law
ETS	European Treaty Series
EWCA Civ	Court of Appeal, Civil Division (England & Wales)
EWCA Crim.	Court of Appeal, Criminal Division (England & Wales)
EWHC	High Court, Administrative Court (England & Wales)
F.2d	Federal Reporter, Second Series (United States)
FCA	Federal Court of Australia
Fed. Reg.	Federal Register
FIDH	Fédération Internationale des Ligues des Droits de l'Homme
FRY	Federal Republic of Yugoslavia (Serbia and Montenegro)
FSIA	Foreign State Immunity Act
GA	General Assembly (United Nations)
GAOR	General Assembly Official Records

Gaz.Pal.	Gazette du Palais
GC I	Geneva Convention (I) for the Amelioration of the Condition of the Wounded and Sick in Armed Forces in the Field of 1949
GC II	Geneva Convention (II) for the Amelioration of the Condition of the Wounded, Sick and Shipwrecked Members of Armed Forces at Sea of 1949
GC III	Geneva Convention (III) Relative to the Treatment of Prisoner of War of 1949
GC IV	Geneva Convention (IV) Relative to the Protection of Civilian Persons in Time of War of 1949
GDR	German Democratic Republic
Hague Convention IV	The 1907 Hague Convention IV Respecting the Laws and Customs of War on Land, 18 October 1907
Hague Regulations (1907)	Regulations Respecting the Laws and Customs of War on Land, 18 October 1907, annexed to the 1907 Hague Convention IV Respecting the Laws and Customs of War on Land
HCA	High Court of Australia
HILJ	Harvard International Law Journal
HL	House of Lords
HLR	Harvard Law Review
HR	Hoge Raad (Dutch Supreme Court)
HRC	Human Rights Committee
HRQ	Human Rights Quarterly
HuV	Humanitäres Völkerrecht
IAComHR	Inter-American Commission of Human Rights
IACtHR	Inter-American Court of Human Rights
ICC	International Criminal Court
ICC RPE	Rules of Procedure and Evidence of the International Criminal Court
ICCPR	International Covenant on Civil and Political Rights
ICESCR	International Covenant on Economic, Social and Cultural Rights
ICJ	International Court of Justice
ICL	International criminal law
ICLQ	International and Comparative Law Quarterly
ICRC	International Committee of the Red Cross
ICT	International Criminal Tribunal
ICTR RPE	Rules of Procedure and Evidence of the International Criminal Tribunal for Rwanda
ICTR	International Criminal Tribunal for Rwanda
ICTY RPE	Rules of Procedure and Evidence of the International Criminal Tribunal for the former Yugoslavia
ICTY	International Criminal Tribunal for the former Yugoslavia
IDI	Institut de Droit International
IHL	International Humanitarian Law
ILA	International Law Association
ILC	International Law Commission
ILM	International Legal Materials
ILPr	International Litigation Procedure
ILR	International Law Reports
ILSA J. Int'l and Comp. L	ILSA Journal of International and Comparative Law
IMT	International Military Tribunal (Nuremberg Tribunal)

IMTFE	International Military Tribunal for the Far East, Tokyo
IRRC	International Review of the Red Cross
IYHR	Israeli Yearbook on Human Rights
J.Bl.	Juristische Blätter
JCP	Jurisclasseur périodique
JICJ	Journal of International Criminal Justice
LCP	Law and Contemporary Problems
LJIL	Leiden Journal of International Law
LNTS	League of Nations Treaty Series
LOPJ	Ley Orgánica del Poder Judicial
LRC	Law Reports of the Commonwealth
LRTWC	Law Reports of Trials of War Criminals, 15 Volumes (London: UN War Crimes Commission, 1949)
LSI	Laws of the State of Israel
Max Planck UNYB	Max Planck Yearbook of United Nations Law
MCCOC	Model Criminal Code Officers Committee
MLR	Military Law Review
MPI	Max Planck Institute
mtg.	Meeting
N.Y.S.	New York State
N.Y.U. L. Rev.	New York University Law Review
NATO	North Atlantic Treaty Organization
NederJ	Nederlandse Jurisprudentie
NELR	New England Law Review
NGO	Non-governmental organisation
NILR	Netherlands International Law Review
No.	Number
NSW	New South Wales
NSWLR	New South Wales Law Reports
NSWR	New South Wales Reports
NYIL	Netherlands Yearbook of International Law
NZLR	New Zealand Law Reports
O.A.S.	Organization of American States
Op. Att'y Gen.	Opinions of the Attorney General
OTP	Office of the Prosecutor
OUP	Oxford University Press
p.	page
P.2d	Pacific Reporter, Second Series
para.	paragraph
PC	Privy Council (United Kingdom)
PCIJ	Permanent Court of International Justice
PKK	Kurdistan's Workers' Party
pmbl.	Preamble
POW	Prisoner of War
PrepCom	Preparatory Committee on the Establishment of an International Criminal Court

PUF	Presses Universitaires de France
QB/QBD	Law Reports Queen's Bench Division (United Kingdom)
RdC	Recueil des Cours de l'Académie de Droit International de La Haye
RDI	Rivista di Diretto Internazionale
RDPC	Revue de Droit Pénal et de Criminologie
Res.	Resolution
Rev. Jur. U.I.P.R.	Revista Juridica de la Universidad Interamericana de Puerto Rico
RGDIP	Revue Générale de Droit Internationale Public
RGMDG	Revue de Droit Militaire et de Droit de la Guerre
RIAA	Reports of International Arbitration Awards
RIDC	Revue Internationale de Droit Comparé
RIDP	Revue Internationale de Droit Pénal
RPE	Rules of Procedure and Evidence
S.D.	Southern District
S.L.T.	Scots Law Times
SA	South African Law Reports
SACJ	South African Journal of Criminal Justice
SACR	South African Criminal Law Reports
SASR	South Australian State Reports
SC	Security Council (United Nations)
SCC	Supreme Court Cases
SCR	Supreme Court Reporter
SCSL	Special Court for Sierra Leone
SDNY	Southern District of New York
Sess.	Session
SFOR	Stabilisation Force for Bosnia and Herzegovina
SIA	State Immunity Act (UK)
StGB	Strafgesetzbuch (German Penal Code)
Sup. Ct.	Supreme Court
Suppl.	Supplement
TIAS	Treaties and other International Acts Series
TILJ	Texas International Law Journal
TLR	Times Law Reports
TRC	Truth and Reconciliation Commission
TWC	Trials of War Criminals before the Nürnberg Military Tribunals under Control Council Law No. 10, 15 Volumes (Washington, DC: US Govt Printing Office, 1950)
U.S.C.	United States Code
U.S.T.	United States Treaties
UCMJ	Uniform Code of Military Justice (United States of America)
UK	United Kingdom
UKHL	House of Lords (United Kingdom)
UN	United Nations
UN Doc.	United Nations Document
UN ESCOR	UN Economic and Social Council Official Records
UN Hum. Rts. Comm	UN Human Rights Commission
UN SCOR	UN Security Council Official Records

UNITA	União Nacional para a Independência Total de Angola
UNMIK	United Nations Interim Administration in Kosovo
UNTAET	United Nations Transitional Administration in East Timor
UNTS	United Nations Treaty Series
UNWCC	United Nations War Crimes Commission
US Restatement Third	The American Law Institute, Restatement of the Law Third, *Restatement of the Law –The Foreign Relations Law of the United States*, Vol. I (St. Paul, Minn.: American Law Institute Publishers, 1987)
US	United States Supreme Court Reports
USCMA	United States Court of Military Appeals
v.	versus
VCLT	Vienna Convention on the Law of Treaties
VJIL	Virginia Journal of International Law
Vol.	Volume
WIM	Wet Internationale Misdrijven (Dutch International Crimes Act)
WLR	Weekly Law Reports (United Kingdom)
WW I	First World War
WW II	Second World War
Y. B. ECHR	Yearbook of the European Convention on Human Rights
YIHL	Yearbook of International Humanitarian Law
YIL	Yearbook of International Law
YILC	Yearbook of the International Law Commission
ZaöRV	Zeitschrift für Ausländisches Öffentliches Recht und Völkerrecht

Part One
Exercising Jurisdiction over International Crimes

Chapter 1
INTRODUCTION

The rapid expansion of the international criminal justice system over the last sixty years and particularly in the last two decades would seem to have had the general effect of casting doubt on the legality of impediments which serve to deny adjudicatory jurisdiction to courts when applied to cases dealing with international crimes. Courts, scholars and international organisations have in recent years and with increasing resoluteness evinced a general presumption that international crimes, due to their particular nature, should be distinguished from 'ordinary crimes' and have different legal consequences, including with regard to jurisdictional obstacles.[1] The desired outcome of such a presumption would appear to be to ensure that prosecution of those accused of serious crimes is unhindered, thereby contributing to ending the 'culture of impunity'[2] which has unquestionably been the rule rather than the exception in international practice with regard to international crimes perpetrated on a massive scale.

The concern of this book lies in discerning the legal basis for such claims, as well as the underlying driving forces for this apparent legal evolution. In other words, what factors have motivated courts, commentators and international organisations such as the United Nations, to reinterpret the legal validity of barriers such as amnesties, statutes of limitation, and immunity for high-ranking officials when applied to cases involving international crimes, and what tools of legal or other argumentation have been utilised in so doing? The central axis of this book is the examination of the claim that different legal consequences result from the exercise of jurisdiction over an international crime. While this claim may well be correct, it is worth examining the legal logic used to reach this conclusion. The mere assumption that international crimes require jurisdictional leeway or the sim-

[1] See, e.g., Ward N. Ferdinandusse, *Direct Application of International Criminal Law in National Courts* (The Hague: T.M.C. Asser Press, 2006), at 202: 'Clearly, current international law contains a strong presumption against amnesties for core crimes, but probably no more than that.'

[2] 'Impunity' has been defined as 'the impossibility, *de jure* or *de facto*, of bringing the perpetrators of human rights violations to account – whether in criminal, civil, administrative or disciplinary proceedings – since they are not subject to any inquiry that might lead to them being arrested, tried and if found guilty, convicted.' "Question of the Impunity of Perpetrators of Violations of Human Rights (civil and political rights)", Final Report prepared by Mr. Joinet pursuant to Sub-Commission Res. 1996/119, UN Doc. E/CN.4/Sub.2/1997/20, 26 June 1997 (hereafter, Joinet Report). The term 'culture of impunity' has uncertain origins, but it is commonly used to describe the situation where a pattern of non-prosecution has become the norm, so that perpetrators do not expect any legal consequences for illegal actions, thus depriving existing criminal sanctions of any effect.

plistic argument that their abhorrent nature dismisses any jurisdictional obstacles only serves to weaken the edifice of international criminal law.

Most commentators writing about the legality of impediments to the exercise of jurisdiction over international crimes utilise the traditional positivist 'problem-solving' approach that focuses its attention on evaluating State practice and *opinio juris*.[3] In broad terms, the 'problem' identified would appear to be that international legal rules requiring the prosecution of persons accused of international crimes stand in tension with existing legal constraints on the ability of courts to exercise adjudicatory jurisdiction. A commonly proposed 'solution' has been to argue that there is a crystallising customary rule requiring that all international crimes be prosecuted, hence invalidating all barriers to legal process.[4] Notably, however, authors rarely conclude that such a rule is already in existence for all serious international crimes.[5] A second way of overcoming the problem has been to argue that exceptions exist, or are in the process of formation, for the treatment of international crimes in terms of each of these barriers to prosecution. Such arguments focus on the particular nature of international crimes as constituting 'attacks on universal values' which entails that no single State can assume the right to decide to 'cancel such crimes, or to set aside their legal consequences.'[6]

Some commentators, concerned with the striking gap between the much heralded international criminal legal regime and its very disappointing, selective and *ad hoc* implementation, have attempted to avoid international law's legitimacy crisis in this regard by identifying and correcting the misalignment by emphasising 'legitimate' limiting techniques to prosecution. These take account of the competing goals as well as practical constraints of transitional societies, but the contours of these views vary significantly from author to author, depending on differences in emphases, approach or even values.[7] While a small number of commentators explicitly set out the methodological premise upon which they make their legal

---

3 For an overview of the positivist approach as applied to the field of international criminal law, see Bruno Simma and Andreas L. Paulus, "The Responsibility of Individuals for Human Rights Abuses in Internal Conflicts: A Positivist View", 93 *AJIL* 302 (1999).

4 See M. Cherif Bassiouni, "The Legacy of Legalism and the Need to combat Impunity for International Crimes", *Menschengerechtes Strafrecht: Festschrift für Albin Eser zum 70. Geburtstag* (München: Beck, 2005), at 705-715.

5 See, e.g., Robert Cryer, *Prosecuting International Crimes: Selectivity and the International Criminal Law Regime* (Cambridge: CUP, 2005), at 108-109.

6 Antonio Cassese, *International Criminal Law* (Oxford: OUP, 2003), at 315 (discussing the rationales behind international practice barring amnesties for international crimes).

7 Compare, e.g., the defined contours of 'legitimate' amnesties which might be accorded international recognition as identified in William W. Burke-White, "Reframing Impunity: Applying Liberal International Law Theory to an Analysis of Amnesty Legislation", 42 *HILJ* 2 (2001), 468 (emphasising the legitimising effect of democratically elected governments enacting amnesties); Michael P. Scharf, "The Amnesty Exception to the Jurisdiction of the International Criminal Court", 32 *Cornell ILJ* 507 (1999) (noting the factors which the ICC should consider in deciding whether to recognise an amnesty: whether an offence attaches to a duty to prosecute, whether the armed conflict would have ended without the recourse to amnesty, and whether the State has instituted a truth mechanism); and John Dugard, "Dealing with Crimes of a Past Regime: Is Amnesty Still an Option?", 12(4) *LJIL* 1001 (1999) (suggesting that amnesties which are accorded by a truth and reconciliation commission such

analysis,[8] most seem to proceed from the standpoint of 'objective' analysis, while consciously or unconsciously imbruing their analysis with value judgments about the role of criminal justice in war torn societies. Attempts to prove coherence between the moral/legalistic principles of international criminal law and contradictory and inconsistent practice prove easy to debunk for those scholars employing a more sceptical line of analysis because of the value or moral-laden character of the debate and the striking dissonance between international legal principles and the reality of practice.[9]

Where the law is indeterminate or where there are conflicting laws and principles at play, as is arguably the case in the field of study forming the basis of this book, a positivist analysis about 'what the law is' provides an insufficient basis upon which decision-makers must make choices. The legal enquiries at the heart of this book are practical questions requiring practical responses from courts and which can be applied in the operational field. For these reasons, an alternative approach to the legal analysis of impediments to the exercise of adjudicatory jurisdiction is suggested in this book which one may term an 'interests-analysis approach.' Ultimately, this approach identifies various 'interests' which courts need to balance when deciding whether or not to exercise jurisdiction when dealing with a case involving serious international crimes and may suggest coherent and reasonable ways to decide whether to continue with the case. The analysis of the impediments under study thus looks both to their historical development and contextual and policy reasons for them, as well as the legal rationales which impact upon a court's decision to exercise jurisdiction.

The theoretical underpinnings of an interests-analysis approach are broadly related to the policy-oriented legal methodology that is sometimes described as the 'Yale school' or the 'New Haven school,' in reference to the views first propounded by Professors Myres S. McDougal and Harold D. Lasswell at the Yale Law School from the early 1950s.[10] McDougal and Lasswell situated their approach generally in the American Realist school which rejects formalist approaches and tends to be sceptical of norms as neutral rules.[11] Instead, the 'New Haven' school is explicitly value-based; the law is viewed as 'a process of authoritative and controlling decision'[12] that aims at the promotion of a free, democratic international society founded upon the fundamental value of human dignity. In their methodology, McDou-

as that in South Africa after investigation 'may contribute to the achievement of peace and justice in a society in transition more effectively than mandatory prosecution').

8 Burke-White, "Reframing Impunity", at 468.

9 See, e.g., Martti Koskenniemi, "Between impunity and show trials", 6 *Max Planck UNYB* 34 (2002); Antoine Garapon, "Three Challenges for International Criminal Justice", 2 *JICJ* 724 (2004).

10 Harold D. Lasswell and Myres S. McDougal, *Jurisprudence for a Free Society: Studies in Law, Science and Policy* (New Haven, Conn.: New Haven Press/Martinus Nijhoff Publishers, 1992).

11 This approach also repudiates naturalism because of its supraempirical claims of validation. *Ibid.*, at 212-7, 220-23, 231-35, 236-42.

12 Siegfried Wiessner and Andrew R. Willard, "Policy-Oriented Jurisprudence and Human Rights Abuses in Internal Armed Conflict: Toward a World Public Order of Human Dignity", 93 *AJIL* 320 (1999).

gal and Lasswell identified eight constituent values that are universally desired by humans – power, wealth, affection, respect, rectitude, skills, enlightenment, and well-being, which help form a 'cognitive map' of any social problem. The central concept is the aspiration to a 'public order of human dignity.' A 'minimum' world public order entails the minimisation of unauthorised violence and coercion,[13] while an 'optimum' world public order refers to an order that maximises all human beings' access to all of the values and the processes that shape such values.[14] The approach suggests 'a rigorous approach to decision, as well as one embedded in social context.'[15]

This methodology is particularly pertinent to the resolution of legal problems involving choices between competing rules or goals. Rosalyn Higgins, a proponent of this approach, has noted that '"the correct legal view" or "rules" can never avoid the element of choice (though it can seek to disguise it), nor can it provide guidance to the preferable decision. In making this choice one must inevitably have consideration for the humanitarian, moral, and social purposes of the law.'[16] Oscar Schachter similarly rejected the idea of simply applying neutral rules as 'a somewhat crude one' and instead held the view that 'each of the opposing general principles will have elements of validity, and that joined together they will provide a more rational guide than either principle standing by itself.'[17] Schachter was particularly mindful of the need for contextual analysis of any given legal problem, and stated that what is important 'is that the context of a legal rule can only be determined in terms of the whole set of consequences that may flow from its application.'[18]

Thus an interests-analysis approach provides an intellectual tool that can be used analytically and prescriptively to deal with issues of conflicting rules that impact upon the decision of whether or not to exercise jurisdiction. The approach encourages decision-makers to deal with value-dependent policy options openly and systematically unlike other approaches which tend to insinuate goals, whether

---

[13] Myres S. McDougal and Siegfried Wiessner, "Law and Minimum World Public Order, Introduction to the Reissue", in Myres S. McDougal and Florentino P. Feliciano, *The International Law of War: Transnational Coercion and World Public Order* (New Haven: New Haven Press, 1994), xix at xxvii.

[14] Myres S. McDougal, Harold D. Lasswell, and Lung-Chu Chen, *Human Rights and World Public Order* (New Haven: New Haven Press, 1980).

[15] Richard Falk, "Casting the Spell: The New Haven School of International Law", 104 *Yale Law Journal* 1991 (1995), at 1992.

[16] Rosalyn Higgins, *Problems and Process: International Law and How We Use It* (Oxford: Oxford Clarendon Press, 1994), at 5.

[17] Oscar Schachter, "Private Foreign Investment and International Organization", 45 *Cornell Law Quarterly* 426 (1959-60).

[18] Oscar Schachter, "Problems of Law and Justice", *Annual Review of United Nations Affairs* 190 (1951). He further noted that 'Law in the United Nations, as elsewhere, has to be viewed more as an institution than as a particular set of rules; it involves not only words and their meanings but also practices, techniques and procedures. It includes as well those broad concepts and standards (in Roscoe Pound's words, the "received ideals" of the legal system) that cannot be reduced simply to rules but that nevertheless shape both conduct and doctrine.' *Ibid.*

consciously or unconsciously into the analysis.[19] Courts should therefore consider all the policy implications of a particular impediment within a specific context in a transparent and engaged analysis with a view to reaching a decision on jurisdiction most likely to bring about a world order based on human dignity.[20] One may note that international crimes perpetrated on a large scale are most often associated with armed conflicts or mass violence resulting from political transition. As a result, the reality remains that 'in post-conflict countries, the vast majority of perpetrators of serious violations of human rights and international humanitarian law will never be tried, whether internationally or domestically.'[21] It is this fact, together with evidence that responses other than, or in addition to, prosecutions may be (more) beneficial to reconciling divided communities that has led to the 'transitional justice' framework.[22] In some ways, this reflects the policy-oriented recognition that the application of law enforcement responses to international crimes needs to take into account a range of goals of the local and international community, including 'restoring minimum order where it has been breached, reducing the expectation of violence, re-establishing practices of a productive civil society, eliminating or mitigating the factors that could, in varying combination, reignite particular conflicts, and deterring the occurrence of comparable offending behaviour in the society at issue and in others that are watching.'[23] An interests-analysis approach encourages

---

19 Higgins, *Problems and Process*, at 5: 'Dealing with them systematically means that all factors are properly considered and weighed, instead of the decision-maker unconsciously narrowing or selecting what he will take into account in order to reach a decision that he has instinctively predetermined is desirable.'

20 In this sense, the approach is similar to a critical knowledge approach, which focuses on deconstructing the problem-solving methods of courts and analysts to expose the links between legal solution and material reality. For a detailed explanation and justification of the use of a critical knowledge approach to legal problems, see Susan Marks, *The Riddle of All Constitutions: International Law, Democracy and the Critique of Ideology* (Oxford: OUP, 2000), at 121-146. See also Deborah Z. Cass, "Navigating the Newstream: Recent Critical Scholarship in International Law", 65 *Nordic Journal of International Law* 341 (1996). For a discussion of how these contrast with traditional 'positivist' approaches, see "Symposium on Method in International Law", 93(2) *AJIL* 291 (1999).

21 "The rule of law and transitional justice in conflict and post-conflict societies", Report of the Secretary-General, UN Doc. S/2004/16, 3 August 2004, para. 46 (hereafter, Rule of law report).

22 The classical example is the Truth and Reconciliation Commission of South Africa, which allowed perpetrators and victims alike to publicly discuss atrocities committed during the Apartheid regime. An Amnesty Commission was authorised to issue a full amnesty to any person who fully disclosed their participation in politically-motivated crimes. See 'Foreword by Chairperson', in Susan de Villiers (ed.), *Truth and Reconciliation Commission of South Africa, Report*, Vol. 1 (1998), at 8-9: 'Certainly, amnesty cannot be viewed as justice if we think of justice only as retributive and punitive in nature. We believe, however, that there is another kind of justice – a restorative justice which is concerned not so much with punishment as with correcting imbalances, restoring broken relationships – with healing, harmony and reconciliation. Such justice focuses on the experience of victims; hence the importance of reparation.'

23 Wiessner and Willard, "Policy-Oriented Jurisprudence and Human Rights Abuses", at 317. See Myres S. McDougal and Florentino P. Feliciano, *The International Law of War: Transnational Coercion and World Public Order* (New Haven: New Haven Press, 1994), at 261-383; Richard Arens and Harold D. Lasswell, *In Defence of Public Order: The Emerging Field of Sanction Law* (1961); W. Michael Reisman, "Institutions and Practices for Restoring and Maintaining Public Order", 6 *Duke Journal of Comparative and International Law* 175 (1995).

courts, when making choices as to whether to exercise jurisdiction, to be expressly mindful of such competing goals in order to reach decisions most likely to satisfy the core values underlying the international legal order.

As for any legal methodology, there have been numerous criticisms of policy-oriented jurisprudence which need be accounted for in the context of this book. Most prevalent among these, the approach has been criticised for 'conflating law, political science and politics' or for 'conflating law with apology for state power'[24] which means that it 'fails to provide the very guidance that real-life decision makers expect from their lawyers.'[25] However, this rather oversimplifies a policy-oriented approach, which does not equate law with processes of power, but rather with the authoritative process of decision-making. Those applying a policy-oriented approach have also been accused of not clearly distinguishing between norms and values, though critics concede that such a tool 'may have considerable value for both the analysis of actual decision-making and the formulation of policy proposals.'[26] This criticism is also inaccurate: while policy considerations might affect the interpretation or scope of a norm, they do not form part of the same typology as rules themselves, though their impact upon norm-creation and enforcement is openly analysed.[27] The view that the introduction of policy considerations leads to arbitrary or partisan legal dealings was firmly countered by Schachter, who pointed out that communal values differ markedly from subjective preferences, and can be validated objectively.[28] Another criticism is that such an approach neglects the need for certainty of the law.[29] On the face of it, a context-specific decision-making process that takes into account numerous goals and values does pose the risk of coming up with myriad possible answers to the same legal question. Along similar lines, Richard Falk, generally an adherent of the New Haven approach, has voiced strong scepticism about the ability of the approach to help policy makers use the law as an instrument to pursue normative goals because the orientation will inevitably lead to 'policy divergences' rather than any common vision.[30]

---

[24] Falk, "Casting the Spell", at 2006, citing Martti Koskenniemi, *From Apology to Utopia* (Cambridge: Cambridge University Press, 1989), at 173-78.

[25] Simma and Paulus, "The Responsibility of Individuals for Human Rights Abuses in Internal Conflicts: A Positivist View", at 305.

[26] *Ibid.*

[27] Law, in the policy-oriented approach, derives only from decisions with policy, or prescriptive, content that are taken from community-wide perspectives of authority and backed up by control intent. Wiessner and Willard, "Policy-Oriented Jurisprudence and Human Rights Abuses", at 319.

[28] Oscar Schachter, "The Place of Policy in International Law", 2 *Georgia Journal of International and Comparative Law* 5 (1972).

[29] Sandra Voos, *Die Schule von New Haven: Darstellung und Kritik einer amerikanischen Völkerrechtslehre* (Berlin: Duncker & Humblot, 2000), at 322, transl. by Siegfried Wiessner, "Book review", 96 *AJIL* 498 (2002).

[30] Falk, "Casting the Spell", at 2000. Falk cites as an example of such divergences the contrasting views of two New Haven adherents *vis-à-vis* the legality of nuclear weapons: W. Michael Reisman, "Deterrence and International Law", 4 *New York Law School Journal of International and Comparative Law* 339 (1983) (arguing that the expectations of politically relevant actors and control intention indicate the effective legality of nuclear weapons) with Burns H. Weston, "Nuclear Weapons and International Law: Prolegomenon to General Illegality", 4 *New York Law School Journal of Interna-*

However, Falk's criticism – shared to some degree by Schachter, who thought it doubtful that political leaders would take into account fundamental values separate from their political manifestations[31] – relates mainly to policy-makers, not to judicial decision-making. In the context of the latter, the danger of creating an unpredictable legal enforcement system is reduced with an approach that encourages courts to openly discuss how they value various policy considerations. In fact, one could well argue that it would be far easier to gage how courts might react to a particular issue if value-based elements were transparently presented and weighed against each other in judgments rather than trying to guess the outcome from an opaque analysis of neutral rules. Moreover, the desire for certainty in the law should never be an excuse for rigidity in the face of changing contexts, values and community expectations otherwise there would never be any legal evolution jurisprudentially. In sum, the criticisms levelled at policy-oriented approaches do not hold when applied to the decision-making process under issue in this book – that is, judicial deliberation upon the issue of jurisdiction over international crimes. Instead, the approach provides courts with a set of intellectual tools that are rooted in realism and logic, while at the same time founded upon the ultimate value of upholding human dignity which lies at the heart of the notion of international criminal justice.[32]

1.1 Impediments to exercising jurisdiction over international crimes

There are a number of barriers to the institution and execution of criminal proceedings for international crimes.[33] This book is concerned with barriers of a *legal* nature which operate to stay the exercise of adjudicatory jurisdiction. While there are many legal obstacles to exercising jurisdiction over international crimes, the study focuses on six principal impediments:

(1) Amnesties
(2) Pardons
(3) Statutes of limitation
(4) Immunity from prosecution
(5) *Ne bis in idem*
(6) Abuse of process

tional and Comparative Law 227 (1983) (arguing that nuclear weapons are incompatible with fundamental bases of international law).

31 "The International Official in a Divided World", 53 *ASIL Proceedings* 344 (1959), at 347.

32 Law is considered as a means to an end (the end being the optimum public order), and not an end in itself. Wiessner and Willard, "Policy-Oriented Jurisprudence and Human Rights Abuses", at 324.

33 Many of the obstacles are of a practical and political nature – from the lack of political will to prosecute those who perpetrated international crimes to the problem of the collection of evidence with scarce resources, the paucity of trained professionals and the need to direct resources towards more immediate needs such as reconstruction and rebuilding in the aftermath of armed conflict.

As well as being arguably the most common of the legal impediments faced by courts considering exercising jurisdiction over international crimes, these impediments share certain characteristics which make a comparative analysis useful. All are obstacles which may be faced by both national and international courts when deciding to exercise jurisdiction over international crimes and are often regulated in the constitutive instruments of the latter. With regard to these six impediments, international law does not appear to provide a clear answer as to their legality when applied to international crimes. As a result, all have produced academic controversy and conflicting jurisprudence. When these prevent the exercise of jurisdiction, these impediments have been charged with contributing to impunity, and hence have been criticised as being out of step with the current trends to exercise jurisdiction over international crimes without exception. Finally, one may argue in relation to all these impediments that in the absence of a clear rule of international rule to determine courts' decisions in this regard, judges would find rational guidance by attempting to balance the interests sought to be protected by these barriers against the interest of prosecution.

There are, of course, a number of other significant jurisdictional obstacles which courts may also face when dealing with international crimes. These include judicially-made doctrines particularly prevalent in Anglo-American systems, such as the political question doctrine, the act of State doctrine, the doctrine of non-justiciability and the doctrine of *forum non conveniens*. While a detailed study of these doctrines falls outside the parameters of this book, a comparative analysis *vis-à-vis* the barriers focused upon is, however, made where possible.

The six barriers under study which all ultimately justify the non-enforcement of otherwise legal rules have disparate historical origins, policy justifications, legal rationales, and interactions with the international criminal system and with the wider system of public international law. Many also share legal rationales or policy justifications. Although there is a large amount of case law and legal literature examining these problems in human rights litigation as discrete subjects, a critical comparison of how courts deal with the various impediments or the question of how each should be treated in the light of the emerging international criminal system has rarely been tackled in international legal literature.[34] The lack of a comprehensive examination of these impediments in regard to international crimes has led to a confusing and at times conflicting array of legal theories and arguments relied upon by courts in cases dealing with serious violations to either justify or negate the application of a particular impediment. Rather than conforming to the commonly posited suggestion that one international legal *rule* should apply to the question

[34] One piece of legal scholarship going in this direction is the useful article of Ronald Slye, "The Legitimacy of Amnesties under International Law and General Principles of Anglo-American Law: Is Legitimate Amnesty Possible", 43 *VJIL* 173-247 (2002). For a comparative analysis of impediments to bringing States before national courts in regard to serious human rights violations, see Andrea Bianchi, "Serious Violations of Human Rights and Foreign States' Accountability before Municipal Courts", in Lal Chand Vohrah, et al. (eds.), *Man's Inhumanity to Man. Essays on International Law in Honour of Antonio Cassese* (The Hague: Kluwer Law International, 2003), at 149.

of their operability in cases of international crimes, this book instead advocates a coherent international law *approach* which courts could apply in dealing with the question of jurisdiction.

Part One of this book examines the key terms and concepts in the title of the book, namely: 'impediments,' 'exercise of adjudicatory jurisdiction' and 'international crimes,' with a view to outlining a framework of analysis for the second part of the book. This analysis seeks to explain that the assessment of adjudicatory jurisdiction over international crimes in the face of impediments is not a straight forward consideration of conflicting rules, but requires courts to properly analyse not only the operation of the legal principles involved, but also the values they seek to uphold and the overall objectives of international criminal processes.

1.2 Impediments

The *Oxford English Dictionary* defines an 'impediment' as 'a hindrance or obstruction.'[35] In the framework of the subject-matter of international crimes, the use of such a term suggests that the proper response to the perpetration of international crimes (i.e., adjudication) is blocked by reason of a conflicting rule. The 'impediments' under study here have been described in legal literature as 'obstacles'[36] and examples of '*la responsibilité pénale en échec*'.[37] However, the negative connotation of the word 'impediment' is not necessarily warranted. The operation of legal rules and principles always has legitimate aims and objectives which need to be balanced against the objectives of international criminal prosecution. In other words, these legal rules and principles are not necessarily 'problems' which need to be 'fixed' when opposed to the prosecution of international crimes. Rather, courts need to take into account the competing forces at play at a nuanced level, if indeed a conflict does exist, in order to properly find a solution consistent with the aims and principles of the international legal order. Therefore, the term 'impediment' should not be read as necessarily implying a problem to the functioning of international criminal law, but as a legal obstacle which should be properly considered by a court when deciding whether to exercise jurisdiction.

There are undoubtedly myriad impediments, in the broad sense of the word, to the exercise of jurisdiction over international crimes, ranging from problems of a practical nature (capturing the accused, gathering evidence, securing credible witnesses, inter-State co-operation), to political difficulties, as well as any number of

---

[35] *Oxford English Dictionary* (Oxford: OUP, 2002). Although the term 'impediment' is not a term of art, it is also commonly used in the sense of a bar to the conclusion of a contract under domestic law such as a marriage.

[36] Micaela Frulli, "Le droit international et les obstacles à la mise en oevre de la responsibilité pénale pour crimes internationaux", in Antonio Cassese & Mireille Delmas-Marty (eds.), *Crimes internationaux et jurisdictions internationales* (Paris: PUF, 2002), at 215.

[37] Mireille Delmas-Marty, "La responsibilité pénale en échec (prescription, amnistie, immunités)", in Antonio Cassese & Mireille Delmas-Marty (eds.), *Jurisdictions Nationales et Crimes Internationaux* (Paris: PUF, 2002), at 613.

legal challenges that may be brought in regard to the case. This book is concerned with a particular type of impediment which may be loosely defined as the operation of a legal rule or principle at the national or international level which prevents a court from exercising adjudicatory jurisdiction. Thus, it is generally at the procedural level that these obstacles arise. Two exceptions to this parameter are made in this book: pardons and functional immunities.

The decision to include the consideration of pardon in the context of adjudicatory jurisdiction may be justified in three ways. First, pardon may act as an impediment to adjudicatory jurisdiction in the technical sense, that is, prior to any trial. The first Argentine pardon issued on 8 October 1989, which applied to 277 people was issued prior to these people being tried.[38] A large number of pardons issued by Presidents of the United States have all happened before any trial.[39] Pardons may also prevent adjudicatory jurisdiction in the context of *ne bis in idem*. A number of national constitutions and laws prevent national courts from adjudicating persons who have been pardoned in foreign jurisdictions. This was the case in *Finta* (though in this case, the Canadian Court found the pardon was an amnesty)[40] and in Spain.[41] Furthermore, the operation of the 'guilty plea' is similar to clemency actions, whereby a person admits to legal liability but receives a reduced sentence in exchange for information, co-operation, and to promote legal efficiency.[42] Secondly, if one applies the principle of effectiveness to the notion of adjudicatory jurisdiction, then it is clear that without punitive consequences in cases of conviction, adjudicative jurisdiction means nothing. In other words, the obligations to 'prosecute and punish' are intimately connected. A failure to fulfil part of one aspect necessarily negates the effectiveness of the other. Thus, without prosecution, there cannot be punishment. Without punishment, prosecution resulting in conviction is pointless. In this sense, pardon can be characterised as an impediment to the whole basis of adjudicative jurisdiction. This is why some commentators have argued that the 'sham prosecution' principle in the *ne bis in idem* provision of the Rome Statute should have included the use of pardon.[43] It may also be argued that the notion of the right to justice also includes adequate punishment. Thirdly, the close connection between pardon and amnesty underlines the relevance of its inclusion. For instance, the South African amnesty can be characterised as a pardon because of the sense of forgiveness that accompanied grants of amnesty, so that there was a sense of liability, even if this didn't involve criminal prosecution. It is instructive to use the elements used to grant legitimate pardons (such as co-operation, remorse,

[38] Decree 1002/89, 6 October 1989.

[39] See *infra*, Chapter 3 'Pardons.'

[40] *Regina* v. *Finta*, Canada [1994] 1 *SCR* 701, Supreme Court of Canada, 24 March 1994; case note by Cotler in 90 *AJIL* 460 (1996).

[41] *Scilingo, Adolfo*, Spain, Central Criminal Court (*Audiencia Nacional*), Order (auto) of 5 November 1998, no. 1998/22605, rec. 173/1998, Case 19/97, in EL DERECHO, at 8.

[42] See *infra*, Chapter 3 'Pardons.'

[43] Christine Van den Wyngaert and Tom Ongena, "Ne bis in idem Principle, Including the Issue of Amnesty", in Antonio Cassese, Paola Gaeta and John R.W.D. Jones (eds.), *The Rome Statute of the International Criminal Court: A Commentary*, Vol. 1 (Oxford: OUP, 2002), at 727.

helping to repay victims) to determine if provisional amnesties could be granted. Finally, the value of the finding of liability may be assessed by comparing the treatment of amnesties to pardons under international law.

The second exception is the examination of functional immunities over international crimes, which is really a substantive defence rather than a procedural obstacle.[44] Given that its operation effectively prevents a court from examining a particular matter, however, it is included in the analysis. Moreover, it is instructive to compare how this impediment operates in comparison with personal immunities, which do circumvent the exercise of adjudicatory jurisdiction.

In an unevenly developed system of international criminal enforcement, courts inclined to prosecute those accused of international crimes may often need to think of creative solutions to overcome jurisdictional hurdles. Belgian judge, Judge Vandermeersch, has criticised those national courts taking a more cautious approach to cases involving international crimes:

> 'National judicial authorities often seek legal reasons to avoid prosecuting crimes against humanity instead of ascertaining whether they can prosecute them under international and national law … Concerning the enforcement of international humanitarian law, too, the risk is not that domestic authorities may overstep their competence but rather that by looking for excuses to justify their alleged lack of jurisdiction, they condone the impunity of one of the most serious crimes … The struggle against impunity of persons responsible for crimes under international law is, therefore, a responsibility of all states. National authorities have, at least, the right to take such measures as are necessary for the prosecution and punishment of crimes against humanity.'[45]

This statement is characteristic of the doctrinal position that favours an assumption of the exercise of jurisdiction when an international crime is involved. The danger of impunity for the perpetrators of international crimes is weighed against the danger of courts overstepping their competence and the former is seen to be far more negative a consequence than the latter. However, a more detailed examination of the impediments under review in this book shows that the assumption of continued exercise of jurisdiction does not always hold even where crimes of such gravity are at stake.

1.3 Jurisdiction

In general terms, 'jurisdiction' refers to 'the particular aspects of the general legal competence of states often referred to as sovereignty.'[46] While jurisdiction may

---

44 Antonio Cassese, *International Criminal Law* (Oxford: OUP, 2003), at 264.

45 Ordonnance, Dossier no. 216/98, Notices no. 30.99.3447/98, Tribunal de première instance, Arrondissement de Bruxelles, Cabinet du juge d'instruction, Damien Vandermeersch, 6 November 1998, at 3.3.3, translated from French.

46 Ian Brownlie, *Principles of Public International Law*, 6th edn. (Oxford: OUP, 2003), at 297. For a comprehensive study of jurisdiction under international law, see Cedric Ryngaert, *Jurisdiction in International Law* (Oxford: OUP, 2008).

be treated as a single concept, some interpretations, such as that adopted by the Restatement (Third) of the Foreign Relations Law of the United States, break down the concept into three distinct categories: prescriptive (legislative), adjudicative (judicial) and enforcement (executive) competence.[47] *Legislative* competence refers to the power of a State's institutions to prescribe laws or rules involving a foreign element, while *executive* competence denotes the power of one State to perform acts in the territory of another State.[48] *Judicial* competence, also referred to as 'adjudicatory jurisdiction,' may be described as the power of an agency (which need not necessarily be a court) to adjudicate disputes.[49] Such jurisdiction has also been described as 'the power of a court to decide a matter in controversy and presupposes the existence of a duly constituted court with control over the subject matter and the parties.'[50]

While the tripartite categorisation is somewhat of an innovation with regard to the traditional view (and for that matter, with the Second Restatement), which generally only distinguishes between prescriptive and enforcement jurisdiction,[51] it provides a useful schema for the purpose of defining what is meant by adjudicative jurisdiction in this thesis. Moreover, given the particular jurisdictional constraints under scrutiny in this field of research which arise only at the stage of adjudication, it seems reasonable to delineate this type of competence from prescriptive or executive competence. The Third Restatement sets out different regimes and limits applicable to each of the three categories. In doing so, the Restatement utilises the application of conflict of laws techniques for the resolution of jurisdictional conflicts at international law.[52] With regard to adjudicative jurisdiction, this entails subjecting the question of whether to exercise jurisdiction to a requirement of reasonableness which is assessed by reference to a number of elements, such as the presence of the person in the forum State's territory, whether a legal person

---

[47] Restatement (Third) of the Foreign Relations Law of the United States, sec. 401, Categories of Jurisdiction: 'Under international law, a state is subject to limitation on (a) jurisdiction to prescribe, i.e. to make its laws applicable to the activities, relations, or status of persons, or the interests of persons in things, whether by legislation, by executive order, by administrative rule or regulation, or by determination of a court; (b) jurisdiction to adjudicate, i.e. to subject persons or things to the process of its courts or administrative tribunals, whether in civil or in criminal proceedings, whether or not the state is a party to the proceedings; (c) jurisdiction to enforce, i.e. to induce or compel compliance or to punish non-compliance with its laws or regulations, whether through the courts or by use of executive, administrative, police, or other nonjudicial action.'

[48] Michael Akehurst, "Jurisdiction in International Law", *BYIL* (1972-1973), at 145.

[49] See Restatement of the Foreign Relations Law of the United States (Revised), § 441 (Tent. Draft No. 2, 1981) (using the term 'jurisdiction to adjudicate').

[50] *Black's Law Dictionary*, 6th edn. (St Paul, MN, 1990), at 853, cited by Judge Shahabuddeen in *Kanyabashi* (ICTR-96-15-A), Dissenting Opinion of Judge Shahabuddeen, 3 June 1999, at 3.

[51] Frederick A. Mann, "The Doctrine of Jurisdiction in International Law", 111 *RdC* (1964-1), at 13, 14.

[52] This resort to conflict of laws theories of jurisdiction probably derives from theories enunciated by Andreas Lowenfeld, "Public Law in the International Arena: Conflict of Laws, International Law, and Some Suggestions for their Interaction", 163 *RdC* 315-445 (1979-II). See also Andrea Bianchi, "Extraterritoriality and Export Controls: Some Remarks on the Alleged Antinomy Between European and U.S. Approaches", 35 *German Yearbook of International Law* 379 (1992).

is doing business in the forum State, or whether the thing that is the subject of the dispute is owned, possessed or used in the forum State.[53] The requirement of reasonableness derives from notions of fair play and substantive justice that have come to characterise the doctrine of jurisdiction in the United States.[54] Arguably, requiring courts to consider whether it is 'reasonable' to exercise jurisdiction in the field of international criminal law would lend itself to an approach which encourages courts to weigh up varying interests and policy considerations in any specific case or context.

However, before one may wholeheartedly embrace this regime of adjudicatory jurisdiction, it is worth pausing to reflect upon the evolution of jurisprudence which led to the adoption of the reasonableness and fairness requirement in American courts, and to consider other theories of adjudicatory jurisdiction in different systems, namely Anglo-Commonwealth jurisdictions and civil law jurisdictions. Generally-speaking, under private international law, justifications for the exercise of adjudicatory jurisdiction have been historically based upon three general theories. Jurisdiction can be viewed as resting: (1) on the relationship of lord (or king) and tenant (or subject), (2) on physical power, or (3) on considerations of convenience, fairness, and justice.[55] The basis of adjudicatory jurisdiction in the feudal systems of medieval Europe was premised on a personal bond between the lord and his tenant. When kings became strong, the concepts of society changed, but 'the notion of the king as the fountain of justice still rested, to some extent, on a personal relation between subject and king.'[56] However, as the Westphalian system of the sovereign State became entrenched, the personal bond or relation between subject and ruler lost its central place in the explanation of adjudicatory jurisdiction. Instead, as famously put by Justice Holmes: 'The foundation of jurisdiction is physical power …'[57] This means that as long as a sovereign State is able to serve process on an individual, i.e., the person is under the power of the sovereign, it may exercise adjudicatory jurisdiction.[58] Service of process has played a crucial role as the foundation of jurisdiction in the common law and is still valid today in Anglo-Commonwealth jurisdictions.[59] An alternative view that the jurisdiction depends

[53] Restatement (Third) of the Foreign Relations Law of the United States, sec. 421.

[54] Bianchi, *supra* n. 52, at 381; Gary B. Born and David Westin, *International Civil Litigation in United States Courts: Commentary and Materials*, 2nd edn. (Deventer: Kluwer Law and Taxation Publishers, 1992).

[55] Arthur Taylor von Mehren, "Adjudicatory Jurisdiction: General Theories Compared and Evaluated", 63(2) *Boston University Law Review* 283 (1983).

[56] *Idem.*, at 283.

[57] *McDonald* v. *Mabee*, 243 US 90 (1917), at 91.

[58] Similar statements have emanated from the House of Lords and the High Court of Australia. See *John Russell & Co Ltd* v. *Cayzer, Irvine & Co Ltd* [1916] 2 AC 298, at 302 *per* Lord Haldane; *Laurie* v. *Carroll* 98 *CLR* 310 (1958), at 328 *per* Dixon CJ, Williams and Webb JJ.

[59] Peter Nygh, "The Common Law Approach", in Campbell McLachlan and Peter Nygh (eds.), *Transnational Tort Litigation: Jurisdictional Principles* (Oxford: Clarendon Press, 1996), at 21. See also Lawrence Collins (ed.), *Dicey and Morris on the Conflict of Laws*, 12th edn. (1993), at 270: '… in England service of the writ or other originating process is the foundation of the court's jurisdiction to entertain an action *in personam*.'

upon the issue rather than on the service of the writ[60] has not been supported by case law.[61] The English courts based the theory directly on the territoriality principle in international law.[62] As a result, the British tradition in the field of jurisdiction in private international law is still based primarily upon the territoriality – and to a lesser extent nationality – principle, although there have been some inroads into this.[63]

Despite the procedural nature of the power theory of jurisdiction in British tradition, considerations of *forum conveniens*, and the need to balance the plaintiff's claim with the perceived infringement of the defendant's right not be prosecuted before a foreign court were always present.[64] This introduced considerations of fairness and justice into the jurisdictional question.[65] This trend towards a fairness requirement continues to erode the primacy of service as the foundation of jurisdiction.[66] This is the case even in those countries such as Australia, Canada and New Zealand which do not have statutory provisions defining jurisdiction generally and which still apply the service of process principle as the primary means of establishing jurisdiction.[67] In other common law countries, such as India, statutory provisions define the necessary connection required to establish international civil jurisdiction, either by reference to the residence of the defendant in the forum or from the cause of action arising in the forum.[68] In England and the Republic of Ireland, where the Brussels/Lugano Conventions apply,[69] jurisdiction depends on a specified connection with the forum rather than service of the writ on the defendant.[70]

In the United States, the courts early on adopted the common law approach of service as the foundation of jurisdiction.[71] An 1878 judgment of the Supreme Court

---

[60] See Clive Schmitthoff, *The English Conflict of Laws*, 3rd edn. (1954), at 428.

[61] Nygh, *supra* n. 59, at 23, citing the Full Court of the Supreme Court of South Australia in *Atco Industries (Aust) Pty Ltd* v. *Ancla Maritima SA* (1984) SASR 408. The High Court of Australia left the question open in *Laurie* v. *Carroll, supra* n. 58, at 328.

[62] Nygh, *supra* n. 59, at 27, citing *Carrick* v. *Hancock* (1895) 12 *TLR* 59.

[63] See, e.g., Oppenheim, *International Law*, 8th edn. (London/New York, 1930); Rosalyn Higgins, "The Legal Bases of Jurisdiction", in Cecil Olmstead (ed.), *Extraterritorial Application of Laws and Responses Thereto* (Oxford, 1984), at 3-14.

[64] Thus, where the plaintiff can be shown to have abused the right to have jurisdiction exercised, a court might still refuse to exercise jurisdiction notwithstanding the fact that the defendant had been properly served. *The Atlantic Star* [1974] AC 436.

[65] *Sim* v. *Rainbow* (1892) 19 R 665, at 668: '... the plea [of *forum conveniens*] can never be sustained unless the court is satisfied that there is some other tribunal, having competent jurisdiction, in which the case may be tried more suitably for the interests of the parties and for the ends of justice.'

[66] Nygh, *supra* n. 59, at 36, citing the suggestion of Rogers CJ in *Pendal Nominees Pty Ltd* v. *M & A Investments Pty Ltd* (1989) 18 *NSWLR* 383, at 394 that jurisdiction is more a question of *forum conveniens* than a discovery of a 'good arguable case' within one of the Ord. 11 provisions.

[67] Dicey and Morris, *The Conflict of Laws*, 12th edn. (1993), r. 22(1), at 270.

[68] Code of Civil Procedure 1908, s. 20 (India).

[69] See *infra*, notes 80-81 and accompanying text.

[70] Peter North and J.J. Fawcett, *Cheshire and North's Private International Law*, 12th edn. (London: Butterworths, 1992), at 180.

[71] Joseph Story, *Commentaries on the Conflict of Laws*, 2nd edn. (1841), at 768-87.

gave the English practice a constitutional basis.[72] This precedent severely strained the jurisdictional reaches of courts for the next 70 years in a federal system with a mobile population. Not only did it encourage an overly wide usage of 'tag jurisdiction,' but it meant that no forum for relief was available for victims of non-resident perpetrators. The precedent was finally replaced in 1945 by the landmark decision of *International Shoe Co* v. *Washington*,[73] in which the US Supreme Court held that service within the forum State was no longer a *sine qua non* for *in personam* jurisdiction. Instead, jurisdiction was founded upon the discovery of a sufficient nexus of the defendant with the forum State, that is: 'minimum contacts … such that the maintenance of the suit does not offend "traditional notions of fair play and substantial justice."'[74] Thus, one may reasonably postulate that in the United States the exercise of adjudicatory authority is explained and justified primarily by considerations of convenience, fairness, and justice.[75] This means that a court will consider the propriety of its assertion of adjudicatory jurisdiction by reference to two factors: the parties' relation to the forum community independent of the underlying controversy, and the underlying controversy's litigational relation to the forum community.[76] A court applying a fairness theory, unlike a power theory, must explicitly weigh the various considerations – including power – that can rationally influence a legal order's decision whether to assert adjudicatory jurisdiction over controversies involving foreign elements.[77]

By requiring a nexus between the forum and the defendant, this 'aligned US jurisdictional notions with those prevailing in civil law countries.'[78] Civil law countries found civil jurisdiction upon statutory provisions which are based upon particular connections between the litigation and the forum.[79] The Convention on Jurisdiction and the Enforcement of Judgments in Civil and Commercial Matters of 1968 (Brussels Convention)[80] and the parallel Convention agreed to at Lugano in 1988 between EU and EFTA States[81] sets down the basic rules of jurisdiction for those States. These conventions reflect the basic approach of civil law countries as to jurisdiction, which focuses upon reasonable connecting factors between the defendant or the subject matter and the forum. The rules for jurisdiction in civil law

---

72 *Pennoyer* v. *Neff* 95 US 714 (1878).

73 *International Shoe Co* v. *Washington* 326 US 310 (1945).

74 *Ibid*., at 316.

75 Von Mehren, "Adjudicatory Jurisdiction", at 283.

76 *Idem*.

77 *Ibid*., at 288.

78 Friedrich K. Juenger, "An Addendum on the United States Approach", in Campbell McLachlan and Peter Nygh (eds.), *Transnational Tort Litigation: Jurisdictional Principles* (Oxford: Clarendon Press, 1996), at 39.

79 Gerhard Walter and Rikke Dalsgaard, "The Civil Law Approach", in McLachlan and Nygh, *supra* n. 78, at 41.

80 Contracting States are Belgium, Denmark, France, Germany, Italy, Luxembourg, the Netherlands, the United Kingdom, the Republic of Ireland, Greece, Spain and Portugal.

81 Member States of the European Free Trade Association are Austria, Finland, Iceland, Liechtenstein, Norway, Sweden and Switzerland. For ratifications of the Lugano Convention, see [1994] ILPr 139.

countries are, however, mandatory, leaving no discretion on the part of courts to refuse to exercise jurisdiction (except for where there are bars on jurisdiction, such as sovereign immunity). This is justified by the argument that the typical interests of both parties have been balanced within the jurisdictional provisions, thus there is 'no need to rebalance these interests in the particular case at the expense of legal certainty.'[82] Some continental European scholars, however, such as Karl Meessen, have argued that States are obligated to balance their mutual interests in any conflict of jurisdictions, an argument that aligns to some degree with the 'balance of interests' approach as seen in American scholarship.[83]

It should be borne in mind that the interest of this book lies in the jurisdictional regime governing international crimes, which is arguably subject to different jurisdictional criteria than other areas of international law.[84] Notwithstanding this observation, the general remarks on adjudicative jurisdiction made above remain pertinent.[85] In particular, one may note that considerations of fairness and substantive justice play a role in the foundation of jurisdiction in all three legal systems mentioned. While the American stance on jurisdiction is the most explicit in this regard, the Anglo-Commonwealth countries have increasingly relied on notions of *forum conveniens* as valid considerations on the question of jurisdiction, while the balancing of different interests are codified in the jurisdictional provisions of the Brussels and Lugano Conventions and in the domestic laws of civil law States. It is reasonable to argue therefore that an interests-analysis approach fits well into the existing principles for deciding upon adjudicatory jurisdiction, whether this applies by way of inherent judicial process or by the formulation of legislation.

Under public international law, in terms of judicial jurisdiction over criminal matters, there exist a number of principles which justify adjudication by a State's courts, some of which refer to the relation between the accused person and the forum community (territoriality, nationality, passive personality) and some of which refer to the relation between the controversy and the forum community (protective principle, universality).[86] However, in deciding whether to act upon these bases it is fair to assume that courts may also consider other elements that can rationally influence their decision to assert adjudicatory jurisdiction. Legal impediments to the exercise of jurisdiction are such elements. Hence, a court's decision to exercise jurisdiction will usually consider questions of fairness, convenience and justice, as well as basic legal entitlement. With regard to the exercise of jurisdiction over international crimes, such considerations need to be carefully weighed in relation to the values underlying the prosecution of offenders. One could make the

[82] Walter and Dalsgaard, *supra* n. 79, at 46.

[83] Karl Meessen, "Antitrust Jurisdiction Under Customary International Law", 78 *AJIL* 783-810 (1984).

[84] Bianchi, *supra* n. 52, at 384: '... the existence of special regimes, especially in as far as crimes against international law are concerned, are envisaged so that the concept of jurisdiction may be broken down depending on the area to which it applies.'

[85] See Ryngaert, *Jurisdiction in International Law*, at 14-20, for a discussion of the interplay between private and public international law rules of jurisdiction and how these are distinguished.

[86] Akehurst, "Jurisdiction in International Law", at 152-166.

observation that with the development of the human rights system in the last fifty years, which has emphasised the rights of victims of serious rights abuses to have justice done, leading to efforts at various levels to close the impunity gap, together with the burgeoning field of international criminal law, the balance of such considerations has shifted towards prosecution. This has been argued to be the case even where valid impediments would normally block such processes for the purpose of protecting other values, such as reconciliation and creating the conditions for negotiating peace. However, courts are still required to enter into consideration of balancing interests, and it is in this balance which this book seeks to clarify the tipping point by applying an interests-analysis approach.

With regard to the jurisdictional principles justifying the exercise of criminal jurisdiction over serious international crimes, only the territoriality and nationality principles are without controversy as heads of jurisdiction. Their continued primacy as justifications for asserting jurisdiction over international crimes has been reaffirmed by the jurisdictional procedures of the Rome Statute of the International Criminal Court (ICC),[87] which sets out as preconditions for the exercise of jurisdiction of the ICC that the crimes to be adjudged be either allegedly committed in the *territory* of a State party or by the *national* of a State party to the Rome Statute.[88] If these States prove unable or unwilling to prosecute the alleged offender, the jurisdiction of the ICC may be exercised.[89] Thus, in a sense the ICC is a substitute court for when the territoriality and nationality principles fail to ensure the effective repression of serious international crimes for political or practical reasons.[90] The continued pre-eminence of the principles of territoriality and nationality as bases for adjudicatory jurisdiction is entirely appropriate as all States bear primary responsibility for crimes committed within their jurisdiction or by persons under their control.[91] Also supporting the pre-eminence of the principles of territoriality or nationality is research into transitional justice processes which has indicated that having the territorial State or State of nationality prosecute serious international crimes may have a more profound impact upon ending impunity and associ-

[87] Rome Statute of the International Criminal Court, 17 July 1998, UN Doc. A/COMF.183/9, corrected by the proces-verbaux of 10 November 1998 and 12 July 1999 (hereafter, ICC Statute).

[88] ICC Statute, Art. 12(2)(a) and (b). Of course, reliance on the other principles of jurisdiction would result in interference with non-party States and therefore would not have been accepted by the negotiating States of the Rome Statute, as well as violating Art. 31 of the 1969 Vienna Convention on the Law of Treaties (VCLT) (1969).

[89] ICC Statute, Art. 17(a).

[90] Speaking to the Rome Conference in 1998, the Secretary-General of the United Nations Kofi Annan set out the rationale of the ICC: '[g]radually the world has come to realise that relying on each State or army to punish its own transgressors is not enough. When crimes are committed on such a scale we know that the State lacks either the power or the will to stop them. Too often, indeed, they are part of a systematic State policy, and the worst criminals may be at the pinnacle of State power.' UN Doc. L/Rom/6.r1.

[91] As asserted by the Institute of International Law in the preamble to its Resolution 'Universal jurisdiction with respect to the crime of genocide, crimes against humanity and war crimes,' Krakow, 26 August 2005.

ated tensions than prosecution in other States and may contribute more directly to efforts towards reconciliation and societal healing.[92]

However, in recent years, State practice with regard to the prosecution of international crimes has evinced a trend towards a stronger reliance on the protective principle[93] (most notably used in the *Eichmann* case),[94] the passive personality principle,[95] particularly in regard to terrorist crimes[96] and the universality principle,[97] although the scope of the latter is still subject to ongoing debate.[98]

The question of jurisdiction is multi-dimensional – with both legal and political elements – and these combine in the grounds for jurisdiction. These variant practices support the idea that the question of exercising adjudicatory jurisdiction is one

[92] Diane Orentlicher, "The Future of Universal Jurisdiction in the New Architecture of Transnational Justice", in Stephen Macedo (ed.), *Universal Jurisdiction: National Courts and the Prosecution of Serious Crimes Under International Law* (Philadelphia, PA: University of Pennsylvania, 2004), at 236: 'Provided they enjoy legitimacy, trials in the territorial state are more likely than prosecutions abroad to inspire a sense of "ownership" by societies recently scourged by atrocious crimes.'

[93] The protective principle refers to the assertion of jurisdiction over a crime committed by an alien abroad which has adverse effects on the security of the State. Although the principle is uncontroversial, the range of crimes to which it applies remains in question. The authoritative 1935 Harvard Research Draft Convention on Jurisdiction with Respect to Crime, in Arts. 7 and 8, refers to crimes against the security, territorial integrity or political independence of the State, and the counterfeiting of the seals, currency, instruments or credit, stamps, passports or public documents issued by the State. Reprinted in 29 *AJIL Supplement* 480 (1935).

[94] Despite the fact that the State of Israel was not in existence at the time the crimes were committed, the District Court took the view that it was entitled to exercise jurisdiction under the 'protective principle,' 'which gives the victim nation the right to try any who assault its existence.' *Attorney-General of Israel* v. *Eichmann*, 36 *ILR* 277 (1968), para. 30. See also para. 38.

[95] The head of jurisdiction is based upon the nationality of the victim of the alleged crime.

[96] Although the First and Second Restatements rejected this head of jurisdiction, the modification of this position in the Third Restatement to admit the possibility of courts exercising jurisdiction based on the nationality of victims of serious crimes was prompted by the adoption of legislation (18 U.S.C. §2331) allowing for jurisdiction to be exercised over terrorists who 'kill, assault or make any violent attack against United States nationals abroad.' See Restatement (Third) of the Foreign Relations of the United States, §402(3) (1987). For the view that the passive personality principle is becoming the dominant practice in national courts dealing with international crimes committed in foreign territory, see, e.g., Chandra Lekha Sriram, *Globalizing Justice for Mass Atrocities: A Revolution in Accountability* (London: Routledge, 2005), at 35.

[97] This head of jurisdiction provides justification for the exercise of jurisdiction by a State's courts over certain crimes committed anywhere in the world regardless of nationality of the offender or the victim. See *Institut de Droit International* Resolution 'Universal jurisdiction with respect to the crime of genocide, crimes against humanity and war crimes' Art. 1, Krakow, 26 August 2005.

[98] State practice indicates ambivalence with regard to the attitude of domestic courts exercising universal jurisdiction over international crimes in the face of impediments. In some instances, courts acting upon this basis have refused to open an investigation or to prosecute in light of the weak jurisdictional link to the crimes allegedly perpetuated. Others have insisted on a subsidiarity requirement, so that such a basis for jurisdiction only becomes operable once it has been established that the primary forum is unable or unwilling to prosecute. See, e.g., *Scilingo, Adolfo*, Spain, Third Section of the Criminal Division (*Audiencia Nacional*), Judgment no. 16/2005 of 19 April 2005, *Sentencia por crímenes contra la humanidad en el caso Adolpho Scilingo*, available at: <http://www.derechos.org/nizkor/espana/juicioral/doc/sentencia.html> (finding that Argentina's continued failure to prosecute those responsible for the atrocities committed by the military junta during the dictatorship years fulfilled the condition of subsidiarity).

related to a number of factors, particularly those relating to the forum State. Thus, for instance, a transnational *ne bis in idem* rule is less likely to be accepted by the territorial State or by the State exercising the protective principle. International and national courts justify not giving effect to amnesties if they are exercising universal jurisdiction, whereas courts in the State of territoriality are more likely to uphold an amnesty. Therefore it is unsurprising that, with one notable exception,[99] every national court that has ruled on the validity of its own government's amnesty laws, has upheld the amnesty.[100] National courts reject functional immunity where universal jurisdiction is provided for in a treaty. Courts operating on the nationality principle often uphold pardons for international crimes whereas courts exercising passive personality are much more likely to reject amnesties. The trends in this regard are still nascent and somewhat difficult to trace, however the idea of courts using a number of factors to assess the reasonableness of exercising jurisdiction in the presence of an impediment is supported by these emergent patterns.

1.4 International crimes

The precise definition of 'international crime' remains a subject of academic controversy.[101] Rather than fully entering into the definitional controversy, the objective of this section is two-fold: first, to identify the key features of such crimes as they relate to the exercise of jurisdiction and second to explain why the so-called 'core crimes' (war cimes, crimes against humanity, genocide) and torture attract these particular jurisdictional consequences.[102]

International crimes may be broadly described as 'breaches of international rules entailing the personal criminal liability of the individuals concerned …'[103] It has been argued that international crimes may also be perpetrated by corporations, however this interesting debate goes beyond the scope of this book,[104] and thus the proceeding discussion will focus on individual criminal liability for violations of international law. Any breach of an international rule entailing the criminal liability

[99] *Resolución del Cavallo* (in which Judge Gabriel Cavallo declared the Argentinian amnesty laws unconstitutional and invalid) available at <http://www.derechos.org/nizkor/arg/ley/juezcavallo-03mar.html>.

[100] See *AZAPO* case, and *Proceedings No. 10-93 of the Supreme Court of El Salvador on the Amnesty Law*, reprinted in 3 *Transitional Justice* (1995), at 549-55.

[101] Definitions of international crimes vary. Wright defines an international crime as 'an act committed with intent to violate a fundamental interest protected by international law or with knowledge that the act will probably violate such an interest, and which may not be adequately punished by the exercise of the normal criminal jurisdiction of any state.' Quincy Wright, "The Law of the Nuremburg Trial", 41 *AJIL* 56 (1947). Dinstein, by contrast, defines international crimes as grave offences which 'harm fundamental interests of the whole international community' and which are translated as such into positive law. Yoram Dinstein, "International Criminal Law", 20 *Israel Law Review* 221 (1985).

[102] See Ryngaert, *Jurisdiction in International Law*, at 115-127.

[103] Cassese, *International Criminal Law*, at 23.

[104] E.g., Andrew Clapham, "Corporations' International Crimes and the Extension of International Criminal Law Beyond the Individual", 6(5) *JICJ* 899-926 (2008).

of the perpetrator, emanating from treaty or custom, is an international crime.[105] This definition begs the question, however, of how to distinguish and to identify these rules from 'other' rules of international law. Dinstein has postulated that it is 'the practice of States [that] is the conclusive determinant in the creation of international law (including international criminal law) and not the desirability of stamping out obnoxious patterns of human behaviour.'[106] While this observation certainly reflects the evidence needed to identify an international crime, it does not explain why certain behaviour has been accorded such a status by States in the international legal system.

According to James Crawford, the 'common core' of international crimes include offences, 'under a norm of international law accepted and recognised by the international community as a whole as being of such a fundamental character that its violation attracts the criminal responsibility of individuals.'[107] This statement, which aligns closely to the International Law Commission's definition of an international crime of State in Article 19 of its Draft Articles on State Responsibility,[108] draws attention to the *fundamental character* of an international rule that is of such gravity that its violation entails individual criminal liability. This suggests that an international crime has a customary law basis, given that it must be accepted and recognised as an international crime by the international community as a whole. Thus, a distinction must be made between those offences set down in certain conventions for which jurisdiction is extended beyond the State of primary jurisdiction in the enforcement regime to the jurisdictions of all the participating States ('treaty crimes') and those offences for which individual criminal liability exists under international law ('international crimes').[109] A similar view was taken by a United States Military Tribunal sitting at Nuremberg in 1948, which defined an 'international crime' as:

> 'such an act universally recognized as criminal, which is considered a grave matter of international concern and for some valid reason cannot be left within the exclusive jurisdiction of the state that would have control over it under ordinary circumstances.'[110]

Dinstein, "International Criminal Law", at 221.

106 *Idem.*

107 James Crawford, "The ILC's Draft Statute for an International Criminal Tribunal", 88 *AJIL* 144 (1994).

108 In 1976, the International Law Commission (ILC) adopted the concept of international crimes of States in Art. 19 of its Draft Articles on State Responsibility. Art. 19(2) of the Draft stipulates: 'An internationally wrongful act which results from the breach by a State of an international obligation so essential for the protection of fundamental interests of the international community that its breach is recognized as a crime by the community as a whole constitutes an international crime.' The Article was deleted in the final draft adopted by the ILC in 2001.

109 Susan Marks & Andrew Clapham, *International Human Rights Lexicon* (Oxford: OUP, 2005), at 47 (noting that offences such as aircraft hijacking to drugs trafficking and the transboundary movement of hazardous waste are 'treaty crimes' which cannot be properly called 'international crimes').

110 *US* v. *List, et al.*, 19 February 1948, *Trials of War Criminals Before the Nuernberg Tribunals under Control Council Law No. 10*, Vol 9 (Washington, DC: US Government Printing Office, 1950), 1230 at 1241.

Notably, this definition adds another justification for 'international crime' status; that is, the need to extend the authorisation to exercise jurisdiction over such offences from the State of primary jurisdiction to other courts, in the case at issue, a military tribunal of an occupying power. The statement emphasises three important elements of the definition of international crime: (1) the need for the act to be universally recognised as criminal; (2) the act being a grave matter of international concern; and (3) the need for universal jurisdiction over such acts for effective enforcement.[111]

One of the reasons that an international law offence would be of such a fundamental character that it would be of international concern is that the commission of such an act endangers international peace and security, or more generally, international relations.[112] Writing shortly before representing the USSR in the drafting of the Nuremberg Charter, Professor Trainin described 'international crime' as:

> 'an infringement of the connection between States and peoples, a connection which constitutes the basis of relations between countries and countries. International crime is directed towards the worsening, the rendering acute, the rupture of those connections. Those guilty of such crimes hold up the stream of trains, ships, people, goods, passing in a broad current from one country to another; they attempt to build up barriers, to set one State against another, one people against another … International crime, consequently, must be defined as an infringement of the foundations of international communion.'[113]

The statutes of the international criminal courts all make explicit or implicit reference to the need for criminal prosecution of those accused of committing and/or orchestrating international crimes in order to restore or maintain international peace and security.[114] Given the apparent link between international criminal law

---

[111] On the establishment of universal jurisdiction more generally, see Luc Reydams, *Universal Jurisdiction: International and Municipal Legal Perspectives* (Oxford: OUP, 2003).

[112] In the *Eichmann* case, in its judgment of 29 May 1962, the Supreme Court of Israel held that: 'Not only do all the crimes attributed to the appellant bear an international character, but their harmful and murderous effects were so embracing and widespread as to *shake the international community to its very foundations*. The State of Israel therefore was entitled, pursuant to the principle of universal jurisdiction and in the capacity of a guardian of international law and an agent for its enforcement, to try the appellant.' See 36 *ILR* 304. [Emphasis added]

[113] A.N. Trainin, edited by A.Y. Vishinski, *Hitlerite Responsibility under Criminal Law*, transl. Rothstein, Andrew (London: Hutchinson & co., 1946; Institute of Law, Academy of Sciences of the U.S.S.R.), at 32.

[114] In the case of the IMT at Nuremberg, although the war was over by the time the Charter was drafted, the Allied Powers justified the judging of matters traditionally considered exclusively the sovereign domain of States by linking the commission of crimes against humanity to international war. It was asserted by the Allies that crimes against humanity were a threat to world peace. Charter of the International Military Tribunal, Art. 6(c), 59 Stat. 1546, 1547 (1945), E.A.S. No. 472, 82 *UNTS* 284. The ICTY and ICTR, both established by the UN Security Charter acting under Chapter VII, were explicitly tied to the need to restore peace and security in the respective territories. SC Res. 827 (1993) establishing the ICTY stated that such a mechanism 'would contribute to the restoration and maintenance of peace' (preambular para. 6); SC Res. 955 (1994) establishing the ICTR stated that such a mechanism 'would contribute to the process of national reconciliation and to the restoration and

and international peace and security, the aim of criminal justice is arguably not only to punish the perpetrators, but also to restore law and order and to contribute to a lasting peace by facilitating reconciliation.[115]

This element of the definition of international crime not only underscores the seriousness of such offences, but also resonates with the logic of an international criminal law. As explained by Gerry J. Simpson, '[g]enerally, it is thought that criminal law is an expression of a community's moral sense. As such, it is public, punitive, retributive and moral in ways that civil law is not. Consequently, violations of criminal law are said to have graver social consequences for the whole society which demands in turn that the community acts through its public enforcement agencies to suppress these breaches.'[116] Similarly, in *U.S.* v. *von Leeb & Others*, the court stated that 'to be held criminally responsible, there must be a breach of some moral obligation fixed by international law, a personal act voluntarily done with knowledge of its inherent criminality under international law.'[117] If the international community of States may be conceived of as a *bona fide* community with a shared set of moral values, at least with regard to the most heinous of acts, then one could very well define an international crime as an infringement of that 'international communion.' Arguably, the shared set of moral values derives from universally recognised fundamental human rights set down in international instruments and/or accepted in custom.[118] In domestic criminal law, the general theory is that 'certain illegal conduct is more dangerous than others in relation to the highest values of society' and for this reason the community reacts strongly to such offences and 'assigns "penalties" expressing those negative feelings.'[119] One

maintenance of peace,' (preambular para. 7). The preamble of the Statute of the ICC also recognizes that 'such grave crimes threaten the peace, security and well-being of the world' and that by ending impunity, such crimes might be prevented. ICC Statute, preambular paras. 3 and 5.

[115] Ilias Bantekas & Susan Nash, *International Criminal Law* (London: Cavendish Publishing, 2003), at 10.

[116] Gerry J. Simpson, "War Crimes: A Critical Introduction", in Timothy L.H. McCormack & Gerry J. Simpson (eds.), *The Law of War Crimes: National and International Approaches* (The Hague: Kluwer Law International, 1997), at 16 citing Williams, "The Definition of a Crime", 8 *Current Legal Problems* 107 (1955).

[117] *U.S.* v. *von Leeb & Others* (Case 12), *TWC*, Vol. 11 (Trials of War Criminals before the Nuremberg Military Tribunals under Control Council Law No. 10, Vols. I-XV, US-GPO, Washington D.C. 1950-1953).

[118] Such values have been laid down in international instruments such as the 1945 UN Charter, 1948 Universal Declaration of Human Rights, 1950 European Convention on Human Rights and Fundamental Freedoms, 1966 ICCPR and ICESCR, 1969 American Convention on Human Rights, 1970 UN Declaration on Friendly Relations and the 1981 African Charter on Human and People's Rights, or may be protected under treaties that prohibits conduct which infringes them, such as the 1948 Genocide Convention, 1949 Geneva Conventions and 1977 Protocols, 1984 Convention against Torture, and treaties prohibiting forms of terrorism. While debate exists over which human rights have achieved customary law status, it is commonly accepted that 'the rules prohibiting arbitrary killing, slavery, torture, detention, and systematic racial discrimination – such as apartheid – are now recognized as rules of customary international law binding on all states.' Andrew Clapham, *Human Rights of Non-State Actors* (Oxford: OUP, 2006), at 86.

[119] Julio Barboza, "International Criminal Law", 278 *RdC* 23 (The Hague) (1999).

could thus characterise international criminal law as the criminal law of the international community: 'a corpus of norms with the description of criminal conduct affecting the highest values of the international ... community.'[120] Naturally, in a horizontal system of authority as the international community of States, the enforcement system of such values cannot emanate from a central police force and judiciary, but must be based upon the collective responsibility of all States to enforce the most important rules which form the foundation of their relations with each other and the relations between the peoples of each State to the State structures themselves.[121]

Hence, one can surmise from this brief analysis that the issue of exercising jurisdiction is central both to the enforcement of a system of international criminal law and to the definition of international crimes. This is despite the fact that a distinction must be made between 'criminalisation' and 'jurisdiction,' the former being the 'the act of outlawing or making illegal certain behaviour'[122] whereas the latter relates to 'the judicial authority to prosecute those criminal acts.'[123] The intertwining of the two concepts is explained in part by the fact that criminal offences are distinct from 'normal' offences in that there are distinct penalties connected to crimes; in other words, crimes may be defined in part by the legal response to them. In fact, some have gone so far as to argue that 'what acts should be characterized as international crimes depends on the machinery by which such acts are to be dealt with' and that since the establishment of the International Criminal Court, 'international crimes are those prosecuted before an international criminal tribunal,

---

[120] *Ibid.*, at 24.

[121] Simpson has questioned whether the international community has such a system of shared social values given that it is 'morally pluralistic and normatively consensual.' Simpson, "War Crimes", at 20. However, Cherif Bassiouni's analysis of twenty-two categories of international crimes revealed that the conventions in which they were contained demonstrated the following penal characteristics, most of which pertain to the method of enforcement rather than shared social values:
(1) Explicit recognition of proscribed conduct as constituting an international crime, or a crime under international law, or as a crime;
(2) Implicit recognition of the penal nature of the act by establishing a duty to prohibit, prevent, prosecute, punish or the like;
(3) Criminalisation of the proscribed conduct;
(4) Duty or right to prosecute;
(5) Duty or right to punish the proscribed conduct;
(6) Duty or right to extradite;
(7) Duty or right to co-operate in prosecution, punishment (including judicial assistance in penal proceedings);
(8) Establishment of a criminal jurisdictional basis (or theory of criminal jurisdiction or priority in criminal jurisdiction);
(9) Reference to the establishment of an international criminal court or international tribunal with penal characteristics (or prerogatives); and
(10) Elimination of the defence of superior orders.
Cherif Bassiouni, *International Criminal Law* (Dobbs Ferry, New York: Transnational, 1986), at 2.

[122] *Delalić and others* (*Čelebići* case) *(appeal)*, ICTY Appeals Chamber, Judgment of 20 February 2001, Case No. IT-96-21-A, para. 163.

[123] *Idem.*

whether *ad hoc* or permanent.'[124] According to this view, '[f]or an individual to be held criminally liable for an act of genocide under international law, he would have to be prosecuted and punished by an international criminal tribunal applying an international criminal statute.'[125] The idea that only an international enforcement mechanism could prosecute persons for international crimes was put forward in 1950 by Schwarzenberger, who argued that international criminal law is 'merely a loose and misleading label for topics which comprise anything but international criminal law' and that whatever the content of these rules, there is no evidence that they are endowed with a prohibitive character and specific penal sanctions.[126] He grounded his argument on the fact that, in the absence of international enforcement mechanisms, the concept of offences against the law of nations was redundant, unless regulated and enforced before a domestic setting. This led him to believe that international criminal law was in fact domestic criminal law.

The view that international crimes may only be prosecuted before international criminal courts or tribunals is rejected in this book. In the light of the significant role that both international and national courts have played since 1950 in the enforcement of international criminal law, the more persuasive view is that international crimes may be prosecuted before either international tribunals or by national courts or military tribunals. The former 'exercise an international jurisdiction by reason of the law applied and the constitution of the tribunal' while the latter exercise international jurisdiction 'by reason of the law applied and the nature of jurisdiction (the exercise of which is justified by international law).'[127]

One final element of the notion of 'international crime' that should be highlighted is the general acceptance that international crimes are usually violations of so-called 'peremptory' norms of international law (*jus cogens*).[128] In 2001, the ICTY stated that 'in human rights law the violation of rights which have reached the

---

[124] Kriangsak Kittichaisaree, *International Criminal Law* (Oxford: OUP, 2001), at 3.

[125] Kittichaisaree, *ibid.*, at 9. Kittichaisaree argues that if a perpetrator of genocide is tried in the domestic court of his State or another State to which he is extradited, either of these courts will be applying its own domestic law.

[126] G. Schwarzenberger, "The Problem of an International Criminal Law", 3 *CLP* 274 (1950).

[127] Ian Brownlie, *Principles of Public International Law*, 6th edn. (Oxford: OUP, 2003), at 561. As Mr. Malek of Lebanon, formerly a member of the UN Office of Legal Affairs and later of the International Law Commission put it during the drafting of the Hostages Convention: '[National courts] had an essentially international character in terms of the functions they were performing. They were called upon to prosecute international offenders on behalf not only of the states to which they belonged but also of all other states. They were carrying out a task that should normally be carried out by an international jurisdiction. Thus they were acting as judicial bodies under an institutionally defective international legal order.' 34 UN GAOR, Sixth Committee, 53rd mtg., at 12, UN Doc. A/C.6/34/53 (1979).

[128] See Stefan Kadelbach, "*Jus Cogens*, Obligations *Erga Omnes* and other Rules – The Identification of Fundamental Norms", in Christian Tomuschat and Jean-Marc Thouvenin (eds.), *The Fundamental Rules of the International Legal Order.* Jus Cogens *and Obligations* Erga Omnes (Leiden/Boston: Martinus Nijhoff Publishers, 2006), at 21; Leila Nadya Sadat, "Individual Progress in International Law: Considering Amnesty", in Russell A. Miller and Rebecca M. Bratspies (eds.), *Progress in International Law*, (Leiden/Boston: Martinus Nijhoff Publishers, 2008), at 342-345.

level of *jus cogens*, such as torture, may constitute international crimes.'[129] A rule which is *jus cogens* '[b]ecause of the importance of the values it protects … enjoys a higher rank in the international hierarchy than treaty law and even "ordinary" customary rules.'[130] While the exact list of *jus cogens* norms remains in dispute,[131] there is ample evidence that at least the prohibitions of 'core international crimes' constitute peremptory norms. Clearly accepted and recognized *jus cogens* norms include the prohibitions of aggression, genocide, slavery, racial discrimination, crimes against humanity and torture.[132] It is now increasingly accepted that war crimes may be included in this category.[133] While not all *jus cogens* prohibitions are international crimes, it may be asserted that all international crimes are *jus cogens* prohibitions. Out of the ILC's list of identified *jus cogens* norms – aggression, genocide, slavery, racial discrimination, crimes against humanity and torture – only racial discrimination is not really considered a crime, though certain mani-

---

[129] *Delalić and others* (*Čelebići* case) *(appeal)*, ICTY Appeals Chamber, Judgment of 20 February 2001, Case No. IT-96-21-A, para. 172, fn. 225.

[130] *Furundžija*, ICTY, Trial Chamber II, Judgment of 10 December 1998, Case No. IT-95-17/1-T; 39 *ILM* (1999), para. 153.

[131] Art. 53 of the Vienna Convention on the Law of Treaties 1969 provides a definition of a *jus cogens* or peremptory norm of international law: 'a peremptory norm of general international law is a norm accepted and recognized by the international community of States as a whole as a norm from which no derogation is permitted and which can be modified only by a subsequent norm of general international law having the same character.' In the *Barcelona Traction* case (Second Phase), the ICJ drew the distinction between obligations of a State arising *vis-à-vis* another State and obligations 'towards the international community as a whole,' saying: '[s]uch obligations derive, for example, in contemporary international law, from the outlawing of acts of aggression, and of genocide, as also from the principles and rules concerning the basic rights of the human person, including protection from slavery and racial discrimination.' ICJ Reports 1970, 3 at 32. See also *East Timor* case, ICJ Reports 1995, 90 at 102.

[132] Commentary to Art. 26 of the ILC Draft Articles on State Responsibility. Report of the ILC, GAOR, Suppl. (No. 10), UN Doc. A/56/10, para. 5, at 208.

[133] In the *Nicaragua* case, the ICJ found that Art. 3 common to the Geneva Conventions represented a customary rule of international law, adding that the rules reflect 'elementary considerations of humanity.' *Military and Paramilitary Activities in and against Nicaragua (Nicaragua* v. *United States)*, 1986 ICJ Reports 14 (1986), at 104. In its opinion on the *Legality of the Threat or Use of Nuclear Weapons*, the Court recognized that the 'fundamental rules [of humanitarian law] are to be observed by all States whether or not they have ratified the conventions that contain them, because they constitute intransgressible principles of customary law.' *Legality of the Threat or Use of Nuclear Weapons*, Advisory Opinion of 8 July 1996, ICJ Reports 1996, at 257, para. 79. Some judges went further and clearly stated in separate opinions that the rules of war have acquired the status of *jus cogens*, see Weeramantry J, at 496, President Bedjaoui, at 273, Koroma J, at 574. In the *Haas and Priebke* cases, Military Court of Appeal of Rome/Supreme Court of Cassation, 7 March 1998/16 November 1998, the judgments describe the principle of the non-applicability of statutory limitations to war crimes as a peremptory norm of general international law, necessarily implying that war crimes also have a *jus cogens* nature. See also, Antonio Cassese, "On the Current Trends towards Criminal Prosecution and Punishment of Breaches of International Humanitarian Law", 9(1) *EJIL* (1998); Hans-Peter Gasser, "International Humanitarian Law", in H. Haug (ed.), *Humanity for all* (Berne: Henry Dunant Institute, Paul Haupt Publishers, 1993), at 556; M. Cherif. Bassiouni, "International Crimes *Jus Cogens* and *Obligatio Erga Omnes*", in C. Joyner and C. Bassiouni (eds.), *Reining in impunity for international crimes and serious violations of fundamental rights* (Ramonville St. Agne: Association Internationale de Droit Penal, 1998), at 267.

festations may amount to international crimes: apartheid is included as a form of crime against humanity in the Rome Statute (Art. 7(1)(j)).[134]

Some commentators have noted that the *Barcelona Traction* case and the work of the ILC is not directly related to international crime. However, although the case itself did not factually involve an international crime,[135] the ICJ seemed to go out of its way in *obiter dictum* to draw the distinction between obligations of a State arising *vis-à-vis* another State and obligations 'towards the international community as a whole,' saying: '[s]uch obligations derive, for example, in contemporary international law, from the outlawing of acts of aggression, and of genocide, as also from the principles and rules concerning the basic rights of the human person, including protection from slavery and racial discrimination.'[136] The ILC itself heavily relied on this passage in its report on Draft Article 19 of the Articles on State Responsibility to show that there are separate regimes of international responsibility depending on the subject matter of the international obligation breached.[137] *Erga omnes* obligations were referred to again in the *East Timor* case (in regard to the right of peoples to self-determination)[138] and in the *Genocide Convention (preliminary objections)* case (with regard to genocide).[139] ILC Special Rapporteur James Crawford noted that 'the developments outlined above confirm the view that within the field of general international law there is some hierarchy of norms, and that the importance of at least a few basic substantive norms is recognized as involving a difference not merely of degree but of kind.'[140] While the ILC finally rejected the idea of distinguishing between international crimes and international delicts, the notion of international crime as previously contained in Draft Article 19 was included in those parts of the Articles dealing with the specific legal consequences that attach to serious breaches of peremptory norms in Article 41. In its 2007 judgment on the *Genocide Convention*, the ICJ refers in the

---

[134] The small number of States parties to the Apartheid Convention suggests that the crime of apartheid *per se* is not an international crime under customary law, despite the obligation incumbent on States parties to prosecute or extradite offenders (Art. V, International Convention on the Suppression and Punishment of the Crime of Apartheid of 1973). As of July 2009, 107 States have ratified the Convention and this number does not include any of the Western Bloc, nor Japan. Therefore, it is difficult to argue that universal jurisdiction over the crime of apartheid is widely accepted.

[135] In fact far from it – Barcelona Traction was a corporation that controlled light and power utilities in Spain and was incorporated in Toronto (Canada) 12 September 1911 by Frederick Stark Pearson. It was operated in Spain, but was owned mostly by Belgians. The government of Spain in the 1960s made business more difficult for foreigners in Spain. The Belgian stockholders lost money and wanted to sue in the International Court of Justice, but the court ruled on the side of the Spanish, holding that only the nationality of the corporation (the Canadians) can sue.

[136] *Barcelona Traction* case (Second Phase), ICJ Reports 1970, 3 at 32.

[137] See Arangio-Ruiz, "Fourth Report on State Responsibility Add. 1-3", *Yearbook of the ILC*, Vol. II, Part One (1992), at 34 et seq., and 43 et seq.

[138] *East Timor (Portugal* v. *Australia)*, ICJ Reports 1995, 90 at 102-105.

[139] *Application of the Convention on the Prevention and Punishment of the Crime of Genocide (Bosnia and Herzegovina* v. *Serbia and Montenegro)*, Preliminary Objections, Judgment of 11 July 1996, para. 31.

[140] James Crawford, "First Report on State Responsibility Add.", GA Doc. A/CN.4/490/Add.2, 5 May 1998, para. 71.

same vein to 'obligations under peremptory norms, or of obligations which protect essential humanitarian values, and which may be owed *erga omnes*,'[141] and to the 'significance of the *jus cogens* character of the relevant norms, and the *erga omnes* character of the relevant obligations.'[142] The Court also recalls that in the case concerning *Armed Activities on the Territory of the Congo (New Application 2002) (Democratic Republic of the Congo* v. *Rwanda)*, it observed that the norm prohibiting genocide was assuredly a peremptory norm of international law *(jus cogens)*.[143] All these developments confirm the importance and relevance of the concept of *jus cogens* to determining what constitutes an international crime and what consequences flow from such a characterisation, which certainly go beyond establishing standing before the ICJ (*Armed Activities on the Territory of the Congo* case) and voiding incompatible treaties (Art. 53, VCLT).

There are three arguments one can posit to substantiate the claim that *jus cogens* crimes have as a consequence 'an entitlement to prosecute.' First, it may be argued that as *jus cogens* norms involve *erga omnes* obligations in terms of enforcement, the community interest in the suppression of international crimes entails the establishment of universal jurisdiction at the national level. In the *Armed Activities on the Territory of the Congo* case, while the ICJ held that the *jus cogens* character of a norm such as the prohibition of genocide did not provide a basis for jurisdiction before the ICJ, which is based on the consent of the parties, this does not take away from the Court's recognition that the *erga omnes* obligations flowing from the prohibition of the norm entail a universal interest in the repression of the behaviour.[144] The strongest example of this reasoning is found in the ICJ's Advisory Opinion in the *Reservations to Genocide Convention* (1951) in which the Court reaffirmed that 'the principles underlying the [Genocide] Convention are principles which are recognized by civilized nations as binding on States, even without any conventional obligation' and that a consequence of that conception is 'the universal character both of the condemnation of genocide and of the co-operation required "in order to liberate mankind from such an odious scourge" (Preamble to the Convention).'[145] As noted in the *Application of the Genocide Convention* case, it follows that 'the rights and obligations enshrined by the Convention are rights and obligations *erga omnes*.'[146] This meant that 'the obligation each State has to prevent and to punish the crime of genocide is not territorially limited by the Convention.'[147] Thus, all

---

[141] *Application of the Convention on the Prevention and Punishment of the Crime of Genocide (Bosnia and Herzegovina* v. *Serbia and Montenegro)*, Judgment, 26 February 2007, para. 147.

[142] *Ibid.*, at para. 185.

[143] *Ibid.*, at para. 161.

[144] *Armed Activities on the Territory of the Congo (Democratic Republic of the Congo* v. *Rwanda)*, Jurisdiction of the Court and Admissibility of the Application, Judgment, 3 January 2006, para. 64.

[145] *Reservations to the Convention on Genocide* (Advisory Opinion), 1951 ICJ Reports 15 (1951), at 12.

[146] *Application of the Convention on the Prevention and Punishment of the Crime of Genocide (Bosnia and Herzegovina* v. *Serbia and Montenegro),* Preliminary Objections, Judgment of 11 July 1996, para. 31.

[147] *Idem.*

States have the right to try the perpetrators of genocide. The same reasoning would surely apply to war crimes, crimes against humanity and torture.

A second argument is that the particular consequences of *jus cogens* crimes under the law of State responsibility could be interpreted to establish universal jurisdiction. Article 41 of the ILC's Articles on State Responsibility provides that the three specific consequences of such violations are: (1) the duty not to recognise as lawful a situation created by breach of a peremptory norm; (2) the duty to bring the situation to an end; and (3) the duty not to condone, authorise or absolve responsibility. All these consquences suggest that all States may exercise jurisdiction over perpetrators. ILC Special Rapporteur Gaetanao Arrangio-Ruiz interpreted 'the obligation not to recognize as "legal"' in the sense of not 'producing legal effects at the international level and in the respective national systems.'[148] It is arguable that 'the general legal consequences of acts of State under international law, such as the personal and functional immunity of State officials from the jurisdiction of foreign courts or State immunity, may be denied if the acts in question constitute genocide or other breaches of *jus cogens* obligations.'[149]

Thirdly, recent national and international jurisprudence supports the assertion that an entitlement to prosecute emanates from the *jus cogens* character of international crimes. The first court to make such a finding explicitly was the ICTY in *Furundžija* (1998), concerning torture as a war crime.[150] The Trial Chamber noted that this *jus cogens* prohibition is designed to produce a deterrent effect, in that it signals to all members of the international community and the individuals over whom they wield authority that the prohibition of torture is an absolute value from which nobody must deviate. The Tribunal further held that 'at the individual level, that is, that of criminal liability, it would seem that one of the consequences of the *jus cogens* character bestowed by the international community upon the prohibition of torture is that every State is entitled to investigate, prosecute and punish or extradite individuals accused of torture, who are present in a territory under its jurisdiction.'[151]

In *Pinochet III* (1999), Lord Hope opined that the status of a norm of *jus cogens* 'compels all states to refrain from such conduct under any circumstances and imposes an obligation *erga omnes* to punish such conduct.'[152] The American Court of Human Rights held on similar grounds in *Barrios Altos* (2001) that the protection of non-derogable rights entailed a duty to investigate and prosecute

---

148 UN Doc. A/CN.4/453/Add.2, 8 June 1993, at 29, para. 50.

149 See Stefan Talmon, "The Duty Not to 'Recognise as Lawful' a Situation Created by the Illegal Use of Force or Other Serious Breaches of a *Jus Cogens* Obligation: An Obligation without Real Substance?", in Tomuschat and Thouvenin (eds.), *supra* n. 128, at 118.

150 *Furundžija*, ICTY, Trial Chamber II, Judgment of 10 December 1998, Case No. IT-95-17/1-T; 39 *ILM* (1999), para. 156.

151 *Idem.*

152 *R* v. *Bow Street Metropolitan Stipendiary Magistrate*, ex parte *Pinochet Ugarte*, United Kingdom, House of Lords Judgment of 24 March 1999, 2 *WLR* 827 (HL 1999); [1999] 2 *All ER* 97, *per* Lord Hope.

these crimes.[153] In *Kallon and Kamara* (2004), the Special Court for Sierra Leone concluded that 'a state cannot sweep such crimes into oblivion and forgetfulness which others have jurisdiction to prosecute by reason of the fact that obligation to protect human dignity is a peremptory norm and has assumed the nature of obligation *erga omnes*.'[154] Finally, in the *Scilingo* case (2005), the Spanish National Court found that the *jus cogens* prohibition of crimes against humanity entails an *erga omnes* authorization on all States to repress such crimes.[155] However, whether jurisdictional consequences of the hierarchically superior status of *jus cogens* crimes override any conflicting impediments remains a controversial and not fully coherent proposition.[156]

To summarise, the following features would appear to characterise an international crime:

- It is a norm of such a fundamental character that its violation attracts the criminal responsibility of individuals
- Individual criminal liability exists at international law
- The act is universally recognised as criminal and is considered a grave matter of international concern, i.e., it is recognised under customary law
- The enforcement of this norm requires universal jurisdiction because it is not sufficient to leave it to the forum of primary jurisdiction
- Such an act endangers international relations (peace and security). In this sense, the exercise of jurisdiction is not just for prosecution's sake, but to fulfil the broader objectives of contributing to international peace and security
- The act breaches a moral obligation fixed by international law
- There is a collective responsibility to enforce such rules
- International crimes are violations of *jus cogens* norms

In this book, it is posited that war crimes (encompassing grave breaches of the Geneva Conventions of 1949 and other serious violations of the laws and customs of war), crimes against humanity, genocide and torture have all these features, which has specific consequences in terms of the exercise of jurisdiction.[157] This does not exclude that other offences such as piracy – which has in recent years re-surfaced as a crime of international concern[158]–, international terrorism – which may be the subject of a comprehensive United Nations convention in the near

---

153 *Barrios Altos (Chumbipuma Aguirre and others* v. *Peru)*, IACtHR (ser. C) (2001), paras. 41-44

154 *Kallon, Morris and Kamara, Brima Bazzy*, SCSL, Appeals Chamber Decision on Challenge to Jurisdiction: Lomé Accord Amnesty, 13 March 2004, Case No. SCSL-2004-15-AR72(E), para. 71.

155 *Scilingo, Adolfo*, Spain, Third Section of the Criminal Division (*Audiencia Nacional*), Judgment no. 16/2005 of 19 April 2005, *Sentencia por crímenes contra la humanidad en el caso Adolpho Scilingo*, available at: <http://www.derechos.org/nizkor/espana/juicioral/doc/sentencia.html>, at 83.

156 See further, Chapters 2 and 5, in this volume.

157 See also Ryngaert, *Jurisdiction in International Law*, at 115-127.

158 See, e.g., Eugene Kontorovich, "International Legal Reponses to Piracy off the Coast of Somalia", 13(2) *ASIL Insights* (6 February 2009).

future[159] –, and enforced disappearances – now criminalised in an international treaty not yet in force[160] – may also eventually come to be added to this list.

1.4.1 War crimes

War crimes encompass grave breaches of the Geneva Conventions of 1949 and other serious violations of the laws and customs of war. Under treaty law, universal jurisdiction is provided for by the grave breaches regime of the Geneva Conventions of 1949 and Additional Protocol I.

1.4.1.1 *Grave breaches*

Articles 50/51/130/147 of the four Geneva Conventions respectively define the conduct constituting grave breaches of the Conventions. Offences amounting to grave breaches include wilful killing, torture or inhuman treatment, and wilfully causing great suffering or serious injury to body or health to persons protected by the Conventions. Universal jurisdiction over 'grave breaches' of the Geneva Conventions of 1949 and Additional Protocol I is provided for under the terms of the treaties.[161] States parties to the four Geneva Conventions of 1949 are obliged 'to enact any legislation necessary to provide effective penal sanctions for persons committing, or ordering to be committed, any of the grave breaches of the present Convention' and 'to search for persons alleged to have committed, or to have ordered to be committed, such grave breaches, and shall bring such persons,

[159] Some commentators have argued that international terrorism may already be a crime under international customary law. See, e.g., Antonio Cassese, *International Criminal Law* (Oxford: OUP, 2003), at 129. Some support for this position may be found in the Restatement (Third) of the Foreign Relations Law of the United States, which takes the position that universal jurisdiction crimes include certain acts of terrorism. Restatement (Third) of the Foreign Relations Law of the United States, § 404 (1986). In addition, a large number of General Assembly resolutions have condemned as criminal all acts, means and practices of terrorism. See, e.g., UN GA Res. 40/61, 9 December 1985, para. 1; UN GA Res. 44/29, 4 December 1989, para. 1; UN GA Res. 42/159, 7 December 1987; UN GA Res. 46/51, 27 January 1992; UN GA Res. 49/60, 9 December 1994; UN GA Res. 51/210, 17 December 1996. The UN Security Council has repeatedly characterised acts of terrorism as a threat to international peace and security, and in UN SC Res. 1373 (2001) provided (at para. 2(e)) that all States have a duty to enact legislation criminalising certain acts of terrorism. Other commentators maintain, however, that 'there is insufficient evidence of State practice and *opinio juris* supporting a customary international definition or crime of terrorism.' Ben Saul, *Defining Terrorism in International Law* (Oxford: OUP, 2008), at 319.

[160] International Convention for the Protection of All Persons from Enforced Disappearances (2006). As of writing, there are 10 parties and 81 signatories to this Convention. Art. 39 of the Convention specifies that, in order to enter into force, at least 20 ratifications or accessions are required.

[161] Art. 85 of the Protocol Additional to the Geneva Conventions of 12 August 1949, and Relating to the Protection of Victims of International Armed Conflicts of 8 June 1977 (hereafter, Additional Protocol I) expands the list of grave breaches to include serious violations of the laws and customs of war (sometimes referred to as 'Hague Law'), when committed wilfully, in violation of the relevant provisions of Protocol I, and causing death or serious injury to body or health.

regardless of their nationality, before its own courts' or 'if it prefers, and in accordance with the provisions of its own legislation' extradite to another State party.[162]

Article 85(1) of Additional Protocol I states that the provisions of the Geneva Conventions relating to the repression of breaches and grave breaches, supplemented by Protocol I, apply equally to the repression of breaches and grave breaches of Protocol I. Article 86 of Protocol I reaffirms State Parties' obligation to repress grave breaches, and adds that States must take measures necessary to suppress all other breaches of the Conventions or of Protocol I which result from a failure to act when under a duty to do so. The ICRC Commentary to the Geneva Conventions states that the obligation to extradite or prosecute in regard to grave breaches is 'absolute.'[163] This conclusion is supported by the fact that States Parties are unable to absolve themselves or any other State Party of any liability incurred in respect of grave breaches.[164] While in the Commentary's view, the latter provision is 'intended to prevent the vanquished from being compelled in an armistice agreement or a peace treaty to renounce all compensation due for breaches committed by persons in the service of the victor,'[165] one may also interpret this provision as preventing States from avoiding their obligation to prosecute those accused of grave breaches, as far as this may form part of war reparations.[166] States party to the instruments must also *suppress* all other violations. Although the obligation to suppress violations does not require the adoption of criminal legislation, States are able to take whatever legislative, administrative or disciplinary measures are deemed appropriate.[167]

As mentioned earlier, on the basis of the universal ratification of the Geneva Conventions[168] and the widespread occurrence of implementing legislation enacted by States around the world,[169] it can be confidently stated that the obligation

---

[162] Arts. 49/50/129/146 common to the four Geneva Conventions of 1949.

[163] J. Pictet (ed.), *Commentary to Geneva Convention IV of 1949*, ICRC, Geneva (hereafter, *Commentary to Geneva Convention IV*) at 602. Furthermore, the Commentary states that: 'The universality of jurisdiction for grave breaches is some basis for the hope that they will not remain unpunished and the obligation to extradite ensures the universality of punishment.' *Ibid.*, at 587.

[164] Arts. 51/52/131/148 common to the four Geneva Conventions of 1949.

[165] *Commentary to Geneva Convention IV*, at 603.

[166] The *Commentary, ibid.*, continues, 'As the law stands today … [o]nly a State can make such claims on another State, and they form part, in general, of what is called "war reparations."' Principle 15 of the "Revised set of basic principles and guidelines on the right to reparation for victims of gross violations of human rights and humanitarian law" proposes that judicial or administrative sanctions or 'a judicial decision restoring the dignity, reputation and legal rights of the victim and/or of persons connected with the victim' may constitute satisfaction as part of reparations. Annex to Sub-Commission on Prevention of Discrimination and Protection of Minorities, Revised set of basic principles and guidelines on the right to reparation for victims of gross violations of human rights and humanitarian law prepared by Mr. Theo van Boven pursuant to Sub-Commission Decision 1995/117, UN Doc. E/CN.4/Sub.2/1996/17, 24 May 1996.

[167] Anna Segall, *Punishing Violations of International Humanitarian Law at the National Level: A Guide for Common Law States* (Geneva: ICRC, 2001), at 30-38.

[168] As of 25 August 2003 there are 203 State Parties to the Geneva Conventions of 1949.

[169] See the ICRC Advisory Service compilation of national implementation mechanisms of international humanitarian law, available at: <http://www.gva.icrc.org/ihl-nat>.

to prosecute or extradite persons accused of grave breaches, as enumerated in the Geneva Conventions, is a customary rule of international law.[170] While State practice has been fairly scant in terms of prosecutions, a number of countries have legislation providing for extra-territorial jurisdiction over grave breaches committed during the course of WW II (often a nexus to the prosecuting State is still required). Some countries provide for universal jurisdiction over all war crimes. Such legislation has become more prevalent since States began adopting or amending legislation pursuant to their implementation of the Rome Statute.

1.4.1.2 *Serious violations of the laws and customs of war*

Serious violations of the laws and customs of war refer primarily to rules deriving from Hague Convention IV of 1907 and its Regulations, some of which are included in the extended list of grave breaches in Article 85 of Additional Protocol I, as well as serious violations of Article 3 common to the Geneva Conventions of 1949 and of Additional Protocol II. Although these instruments do not by their terms provide for a system of repression,[171] State practice and *opinio juris* have evolved in recent years to recognise a customary entitlement to exercise universal jurisdiction over these crimes.[172]

The Hague Conventions and Regulations contain no provision dealing with individual responsibility for violations of the rules contained therein, nor do they specify a duty for States Parties to prosecute those who have breached even the most serious of the laws.[173] Nevertheless, the International Military Tribunal at Nuremburg found no obstacle to attaching individual criminal responsibility to serious violations of these laws, noting that: '[c]rimes against international law are committed by men, not by abstract entities, and only by punishing individuals

[170] Interestingly, the ICRC Study on Customary International Law does not specifically confirm this as a rule of customary international law. Instead, it finds that the more general principle that 'States have the right to vest universal jurisdiction in their national courts over war crimes' is a rule of customary international law. See Jean-Marie Henckaerts and Louise Doswald-Beck, *Customary International Humanitarian Law*, Vol. I. (Cambridge: CUP, 2005), Rule 157, at 604. Rule 158 sets down a more affirmative obligation which the Study finds as applicable in both international armed conflicts and non-international armed conflicts: 'States must investigate war crimes allegedly committed by their nationals or armed forces, or on their territory, and, if appropriate, prosecute the suspects. They must also investigate other war crimes over which they have jurisdiction and, if appropriate, prosecute the suspects.' *Ibid.*, at 607.

[171] Although Additional Protocol I extends the list of grave breaches (and hence the system of grave breaches) to other serious violations of the laws and customs of war when committed wilfully and with the result of causing death or serious injury (Art. 85(3)), the customary character of these rules remains in dispute.

[172] Jean-Marie Henckaerts and Louise Doswald-Beck, *Customary International Humanitarian Law*, Vol. I. (Cambridge: CUP, 2005), Rule 157, at 604 ('States have the right to vest universal jurisdiction in their national courts over war crimes'). Rule 156 finds a customary rule that 'Serious violations of international humanitarian law constitute war crimes.' *Ibid.*, at 568.

[173] Art. 3 of Hague Convention IV concerning the Laws and Customs of War of 1907 does, however, specify a duty for the State to pay compensation for violations committed by persons in its armed forces.

who commit such crimes can the provisions of international law be enforced.'[174] The Statute of the ICTY provides for jurisdiction over 'violations of the laws and customs of war.'[175] During the negotiations on war crimes at Rome for the Statute of the International Criminal Court, there was no disagreement that the norms laid down in the Hague Conventions and Regulations gave rise to individual criminal responsibility under customary international law.[176] This was not, however, the case for the extended list of grave breaches laid down in Additional Protocol I.[177] Nonetheless, with the inclusion of the bulk of serious violations of the laws and customs of war in the authoritative list of 'war crimes' in the jurisdiction of the International Criminal Court,[178] one may definitively attest that there exists at least a universal permissive right to prosecute those accused of these crimes under customary international law.[179]

Serious violations of common Article 3 to the Geneva Conventions and other serious violations of the laws and customs of war committed in non-international armed conflict have traditionally not been considered criminal offences attracting universal jurisdiction or a duty to prosecute and punish under international law.[180] Neither common Article 3 of the Geneva Conventions nor Additional Protocol II contains provisions on grave breaches or enforcement. However, recent developments in the law, largely in response to the atrocities committed in the former Yugoslavia and Rwanda during the armed conflicts which took place in

---

[174] Trial of the Major War Criminals before the International Military Tribunal, Nuremburg, 14 November 1945-1 October 1946, Official Documents 223 (1947), reprinted in the 41 *American Journal of International Law* (1947), at 220-221.

[175] Statute of the International Tribunal for the Prosecution of Persons Responsible for serious Violations of International Humanitarian Law Committed in the Territory of the Former Yugoslavia Since 1991, UN Security Council Res. 827 (1993), UN Doc. S/RES/827, 25 May 1993 (hereafter, ICTY Statute), Art. 3.

[176] See 1995 Ad Hoc Committee Report, para. 74 and 1996 PrepCom Report, Vol. I, para. 81.

[177] During the negotiations at Rome over the list of war crimes to be included in the Statute of the International Criminal Court, States strongly disagreed on the customary status of Additional Protocol I. See 1995 Ad Hoc Committee Report, para. 74 and 1996 PrepCom Report, Vol. I, para. 81, cited in R.S. Lee (ed.), *The International Criminal Court: The Making of the Rome Statute, Issues, Negotiations, Results* (The Hague: Kluwer Law International, 1999), at 104.

[178] Some norms were deleted from the Statute on the basis that a violation of the rule was not serious enough to come before the Court. For example, the prohibition of 'unjustifiable delay in the repatriation of prisoners of war or civilians' which is a grave breach under Art. 84(4)(b) of Additional Protocol I. See 1995 Ad Hoc Committee Report, para. 72 and 1996 PrepCom Report Vol. I, para. 74, at 104.

[179] See 1995 Ad Hoc Committee Report, para. 74 and 1996 PrepCom Report, Vol. I, para. 81.

[180] D. Plattner, "The Penal Repression of Violations of International Humanitarian Law Applicable in Non-International Armed Conflict", 30 *IRRC* 414 (1990). However, there are some historical examples of war crimes prosecutions for offences of the laws and customs of war committed in internal conflicts. For instance, Captain Henry Wirz was prosecuted and found guilty of war crimes perpetrated in the prisoner of war camp of which he was in charge during the American Civil War. H.S. Levie (ed.), *Documents on Prisoners of War* (Newport, Rhode Island: United States Naval War College, 1979), at 46-56.

the early 1990s, have undoubtedly challenged this position.[181] The International Criminal Tribunal for Rwanda (ICTR) was specifically given the subject matter jurisdiction over serious violations of common Article 3 and Additional Protocol II.[182] Although the ICTY was not given the same specific competence, the Tribunal decided in the *Tadić* case that customary international law imposes criminal liability for serious violations of common Article 3 and that it had jurisdiction over such violations.[183] However, as both these courts are international in character and have been specifically assigned jurisdiction over certain offences in their Statutes, it does not automatically follow that the recognition of serious violations of common Article 3 as an international crime by the ICTY means that domestic courts can exercise universal jurisdiction over such offences. In fact, the basis for the jurisdiction of these *ad hoc* tribunals may be more easily ascribed to the principle of territoriality, rather than universality, given the respective geographic focus of the two tribunals.

Nonetheless, there is additional support for the notion that universal jurisdiction may be exercised over serious violations of common Article 3 and Additional Protocol II. One argument is that the fact that the obligations in common Article 3 and AP II are addressed to parties to the conflict 'is not dispositive of the penal responsibility of individuals, if individuals clearly must carry out that obligation.'[184] Moreover, since common Article 3 clearly prohibits fundamental offences such as murder and torture, that means that such acts 'were intended to be criminalised in 1949, as they were clearly intended to be illegal within the international legal order.'[185] The Rome Statute provides for jurisdiction over serious violations of the rules applicable in internal armed conflicts.[186] These rules are derived from a range of sources including the Hague Regulations, the Geneva Conventions and Additional Protocol II. The inclusion of most of the 'Hague' rules in Article 8(2)(e) reflects the view that these norms are also applicable in non-international conflicts. Most of the provisions in section (e) also find support in Additional Protocol II. Given the complementarity principle enshrined in the Rome Statute, one may assume that domestic courts would also have jurisdiction over these offences once enabling legislation has been passed which provides for domestic jurisdiction over war crimes in the Rome Statute. Dutch courts have prosecuted serious

[181] Thomas Graditzky, "Individual Criminal Responsibility for Violations of International Humanitarian Law Committed in Non-International Armed Conflicts", 322 *IRRC* 29-56 (1998); Theodor Meron, "International Criminalization of Internal Atrocities", 89 *AJIL* 554 (1995). The ICJ in the *Nicaragua* case in 1986 noted the customary character of common Art. 3 of the Geneva Conventions. *Military and Paramilitary Actitivies in and against Nicaragua (Nicaragua* v. *United States of America)*, Merits, Judgment of 27 June 1986, ICJ Reports 1986, at 114, para. 220.

[182] ICTR Statute, Art. 4, Annex to Security Council Res. 955 (1994), S/RES/955 (1994), 8 November 1994.

[183] *Prosecutor* v. *Dusko Tadić*, ICTY Appeals Chamber, Judgment, 2 October 1995, para. 137, 35 *ILM* 32 (1996).

[184] Meron, "International criminalization of internal atrocities", at 562.

[185] *Delalić and others* (*Čelebići* case), ICTY, Appeals Chamber, Judgment of 20 February 2001, Case No. IT-96-21-A, para. 163.

[186] ICC Statute, Art. 8(2)(c) and (e).

violations of common Article 3 as war crimes in relation to the torture of civilians by the Soviet-backed government's Intelligence Unit in Afghanistan during the Afghan Civil War.[187] Other national courts have also relied upon customary universal jurisdiction to prosecute persons accused of war crimes in non-international armed conflicts.[188]

It is also worth noting that the Special Court for Sierra Leone, dealing with the civil war in that country, was given jurisdiction over serious violations of common Article 3 as well as three types of 'serious violations of international humanitarian law' that had no basis in conventional law.[189] In a decision of the Special Court in the *Norman* case, it held that one of these rules (the prohibition of recruiting child soldiers) had crystallised into a rule of customary law prior to 1996, thereby fulfilling the principle of legality in terms of the jurisdiction of the Court to examine this crime.[190]

1.4.2 **Crimes against humanity**

Crimes against humanity refer to particularly odious offences constituting serious attacks on human dignity of one or more human beings, as part of a widespread or systematic practice of atrocities tolerated, condoned, or acquiesced by a State or de facto authority, perpetrated against civilians,[191] whether in time of war or peace. The 1998 Rome Statute defines the crime as a number of acts including murder,

[187] The two judgments of The Hague District Court were issued on 9 February and 13 February 2005 respectively. For a comment (critical of the Court's recognition of universal jurisdiction over violations of common Art. 3), see Guénaël Mettraux, "Dutch Courts' Universal Jurisdiction over Violations of Common Article 3 *qua* War Crimes", 4(2) *JICJ* (2006), at 362-371.

[188] See, e.g., "Butare Four Case", Belgium, Cour d'Assises de l'Arrondissement Administratif de Bruxelles-Capitales, 8 June 2001, available at: <http://www.asf.be/AssisesRwanda2/fr/fr_VERDICT_verdict.htm>. See Luc Reydam, "Belgium's First Application of Universal Jurisdiction: The Butare Four Case", *JICJ* 1 (2002); *Niyonteze*, Switzerland, *Tribunal Militaire de Division* 2, Lausanne, Judgment of 30 April 1999.

[189] SCSL Statute, Art. 4: 'a. Intentionally directing attacks against the civilian population as such or against individual civilians not taking direct part in hostilities; b. Intentionally directing attacks against personnel, installations, material, units or vehicles involved in a humanitarian assistance or peacekeeping mission in accordance with the Charter of the United Nations, as long as they are entitled to the protection given to civilians or civilian objects under the international law of armed conflict; c. Conscripting or enlisting children under the age of 15 years into armed forces or groups or using them to participate actively in hostilities.'

[190] *Norman, Sam Hinga*, SCSL, Case No. SCSL-2003-14-AR72(E), Decision on Preliminary Motion based on Lack of Jurisdiction (Child Recruitment), 31 May 2004.

[191] Some disagreement exists as to whether enemy combatants not or no longer taking part in hostilities and those *hors de combat* may also be the victims of crimes against humanity. The ICC Statute, ICTY Statute and ICTR Statute define the crime as only directed against civilians. Cassese has argued that this may be an undue restriction on the customary scope of the crime. See Cassese, *International Criminal Law*, at 64. In *Mrškić*, the ICTY Appeals Chamber authoritatively held that so long as an attack is directed against a 'civilian population,' there is no requirement nor is it an element of crimes against humanity that the victims of the underlying crimes be 'civilians.' *Mrškić*, ICTY, Appeals Chamber, Case No. IT-95-13/1-A, Judgment of 5 May 2009, para. 32.

torture and persecution 'when committed as part of a widespread or systematic attack directed against any civilian population, with knowledge of the attack.'[192]

There is no convention that specifically requires States parties to criminalise or to prosecute or extradite alleged offenders of crimes against humanity. However, it is commonly contended that crimes against humanity attract universal jurisdiction under international law.[193] Historically, the origin for calls for the prosecution of the authors of these types of crimes may be traced to the joint declaration of the French, British and Russian Governments on 18 May 1915 in response to the mass killings of Armenians in the Ottoman Empire, which stated:

> 'In view of these new crimes of Turkey against humanity and civilization, the Allied governments announce publicly to the Sublime Porte that they will hold personally responsible [for] these crimes all members of the Ottoman Government and those of their agents who are implicated in such massacres.'

The original proposal from the Russian Foreign Minister Sazanov was the expression 'crimes against Christianity and civilisation.' However, the French Foreign Minister Delcassé rejected this language, fearing a negative response from the Muslim populations under French and British colonial dominion. Thus, he proposed the words 'crimes against humanity' and this term was accepted by the British and Russian Ministers.[194] Although an attempt was made to get the Ottoman Government to hand over alleged perpetrators of these crimes by the terms of the 1920 Peace Treaty of Sèvres (the Allies reserving the right to 'designate' the tribunal which would try them), this Treaty was never ratified and its replacement, the Peace Treaty of Lausanne, of 24 July 1923, provided for a complete amnesty for crimes committed between 1914 and 1922.

In the aftermath of WW I, the Commission on the Responsibility of the Authors of the War and on the Enforcement of Penalties proposed in its report to the Versailles Conference that an international criminal tribunal be set up with jurisdiction

---

[192] Art. 7 ICC Statute. The other acts enumerated are extermination; enslavement; deportation or forcible transfer of population; imprisonment or other severe deprivation of physical liberty in violation of fundamental rules of international law; rape, sexual slavery, enforced prostitution, forced pregnancy, enforced sterilisation, or any other form of sexual violence of comparable gravity; enforced disappearance of persons; apartheid; or any other inhumane acts of a similar character intentionally causing great suffering, or serious injury to body or to mental or physical health.

[193] See, e.g., Christian Tomuschat, "Universal Criminal Jurisdiction with Respect to the Crime of Genocide, Crimes against Humanity and War Crimes", *Annuaire de l'Institut de Droit International*, 71, 1 (2005), 213-388; Christopher A. Amerasinghe, "The Domestic Tribunals' Universal Jurisdiction for War Crimes and Crimes against Humanity: from *Finta* to today", in *La voie vers la Cour Pénale Internationale : tous les chemins mènent à Rome : les Journées Maximilien-Caron 2003 : all roads lead to Rome* (Montréal: Thémis, 2004), at 491; Christopher Keith Hall, "Universal jurisdiction: new uses for an old tool", in Mark Lattimer and Phillipe Sands QC (eds.), *Justice for Crimes Against Humanity* (Oxford/Portland: Hart Publishing, 2003), at 47; John Dugard, "Universal jurisdiction for crimes against humanity", *Africa Legal Aid Quarterly* (April-June 2000), at 7-9.

[194] Cassese, *International Criminal Law*, at 67, citing the Russian despatch of 11 May 1915, published in A. Beylerian, *Les Grandes Puissances, l'Empire Ottoman et les Arméniens dans les archives françaises (1914-1918) – Recueil de documents* (Paris, 1983), at 23 (doc. No. 29).

over 'offences against the laws of humanity.'[195] This language derived from the preamble of the 1907 Hague Convention IV, which laid down the rule commonly known as the Martens Clause whereby 'in cases not included in the Regulations adopted by them, the inhabitants and the belligerents remain under the protection and the rule of the principles of the law of nations, as they result from the usages established among civilized peoples, from the *laws of humanity*, and the dictates of the public conscience.'[196] However, the representatives of the Unites States, Robert Lansing and James Brown Scott strongly disagreed with this idea, arguing that the 'laws and principles of humanity are not certain, varying with time, place and circumstance, and according, as it may be, to the conscience of the individual judge. There is no fixed and universal standard of humanity.'[197] The Americans felt that this 'if for no other reason, should exclude them from consideration in a court of justice, especially one charged with the administration of criminal law.'[198] As a result of this opposition, crimes against humanity did not figure in the final proposals.

The atrocious crimes committed systematically on massive scale against civilians by the Nazis and collaborators before and during WW II prompted renewed calls for the prosecution of crimes which went beyond the laws of warfare, which only proscribed violations involving the adversary or enemy populations. The crimes committed by the Germans were perpetrated against their own citizens – mainly Jews, but also trade union members, social democrats, communists, gypsies and members of the church – as well as other persons not protected under the law of armed conflict.[199] Such acts as mere persecution for political or racial purposes were similarly not prohibited under the laws of war even when directed against civilians of occupied territories. Thus, the London Agreement embodying the Charter of the IMT included for the first time in positive international law a provision to punish persons found guilty of 'crimes against humanity,' defined as:

> 'murder, extermination, enslavement, deportation, and other inhumane acts committed against any civilian population, before or during the war, or persecution on political, racial or religious grounds in execution of or in connexion with any crimes within the jurisdiction of the Tribunal [i.e. crimes against peace or war crimes], whether or not in violation of the domestic law of the country where perpetrated.'[200]

---

[195] "Report presented to the preliminary Peace Conference by the Commission on the Responsibility of the Authors of the War and on the Enforcement of Penalties", in Carnegie Endowment for International Peace, Division of International Law, Pamphlet No. 32, *Violations of the Laws and Customs of War, Report of the Majority and Dissenting Reports of American and Japanese Members of the Commission of Responsibilities, Conference of Paris 1919* (Oxford: Clarendon Press, 1919), at 25-6.

[196] Convention (IV) respecting the Laws and Customs of War on Land and its annex: Regulations concerning the Laws and Customs of War on Land. The Hague, 18 October 1907, preamble. [Emphasis added]

[197] *Supra* n. 195, at 73.

[198] *Ibid.*, at 64.

[199] E.g, citizens of the Allies (France), nationals of States not formally under German occupation (Austria, Czechoslovakia), stateless Jews and gypsies.

[200] The Charter of the International Military Tribunal (IMT), annexed to the London Agreement for the Prosecution and Punishment of Major War Criminals of the European Axis, of 8 August 1945, Art. 6(c).

Given that crimes against humanity could only be prosecuted when committed in connection with crimes against peace or war crimes, this effectively limited the offence to the context of a war.[201] As has been pointed out, this meant that only those criminal activities which 'directly affected the interests of other States were punished,'[202] indicating that 'in 1945 the Allies did not feel that they should "legislate" in such a way as to prohibit inhuman acts regardless of their consequences or implications for third States.'[203] Nonetheless, more universal acceptance and understanding of this category of international crime was forthcoming when on 13 February 1946, the UN GA passed resolution 3(1) recommending the extradition and punishment of persons accused of crimes provided for in the Nuremberg Charter, although the resolution only foresaw the actual prosecution in the territories where the offences occurred (i.e., on the basis of territorial jurisdiction).[204] Later in the same year, the UN GA unanimously adopted a resolution affirming the principles of the IMT Charter and its judgment.[205] A number of Peace Treaties with Italy, Romania, Hungary, Bulgaria and Finland also provided terms for the punishment of the crimes in the IMT Charter.[206] The Nuremburg Charter was subsequently codified by the International Law Commission in 1950,[207] thereby further developing the customary legal basis for prosecutions of this crime.

The need for a nexus between the commission of crimes against humanity and a war context was dropped as early as 20 December 1945 when the four victorious Powers passed Control Council Law No. 10 and this was confirmed in subsequent

[201] The IMT stated that '[t]o constitute crimes against humanity, the acts relied on before the outbreak of war must have been in execution of, or in connection with, any crime within the jurisdiction of the Tribunal. The Tribunal is of the opinion that revolting and horrible as many of these crimes were, it has not been satisfactorily proved that they were done in execution of, or in connection with, any such crime. The Tribunal therefore cannot make a general declaration that the acts before 1939 were crimes against humanity within the meaning of the Charter', Judgement of the International Military Tribunal for the Trial of German Major War Criminals, Nuremberg, 30 September and 1 October, 1946, London, His Majesty's Office, Cmd. 6964, reprinted in *Trial of German Major War Criminals* (Buffalo/New York: William S. Hein & Co., Inc., 2001), at 65.

[202] E. Schwelb, "Crimes Against Humanity", 23 *BYIL* (1946), at 207.

[203] Cassese, *International Criminal Law*, at 69.

[204] UN GA Res. 3(1), of 13 February 1946. The preamble takes note of the definition of war crimes and crimes against peace and against humanity contained in the Charter of the IMT dated 8 August 1945 and recommends 'that Members of the United Nations forthwith take all the necessary measures to cause the arrest of those war criminals who have been responsible for or have taken a consenting part in the above crimes, and to cause them to be sent back to the countries in which the abominable deeds were done, in order that they may be judged and punished according to the laws of those countries.'

[205] UN GA Res. 95(I), of 11 December 1946. In this resolution, the GA directs the committee on the codification of international law established by a resolution of the same day (94(I)) to 'treat as a matter of general importance plans for the formulation, in the context of a general codification against the peace and security of mankind, or of an International Criminal Code, of the principles recognized in the Charter of the Nürnberg Tribunal and in the judgment of the Tribunal.'

[206] E.g., Art. 45 of the Peace Treaty with Italy, Art. 6 of the Treaty with Romania, and Art. 5 of the Peace Treaty with Bulgaria.

[207] International Law Commission Report on Principles of the Nuremburg Tribunal, 29 July 1950, 5 UN GAOR Suppl. (No. 12), at 11, UN Doc. A/1316 (1950).

proceedings before the military tribunals in the respective occupied zones.[208] Several States have national legislation providing for the prosecution of crimes against humanity without the nexus to war.[209] The Secretary-General of the United Nations in his report accompanying the draft Statute of the ICTY also made clear that crimes against humanity do not require a nexus to war.[210] The ICC Statute does not require any connection to war in its jurisdiction over crimes against humanity.[211]

The adoption of the Convention on the Non-Applicability of Statutory Limitations to War Crimes and Crimes against Humanity by the UN General Assembly on 26 November 1968 signified an important legal development for crimes against humanity 'whether committed in time of war or time of peace,'[212] since the Convention defines the crime, adding a number of specific acts to the definition provided in the IMT Charter to include genocide as well as modern manifestations of the crime,[213] and by requiring States parties to abrogate any legislation providing a

---

[208] See, e.g., *Ohlendorf and others* (*Einsatzgruppen* case), United States, US Military Tribunal sitting at Nuremberg, Judgment of 10 April 1948, in *TWC*, Vol. 4, at 3-596, 1 Official Documents 223 (1947), reprinted in 41 *AJIL* 49 (1947); *Altstötter and others* (*Justice* case), US Military Tribunal sitting at Nuremberg, Judgment of 4 December 1947, in *TWC*, Vol. 3, 954-1201 at 974. But see *Flick and others*, US Military Tribunal sitting at Nuremberg, Judgment of 22 December 1947, *TWC*, Vol. 6, 1187-1223 at 1213 and the *Ministries* case (*Weizaecker*), United States, US Military Tribunal sitting at Nuremberg, Decision of 12 December 1949, in *TWC*, Vols. 12-14, at 308-942; Case No. 11, XIII CCL Trials (1948), at 112.

[209] E.g., Canada (Criminal Code, Section 7(3.71), Israel (Nazi and Nazi Collaborators (Punishment) Law, 1 August 1950, 4 LSI, No. 64, at 154), Germany (Criminal Code, Art. 212), France (Criminal Code, Art. 212-1), Belgium (Act Concerning the Punishment of Serious Violations of International Humanitarian Law, as amended, Section 7) and Switzerland (see Christian Favre, Marc Pellet and Patrick Stoudmann, Code Penal Annote (1997)).

[210] This is despite the fact that Art. 5 of the Statute of the ICTY provides in relation to crimes against humanity that the tribunal 'shall have the power to prosecute persons responsible for the following crimes *when committed in armed conflict* whether international or internal in character, and directed against any civilian population' [emphasis added]. It is possible to read the Article merely as a jurisdictional limitation on the tribunal rather than as part of the definition. See D. Orentlicher, "Yugoslavia War Crimes Tribunal", 1 *ASIL Focus* (1993) and T. Meron, "War Crimes in Yugoslavia and the Development of International Law", 88 *AJIL* 78 (1994).

[211] ICC Statute, Art. 7.

[212] The Convention on the Non-Applicability of Statutory Limitations to War Crimes and Crimes Against Humanity was adopted by UN GA Res. 2391 (XXIII) of 26 November 1968. It entered into force on 11 November 1970. As of July 2009, there are 53 States parties to the Convention.

[213] Art. I of the Convention provides: 'No statutory limitation shall apply to the following crimes, irrespective of the date of their commission: … (b) Crimes against humanity whether committed in time of war or in time of peace as they are defined in the Charter of the International Military Tribunal, Nurnberg, of 8 August 1945 and confirmed by resolutions 3 (I) of 13 February 196 and 95 (I) of 11 December 1946 of the General Assembly of the United Nations, *eviction by armed attack or occupation* and *inhuman acts* resulting from the policy of *apartheid*, and the crime of *genocide* as defined in the 1948 Convention on the Prevention and Punishment of the Crime of Genocide, even if such acts do not constitute a violation of the domestic law of the country in which they were committed' [emphasis added]. The Arab States wished to include in the convention a reference to the crimes against humanity which they said had occurred as a result of the occupation of Arab territories in the Middle East by Israel. See UN Doc. A/C.3/SR/1523, at 319, *per* the Iraqi delegate. The African-Asian States wanted to include inhuman acts resulting from the policy of apartheid, as a modern type of crime against humanity. See UN Doc. A/C.3.SR/1547, at 473 for the statement of the representative of Somalia.

statute of limitations over these crimes. Article 3 of the Convention requires State parties to take all necessary measures, legislative or otherwise, to make extradition of persons accused of such crimes possible, while Article 4 stipulates that the States Parties to the Convention shall adopt any legislative or other measures necessary to ensure that statutory or other limitations shall not apply to the prosecution and punishment of such crimes.

However, it is difficult to infer universal jurisdiction over crimes against humanity from the provisions of this Convention, which was acrimoniously debated for four years before its adoption by the GA (58 votes in favour, 7 against, with 36 abstentions).[214] The Convention does not require the criminalisation of crimes against humanity at the national level or that States parties prosecute or extradite a person accused of such offences when found on their territory. It has been argued that the Convention 'by necessary implication' entails an obligation on States to prosecute war crimes and crimes against humanity by requiring States not to apply statutory limitations to such crimes.[215] However, at least one national court has ruled that the Convention does not by itself establish adjudicatory jurisdiction over crimes against humanity.[216]

If the Convention could be interpreted as implying a duty to prosecute crimes against humanity, this would probably only be with regards to the State where the crimes were committed. Although the Convention is concerned about ensuring that those accused of grave international crimes should not escape punishment by the expiry of statutory time limits, it does not extend this concern to an obligation to prosecute alleged offenders should they be found on a State party's territory. In fact, the emphasis would appear to be on ensuring that no obstacles to extradition to the country of primary jurisdiction (i.e., either the territorial State or State of nationality) are in place. As one commentator observed, 'the effectiveness of the convention depends on the real and practical possibility of bringing accused or condemned persons within the jurisdiction of the authorities competent to try them or enforce their sentences.'[217] The Convention does not incorporate an obligation to extradite on States parties – the decision is left to each particular State under Article 3. It simply obliges States parties to make sure that their legislation permits extradition.[218]

Five years after the adoption of the Convention, the General Assembly adopted the Principles of International Cooperation in the Detection, Arrest, Extradition, and Punishment of Persons Guilty of War Crimes and Crimes Against Humani-

---

[214] It is notable that more opposing votes were cast against the adoption of this convention than were voted in opposition to any prior international human rights instrument. Robert H. Miller, "The Convention on the Non-Applicability of Statutory Limitations to War Crimes and Crimes Against Humanity", 65 *AJIL* 478 (1971).

[215] John Dugard, "Possible Conflicts of Jurisdiction with Truth Commissions", in Antonio Cassese, Paola Gaeta and John R.W.D. Jones (eds.), *The Rome Statute of the International Criminal Court: A Commentary*, (Oxford: OUP, 2002), at 696.

[216] *Javor and others*, France, Cour de Cassation, 26 March 1996, in *Bull. crim.*, no. 132 1996.

[217] Miller, "The Convention on the Non-Applicability of Statutory Limitations", at 495.

[218] *Idem.*

ty.[219] The Principles establish a duty to prosecute, and indicate that 'crimes against humanity, wherever they are committed, shall be subject to investigation and the persons against whom there is evidence ... shall be subject to tracing, arrest, trial and, if found guilty, to punishment.'[220] The Draft Code of Crimes Against the Peace and Security of Mankind, adopted by the International Law Commission in 1996,[221] embodies an obligation to extradite or prosecute offenders of crimes against the peace and security of mankind,[222] which include crimes against humanity (adding torture and rape to the list of acts which may amount to such a crime). The Code makes clear that individuals who commit offences are liable to punishment,[223] and that individual responsibility does not preclude State responsibility.[224] While these two latter instruments are not binding on States, they nonetheless reflect the growing expectation of the international community that crimes against humanity entail judicial consequences for perpetrators and that States are primarily responsible for seeing this done. They could also be evidence of an *opinio juris* regarding the customary character of universal jurisdiction over crimes against humanity.

The Statutes of the ICTY and the ICTR both of which purport to apply only 'rules of international humanitarian law which are beyond doubt part of customary law' include crimes against humanity in their list of offences,[225] as does the Statute of the Special Court for Sierra Leone (Art. 2), the UNTAET Regulation 2000/15 establishing the Special Panels with jurisdiction over Serious Crimes in East Timor (Section 10) and the Law on the Establishment of the Extraordinary Chambers in the Courts of Cambodia for the Prosecution of Crimes Committed during the Period of Democratic Kampuchea (as amended) (Art. 5). The definition of crimes against humanity is slightly different in all these constitutive instruments.[226]

---

[219] Principles of International Cooperation in the Detection, Arrest, Extradition, and Punishment of Persons Guilty of War Crimes and Crimes Against Humanity, GA Res. 3074, 28 UN GAOR Suppl. (No. 12), at 11, UN Doc. A/9030 (1973).

[220] *Ibid.*, principle 1.

[221] Draft Articles on the Draft Code of Crimes Against the Peace and Security of Mankind, Report of the International Law Commission on the work of its Forty-Eighth Session, UN Doc. A/48/10, *Yearbook of the International Law Commission*, Vol. II(2) (1996). The offences falling within the scope of the Articles are the crime of aggression (Art. 16), the crime of genocide (Art. 17), crimes against humanity (Art. 18), crimes against United Nations and associated personnel (Art. 19), and war crimes (Art. 20).

[222] *Ibid.*, Art. 9.

[223] *Ibid.*, Art. 3.

[224] *Ibid.*, Art. 4.

[225] ICTY Statute Art. 5, ICTR Statute Art. 3.

[226] While the UNTAET Regulation repeats verbatim the definition in the ICC Statute (and states that the Special Panels exercise universal jurisdiction), the Sierra Leone Statute contains a slightly different version but with essentially the same elements. The SCSL Statute omits the words 'with knowledge of the attack' and provides a simpler explanation of persecution than the ICC Statute. The Law on the Extraordinary Chambers for Cambodia provides a more restricted definition, limiting the crime to those attacks committed against civilians 'on grounds of national, political, ethnical, racial or religious grounds,' as does the Statute of the ICTR. See *Bagilishema*, ICTR, Trial Chamber, Judgment of 7 June 2001, Case No. ICTR-95-1A-T, at para. 81: 'The Statute contains a requirement that, the broader attack must be conducted on national, political, ethnic, racial, or religious grounds. The

There have been a number of trials for crimes against humanity before national courts, although universal jurisdiction has often been bolstered by reliance on other bases of jurisdiction in conjunction, especially passive personality, or a territorial or nationality link by the fact that the alleged offender is a resident of the prosecuting country. The most well-known example of a national court relying on both universal and passive personality jurisdiction is the *Eichmann* case.[227] In the 1980s, the United States Court of Appeal for the 6th circuit accepted Israel's right to act on this basis in the *Demjanjuk* case.[228] In this instance, the Court allowed the extradition to Israel of a German concentration camp guard on the basis of universal jurisdiction, noting: 'international law does not generally prohibit the application of national laws over non citizens for acts committed outside its territory.' The Court went on to say that 'Israel has brought charges … asserting jurisdiction based on a statute that penalizes "war crimes" and "crimes against humanity" among other acts. The international community has determined that these offenses are crimes over which universal jurisdiction exists.'[229]

In the *Finta* case, concerning a captain in the Royal Hungarian Gendarmerie, who was the commander of an investigative unit at Szeged when 8,617 Jewish persons were detained in a brickyard, forcibly stripped of their valuables and deported to concentration camps as part of the Nazi regime's 'final solution,' the Canadian Supreme Court recognized the constitutionality of the impugned provisions of the Criminal Code while establishing a high standard of proof for prosecution of war

Chamber is of the view that the qualifier "on national, political, ethnic, racial or religious grounds", which is peculiar to the ICTR Statute should, as a matter of construction, be read as a characterisation of the nature of the "attack" rather than of the *mens rea* of the perpetrator. The perpetrator may well have committed an underlying offence on discriminatory grounds identical to those of the broader attack; but neither this, nor for that matter any discriminatory intent whatsoever, are prerequisites of the crime, so long as it was committed as part of the broader attack.' In this regard, it is worth noting that while a restrictive definition may have been appropriate for the work of the ICTR, which deals with a context in which one ethnic group (Tutsi) was clearly targeted by another (Hutu), this categorisation of target groups does not easily explain the Cambodian experience. Although it has been documented that the Khmer Rouge did target some ethnic or religious groups such as the Cham Muslim minority and Buddhist monks, these attacks do not account for the estimated 1.7 million deaths of Cambodians attributed to the acts and policies of the Khmer Rouge. (It has been estimated that some 90,000 Cham Muslims were killed by the Khmer Rouge from 1975 to 1979, which amounted to 36 per cent of the 1975 Cham population. Ben Kiernan, "The Demography of Genocide in Southeast Asia: The Death Tolls in Cambodia, 1975-79, and East Timor, 1975-80", 34(4) *Critical Asian Studies* 590 (2003)). While the definition of crimes against humanity in the Cambodian Law on the establishment of the Extraordinary Chambers does allow for a broader range of crimes to be prosecuted than the charge of genocide (for which the *mens rea* is even more restrictive), notably by including political grounds as a motive, it is unfortunate that the Extraordinary Chambers will be forced to consider a discriminatory motive element to its deliberations on crimes against humanity, probably beyond what is required in international customary law.

[227] *Eichmann*, Israel, District Court of Jerusalem, Judgment of 12 December 1961, English translation in 36 *ILR* 5-276; *Eichmann*, Israel, Supreme Court, Judgment of 29 May 1962, English translation in 36 *ILR* 277-324.

[228] *Demjanjuk* v. *Petrovsky*, United States, 776 F.2d 571 (6th Cir. 1985); cert. den. 475 US 1016 (1986), 628 F. Suppl. 1370; 784 F.2d 1254 (1986).

[229] *Ibid.*, at 582.

crimes and crimes against humanity.[230] With regard to jurisdiction, the Court held that:

> 'Canadian courts have jurisdiction to try individuals *living in Canada* for crimes which they allegedly committed on foreign soil only when the conditions specified in s. 7(3.71) are satisfied. The most important of those requirements, for the purposes of the present case, is that the alleged crime must constitute a war crime or a crime against humanity. It is thus the *nature of the act* committed that is of crucial importance in the determination of jurisdiction. Canadian courts may not prosecute an ordinary offence that has occurred in a foreign jurisdiction. The only reason Canadian courts can prosecute these individuals is because the acts alleged to have been committed are viewed as being war crimes or crimes against humanity. A war crime or a crime against humanity is not the same as a domestic offence. There are fundamentally important additional elements involved in a war crime or a crime against humanity.'[231]

National courts have proved most willing to prosecute persons accused of crimes against humanity when the crimes have been committed in their territorial jurisdiction, as in the cases arising from WW II in Nazi-occupied areas such as *Barbie*,[232] *Papon*[233] and *Touvier*[234] in France and the *Hass and Priebke* case in Italy,[235] though the definition of crimes against humanity has varied considerably in case law from that contained in the instruments cited above, sometimes to suit national interests or circumstances.[236] However, there are a handful of cases where no such (or not just) national interest has been present, though with less than successful results. Spanish courts have recognised universal jurisdiction over crimes against humanity in the *Fidel Castro* case, although the court declined to exercise jurisdiction based on his immunity as a serving Head of State.[237] In Belgium, courts have recognised the possibility of prosecuting crimes against humanity under its

---

230 Finta's acquittal by jury at the Trial Chamber stage was upheld by the Supreme Court.

231 *Regina* v. *Finta*, Canada [1994] 1 SCR 701, Supreme Court of Canada, 24 March 1994 [emphasis added]; case note by Cotler in 90 *AJIL* 460 (1996).

232 *Barbie*, France, *Cour de cassation*, decision of 20 December 1985, JCP 1986, II, no. 20655; *Bull. crim.* 1985, at 1038-55. English translation in 78 *ILR* 136-47.

233 *Papon*, France, *Cour de cassation*, decision of 23 January 1997, no. 502, at 15.

234 *Touvier*, France, *Cour de cassation*, decision of 1 June 1995, *Bull. crim.* 1995, at 547-58.

235 *Hass and Priebke (Appeal)*, Italy, Military Court of Appeal of Rome, Judgment of 7 March 1998, in *L'Indice Penale* (1998), at 959-1000.

236 For instance, the *Cour de cassation* in the *Barbie* case in 1985 held that crimes against humanity were 'all inhuman acts and persecutions which, in the name of a state practising a policy of ideological hegemony, have been committed systematically, not only against persons because of their membership in a racial or religious group, but also against the opponents of this policy, whatever the form of their opposition.' Judgment of 20 December 1985. JCP 1986, II, no. 20655; *Bull. crim.* 1985, at 1038-55. English translation in 78 *ILR* 136-47.

237 *Fidel Castro*, Spain (*Audiencia nacional*), Order (auto) of 4 March 1999, no. 1999/2723, in CD Rom, EL DERECHO, 2002, Criminal case law.

universal jurisdiction law and customary law[238] in the *Pinochet* litigation[239] and in the *Sharon* case,[240] although head of State immunity again precluded the exercise of jurisdiction over the incumbent Israeli President Sharon in the latter case. Jurisdiction over the remaining defendant in the *Sharon and others* case, Yaron, was subsequently found lacking after the amendment of the 1993 Law on 23 June 2003, effectively limiting the exercise of universal jurisdiction to cases concerning Belgian nationals or residents (as perpetrators or victims) or where the country of the nationality of the perpetrator does not consider war crimes as crimes or cannot guarantee a fair procedure. Although some commentators have interpreted this alteration of the law as signalling the end of universal jurisdiction *in absentia*,[241] this assumes that Belgium's actions had been motivated by the belief that such an exercise of jurisdiction is unlawful. In fact, the stated reason for such a restriction to the exercise of universal jurisdiction was because lawmakers felt that the legislation had been abused.[242]

In France, there has been an attempt to prosecute crimes against humanity on the basis of universal jurisdiction in the so-called *Disappeared on the Beach* case, concerning the alleged forced disappearance of a number of individuals, mostly young men, on 4-5 May 1999 being voluntarily repatriated from refugee camps in the Democratic Republic of the Congo to the Republic of Congo at Brazzaville Beach by Congolese forces. On 7 December 2001, a complaint was lodged in France which expressly implicated Denis Sassou Nguesso, President of the Republic of the Congo, along with four other high-ranking individuals, in the affair. This complaint was lodged on the principle of universal jurisdiction for torture, forced

---

[238] The authority to exercise universal jurisdiction was said to be derived from customary international law, which gives each State the right to exercise universal jurisdiction over crimes against humanity. *Pinochet*, Belgium, Brussels Investigating Judge (*juge d'instruction*), order of 16 November 1998, in 79 *RDPC* (1999), at 309-311 (customary international law concerning crimes against humanity is directly applicable in the Belgian domestic legal order, including the creation of universal jurisdiction). At this time, the 1999 amendments had not yet been adopted.

[239] *Pinochet*, Belgium, Brussels Investigating Judge (*juge d'instruction*), order of 16 November 1998, in 79 *RDPC* (1999), at 281-288. The Judge found that universal jurisdiction existed with regard to crimes against humanity even before the 1999 amendment to the 1993 Law granting jurisdiction over these crimes. The authority to exercise universal jurisdiction was said to be derived from customary international law, which gives each State the right to exercise universal jurisdiction over crimes against humanity. *Ibid.*, at 309-311. In Belgium, under the Law of 16 June 1993, courts have jurisdiction over grave breaches of the 1949 Geneva Conventions and 1977 Protocols, no matter where such offences are committed, by whom or against whom they are committed, and whether or not the offender is on Belgium territory. A law of 3 February 1999 added genocide and crimes against humanity to the international crimes over which Belgian courts possess universal jurisdiction.

[240] *Sharon Ariel and others,* Belgium, Appeals Court of Brussels, Decision of 26 June 2002, available at: <www.sabra-shatila.be/documents/arrest020226.pdf>; *Sharon Ariel and others*, Belgium, Court of Cassation, Judgment of 12 February 2003, available at: <www.cass.be/cgi-juris/juris-cass-a1.pl>.

[241] Antonio Cassese, "Is the Bell Tolling for Universality? A Plea for a Sensible Notion of Universal Jurisdiction", 1 *JICJ* 589 (2003).

[242] Luc Reydams, "Belgium Reneges on Universality: The 5 August 2003 Act on Grave Breaches of International Humanitarian Law", 1 *JICJ* 679 (2003).

disappearances as a crime constituting torture, and for crimes against humanity.[243] It highlighted the fact that General Norbert Dabira, one of the five indictees, was known to be resident in France at the time the complaint was lodged thus constituting sufficient grounds on which to base the jurisdiction of the French authorities. On 18 September 2002, the Meaux investigating judge, in conformity with Article 656 of the Code of Criminal Procedure, addressed a request to the French Ministers of Justice and Foreign Affairs, demanding a 'written deposition' from the Congolese President, on the occasion of his State visit to France. Subsequently, at the beginning of December 2002, the Congolese Government lodged an official request with the ICJ to declare that the French Republic 'shall cause to be annulled the measures of investigation and prosecution taken by the prosecutor of the Meaux Tribunal.' The complaint against France was that, *inter alia*,

> 'by attributing to itself universal jurisdiction in criminal matters and by arrogating to itself the power to prosecute and try the Minister of the Interior of a foreign State for crimes allegedly committed by him in connection with the exercise of his powers for the maintenance of public order in his country,' France violated 'the principle that a State may not, in breach of the principle of sovereign equality … exercise its authority on the territory of another State.'[244]

On 27 September 2004, the Paris Court of Appeals annulled the overall procedure in France concerning the Beach Affair, on the basis that the complaint was too general to provide a basis to apply the principle of universal jurisdiction before French courts. This decision was overturned by the French Supreme Court on 10 January 2007 which remitted the case to the Court of Versailles.[245] It remains to be seen how the International Court of Justice will rule in the *Certain Criminal Proceedings* case, but the judgment will almost certainly be instructive as to the legality of national courts exercising universal jurisdiction over crimes against humanity.

Apart from *Eichmann*, there has been one truly successful, albeit criticised, case of prosecuting crimes against humanity under universal jurisdiction and this is the landmark *Scilingo* case, decided in Spain on 19 April 2005.[246] This case concerned

---

[243] Art. 689-1 and 689-2 of the French Code of Criminal Procedure and the Convention against Torture, and further as a crime against humanity (under Art. 212-1 of the Criminal Code).

[244] It is further asserted by the Republic of Congo that, in issuing an arrest warrant instructing police officers to examine the President of the Republic of the Congo as a witness in the case, France violated 'the criminal immunity of a foreign Head of State – an international customary rule recognized by the jurisprudence of the Court.' *Certain Criminal Proceedings in France (Republic of the Congo* v. *France),* International Court of Justice Press Release 2003/21, 16 July 2003.

[245] FIDH, "Case of the 'Disappeared on the Beach': An important victory for victims", 10 January 2007, available at: <http://www.fidh.org/article.php3?id_article=3947>.

[246] *Scilingo, Adolfo*, Spain, Third Section of the Criminal Division (*Audiencia Nacional*), Judgment no. 16/2005 of 19 April 2005, *Sentencia por crímenes contra la humanidad en el caso Adolpho Scilingo*, available at: <http://www.derechos.org/nizkor/espana/juicioral/doc/sentencia.html>. For commentary, see Alicia Gil Gil, "The Flaws of the Scilingo Judgment", 3(5) *JICJ* (2005) and Christian Tomuschat, "Issues of Universal Jurisdiction in the Scilingo Case", 3(5) *JICJ* (2005); Giulia Pinzauti, "An Instance of Reasonable Universality: The Scilingo Case", 3(5) *JICJ* (2005).

a former Argentinean army officer, Adolfo Francisco Scilingo, who had worked at the infamous *Escuela Mecánica de la Armada* (ESMA), a naval mechanics school which had functioned as a torture centre for the military junta which held power in Argentina from March 1976 to December 1983.[247] The National Court reached a conviction of one count of crimes against humanity, and sentenced Scilingo to 640 years imprisonment.[248] The Court justified its exercise of universal jurisdiction over crimes against humanity by reliance on (1) the customary character of crimes against humanity in international law, particularly the *jus cogens* nature of the prohibition which entails an *erga omnes* authorisation on all States to repress such crimes and (2) a provision of Spanish legislation, the *Ley Orgánica del Poder Judicial* (LOPJ, Organic Law of the Judicial Branch), enacted in 1985.[249] In terms of the first basis, the Court implied both procedural and substantive consequences from the customary prohibition of crimes against humanity.[250] Universal jurisdiction was held to be an inherent corollary of the customary norm prohibiting such crimes.[251] The National Court found that universal jurisdiction has a subsidiary role and operated when the country of primary jurisdiction is passive. Due to Argentina's continued failure to prosecute those responsible for the atrocities committed by the military junta during the dictatorship years, the Court found that this condition had been fulfilled.[252]

---

[247] As published in the book 'El Vuelo' (Horacio Verbitsky, *The Flight: Confessions of an Argentine Dirty Warrior*), Adolfo Scilingo in 1995 admitted his part in the atrocities. He is quoted as recalling of the operation that, 'They [the victims] were unconscious. We undressed them and as soon as the aircraft commander issued the order, we opened the hatches and threw them, naked, one after the other, out into the open air.'

[248] The sentence of 640 years was arrived at by the addition of the penalties corresponding to each conviction. In this regard, it has been observed that the Court erred in finding only one count of crimes against humanity, when it should have considered that there were 32 counts of crimes against humanity committed, as seems to be implied by the sentencing. See Gil Gil, "The Flaws of the Scilingo Judgment", at 1084.

[249] *Ley Orgánica* 6/1985, B.O.E. 1985, at 157, available at: <http://www.juridicas.com/base_datos/Admin/lo6-1985.l1tl.html>.

[250] Tomuschat, "Issues of Universal Jurisdiction in the Scilingo Case", at 1078: '[The Court] is of the view that individual criminal responsibility and universal jurisdiction go hand in hand, and that a twofold consequence derives from the categorization of a crime as a crime against humanity, namely on the level of substantive criminal responsibility as well as on the level of procedure.'

[251] *Scilingo*, April 2005 Judgment, at 83 ('*la norma penal internacional ... finalmente tiene capacidad para legitimar y dar cobertura a la actuación extraterritorial de los Tribunales nacionales*').

[252] It may be recalled that Spain has never prosecuted those atrocities committed during the Spanish Civil War and 'there seems to be a national consensus to the effect that this Pandora's box should not be opened.' Tomuschat, "Issues of Universal Jurisdiction in the Scilingo Case", at 1080. Hence, the notion of passivity of the State of primary jurisdiction as applied by the Spanish National Court seems to be somewhat of a double standard and perhaps also unwarranted given the judicial and legislative activism in Argentina in this regard in recent years, especially in hindsight of the judgment of the Argentine Supreme Court of 14 June 2005 and subsequent trials. After a trial which began in late June 2005, Julio Simon was sentenced in August 2006 to 25 years in prison for the disappearance of Jose Poblete and his wife in 1978, and the abduction of their baby daughter, Claudia. Another trial is underway of former police investigator Miguel Osvaldo Etchecolatz on murder, kidnapping and torture charges. The trial began in early June 2005, making him the first former government official to stand trial for crimes committed during the Dirty War in 20 years. Jaime Jansen, "Argentina

In summary, it may be posited that crimes against humanity are prohibited under customary international law. While it remains somewhat unclear whether there is a customary international law entitlement for national courts to exercise universal jurisdiction over crimes against humanity, there would not appear to be any international legal rule preventing national courts from exercising universal jurisdiction over such crimes.

1.4.3 **Genocide**

Genocide emerged as a crime in international law with the adoption by the UN General Assembly of the Convention on the Prevention and Punishment of the Crime of Genocide in 1948 (hereafter, Genocide Convention).[253] The term 'genocide' was originally coined by Raphael Lemkin from the root words 'genos' (Greek for family, tribe or race) with '-cide' (Latin for killing) in his book published in 1944, which provided a legal analysis of Axis rule in countries occupied by Nazi Germany during the course of World War II.[254] However, the conception of genocide by Lemkin traced back to earlier events. In 1933 Lemkin presented before the Legal Council of the League of Nations conference on international criminal law in Madrid an essay on the *Crime of Barbarity* as a crime against international law. The concept of the crime, which later evolved into the idea of genocide, was based mostly on the experience of Arameans massacred in Iraq during the early 1930s and on the Armenian Genocide during World War I. Lemkin proposed the creation of a multilateral convention making the extermination of human groups an international crime.[255] Unfortunately it took the experience of the systematic annihilation of some six million Jews by the Axis powers during WW II to convince the international communitiy that such a proposal may have merit.

In terms of the criminalisation of genocide in international instruments, the crime of genocide was first conceived as a sub-category of crimes against humanity. Neither Article 6(c) of the IMT Charter, Article 5(c) of the IMTFE Charter, nor Article II(1)(c) of Allied Control Council Law No. 10 explicitly listed genocide as a separate category of offence, although the crime was certainly covered under the elements of crimes against humanity, particularly 'extermination' and 'persecu-

---

court hands down first 'Dirty War' sentence since amnesty laws scrapped", *Jurist – Legal News and Research*, 7 August 2006, available at: <http://jurist.law.pitt.edu/paperchase/2006/08/argentina-court-hands-down-first-dirty.php>.

[253] Convention on the Prevention and Punishment of the Crime of Genocide, Approved and proposed for signature and ratification or accession by General Assembly Resolution 260 A(III) of 9 December 1948, entered into force 12 January 1951. As of July 2009, there are 140 States parties.

[254] Raphael Lemkin, *Axis Rule in Occupied Europe: Law of Occupation, Analysis of Government, Proposal for Redress* (Washington, D.C: Carnegie Endowment for International Peace, 1944), at 79.

[255] *Les actes constituant un danger general (interétatique) consideres comme delites des droit des gens* (Paris: A. Pedone, 1933). Art. 1 of the proposed legislative text stated: 'Whoever, out of hatred towards a racial, religious or social collectivity or with the goal of its extermination, undertakes a punishable action against the life, the bodily integrity, liberty, dignity or the economic existence of a person belonging to such a collectivity, is liable, for the offense of barbarity, to a penalty … unless punishment for the action falls under a more severe provision of the given Code.'

tions on political, racial or religious grounds in execution of or in connection with any crime within the jurisdiction of the Tribunal, whether or not in violation of the domestic law of the country where perpetrated.'[256] In their judgments, the IMT and IMTFE did not mention genocide in the parts dealing with the extermination of the Jews or other religious or ethnic groups; they mostly referred to the crime of persecution.[257] However, genocide was mentioned by a Polish court in the *Hoess* case in 1947[258] and by a United States Military Tribunal sitting at Nuremberg in *Greifelt and others* in 1948.[259]

The emergence of genocide as an autonomous crime occurred at the end of 1948 with the adoption of the Genocide Convention. The principal objective of the Convention was to prevent a recurrence of the atrocities committed in World War II by assuring the punishment of offenders.[260] According to Article I, Contracting Parties 'confirm … that genocide is a crime under international law which they undertake to prevent and punish.' The definition of genocide is provided in Article II, [261] while Article III sets out the types of participation in acts of genocide that 'shall be punishable.'[262] It is provided in Article IV that persons 'committing genocide or any of the other acts enumerated in Article III shall be punished, whether they are constitutionally responsible rulers, public officials or private individuals.' Contracting Parties are required to enact legislation necessary to give effect to the Convention, 'and, in particular, to provide effective penalties for persons guilty of genocide.'[263]

In terms of jurisdiction, the original draft resolution on genocide in the UN GA, proposed in 1946, said: '*Whereas* the punishment of the very serious crime of genocide when committed in time of peace lies within the exclusive territorial jurisdiction of the judiciary of every State concerned, while crimes of a relatively lesser importance such as piracy, trade in women, children, drugs, obscene publications are declared as international crimes and have been made matters of pub-

---

[256] IMT Charter, Art. 6(c).

[257] Cassese, *International Criminal Law*, at 98.

[258] *Hoess Rudolf Ferdinand*, Poland, Supreme National Tribunal, March 1947, in *LRTWC*, Vol. 7, 11 at 25.

[259] *Greifelt and others*, United States Military Tribunal sitting at Nuremberg, Judgment of 10 March 1948, in *TWC*, Vol. 5, at 88-169.

[260] See UN Doc. E/AC.25/3, at 8 (remarks of Secretary General). A second purpose was to correct what was viewed by many as a serious deficiency of the Nuremburg prosecutions which was the IMT's determination that it could convict Nazis of crimes against humanity only when the offences were 'in execution of or in connection with' crimes against peace or war crimes.

[261] According to Art. II of the Genocide Convention, genocide means any of the following acts committed with intent to destroy, in whole or in part, a national, ethnical, racial or religious group, as such: (a) Killing members of the group; (b) Causing serious bodily or mental harm to members of the group; (c) Deliberately inflicting on the group conditions of life calculated to bring about its physical destruction in whole or in part; (d) Imposing measures intended to prevent births within the group; (e) Forcibly transferring children of the group to another group.

[262] Namely: (a) Genocide; (b) Conspiracy to commit genocide; (c) Direct and public incitement to commit genocide; (d) Attempt to commit genocide; (e) Complicity in genocide.

[263] Art. V Genocide Convention.

lic concern.'[264] This language signified a desire to recognise universal jurisdiction over genocide. However, the clause was deleted in the final draft, and the result was that universal jurisdiction was not included in the 1948 Convention. Instead, Article VI of the Convention provides that 'Persons charged with genocide or any of the other acts enumerated in article III shall be tried by a competent tribunal of the State in the territory of which the act was committed, or by such international penal tribunal as may have jurisdiction with respect to those Contracting Parties which shall have accepted its jurisdiction.'[265] This provision demonstrates that territorial jurisdiction is the primary basis for prosecuting the crime of genocide under the Convention, unless the States parties have consented to allow an international penal tribunal to conduct proceedings. It has been observed that the jurisdictional preference for the territorial State in the Convention meant that any prosecutions for genocide would certainly be unlikely, given that genocide is most often perpetrated by the government of the territorial State against a segment of its own population.[266] History seems to have borne this out, at least in countries where structures of power have remained unchanged following a genocidal campaign, such as in Guatemala.[267] In States with dualist systems of law, courts have held that in the absence of enabling legislation, no person may be tried for genocide.[268] In those countries where governments accused of perpetrating genocide have been overthrown, some prosecutions have been brought, but even these examples are few and far between. One example is the *in absentia* trial in Cambodia in 1979 of Pol Pot and Ieng Sary for the genocide committed during the reign of the Khmer

[264] UN Doc. A/BUR/50. The GA included the point in its agenda (UN Doc. A/181), and referred the matter to the Sixth Committee (UN Doc. A.C.6/64).

[265] Art. VI Genocide Convention. The 'international penal tribunal' has now arguably been created with the adoption and entry into force of the Rome Statute, although strictly speaking, States Parties to the Genocide Convention will have to explicitly accept the jurisdiction of the ICC before it may try people for offences under the Genocide Convention. However, the principle of complementarity in the Rome Statute means that domestic courts will remain the primary forums for prosecutions of genocide, unless they are 'unable or unwilling' to carry out the prosecutions. See preambular paragraph 10, Arts. 1 and 17 ICC Statute.

[266] Cassese, *International Criminal Law*, at 97.

[267] The Commission for Historical Clarification in Guatemala found that in certain regions and against people of certain ethnicities (indigenous and *ladinos*) the army committed genocide. See the Final Report of the Commission for Historical Clarification in Guatemala "Guatemala: Memory of Silence", Guatemala, CEH, February 1999, available at: <http://www.hrdata.aaas.org/ceh> (hereafter, Commission for Historical Clarification Final Report). On 6 June 2001, a criminal complaint against Efrain Rios Montt, the chief of the military junta in Guatemala during the genocidal campaign, concerning 'acts of genocide and crimes against humanity' was submitted in the name of the Association for Justice and Reconciliation (AJR), a collective of 23 Maya associations and survivors of the massacres. The case is still under investigation. Proceedings against Montt are also underway in Spain.

[268] *Nulyarimma and others* v. *Thompson*, Federal Court of Australia, Full Court, 1 September 1999, 39 *ILM* 20 (2000). Swiss Courts have also refused to try a Rwandan citizen accused of genocide on the same basis. He was, however, convicted of murder, attempted murder, incitement to murder and war crimes committed in Rwanda in 1994. *En la cause Fulgence Niyonteze*, Tribunal militaire de division 2, Lausanne, 30 April 1999; *En la cause Fulgence Niyonteze*, Tribunal militaire d'appel 1a, Geneva, 26 May 2000; Tribunal militaire de cassation, Yverdon-les-Bains, 27 April 2001.

Rouge.[269] Another example is the trials in Ethiopia under way for several years against members of the former Derg regime who are charged with genocide.[270] In December 2006, Mengistu, the former Head of State, was found guilty of genocide and in January 2007 was sentenced to life in prison.[271] The *ad hoc* international criminal tribunals for the former Yugoslavia and Rwanda, both of which have jurisdiction over genocide, are also arguably based upon territorial jurisdiction.[272] The International Criminal Court also has jurisdiction over genocide (Art. 6), defined in almost the same terms as Article II of the Genocide Convention.[273] However, the jurisdiction of the ICC may be said to be only properly universal where the Security Council refers a case to the Court; otherwise, it is probably a form of delegated territorial or nationality-based jurisdiction. The other enforcement mechanism in the Genocide Convention provided for in Article VIII, which authorises any State party to 'call upon the competent organs of the United Nations to take such action' under the Charter 'as they consider appropriate' for the prevention and suppression of genocide, has only been used once, in the case of *Sabra and Shatila*, when the GA characterised the massacre perpetrated there by Christian falangist troops as 'an act of genocide.'[274] However, this action by the GA has been viewed as a political, rather than legal, characterisation, aimed to hurt the sensitivities of the Israeli population, by accusing them of perpetrating the same acts of which the Jewish population have historically been victims.[275]

Despite this apparent bias towards territorial or international enforcement of the crime of genocide in the Genocide Convention, it is commonly posited that customary law establishes universal jurisdiction over genocide.[276] Support for this

---

[269] See the discussion on this trial and its potential consequences for the Extraordinary Chambers for Cambodia below, in Chapter 6.

[270] The trial of 68 members of the former ruling military council, including former dictator Mengistu Hailemariam, in exile in Zimbabwe since the fall of his regime in May 1991, has been in progress since October 1994. They face 210 counts involving genocide, crimes against humanity and systematic human rights violations during the 17-year rule of Mengistu's military-Marxist regime in Ethiopia from 1974-1991.

[271] It is, however, unlikely that this sentence will ever be carried out against Mengistu, who remains in exile in Zimbabwe.

[272] ICTY Statute, Art. 4; ICTR Statute, Art. 2.

[273] There is one important inconsistency between the two instruments. While the Genocide Convention prohibits and makes punishable 'conspiracy to commit genocide,' Art. 6 of the ICC Statute does not contain a similar prohibition. Conspiracy did not find the support of all the civil law countries during the negotiations of the Statute in Rome. Other forms of responsibility are laid out in general terms (i.e., for all the crimes) in Art. 25(3)(c), (d), (e), and (f) ICC Statute.

[274] UN GA Res. 37/123 of 16 December 1982.

[275] William A. Schabas, "The Genocide Convention at Fifty", *The United States Institute for Peace*, 7 January 1999, Special Report No. 41 ('In 1982, the General Assembly denounced the massacres of hundreds at the Palestinian refugee camps of Sabra and Shatila as genocide. But there was significant, vocal opposition, and there can be no doubt that the term was stretched in order to wound Israel's Jewish population, the crime's great historic victims, by suggesting that they had become its perpetrators').

[276] *Attorney General of Israel* v. *Eichmann*, 36 *ILR* 18, at 39 (Isr. Dist. Ct. – Jerusalem 1961), affirmed in 36 *ILR* 227 (Isr. Sup. Ct. 1962); *Restatement (Third) of the Foreign Relations Law of the United States* (1987), § 702 comment d.

contention may be partly gleaned from the drafting history of the Genocide Convention, during which the majority of the drafting Committee adopted a statement that, 'The first part of Article VI contemplates the obligation of the State in whose territory acts of genocide have been committed. Thus, in particular, it does not affect the right of any State to bring to trial before its own tribunals any of its nationals for acts committed outside the State.'[277] Although this statement would appear to be referring to preserving the principle of nationality in regards to exercising jurisdiction, the use of the words 'in particular' suggests that this was not the only head of jurisdiction which would remain operative in customary international law, notwithstanding the jurisdictional obligation in the Genocide Convention.

One advisory opinion and one judgment of the International Court of Justice (ICJ) also lend support to the notion that customary international law recognises universal jurisdiction over genocide. In its Advisory Opinion on reservations to the Genocide Convention, the ICJ asserted that the principles underlying the Genocide Convention 'are recognized by civilized nations as binding on States, even without any conventional obligation.'[278] Although the Opinion does not specify which obligations reflect customary rules, it is highly likely that those requiring the prosecution and punishment of those accused of genocide pursuant to the territorial principle would be included. The Court further noted 'the universal character both of the condemnation of genocide and of the co-operation required "in order to liberate mankind from such an odious scourge" (Preamble to the Convention).'[279] This comment would seem to point towards the need for universal jurisdiction over the crime of genocide, if not the recognition of it. The Court went further in the case concerning the *Application of the Genocide Convention (Preliminary Objections)*, the first time in which Article IX of the Convention has been invoked,[280] which confers on the ICJ disputes between States concerning the interpretation, application or fulfilment of the Convention. The case concerned the alleged acts of genocide by Serbia and Montenegro against (Muslim) segments of the population of Bosnia-Herzegovina.[281] In 1996, the ICJ affirmed that the 'rights and obligations enshrined by the Convention are rights and obligations *erga omnes*.'[282] From this observation, the Court concluded that 'the obligation each State thus

[277] UN Doc. A/C.6/SR 134, at 5.

[278] *Reservations to the Convention on the Prevention and Punishment of the Crime of Genocide*, 1951 ICJ Reports 15, at 23.

[279] ICJ Opinion of 28 May 1951, ICJ Reports 1951, at 23.

[280] Art. IX of the Genocide Convention provides: 'Disputes between the Contracting Parties relating to the interpretation, application or fulfilment of the present Convention, including those relating to the responsibility of a State for genocide or for any of the other acts enumerated in article III, shall be submitted to the International Court of Justice at the request of any of the parties to the dispute.'

[281] The case was initiated by Bosnia-Herzegovina on 20 March 1993. Subsequently, on 2 July 1999, the Republic of Croatia instituted proceedings before the ICJ against the Federal Republic of Yugoslavia (FRY) for violations of the 1948 Genocide Convention alleged to have been committed between 1991 and 1995, basing the jurisdiction of the Court upon Art. IX of the Genocide Convention.

[282] *Application of the Convention on the Prevention and Punishment of the Crime of Genocide (Bosnia and Herzegovina* v. *Yugoslavia (Serbia and Montenegro),* Preliminary Objections, Judgment of 11 July 1996, para. 31.

has to prevent and to punish the crime of genocide is not territorially limited by the Convention.'[283] In its 2007 judgment on the merits, however, the Court takes a more strict interpretation of Article VI, finding that '[t]he obligation to prosecute imposed by Article VI is by contrast [to Articles I and III] subject to an express territorial limit. The trial of persons charged with genocide is to be in a competent tribunal of the State in the territory of which the act was committed ... or by an international penal tribunal with jurisdiction ...'[284] However, the Court later notes that this does not prevent States from legislating a more expansive jurisdictional basis for the crime of genocide.[285] The *Restatement (Third) of the Foreign Relations Law of the United States* would also appear to support the notion of universal jurisdiction over genocide: 'A state violates customary law if it practices or encourages genocide, fails to make genocide a crime or to punish persons guilty of it, or otherwise condones genocide.'[286]

Generally speaking, State practice, though scant, has tended to affirm universal jurisdiction over genocide, although the acceptance of exercising jurisdiction is often been found to be contingent on various conditions relating to the territorial State, which would normally exercise jurisdiction according to the terms of the Genocide Convention. For instance, in the *Cvjetković* case in Austria, the court implied universal jurisdiction into the Genocide Convention when there is no functioning territorial judiciary.[287] Similarly, in the case before Spanish courts concerning the genocide in Guatemala,[288] the investigating judge on 27 March 2000 agreed to open an investigation, noting that several of the victims were Spanish or had died on Spanish territory,[289] thereby making Spanish jurisdiction appropriate because the local courts had not acted. In December 2000, the *Audiencia Nacional* held that Spanish courts could act only if there were clear legal impediments to prosecution in the territorial state or if judges there were 'subject to pressure from official or *de facto* powers that create a climate of intimidation or fear making it impossible to carry out the judicial function with the serenity and impartiality required.' Given

---

[283] *Idem.*

[284] *Application of the Convention on the Prevention and Punishment of the Crime of Genocide (Bosnia and Herzegovina* v. *Serbia and Montenegro)*, Judgment, 26 February 2007, para. 184. Following from this reasoning, the Court finds that Serbia and Montenegro was under no obligation to prosecute persons accused of participating in the genocide at Srebrenica before its own courts. However, by not complying with requests from the ICTY – an international penal tribunal with jurisdiction – to hand over suspects, in particular, General Mladić, it nonetheless violated Art. VI of the Genocide Convention. *Ibid.*, para. 448-450.

[285] *Ibid.*, para. 442: 'Article VI only obliges the Contracting Parties to institute and exercise territorial criminal jurisdiction; while it certainly does not prohibit States, with respect to genocide, from conferring jurisdiction on their criminal courts based on criteria other than where the crime was committed which are compatible with international law, in particular the nationality of the accused, it does not oblige them to do so.'

[286] The *Restatement (Third) of the Foreign Relations Law of the United States* (1987), § 702.

[287] *Cvetjković, Dusko*, Austria, Beschluss des Oberstern Gerichtshofs Os99/94-6, 13 July 1994.

[288] The suspects included five generals, two police chiefs, and a colonel. This group included former presidents and defense and interior ministers.

[289] One set of allegations referred to the firebombing of the Spanish Embassy in Guatemala City in January 1980, in which several protesters died.

that there was insufficient evidence that the Guatemalan courts were unable or unwilling to proceed with the prosecutions,[290] Spanish courts should not exercise universal jurisdiction.[291] In coming to this decision, the Court took into account Article VI of the Genocide Convention, which it felt had the effect of giving precedence to the territorial State and drew a parallel with the complementarity provisions of the Rome Statute.[292] The Supreme Court in 2003 (by 8-7) allowed the appeal in part, the majority finding that 'the Spanish judiciary is competent to investigate the circumstances that led to the attack on the embassy and to examine the murder of Spanish priests by the Guatemalan army.'[293] Although the Spanish judiciary 'condemns the crimes perpetrated against the Guatemalan Maya,' it declares itself incompetent to judge them.[294] In its 26 September 2005 judgment, the Spanish Constitutional Court re-asserted the competence of Spanish courts to exercise universal jurisdiction over the crime of genocide, pursuant to the LOPJ,

[290] The Court recalled that the UN-sponsored truth commission had only recently finished its work in Guatemala and that the Guatemalan Law of National Reconciliation expressly permitted genocide prosecutions.

[291] Decision of the *Audiencia Nacional* (Sala de lo penal) of 13 December 2000 (genocide in Guatemala), summary available at: <www.icrc.org/ihl-nat.nsf>.

[292] Although this principle does not apply as a matter of law to inter-State overlaps of jurisdiction, the idea of universality principle being subsidiary to the other principles has been suggested as one way to define the parameters of universal jurisdiction. See, e.g., Institute of International Law, Seventeenth Commission, Resolution 'Universal jurisdiction with respect to the crime of genocide, crimes against humanity and war crimes,' Krakow, 26 August 2005. Art. 3(c) requires the prosecuting State to inquire whether the State of nationality or territoriality wishes to prosecute before taking action, while Art. 3(d) requires the prosecuting State to carefully consider any request for extradition of the offender from a State with a significant link to the crime.

[293] The majority opined that extraterritorial jurisdiction, when not authorised by the United Nations or specifically regulated by treaty, required a nexus to national interests, citing cases from the German and Belgian courts, as well as the International Court of Justice's *Arrest Warrant* case in support of this proposition. In addition, the Court reasoned, the 'extradite or prosecute' provisions of a number of treaties require the presence of the defendant to proceed when there is no other type of national interest (such as the protective principle or the active or passive personality principles) involved. Moreover, 'a connection to a state interest creates legitimacy and rationality in international relations and also expresses respect for the non-intervention principle.' Roht-Arriaza, "Guatemala Genocide Case", 100 *AJIL* (2006), at 210, citing the judgment at sec. 13. The dissenting judges felt that a link to Spain was merely an element in applying a rule of reason to accommodate practical concerns in the investigation of such crimes, not a jurisdictional prerequisite. Such a rule of reason would be satisfied by the many links to Spain in the case. They underscored that this was 'a paradigmatic example of those [cases] in which Spain should exercise its jurisdiction: there would never be a more compelling case. "If there is no nexus in this case, then a nexus requirement becomes a mere pretext to exclude or suppress universal jurisdiction in all genocide cases."'

[294] The Court rejected the test of subsidiarity, the majority noting that basing this test '"on the real or apparent inactivity of local courts implies a judgment of one state's courts about the ability to administer justice of the similarly situated organs of another sovereign state" (sec. II[6]); while such an "unable or unwilling" inquiry might be appropriate for the International Criminal Court, national courts should not be making these kinds of judgments, which could have an important effect on foreign relations and should be left to the political branches.' Naomi Roht-Arriaza, "Guatemala Genocide Case", 100 *AJIL* 208-209 (2006).

without any restrictions based on a link to Spain.[295] The Constitutional Tribunal construed that according to the plain language and legislative intent of Article 23(4) of the LOPJ, there is only a single limitation on the exercise of such jurisdiction: the suspect cannot have been convicted, found innocent, or pardoned abroad. The legislation contains no implicit or explicit hierarchy of potential jurisdictions and focuses only on the nature of the crime, not on any ties to the forum. Moreover, the Tribunal found that 'the subsidiarity requirement imposed by both the *Audiencia Nacional* and the Supreme Tribunal put complainants in an untenable position, requiring that they prove that no case could be brought at home.'[296] The Tribunal also reasoned that the obligations to avoid impunity found in customary international law are incompatible with a limited reading of Article VI of the Convention.

Significantly, the Constitutional Tribunal found that although the defendant's presence was necessary for *trial* (Spain forbids trial *in absentia*), it was not needed to *open* the case. Rather, Spain could make use of extradition procedures to prosecute persons under universal jurisdiction.[297] The Tribunal also held that 'it is highly debatable that the requirement of a link [to the prosecuting State] is to be found in customary international law.'[298]

Spanish courts have also sought to rely on universal jurisdiction to prosecute the crime of genocide in the *Pinochet* litigation (concerning crimes in Chile), the *Scilingo* and *Cavallo* cases (concerning crimes in Argentina), and in proceedings against Fidel Castro (for crimes in Cuba). In the *Pinochet* case, a ruling by an investigative judge in 1998 that Spain has jurisdiction to hear allegations of genocide and torture that took place under Pinochet's leadership[299] was upheld by the Criminal Division of the Spanish National Court.[300] The Court determined that the acts alleged in the complaint, bolstered by the Chilean truth commission's report and a 1982 Spanish parliamentary investigation could constitute, *inter alia*, genocide, that is subject to judicial action under domestic[301] and international law and is subject to universal jurisdiction. Furthermore, the Organic Law of the Judicial

---

[295] See also, *Sentencia* 237/2005, *Recursos de amparo promovido por Rigoberta Menchu y otros*, 5 October 2005, available at: <www.icrc.org/ihl-nat.nsf>.

[296] Roht-Arriaza, "Guatemala Genocide Case", at 210.

[297] One may note that precisely this procedure had been adopted with technical, if not material, success in the *Pinochet* litigation.

[298] The Tribunal, echoing the minority's views of the *Audiencia Nacional*, found that the cited German cases had been superseded, that the *Arrest Warrant* case had been explicitly limited to the issue of the immunity of a sitting foreign minister, and that the *Sharon* case had not only been similarly limited, but actually embraced a broad view of universal jurisdiction. The Tribunal then noted that numerous other countries have broad jurisdictional competences that do not require any link.

[299] "Spain-Chile: Writ of the Instructing Court accepting the Jurisdiction of the Pinochet case" (20 September 1998), available at: <www.derechos.org.nizkor.chile/juicio/jurie/html>.

[300] "Auto de la Sala de lo Penal de la Audienca Nacional confirmando la jurisdicción de España para conocer de los crimenes de genecidio y terrorismo cometidos durante la dictadura chilena" (5 November 1998), available at: <www.derechos.org.nizkor.chile/juicio/audi.html>; "*In re* Pinochet: Spanish National Court; Criminal Division (Plenary Session). Case 19/97, November 4, 1998; Case 1/98, November 5, 1998", 93(4) *AJIL* (July 1999), at 690-93.

[301] Spanish Penal Code, Art. 607.

Branch (LOPJ) established Spanish competence to examine certain acts proscribed by international conventions (such as the Genocide Convention) whether committed by Spaniards or foreigners extraterritorially.[302] Although the charge of genocide was initially considered by the UK House of Lords in deciding upon the validity of extraditing Pinochet to Spain,[303] it was later dropped from the case after the Home Secretary decided that genocide would not be considered as a charge for the grounds of extradition.[304]

Encouraged by the proceedings against Pinochet, in late 1998 a Cuban exile group filed suit in Spain accusing Cuban leader Fidel Castro of genocide, terrorism and torture.[305] The case was not admitted. An identical complaint was lodged on 14 October 2005 in Spain by the 'Fundación para los Derechos Humanos en Cuba' (FDHC) and Cuban citizens. The same judge, Ismael Moreno of the *Audiencia Nacional*, dismissed the complaint on 4 November 2005 by reason of Castro's head of State immunity from prosecution under international law. This aspect of the ruling does not necessarily suggest that the Spanish court would not have had jurisdiction over the case in the absence of that exception from the principle of adjudicatory jurisdiction. However, the judge also found that the crimes of which Castro is accused do not constitute acts of genocide or terrorism.

In the *Cavallo* case, a Mexican court approved of the Spanish request for the former Argentine navy officer's extradition to Spain on charges of genocide and terrorism.[306] However, the Mexican court made no explicit comment upon the basis for Spain's jurisdiction. The Court merely ruled upon whether, by acceding to the extradition request pursuant to the 1978 Extradition Treaty between Mexico and Spain, Mexico would be acting in violation of its constitution, which it found it would not. In particular, the court held that the ratification of the 1948 Genocide Convention did not violate either the principle of self-determination or the principle of non-intervention in the internal affairs of a foreign State, which are inscribed in the Mexican constitution. On 11 January 2006, a Spanish prosecutor formally charged Cavallo with genocide, organised terrorism, crimes against humanity and murder.[307] However, on 20 December 2006, a Spanish court decided it had no jurisdiction over Cavallo because he had also been indicted by courts in Argentina and

---

[302] Law on Judicial Power (Spain), Art. 23.4.

[303] *R* v. *Bow Street Metropolitan Stipendiary Magistrate,* ex parte *Pinochet Ugarte*, United Kingdom, House of Lords Judgment of 25 November 1998, 3 *WLR* 1456 (HL 1998), *per* Lord Slynn of Hadley.

[304] *Pinochet III*: *R* v. *Bow Street Metropolitan Stipendiary Magistrate*, ex parte *Pinochet Ugarte*, United Kingdom, House of Lords Judgment of 24 March 1999, 2 *WLR* 827 (HL 1999) ; [1999] 2 *All ER* 97, *per* Lord Browne Wilkinson, at 272.

[305] Ciaran Giles, "Castro Sued for Genocide, Terrorism", *AP*, 5 November 1998.

[306] *Cavallo, Ricardo Miguel*, Mexico, Extradición Ricardo Miguel Cavallo, Suprema Corte de Justicia de la Nación, Amparo en Revisión 140/2002, 10 June 2003, <http://www.scjn.gob.mx/Asuntos/2003/CAVALLOENGROSE(X)2.pdf>.

[307] See profile for Ricardo Miguel Cavallo on Trial Watch, available at: <http://www.trial-ch.org/en/trial-watch/profile/db/legal-procedures/ricardo-miguel_cavallo_48.html>.

instead invited Argentina to apply for his extradition.[308] Cavallo had to be released 40 days later due to the expiry of a time limit in the course of which an Argentinean extradition order should have arrived in Spain. The following day – the extradition order having finally arrived – he was arrested again. On 28 February 2008, the Spanish government authorised his extradition to Argentina, a decision taken after the Mexican authorities had approved his re-extradition to Argentina.[309] Cavallo was extradited to Argentina on 31 March 2008. He was handed over to Argentinean officials after the Third Section of the Spanish Criminal Court officially closed the case against him to enable his trial in Argentina. An Argentinean court recently characterised the crimes committed against opponents of the military regime in Argentina from 1976 to 1983 as genocide in a trial concerning former police officer Miguel Etchecolatz.[310]

In the landmark *Scilingo* case in Spain, as noted, the charge of genocide was found to be unsupported by the facts, in particular with regard to the required 'intent to destroy, in whole or in part, a national, ethnical, racial or religious group, as such,' however the Spanish Court did find that it had the competence to exercise jurisdiction over the crime on the basis of universal jurisdiction.[311] In its Order of 4 November 1998, in Legal Ground no. 2, the Court held that it was contrary to the spirit of the Genocide Convention to interpret Article VI of this Convention (requiring the territorial State or an international penal tribunal to exercise jurisdiction over genocide cases) to the effect that such a provision would limit the jurisdiction of other States. This interpretation would run counter to the fact that genocide is 'regarded as a crime of extreme gravity in the whole world and affects directly the international community, indeed all humanity, as is intended by the same Convention.'

German courts have convicted two Bosnian Serbs of genocide committed against Muslims in Bosnia on the basis of universal jurisdiction.[312] Notably, however, one defendant, Jorgić, had had a permanent residence in Germany since

---

[308] *Cavallo Ricardo Miguel*, Spain (*Audiencia nacional*), Order (auto) of 20 December 2006, no. 139/1997, available at: <http://www.trial-ch.org/fileadmin/user_upload/documents/trialwatch/Decision_AN_incompetencia_caso_Cavallo.doc>. In a separate trial against Juan Carlos Fotea, accused of kidnapping Argentine writer and journalist Rodolfo Walsh in 1977, a Spanish judge similarly declined to exercise jurisdiction on the basis that an extradition request had come from Argentina. "Spain to extradite Argentine over writer killing", *Reuters*, 26 January 2007.

[309] "Spanish judge asks Mexico for go-ahead to extradite 'dirty war' suspect to Argentina", *AP*, 21 February 2007.

[310] *Etchecolatz, Miguel*, Argentina, Judgment of the Court of La Plata, 20 September 2006. Etchecolatz had in 1986 been sentenced to 23 years imprisonment for illegal detention and forced disappearances but was released pursuant to the amnesty laws in force at the time.

[311] *Scilingo, Adolfo*, Spain, Third Section of the Criminal Division (*Audiencia nacional*), Judgment no. 16/2005 of 19 April 2005, Sentencia por crímenes contra la humanidad en el caso Adolpho Scilingo, available at: <http://www.derechos.org/nizkor/espana/juicioral/doc/sentencia.html>.

[312] *Prosecution* v. *Novislav Djajic*, Bayerisches Oberstes Landesgericht, 23 May 1997, 19 *Neue Juristische Wochenschrift* 392 (1998); *Prosecution* v. *Nikola Jorgic*, Oberlandesgericht Düsseldorf, 26 September 1997; *Prosecution* v. *Nikola Jorgic*, Bundesgerichtshof, 30 April 1999, *Neue Zeitschrift für Strafrecht* (1999), at 396.

May 1969 and the second, Djadic, had also been living and working in Germany. Belgium's Court of Cassation, in its decision on the indictment of *Sharon, Ariel; Yaron, Amos and others*,[313] after recognising that international customary law is opposed to the idea that current heads of State and Government should be judged by foreign tribunals in the absence of treaty or customary rules that oblige the States concerned to lift immunities, has ruled that the exclusion of immunity established in Article IV of the Genocide Convention is only applicable in respect to the competent courts according to the Convention itself (i.e., the territorial State or an international penal tribunal). Similarly, Article 27(2) of the ICC Statute, which removes the bar of immunity before the ICC, does not affect or prevent the application of the customary rule on immunities when a court is exercising 'universal jurisdiction by default.' Thirdly, Article 5(3) of the 1993 Belgian law (which states that the official status of a person accused of international crimes does not preclude his prosecution) does not impose prosecution of incumbent heads of states or governments. Rather, this provision merely entails that the nature of a State organ is not a ground for exemption from criminal responsibility when international crimes are involved.[314] This case thus arguably recognises a customary entitlement to prosecute the crime of genocide, subject to the exception of personal immunity of incumbent heads of State.

1.4.4 **Torture**

Torture has long been considered as a serious crime by almost all nations. However, it is worth recalling that the practice of torture was not always considered as illegal, but was historically used in all parts of the world as a recognised component of warfare (in the treatment of captured belligerents or occupied civilians), law enforcement (for obtaining confessions, aiding investigations and meting out punishment), or the destruction of political opponents.[315] The practice was abolished in England in about 1640 (except *peine forte et cure* which was only abolished in 1772), in Scotland in 1708, in Prussia in 1740, in Denmark around 1770, in Russia in 1801. In France, the 1789 Declaration of the Rights of Man and of the Citizen, which has constitutional status, prohibits submitting suspects to any hardship not necessary to secure his person. Moreover, statute law explicitly makes torture a crime and prohibits the police or justice from interrogating suspects under oath. In

---

[313] *Sharon Ariel and others*, Belgium, Court of Cassation, Judgment of 12 February 2003, available at: <www.cass.be/cgi-juris/juris-cass-a1.pl>.

[314] Antonio Cassese, "The Belgium Court of Cassation v. the International Court of Justice: the *Sharon and others* Case", 1 *JICJ* (2003), at 439-440.

[315] See the description of torture in its historical and geographic perspective in Daniel H. Derby, "Torture", in M. Cherif Bassiouni (ed.), *International Criminal Law*, 2nd edn. (Ardsley, New York: Transnational Publishers, Inc., 1999), at 705-712. Torture has been traced back to practices in ancient Egypt as a coercive form of tax collection and in Ancient Greece where slaves were subjected to it to obtain information, a practice condoned by Aristotle and Demosthenes. In ancient Rome, laws relating to torture were codified, mostly under the titles *De quaestionibus*, in the Digest and the Code.

the United States, the 1789 Constitution banned the coercion of confessions,[316] and the Fifth Amendment serves as the basis of the Miranda warning that is issued to individuals upon their arrest, in order to prevent the circumstances that allow the practice to occur.[317] China officially abolished torture at the beginning of the 20th century.[318] Virtually all nations have now officially banned the use of torture.

Torture was first criminalised at the international level as a war crime or a crime against humanity. The Commission on Responsibilities, established at the Paris Peace Conference in 1919 included 'torture of civilians' as one particular violation of the 'laws and customs of war.'[319] Torture as a war crime was identified by the Commission taking into account 'explicit regulations,' 'established customs' and 'the clear dictates of humanity.'[320] One such source of the rule was the 1863 US Lieber Code, which operated during the American Civil War, Article 16 of which declared: 'Military necessity does not admit of cruelty – that is, the infliction of suffering for the sake of suffering or for revenge, nor of maiming or wounding except in fight, nor of torture to extort confessions.'[321] Some cases of the Leipzig trials dealt with cruelty to prisoners of war, though sentences tended to be lenient.[322] Although the word 'torture' does not appear in the Nuremberg Charter, it was undoubtedly covered by 'ill-treatment … of civilian population of or in occupied territory, murder or ill-treatment of prisoners of war' in Article 6(b) (defining war crimes) and 'other inhumane acts committed against any civilian population, before or during the war' in paragraph (c) (defining crimes against humanity). The judgment of Nuremberg uses the term 'torture' to describe some of the proscribed acts amounting to war crimes or crimes against humanity.[323] Torture is explicitly referred to in Control Council Law No. 10 under the definition of crimes against humanity, adopted in December 1945 for trials carried out subsequent to the IMT by the allied military tribunals and German national courts.[324] In their judgments,

---

[316] US Constitution, Amendment VIII.

[317] See *Miranda* v. *Arizona*, 384 US 436 (1966).

[318] Derby, "Torture", at 709-710.

[319] "Report presented to the preliminary Peace Conference by the Commission on the Responsibility of the Authors of the War and on the Enforcement of Penalties", in Carnegie Endowment for International Peace, Division of International Law, Pamphlet No. 32, *Violations of the Laws and Customs of War, Report of the Majority and Dissenting Reports of American and Japanese Members of the Commission of Responsibilities, Conference of Paris 1919* (Oxford: Clarendon Press, 1919), at 17, and in 14 *AJIL* 95 (1920), at 114.

[320] *Ibid.*, reprinted in 14 *AJIL* 95 (1920), at 113.

[321] Adjutant General's Office, US War Dep't, Gen. Orders No. 100, Instructions for the Government of Armies of the United States in the Field, Art. 16 (1863).

[322] See, e.g., In re *Muller*, translated in 16 *AJIL* 684 (1922), at 688-89.

[323] See, e.g., *Kaltenbrunner*, Judgment of the International Military Tribunal for the Trial of the German Major War Criminals, Nuremberg, 30 September and 1 October, 1946. London: HMSO, Cmd. 6964, Reprinted 1966, at 92-94 ('During the period in which Kaltenbrunner was Head of the RHSA, the Gestapo and SD in occupied territories continued the murder and ill-treatment of the population, using methods which included the *torture* and confinement in concentration camps, usually under orders to which Kaltenbrunner's name was signed'). [Emphasis added]

[324] Allied Control Council Law No. 10, Punishment of Persons Guilty of War Crimes, Crimes Against Peace and Against Humanity, Art. 2(1)(c), 20 December 1945, 3 *Official Gazette Control Council for Germany* 50-55 (1946).

the military tribunals referred to the crime of torture as both war crimes and crimes against humanity.[325]

With the adoption of the 1949 Geneva Conventions, torture was explicitly listed as a grave breach, subject to the universal system of repression, when committed against protected persons[326] in an armed conflict between two High Contracting Parties.[327] It is also listed as a proscribed act in common Article 3 in non-international armed conflicts when committed against persons taking no active part in hostilities.[328] In the Additional Protocol I of 1977, which extends the grave breaches regime of the GCs as well as the notion of international armed conflict, torture is prohibited whether committed by civilians or by the military at any time and in any circumstances whatsoever.[329] The Second Additional Protocol of 1977 prohibits the torture of any person who is not or no longer taking part in hostilities at any time and in any circumstances whatsoever.[330] There is no system of enforcement in Protocol II, however, the ICTY and the ICTR have held that such prohibitions amount to violations of the laws and customs of war,[331] from which one could imply universal jurisdiction over torture committed in both international and non-international armed conflicts, committed by civilians or military, regardless of the situation. Support for this proposition may be found partially in the case of *Kadić* v. *Karadžić* before US courts, in which torture as a war crime and crime against humanity, among other acts, founded the civil jurisdiction of the US to assess the claims of victims of the war in the former Yugoslavia, based upon the Alien Torts Claims Act.[332]

---

325 See, e.g., *Trial of Öbersturmbannführer Rudolf Franz Ferdinand Hoess*, Supreme National Tribunal of Poland, 11-29 March 1947, *Law-Reports of Trials of War Criminals, The United Nations War Crimes Commission, Volume VII*, London, HMSO, 1948; The Doctor's Trial, *Trials of War Criminals before the Nuremberg Military Tribunals under Control Council Law No. 10. Nuremberg, October 1946-April 1949* (Washington, D.C.: U.S. G.P.O, 1949).

326 Under GC I, protected persons are wounded and sick members of the armed forces or other groups entitled to POW status (Art. 13, GC I). Under GC II, protected persons are wounded, sick and shipwrecked at sea members of the armed forces or other groups entitled to POW status (Art. 13, GC II). Under GC III, protected persons are those entitled to POW status (Art. 4, GC III). Under GC IV, proteced persons are those who, at a given moment and in any manner whatsoever, find themselves, in case of a conflict or occupation, in the hands of a Party to the conflict or Occupying Power of which they are not nationals. Excluded from this category are those nationals of States not bound by the Convention, and nationals of neutral States and co-belligerent States with normal diplomatic representation in the State in whose hands they are (Art. 4, GC IV).

327 GC I, Art. 50, GC II, Art. 51, GC III Art. 130, GC IV, Art. 147.

328 Common Art. 3(1)(a) GC's of 1949.

329 AP I, Art. 75(2)(a)(ii).

330 AP II, Art. 4(2)(a).

331 See, e.g., *Furundžija*, ICTY, Trial Chamber II, Judgment of 10 December 1998, Case No. IT-95-17/1-T; 39 *ILM* (1999); *Delalić, et al.*, ICTY, Case No. IT-96-21, Trial Judgment, at 494 (16 November 1998), ICTR Statute, 4(a) and (e). *Akayesu*, ICTR Trial Chamber, 2 September 1998, paras. 593-595, 681.

332 *Kadić* v. *Karadžić*, 70 F. 3d 232, 248 (2d Cir. 1995). In this case, filed against Radovan Karadžić, the leader of the self-proclaimed Republica Srpska, the Second Circuit refused to recognise Karadžić's claim to head of state immunity as he was never recognised by the US government as 'the head of a friendly nation.'

The Statutes of the ICTY and ICTR both include torture as a form of crime against humanity and of war crimes (committed in both international and non-international armed conflicts) and as an act of genocide,[333] drawing no doubt upon the enumeration of crimes under Control Council Law No. 10.[334] A number of judgments have been issued by the two tribunals with regard to torture amounting to a war crime, a crime against humanity or an act of genocide, producing a wealth of jurisprudence on the subject.[335] The Rome Statute of the International Criminal Court lists (and defines) torture as an act falling under crimes against humanity[336] and as a war crime when committed in both international and non-international armed conflict.[337] Torture would probably also be covered by the act of '[c]ausing serious bodily or mental harm' as part of the crime of genocide, provided all the other conditions were satisfied, in Article 6(c) of the ICC Statute.

None of the international criminal tribunals include the crime of torture as a discrete crime in their subject-matter jurisdiction. With regard to the 'hybrid' tribunals which have been established, only two of these – the Extraordinary Chambers in Cambodia and the Special Panels in East Timor – have jurisdiction over the crime of torture *per se*.[338] The 2001 Law establishing the Extraordinary Chambers includes the crime of torture as one of three crimes derived from the 1956 Penal Code of Cambodia. The Special Panels over Serious Crimes in East Timor stands

---

[333] ICTY Statute, Art. 2(b) lists torture as a grave breach of the Geneva Conventions, Art. 4(b) provides that 'causing serious bodily or mental' harm may amount to an act of genocide, Art. 5(f) lists torture as a crime against humanity if perpetrated in an armed conflict whether international or non-international, against the civilian population. In the *Tadić (Jurisdiction)* case, the ICTY Appeals Chamber held that serious violations of Art. 3 common to the Geneva Conventions, which prohibits acts of torture in paragraph 1(a) are violations of the laws and customs of war and hence covered under Art. 3 of the Statute. *Tadić (Decision on the defence motion for Interlocutory Appeal on Jurisdiction)*, ICTY, Appeals Chamber, Decision of 2 October 1995, Case No. IT-94-1-AR72, 35 *ILM* 32 (1996). The ICTR Statute provides jurisdiction over torture under Art. 2(2)(b) for genocide (acts causing bodily and mental harm), Art. 3(f) as a crime against humanity, when perpetrated as part of a widespread or systematic attack against any civilian population on national, political, ethnic, racial or religious grounds, and Art. 4(a) as a serious violation of common Art. 3 of the Geneva Conventions of 1949.

[334] William A. Schabas, "The Crime of Torture and the International Criminal Tribunals", 37(2&3) *Case Western Reserve Journal of International Law* (2006), at 351.

[335] See, e.g., *Akayesu*, ICTR, Trial Chamber I, Judgment of 2 September 1998, Case No. ICTR-96-4-T; *Delalić and others* (*Čelebići* case), ICTY Trial Chamber II, Judgment of 16 November 1998, Case No. IT-96-21.T; *Furundžija*, ICTY, Trial Chamber II, Judgment of 10 December 1998, Case No. IT-95-17/1-T; 39 *ILM* (1999); *Kvočka*, ICTY, Trial Chamber, Judgment of 2 November 2001, Case No. IT-98-30/1-T ('the state actor requirement imposed by international human rights law is inconsistent with the application of individual criminal responsibility for international crimes found in international humanitarian law and international criminal law' (at 139).

[336] ICC Statute, Art. 7(2)(e) ('"Torture" means the intentional infliction of severe pain or suffering, whether physical or mental, upon a person in the custody or under the control of the accused; except that torture shall not include pain or suffering arising from, inherent in or incidental to, lawful sanctions').

[337] ICC Statute, Arts. 8(2)(a)(ii), 8(2)(c)(i).

[338] Torture has been included as a crime against humanity or as a war crime in all of the constituent instruments of these bodies.

apart as the only quasi-international criminal court with explicit 'universal jurisdiction' over the crime of torture *per se*.[339]

In the aftermath of WW II, torture slowly emerged as a discrete crime in international law both under customary and conventional law, distinct in scope and context from torture as a war crime or as a crime against humanity. In 1948, the Universal Declaration of Human Rights was adopted by the UN General Assembly, stating that: 'No one shall be subjected to torture or to cruel, inhuman or degrading treatment or punishment.'[340] A similar human right is guaranteed under the 1966 ICCPR[341] and its regional counterparts.[342] Although these instruments do not impose an obligation on States parties to prosecute or extradite offenders of such offences, regional international courts have held that the lack of investigation of crimes such as torture by State officials is a violation of an individual's right to an effective remedy, guaranteed under the human rights conventions.[343] In December 1975, the UN General Assembly adopted the Declaration on the Protection of All Persons from Being Subjected to Torture and Other Cruel, Inhuman or Degrading Treatment or Punishment,[344] which defines the crime,[345] referring to the Standard Minimum Rules for the Treatment of Prisoners of 1955,[346] and requires States to criminalise torture and investigate any instance of the act that has come to the attention of the authorities whether a complaint has been lodged or not.[347] The Declaration is silent as to any jurisdictional nexus required for a State to investigate and prosecute a suspected torturer. On 10 December 1984, the Convention against Torture and Other Cruel, Inhuman or Degrading Treatment or Punishment was adopted by the General Assembly.[348] The Convention entered into force on 26 June 1987.[349]

---

339 UNTAET Regulation No. 2000/11, 6 March 2000, Section 10; UNTAET Regulation 2000/15, Section 2 ('2.1 With regard to the serious criminal offences … as specified in Sections 4-7 of the present regulation [genocide, crimes against humanity, war crimes and torture], the panels shall have universal jurisdiction.')

340 Universal Declaration of Human Rights, adopted by GA Res. 217 A(III) of 10 December 1948, Art. 5.

341 ICCPR, adopted by GA Res. 2200A (XXI) of 16 December 1966, Art. 7.

342 ECHR, adopted in Rome, 4 November 1950, Art. 3; ACHR, adopted in San Jose, 22 November 1969, Art. 5(2); African Charter of Human and People's Rights, adopted 27 June 1981, Art. 5.

343 See, e.g., *Zeki Aksoy* v. *Turkey*, ECtHR (judgment), 18 December 1996, No. 100/1995/606/694.

344 UN GA Res. 3452 (XXX) of 9 December 1975.

345 Torture is defined in Art. 1 as 'any act by which severe pain or suffering, whether physical or mental, is intentionally inflicted by or at the instigation of a public official on a person for such purposes as obtaining from him or a third person information or confession, punishing him for an act he has committed or is suspected of having committed, or intimidating him or other persons. It does not include pain or suffering arising only from, inherent in or incidental to, lawful sanctions to the extent consistent with the Standard Minimum Rules for the Treatment of Prisoners.'

346 Adopted by the First United Nations Congress on the Prevention of Crime and the Treatment of Offenders (1955), reproduced in its report, UN publication, Sales No. 1956 IV.4; approved by resolution 663 (XXIV) of 31 July 1957 of the Economic and Social Council.

347 Declaration on the Protection of All Persons from Being Subjected to Torture and Other Cruel, Inhuman or Degrading Treatment or Punishment, Arts. 1, 7 and 9 respectively.

348 GA Res. 39/46 of 10 December 1984. The Convention entered into force on 26 June 1987.

349 As of July 2009, there are 146 States parties and 76 signatories.

The Convention Against Torture imposes an explicit duty on States parties to prosecute acts it defines as criminal.[350] States Parties are bound to 'ensure that all acts of torture are offences under [their] criminal law,'[351] and to undertake measures to establish jurisdiction over such offences.[352] Under Article 7, State Parties are required to either extradite an alleged torturer or 'submit the case to [their] competent authorities for the purpose of prosecution.' The object of this provision was to ensure that 'no offender would have the opportunity to escape the consequences of his acts of torture.'[353] Article 7 was meant to be a practical and effective means of suppressing torture. While the Convention focuses on domestic measures to prevent torture,[354] the treaty also sets up a form of universal jurisdiction to ensure punishment in the event that a State Party fails to prosecute offenders. Article 5 provides that, in addition to territorial, nationality and passive personality jurisdiction, 'each state party shall likewise take such measures as may be necessary to establish jurisdiction over such offences in cases where the alleged offender is present in any territory under its jurisdiction and it does not extradite him.' Therefore, according to Bassiouni, the Torture Convention 'implicitly allows universal jurisdiction.'[355] One of the considerations that led to the establishment of such a 'universal jurisdiction' system was the recognition that national laws are administered by the very authorities who might engage in or tolerate torture in an effort to support a government against its enemies.[356]

However, the Convention does not go as far in establishing torture as an international crime with its attendant consequences as was proposed in some of the drafts.[357] Unlike the draft convention proposed by the International Association of Penal Law, the Convention against Torture does not bar the application of the political offence exception to extradition, it does not require States that extradite

---

[350] 'Torture' is defined in Art. 1 as any act by which severe pain or suffering, whether physical or mental, is intentionally inflicted on a person for such purposes as obtaining from him or a third person information or a confession, punishing him for an act he or a third person has committed or is suspected of having committed, or intimidating or coercing him or a third person, or for any reason based on discrimination of any kind, when such pain or suffering is inflicted by or at the instigation of or with the consent or acquiescence of a public official or other person acting in an official capacity. It does not include pain or suffering arising only from, inherent in or incidental to lawful sanctions.

[351] Convention Against Torture, Art. 4.

[352] *Ibid.*, Art. 5.

[353] Report of the Working Group on a Draft Convention Against Torture and Other Cruel, Inhuman or Degrading Treatment or Punishment, 36 UN ESCOR Commission on Human Rights, at 11, para. 61, UN Doc. E/CN.4/1367 (1980).

[354] See for example, Art. 14 (providing for civil remedies for torture) and Art. 10 (providing for the training of law enforcement personnel).

[355] M. Cherif Bassiouni, "The History of Universal Jurisdiction and Its Place in International Law," in Stephen Macedo (ed.), *Universal Jurisdiction: National Courts and the Prosecution of Serious Crimes under International Law* (Philadelphia: University of Pennsylvania Press, 2004), at 56.

[356] Derby, "Torture", at 727.

[357] Draft conventions were submitted by the International Committee of Experts, the International Association of Penal Law and Sweden. See Draft Convention for the Prevention and Suppression of Torture, UN ECOSOC Doc. E/CN.4/NG0-213 (1978); Draft Convention for the Prevention and Suppression of Torture, UN ECOSOC Doc. E/CN.4/1285 (1978).

only on the basis of treaties to use the convention itself for a basis, it does not bar application of statutes of limitation and it does not explicitly declare torture to be an international crime and therefore suitable for the exercise of universal jurisdiction.[358] For these reasons, the 'extradite or prosecute' clause has been viewed as less an expression of universal jurisdiction and more of 'an obligatory territorial jurisdiction over persons, albeit in relation to acts committed elsewhere.'[359] However, universal jurisdiction over the crime of torture can also arguably be based upon customary law. According to the ICTY, the definition in Article 1(1) of the CAT should not be read as an exhaustive statement of what counts as torture for all international legal purposes.[360] In the Tribunal's assessment, the definition in Article 1(1) does not 'wholly [reflect] customary international law regarding the meaning of the crime of torture generally.' In particular, 'the public official requirement is not a requirement under customary international law in relation to the criminal responsibility of an individual for torture outside the framework of the Torture Convention.'[361] Such a perspective would mean that 'extradite or prosecute' obligation under the CAT would only apply in a limited set of situations,[362] while arguably the authorisation under customary law to prosecute would apply to a broader range of offences.

The Torture Convention limits the obligation to exercise jurisdiction over extraterritorial crimes committed by non-nationals to where the alleged offender is found on territory under the State's jurisdiction. Courts in some countries have interpreted this as meaning that jurisdiction is founded by the presence of the offender; in other words, that jurisdiction over the crime of torture does not arise until the alleged offender is on the territory of the prosecuting State,[363] although

[358] Derby, "Torture", at 733: 'As a result, extradition under the 1984 convention would not be required if the requesting state did not fit one of three jurisdictional categories – state within whose territory the conduct occurred; state of citizenship of the accused; or state of citizenship of the victim. Because many tortures take place within the state of nationality of both the accused and the victim, there is often only one state that fits the above criteria, and extradition to such a state may be either impossible because that state does not request his extradition or it may be barred by the danger that an accused would himself be subject to torture or to persecution there.'

[359] *Arrest Warrant of April 11th 2000 (Democratic Republic of the Congo* v. *Belgium)*, Judgment, Merits, 41 *ILM* 536 (2002), Separate Opinion of Judges Higgins, Kooijmans and Buergenthal, para. 41.

[360] *Prosecutor* v. *Kunarac, Kovac and Vukovic* (Case Nos. IT-96-23 & IT-96-23/I-A), Judgment of the ICTY (Appeals Chamber), 12 June 2002, para. 147.

[361] *Ibid.*, para. 148.

[362] See also Susan Marks & Andrew Clapham, *International Human Rights Lexicon* (Oxford: OUP, 2005), at 233.

[363] In France, for example, courts have found a lack of jurisdiction over claims of torture brought by Bosnian citizens residing in France against a non-disclosed person concerning events in 1992 in Bosnia-Herzegovina because the alleged perpetrators of the acts had not been found on French territory. The complainants, Elvir Javor, Kasim Kusuran, Munib Softic, Sénada Softic and Meho Mujdzic, claimed to be victims of crimes committed by representatives of Serb forces committed as part of the policy of ethnic cleansing, which took place in the town of Kozarac and in the surrounding villages. The Appeals Chamber found that 'the competence of the French jurisdiction, as spelled out by articles 689-1 and 689-2 of the French code of criminal procedure, are triggered by an objective element and

it would appear that such jurisdictions accept that a trial *in absentia* may be possible for the crime of torture if the alleged perpetrator was in the forum at the time the charges were filed.[364] Countering the view that presence of the offender is necessary for national courts to exercise jurisdiction against suspected torturers are the large number of investigations and extradition requests for Pinochet and other high-ranking military officials in Chile, Argentina and other Latin American countries with repressive pasts in Spain and other European countries to stand trial for torture and other international crimes. In order to issue the extradition requests, courts already need to have determined whether they have jurisdiction over the crimes in question in order to begin the investigation. In the *Pinochet* case, the Spanish National Court found jurisdiction over acts of torture based on Article 23(4)(g) of the Organic Law 6/1985, which grants universal jurisdiction over specific crimes, on the strength of the 1984 Torture Convention.[365] As noted, the view that jurisdiction is only triggered where the alleged torturer is on the territory of the forum State makes little sense from the point of view of acts of investigation or extradition requests. The more plausible explanation would seem to be that while customary international law entitles all States to exercise universal jurisdiction over torture, where the alleged offender is on the territory of a State party to the Convention against Torture, that State is *obliged* to either extradite him to a country that will prosecute (such as a country that has requested his extradition), or has to prosecute him before its own courts. In other words, presence of the alleged

a material element of connection to the country, which consists of the presence of the alleged perpetrators on French territory.' *Javor and others*, France, Paris Court of Appeal, *Quatrième Chambre d'accusation*, decision of 24 November 1994, no. A 94/02071, unreported. For this reason the Appeals Chamber rejected French jurisdiction in order to adjudicate the reported crimes based on the 1984 Convention against Torture. This decision was upheld in principle by the *Cour de Cassation*. *Javor and others*, France, Cour de Cassation, 26 March 1996, in *Bull. crim.*, no. 132 1996.

[364] This was the case in *Ely Ould Dah*, which concerned charges of torture against a Mauritanian intelligence officer during a governmental campaign of repression in 1990. In May 1993, an amnesty law was passed in Mauritania, preventing any investigation or prosecution of persons responsible for crimes committed in that period. Ely Ould Dah was arrested in France on 1 July 1999 when he was participating in a training program in Montpellier, and was subsequently indicted for torture and put under house arrest. On 5 April 2000, Ely Ould Dah escaped to Mauritania – an event that has caused an investigation to be opened. After a series of legal wrangles, during which the *Cour de Cassation* recognised the competence of French courts to exercise jurisdiction over the crime of torture committed in Mauritania notwithstanding the amnesty law, the trial *in absentia* opened on 30 June 2005 before the *Cour d'assises* of Nîmes. On 25 July 2005, the court sentenced the Mauritanian Captain to ten years in prison, the maximum term for the charges of torture. *Ely Ould Dah*, France, Court of Cassation, Criminal division, decision of 23 October 2002, *Bulletin criminel* 2002 no. 195 at 725. The decision was upheld by the European Court of Human Rights. *Decision on the Admissibility in the case of Ould Dah* v. *France* (No. 13113/03), 30 March 2009. See also *Bouterse, Desi*, Supreme Court [*Hoge Raad*], Criminal Chamber, judgment of 18 September 2001, No. 00749/01 (CW 2323), summary available at: <http://www.icrc.org/ihl-nat.nsf/39a82e2ca42b52974125673e00508144/07c5ae1b4a999f1cc1256da200518c91?OpenDocument>.

[365] *Pinochet*, Spain, Central Criminal Court (*Audiencia nacional*), Order (auto) of 5 November 1998, no. 1998/22605, rec. 84/1998. This order was confirmed in the decision of the *Audiencia nacional* of 24 September 1999, no. 1999/28720, rec. 84/1999.

offender in a State does not provide the basis for universal jurisdiction; it obliges the country to act upon its entitlement.[366]

As discussed above, the seminal case on torture as an international crime and the legal consequences thereof is the *Furundžija* case, decided by a Trial Chamber of the ICTY on 10 December 1998.[367] As well as finding that torture was a war crime based upon the prohibition of torture in common Article 3 of the Geneva Conventions and in 4(2) of Additional Protocol II,[368] the Trial Chamber found that a 'general prohibition against torture has evolved in customary international law,' basing this claim upon the IHL sources cited above, as well as Control Council Law No. 10. The court also noted the evolution of the human right to be free from torture. It concluded that '[be]cause of the importance of the values it protects, this principle has evolved into a peremptory norm or *jus cogens*, that is, a norm that enjoys a higher rank in the international hierarchy than treaty law and even "ordinary" customary rules.'[369] The court proceeded to articulate the inter-State and individual consequences of a violation of a *jus cogens* norm.

There is a reasonable number of cases of national courts exercising universal jurisdiction over the crime of torture perhaps because of the clear conventional basis provided by the Convention against Torture and also because just one act of torture, as defined in the 1984 Convention, is sufficient to trigger universal jurisdiction over this crime.[370] Even before the adoption of the 1984 Convention, torture was arguably recognised as a crime under customary law to which univer-

---

366 One explanation for this is that in this circumstance, there exists a *duty* to prosecute, since 'it is nonsensical to speak of a duty to prosecute all offences everywhere on every State party to the Convention.' For this reason, it has been argued that the voluntary presence of the accused in the jurisdiction of the prosecuting State is not 'an inherent aspect' of universal jurisdiction. Cryer, *Prosecuting International Crimes*, at 86.

367 The case concerned the events surrounding the interrogation by the accused, a local commander of 'the Jokers,' a special unit within the armed forces of the Croatian Community of Herzeg-Bosna, known as the Croatian Defence Council, of a Bosnian Moslem woman who was subjected to multiple rape and sexual assault by another soldier (who was tried separately) during the course of the interrogation in front of a large number of other soldiers. Although Furundžija did not participate in the sexual attacks, he did nothing to prevent or stop them from happening and his line of interrogation was carried out in conjunction with the physical attacks, as a way of eliciting information from the woman. *Furundžija*, ICTY, Trial Chamber II, Judgment of 10 December 1998, Case No. IT-95-17/1-T; 39 *ILM* (1999), para. 281: '[T]he accused's role in the tortures was that of fellow perpetrator. His function was to interrogate Witness A in the large room and later in the pantry where he also interrogated Witness D, while both were being tortured by Accused B. In such situations, the fellow perpetrator plays a role every bit as grave as the person who actually inflicts the pain and suffering.'

368 The Trial Chamber relied on the *Tadić Jurisdiction* case to come to this decision.

369 *Furundžija*, ICTY, Trial Chamber II, Judgment of 10 December 1998, Case No. IT-95-17/1-T; 39 *ILM* (1999), para. 153.

370 However, see the arguments of Lord Hope in *Pinochet III* that single acts of torture are not international crimes, and therefore not subject to universal jurisdiction, because the risks to former heads of State 'of being detained in foreign states' would be so great that governments could not have agreed to this. This argument is difficult to reconcile with the terms of the Convention against Torture which clearly require States parties to criminalise single acts of torture and to apply the 'extradite or prosecute' provision to all acts of torture, not just those part of a systematic and widespread practice. Michael Ratner, "The Lords' Decision in Pinochet III", in Reed Brody and Michael Ratner (eds.),

sal jurisdiction was attached. In the landmark *Filartiga* v. *Peña-Irala* case in the United States, concerning a civil law claim regarding acts of torture perpetrated by a Paraguayan official against a Paraguayan citizen in Paraguay, a US court held that 'the torturer has become, like the pirate or the slave trader before him, *hostis humanis generis*, an enemy of all mankind' (at 980) and granted civil jurisdiction over the crime pursuant to the 1789 Alien Torts Claim Act.[371] This statute provides US district courts with 'original jurisdiction of any civil action by an alien for a tort only (committed) in violation of the law of nations or a treaty of the United States.'[372] Since the Convention against Torture had not yet come into existence, the court was clearly relying on the characterisation of torture as a violation of the law of nations: 'we find that an act of torture committed by a state official against one held in detention violates established norms of the international law of human rights, and hence the law of nations' (at 11). In coming to this conclusion, the court relied heavily on the 1975 UN Declaration, as well as the Universal Declaration of Human Rights and the treaty provisions in human rights treaties cited above. Although the *Filartiga* case concerns civil jurisdiction, the case nonetheless supports the principle that the crime of torture is universally condemned and that all nations have an interest in the repression of such crimes, regardless of the nationalities of the parties involved or where the crime took place. Further support may be found in the dictum of the 1990 decision of the Committee Against Torture concerning the Argentinean amnesty laws, that 'even before the entry into force of the Convention against Torture, there existed a general rule of international law which should oblige all states to take effective measures to prevent torture and to punish acts of torture.'[373] While the use of the word 'should,' might indicate that the Committee 'indicated that its statement was aspirational rather than a declaration of binding law,'[374] it definitely confirms that States are *able* to prosecute and in fact *should* do so.

The *Pinochet* case before the courts of the United Kingdom is perhaps the most famous case of the application of the Convention against Torture provisions on jurisdiction, as well as whether or to what extent these provisions reflect customary law. In regard to the issue of universal jurisdiction over torture, the Law Lords approached the issue in very different ways.[375] For instance, Lord Browne-Wilkinson, the presiding judge, argued that torture committed on a systematic or widespread scale was a crime against humanity which has a *jus cogens* status, thereby justifying all States to assert jurisdiction over acts of torture wherever committed. Lord Millet went further, stating that crimes of *jus cogens* which are on a scale as

The Pinochet Papers: The Case of Augusto Pinochet in Spain and Britain (The Hague: Kluwer Law International, 2000), at 47-48.

[371] *Filatiga* v. *Pena-Irala,* United States, 630 F.2d 876 (1980).

[372] Judiciary Act of 1789, Ch. 20, § 9(b), 1 Stat. 73, 77 (1789), codified at 28 U.S.C. § 1350.

[373] *Report of the Committee Against Torture*, UN GAOR, 45th Sess., Suppl. (No. 44), Annex V, at 109-13, UN Doc. A/45/44 (1990).

[374] Michael P. Scharf, "Swapping Amnesty for Peace: Was there a duty to prosecute international crimes in Haiti?", 31(1) *Texas International Law Journal* 25 (1996).

[375] See Chapter 5 *infra* for a breakdown of the various legal paths taken by the Lords.

to be regarded as an attack on the international legal order entail universal jurisdiction under customary law. It would appear that although the majority of judges in *Pinochet III* relied on the Torture Convention as the basis to refute the claim to immunity, the Convention was also generally viewed as having either codified or crystallised an emerging international consensus on the customary right of all States to prosecute suspected torturers no matter what their nationality or where the crime was committed, based on the *jus cogens* character of the prohibition under international law. The obligation to prosecute or extradite suspected torturers under the principle of universal jurisdiction (as codified in the Torture Convention) was viewed as either inconsistent with immunity and was therefore an exception to the general rule or constituted an implied waiver of immunity on the part of States parties. In this sense, universal jurisdiction may be seen as a fundamental consequence of serious international crimes, with immunity-stripping power. One may observe, for example, that Pinochet was found to retain immunity for one of the three remaining charges – conspiracy to commit murder in Spain – which was based on the principle of territoriality.[376]

Universal jurisdiction over torture as codified in the Convention against Torture has been the central issue in the efforts to prosecute Hissène Habré, the former Chadian head of State, who has been residing in Senegal since 1990, for atrocities committed mainly against political opponents during his reign (1982-1990). While the Senagalese Supreme Court dismissed the case against Habré in March 2001, citing lack of universal jurisdiction over acts of torture committed abroad by foreigners under the existing provisions of the Senegalese Criminal Code,[377] after protracted legal wrangling involving an extradition request from Belgium,[378] consideration of the case by a Committee of Eminent African Jurists on the Case of Hissene Habré,[379] and criticisms of the United Nations Committee against Torture (CAT),[380] it was decided by the African Union in July 2006 that Senegal should

[376] *Pinochet III, per* Lord Browne-Wilkinson.

[377] *Habré, Hissène*, Senegal, Supreme Court, 20 March 2001, available at: <www.icrc.org/ihl-nat.nsf>.

[378] On 19 September 2005, Belgian Judge Fransen issued an arrest warrant against Hissène Habré. An extradition request from Belgium was then forwarded to the Senegalese authorities, based on its universal jurisdiction law. On 16 November 2005, Hissène Habré was detained in anticipation of the decision on Belgian's extradition request. At the extradition hearing on 25 November 2005, the Appeals Court in Dakar declared itself 'not competent' to rule on Belgium's request for extradition of Hissène Habré. The Court's reasoning seemed to be based on Habré's 'immunity' as a former head of State, despite the fact that Chad had appeared to have waived such immunity by the letter of the Minister of Justice.

[379] *Report of the Committee of Eminent African Jurists on the Case of Hissene Habré*, available at: <http://www.hrw.org/justice/habre/CEJA_Repor0506.pdf>, para. 1. The other factors taken into consideration were: (a) adherence to the principles of the total rejection of impunity; (b) adherence to international standards of fair trial; (c) jurisdiction of the alleged crimes for which Habré should be tried; (d) efficiency in terms of cost and time of the trial; and (e) accessibility to the trial by alleged victims and of witnesses.

[380] See UN Doc. CAT/C/36/D/181/2001, Communication No. 181/2001, 19 May 2006.

serve as the location of Habré's trial.[381] New legislation allowing for the prosecution of genocide, crimes against humanity, war crimes and torture, even when committed in another country, was passed on 31 January 2006 and a trial is expected to take place in the next few years.[382]

A number of cases based on universal jurisdiction involving somewhat lower level offenders living in Europe have taken place since the *Pinochet* litigation. In the Netherlands, three individuals, one former colonel in the Zairian army under Mobutu[383] and two Afghan war criminals have been convicted for torture on the basis of the Dutch Torture Convention Implementation Act of 1988,[384] the International Crimes Act of 2003, the Dutch Criminal Code[385] and the Criminal Law in Wartime Act.[386] In all of these cases, the offenders had applied for asylum in the Netherlands and been rejected on the basis that they were suspected of having committed serious international crimes pursuant to Article 1F of the 1951 Refugee Convention.[387] In the United Kingdom, an Afghan warlord was found guilty of

[381] Decision On The Hissene Habre Case And The African Union Doc. Assembly/Au/3 (Vii), July 2006, available at: <http://www.hrw.org/english/docs/2006/08/02/chad13897.htm>.

[382] Belgium had stated that should Senegal not act upon its obligations, it would invoke Art. 30 of the Torture Convention which allows States parties to proceed to arbitration where there is a dispute between parties concerning the interpretation or application of the Convention, and then to apply to the ICJ, if the organisation of the arbitration cannot be agreed upon. Convention against Torture, Art. 30(1). See Reed Brody, "Senegal: New Law Will Permit Habré's trial", *Universal Jurisdiction Digest Number 489*, 5 February 2007.

[383] In the *Nzapali* case, the former colonel of the Zairian army and member of the Presidential Guard known as the 'king of the beasts' to his fellow officers, who allegedly led death squads between 1990 and 1995 in Kinshasa, was arrested in September 2003 on charges of torture and rape committed in 1995 and 1996. He had applied for asylum in the Netherlands in 1998, but after a victim informed the police of his criminal past, an investigation was commenced into his possible involvement in war crimes led by the Netherlands National Investigation Team for War Crimes [*Nationaal Opsporingsteam Voor Oorlogsmisdrijven*, NOVO], which was set up in 1998 and is responsible for investigating '1F' files. On 7 April 2004, the District Court of Rotterdam convicted him for torture, acquitted him on the rape charge, and sentenced him to two and a half years of prison. It was judged that 'the accused, at some time in or around October 1996, in Matadi (Bas-Zaïre), jointly and in conjunction with others, as civil servant, i.e. as member of the Garde Civile and in the performance of his duties, repeatedly and intentionally inflicted (grievous) bodily harm on someone who was deprived of his freedom, the sole object being to punish him and force him into compliance with his wishes.'

[384] Torture Convention Implementation Act of 1989 (Netherlands), Art. 1.

[385] Arts. 47 and 57.

[386] Criminal Law in Wartime Act of 1952, Arts. 8 and 9. The judgments were published on 9 and 13 February 2006. For a comment, see Guénaël Mettraux, "Dutch Courts' Universal Jurisdiction over Violations of Common Article 3 *qua* War Crimes", 4(2) *JICJ* (2006). Habibullah Jalalzoy and Heshamuddin Hesam, under the regime of Soviet-backed president Najibullah (1979-1992), had both worked in the military intelligence of the KhAD (*Khedamat-e Etelea'at-e Dawlati*), the regime's secret police set up in 1980 to suppress its internal opponents, Hesam as the head of the Afghan military intelligence (he was later the secretary of State attached to the security ministry before going to Moscow as a military attaché) and Jalalzoy as the head of a unit charged with interrogations. Reports of human rights groups allege that Afghan intelligence officials tortured more than 200,000 people during that period, around 50,000 of whom were killed.

[387] The Convention relating to the Status of Refugees of 28 July 1951, Art. 1F, provides that the provisions of the Convention shall not apply to 'any person with respect to whom there are serious reasons for considering that: (a) He has committed a crime against peace, a war crime, or a crime

torture in Afghanistan in the 1990s on the basis of the Convention against Torture, as implemented in domestic legislation, section 134 of the Criminal Justice Act in 1988.[388] In France, two Algerian brothers,[389] also citizens of France, members of the Algerian Relizane Militias,[390] were indicted on 30 March 2004 by a Nîmes investigating judge for torture and crimes against humanity allegedly committed between 1994 and 1997, during a terror campaign against civilians, aimed at finding out information about subversive groups. They have been released on bail awaiting trial.

However, this trend towards investigating and prosecuting alleged torturers seems to be limited to cases where the suspected persons are living on the territory of the investigating country. In Germany, for instance, on 31 March 2006, Federal Prosecutor Kay Nehm issued his decision not to go forward with an investigation against Zakirjon Almatovich Almatov, the Interior Minister of Uzbekistan, for crimes against humanity (tied to the Andijan massacre of 13 May 2005) and systematic torture committed in Uzbekistan's prisons. A complaint had been filed against Almatov and 11 other government officials by eight Uzbek victims, with the support of human rights groups, in December 2005, when Almatov was visiting Germany to receive medical treatment for cancer in a specialised hospital in Hannover.[391] Under the 2002 German Code of Crimes against International Law, genocide, war crimes and crimes against humanity may be investigated and prosecuted under the principle of universal jurisdiction.[392] Although presence of the offender

against humanity, as defined in the international instruments drawn up to make provision in respect of such crimes; (b) He has committed a serious non-political crime outside the country of refuge prior to his admission to that country as a refugee; (c) He has been guilty of acts contrary to the purposes and principles of the United Nations.

388 In the case of *Faryadi Sarwar Zardad*, the accused was a member of a group of warlords Gulbuddin Hekmatyar known as the Hezb-I-islami, the Islamic party, in Afghanistan. Since 1992 he was in control of a checkpoint located in Sarobi on the route between Kabul and Pakistan. Known as Commander Zardad or Zardad Khan, he controlled more than a thousand men who terrorised, tortured, imprisoned, blackmailed and killed civilians passing by this important route. When the Taliban rose to power in Afghanistan in 1996, Zardad sought asylum in the United Kingdom in 1998 using a fake passport. He was living in Kent, at the south of London and was running a pizzeria when he was arrested in July 2003. The first jury could not reach a verdict, however new evidence was brought at the retrial, which began on 8 June 2005, and on 18 July 2005, the second jury found Zardad guilty of torture and of hostage taking. He was sentenced to 20 years imprisonment.

389 The brothers' names are Hocine 'Adda' Mohamed and Abdelkader Mohamed.

390 These government-supported 'self defence groups' were charged with rooting out subversive elements in the population.

391 The European Union imposed sanctions, including a ban on travel to EU countries for 12 Uzbek officials it considers responsible for the indiscriminate and excessive use of force in Andijan. Almatov is on the top of that list. However, days before the EU released the 12 names subject to the visa ban, German authorities granted Almatov a visa on humanitarian grounds to undergo treatment for cancer.

392 Act to Introduce the Code of Crimes against International Law of 26 June 2002, available at: <http://www.iuscomp.org/gla/statutes/VoeStGB.pdf>, Art. 1, Part 1, Section 1: 'This Act shall apply to all criminal offences against international law designated under this Act, to serious criminal offences [2] designated therein even when the offence was committed abroad and bears no relation to Germany.'

on German territory is not a formal requirement for the exercise of jurisdiction, the public prosecutor is not *required* to prosecute if the suspect is not present on German territory and such presence is not to be anticipated.[393] The prosecutor justified his decision not to open an investigation based primarily on the argument that the likelihood of a successful investigation and prosecution was 'non-existent,' given that Uzbekistan was unlikely to co-operate and an investigation in Uzbekistan would be necessary.[394] The Torture Convention makes no exception to the obligation 'to extradite or prosecute' where co-operation of the State of territoriality would be difficult to secure, so long as the alleged offender is able to receive a fair trial.[395] In fact, the system of universal jurisdiction would seem to have been included in the Torture Convention precisely because of the recognition that perpetrators may be unlikely to be prosecuted by their State of nationality, usually also the State where the crimes were committed. Moreover, prosecution of Almatov in Germany had been urged by both the former and current UN Special Rapporteur on Torture, Theo Van Boven and Manfred Novak, respectively,[396] which may further indicate the legitimacy of Germany's exercise of jurisdiction over Almatov in international and German law.[397] It thus seems likely that the decision of the Prosecutor not to proceed with the case was based on policy considerations related to Germany's foreign relations with Uzbekistan rather than legal obstacles. In an interests-analysis approach to the issue, such considerations would have been transparently formulated and weighed against the legal and moral imperative of prosecution.

One may conclude that universal jurisdiction is recognised for torture as an international crime both under customary international law and as implied in the Torture Convention. Due to the particular formulation of the basis for universal jurisdiction in the Torture Convention, States often interpret the universality possibility of jurisdiction as requiring the presence of the alleged offender on their territory before commencing an investigation or prosecution. However, it is unlikely that this is a requirement under customary international law or under the Torture Convention, at least as far as acts of investigation and requests for extradition are concerned. The more plausible interpretation is that presence of the offender on the territory of a State party to the Torture Convention mandates that State to act upon their existing customary entitlement to prosecute (or extradite) suspected torturers.

[393] *Ibid.*, Art. 3, s. 153f. The prosecutor may also dispense with prosecuting if the suspect is not a German national, the offence was not committed against a German, or the suspect is being prosecuted by an international criminal tribunal or by the State of territoriality, nationality or passive personality.

[394] He also noted that some of the alleged acts of torture took place before the entry into force of the 2002 German Code of Crimes against International Law.

[395] See Torture Convention, Art. 7(3).

[396] See Gulnoza Saidazimova, "Uzbekistan: Germany Under Pressure To Reopen Andijon Case", *Radio Free Europe*, 23 June 2006, available at: <http://rfe.rferl.org/featuresarticle/2006/06/B7311ACB-04E8-45D3-AE57-30C34A1CCD1F.html>.

[397] For a critical analysis, see also Salvatore Zappalà, "The German Federal Prosecutor's Decision not to Prosecute a Former Uzbek Minister Missed Opportunity or Prosecutorial Wisdom?", 4(3) *JICJ* 602 (2006).

Part Two
Impediments

Chapter 2
AMNESTIES

Hannah Arendt famously described the types of international crimes committed by the Nazis during WW II as 'those crimes which can neither be punished nor forgiven.'[1] There is no totally perfect response to the perpetration of crimes which strike at the very heart of the notion of humanity. Sometimes, societies deem it better to simply wipe the slate clean and, as Aristotle suggested, to use misfortune politically as the starting point for consensus.[2] Amnesties over international crimes represent one way of accommodating such concerns – unlike pardons, there is no sense of forgiveness in an amnesty law; political expediency is deemed to have created an exception to the normal rules of punishment.[3] But as the value of international criminal justice has risen in stature since the trials of Nuremberg and Tokyo and particularly in the last two decades and the rights of victims gained substantive legal weight, the legality of such measures of forced amnesia has increasingly come under question. Despite these trends, international law remains subject to interpretation as to the question of whether amnesties for international crimes are authorised, making an interests-analysis approach particularly pertinent as a nuanced means to resolve the dilemma.

2.1 Definition and historical context

Amnesties[4] designed to preclude the prosecution of persons suspected or accused of international crimes usually take the form of legislative or constitutional acts of States, are contained in treaties or political agreements, or may be declared as

---

[1] Hannah Arendt, *Eichmann in Jerusalem: A Report on the Banality of Evil* (New York: Penguin Books, 1994 (first published by Viking Press in 1963)), at 241.

[2] *Constitution of Athens* (40), cited in Barbara Cassin, "'Removing the perpetuity of hatred': on South Africa as a role model", 862 *IRRC* 238 (June 2006).

[3] *Black's Law Dictionary* defines amnesty as '[a] pardon extended by the government to a group or class of persons, usually for a political offense; the act of a sovereign power officially forgiving certain classes of persons who are subject to trial but have not yet been convicted … Unlike an ordinary pardon, amnesty is usually addressed to crimes against state sovereignty – that is, to political offenses with respect to which forgiveness is deemed more expedient for the public welfare than prosecution and punishment.' Bryan A. Garner, *Black's Law Dictionary*, 8th edn. (St. Paul, Minn: West Group, 2004), at 93.

[4] Amnesty literally means '[f]orgetfulness, oblivion; an intentional overlooking.' *Oxford English Dictionary*, 2nd edn. (1989). Legally, it means foreclosing criminal prosecution for past offences. This pre-conviction measure may be distinguished from a pardon, which officially recognises the guilt

an exercise of executive power. Amnesties for war crimes and other international crimes come into being mainly when States are going through periods of transition, often from war to peace, and of extreme political upheaval, for example, the handing over of power from dictatorial military regimes to democratic civilian governments. Most States have the possibility of granting amnesties within the framework of their constitution for crimes committed in their national legal orders. However, may States also issue amnesties for crimes against the international legal order?

The granting of amnesty for serious crimes, particularly those committed during war, has a long and varied history.[5] The oldest record of a peace treaty – that ending the battle of Kadesh between the Egyptians (under the pharaoh Ramses II) and the Hittites of 1286 B.C. – may have included a form of amnesty for repatriated refugees.[6] An amnesty law was passed by Thrasybulus in the aftermath of the civil war in Athens in 404 B.C. which covered both sides, except for the leaders of the defeated side (the 'Thirty') and their worst agents.[7] Roman commanders also appeared to have used amnesties to quell their opponents, as did Julius Caesar, and the practice gradually became a common feature of peace treaties. European history of the seventeenth to nineteenth centuries shows that amnesties were most likely to be inserted in peace treaties when there was no clear victor or when the parties to the conflict had a genuine desire to create a stable and long-lasting peace.[8] The practice of granting amnesties appears to have been a peculiarly European practice up until the twentieth century, although the early government of the United States incorporated an amnesty in Article I of the Treaty with the Delawares of 1778 with indigenous groups,[9] and a number of peace treaties between Great Britain and non-European countries also contained amnesties.[10]

In the twentieth century, the two major inter-State wars ended with decisive victories for one side and hence efforts for prosecution of the defeated side were

---

of the offender but foregoes the sentence. The word 'amnesty' is derived from the Greek '*amnestia*' meaning oblivion or not remembering.

[5] For a thorough discussion, see Andreas O'Shea, *Amnesty for Crime in International Law and Practice* (The Hague: Kluwer Law International, 2002), at 5-33.

[6] One of the inscriptions has been interpreted by archeologists as: 'But as for the man who shall be brought to the great ruler of Egypt, do not cause that his crime be raised against him; do not cause that his wife or his house or his children be destroyed; do not cause that he be slain; do not cause that injury be done to his eyes, ears, arms, mouth or legs.' Quoted in *ibid.*, at 5.

[7] *Ibid.*, at 6, citing N.G.L. Hammond, *A History of Ancient Greece to 322 B.C.*, 3rd edn. (1986), at 444.

[8] *Ibid.*, at 15, comparing, e.g., the amnesty clause inserted in Art. 2 of the Treaty of Westphalia of 1648, ending the Thirty Years War, as well as other treaties, and the lack of amnesty clauses in most treaties concluded during the Napoleonic wars.

[9] Art. I of the Treaty with the Delawares of 1778 provided, 'That all offences or acts of hostilities by one, or either of the contracting parties against the other, be mutually forgiven, and buried in the depths of oblivion, never more to be had remembrance.'

[10] E.g., the Treaty of Nanking of 1842 (Great Britain and China) and the Treaty of Vereeniging of 1902 ending the Boer war (Great Britain and burgher [Boer] forces).

the foremost concern.[11] In addition, the outlawing of the resort to aggressive war and the setting up of a collective security system made the use of amnesties in peace agreements a less obvious option.[12] However, a declaration of amnesty was attached to the Treaty of Lausanne of 1923 to the Turks covering the massacre of the Armenians,[13] overriding the earlier Treaty of Sèvres of 1920 which provided for prosecution of these crimes.[14] An informally agreed to amnesty was linked to the accord between Germany and Austria of 11 July 1936, which granted amnesty to all Nazis, except those convicted for the most serious crimes.[15] At the end of WW II, prosecution became the focus for dealing with Nazi war criminals leading to the Nuremberg trial and subsequent prosecutions and armistice agreements concluded with Axis countries did not contain amnesty clauses.[16]

On the other hand, General Douglas MacArthur, Supreme Commander of the Allied Occupation Forces in Japan pardoned some Japanese officials who had been sentenced to death and also amnestied the Emperor of Japan, a move which has been said to have contributed to reconciliation between the US and Japan,[17] but which angered many of those who viewed Hirohito as a major mastermind behind the Japanese war of aggression and related war crimes. In a secret deal, MacArthur also offered immunity from prosecution to the military commander and staff of the infamous biological Unit 731, responsible for conducting biological experiments in relation to chemical and biological weapons development on live prisoners of war and used in biological warfare against the Chinese,[18] in return for their research.[19] Despite noting that trials against Nazi doctors who had engaged

---

[11] Efforts to prosecute war criminals made at the end of WW I were less than successful. The Treaty of Versailles in Art. 227 provided for the prosecution of Kaiser William II, however this never came to pass due to the Netherlands' refusal of his extradition. A small number of German officials were prosecuted before the court in Leipzig, constituting a fraction of the number of persons listed by the Allies as having been accused of war crimes.

[12] O'Shea, *Amnesty for Crime in International Law and Practice*, at 15.

[13] See Declaration of Amnesty and Protocol, 24 July 1923, Australian Treaty Series 1924 No. 13, Department of Foreign Affairs and Trade, Canberra, available at: <http://www.austlii.edu.au/au/other/dfat/treaties/1924/13.html>; Treaty of Peace with Turkey Signed at Lausanne, 24 July 1923, *The Treaties of Peace 1919-1923, Vol. II*, Carnegie Endowment for International Peace, New York, 1924, text available at: <http://net.lib.byu.edu/~rdh7/wwi/1918p/lausanne.html>.

[14] See Arts. 226-228 Peace Treaty of Sèvres, 10 August 1920, text available at: <http://net.lib.byu.edu/~rdh7/wwi/versa/sevres1.html>.

[15] *Nuremberg Trial Proceedings*, Vol. I, Indictment, Count One at IV(F)3(b).

[16] See, e.g., the armistice agreements with Italy in 1943, Romania in 1944, Bulgaria in 1944 and Hungary in 1945, available at: <www.yale.edu/lawweb/avalon.wwii>.

[17] O'Shea, *Amnesty for Crime in International Law and Practice*, at 16.

[18] There were no survivors of Unit 731. An estimated 300,000 Chinese peasants were killed by germ warfare launched by the Japanese. Sheldon D. Harris, *Factories of Death: Japanese Biological Warfare, 1932-1945 and the American Cover Up* (London: Routledge, 1994).

[19] Bernard V.A. Röling and Antonio Cassese, *The Tokyo Trial and Beyond* (Cambridge: Policy, 1992), at 18. Nicholas D. Kristof, "Unmasking Horror – A special report; Japan Confronting Gruesome War Atrocity", *New York Times*, 17 March 1995, available at: <http://query.nytimes.com/gst/fullpage.html?sec=health&res=990CE2D71630F934A25750C0A963958260 >; "How the United States Protected Japanese War Criminals and Facilitated Japan's Denial of War Guilt and War Crimes", <http://www.users.bigpond.com/battleforaustralia/JapWarCrimes/USWarCrime_Coverup.html>; Anita Mc-

in similar activity were currently underway before the IMT in Nuremberg, the Sub-Committee for the Far East of the State-War-Navy Co-ordinating Committee at Washington concluded that, '[t]he value to the U.S. of Japanese BW data is of such importance to national security as to far outweigh the value accruing from war crimes' prosecution.'[20]

Although a number of major inter-State peace agreements post WW II did not contain amnesty clauses,[21] decisions not to prosecute persons charged with international crimes were agreed to in the Evian Accord of 1962 concerning atrocities committed by French military officials and Algerian independence fighters,[22] as well as after the Bangladesh war of 1971 when India and Bangladesh agreed not to prosecute Pakistani soldiers charged with genocide and crimes against humanity in exchange for political recognition of Bangladesh by Pakistan and the withdrawal of Pakistan's case against India before the International Court of Justice.[23]

Amnesties have been employed by governments as a means of ending civil wars or insurrections since at least the eighteenth century.[24] This trend continued and intensified in the twentieth century in countries from almost every region of the world, increasingly by the passing of amnesty laws, as opposed to exercises of presidential discretion.[25] Although some countries opted for a policy of prosecu-

Naught, "Unit 731: Japan's biological force", *BBC*, 1 February 2002, available at: <http://news.bbc.co.uk/2/hi/programmes/correspondent/1796044.stm>.

[20] The US State Department was stringently opposed to this deal, which it regarded as contrary to international law and human morality, and would also be a source of embarrassment to the US once revealed. See Yuki Tanaka, *Hidden Horrors: Japanese War Crimes in World War II* (Boulder: Westview, 1998), 154; Harris, *supra* n. 18, at 208-221.

[21] For example, the Agreements of the Cessation of Hostilities in Cambodia, Laos and Vietnam of 1954, the Camp David Accords of 1978 and the Dayton Peace Accords of 1995.

[22] One may note, however, that French courts, in cases challenging the amnesty law have gone to great pains to distinguish the crimes at issue from crimes against humanity, the implication being that the latter cannot be subject to an amnesty law. See *Aussaresses*, France, Criminal Chamber of the Court of Cassation, Judgment of 17 June 2003, *Bull. crim.* (2003) 122, at 465-469. See also *Boudarel*, France, Cass. Crim. 1 April 1993 (*Association Nationale des Anciens Prisonniers-internés d'Indocine contre G. Bouderal*), *Bull. Crim.* (1993) 143, at 354-5.

[23] Michael P. Scharf, "Swapping Amnesty for Peace: Was there a duty to prosecute international crimes in Haiti?", 31(1) *Texas International Law Journal* 36-37 (1996). An estimated one million East Pakistanis were killed by West Pakistani troops during the war over Bangladesh's independence. India and Bangladesh initially agreed to prosecute 195 persons charged with genocide and crimes against humanity out of the 10,000 troops who had been captured by India. Pakistan filed a case with the ICJ in a bid to compel India to repatriate the Pakistani troops. The charges and the case were dropped in the 1973 deal.

[24] Art. 6 of the Paris Peace Treaty of 1783 ending the American war of independence provided for a broad amnesty. In 1784, Emperor Joseph II of modern-day Romania granted a general amnesty to all the participants of a feudal rebellion except for the leaders. Proclamations of amnesty were issued at the end of the American Civil War in 1865 and 1868, the first being conditional and the second unconditional. In Brazil in 1894, President Jose de Marais negotiated the end of a war in the south using amnesty as a bargaining tool with the rebels. O'Shea, *Amnesty for Crime in International Law and Practice*, at 20-21.

[25] Amnesties have been passed as part of the peace process in internal conflicts in Albania, Algeria, Angola, Argentina, Burundi, Bhutan, Bolivia, Brazil, Bulgaria, Cambodia, Chad, Chile, Colombia, the Comoros, Croatia, Cyprus, Democratic Republic of the Congo, Ecuador, El Salvador, Ghana, Gua-

tion in the aftermath of military dictatorships, notably Greece in the mid-1970s[26] and Ethiopia,[27] the use of amnesties in political transitions became increasingly used and gained notoriety in the 1970s and 1980s when a host of military juntas in various countries in Latin America granted themselves amnesties for all the crimes committed by their agents during their reigns before handing over power to civilian governments or compelled the new governments to do so.[28] In response to these flagrantly self-serving manoeuvres, which were then copied by various governments in Africa,[29] human rights organisations and victims groups began demanding justice, truth and reparations from the new governments in relation to past atrocities. In particular, family members of those who had been forcibly 'disappeared' under the military regimes opposed the amnesties which foreclosed investigations into what had happened to their loved ones, leaving them in a state of perpetual pain and doubt.[30] Some governments sought to respond to such pressures by instituting truth commissions, which would investigate events and the

---

temala, Haiti, Jordan, Mauritania, Mauritius, Mozambique, Nepal, Oman, Poland, Romania, Russia, Sierra Leone, South Africa, Spain, Sri Lanka, Syria, Serbia and Uruguay. Naomi Roht-Arriaza, "State Responsibility to Investigate and Prosecute Grave Violations of Human Rights in International Law", 78 *California Law Review* 458-61 (1990); U.S. Delegation Draft, "State Practice Regarding Amnesties and Pardons" (1 August 1997), available at: <http://www.iccnow.org/documents/USDraftonAmnestiesPardons.pdf>; O'Shea, *Amnesty for Crime in International Law and Practice*, at 22.

[26] After the Colonels lost power in 1974, the civilian regime tried the military leaders of the former regime as well as hundreds of lower-ranking military officers accused of torture. Carla Edelenbos, "Human Rights Violations: A Duty to Prosecute?", 7(5) *LJIL* 13 (1994).

[27] Trials of some 3,000 members of the Mengistu regime began in the mid-1990s. According to Amnesty International, using official statistics made available in mid-2003, since the beginning of the trials in 1994, 1,017 persons have been tried, 552 of whom have been sentenced and 3,426 others are still awaiting to be brought to trial. In the course of 2003, six of the Accused were condemned to death and others had received prison sentences. The lengthy trial against Mengistu and 72 other senior leaders of the Derg regime came to an end when the court rendered its verdict in December 2006.

[28] Argentina (Full Stop Law 23492 of 1986 and Due Obedience Law 23521 of 1989, and Presidential Pardons of 1989 and 1990), Chile (1978 Amnesty law 2191, upheld by Supreme Court in 1990), Brazil (1979 Amnesty law 6683), El Salvador (Law of National Reconciliation 1992, excludes those already convicted in jury trial and those 'serious acts of violence whose impact on society requires, with greater urgency public knowledge of the truth'; General Amnesty Law for the Consolidation of Peace of 1993), Guatemala (Amnesty Decree 8-86, of 1986), Uruguay (1984 Naval Pact; Ley de Caducidad de la Pretension Punitiva del Estado por Delitos de Militares y Policias durante el Regimen de Facto, Law 15848, 1986; Texto de Acuerdo entre las Fuerzas Armadas y Politicos en el Que Se Acuerda el Nuevo Proceso Democratico, 1984, reaffirmed in 1989 plebiscite).

[29] E.g., Zimbabwe (Amnesty Ordinance 3 of 1979 and the Amnesty (General Pardon) Ordinance 12 of 1980; Clemency Order No. 1 of 1988 and of 2000), Lesotho (Amnesty Act No. 7 of 1980), Uganda (Amnesty Act of 2000).

[30] Emblematic of these groups was the *Asociación Madres de Plaza de Mayo*, an association of Argentine mothers and grandmothers whose children 'disappeared' under the military dictatorship between 1976 and 1983, who would walk around the Plaza de Mayo in Buenos Aires every Thursday, wearing white headscarves and bearing pictures of their children or grandchildren, in order to press the government into finding out what had happened to those kidnapped.

causes of conflicts, without necessarily attributing responsibility to individuals or handing out sanctions.[31]

During this period, the Inter-American Commission on Human Rights began to receive complaints from individuals from a range of Latin American countries asserting that the amnesties passed by the military regimes violated basic human rights guaranteed under the American Convention on Human Rights, principally – the right to judicial protection and the right to an effective remedy.[32] The Inter-American Court of Human Rights also recognised that investigation and punishment should follow serious violations of fundamental rights under the Convention[33] and that certain amnesty laws violated these.[34] Following suit, the UN Human Rights Committee came to similar conclusions with regard to the duty to investigate serious crimes, to ensure freedom from such acts and to guarantee the right to the remedy under the ICCPR.[35] Other bodies of the UN concerned with human

[31] Argentina, Chile, El Salvador, Guatemala, Haiti, and Peru established truth commissions as a mechanism to address massive human rights violations in the recent past. For a schematic overview of many of the truth commissions that have existed in all regions of the world, see Priscilla B. Hayner, "Truth Commissions: A schematic overview", 88(862) *IRRC* (Cambridge) 295 (June 2006).

[32] See IAComHR, Report No. 26/92 (El Salvador), 82nd Sess., OEA/ser.L/V/II/82 (24 September 1992); Report No. 29/92 (Uruguay), 82nd Sess., OEA/ser.L/V/II.82, Doc. 25 (2 October 1992); Report No. 24/92 (Argentina), 82nd Sess., OEA/ser.L/V/II.82, Doc. 24 (2 October 1992).

[33] IACtHR, Case *Velasquez Rodriguez*, Judgment of 29 July 1988 (ser. C), No. 4, para. 174; Case *Neira Alegra and others*, Judgment of 19 January 1995 (ser. C), No. 20, para. 69; Case *Caballero Delgado and Santana*, Judgment of 8 December 1995 (ser. C), No. 22, para. 56; Case *Blake*, Preliminary Exceptions, Judgment of 2 July 1996 (ser. C), No. 27, para. 39; Case *Castillo Paez*, Judgment of 3 November 1997 (ser. C), No. 34, para. 90; *Barrios Altos* case *(Chumbipuma Aguirre, et al.,* v. *Peru)* 14 March 2001; *Almonacid-Arellano, et al.,* v. *Chile*, Preliminary Objections, Merits, Reparations and Costs. Judgment of 26 September 2006 (ser. C), No. 154 (hereafter, *Barrios Altos* case); *Case of La Cantuta* v. *Peru*. Merits, Reparations and Costs. Judgment of 29 November 2006 (ser. C), No. 162.

[34] *Consuelo* v. *Argentina*, Cases 10.147, 10.181, 10.240, 10.262, 10.309, 10.311, IACtHR 28, OEA/ser.L/V./II.83, doc. 4, at 41 (1993) paras. 38-39; *Mendoza* v. *Uruguay*, Cases 10.029, 10.036, 10.145, 10.305, 10.372, 10. 373, 10.374, and 10.375, IACtHR 29, OEA/ser.L/V./II.83, doc. 14 at 14 (1993), paras. 47-49; *Hermosilla*, Case 10.843, IACtHR 36 at paras. 68-72); *Almonacid-Arellano, et al.,* v. *Chile*, IACtHR, Preliminary Objections, Merits, Reparations and Costs. Judgment of 26 September 2006 (ser. C), No. 154; *Case of La Cantuta* v. *Peru*, IACtHR, Merits, Reparations and Costs. Judgment of 29 November 2006 (ser. C), No. 162.

[35] *Rodriguez* v. *Uruguay*, Communication No. 322/1988, UN Human Rights Committee, 19 July 1994; Human Rights Committee General Comment No. 20 on Art. 7 (replacing General Comment 7 concerning prohibition of torture and cruel treatment or punishment, 10 March 1992 (finding that amnesties are 'generally incompatible' with the duty to investigate acts such as torture, to guarantee freedom from such acts and to ensure an effective remedy to victims). The HRC reaffirmed its position with regard to amnesty laws in Chile (HRC "Concluding Observations" to Chile in 1999, UN Doc. CCPR/C/79/Add.104, para. 7), France (UN Doc. CCPR/C/79/Add.80, para. 13), Lebanon (UN Doc. CCPR/C/79/Add.78, para. 12), El Salvador (UN Doc. CCPR/C/79/Add. 34, para. 7), Haiti (UN Doc. A/50/40, paras. 224-241), Peru (UN Doc. CCPR/C/79/Add.67, para. 9), Uruguay (UN Doc. CCPR/C/79/Add.19, paras. 7 and 11; CCPR/C/79/Add.90, Part "C. Principal subjects of concern and recommendations"; and the Decision of 9 August 1994 in the case of Hugo Rodríguez (Uruguay), Communication No. 322/1988, CCPR/C/51/D/322/1988, para. 12.4), Yemen (UN Doc. A/50/40, paras. 242-265) and Croatia (Concluding Observations of the Human Rights Committee: Republic of Croatia, 4 April 2001, UN Doc. CCPR/CO/71/HRV, para. 11)

rights – the GA[36] and the Commission on Human Rights (CHR),[37] including its various Special Rapporteurs and Working Groups with related mandates[38] – issued resolutions and reports condemning the 'culture of impunity' in relation to mass international crimes and called upon States to bring the perpetrators to justice. A wave of academic writing began to emerge in support of the these findings, arguing that a duty to prosecute grave human rights offences existed at international law and that States violated this duty as well as a number of essential human rights by passing blanket amnesty laws.[39] Contrary to the earlier observation that an amnesty in a peace deal (at least between States) signalled a genuine desire on the part of the parties for lasting peace by removing sources of enmity, a body of literature

---

[36] See for example, GA Res. 37/185, para. 10 (1982) (urging El Salvador to 'assume its obligation to … prosecute and to punish those found responsible for assassinations, acts of torture and other forms of cruel, inhuman or degrading treatment'); GA Res. 36/157, para. 4(e) (1981) (urging Chile to 'prosecute and punish those responsible for … disappearances'). In 1985, the GA adopted the Declaration of Basic Principles of Justice for Victims of Crime and Abuse of Power, which calls on States to 'enact and enforce legislation proscribing acts that violate internationally recognized norms relating to human rights.' In 1989 the GA endorsed ECOSOC Res. 1989/65 which adopted the 'Principles on the Effective Prevention and Investigation of Extra-Legal, Arbitrary and Summary Executions.' Principle 19.2 provides that: 'In no circumstances, including a state of war, siege or other public emergency, shall blanket immunity from prosecution be granted to any person allegedly involved in extra-legal, arbitrary or summary executions.' UN Doc. A/Res/44/162. In 1992, the GA adopted the Declaration on the Protection of All Persons from Enforced Disappearance, which provides that those responsible for this crime 'shall not benefit from any special amnesty law or similar measures that might have the effect of exempting them from any criminal proceedings or sanction.' Art. 18 Declaration on the Protection of All Persons from Enforced Disappearance, UN GAOR Res. 47/133, 18 December 1992. This firm stance is slightly tempered by Art. 18(b) which allows States the right of pardon so long as the extreme seriousness of acts of enforced disappearance are taken into account.

[37] Commission on Human Rights Res. 2002/79, para. 2: 'amnesties should not be granted to those who commit violations of international humanitarian and human rights law that constitute serious crimes and urges States to take action in accordance with their obligations under international law.'

[38] See Report prepared by the Special Rapporteur on the situation of human rights in Chile in accordance with paragraph 11 of the Commission on Human Rights resolution 1983/38 of 8 March 1983, UN Doc. A/38/385, para. 341 (1983); Final report on the situation of human rights in El Salvador submitted to the Commission on Human Rights by Mr. José Antonio Pastor Ridruejo in fulfilment of the mandate conferred under Human Rights CHR Resolution 1986/39, 42 *UN Hum. Rts. Comm* at 85, para. 312, UN Doc. E/CN.4/1989/18; Report of the Working Group on Enforced or Involuntary Disappearances, 47 *UN Hum. Rts. Comm* at 86, para. 406. See also Principle 15, Basic Principles and Guidelines on the Right to Reparation for Victims of Gross Violations of Human Rights and Humanitarian Law; Final report of the Study concerning the right to restitution, compensation and rehabilitation for victims of gross violations of human rights and fundamental freedoms. "Question of the Impunity of Perpetrators of Violations of Human Rights (civil and political rights)", Final Report prepared by Mr. Joinet pursuant to Sub-Commission Resolution 1996/119, E.CN.4/Sub.2/1997/20, 26 June 1997.

[39] Naomi Roht-Arriaza, "State Responsibility to Investigate and Prosecute Grave Violations of Human Rights in International Law", 78 *California Law Review* 451 (1990) (urging the necessity of an international duty to investigate serious human rights violations); Diane F. Orentlicher, "Settling Accounts: The Duty to Prosecute Human Rights Violations of a Prior Regime", 100 *Yale Law Journal* (1991) (analysing the law generated by the Nuremberg trials and the UN's actions affirming that law to 'require punishment of crimes against humanity'); M. Cherif Bassiouni, "International Crimes: Jus Cogens and Obligatio Erga Omnes", 59 *Law and Contemporary Problems* 63 (1996) (arguing that *jus cogens* crimes entail a duty to prosecute).

arose asserting that amnesties undermined the very principles needed to create a democratic and stable society based on the rule of law.[40]

Although amnesties continued to be passed as a means of negotiating peace deals, often with the tacit or explicit support of the United Nations, notably in Haiti in 1993,[41] Angola in 1994,[42] South Africa in 1995,[43] Sierra Leone in 1996[44] and Algeria in 1999[45] and 2006,[46] a general presumption of illegality of amnesties for international crimes eventually found its way into the doctrine and practice of the United Nations.[47] When signing the Lomé Peace Agreement of 1999 which established a framework for ending the civil war in Sierra Leone, including by offering a blanket amnesty, the UN Secretary-General's special representative to Sierra Leone appended to his signature a statement that the UN holds the understanding that the amnesty provisions of the Agreement shall not apply to war crimes, other serious violations of international humanitarian law, crimes against humanity and genocide.[48] In 2002, when the Luena Memorandum ending the civil war in Angola provided for an amnesty, the special representative of the UN Secretary-General again made a hand-written disclaimer to the effect that the UN 'does not recognise amnesties for crimes against humanity and war crimes.'[49] In his 2004 report

[40] See, e.g., Ruti Teitel, "Transitional Jurisprudence: The Role of Law in Political Transformation", 106(7) *Yale Law Journal* 2009 (1997); Orentlicher, "Settling Accounts", at 2547.

[41] See *United Nations, The Situation of Democracy and Human Rights in Haiti: Report of the Secretary-General*, UN Doc. A/47/97-S/26063 (1993), reproducing the text of the Governors Island Agreement.

[42] Protocolo de Lusaka, 21 de Novembro de 1994 (Lusaka Protocol), UN Doc. S/1994/1441, annex (1994). The 1994 Lusaka Protocol was signed under the auspices of the United Nations and included a blanket amnesty. See also SC Res. 1055, 8 May 1996, para. 9 (welcoming the proclamation by the National Assembly of Angola of amnesty arrangements) and SC Res. 1064, 11 July 1996, para. 9 (commending the Angolan government for the proclamation of an amnesty law).

[43] Promotion of National Unity and Reconciliation Act, No. 34 of 1995 (South Africa).

[44] *Peace Agreement between the Government of the Republic of Sierra Leone and the Revolutionary United Front of Sierra Leone (RUF)*, 20 November 1996.

[45] Civil Concord Law, June 1999 (Algeria).

[46] Charter of National Reconciliation and Peace of 2006 (Algeria). For a discussion, see George Joffé, "National Reconciliation and General Amnesty in Algeria", in Sune Haugbolle and Anders Hastrup (eds.), *The Politics of Violence, Truth and Reconciliation in the Arab Middle East* (Oxon/New York: Routledge, 2009), at 63-76; Laura Scully, "Neither Justice, Nor Oasis: Algeria's Amnesty Law", 33 *Brooklyn Journal of International Law* 975-1035 (2007-2008).

[47] Such a position may be contrasted to the negative response of UN Secretary-General Kofi Annan to Angola's issuing of an arrest warrant on 24 July 1999 against Savimbi, leader of UNITA, for charges of rebellion, sabotage, murder and torture, which was to state that the warrant was 'wrong' and that 'you make peace with enemies, and to make peace you have to have communications, either directly or through third parties.' A. Vines, *Angola unravels, The rise and fall of the Lusaka Peace Process* (New York: Human Rights Watch, 1999), at 29.

[48] See UN Doc. S/1999/836, at 2, para. 1. See also SC Res. 1315, 14 August 2000, preamble. For legal analysis as to the legal effect of the disclaimer, see Avril McDonald, "Sierra Leone's Uneasy Peace: The Amnesties Granted in the Lomé Peace Agreement and the United Nations' Dilemma", 13(1) *Humanitares Volkerrecht* 11 (2000); Carsten Stahn, "United Nations peace-building, amnesties and alternative forms of justice: A change in practice?", 84(845) *IRRC* 191 (March 2002).

[49] José Doria, "Angola: A Case Study in the Challenges of Achieving Peace and the Question of Amnesty or Prosecuting of War Crimes in Mixed Armed Conflicts", 5 *YIHL* 47 (2002).

on transitional justice and the rule of law, the Secretary-General stated that peace agreements and Security Council resolutions and mandates should '[r]eject any endorsement of amnesty for genocide, war crimes, or crimes against humanity, including those relating to ethnic, gender and sexually based international crimes, [and] ensure that no such amnesty previously granted is a bar to prosecution before any United Nations-created or -assisted court.'[50] This change in practice by the UN paralleled the adoption of the Rome Statute of the International Criminal Court in 1998, signalling that States, by voluntarily accepting criminal prosecution for the gravest international crimes under the principle of complementarity, were in favour of prosecution rather than forgetting in the aftermath of conflict.[51] Nonetheless, the controversy in Rome over how the issue of amnesty should be dealt with in the ICC Statute and the resulting silence in the Statute illustrated the continuing ambiguous international attitude with regard to the legality of amnesties.

Most national courts which have adjudicated the validity of their own amnesty laws have found them to be valid.[52] A notable exception to this practice was the 2001 decision of the Federal Court of Buenos Aires, which found the amnesty laws in Argentina[53] to be unconstitutional and invalid,[54] a decision upheld by the Supreme Court in 2005.[55] Where third States have evaluated a foreign State's amnesty law, courts have refused to give the amnesty any legal effect.[56] The Sierra Leone Special Court, the only international criminal court to have directly faced the issue to date, held in 2004 that the Lomé amnesty had no effect *vis-à-vis* its jurisdiction.[57]

---

[50] *Report of the Secretary-General on the Rule of Law and Transitional Justice in Conflict and Post-Conflict Societies,* UN Doc. S/2004/16 (23 August 2004), para. 64.

[51] See *infra*, notes 71-96 and accompanying text, the discussion on amnesties and the Rome Statute of the International Criminal Court.

[52] See *Azanian People's Organisation and Others* v. *The President of the Republic of South Africa and Others*, South Africa, 1996 (4) SA 671 (CC), 1996 (8) BCLR 1015 (CC) (hereafter, *AZAPO* case); *Proceedings No. 10-93 of the Supreme Court of El Salvador on the Amnesty Law*, reprinted in 3 *Transitional Justice* (1995), at 549-55; *Camps*, Argentina, Supreme Court, 310:1162, 1301-3 (22 June 1987) (declararing the Due Obedience Law and the Full Stop Law to be valid).

[53] Although neither of the two laws were explicitly amnesty laws, the Full Stop Law and Due Obedience Law were held to effectively amount to amnesty laws in a decision of the Argentine Supreme Court in 1987. *Camps*, Argentina, Supreme Court, 310:1162, 1301-3 (22 June 1987).

[54] *Resolución del Cavallo*, Argentina, Decision of 6 March 2001, available at: <http://www.derechos.org/nizkor/arg/ley/juezcavallo03mar.html> (in which Judge Gabriel Cavallo declared the Argentinian amnesty laws unconstitutional and invalid).

[55] *Simón, Julio Héctor y otros s/privación ilegítima de la libertad*, Argentina, Case S. 1767. XXXVIII (14 June 2005). For commentary, see Christine A.E. Bakker, "A Full Stop to Amnesty in Argentina: The Simón Case", 3(5) *JICJ* 1106 (2005); Santiago Legarre, "Crimes against Humanity, Reasonableness and the Law: the *Simon* case in the Supreme Court of Argentina", 5(3) *Chinese Journal of International Law* 723 (2006).

[56] For example, in several cases involving the forcible disappearance of Spanish citizens in Argentina it has been held that Argentina's domestic amnesty is not binding on Spanish courts. See *Fortunata Galtieri* case, Judgment of March 1997, available at: <http:www.derechos.org/nizkor/arg/espana/authgalt.html>; *Ely Ould Dah*, France, Court of Cassation, Criminal division, decision of 23 October 2002, *Bulletin criminel* 2002 No. 195 at 725 (refusing to recognise the Mauritanian amnesty).

[57] *Kallon, Morris and Kamara, Brima Bazzy*, SCSL, Appeals Chamber Decision on Challenge to Jurisdiction: Lomé Accord Amnesty, 13 March 2004, Case No. SCSL-2004-15-AR72(E) (hereafter,

Despite the emergence of an international system of prosecution for dealing with international crimes, the reasons for offering amnesties have not diminished and some countries in the midst of violence have continued to rely on promises of non-prosecution as a means to bring all parties to a conflict to the negotiating table or to begin a process of demobilisation, reintegration or reconciliation.[58] Thus, the members of the International Truth and Reconciliation Commission for Sierra Leone concluded that they were:

> '… unable to condemn the resort to amnesty by those who negotiated the Lomé Peace Agreement. The explanations given by the Government negotiators, including in their testimonies before the Truth and Reconciliation Commission, are compelling in this respect. In all good faith, they believed that the RUF would not agree to end hostilities if the Agreement were not accompanied by a form of pardon or amnesty … The Commission is unable to declare that it considers amnesty too high a price to pay for the delivery of peace to Sierra Leone, under the circumstances that prevailed in July 1999.'[59]

Reflecting a need to reconcile this difficult reality with the forceful rhetoric of international criminal law theory and taking into account the progressive conditional amnesty in South Africa, which even critics of amnesties have been unable to de-legitimise,[60] a new wave of academic writing on the subject has striven to identify certain conditions or circumstances that may legitimise an amnesty covering international crimes without violating international law or the principles of international criminal justice – principally those of justice, truth and reparation.[61]

Kallon and Kamara Decision on Amnesty case), quoting Antonio Cassese, *International Criminal Law* (2003), at 315.

[58] For example, on 27 February 2006, Algeria's full cabinet, with President Abdelaziz Bouteflika presiding, approved the 'Decree Implementing the Charter for Peace and National Reconciliation,' which provides for a broad amnesty excluding those who 'committed, or were accomplices in, or instigators of, acts of collective massacres, rape, or the use of explosives in public places.' In Colombia, Law 975, known as the 'Justice and Peace Law,' regulating Decree 4760 of 2005, provides for the suspension, interruption or abandoning of a criminal investigation in cases included in Art. 324 of the Criminal Procedure Code in exchange for demobilisation of paramilitaries. See Office in Colombia, OHCHR, "The regulations regarding the 'Law on Justice and Peace' do not adequately ensure due respect for the rights of victims", 4 January 2006. In Burundi, the 'Law of 21 November 2003 relating to the judicial proceedings for provisional immunity of political leaders returning from exile' provided provisional immunity to political leaders allegedly involved in crimes with a 'political' element, on the understanding that in the future the truth would be established and the perpetrators would be held to account for their crimes. In Angola, an amnesty law of 2000 granted amnesty to all those who deposed of their arms and intended to embrace the peace process (Lei de Amnistia No. 7/00, de Dezembro de 2000, Diário da República, I Série – No. 53). In Sierra Leone the Lomé Peace Agreement of 8 July 1999 granted a blanket amnesty to all those fighting in the civil war. The Mozambique Peace Agreement of 1994 provided for blanket amnesties as did the 1996 amnesty law adopted in Angola.

[59] *Witness to Truth: Report of the Sierra Leone Truth and Reconciliation Commission* (5 October 2004), available at: <http://www.trcsierraleone.org/drwebsite/publish/index.shtml>, at 365.

[60] Jeremy Sarkin, "An Evaluation of the South African Amnesty Process", in Audrey R. Chapman and Hugo van der Merwe (eds.), *Truth and Reconciliation in South Africa* (Pennsylvania: University of Pennsylvania, 2008), at 93.

[61] Scharf, "Swapping Amnesty for Peace" (arguing that there was no duty to prosecute crimes against humanity in Haiti and noting the short term beneficial effects of the amnesty); John Dugard,

The terms 'transitional justice' or 'restorative justice' have sometimes been used to describe these alternative approaches to the notion of criminal justice while incorporating limited or conditional amnesties.[62] Nonetheless, not all South Africa style amnesty-for-truth schemes have gained legitimacy. The Commission of Truth and Friendship established by Indonesia and Timor-Leste in March 2005, which offers an amnesty to those involved in human rights violations committed in 1999 'who cooperate fully in revealing the truth' has not garnered much international support and the United Nations has refused to participate.[63]

2.2. Amnesties and international and hybrid criminal courts and tribunals

The treatment of amnesties by international and hybrid criminal court and tribunals reveals an interesting dichotomy. While the constitutive instruments of international courts tend to be absent any specific provision on the legal effect of an amnesty law, the statutes of hybrid tribunals have often faced the issue head on, with an explicit provision stating that the amnesty would have no effect on the jurisdiction of the court.

"Dealing with Crimes of a Past Regime: Is Amnesty Still an Option?", 12(4) *LJIL* 1001 (1999) (arguing that while unconditional amnesties should be considered illegal, amnesties given after an investigation such as the South African Truth and Reconciliation Commission may contribute to the achievement of peace and justice in a transitional society more than mandatory prosecution); William W. Burke-White, "Reframing Impunity: Applying Liberal International Law Theory to an Analysis of Amnesty Legislation", 42(2) *HILJ* (2001) (arguing that amnesties which have been enacted through the democratic process have more legitimacy); Ronald Slye, "The Legitimacy of Amnesties under International Law and General Principles of Anglo-American Law: Is Legitimate Amnesty Possible", 43 *VJIL* (2002) (arguing that those amnesties made conditional on disclosure and accompanied by other accountability measures should be considered legitimate); Michael P. Scharf, "From the eXile Files: An Essay on Trading Justice for Peace", 63(1) *Washington and Lee Law Review* (2006) (arguing that amnesties for crimes for which there is no treaty-based duty to prosecute are valid under international law and noting the importance of amnesties to use as an incentive to end violent confrontations); O'Shea, *Amnesty for Crime in International Law and Practice* (arguing that certain conditional amnesties should be given recognition in circumstances where the amnesty is necessary to secure a peace deal and prevent or provoke further bloodshed); Louise Mallinder, *Amnesty, Human Rights and Political Transitions: Bridging the Peace and Justice Divide* (Oxford/Portland Oregon: Hart Publishing, 2008), at 413 (arguing that 'it is necessary to privilege pragmatism, rather than attempting to apply ill-suited universal models to the complexities faced by individual transitional states').

[62] 'Transitional justice' has been described by the Secretary-General as comprising 'the full range of processes and mechanisms associated with a society's attempts to come to terms with a legacy of large-scale past abuses, in order to ensure accountability, serve justice and achieve reconciliation.' 'The rule of law and transitional justice in conflict and post-conflict societies,' Report of the Secretary-General, UN Doc. S/2004/16, 3 August 2004, para. 8. 'Restorative justice' refers to the focus on the normative, rather than punitive aspects of criminal law.

[63] Terms of Reference for the Commission of Truth and Friendship, Established by the Republic of Indonesia and the Democratic Republic of Timor-Leste, 10 March 2005, Art. 14(c)(i). AP, "UN boycotts East Timor truth commission over amnesty concerns", *International Herald Tribune*, 27 July 2007.

The Statute of the IMT sitting in Nuremberg set up by the four Allies was annexed to and formed an integral part of the London Agreement of 8 August 1945.[64] By contrast, the IMTFE sitting in Tokyo was established in 1946 through proclamation by US General Douglas MacArthur.[65] Both the IMT and IMTFE are silent on the issue of amnesties. By contrast, Control Council Law No. 10,[66] which established the courts of the four Allied nations in the occupied German territory in order to prosecute the lesser war criminals,[67] explicitly stated in Article 5 that any amnesty granted under the Nazi regime would not be admitted as a bar to trial or punishment.

The *ad hoc* international criminal tribunals for the former Yugoslavia[68] and Rwanda,[69] established in 1993 and 1994 respectively by the UN Security Council pursuant to its powers under Chapter VII of the Charter of the United Nations, are also silent on amnesties, although the clear implication is that no national amnesty would constitute a bar to proceedings since this would defeat the object and purpose of the Tribunals. Interestingly, the only country of the former Yugoslavia to have adopted an amnesty law – the Former Yugoslav Republic of Macedonia, in relation to the internal armed conflict in 2001 between governmental forces and the National Liberation Army (NLA) – contained an exception for crimes falling within the jurisdiction of the ICTY.[70] This supports the contention that the ICTY would not countenance an amnesty law as a barrier to its exercise of jurisdiction.

As noted above, the Rome Statute is similarly absent any provision on amnesties, despite the issue being on the agenda of the Rome Diplomatic Conference and having been considered in the *travaux préparatoires*,[71] leaving the text in a state

---

[64] Charter of the International Military Tribunal (IMT), annexed to the London Agreement for the Prosecution and Punishment of Major War Criminals of the European Axis, of 8 August 1945, 82 *UNTS* 279, at 288; 59 Stat. 1544. The IMT Charter was annexed to the London Agreement and constituted an integral part thereof (hereafter, IMT Charter).

[65] 19 January 1946, *TIAS* No. 1589 at 3, 4 Bevans 20; amended 26 April 1946, *TIAS* No. 1589 at 11, 4 Bevans 27 (hereafter, IMTFE Amended Charter).

[66] Allied Control Council Law No. 10, Punishment of Persons Guilty of War Crimes, Crimes Against Peace and Against Humanity, 20 December 1945, *Official Gazette of the Control Council for Germany*, No. 3, Berlin, 31 January 1946.

[67] Allied Control Council Law No. 10, preamble (stating that these trials sought 'to give effect to the terms of the Moscow Declaration of 30 October 1943 and the London Agreement of 8 August 1945, and the Charter issued pursuant thereto … in order to establish a uniform legal basis in Germany for the prosecution of war criminals and other similar offenders, other than those dealt with by the International Military Tribunal …').

[68] SC Res. 808 (1993), annexed to Report of the Secretary-General Pursuant to Paragraph 2 of UN SC Res. 808 (1993), UN Doc. S/2-5704 and Add. 1 (1993).

[69] SC Res. 955 (1994), Annex, UN Doc. S/RES/955 (1994).

[70] Amnesty law of 8 March 2002, passed for the 'promotion of peace and overcoming the crisis [of 2001],' cited in *Boškoski and Tarčulovski*, ICTY, Trial Chamber, Case No. IT-04-82-T, Judgment, 10 July 2008, para. 238.

[71] There was no plenary discussion of the issue, given the complexity and controversy of the debate. One commentator observes that the discussion of amnesties at Rome was 'so controversial that it was unlikely to provide a compromise.' Jessica Gavron, "Amnesties in the light of developments in international law and the establishment of the International Criminal Court", 51(1) *ICLQ* 107 (2002). Both amnesty and pardon were rejected in the context of the defence of *ne bis in idem*. *Report of the*

of 'creative ambiguity.'[72] A number of commentators have argued that an 'amnesty exception' may be inferred from several provisions of the Rome Statute.[73] There are essentially three different ways that have been identified under ICC Statute to provide such leeway: (1) by reason of inadmissibility of a case due to an amnesty following an investigation by the State of territoriality or nationality; (2) by the Prosecutor deciding not to proceed to an investigation 'in the interests of justice'; and (3) by the Security Council deferring proceedings as a measure to maintain or restore peace and security.

Under the first possibility, the argument is that the Prosecutor may decide that a case is inadmissible under Article 17,[74] because an amnesty has been granted following an investigation. Article 17(1)(b) provides that the ICC will declare a case inadmissible where the State which has jurisdiction over the case has investigated and decided not to prosecute the accused, unless the decision resulted from the unwillingness or inability of the State genuinely to prosecute. The Statute does not specify that the State must have conducted a 'criminal investigation,' arguably leaving it open for the Prosecutor to find that a conditional amnesty combined a truth and reconciliation commission amounts to an 'investigation,'[75] although such an investigation would have to be sufficiently linked to crimes committed for it to be the basis of a decision not to prosecute.[76] Thus an amnesty law that is granted without any investigation or which prevents prosecution without conditions would never make a case inadmissible before the ICC.[77] Unwillingness to prosecute genuinely is determined, *inter alia*, by considering whether the decision

---

Preparatory Committee on the Establishment of an International Criminal Court, Vol. 1, at 40, para. 174 (Proceedings of the Preparatory Committee during March-April and August 1996) GAOR, 51st Sess., Suppl. (No. 22), UN Doc. A/51/22); UN Doc. A/CONF./283/2/Add. 1 (1998), Art. 19. The United States circulated a 'non-paper' which suggested that a responsible decision by a democratic regime to allow an amnesty should be taken into account in judging the admissibility of a case. U.S. Delegation Draft, "State Practice Regarding Amnesties and Pardons" (1 August 1997), available at: <http://www.iccnow.org/documents/USDraftonAmnestiesPardons.pdf>.

[72] Scharf, "From the eXile Files", at 367.

[73] On a discussion of these possible ways to accommodate amnesties into the Rome Statute, see also generally, Ruth Wedgwood, "The International Criminal Court: An American View", *EJIL* 10 (1999) 97; Gerhard Hafner, Kristen Boon, Anne Rübesame and Jonathan Huston, "A Response to the American View as Presented by Ruth Wedgwood", *EJIL* 10 (1999) 107; Michael P. Scharf, "The Amnesty Exception to the Jurisdiction of the International Criminal Court", 32 *Cornell International Law Journal* 507 (1999).

[74] Such a decision on the part of the Prosecutor may be subject to review by the Pre-Trial Chamber if so requested by the State making a referral under Art. 14 or by the Security Council. However, the Pre-Trial Chamber may only 'request' the Prosecutor 'to reconsider that decision.' ICC Statute, Art. 53(3).

[75] Carsten Stahn, "Complementarity, Amnesties and Alternative Forms of Justice: Some Interpretative Guidelines for the International Criminal Court", 3 *JICJ* 697 (2005).

[76] See John Dugard, "Possible Conflicts of Jurisdiction with Truth Commissions", in Antonio Cassese, Paola Gaeta and John R.W.D. Jones (eds.), *The Rome Statute of the International Criminal Court: A Commentary* (Oxford: OUP, 2002), at 702 (commenting that such an interpretation of 'investigation' would be unlikely given the second part of the provision).

[77] Stahn, "Complementarity, Amnesties and Alternative Forms of Justice", at 709: 'An amnesty law which impedes prosecution or which does not provide for an investigation cannot invoked as a bar

not to prosecute was taken with the purpose of shielding the person from criminal responsibility for crimes within the jurisdiction of the Court.[78] Thus, the crux of the matter is whether the issuing of an amnesty had as its purpose shielding the person from criminal responsibility. Although the *legal consequence* of all amnesties is the exemption of persons from criminal and/or civil liability, it is possible to argue that amnesties tied to the requirement of full disclosure of the facts surrounding the perpetration of international crimes do not have the purpose of shielding the person from criminal responsibility. Rather, such conditional amnesties have as their purpose the discovery of the truth about the circumstances in which crimes were committed and the underlying causes of the conflict, as well as reconciliation and even the restoration of peace. The use of the word 'shielding' suggests a devious intent on the part of the State to prevent a genuine prosecution. Clearly, self-granted amnesties were in the minds of the drafters when the provision was adopted. However, those amnesties adopted as part of peace deals reached after a proper negotiation between parties to the conflict, often with the mediation or support of the UN or other States, do not carry such an intent. The fact that alleged perpetrators may still face criminal prosecution in the event that they fail to fulfil the conditions attaching to the amnesty means that there is no devious intent *to shield* the person from criminal responsibility, although the person may qualify for an exemption from prosecution, and could suggest that the ICC should defer to the national decision not to prosecute.[79]

The second possibility to recognise an amnesty under the ICC Statute arguably emanates from the determination of the Prosecutor that there is no reasonable basis to proceed to an investigation under Article 53, based on the consideration that 'taking into account the gravity of the crime and the interests of the victims, there are nonetheless substantial reasons to believe that an investigation would not serve the interests of justice.'[80] The problem lies in interpreting what is meant by 'the interests of justice.' The term is left undefined, although some elements are mentioned that should guide the Prosecutor in this regard: the gravity of the offence, the interests of the victims, the age or infirmity of the perpetrator and the role he or she played.[81] The use of the words 'taking into account all circumstances, *including* …' means that this list is not exhaustive.[82] In fact, one commentator has argued that the

---

to ICC proceedings because it does not even meet the basic requirements for inadmissibility under Art. 17(1)(a) or (b).' Footnotes omitted.

[78] ICC Statute, Art. 17(2)(a). Where proceedings have taken or are taking place, unwillingness to genuinely prosecute may also be evidenced by an unjustifiable delay which in the circumstances is inconsistent with an intent to bring the person to justice or by proceedings not undertaken impartially or independently or otherwise in a manner inconsistent with an intent to bring the person to justice. Art. 17(2)(b) and (c) respectively.

[79] Stahn, "Complementarity, Amnesties and Alternative Forms of Justice", at 711: 'an alternative interpretation [of Art. 17(1) and (2)] … allows deference in the case of investigations only where these investigations may potentially lead to criminal prosecution.'

[80] ICC Statute, Art. 53(1)(c).

[81] ICC Statute, Art. 53(1)(c) and (2)(c).

[82] Gavron makes the point that while it is potentially arguable that a prosecution that is likely to spark further atrocities is not in the interests of justice, this involves speculating about future events

formulation of the provision in this way suggests that the Prosecutor could apply a broader concept of justice and hence justify non-prosecution on the basis of amnesties or other alternative methods of providing justice.[83] One may note in this regard that the 'right to justice' has been interpreted as encompassing a wider notion than merely criminal retribution.[84] This suggests that a limited amnesty together with an effective truth commission could satisfy 'the essential purpose of the right to justice.'[85] On the other hand, if 'justice' is interpreted in a narrow way by the ICC, as referring only to criminal justice, then such extra-judicial proceedings are unlikely to persuade the Prosecutor from refraining to investigate.

Although some commentators have interpreted Article 53(1)(c) and (2)(c) as vesting the Prosecutor with 'unlimited political discretion as to decide whether or not amnesty laws constitute an exception to the jurisdiction of the Court,'[86] this is probably not an accurate reflection of the Prosecutor's powers. The elements which the Prosecutor must take into account in deciding if a prosecution is in the interests of justice (i.e., gravity of the crime, interests of victims, age or infirmity of the alleged perpetrator) are very much 'linked to justice in a specific case (*Einzelfallgerechtigkeit*), rather than general policy considerations.'[87] This suggests that it is not clearly open for the Prosecutor to consider issues such as reconciliation or the need for amnesties in peace negotiations in deciding if a prosecution is 'in the interests of justice.' Rather, the considerations in this regard are more likely to be linked to the precise elements of a case. Moreover, the notion of 'justice' has to be interpreted within the context of the Rome Statute, which is concerned first and foremost with criminal justice. Thus, it is more likely that the drafters had in mind a narrow concept of justice in the retributive sense, rather than a vague concept linked to broader issues of peace-making and reconciliation. In fact, it may even be dangerous to accord the Prosecutor the authority to determine what is in the 'interests of justice' in such a broad sense. In any case, there is a substantial check on the Prosecutor's decision not to proceed on this basis. If the Prosecutor decides not to proceed 'in the interests of justice,' he or she is obliged to inform the Pre-Trial Chamber, as well as the State which referred the case or the Security Council.[88] The Pre-Trial Chamber is able to review the Prosecutor's decision on its own initiative and if this occurs, the Prosecutor's decision will not be effective

---

and contradicts the deterrence argument. Gavron, "Amnesties in the light of developments in international law", at 111.

[83] Stahn, "Complementarity, Amnesties and Alternative Forms of Justice", at 698.

[84] Mr Joinet, in his "Final Report on the question of the impunity of perpetrators of violations of human rights" proposed under Principle 19 – Purpose of the Right to Justice, that: 'There can be no just and lasting reconciliation … without an effective response to the need for justice; the prerequisite for any reconciliation is forgiveness, which is a private act that implies that the victim knows the perpetrator of the violations and that the latter has been able to show repentance. Over and above any verdict, that is the essential purpose of the right to justice.' Joinet Report, Principle 19.

[85] See Gavron, "Amnesties in the light of developments in international law", at 111.

[86] H. Olásolo, "The Prosecutor of the ICC Before the Initiation of Investigations: A Quasi-Judicial or a Political Body?", 3 *International Criminal Law Review* 87 (2003), at 141.

[87] Stahn, "Complementarity, Amnesties and Alternative Forms of Justice", at 718.

[88] ICC Statute, Art. 53(3)(c).

until the Pre-Trial Chamber confirms it.[89] In this regard, it should be noted that the Court is obliged to interpret and apply the Statute in conformity 'with internationally recognized human rights' under Article 21(3), which could be taken to mean that only those amnesties not incompatible with fundamental human rights (such as the right to an effective remedy or to reparations) could be contemplated by the ICC as relevant to the decision of the Prosecutor not to proceed 'in the interests of justice.'[90]

Finally, a possibility for the ICC to recognise an amnesty has been inferred from Article 16, which grants the Security Council, acting under Chapter VII of the UN Charter, the power to defer proceedings for a period of 12 months if it so requests. Such a request may be renewed by the Council under the same conditions. This provision appears to recognise that peace and justice may conflict at certain moments in time, and if the Security Council determines that a prosecution by the ICC might threaten international peace and security, it may stay the prosecution for as long as that threat remains. However, such a deferral remains a temporary measure and requires the Security Council to make a difficult political judgment that prosecution of the most serious international crimes threatens international peace and security, thus making it unlikely to provide for the permanent recognition of a domestic amnesty.[91] The recent hard-line policy of the UN not to recognise amnesties for international crimes in any circumstances would also make such a resolution even more difficult to conceive.[92]

In order to clarify the legal situation *vis-à-vis* amnesties and the ICC, one academic writer has proposed a protocol to the ICC, which would set out reasonable parameters for the Court to admit the operation of some conditional amnesties.[93] Another commentator has set out interpretative guidelines to aid the ICC in determining whether or not to recognise an amnesty.[94] However, the prevailing view among commentators and from the UN would seem to be that the prospect of negotiating impunity is no longer viable for crimes in the ICC subject-matter jurisdic-

---

89 ICC Statute, Art. 53(3)(b).

90 Stahn, "Complementarity, Amnesties and Alternative Forms of Justice", at 704. The case law of the Inter-American Commission and Court of Human Rights, in particular, would be relevant for the ICC to help identify which amnesties are in incompatible with fundamental human rights. See, e.g., *Barrios Altos* case, para. 53.

91 Concurring, Stahn, "Complementarity, Amnesties and Alternative Forms of Justice", at 717 and Gavron, "Amnesties in the light of developments in international law", at 109.

92 See "The rule of law and transitional justice in conflict and post-conflict societies", Report of the Secretary-General, UN Doc. S/2004/16, 3 August 2004.

93 O'Shea, *Amnesty for Crime in International Law and Practice*, at 330.

94 See generally, Stahn, "Complementarity, Amnesties and Alternative Forms of Justice", at 695-720. Stahn proposes the following guidelines: (1) the ICC has judicial autonomy in deciding if an amnesty is permissible under the Statute; (2) Exemptions from criminal responsibility for the crimes within the jurisdiction of the Court by amnesties are generally incompatible with the Statute; (3) Prosecution by States and by the Court may be limited to the most serious crimes and the most responsible perpetrators (targeted prosecution); and (4) Amnesties should, if at all, only be permitted in exceptional cases, namely when they are conditional and accompanied by alternative forms of justice.

tion.[95] Nonetheless, commentators have suggested that amnesties or participation of convicted perpetrators in truth and reconciliation procedures at the national level could be taken into account in mitigation of sentence by the ICC.[96]

With regard to the hybrid tribunals, there are more explicit pronouncements on the amnesty issue. The Law on the Establishment of the Extraordinary Chambers in the Courts of Cambodia for the Prosecution of Crimes Committed during the Period of Democratic Kampuchea (as amended)[97] obliges the Government of Cambodia to refrain from enacting any amnesty or pardon for the international crimes in the subject-matter jurisdiction and gives the Chambers the power to review the scope of any amnesty or pardon promulgated before the enactment of the Law.[98] This suggests that the Chambers would be able to either override or at least reduce the scope both of the 1994 law that promised amnesty to members of the Khmer Rouge in return for complete surrender[99] and the royal pardon granted in 1996 to Ieng Sary, Brother No. 3 – Deputy Prime Minister and Minister for Foreign Affairs and Central and Standing Committee member of the Khmer Rouge regime, for a conviction of genocide that had been handed down in Phnom Penh in 1979 by a Vietnamese-sponsored court.[100] The pardon/amnesty was granted in return for his defection from the Khmer Rouge to the government, along with hundreds of rebels. However, given that the 1994 amnesty did not apply to senior leaders,[101] it is unlikely that those who benefited from it would come within the personal jurisdiction of the Chambers, unless they took a particularly zealous role in committing

[95] It has been contended that the failure of the Rome Statute to recognise amnesty as a valid alternative to prosecution illustrates that amnesty has lost favour in the contemporary international legal order. This is Dugard's view, although he argues that while unconditional amnesties should be considered illegal, amnesties given after an investigation such as the South African Truth and Reconciliation Commission, may contribute to the achievement of peace and justice in a transitional society more than mandatory prosecution. Dugard, "Dealing With Crimes of a Past Regime", at 1001.

[96] Dugard, "Possible Conflicts of Jurisdiction with Truth Commissions", at 703.

[97] See *Law on the Amendments to the Law on the Establishment of the Extraordinary Chambers in the Courts of Cambodia for the Prosecution of Crimes Committed during the Period of Democratic Kampuchea, Kram* NS/RKM/1004/006, 27 October 2004.

[98] 2001 Law (as amended), Chapter XII, Art. 40.

[99] The Law on Outlawing the Group of Democratic Kampuchea, Art. 5 (7 July 1994), reprinted in the *Phnom Penh Post* (21-28 July 2004). See Kassie Neou and Jeffrey C. Gallup, "Human Rights and the Cambodian Past: In Defence of Peace Before Justice", *Carnegie Council on Ethics and International Affairs* (New York: 2006).

[100] The decree read: 'Amnesty is granted to Mr. Ieng Sary, former Deputy Prime Minister responsible for Foreign Affairs in the Government of Democratic Kampuchea, who was sentenced to death and confiscation of all property by order of the People's Revolutionary Court of Phnom Penh dated 19 August 1979 and with regard to penalties stipulated by the Law on the Outlawing of the Democratic Kampuchea Group which was promulgated by Royal Proclamation no. 01 BM 94 dated 15 July 1994.' For a legal analysis, see Ronald C. Slye, "The Cambodian Amnesties: Beneficiaries and the Temporal Reach of Amnesties for Gross Violations of Human Rights", *ExpressO Preprint – Service Working Paper* 33 (available at: <http://law.bepress.com/cgi/viewcontent.cgi?article=1063&context=expresso>) (2003). For an overview of the trial which convicted Ieng Sary and Pol Pot and its primary documents, see H.J. De Nike, J. Quigley & K.J. Robinson (eds.), *Genocide in Cambodia: Documents from the Trial of Pol Pot and Ieng Sary* (Philadelphia: University of Pennsylvania Press, 2000).

[101] Art. 6 provided that 'For leaders of the "Democratic Kampuchea" group, the amnesty described above does not apply.'

atrocities. With regard to the 1996 pardon, the Chambers may well decide that a pardon may not be given for the crime of genocide and is thus invalid.[102]

The Special Court for Sierra Leone, whose jurisdiction is founded on an international treaty between a Sierra Leone and the United Nations,[103] rejects amnesty as a bar to prosecution for any person charged with crimes falling into Articles 2-4 of the Statute (i.e., international crimes).[104] This provision was inserted in the Statute specifically to counter the effect of the Lomé Peace Agreement, which contained a sweeping amnesty for all crimes.[105] As previously noted, the UN Secretary-General's Special Representative had objected to the amnesty clause in the Lomé Peace Agreement[106] and had added a disclaimer to that effect.[107] In the case involving the question of amnesty, the decision turned on the fact that the Special Court, as an 'international court,' has jurisdiction over the international crimes listed in Articles 2-4 of its Statute by virtue of universal jurisdiction,[108] and that a domestic amnesty law has no effect on the universal jurisdiction of foreign courts or international courts.[109]

The Special Crimes Unit for East Timor, established by the UN Transitional Administration in East Timor (UNTAET), set up the Panels with Exclusive Jurisdiction Over Serious Criminal Offences in East Timor.[110] Amnesties are not overtly

---

[102] The Genocide Conventions obliges States parties to ensure that those convicted of genocide receive 'an effective penalty,' which a pardon would seem to violate. Genocide Convention, Arts. 1 and 5. Cambodia has been a party to the Genocide Convention since 1950. See Chapter 3, in this volume.

[103] The treaty establishing the SCSL would be governed by the 1986 Vienna Convention on the Law of Treaties Between States and International Organisation or Between Organisations. Agreement between the United Nations and the Government of Sierra Leone on the Establishment of a Special Court for Sierra Leone, 16 January 2002 (hereafter, UN-Sierra Leone Agreement). The Statute of the Special Court is annexed to the Agreement (hereafter, SLSR Statute). See also The Special Court Agreement, 2002, Ratification Act, 2002, Supplement to the *Sierra Leone Gazette*, Vol. 80, No. 2, dated 7 March 2002.

[104] Art. 10 SCSL Statute.

[105] Schabas notes that Art. 10 was probably unnecessary because the SCSL would not be bound by any legislation of Sierra Leone or by agreements reached between the government of Sierra Leone and third parties. William A. Schabas, *The UN International Criminal Tribunals: The Former Yugoslavia, Rwanda and Sierra Leone* (Cambridge: CUP, 2006), at 338.

[106] "Report of the Secretary-General on the Establishment of a Special Court for Sierra Leone", UN Doc. S/2000/915, paras. 22-24.

[107] The Secretary-General, in his report on the draft SCSL Statute, stated that, '[w]hile recognising that amnesty is an accepted legal concept and a gesture of peace and reconciliation at the end of a civil war or an internal armed conflict, the United Nations has consistently maintained the position that amnesty cannot be granted in respect of international crimes, such as genocide, crimes against humanity or other serious violations of international humanitarian law.' *Ibid.*

[108] The SCSL also cites the ICJ in its *Congo* v. *Belgium* Decision (para. 61) for the proposition that certain international courts have jurisdiction over international crimes. *Kallon and Kamara* Decision on Amnesty case, para. 70.

[109] The SCSL identifies the primary question as 'whether the crimes within the competence of the Court are crimes susceptible to universal jurisdiction.' *Kallon and Kamara* Decision on Amnesty case, para. 69. It goes on to note that '[o]ne consequence of the nature of grave international crimes against humanity is that States can, under international law, exercise universal jurisdiction over such crimes.' *Kallon and Kamara* Decision on Amnesty case, para. 70.

[110] UNTAET Regulation 2000/15.

dealt with in the regulations setting up the Special Panels. A limited amnesty is offered to persons under the Community Reconciliation Procedures (CRAs) pursuant to Regulation No. 2001/10 which establishes the Commission for Reception, Truth and Reconciliation who voluntarily make an admission of responsibility for criminal or non-criminal acts committed in the context of the political conflicts in East Timor between 25 April 1974 and 25 October 1999.[111] However, the Regulation makes clear that '[i]n no circumstances shall a *serious criminal offence* be dealt with in a Community Reconciliation Process.'[112] The term 'serious criminal offence' is defined in Part 1, section 1(m) as the crimes listed in Sections 4-9 of UNTAET Regulation 2000/15, namely genocide, crimes against humanity, war crimes, torture, murder and sexual offences.[113] Furthermore, the Regulation specifies that the CRA program does not in any way prejudice the prosecution of serious crimes under Section 14 of UNTAET Regulation No. 2000/16 nor the exclusive jurisdiction over serious criminal offences of the Serious Crimes Panel.[114] Despite these clear indications of the rejection of amnesty for international crimes, high-level politicians in Timor Leste have repeatedly called for amnesties to further a policy of reconciliation.[115] This view has become more entrenched since the Serious Crimes Unit closed on 12 May 2005, due to the fact that two thirds of the persons indicted by the Special Panels remain outside the territorial jurisdiction of Timor Leste (mostly in Indonesia).[116]

2.3 Contextual and policy considerations

Contextual and policy considerations *vis-à-vis* the granting of amnesties have taken on a particular significance in the legal analysis of amnesties for international

[111] UNTAET Regulation No. 2001/10 on the Establishment of a Commission for Reception, Truth and Reconciliation in East Timor, UNTAET/REG/2001/10, 13 July 2001, Sections 22.4 (admission requirement) and 32 (immunity upon completion of CRA obligations).

[112] *Ibid.*, Schedule 1(4). Section 32 of the Regulation (conferring immunity) also states that 'no immunity conferred by operation of this or any other provision of the present Regulation shall extend to a *serious criminal offence*.' An earlier draft of the Regulation provided an amnesty for all politically motivated crimes. See Human Rights Watch, "Unfinished Business: Justice for East Timor", *Press Backrounder*, August 2000, at 13.

[113] Cases involving these crimes will be passed on to the General Prosecutor.

[114] *Supra* note 111, Section 22.2.

[115] "Xanana Gusmao wins East Timor presidential race", *Agence France-Press*, 17 April 2002; "Gusmao calls East Timor refugees home", *BBC News*, 4 April 2002; V. England, "Amnesties split leaders on eve of crucial poll", *South China Morning Post*, 29 August 2001; Human Rights Watch, "East Timor: Draft Amnesty Law", *Letter to José Alexandre Gusmão, President – Democratic Republic of East Timor*, 16 July 2002, available at: <http://hrw.org/press/2002/07/timor-ltr0716.htm>.

[116] Judicial System Monitoring Programme, *Overview of Timor Leste Justice Sector 2005*, January 2006, at 33, available at: <http://www.jsmp.minihub.org/Reports/2006/Final%20Overview%20 Report%202005%20(e).pdf>. Prime Minister Jose Ramos-Horta has been reported as calling for the Dili Parliament to consider an amnesty for convicted and imprisoned Timorese militiamen, arguing that: 'If it is not possible to punish the true culprits – the Indonesian military – why should Timorese militiamen be tried and sentenced?' "Horta 'saddened' by upholding of jail term of militia boss", ASAP, *East Timor News Digest*, 15 March 2006.

crimes because of the persistently grey contours of their (il)legality under international law and because of the fact that the issue of amnesties straddles the complex legal and political crossroads of conflict resolution and human rights. Reflecting a (probably unconscious) New Haven approach to legal interpretation,[117] courts faced with the question of exercising jurisdiction when facing an amnesty law have often turned to policy considerations to help decide the issue.[118]

There are two broad schools of thought which impact upon the interpretation of policy elements. One school of thought, which one may equate generally to a 'realist' approach (based on notions of power and consent), emphasises the value of stopping violence immediately through the application of concrete bargaining tools, advocates that criminal prosecution should not disrupt processes towards peace, and questions the ability of international criminal law to contribute to reconciliation or lasting peace. The second school of thought, which one may equate to a generally 'liberalist' approach (with an emphasis on the building of ethical legal processes), focuses upon the rights of victims to have redress for violations and focuses upon the role of criminal prosecution as a means to secure this.[119] Thus while the former school of thought turns its attention to preventing further violations, the second school of thought emphasises the need to provide accountability for existing victims of violations. This has sometimes been characterised as the tension between peace and justice. However, this is somewhat of a simplification of the policy debate, as both schools of thought acknowledge the intrinsic relationship between these two objectives. At present there remains a lack of anecdotal evidence to confirm or disprove any of the assumptions underlying either of these schools of thought, and whether such elements as truth, accountability, acknowledgement, participation and reparations really lead to a stable peace. Nonetheless these 'legitimating indicia' may be useful pointers for courts when navigating the murky waters of amnesties for international crimes.[120] As pointed out by Rosalyn

[117] As noted in the introduction, the 'New Haven' school of thought draws attention to the impact of policy considerations on decision-makers when faced with conflicting principles of international law. See Richard Falk, "Casting the Spell: The New Haven School of International Law", 104 *Yale Law Journal* (1995), at 1991.

[118] The policy questions surrounding the debate over the value of prosecution in the aftermath of mass violations also have relevance for courts when considering exercising jurisdiction in the presence of the other principal legal impediments under consideration in this study. Hence, this section may be considered equally relevant for the subsequent chapters.

[119] See A.C. Arend, "Do Legal Rules Matter? International Law and International Politics", 68 *VJIL* 107 (1998); S.D. Krasner, "Realist Views of International Law", in Proceedings of the Ninety Sixth Annual Meeting of the ASIL, 96 *ASIL Proceedings* 206 (2002), at 265. Hans Morgenthau, a prominent realist, was highly critical of the concept of international criminal justice when dealing with highly political contexts.

[120] Diane Orentlicher refers to amnesties which satisfy 'generally-accepted indicia of legitimacy' to describe those bars which domestic courts should defer to even where they are not bound to so under international law. Orentlicher, "The Future of Universal Jurisdiction", at 238.

Higgins, a legal analysis of a particular problem does not require ignoring everything that is not 'rules.'[121]

2.3.1 The need to secure the peace and maintain the peace

The two broad schools of thought account for the differing theories in regard to the role of criminal prosecutions in the achievement and maintenance of peace. While the 'realist' approach views a policy of non-prosecution as often being the only way to induce warring parties to come to the negotiating table, the 'liberalist' approach claims that a lasting peace must be predicated upon a sense of justice.

The main argument in favour of granting amnesties is that they represent a useful tool to end civil wars or military stand-offs and therefore prevent further bloodshed. In fact, some would view amnesties as a *political necessity* in the resolution of certain peace agreements, where no other inducements appear viable. Until just a few years ago, such justifications were used by the United Nations in pressing governments to enact amnesty laws. For example, in Haiti, the United Nations and the United States pressured President Aristide to grant a full amnesty as part of the Governors Island Agreement[122] to the members of General Cedras' and Brigadier General Biamby's military regime which was responsible for killing and torturing over 3000 civilian political opponents from 1990 to 1994.[123] The Security Council gave its full support to the Agreement which it described as 'the only valid framework for resolving the crisis in Haiti.'[124] The result was that the amnesty deal permitted the return of civilian government and most of the human rights abuses ended.[125] Most commentators believe that the amnesty deal in South Africa prevented a potential civil war,[126] a view shared by the Constitutional Court

121 Rosalyn Higgins, *Problems and Process: International Law and How We Use It* (Oxford: Oxford Clarendon Press, 1994), at 9.

122 "The Situation of Democracy and Human Rights in Haiti", Report of the Secretary-General, UN GAOR, 47th Sess., Annex 1, Agenda Item 22, at 4, UN Doc. A/47/975, S/26063 (1993) (reproducing the Governors Island Agreement).

123 Scharf, "Swapping Amnesty for Peace", at 1-42.

124 Statement of the President of the Security Council, UN SCOR, 48th Sess., 3298th mtg., at 26, UN Doc. S/INF/49 (1993). When the military leaders failed to comply with the agreement, the Security Council took the extreme action of authorising an invasion of Haiti. UN SCOR, 49th Sess., 3413th mtg., UN Doc. S/RES/940 (1994). General Cedras withdrew his troops on the eve of the invasion, only when a general amnesty was passed by the Haitian parliament.

125 A recent case in the United States granting relief in response to a civil law claim for the tort of torture and extrajudicial killings in Haiti against Colonel Carl Dorélien, a former member of Haiti's High Command during the period the military regime held power, demonstrates, however, the penetrability of the amnesty at least in so far as civil claims go. *Jean* v. *Dorélien*, Complaint for Extrajudicial Killing and Crimes Against Humanity, Jury Trial Demanded, United States District Court, Southern District of Miami, 24 January 2003, available at: <http://www.cja.org/cases/Dorelien_docs/Dorelien%20Complaint.htm>; "Haitian Colonel and Member of the High Command Ordered to Pay $4.3 Million for Human Rights Abuses", The Center for Justice and Accountability, *Press Release*, 23 February 2007, available at: <http://www.cja.org/cases/Dorelien_News/dorelienverdict.pdf>.

126 See for example, Scharf, "The Amnesty Exception to the Jurisdiction of the International Criminal Court", at 510.

of South Africa, which found that 'but for a mechanism for amnesty, the "historic bridge" [the negotiated transition to democratic rule] itself might never have been erected.'[127] Similar arguments about the political necessity of amnesty laws have been made in relation to the political transitions in Argentina, Uruguay, Chile and El Salvador.

On the other hand, criminal indictments may serve to shorten the political future of dangerous political players and remove them from existing power structures. The exile of Charles Taylor to Nigeria and eventual transference to The Hague to face charges before the SCSL is one example of this occurrence. It is hoped that a similar result will occur in relation to the indictments of the ICC against Joseph Kony, leader of the Lord's Resistance Army (LRA), and four of his top commanders in northern Uganda. However, many have argued (in line with the 'realist' approach) that an immediate end to the war in Uganda in the form of a peace treaty will require the ICC to relinquish or suspend its indictments (as Kony himself has demanded as a condition to returning to the peace negotiations), thereby providing Kony and his top commanders with a *de facto* amnesty.

There is the fear that fragile countries in the aftermath of war or regime change may not be able to survive the destabilising effects of politically charged trials.[128] When States emerge from dictatorships or wars, in particular those which are internal, they are often unstable, and the community sharply polarised. Prosecutions can have the effect of further fracturing the society. The prosecution of past violations may provoke rebellions or other confrontations which may weaken the power of the civilian authority[129] which will lead to more human rights violations.[130] By contrast, it may be necessary or expedient to obtain the co-operation of the key figures in the former government or other official structures to ensure a smooth transition – co-operation which may be induced by an amnesty.[131] Therefore some proponents argue that under these conditions, democratic consolidation can be bet-

---

[127] *AZAPO* case, para. 19 (*per* Mahomed J).

[128] Orentlicher, "Settling Accounts", at 2544. When the Allies at the end of WW I called for the prosecution of German war criminals before their own tribunals pursuant to the Versailles Treaty, the Germans soon reneged on their promise to deliver their nationals, arguing that '[t]he mere proposal of an order of this kind would create such a storm of indignation that the entire peace structure would be gravely threatened.' Head of the Peace Division of the German Foreign Office and Baron von Lersner, President of the German Peace Delegation in discussion with Allied diplomats in Paris, November 1919, quoted in Sheldon Glueck, *War Criminals: Their Prosecution and Punishment* (New York: Alfred A. Knopf, 1944).

[129] The three rebellions in Argentina in 1988-1989 have been explained as being largely the result of dissatisfaction with the prosecution of military officers for past human rights violations instituted by the government of President Raul Alfonsin. See "Revolt by 400 Argentine troops quelled", *New York Times*, 3 December 1988, at 3. In Uruguay, in late 1986, when military defendants refused to answer to summonses relating to rights violations in the 1970s, the government of Uruguay passed an amnesty law covering the prosecutions to avoid a challenge to the supremacy of the civilian administration. See Americas Watch, "Challenging Impunity: The Ley de Caducidad and the Referendum Campaign in Uruguay" (1989), at 14-15.

[130] Orentlicher, "Settling Accounts", at 2546.

[131] O'Shea, *Amnesty for Crime in International Law and Practice*, at 23.

ter furthered by implementing a policy of reconciliation embodied in an amnesty law covering past violations.[132]

Such concerns underlie the 'liberalist' approach, which is based on the view that '[t]here can be no peace without justice, and there can be no justice without accountability.'[133] The argument is that a new democratic regime or a fragile State in the aftermath of an armed conflict built on foundations of impunity and a forgotten record of human rights atrocities will not be tenable and will inevitably disintegrate or at least hamper the collective psychological rebuilding process of the society.[134] There are certainly numerous examples of peace agreements incorporating amnesties being unsuccessful at achieving lasting peace. In Angola, for example, UN-endorsed amnesties were granted in four peace agreements over 41 years of

---

[132] See for example, Mark Osiel, "Why Prosecute? Critics of Punishment for Mass Atrocity", 22 *Human Rights Quarterly* 118 (2000). See, e.g., the view of the Constitutional Court of South Africa that: 'Although the mechanisms adopted to facilitate that [democratic] process have differed from country to country and from time to time, the principle that amnesty should, in appropriate circumstances, be accorded to violators of human rights in order to facilitate the consolidation of new democracies was accepted in all these countries …' *AZAPO* case, para. 22. The countries the Court was referring to were Chile, Argentina and El Salvador. In Argentina, large scale revolts by the military which threatened to destabilise the political transition to democratic rule led to the government of President Raúl Alfonsin adopting two amnesty laws in 1986 and 1987 which put an end to the trials of over 1,000 officers. Proponents of the broad amnesty law passed by both houses of parliament in Afghanistan, which covers all crimes committed by all parties to the two decade long civil war, have argued that such a law is necessary to forge reconciliation and national unity among groups with long-held animosities towards one another. Around 25,000 Afghans marched in support of the amnesty on 23 February 2007. However, a nation-wide survey conducted by the Afghan Independent Human Rights Commission has suggested that the majority of Afghans want justice for past atrocities, and see this as a pre-condition for lasting peace. President Karzai, for his part, and with considerable pressure from the international community, has refused to sign the amnesty law. See J Alexander Thier and Scott Worden, "Path to peace, justice in Afghanistan: Healing the wounds of the civil war requires both reconciliation and accountability", *Christian Science Monitor*, 13 March 2007, available at: <http://www.csmonitor.com/2007/0313/p09s02-coop.html>; Amin Tarzi, "Afghanistan: Amnesty Deal Places Karzai in Dilemma", *Radio Free Europe/Radio Liberty*, 23 February 2007; "Afghans rally for Mujahedeen", *International Herald Tribune*, 24-25 February 2007, at 6; Afghan Independent Human Rights Commission, *A Call for Justice: A National Consultation on Past Human Rights Violations in Afghanistan* (January 2005), available at: <http://www.aihrc.org.af/Rep_29_Eng/rep29_1_05call4justice.pdf>. 75.9% of those surveyed said that justice was important for them. 76.4% said that prosecuting war criminals would increase stability and bring security. 90.3% felt that human rights abusers should be removed from public posts. 87.6% responded that without accountability, people would seek revenge.

[133] Christopher Joyner, "Redressing Impunity for Human Rights Violations: The Universal Declaration and the Search for Accountability", 26(4) *Denver Journal of International Law and Policy* 609 (1998).

[134] As Goldstone points out: exposure of the truth individualises guilt, thus avoiding collective guilt; justice brings public and official acknowledgment to the victims; public exposure to the facts ensures that history is recorded more accurately; and the exposure of the nature and extent of human rights violations may reveal a systematic and institutional pattern of gross human rights violations. Richard Goldstone, "Justice as a Tool for Peace-making: Truth Commissions and International Criminal Tribunals", 28(3) *New York Journal of International Law and Politics* 488-490 (Spring, 1996). See also J. Van Dyke, "The Fundamental Human Right to Prosecution and Compensation", 29(2) *Denver Journal of International Law and Policy* 77 (1999).

permanent fighting but these measures never succeeded in stopping the violence.[135] Although an amnesty was included in the Luena Memorandum of Understanding of 4 April 2002 – the agreement that finally ended the war – its success was arguably due more to the cessation of foreign intervention in the conflict rather than the granting of the amnesty.[136] The experience of Sierra Leone with regard to its two amnesties, contained in the 1996 Abidjan Agreement and in the 1999 Lomé Peace Agreement, also indicates that the granting of amnesties does not necessarily lead to a lasting peace.[137] However, it is arguable that the latter Agreement, while not immediately returning peace to Sierra Leone, did provide 'the framework for a process that pacified the combatants and, five years later, has returned Sierra Leoneans to a context in which they need not fear daily violence and atrocity.'[138] The examples of post-Franco Spain, the USA in the aftermath of the Civil War and even Cambodia[139] to some extent also show that decisions not to prosecute and to deliberately not acknowledge atrocities do not necessarily lead to vigilantism and an unstable peace.

2.3.2 **The need for a public accounting of the truth**

Most commentators and courts have underlined the importance of a society which has undergone serious violations of human rights to come to grips with its past in a public accounting of the truth. The evolution of this concern together with the recognition of the rights of victims to know what happened into a possible 'right to the truth' in international law suggests that this aspect has both a policy and legal imperative.[140] However, again there are arguments on both sides as to whether the penal process is the most effective one at fulfilling this need.

Where truth commissions have been set up in transitional societies, amnesties may be the only incentive to induce those responsible for crimes to expose or acknowledge facts about the past, and thereby provide some form of redress to victims. The best example of this is in South Africa, where a quasi-judicial Amnesty Commission was established under the Promotion of National Unity and Recon-

---

[135] José Doria, "Angola: A Case Study in the Challenges of Achieving Peace and the Question of Amnesty or Prosecuting of War Crimes in Mixed Armed Conflicts", 5 *YIHL* 7 (2002).

[136] *Ibid.*, at 7.

[137] See Report of the UN Secretary-General on the protection of civilians in armed conflict, UN Doc. S/2001/331, 30 March 2001, para. 10 ('[T]he granting of amnesties to those who committed serious violations of international humanitarian and criminal law is not acceptable. The experience of Sierra Leone has confirmed that such amnesties do not bring about lasting peace and reconciliation.')

[138] *Witness to Truth: Report of the Sierra Leone Truth and Reconciliation Commission* (5 October 2004), available at: <http://www.trcsierraleone.org/drwebsite/publish/index.shtml>, at 365.

[139] But see Report of the Special Representative of the Secretary-General for Human Rights in Cambodia, Mr. Peter Leuprecht, E/CN.4/2001/103, para. 80, in which Mr. Peter Leuprecht expressed his view that the preconditions for healing and consolidating peace include justice and the discovery of truth.

[140] For a more detailed discussion of the evolution of this 'right,' see Yasmin Naqvi, "The right to the truth in international law: Fact or fiction?", 88(862) *IRRC* 246 (June 2006).

ciliation Act to consider applications for amnesty.[141] The Commission could grant amnesty if it was satisfied that the applicant who had committed an act constituting a 'gross violation of human rights' had made 'a full disclosure of all relevant facts,' and that the act to which the application related was 'an act associated with a political objective committed in the course of conflicts of the past.'[142] Those who failed to obtain amnesty faced prosecution.[143] A total 7,116 individuals applied for amnesty, resulting in the granting of 1,167 amnesties. 5,143 of the applications were refused administratively without a hearing.[144] While the numbers of people who applied for amnesty was relatively small, the amnesty process itself led to truth-finding, as opposed to truth-hiding. A number of amnesty laws have also been made conditional upon a person showing repentance for his or her acts.[145]

In addition, criminal trials generally focus on one individual and sometimes just one act at a time, whereas a truth commission seeks to document a whole picture of abuse and systematic violations which may shed more light on the causes of the conflict or the practices of the previous regime and can therefore address institutional as well as individual accountability.[146] A court's necessary compliance with rules of evidence means that many facts are not exposed, leading to only a partial explanation of past events. Truth commissions, by contrast, are more suited to creating a collective memory of the past thereby contributing to reconciliation.[147] In addition, the process of testifying at a truth commission often has a cathartic effect, for victims and perpetrators alike, and may help all actors in a society to come to a sense of acknowledgment and closure. The experience of Sierra Leone (and to a lesser extent Timor Leste) demonstrates that a truth commission may act concurrently with prosecutions, thereby fulfilling this truth-seeking function while not replacing criminal justice mechanisms, suggesting the two institutions can and

---

141 See sections 10(1), 19(3)(b)(iii) of Act 34 of 1995.

142 Section 20 of Act 34 of 1995. Dugard, "Dealing With Crimes of a Past Regime", at 1009.

143 Judge Mahomed, in the *AZAPO* case, framed the justification for such amnesty for truth deals in the following terms: 'That truth, which the victims of repression seek so desperately to know is … much more likely to be forthcoming if those responsible for such monstrous misdeeds are encouraged to disclose the whole truth with the incentive that they will not receive the punishment which they undoubtedly deserve if they do.' *AZAPO* case, at 683-685.

144 Sarkin, *supra* n. 60, at 94.

145 See, e.g., the laws passed by the Peruvian Congress between 1987 and 1993: the Law on Terrorism (1987), the Law on the Mitigation, Exemption or Remission of Punishment of Terrorism (1989), the Decree on Terrorism (1991), the Decree-Law on the Conditions for Mitigation, Exemption, Remission or Reduction of Punishment for Terrorism (1992) and the Decree on Repentance for Terrorism (1993).

146 Priscilla Hayner, *Unspeakable Truths: Confronting State Terror and Atrocity* (London: Routledge, 2001), at 100-101.

147 Since 1974, there have been more than 20 truth commissions established to inquire in the 'truth' of past events, including in Chile, Argentina, El Salvador, South Africa and Guatemala. Priscilla B. Hayner, "Fifteen truth commissions – 1974 to 1994: A comparative study", 15 *Human Rights Quarterly* 597 (1994); Hayner, "Truth Commissions: A schematic overview", 862 *IRRC* 295 (June 2006).

indeed should work in concert. Apart from one instance of dispute between the two bodies,[148] the experience of the Sierra Leone Special Court and the Truth Commission working in parallel was generally mutually beneficial and complementary.[149]

Those adopting a 'liberalist' approach tend to argue that the best version of the truth is that obtained through the evidence vigorously debated in a criminal trial and carefully weighed in a judgment. A commonly posited justification for prosecution instead of amnesty at the end of periods of protracted violence is that such trials may contribute to an accurate historical record of the period, thereby countering revisionist versions of events and making it more difficult for perpetrators to deny the factual actuality of atrocities.[150] Thus, chief US Prosecutor at Nuremberg Robert Jackson famously justified the Nuremberg trials by the need to 'establish incredible events by credible evidence' in order that future generations could not doubt that such events took place.[151]

However, criminal trials have also been criticised for distorting the truth of complex political struggles. Professor Koskenniemi, for example, has described how in trials seeking to deal with international crimes perpetrated in highly political contexts, '[t]he line between justice, history and manipulation tends to become all but invisible.'[152] Such an analysis falls in line with Hans Morgenthau's scepticism about the ability of international legal process to deal with large events of

[148] A decision of the Special Court for Sierra Leone (SCSL) rejected the application for Samuel Norman to appear at the Truth and Reconciliation Commission (TRC) before his trial at the SCSL, on the basis of the lack of procedural safeguards of the accused. *Decision on the Request of the Truth and Reconciliation Commission of Sierra Leone to Conduct a Public Hearing with Samuel Hinga Norman* (SCSL-2003-08-PT) [3257-3264], 29 October 2003. The implication was that fair trial rights of the accused would override the truth-seeking function of the TRC. On appeal, Justice Robertson put forward a compromise solution, allowing Norman to give written evidence or to meet with the TRC in private, but denying a public hearing at the TRC. *Decision on Appeal by the Truth and Reconciliation Commission of Sierra Leone ('TRC' or 'The Commission' and Chief Samuel Hinga Norman JP against the Decision of His Lordship, Mr. Justice Bankole Thompson, delivered on 20 October 2003, to Deny the TRC's Request to Hold a Public Hearing with Chief Hinga Norman JP* (SCSL-2003-08-PT), 28 November 2003.

[149] William A. Schabas, "A Synergistic Relationship: The Sierra Leone Truth and Reconciliation Commission and the Special Court for Sierra Leone", William A. Schabas & Shane Darcy (eds.), *Truth Commission and Courts: The Tension between Criminal Justice and the Search for Truth*, 3 (Dordrecht: Kluwer Academic Publishers, 2004), at 53: 'The lessons of the Sierra Leone experience suggest that it is not unreasonable for the two bodies to operate in parallel. Fears that the threat of prosecution may discourage perpetrators from testifying are simply a fact with which we shall have to live. But experience in Sierra Leone suggests that such fears are more imaginary than real.'

[150] Those advocating trials at the end of WW II argued that 'under the influence of prejudice and propaganda many persons will regard the unspeakable brutalities chargeable to the Germans … as "mere atrocity tales."' Glueck, *War Criminals*, at 66.

[151] Report of Robert H. Jackson, to the President on Atrocities and War Crimes, 7 June 1945, *Department of State Bulletin*, 10 June 1945, at 1071. When the *Milošević* case before the ICTY was suddenly terminated as a result of the death of the former Yugoslav president, Svetozar Marovic, the President of Serbia-Montenegro lamented that, '[w]ith his death, history will be deprived of the full truth.' See "Former Yugoslav President Slobodan Milosevic has died in the detention centre at The Hague tribunal: Reaction to the news", *BBC News*, 12 March 2006.

[152] Martti Koskenniemi, "Between impunity and show trials", 6 *Max Planck UNYB* (2002), at 34. He argues that the objective of '"educating" people of "historical truths" through law emerges from

international politics because of the inevitable distortion that occurs when political contexts are subject to legal process.[153] Koskenniemi also argues that the very structure of a tribunal designed to try perpetrators for such crimes is implicitly grounded in pre-conceived notions about the (contested) context in which the crimes were committed, making a 'show trial' almost inevitable.[154] Other commentators have also warned about the 'moralizing over-simplification' of international criminal law, which 'runs the risk of falling into Manichaean approaches.'[155] Hannah Arendt criticised the *Eichmann* trial for introducing historical, political and educational objectives into it:

> 'The purpose of the trial is to render justice, and nothing else; even the noblest ulterior purposes – "the making of a record of the Hitler regime ..." can only detract from the law's main business: to weigh the charges brought against the accused, to render judgment and to mete out due punishment.'[156]

In addition, the question of what kind of truth is owed to victims and to society may also determine the legitimacy of an amnesty. For instance, those amnesties excluding leaders might allow criminal trials to illuminate the truth about the policy and objectives behind a regime's violent measures, which may satisfy the societal need to know about the causes and consequences of a conflict.[157] However, by not prosecuting lower level perpetrators, the factual and forensic details of the actual crimes themselves may never come to light (unless the amnesty was conditional upon the perpetrator divulging this information before a truth and reconciliation commission).[158]

---

our contemporary wish to accommodate the Realist insight about the need to take into account of the context but also from our rejection of the Realists' conclusion – namely that law cannot be of use here.'

[153] See the discussion on Morgenthau's argument as enunciated in *Die internationale Rechtspflege, ihr Wesen und ihre Grenzen* (1929), at 62-72 in Martti Koskenniemi, *The Gentle Civilizer of Nations. The Rise and Fall of International Law 1870-1960* (Cambridge: CUP, 2002), at 440-445.

[154] Thus, Koskenniemi points out that in the case of the *Milošević* trial in The Hague, '... because the context is part of the political dispute, the trial of Milosevic can only, from the latter's perspective, be a show trial participation which will mean the admission of Western victory.' Koskenniemi, "Between impunity and show trials", at 17-18.

[155] Antoine Garapon, "Three Challenges for International Criminal Justice", 2 *JICJ* 724 (2004).

[156] Because of its overtly didactic purposes, Arendt felt that the *Eichmann* trial had become a show trial staged by the Israeli Prime Minister, David Ben-Gurion, to support political motives, linked to justifying and unifying the State of Israel. Arendt, *Eichmann in Jerusalem*, at 251.

[157] Cambodia's 1994 amnesty law was such a law excluding leaders of the Democratic Republic of Kampuchea group.

[158] The Truth and Reconciliation Commission of South Africa identified at least four differing types of truth: factual and forensic truth; personal and narrative truth; social truth; and hearing and restorative truth. *Truth and Reconciliation Commission of South Africa Report*, 21 March 2003, available at: <http://www.info.gov.za/otherdocs/2003/trc/>. See also *Witness to Truth: Report of the Sierra Leone Truth & Reconciliation Commission*, Vol. I, Chapter 3, 'Categories of Truth,' 5 October 2004. Victims might also feel that justice has not been done until, for example, they see their own torturer on trial, even if a different person ordered the torture.

2.3.3 The need to strengthen the rule of law and uphold the principle of legality

A corollary to the liberalist argument that justice is the foundation of lasting peace is the argument that the consequences of the failure to punish atrocious crimes committed by a prior regime vitiates the authority of the law and undermines the very principles the new democratic regime is trying to establish.[159] The effect of impunity is exacerbated when prosecutions are prevented by an amnesty law because it demonstrates that the law is not independent from gross manipulation by political or military factors.[160] It is argued that trials, by contrast, can advance a nation's transition to democracy. By showing that no person or institution is above the law, prosecutions for grave human rights violations can foster respect for democratic institutions. It is further posited that in fact prosecutions strengthen fragile democracies because the rule of law is integral to democracy itself.

It has been noted that the examples of Chile and Argentina suggest that attempts to prevent accountability in the name of social stability will not work. Recent events in these countries show that the short term amnesty eventually may give way to individual accountability.[161] On the basis of such practice, Professor Ronald Slye has suggested instituting 'probationary' limited amnesty periods, during which a beneficiary would need to show their commitment to human rights and the rule of law.[162] At the end of the probationary period, a permanent amnesty could be awarded on the basis of certain conditions, such as participation in a truth commission and/or otherwise assisting in investigations.[163] If a permanent amnesty is not awarded, any actions undertaken during the probationary period could assist in mitigation of sentence.[164] In this way, justice is delayed, but not foreclosed, in a similar way to what happens with the personal immunities of high-ranking State officials which cease to operate when the person leaves office.[165]

While the idea of probationary amnesty periods may be one way to induce beneficiaries to adopt rights-respecting behaviour (and deter future violations) without

---

[159] Orentlicher, "Settling Accounts", at 2542-2544. See generally Teitel, "Transitional Jurisprudence".

[160] This was the view of the Human Rights Committee, monitoring body of the International Covenant of Civil and Political Rights, in relation to the Uruguayan amnesty law: 'the [C]ommittee is concerned that, in adopting this law, the [S]tate party has contributed to an atmosphere of impunity which may undermine the democratic order and give rise to further grave human rights violations.' *Hugo Rodriguez* v. *Uruguay*, Comm. No. 322/1988, Views of 19 July 1994, UN Doc. CCPR/C/51/D/322/1988 (1994), para. 12.4.

[161] However, note the 1989 Uruguayan referendum in which the Uruguayan public rejected by 53 to 40% to overturn an amnesty passed 4 years earlier.

[162] Slye, "The Cambodian Amnesties", at 24.

[163] The amnesty contained in Algeria's Law on Civil Harmony, No. 99-08, 13 July 1999, is an example of an amnesty with a probationary period of 3-10 years during which behaviour of the beneficiary was monitored and during which the amnesty could be revoked, after which a general permanent amnesty could become effective.

[164] Slye, "The Cambodian Amnesties", at 25.

[165] *Ibid.*, at 29.

the use of criminal sanctions and has the merit of allowing other goals such as truth-telling to occur, such a practice may have the effect of reducing the attractiveness of 'amnesty for peace' deals with only provisional immunity on offer. The experience of Burundi, which in the Law of 21 November 2003 provided for provisional immunity of political leaders allegedly involved in crimes with a 'political' element returning from exile, on the understanding that in the future the truth would be established and the perpetrators would be held to account for their crimes, indicates that a provisional amnesty might be a sufficient inducement for some warring factions to negotiate a peace.[166] Notably, however, the extreme Hutu group Palipehutu-FNL refused to enter into the 2003 negotiations and continued to commit atrocities afterwards.[167] This is despite the fact that efforts led by the UN are currently being made to institute international criminal proceedings by way of a special chamber in the court system of Burundi and to set up a truth commission.[168]

2.3.4 The question of deterrence

A further argument in favour of criminal prosecution, based on the theory of deterrence, is that criminal punishment is considered the most effective insurance against future repression.[169] It is often recalled that in a 1939 speech to his General Staff, Hitler remarked, 'Who after all is today speaking about the destruction of the Armenians?,' in an apparent reference to the non-prosecution of the Turks for the genocidal campaign against the Armenians under the terms of the 1923 Treaty of Lausanne to which a Declaration of Amnesty was attached.[170] Richard Goldstone, former Prosecutor of the ICTY, has asserted that 'the failure of the international community to prosecute Pol Pot, Idi Amin, Saddam Hussein and Mohammed Aidad, among others, encouraged the Serbs to launch their policy of

[166] Law on Provisional Immunity from Prosecution of Political Leaders Returning from Exile, Protocol III, Art. 22(1)(1): 'Amnesty shall be granted to all combatants of the political parties and movements for crimes committed as a result of their involvement in the conflict, *but not for acts of genocide, crimes against humanity or war crimes*, or for their participation in coups d'état.' [Emphasis added]

[167] It is reported that in August 2004, the group massacred 152 Congolese Tutsi refugees at the Gatumba refugee camp in western Burundi. In response to the attack, the Burundian government issued arrest warrants for the FNL leaders Agathon Rwasa and Pasteur Habimana, and declared the group a terrorist organisation.

[168] *Report of the assessment mission on the establishment of an international judicial commission of inquiry for Burundi*, UN Doc. S/2005/158, 11 March 2005.

[169] See, e.g., Anthony D'Amato, "Law and War: A Doctrine of Deterrence", *UN Chronicle* 35, Code A982 (1998) (stating that his 'own view is that the laws of war are significant because of the oldest theory of criminal jurisprudence: deterrence'). In this vein, Robertson asserts that '[t]he doctrine of universal jurisdiction over crimes against humanity is justified because [for example] it may make some torturer pause at the prospect that some time somewhere some prosecutor may feel strongly enough to put him on trial.' Geoffrey Robertson, *Crimes Against Humanity* (Victoria: Penguin Books, 2000), at 242.

[170] Adolf Hitler, Speech to Chief Commanders and Commanding Generals (22 August 1939), quoted in Scharf, "From the eXile Files", at 349.

ethnic cleansing in the former Yugoslavia in the expectation that they would not be held accountable for their international crimes.'[171]

The deterrence theory in criminal law is based on the assumption that a person will be averse to taking actions that put him at personal risk. People are deterred when the degree of risk (of prosecution or some other form of retribution) is more than the degree of reward from performing the action.[172] This assumes that the person is a rational actor, who freely chooses *all* behaviour, both conforming and deviant, based on his rational calculations. Deterrence theorists usually point to the *swiftness, severity*, and *certainty* of punishment as the key elements in understanding a law's ability to control human behaviour.[173] Thus, the argument is that prosecution in the aftermath of conflicts will deter those in future wars from committing atrocities because the degree of risk of punishment outweighs the reward in committing in the act. Advocates of international criminal justice point out that the traditional system of dealing with violations of the laws and customs of war set up under the Hague Conventions, that is, post-war compensation by the guilty belligerent State to the injured belligerent State, is an inadequate remedy because there is no deterrent to military officers because 'the remote possibility of a guilty State having to pay a monetary compensation at the close of a war it expects to win is too vague and generalised prospective punishment; therefore not the sort of threat which is psychologically likely to influence the behaviour of individual offenders.'[174]

However, studies on the behaviour of combatants in war have shown that the idea that the combatant is morally autonomous is mistaken.[175] Combatants are subject to group conformity phenomena such as depersonalisation, loss of independence and a high degree of conformity, which favours the dilution of the sense of individual responsibility of the combatant within the collective responsibility of his combat unit.[176] While those committing international crimes may still be considered to be rational beings, they are often subject to severe moral disengagement which results in the dehumanising of the enemy and the justifying of violations.[177] If how a combatant behaves is more closely connected to the will to obey an order than any moral or rational decision about the risk/reward calculations of a certain act and if such moral choices are anyway distorted by the violent paradigms of war, the deterrence theory is less suited to international criminal law, at least in its classical form.

Even where combatants are consciously aware that they are committing international crimes for which punishment is warranted, the sketchy implementation of

---

[171] Scharf, "From the eXile Files", at 349.

[172] D'Amato, "Law and War".

[173] Robert Keel, "Rational Choice and Deterrence Theory", *Sociology of Deviant Behaviour*, available at: <http://www.umsl.edu/~rkeel/200/ratchoc.html>.

[174] Glueck, *War Criminals*, at 72.

[175] Daniel Muñoz-Rojas and Jean-Jacques Frésard, ICRC, *The Roots of Behaviour in War: Understanding and Preventing IHL Violations* (Geneva: ICRC, October 2004), at 6-10.

[176] *Idem*.

[177] *Ibid*., at 10.

international criminal law throughout history indicates that most lower-level perpetrators are unlikely to be indicted for war crimes. For this reason, some commentators have criticised the recent trend of advocating 'exemplary' trials, focusing on only those 'most responsible,' because the deterrence value is likely to remain low where the risk of prosecution is minimal.[178] Certainly, international criminal justice, at least as administered by the international tribunals, is anything but *swift*, may be less *severe* in punishment than at the national level,[179] and is by no means *certain*, being highly dependant on prosecutorial discretion as well as practical and political considerations. Proceedings at the national level fare little better against these indicators.

While there remains a lack of empirical evidence of the deterrent effect of war crimes trials,[180] history shows little evidence that criminal sanctions have a direct impact on the future behaviour of State officials.[181] More recently, commentators have observed that atrocities committed against civilians in Darfur, Sudan, continue unabated, despite the fact that the Security Council referred the situation to the ICC in March 2005.[182] On the other hand, it should be borne in mind that international criminal law is still an evolving system and if the complementarity regime really does impel States parties of the Rome Statute to prosecute or transfer suspects to The Hague, prosecution at the international or national level should slowly become a more rapid, severe and certain response to international crimes, thereby increasing the deterrent value of international criminal law.

---

[178] Colm Campbell, "Peace and the laws of war: the role of international humanitarian law in the post-conflict environment", 839 *IRRC* 630 (2000).

[179] None of the international tribunals provide for the death penalty. Life imprisonment is the harshest penalty given.

[180] Payam Akhavan, "Beyond Impunity: Can International Criminal Justice Prevent Future Atrocities?", 95(1) *AJIL* 7 (2001); Tom J. Farer, "Restraining the Barbarians: Can International Criminal Law Help?", 22(1) *Human Rights Quarterly* 90 (2000); Michael L. Schmidt, "The International Criminal Court: An Effective Means of Deterrence?", 167 *Military Law Review* 156 (2001); David Wippman, "Atrocities, Deterrence, and the Limits of International Justice", 23 *Fordham International Law Journal* 473 (1999).

[181] Even after the Allies announced their intention to pursue the perpetrators 'to the uttermost ends of the earth' in 1943, the Nazis continued to commit atrocities. "Declaration of German Atrocities", 1 November 1943, 9 *Dep't St. Bull.* 310 (1943), at 311. The International Law Association has pointed out that the deterrent effect should not be overstated, noting that serious crimes on a massive scale continued to be committed in Kosovo after the Chief Prosecutor of the ICTY had announced her intention of investigating and prosecuting these crimes in a letter addressed to President Milošević and other senior officers. Letter from Justice Louise Arbour to President Milošević and other senior officials, ICTY press release JL/PIU/389, 26 March 1999, quoted in International Law Association, *Final Report on the Exercise of Universal Jurisdiction in Respect of Gross Human Rights Offences*, Committee on International Human Rights Law and Practice, London Conference 2000, at 4, available at: <http://www.ila-hq.org.>.

[182] SC Res. 1593, 31 March 2005. The OTP opened an investigation into the situation of Darfur, Sudan, on 1 June 2005. Pablo Castillo, "Rethinking Deterrence: The International Criminal Court in Sudan", *UNISCI Discussion Papers* 13 (January 2007), at 167.

2.3.5 The need for reconciliation

The impact of amnesty on the goal of reconciliation has merited special consideration in the context of policy analysis. The realist school of thought postulates that prosecution threatens peace and further fractures divided societies, thereby hampering efforts to foster reconciliation.[183] The liberalist school of thought posits that 'justice is the precondition for reconciliation, and advocates the formalization of such a link.'[184] A third school, which combines elements of the realist and liberalist approaches, recognises the restorative effect of trials, but sees this as just one aspect of a number of mechanisms that need to be instituted to allow a society to heal and move forward.[185]

The impact of the ICTR trials upon reconciliation in Rwanda provides an interesting, if not conclusive, case study. The Security Council resolution establishing the ICTR maintained that 'the prosecution of persons responsible for serious violations of international humanitarian law would ... contribute to the process of national reconciliation and to the restoration and maintenance of peace.'[186] It may be noted that while the government of Rwanda initially asked to United Nations to set up an international tribunal to prosecute perpetrators of the 1994 genocide, it was the only member of the Security Council to vote against the resolution establishing such a tribunal,[187] based on the belief that the modalities and structure of the ICTR as set out under the resolution meant that the tribunal was unlikely to contribute to reconciliation.[188] While it still may be too early to fully assess the

---

[183] For instance, Peter Penfold, the former British high commissioner to Freetown, has said that prosecutions threaten a fragile peace, reported in Chris McGreal, "African search for peace throws court into crisis: Uganda fears first crucial test for tribunal could prolong brutal 20-year civil war", *The Guardian Unlimited*, 9 January 2007, available at: <http://www.guardian.co.uk/frontpage/story/0,,1986047,00.html#article_continue>.

[184] Jean Marie Kamatali, "The Challenge of Linking International Criminal Justice and National Reconciliation: the Case of the ICTR", 16(1) *LJIL* 115 (March 2003), citing P. Akhavan, "Justice in the Hague, Peace in the Former Yugoslavia? A Commentary on the United Nations War Crimes Tribunal", 20 *HRQ* 737 (1998).

[185] Andrew Rigby, *Justice and Reconciliation: After the Violence* (Boulder, C.O: Lynne Rienner, 2001), at 180.

[186] SC Res. 995 (1994), preamble. Some Security Council members voiced some dissention on this point, noting that 'the Tribunal might become a vehicle of justice, but it is hardly designed as a vehicle of reconciliation.' Security Council, The Establishment of an International Tribunal for the Prosecution of Persons Responsible for Serious Violations of International Humanitarian Law Committed in the Territory of Rwanda and Rwandan Citizens Responsible for Such Violations Committed in the Territory of Neighbouring States, Provisional Verbatim Record, 3453rd meeting, 8 November 1994, S.PV.3453, at 7.

[187] At the time, Rwanda was a non-permanent member of the Security Council.

[188] Kamatali, "The Challenge of Linking International Criminal Justice and National Reconciliation", at 117. In particular, the Rwandan government was concerned about the restricted temporal jurisdiction of the conflict which meant that earlier events would not be considered; the lack of its own appeals chamber and prosecutor signalled that it would be an ineffective court designed only to appease the conscience of the international community; the lack of priority in the subject matter could denigrate the significance of the crime of genocide; those countries which had participated in the civil war in Rwanda were not precluded from proposing or electing judicial candidates; the possibility of

impact of the work of the ICTR upon the process of reconciliation in Rwanda, commentators have been fairly critical of the ICTR in this respect.[189]

One of the driving assumptions of those proclaiming criminal justice to be crucial to national reconciliation is the idea that by punishing individuals, collective responsibility of a particular ethnic, racial, religious or social group is avoided, and hence lasting feelings of resentment and hatred towards particular segments of society may be diminished. The ICTR experience demonstrates, however, that in particular conflicts involving mass atrocities it is difficult to distinguish between individual and collective responsibility.[190] It proved particularly problematic for the Tribunal to determine individual responsibility without identifying particular groups, such as the 'Hutu' and the 'Interahamwe' as being authors of the genocide.[191] Even if a distinction between individual and collective responsibility could be achieved in a criminal trial, this may not be conducive to national reconciliation. For example, while the ICTR positively identified the Tutsi as an ethnic group for the purpose of attributing the crime of genocide to individual perpetrators,[192] the national reconciliation policy in Rwanda has been based on deconstructing such groupings.[193] Thus, contrary to the national reconciliation policy, the ICTR positively identified the Tutsi as the ethnic group targeted in the genocide, and Hutu as the ethnic group responsible.

Indeed, some have argued that in situations of mass atrocities, the whole notion of individual criminal responsibility, based as it is on Kantian conceptions of individual free will and the ability to make rational self-interested choices for which

---

foreign countries deciding about detention of detainees took away the right of Rwandan people to decide on this issue; by ruling out capital punishment, it meant that high level perpetrators would escape the death penalty while lower level perpetrators tried in Rwanda would be subject to this penalty as provided for in the Rwandan penal code; and finally, the fact that the tribunal would not be geographically placed in Rwanda meant that its work was unlikely to bring about reconciliation.

[189] Kamatali, "The Challenge of Linking International Criminal Justice and National Reconciliation", at 115.

[190] *Ibid.*, at 118.

[191] *Clement Kayishema and Obed Ruzindana*, Case No. ICTR-95-I-T, para. 289: ('… the Trial Chamber finds that the massacres of the Tutsi population indeed were "meticulously planned and systematically co-ordinated" by top-level Hutu extremists in the former Rwandan government at the time in question.'); *Ignace Bagirishema*, ICTR-95-IA-T, para. 62: ('In all events, witnesses identified the Abakiga by their distinctive dress and testified that they attacked in large numbers, often in the hundreds'); *Akayesu*, ICTR, Trial Chamber I, Judgment of 2 September 1998, Case No. ICTR-96-4-T, at para. 657: ('The Chamber finds beyond a reasonable doubt that the *Interahamwe*, acting on the orders from the Accused, killed these eight refugees at the bureau command in the presence of the Accused.')

[192] *Akayesu, supra*, paras. 702-703: '… the Chamber is of the opinion that, in Rwanda in 1994, the Tutsi constituted a group referred to as "ethnic" in official classifications … the Chamber finds that, in any case, at the time of the alleged evens, the Tutsi did indeed constitute a stable and permanent group and were identified as such by all.'

[193] A definitive answer as to whether Tutsis and Hutus are in fact separate ethnic groups has not been given. See the Report of the National Summit of Unity and Reconciliation held in Kigali on 18-20 October 2000, available at: <www.nurc.org.rw/archives.htm>. The first policy adopted by the new government in Rwanda after the genocide was to erase the mention of 'ethnic group: Hutu, Tutsi or Twa' from identity cards and to start teaching Rwandans that these are not ethnic groups.

one can be held accountable, loses its suitability.[194] Koskenniemi has also pointed out that 'individualisation' of international criminal guilt may provide an alibi to a criminal state system (and abiding population).[195] In such situations, a restorative justice approach that looks to collective responsibility that communities may acknowledge and thereby restore relationships, may do more to facilitate reconciliation.[196] Studies conducted on traditional healing and social reintegration methods in certain African countries which have undergone severe and harmful wars have demonstrated that reconciliation efforts centre on how a community is able to come to terms with accepting back those persons involved in war brutalities.[197] Traditional healing methods in Angola and Mozambique, for example, focus upon purification rituals, symbolic of making a break with the past and starting afresh.[198] In many cases, this means not talking about the past; in fact, in some tribal cultures talking about the past is viewed as opening a possibility for malevolent spirits or human beings to intervene again. In this sense, avoiding verbal exteriorisation of past affliction is a way to overcome trauma. This indicates that reconciliation is not necessarily dependent upon talking about the past; in fact, such measures (such as testifying in a criminal trial or before a truth commission) could complicate the process of reconciliation as understood by some cultures.[199]

In South Africa, the traditional concept of *ubuntu* – encompassing a sense of humanity in relations with others[200] – was laid down as one of the keys to reconciliation after the apartheid regime handed over power.[201] The decision to issue a general amnesty to perpetrators in return for their testifying before the TRC instead of prosecution was justified by the national choice of 'understanding over venge-

---

[194] Kamatali, "The Challenge of Linking International Criminal Justice and National Reconciliation", at 125.

[195] Koskenniemi, "Between impunity and show trials", at 32.

[196] A. Sachs, "Truth and Reconciliation", quoted in L. McGregor, "Individual Accountability in South Africa: Cultural Optimism or Political Façade?", 95(7) *AJIL* 37 (2001).

[197] Alcinda Honwana, "Healing and Social Reintegration in Mozambique and Angola", in E. Skaar, S. Gloppen & A. Suhrke (eds.), *Roads to Reconciliation*, (Oxford: Lexington Books, 2005), 83 at 84 ('Here, the emphasis is not only placed on the individual self as such, but also on the wider collective body which can interfere and affect the health and well-being of the person, in ways that she or he can't control.')

[198] Honwana, "Healing and Social Reintegration in Mozambique and Angola". The author describes such rituals as the chief of a village in Angola lighting a new fire, sparked out of the friction between two stones, at the centre of the village and then each village household putting the flames of this new fire in place of the extinguished one. War affected children, especially child soldiers are put through purification rituals such as burning the clothes he wore during the war and any instruments he might have had, as well as sacrificing a chicken to appease the spirits of the dead and bathing him in water. Often, the child is not allowed to interact with family members until the rituals are performed.

[199] Honwana, "Healing and Social Reintegration in Mozambique and Angola", at 98.

[200] Archbishop Desmond Tutu has defined *ubuntu* in the following way: 'A person with ubuntu is open and available to others, affirming of others, does not feel threatened that others are able and good, for he or she has a proper self-assurance that comes from knowing that he or she belongs in a greater whole and is diminished when others are humiliated or diminished, when others are tortured or oppressed.'

[201] Promotion of National Unity and Reconciliation Act, No. 34 of 1995 (South Africa), preamble.

ance, reparation over retaliation, *ubuntu* over victimisation.'[202] In addition, as a result of the strong Christian influence over proceedings before the TRC, presided by Archbishop Desmond Tutu, the idea of forgiveness became central to the notion of reconciliation in South Africa.[203] In Angola, forgiveness also played a part in the process of reconciliation.[204]

However, forgiveness is not necessarily the precursor to all reconciliation policics. Another approach advocated is simply the 'normalization of social relations.'[205] This may not require victims to forgive but may carry an imperative for victims and society to know what happened and for such facts to be publicly acknowledged.[206] Acknowledgement has been described as 'what happens to knowledge when it becomes officially sanctioned and enters the public discourse.'[207] This entails some civic education about past events which 'should include a discussion course on linguistic morality' in order to counter revisionist accounts, indifference or silence.[208] However, acknowledgment also recognises that 'remembering always has an aspect of forgetting, and that therefore involved parties need to sort out what must be remembered and what can be forgotten without causing offense to victims.'[209] The South African TRC noted, for example, that their work was not about constructing a history of apartheid as would a historian, but about obtaining 'enough of the truth' to live together.[210]

In addition, policies of reconciliation are also determined by the nature of the conflict which caused the animosities between groups. With regard to the war in Bosnia-Herzegovina in 1992-1995 – a war predicated on changing the ethnic demography of the country – reconciliation has been argued to be hinged on 'a

---

202 *AZAPO* case, para. 48, quoting *ibid.*

203 Audrey R. Chapman, "Perspectives on the Role of Forgiveness in the Human Rights Violations Hearings", in Audrey R. Chapman and Hugo van der Merwe (eds.), *Truth and Reconciliation in South Africa* (Pennsylvania: University of Pennsylvania Press, 2008), at 63-89. Four of the seventeen commissioners were Christian ministers.

204 In September 1998, a pardon was offered by the government of Angola to Jonas Savimbi, head of UNITA 'if he were to ask for it and ask for the forgiveness of the Angolan people.' "Angola Government Offers Savimbi Pardon", *AfrolNews*, 2 September 1998, <www.afrol.com>. In 2003, UNITA publicly apologised to the Angolan people and asked for their forgiveness for crimes committed during the war. "UNITA apologises for partaking in Angolan war", *AfrolNews*, 8 January 2003, <www.afrol.com>.

205 Tone Bringa, "Reconciliation in Bosnia-Herzegovina", in E. Skaar, S. Gloppen and A. Suhrke (eds.), *Roads to Reconciliation* (Maryland: Lexington Books, 2005), at 196.

206 *Idem.*

207 Stanley Cohen, *States of Denial: Knowing about Atrocities and Suffering* (London: Polity Press, 2001), at 225.

208 *Ibid.*, at 240; Bringa, "Reconciliation in Bosnia-Herzegovina", at 197. In the TRC Report of South Africa, Archbishop Tutu noted that 'It is commonplace to treat language as mere words, not deeds … The Commission wishes to take a different view here. Language, discourse and rhetoric, *does* things: it constructs social categories, it gives orders, it persuades us, it justifies, explains, gives reasons, excuses. It constructs reality. It moves certain people against other people.' *Report of the Truth and Reconciliation Commission of South Africa*, Vol. I, at 70. See also Cassin, "Removing the perpetuity of hatred", at 241.

209 Bringa, "Reconciliation in Bosnia-Herzegovina", at 198.

210 *Report of the Truth and Reconciliation Commission of South Africa*, Vol. 1, at 70.

process of reintegration.'[211] A number of amnesty laws (excluding those accused of war crimes) were passed in the aftermath of the conflict, with encouragement of the United Nations, to help the reintegration process.[212]

In summary, reconciliation policies in societies which have undergone serious violence should be based upon local understandings of war trauma, of healing and of community cohesion. Notably, these factors may not always be satisfactorily accommodated by an absolute policy of prosecution or even by the institution of a truth and reconciliation commission.[213] There would, however, appear to be a universal need for acknowledgment of suffering in some public form, suggesting that unconditional amnesties would do little to help reconciliation and may indeed hamper such a process.

2.4 Legal rationales with regard to the exercise of jurisdiction in the face of amnesties

As there is no clear rule of international law prohibiting amnesties over international crimes, courts rely primarily on three main legal rationales which may affect the decision to exercise jurisdiction. These centre on: (1) the scope of the obligation to prosecute international crimes; (2) whether victims' fundamental human rights vitiate the validity of an amnesty law; and (3) whether States are constrained not to amnesty international crimes due to the peremptory character of international crimes.

2.4.1 The scope of the obligation to prosecute international crimes

The strongest evidence of an obligation to prosecute an international crime is where such a duty is incorporated in a treaty. The claim that an obligation to prosecute international crimes may also be found in customary law has also generated some support.[214] While State practice would not seem to support this view, there is on the other hand an unmistakable trend towards a norm of this character.

---

[211] Bringa, "Reconciliation in Bosnia-Herzegovina", at 189.

[212] See Bosnia and Herzegovina, Federation, Amnesty Law as amended (1996), Art. 1; Bosnia and Herzegovina, Federation, Law on Amnesty (1999), Art. 1; Bosnia and Herzegovina, Republika Srpska, Law on Amnesty as amended (1996), Art. 1. In 1997, in a statement by its President, the UN SC encouraged the government of Croatia 'to take steps as are needed to promote goodwill, build confidence, and provide assurances of a safe, secure and stable environment to all people in the region. These steps should include full implementation of its Law on Amnesty.' UN SC, Statement by the President, UN Doc. S/PRST/1997/15, 6 March 1997, at 2.

[213] See Rama Mani, "Does power trump morality? Reconciliation or transitional justice?", in Edel Hughes, William A. Schabas and Ramesh Thakur (eds.), *Atrocities and International Accountability: Beyond Transitional Justice* (Tokyo/New York/Paris: United Nations University Press, 2007), at 23.

[214] This view has been particularly prominent among NGOs. See, e.g., Amnesty International, *Universal Jurisdiction: The duty of states to enact and implement legislation* (London: AI International Secretariat, 2001).

International treaties prohibiting genocide,[215] grave breaches of the Geneva Conventions of 1949 and of AP I[216] and torture[217] oblige States parties to prosecute individuals accused of committing those crimes. While the grave breaches regimes and the Torture Convention would seem to provide for universal jurisdiction, the obligation to prosecute or extradite would only come into play when the suspect is on the territory of the State party.[218] The obligation to prosecute contained in the Genocide Convention only relates to the State of territoriality.[219] The judgment of the ICJ in the *Application of the Genocide Convention* has confirmed that this obligation is territorially limited to the State where the crimes were committed, although it recognises that States *may* legislate to allow for a wider jurisdictional basis.[220] An amnesty law passed by the State of territoriality covering these crimes would therefore likely constitute a violation of such duties and would not be accorded recognition by a court at the international or national lev-

---

[215] Genocide Convention, Art. IV provides that persons 'committing genocide or any of the other acts enumerated in article III shall be punished, whether they are constitutionally responsible rulers, public officials or private individuals.' Contracting parties are required to enact legislation necessary to give effect to the Convention, 'and, in particular, to provide effective penalties for persons guilty of genocide' (Art. V). It is widely accepted that customary international law establishes universal jurisdiction over genocide. *Attorney General of Israel* v. *Eichmann*, 36 *ILR* 18, at 39 (Isr. Dist. Ct. – Jerusalem 1961), affirmed in 36 *ILR* 227 (Isr. Sup. Ct. 1962); *Restatement (Third) of the Foreign Relations Law of the United States* (1987), § 702 comment d. *Reservations to the Convention on the Prevention and Punishment of the Crime of Genocide*, 1951 ICJ Reports 15, at 23.

[216] Arts. 49/50/129/146 of the four Geneva Conventions of 1949 provide: 'Each High Contracting Party shall be under the obligation to search for persons alleged to have committed, or to have ordered to be committed, such grave breaches, and shall bring such persons, regardless of their nationality, before its own courts. It may also, if it prefers, and in accordance with its own legislation, hand such persons over for trial to another High Contracting Party concerned, provided such High Contracting Party has made out a … *prima facie* case.' Geneva Convention for the Amelioration of the Condition of the Wounded and Sick in Armed Forces in the Field, 12 August 1949, 75 *UNTS* 31; Geneva Convention for the Amelioration of the Condition of the Wounded, Sick and Shipwrecked Members of Armed Forces at Sea, 12 August 1949, 75 *UNTS* 85; Geneva Convention relative to the Treatment of Prisoners of War, 12 August 1949, 75 *UNTS* 135; Geneva Convention relative to the Protection of Civilian Persons in Time of War, 12 August 1949, *UNTS* 287. AP I, Art. 85 significantly extends the list of grave breaches as found in the GCs. Under Art. 86(1), the obligation to repress grave breaches extends to grave breaches which result from a failure to do so. Protocol Additional to the Geneva Convention of 12 August 1949, and Relating to the Protection of Victims of International Armed Conflicts (Protocol I), of 8 June 1977, 1125 *UNTS* 3.

[217] Convention against Torture, Art. 7 provides: 'The State Party in the territory under whose jurisdiction a person alleged to have committed any offence referred to in article 4 is found shall in the cases contemplated in article 5, if it does not extradite him, submit the case to its competent authorities for the purpose of prosecution.'

[218] Jean S. Pictet, *Commentary to IV Geneva Convention Relative to the Protection of Civilian Persons in Time of War* (Geneva: ICRC, 1958), at at 593: 'As soon as a Contracting Party realizes that there is on its territory a person who has committed such a breach, its duty is to ensure that the person concerned is arrested and prosecuted with all speed.'

[219] Arts. IV and VI both provide that genocidaires 'shall be' tried by the territorial State.

[220] *Application of the Convention on the Prevention and Punishment of the Crime of Genocide (Bosnia and Herzegovina* v. *Serbia and Montenegro)*, Judgment, 26 February 2007, para. 184.

el.[221] National courts have found that amnesties covering such crimes violate a State's international obligations under the treaties.[222] The ICTY has also observed that a domestic amnesty covering torture, whose prohibition has the status of *jus cogens*, 'would not be accorded international recognition' where the recognition would amount to authorising, condoning or absolving the behaviour of perpetrators.[223] Similar conclusions have been held by domestic courts considering the legal effect on their own exercise of jurisdiction over amnesty laws covering such crimes in third States.[224] The European Court of Human Rights upheld the decision of France's *Cour de Cassation* in the case of *Ould Dah* v. *France*, finding that the prohibition of torture occupied a prominent place in international law and that the

[221] The ICRC *Commentary to the Geneva Conventions* confirms that the obligation to prosecute grave breaches is 'absolute,' meaning that States parties may under no circumstances avoid fulfilling this obligation by providing immunity by way of an amnesty law. Pictet, *Commentary to IV Geneva Convention*, at 160. Art. I of the Genocide Convention provides that 'The Contracting Parties confirm that genocide, whether committed in time of peace or in time of war, is a crime under international law which they undertake to prevent and to punish,' while Art. V obliges States to 'provide effective penalties for persons guilty of genocide.' The whole object and purpose of the Genocide Convention was to prevent the recurrence of genocide (as perpetrated in WW II) by assuring the punishment of offenders. See UN Doc. E/AC.25/3, at 8 (remarks of Secretary General). Therefore an amnesty law would be manifestly inconsistent with the basic obligations under the Convention, as well as its object and purpose. The object of the Torture Convention was also to ensure that 'no offender would have the opportunity to escape the consequences of his acts of torture.' Report of the Working Group on a Draft Convention Against Torture and Other Cruel, Inhuman or Degrading Treatment or Punishment, 36 UN ESCOR Commission on Human Rights, at 11, para. 61, UN Doc. E/CN.4/1367 (1980).

[222] *Videla,* Chile, Appeal Court of Santiago (Third Criminal Chamber), Judgment, 26 September 1994 (finding that grave breaches are 'unamenable to amnesty'). In the *AZAPO* case, the Constitutional Court found that the grave breaches regime did not apply to the situation prevailing in South Africa, therefore the amnesty remained valid. By contrast, the Constitutional Court in the *Basson* case, invoving allegations of war crimes committed by a South African doctor in Namibia, were considered to have raised the obligation of South Africa to prosecute pserons charged with grave breaches, inspite of an Amnesty Law prevailing in Namibia. *S.* v. *Basson*, South Africa, Constitutional Court, 10 March 2004, Published in 2004 (6) BCLR 620 (CC); case note in *YIHL* (2004), at 588. The National Court of Appeal for Federal Criminal and Correctional Cases of Argentina upheld a federal judge's March 2001 ruling declaring invalid the Full Stop Law, Law No. 23,492 of 12 December 1986 and the Due Obedience Law, Law No. 23,521 of 4 June 1987, which had barred further prosecutions of military officers for human rights violations (including, notably, torture and enforced disappearances) committed during the previous military regime. *Resolución del Cavallo*, Argentina, Decision of 6 March 2001, Case 8686/2000, *Juzgado Nacional en lo Criminal y Correccional Federal*, No. 4 (6 March 2001), available at: <http://www.derechos.org/nizkor/arg/ley/juezcavallo03mar.html>.

[223] *Furundžija*, ICTY, Trial Chamber II, Judgment of 10 December 1998, Case No. IT-95-17/1-T; 39 *ILM* (1999), para. 155. For further analysis of the judgment in the context of recognising amnesties, see Yasmin Naqvi, "Amnesty for war crimes: Defining the limits of international recognition", 85(851) *IRRC* (September 2003), at 609-614.

[224] In Spain, the *Audiencia Nacional* held that Spanish jurisdiction (over charges of charges of genocide, terrorism, torture and enforced disappearances) was not precluded by the 1978 Chilean amnesty law. Order of the Criminal Chamber, Appeal 173/98 (5 November 1998). In France, the *Cour de cassation* upheld a decision that had rejected application by French courts of a 1993 Mauritanian amnesty covering torture, stating that recognising the applicability of the amnesty would be tantamount to a violation by the French authorities of their international obligations and would deprive the principle of universal jurisdiction of its purpose. *Ely Ould Dah* case, Crim. 23 October 2002, Bull. Crim. No. 195, at 725. For a summary, see <www.universaljurisdiction.info/index/Cases/Cases/France>.

prohibition was binding.[225] It observed that at the material time the UN Convention against Torture had come into force and had been incorporated into French law, and that the 'absolute necessity' of prohibiting and penalising torture justified, in the exercise of universal jurisdiction, not only that the French courts had jurisdiction over the case, but that they would apply French law.[226] The Mauritanian amnesty law would otherwise deprive the universal jurisdiction provided for by the UN Convention against Torture of its substance. It also considered that an amnesty law was generally incompatible with the duty of States to investigate acts of torture.[227]

While there is no conventional obligation to prosecute crimes against humanity or serious violations of IHL, customary law entitles every State to do so.[228] However, the permissive nature of the jurisdiction over such crimes means that States would not breach customary law by not prosecuting by reason of an amnesty law.[229] As noted by the SCSL in regard to the Lomé amnesty, there was no 'general obligation for States to refrain from amnesty laws on these crimes [crimes against humanity, serious violations of common Article 3 and AP II and other serious violations of IHL] … [and that] [c]onsequently, if a State passes any such law, it does not breach a customary rule.'[230] Notably, in the *Kondewa* case, Justice Robertson concluded in a separate opinion that a customary rule did exist that 'invalidates amnesties offered under any circumstances to persons most responsible for crimes against humanity (genocide and widespread torture) and the worst war crimes (namely those in Common Article 3 of the Geneva Conventions).'[231] A number of international bodies as well as commentators have asserted that there is an obligation to prosecute these types of crimes under customary law. Some commenta-

---

[225] *Ould Dah* v. *France*, Admissibililty, Requête no. 13113/03, Council of Europe: European Court of Human Rights, 17 March 2009.

[226] *Ibid.*, at 16-17.

[227] *Ibid.*, at 17.

[228] See Willard B. Cowles, "Universal Jurisdiction over War Crimes", 33 *California Law Review* 177 (1945); Anna Segall, *Punishing Violations of International Humanitarian Law at the National Level* (Geneva: ICRC, 2001), especially at 30-38. In the *Tadić* case, the Appeals Chamber declared in relation to the principle of universal jurisdiction: 'This is all the more so [justified] in view of the nature of the offences alleged against the Appellant, offences which, if proven, do not affect the interests of one State alone but shock the conscience of mankind. As early as 1950, in the case of *General Wagener*, the Supreme Military Tribunal of Italy held: … The solidarity among nations, aimed at alleviating in the best possible way the horrors of war, gave rise to the need to dictate rules which do not recognize borders, punishing criminals wherever they may be … Crimes against the laws and customs of war cannot be considered political offences, as they do not harm a political interest of a particular State, nor a political right of a particular citizen. They are, instead, crimes of *lese-humanite* (reati di lesa umanita) and, as previously demonstrated, the norms prohibiting them have a universal character, not simply a territorial one. (13 March 1950, in *Rivista Penale* 753, 757 (Sup. Mil. Trib., Italy 1959; unofficial translation),' *Tadić* (Decision on the defence motion for Interlocutory Appeal on Jurisdiction), ICTY, Appeals Chamber, Decision of 2 October 1995, Case No. IT-94-1-AR72, 35 *ILM* 32 (1996), at 57.

[229] Mallinder, *supra* n. 61, at 129-135.

[230] *Kallon and Kamara* Decision on Amnesty case, quoting Antonio Cassese, *International Criminal Law* (2003), at 315.

[231] *Kondewa*, SCSL, Case No. SCSL-2004-14-AR72(E), Separate Opinion of Justice Robertson on the Decision on Lack of Jurisdiction/Abuse of Process: Amnesty Provided by the Lomé Accord, 25 May 2004, para. 51.

tors have argued that the trends with respect to international criminal law show a movement from permissive to mandatory jurisdiction and '[t]aken together, these provisions provide one basis for an emerging consensus that these human rights violations must be investigated and prosecuted.'[232]

However, the sources relied upon by those arguing that a customary duty to prosecute international crimes exists are not fully persuasive. In order for a rule to be recognised as customary, there must be evidence of 'a general practice accepted as law.'[233] For a customary duty to prosecute international crimes to exist, the States exercising jurisdiction on this basis must '... feel that they are conforming to what amounts to a legal obligation.'[234] The ICJ in the *North Sea Continental Shelf* case explained that 'State practice, including that of States whose interests are specially affected, should ... [be] both extensive and virtually uniform.'[235] In *Nicaragua* (Merits), the Court clarified that State practice does not have to be absolutely uniform and that individual deviations may in fact confirm the existence of a rule, rather than show that no rule has crystallised, either because they are regarded as breaches of the rule or the State concerned claims that its conduct was justified by exceptional circumstances.[236] Some of those arguing that the duty to prosecute international crimes is customary assert that 'even those states which have adopted amnesty laws and thereby allowed impunity do not deny the existence, in principle, of an obligation to prosecute, but invoke countervailing considerations, such as national reconciliation or the instability of the democratic process.'[237] In addition, although evidence of inconsistent State practice would normally point against the existence of a customary rule, the ICJ has found that it carries less weight in the field of human rights or humanitarian law. In such matters, the Court has focused instead on verbal statements of governments to international organisations, the content of resolutions and declarations adopted by these organisations, and the consent of States to such instruments.[238] These sources show that States are unwilling to say publicly that they are not under an obligation to prosecute human rights violators.[239]

---

[232] Naomi Roht-Arriaza, "Sources in International Treaties of an Obligation to Investigate, Prosecute, and Provide Redress", in Naomi Roht-Arriaza (ed.), *Impunity and Human Rights in International Law and Practice* (Oxford: OUP, 1995), at 28.

[233] ICJ Statute, Art. 38(1)(b).

[234] *North Sea Continental Shelf (West Germany* v. *Denmark; West Germany* v. *the Netherlands)*, 1969 ICJ Reports 3 (20 February 1969), at para. 77.

[235] *Ibid.*, at para. 74.

[236] *Military and Paramilitary Activities in and against Nicaragua (Nicaragua* v. *United States)*, 1986 ICJ Reports 14 (1986), para. 186.

[237] Carla Edelenbos, "Human Rights Violations: A Duty to Prosecute?", 7(5) *LJIL* 21 (1994); Naomi Roht-Arriaza, "State Responsibility to Investigate and Prosecute Grave Violations of Human Rights in International Law", 78 *California Law Review* 496-97 (1990). See also *Filatiga* v. *Pena-Irala,* United States, 630 F.2d 876 (1980), at para. 186 (noting that the prohibition of torture remains valid despite the fact that States often violate it).

[238] *Military and Paramilitary Activities in and against Nicaragua* (*Nicaragua* v. *United States*), 1986 ICJ Reports 14 (1986), at 98-108.

[239] For example, the Uruguayan civilian government assured the Commission that it would investigate human violations committed under the previous regime and prosecute those alleged of com-

The evidence relied upon to argue for a customary duty to prosecute international crimes consists for the most part of treaties that are not widely ratified, nonbinding GA and CHR resolutions and declarations of international conferences. For instance, the Convention on the Non-Applicability of Statutory Limitations to War Crimes and Crimes Against Humanity of 1968 obliges States parties to remove 'statutory or other limitations' for prosecutions involving these crimes.[240] The treaty falls short of requiring States parties to prosecute or extradite such crimes though logically this could be inferred from the obligation to remove any statute of limitations.[241] If States were not required to prosecute crimes against humanity or war crimes, then prosecutions could simply not be initiated at all and there would be no need to adjust laws on temporal restrictions.[242] The Argentine Supreme Court has interpreted the Convention as implying that amnesties for such crimes – another type of 'limitation' – should also be abolished. Largely as a result of that interpretation,[243] the Court declared Argentina's two amnesty laws of 1986 and 1987 constitutionally invalid and without legal effect.[244] Such an interpretation is probably exceeding the intentions of the drafters, whose objective was merely to ensure that prosecutions could not be time-barred, but a progressive interpretation in this direction does not distort the meaning of the convention either. Nonetheless, as of July 2009 only 53 States are party to the treaty and it cannot be taken to expound a general rule of customary law.[245]

The GA has passed a number of resolutions which assert or infer an obligation to prosecute international crimes,[246] the clearest being Resolution 3074 which

---

mitting them, despite the fact that it had enacted a virtual amnesty. See Americas Watch, *Challenging Impunity* (New York: Americas Watch, 1988), at 12.

[240] Convention on the Non-Applicability of Statutory Limitations to War Crimes and Crimes Against Humanity, of 26 November 1968 (entered into force 11 November 1970), Art. 1: 'The States Parties to the present Convention undertake to adopt, in accordance with their respective constitutional processes, any legislative or other measures necessary to ensure that statutory or other limitations shall not apply to the prosecution and punishment of the crimes referred to in articles 1 and 2 of this Convention and that, where they exist, such limitations shall be abolished.'

[241] Dugard, "Possible Conflicts of Jurisdiction with Truth Commissions", at 696.

[242] This argument was rejected in *Javor and others*, France, Cour de Cassation, 26 March 1996, in *Bull. crim.*, no. 132 1996, where the Court held that the Convention does not by itself establish adjudicatory jurisdiction over crimes against humanity.

[243] The Court also considered that the amnesty laws violated Art. 15(2) of the ICCPR, several provisions of the ACHR and obligations arising as a result of *jus cogens* norms. See Case *Simón*, Judge Maqueda at Sections 49, 57, 62, 56, 88 and 89, Judge Boggiano at Sections 28 and 40-43, Judge Lorenzetti at Section 32, and Judge Highton de Nolasco, at Section 32. For a critical analysis of the case within its political context, see Jose Sebastian Elias, "Constitutional Changes, Transitional Justice, and Legitimacy: The Life and Death of Argentina's 'Amnesty Laws'", 31 *Hastings International and Comparative Law Review* (2008), at 628-646.

[244] *Simón, Julio Héctor y otros s/privación ilegítima de la libertad*, Argentina, Case S. 1767. XXXVIII (14 June 2005). See also Corte Suprema de Justicia [CSJN], 24/08/2004, *Arancibia Clavel, Enrique Lautaro y otros*, Colección Oficial de Fallos de la Corte Suprema de Justicia de la Naćion [Fallos] (2004-327-3294) (Arg.).

[245] See the status of ratifications, available at: <http://www.ohchr.org/english/countries/ratification/6.htm>.

[246] Declaration on Territorial Asylum, GA Res. 2312 (XXII), Art. 4, 22 UN GAOR, Suppl. (No. 16), UN Doc. A/6716 (1 December 1967); Question of the Punishment of War Criminals and

laid down the Principles of International Cooperation in the Detection, Arrest, Extradition, and Punishment of Persons Guilty of War Crimes and Crimes Against Humanity which stated that 'war crimes and crimes against humanity, wherever they are committed, shall be subject to investigation and the persons against whom there is evidence … shall be subject to tracing, arrest, trial and, if found guilty, to punishment.'[247] The UN CHR has also recognised a duty to prosecute international crimes, including war crimes committed in non-international armed conflicts and crimes against humanity.[248] Reports by Special Rapporteurs, Special Representatives, and Working Groups appointed by the CHR to report on human rights conditions in particular countries or on particular types of human rights violations have repeatedly condemned governments' failure to institute prosecutions for serious human rights violations. It is often asserted in the reports that a State's failure to prosecute and punish repeated violations of human rights encourages further violations.[249] The GA has endorsed many of the reports' conclusions concerning the duty to prosecute and punish persons responsible for serious violations of human rights.[250] The Security Council has, in various Presidential Statements, underlined

of Persons Who Have Committed Crimes Against Humanity, GA Res. 2712 (XXV), para. 3, 25 UN GAOR, 25th Sess., Suppl. (No. 28), UN Doc. A/8028 (15 December 1970); Question of the Punishment of War Criminals and of Persons Who Have Committed Crimes Against Humanity, GA Res. 2840 (XXVI), para. 4, 26 UN GAOR, Suppl. (No. 29), UN Doc. A/8429 (18 December 1971); Declaration on the Protection of All Persons from Enforced Disappearances, GA Res. 47/133 pmbl., Art. 14, UN Doc. A/47/49 (18 December 1992).

[247] Principles of International Cooperation in the Detection, Arrest, Extradition, and Punishment of Persons Guilty of War Crimes and Crimes Against Humanity, GA Res. 3074 (XXVIII), 28 UN GAOR Suppl. (No. 12), at 11, UN Doc. A/9030 (3 December 1973), principle 1.

[248] UN CHR Res. 1999/1, 6 April 1999 (reminding all factions in Sierra Leone 'that in any armed conflict, *including an armed conflict not of an international character*, the taking of hostages, wilful killing and torture or inhuman treatment of persons taking no active part in the hostilities constitute grave breaches of international humanitarian law, and that all countries are under the obligation to search for persons alleged to have committed, or to have ordered to be committed, such grave breaches and to bring such persons, regardless of their nationality, before their own courts' [Emphasis added]; In CHR Res. 2002/79, the Commission stated that 'amnesties should not be granted to those who commit violations of international humanitarian and human rights law that constitute serious crimes and urges States to take action in accordance with their obligations under international law' (para. 2). Para. 11 of the resolution states that 'crimes such as genocide, crimes against humanity, war crimes and torture are violations of international law and that perpetrators of such crimes should be prosecuted or extradited by States, and urges all States to take effective measures to implement their obligations to prosecute or extradite perpetrators of such crimes.'

[249] See for example, Report prepared by the Special Rapporteur on the situation of human rights in Chile in accordance with paragraph 11 of the Commission on Human Rights resolution 1983/38 of 8 March 1983, UN Doc. A/38/385, para. 341 (1983); Final report on the situation of human rights in El Salvador submitted to the Commission on Human Rights by Mr. José Antonio Pastor Ridruejo in fulfilment of the mandate conferred under Human Rights Commission resolution 1986/39, 42 *UN Hum. Rts. Comm* at 85, para. 312, UN Doc. E/CN.4/1989/18; Report of the Working Group on Enforced or Involuntary Disappearances, 47 *UN Hum. Rts. Comm* at 86, para. 406.

[250] See for example, GA Res. 37/185, para. 10 (1982) (urging El Salvador to 'assume its obligation to … prosecute and to punish those found responsible for assassinations, acts of torture and other forms of cruel, inhuman or degrading treatment'); GA Res. 36/157, para. 4(e) (1981) (urging Chile to 'prosecute and punish those responsible for … disappearances'); UN Doc. A/Res/44/162, endors-

the need to prosecute those responsible for criminal violations of human rights and humanitarian law.[251] At the June 1993 World Conference on Human Rights, States adopted the Declaration and Programme of Action which affirms that 'States should abrogate legislation leading to impunity for those responsible for grave violations of human rights such as torture and prosecute such violations, thereby providing a firm basis for the rule of law.'[252] Although many of the Declaration's provisions were controversial, there was little disagreement between States on this point.[253] An obligation to prosecute or extradite war crimes and crimes against humanity was also laid down in the Draft Code of Crimes Against the Peace and Security of Mankind, adopted by the ILC in 1996.[254]

It is axiomatic that none of these instruments are binding as a matter of law.[255] Commentators disagree on how much weight may be placed on these sources as evidence of State practice or *opinio juris*. The ICJ explained the significance of GA resolutions in its opinion on the *Legality of the Threat or Use of Nuclear Weapons*:

> 'General Assembly Resolutions, even if they are not binding, may sometimes have normative value. They can, in certain circumstances, provide evidence important for establishing the existence of a rule or the emergence of an *opinio juris*. To establish whether this is true of a given General Assembly Resolution, it is necessary to look at its content and the conditions of its adoption; it is also necessary to see whether an *opinio juris* exists as to its normative character.'[256]

---

ing ECOSOC Resolution 1989/65 which adopted the Principles on the Effective Prevention and Investigation of Extra-Legal, Arbitrary and Summary Executions. Principle 19.2 provides that: 'In no circumstances, including a state of war, siege or other public emergency, shall blanket immunity from prosecution be granted to any person allegedly involved in extra-legal, arbitrary or summary executions.' Principle 18 provides that: '[g]overnments shall ensure that persons identified by the investigation as having participated in extra-legal, arbitrary and summary executions in any territory under their jurisdiction are brought to justice. Governments shall either bring such persons to justice or co-operate to extradite such persons to other countries wishing to exercise jurisdiction.'

[251] In a Presidential Statement on children in armed conflict: 'the Council stresses the obligation of all States to prosecute those responsible for grave breaches of international humanitarian law.' S/PRST/1998/18 of 29 June 1998. On the protection of civilians in armed conflicts: 'The Council affirms the need to bring to justice, in an appropriate manner, individuals who incite or cause violence against civilians in situations of armed conflict or who otherwise violate international humanitarian and human rights law.' S/PRST/1999/6 of 12 February 1999.

[252] Vienna Declaration and Programme of Action, UN Doc. A/CONF.157/23, 12 July 1993, Art. 60.

[253] World Conference on Human Rights, Declaration and Programme of Action, Vienna, June 1993, UN Doc. A/Conf./57/23, second part.

[254] Draft Articles on the Draft Code of Crimes Against the Peace and Security of Mankind, Report of the International Law Commission on the work of its Forty-Eighth Session, UN Doc. A/48/10, II(2) *Yearbook of the International Law Commission* (1996), Arts. 3 and 9. The offences falling within the scope of the Articles are the crime of aggression (Art. 16), the crime of genocide (Art. 17), crimes against humanity (Art. 18), crimes against United Nations and associated personnel (Art. 19), and war crimes (Art. 20).

[255] The resolutions of the GA, ECOSOC and the CHR (a subsidiary body of ECOSOC) have a recommendatory power only. See UN Charter, Arts. 10-14, 62 and 68.

[256] *Legality of the Threat or Use of Nuclear Weapons*, Advisory Opinion of 8 July 1996, ICJ Reports 1996, para. 70.

Analysing the above-mentioned resolutions with regard to their use of language and their voting record reveals a continuing ambivalence with regard to an obligation to prosecute international crimes. None of the resolutions proclaim to be declaratory of international law. While some of the resolutions, such as GA Resolution 3074 use imperative language such as 'perpetrators shall' be subject to trial, this is followed by the words 'as a general rule.' Most of the resolutions adopt the word 'should' in relation to prosecuting those accused of international crimes, reflecting the recommendatory nature of the resolutions.[257] Many of the resolutions were adopted with large numbers of abstentions, signalling that not all States accepted the principles contained therein.[258] Therefore, it is problematic to rely heavily upon these resolutions and statements as evidence of a customary duty to prosecute international crimes.

State practice also militates against a customary duty to prosecute international crimes, even if one takes into account a trend in this direction and the ICJ's comments in *Nicaragua* about deviating behaviour sometimes confirming the rule if justified by situations of exception. The continued reliance on amnesties by some countries suggests that States do not generally consider such practice to be manifestly incompatible with their duties under international law.[259] While some countries that have granted amnesties have justified this action as an exception to the rule,[260] the majority of States have not mentioned the existence of such a rule. The United Nations itself has supported amnesties covering international crimes in certain situations, though there would appear to be a change in practice in this regard in recent years.[261] Taking into account this contrary practice, Michael P. Scharf in 1996 argued that 'a "rule" that is so divorced from the realities of State practice is unlikely to achieve substantial compliance in the real world, and, therefore, cannot be said to be a binding rule at all, but rather an aspiration.'[262] It may be observed that in the Security Council's debate on the Secretary-General's 2004 report on Transitional Justice, which stated that the UN should reject amnesties for international crimes and that no such amnesty should be a bar to prosecution before any UN-created or assisted court, there was no consensus about this recommendation and only two States supported it,[263] while some opposed it.[264]

E.g., CHR Res. 2002/79.

[258] GA Res. 2712 (XXV) was adopted 55-4, with 33 abstentions; GA Res. 2840 (XXVI) was adopted 71-0 with 42 abstentions; GA 3074 (XXVIII) was adopted 94-0 with 29 abstentions.

[259] Cryer, *Prosecuting International Crimes*, at 107.

[260] Roht-Arriaza, "State Responsibility to Investigate and Prosecute", citing Chile in 1984, Uruguay in 1986, Argentina in 1987 and El Salvador in 1987.

[261] Stahn, "United Nations peace-building, amnesties and alternative forms of justice: A change in practice?".

[262] Scharf, "Swapping Amnesty for Peace", at 41. His view has not changed much. In an article published in 2006, he stated that 'there is scant evidence that a rule prohibiting amnesties or asylum in cases of crimes against humanity has ripened into a compulsory norm of customary international law.' Scharf, "From the eXile Files", at 360.

[263] Brazil and Costa Rica: UN 59 SCOR, 5052nd mtg., at 14, UN Doc. S/PV.5052 (6 October 2004) and UN 59 SCOR, 5052nd mtg., Resumption 1, at 26.

[264] See, e.g., the remarks of the representative of South Africa recalling its amnesty for truth process that helped lead to reconciliation in South Africa, indicating that each specific context should be

In the *Arrest Warrant* case, although Belgium originally submitted to the ICJ that there was a 'general obligation on States under customary international to prosecute perpetrators of crimes,' it conceded that where the perpetrators were non-nationals and the crimes were committed outside of its territory, there was no obligation but rather 'an available option.'[265] The ILA has opined that 'international practice offers considerable, but not yet conclusive, support for' the argument that amnesties will always violate international law.[266] During the negotiations of the Rome Statute, the proposal to include a statement that prosecution was the only appropriate response to international crimes was not accepted by all States.[267] The SCSL, in its *Decision on Amnesty*, did recognise 'that there is a crystallising international norm that a government cannot grant amnesties for serious violations of crimes under international law [which] is amply supported by materials placed before the Court [but the view] that it has crystallised may not be entirely correct ... it is accepted that such a norm is developing under international law.'[268] Arguments tied to an obligation to prosecute still rely predominantly on territorial jurisdiction. All commentators concede that there is almost no State practice supporting mandatory universal jurisdiction over international crimes.[269]

The argument that such a duty may be inferred from the complementarity principle enshrined in the Rome Statute is not entirely convincing despite the claim in the preamble that 'it is the duty of every State to exercise its criminal jurisdiction over those responsible for international crimes.'[270] As States are normally reticent to recognise implied obligations under customary law by reason of their ratification of a new legal instrument, the final list of crimes under the ICC Statute is much more likely to represent simply the serious violations of international humanitarian law to which individual criminal responsibility is attached under customary international law rather than a list of crimes which entail mandatory universal jurisdiction.[271] A cautious interpretation of the Rome Statute is particularly warranted in relation to crimes committed in non-international armed conflicts, given the historic reluctance of States to assume precise duties in relation to the law of armed

assessed differently rather than be subject to any common strategy. The Indian representative noted that the balance between retributive justice and the need for reconciliation through an amnesty should be determined strictly by pragmatic considerations of establishing an enduring peace. See UN 59 SCOR, 5052nd mtg., Resumption 1, at 13 and 23, UN Doc. S/PV.5052 (6 October 2004). No mention is made of the rejection of amnesties in the final statement approved by the Council. *Ibid.*, at 37-38.

265 *Arrest Warrant of April 11th 2000 (Democratic Republic of the Congo* v. *Belgium)*, Judgment, Merits, 41 *ILM* 536 (2002), Separate Opinion of Higgins, Kooijmans and Buergenthal, para. 8.

266 International Law Association Committee on International Human Rights Law and Practice (Menno Kamminga), "Final Report on the Exercise of Universal Jurisdiction in Relation to Gross Human Rights Abuses", in ILA, *Report of the Sixty-Ninth Conference, Held in London* (London: ILA, 2000), 403 at 416.

267 Dugard, "Possible Conflicts of Jurisdiction with Truth Commissions", at 693.

268 *Kallon and Kamara* Decision on Amnesty case.

269 Bassiouni, "International Crimes", at 45.

270 ICC Statute, preambular, para. 6.

271 Naqvi, "Amnesty for war crimes: Defining the limits of international recognition", at 600-601.

conflict in conflicts of a non-international character.[272] At the same time, the principle of complementarity does suggest that these serious international crimes cannot be without judicial consequence, either at the national level or the international. The policy paper of the Office of the Prosecutor of the ICC states that: '... the system of complementarity is principally based on the recognition that the exercise of national criminal jurisdiction is not only a right but also a duty of States.'[273] One may well question the wisdom of the OTP second-guessing a State in its decision to adopt an amnesty law to end a long and protracted civil war particularly as the Office will have to plead that a State's granting of amnesty is 'for the purpose of shielding the person from criminal responsibility for crimes within the jurisdiction of the Court referred to in Article 5.'[274]

A duty to prosecute all serious violations of IHL has also been inferred from the obligation to 'respect and ensure respect' for the Geneva Conventions.[275] Since one of the most effective ways of ensuring respect for the Conventions or their Protocols is to have a system of enforcement, including penal sanctions, for serious violations of the rules contained therein, a certain expectation of criminal repression arises.[276] The ICJ in the *Nicaragua* case found that the obligation to 'respect and ensure respect' forms part of customary international law,[277] a finding re-affirmed in its advisory opinion on the *Legality of the Threat or Use of Nuclear Weapons*.[278] Moreover, the ICJ found that such rules were 'intransgressible principles of international customary law,'[279] implying that 'no circumstance may justify a

272 Most commentators on the negotiations of the Rome Statute note that the list of crimes relating to internal armed conflicts was among the most controversial issues to be decided on. While the inclusion of common Art. 3 was eventually able to achieve general acceptance at the Rome Conference, there was continued opposition to the inclusion of most of the other norms. Herman von Hebel and Darryl Robinson, "Crimes within the jurisdiction of the Court", in Roy S. Lee (ed.), *The International Criminal Court, The Making of the Rome Statute: Issues, Negotiations, Results* (The Hague: Kluwer Law International, 1999), at 125.

273 "Paper on some policy issues before the Office of the Prosecutor", available at: <http://www.icc-cpi.int/library/organs/otp/030905-Policy-Paper.pdf>.

274 Dan Sarooshi, "Prosecutorial Policy and the ICC: Prosecutor's *Proprio Motu* or Self-Denial?", 2 *JICJ* 943 (2004).

275 Art. 1 common to the four Geneva Conventions of 1949. *Contreras Sepúlveda, Juan y otros (crimen) cascación fondo y forma*, Chile, Corte Suprema, 517/2004, Resolución 22267, available at: <www.derechos.org/nizkor/chile/doc/krassnoff.html> (in which the Supreme Court of Chile held that the obligation to ensure the protections of common Art. 3 of the Geneva Conventions entailed the illegality of any measure intended to shield persons from criminal liability arising from a violation of those protections).

276 Common Art. 1 also applies to non-international armed conflicts, as it includes ensuring respect for common Art. 3 of the Geneva Conventions. Additional Protocol II which develops and supplements common Art. 3 could also indirectly be covered by the principle. Laurence Boisson de Chazournes and Luigi Condorelli, "Common Article 1 of the Geneva Conventions Revisited: Protecting Collective Interests", 82(837) *IRRC* 69 (March 2000).

277 *Military and Paramilitary Activities in and against Nicaragua (Nicaragua* v. *United States)*, 1986 ICJ Reports 14 (1986), para. 220.

278 *Legality of the Threat or Use of Nuclear Weapons*, Advisory Opinion of 8 July 1996, ICJ Reports 1996, para. 79.

279 *Idem.*

"transgression" of such rules.'[280] However, the obligation of ensuring 'respect' is somewhat broader and more vague than the duty contained in the international and regional human rights conventions to ensure 'rights,' which has been interpreted by authoritative bodies to require governments to investigate and prosecute persons suspected of gross human rights violations.[281] It is conceivable, for example, that a limited amnesty law covering those 'least responsible' for the commission of war crimes on condition of full disclosure, enacted for the purpose of ending a civil war, could still be consistent with a State's obligation to 'respect and ensure respect' for the Geneva Conventions.

With respect to internal armed conflicts 'amnesties are not only permitted, but are encouraged by Article 6(5) of Additional Protocol II,'[282] which provides that at the end of the hostilities, 'the authorities in power shall endeavour to grant the broadest possible amnesty to persons who have participated in the armed conflict …' Several national courts have relied on this provision to support their findings that general amnesties are valid under international law.[283] Their conclusions are bolstered by stressing the need for reconstruction and reconciliation after violent civil wars, which is interpreted as the rationale behind Article 6(5).[284]

However, the normal rules of treaty interpretation counter the applicability of the provision to war crimes.[285] AP II was designed to ensure more protection for the victims of non-international armed conflicts by developing and supplementing Article 3 common to the Geneva Conventions.[286] If Article 6(5) allowed amnesties which prevented prosecution for the most egregious human rights abuses during armed conflict, the provision would be inconsistent with the primary objective of the Protocol. One may interpret the words 'shall endeavour to grant the broadest possible amnesty' in the sense that Article 6(5) should be employed only when it can be implemented without infringing on other binding international treaties or compliance with customary international law.[287] The International Committee of

280 Boisson de Chazournes & Condorelli, "Common Article 1 of the Geneva Conventions", at 75.

281 See section 2.4.2 *infra*, on how the obligation to ensure rights might vitiate amnesty laws.

282 Protocol Additional to the Geneva Convention of 12 August 1949, and Relating to the Protection of Victims of Non-International Armed Conflicts (Protocol II), of 8 June 1977, 1125 *UNTS* 609 (hereafter, AP II). See Scharf, "From the eXile Files", at 352.

283 For example, *Guevara Portillo* case, Salade lo Penal de la Corte Suprema de Justicia, San Salvador (16 August 1995), at 11; *Romo Mena* case, Corte Surprema de Chile (26 October 1995), at 12; *AZAPO* case, para. 30.

284 The ICRC Commentary to the Protocol supports this interpretation to some degree, noting that '[t]he object of this sub-paragraph is to encourage gestures of reconciliation which can contribute to re-establishing normal relations in the life of a nation which has been divided.' ICRC Commentary on Art. 6 of Protocol II of 1977 to the Geneva Conventions of 1949, available at: <http://www.icrc.org> at paras. 4617 and 4618 respectively.

285 Art. 31(1) Vienna Convention on the Law of Treaties 1969 directs States Parties to interpret in good faith in accordance with the ordinary meaning to be given to the terms of the treaty in their context and in the light of its object and purpose.

286 Art. 1 and preambular para. 1 Additional Protocol II.

287 Roht-Arriaza and Gibson also argue that the phrase could be interpreted as meaning '"the broadest possible amnesty" without destroying victim's hopes and needs for retribution and denunciation, or "the broadest possible amnesty" without causing social unrest because of the injustice in

the Red Cross (ICRC) has also interpreted Article 6(5) of the Protocol narrowly. Confirming a previously held position,[288] in an official letter from the Head of the Legal Division to the ICTY Prosecutor dated 1995, the ICRC stated that Article 6(5) essentially provides for 'combatant immunity' which ensures that a combatant cannot be punished for the mere fact of taking part in hostilities, 'including killing enemy combatants, as long as he respected international humanitarian law …'[289] This conclusion was based partly on the drafting history of Article 6(5) which indicates that 'the provision aims at encouraging amnesty, i.e. a sort of release at the end of hostilities, for those detained or punished for the mere fact of having participated in hostilities. It does not aim at an amnesty for those having violated international humanitarian law.'[290] This interpretation has subsequently been affirmed by the Inter-American Commission of Human Rights[291] and the Human Rights Committee.[292] It has also been used as a rationale in much earlier cases in the United States for not recognising amnesties for serious violations in internal conflicts.[293]

Notwithstanding the fact that Article 6(5) might not encourage the use of amnesties for international crimes at the end of an internal armed conflict, there is no clear prohibition in this regard either. Proposals to explicitly exempt war crimes from the purview of Article 6(5) amnesties failed during negotiations of AP II.[294]

---

letting these criminals go free.' See Naomi Roht-Arriaza and Lauren Gibson, "The Developing Jurisprudence on Amnesty", 20 *Human Rights Quarterly* 866 (1998).

[288] ICRC, Statement at the Humanitarian Liaison Working Group, Geneva, 19 June 1995 (noting that given 'the preparatory works and the context,' this provision could not be invoked in favour of war criminals, since it only applied to prosecution for the sole participation in hostilities).

[289] Letter from Toni Pfanner, Head of the ICRC Legal Division to the ICTY Prosecutor of 24 November 1995 and to the Department of Law at the University of California of 15 April 1997 (referring to CDDH, Official Records, Vol. IX (1997), at 319).

[290] *Idem.* During the debate at the Diplomatic Conference negotiating Protocol II, the delegate for the Soviet Union stated that Draft Art. 10 (which became Art. 6) of Protocol II 'could not be constructed as enabling war criminals, or those guilty of crimes against peace and humanity, to evade severe punishment in any circumstances whatsoever.' *Official Records of the Diplomatic Conference on the Reaffirmation and Development of International Humanitarian Law Applicable in Armed Conflicts, Geneva, 1974-1977*, Vol. 9 (Berne, 1978), at 319.

[291] Inter-American Commission on Human Rights, Report No. 199, Case 10,480, *Lucio Parada Cea and others* (El Salvador), 27 January 1999, para. 115.

[292] UN Doc. CCPR/C/79/Add.78, para. 12 (concerning the amnesty for human rights violations committed against civilians during the civil war in Lebanon).

[293] *Ex parte Mudd*, manuscript opinion of Judge Boynton, 9 September 1868, 17 F. Cas. 954 (S.D. Fla. 1868) (No. 9, 899). (concerning petition for *habeus corpus* for civilians convicted by military commission for complicity of assassination of President Lincoln). In response to the petitioner's contention concerning the presidential proclamation of amnesty of 4 July 1868, the court stated, 'But that proclamation plainly excludes … petitioners, whether they have been convicted or not. It pardons the crime of treason … but it pardons no person who has transgressed the laws of war – no spy, no assassin, no person who has been guilty of barbarous treatment to prisoners … Such a provision would refer to those prisoners who had made open and honorable war and transgressed the fearfully wide rules which war allows to be legal.'

[294] See K. Gallagher, "No Justice, No Peace: The Legalities and Realities of Amnesty in Sierra Leone", 23 *T. Jefferson L. Rev.* 149 (2000), at 177 n. 196, noting the rejection by the negotiating parties of a Soviet proposal to make clear that the amnesty encouraged in Art. 6(5) was not to apply to crimes against humanity.

Nonetheless, the ICRC Customary Law Study found as a rule of customary law an exception for the granting of amnesties at the end of hostilities in non-international armed conflicts to those suspected of, accused of, or sentenced for war crimes.[295] It based the confirmation of this as a customary exception on the interpretation of State practice in relation to Article 6(5) in recent years, as noted above.[296] Certainly, the rule would seem to affirm the trend of recognising an exception in this regard, but it is still somewhat doubtful whether clear and consistent State practice and *opinio juris* exists with respect to an obligation to exempt war crimes from the purview of such amnesties.

By way of summary, a positive obligation to prosecute (or extradite) would only arise where a person accused of grave breaches of the GCs or AP I or of torture was found on the territory of a State party to the GCs, AP I or Torture Convention, or where a suspected *genocidaire* was arrested in the State where the genocide was committed. Any amnesty enacted by these States would likely violate such obligations, unless the obligation could be held to be fulfilled by way of exemplary trials whereby not all instances of violation need be prosecuted.[297] For crimes against humanity and other serious violations of IHL, customary international law entitles all States to prosecute persons accused of such crimes, but this remains a permissive right, not a mandatory duty. Hence, a State would not be in violation of international law by passing an amnesty law or otherwise not prosecuting a person accused of such crimes, so long as by not prosecuting the State was not violating other rules of international treaty or customary law. There may well be a strong community expectation of prosecution of such crimes which might weigh on a court's decision to exercise jurisdiction.[298] In addition, it is clear that a State would be under no obligation to recognise an amnesty law granted by another State.[299] However, there are no instances of State practice whereby a national court has acted upon a customary entitlement to prosecute where an amnesty law in the State

---

[295] Jean-Marie Henckaerts and Louise Doswald-Beck, *Customary International Humanitarian Law*, Vol. I. (Cambridge: CUP, 2005), Rule 159, at 611.

[296] *Ibid.*, at 612-614.

[297] See the arguments notes 428-434 and accompanying text, *infra*.

[298] Paust has argued that: '[i]nternational law is based upon common expectations of the human community and does not solely become operative when in conformity with one state's notions of "just wars" or other political conclusions of a nation ... This is due to the fact that international legal norms have a universal character or value content, and these human expectations cannot be ignored on the basis of local self interest ... Today, as the human society is forced to exist on the basis of the sovereign state system it can be argued that it is the duty of the sovereign to execute community legal expectations.' Jordan Paust, "My Lai and Vietnam: Norms, Myths and Leader Responsibility", 57 *Military Law Review* 118 (1972).

[299] In principle, States are bound only by their internal law, treaty obligations which they have entered into, and rules of customary international law. As Brownlie writes: '... the state must be independent of other state legal orders, and any interference by such legal orders, or by an international agency, must be based on a title of international law.' Ian Brownlie, *Principles of Public International Law*, 5th edn. (Oxford: Clarendon Press, 1998), at 72. See also Roman Boed, "The Effect of a Domestic Amnesty on the Ability of Foreign States to Prosecute Alleged Perpetrators of Serious Human Rights Violations", 33(3) *Cornell International Law Journal* (2000), at 323.

of territoriality precludes such trials. The SCSL *Kallon and Kamara* case is the first time a court with jurisdiction over crimes under customary international law (hence in the absence of a duty to prosecute) has proceeded to exercise jurisdiction in spite of a domestic amnesty operating in the State of territoriality.[300] This may set an important precedent in this respect. However, as a UN-assisted international criminal court, set up with the agreement of the State of territoriality with the precise objective of overriding the Lomé amnesty, the SCSL obviously operates without the need to balance competing jurisdictional issues that might be incumbent on national courts in the same predicament.

2.4.2 Whether victims' fundamental rights vitiate the validity of amnesty laws

National and international courts that have addressed the legality of amnesties have also approached the issue by examining whether victims' fundamental human rights in the aftermath of serious human rights violations preclude or minimise the scope of a permissible amnesty. While comprehensive human rights conventions do not contain any positive obligation to prosecute those accused of human rights violations, such a duty has been inferred from the rights contained therein, in particular, the right to 'respect and ensure' the rights,[301] and the right to an effective remedy.[302] Other 'rights' such as the right to justice,[303] the right to truth (or obligation to investigate),[304] and the right to judicial guarantees (or right to fair trial or hearing)[305] have also been inferred from obligations under human rights conventions.

---

[300] *Kallon and Kamara* Decision on Amnesty case.

[301] Art. 2(1) ICCPR; Art. 1(1) ACHR; and Art. 1 ECHR. The African Charter on Human and Peoples' Rights of 27 June 1981, OAU Doc. CAB/LEG/67/3 rev. 5, 21 *ILM* 58 (1982), *entered into force* 21 October 1986, provides in Art. 1 that: 'The Member States of the Organization of African Unity parties to the present Charter shall recognize the rights, duties and freedoms enshrined in this Chapter and shall undertake to adopt legislative or other measures to give effect to them.'

[302] Art. 2(3) ICCPR; Art. 2 ACHR; and Art. 13 ECHR. Notably, the Universal Declaration of Human Rights provides for the right to a remedy in Art. 8: 'Everyone has the right to an effective remedy by the competent national tribunals for acts violating the fundamental rights granted to him by the constitution or by law.' Universal Declaration of Human Rights, adopted and proclaimed by General Assembly Resolution 217A(III) of 10 December 1948. See *Romero*, para. 74; *Parada Cea* v. *El Salvador*, IACtHR 1, OEA/ser.L./V./II.12, doc. 6 (1999), para. 125; see also *Compilation of General Comments and General Recommendations Adopted by Human Rights Treaty Bodies*, UN Human Rights Committee, General Comment 20, regarding Article 7 (44th Sess.), UN Doc. HRI/GEN/1/Rev.1, at 30 (1994); *Lewenhoff* v. *Uruguay*, UN HRC No. 30/1978, UN Doc. CCPR/C/OP/1 (1985).

[303] ACHR, Arts. 1(1) and 2, as interpreted by the Inter-American Commission on Human Rights in *Hermosilla* v. *Chile*, at 156, paras. 58-61 and *Ellacuria*, Case 10.488, IACtHR 136 at para. 198.

[304] *Barrios Altos* case, para. 42; *Lincoleo*, para. 62, *Ellacuria*, para. 223, *Romero*, para. 144. See also *Yasa* v. *Turkey*, ECtHR No. 63/1997/847/1054, para. 100 (finding the obligation of a State under the European Convention on Human Rights to carry out an effective investigation after a murder).

[305] ACHR, Arts. 1(1) and 8(1), as interpreted by the Inter-American Commission on Human Rights in *Barios Altos*, para. 42; *Consuelo* Cases 10.147, 10.181, 10.240, 10.262, 10.309, 0.311, IACtHR 28

The UN CHR, which drafted the ICCPR, extensively debated the nature of a State Party's duty under Article 2(3) to provide an 'effective remedy' for violations of the Covenant, including considering the possibility of explicitly requiring States Parties to prosecute and punish violators. However, a proposal to add a new subparagraph to Article 2(3), providing that 'violators shall swiftly be brought to the law, especially when they are public officials,'[306] was rejected; the Commission instead sought to ensure the broadest range of remedies for violations of human rights so that it did not appear that judicial remedies were the only remedies contemplated by the Covenant.[307] In fact, Article 2(3) was designed principally to ensure that States provided non-criminal remedies, such as restitution or an order to desist the illicit activity.[308] Despite this drafting history, the UN Human Rights Committee which monitors compliance with the Covenant has repeatedly stressed that States Parties must investigate serious violations of human rights; prosecute and punish those found responsible; and provide compensation to victims.[309] In its General Comment 20 concerning Article 7 (the right to be free from torture), the Committee stated that:

> 'Amnesties are generally incompatible with the duty of States to investigate such acts; to guarantee freedom from such acts within their jurisdiction; and to ensure that they do not occur in the future, States may not deprive of individuals of the right to an effective remedy, including compensation and such full rehabilitation as may be possible.'[310]

This conclusion was based on the assertion that:

> '[I]t is not sufficient for the implementation of [article 7] to prohibit [torture or other cruel, inhuman or degrading] treatment or punishment or to make it a crime. Most States have penal provisions which are applicable to cases of torture or similar practic-

---

at paras. 32-37; *Mendoza* v. *Uruguay*, Cases 10.029, 10.036, 10.145, 10.305, 10.372, 10.373, 10.374 and 10.375, IACtHR 29, OEA/ser.L/V./II.83 at paras. 35-46; *Hermonsilla*, paras. 62-67.

306 This was proposed by the delegation of the Philippines. 6 *UN ESCOR Commission on Human Rights* at 6, para. 24, UN Doc. E/CN.4/365 (1950).

307 The initial draft providing for 'an effective remedy before the competent national tribunals' was opposed by the Chairwoman of the Commission, Eleanor Roosevelt, because it 'appeared to imply that all violations of the Covenant would take the form of justiciable issues subject to adjudication by the courts or by the judicial process, with the usual relief given by courts, such as damages or injunctions' whereas the most effective remedy for violations might sometimes lie in the political domain. 6 UN ESCOR Commission on Human Rights, at 20-21, para. 74, UN Doc. E/CN.4/SR.138 (1950).

308 See 18 UN GAOR 3rd Commission, at 247, para. 8, UN Doc. A/C.3/SR.1259 (1963).

309 These comments by the Human Rights Committee may be contrasted with its more characteristic approach of granting States discretion to determine how they will implement the Covenant and to provide an appropriate remedy when found in breach of a treaty obligation. See CCPR/C/21, General Comment 3, para. 1 (Human Rights Committee observes that the International Covenant 'generally leaves it to the States Parties concerned to choose their method of implementation …').

310 General Comment 20 concerning Art. 7, replaces General Comment 7 concerning prohibition of torture and cruel treatment or punishment, 10 April 1992.

es. Because such cases nevertheless occur, it follows from article 7, read together with article 2 of the Covenant, that States must ensure an effective protection through some machinery of control. Complaints about ill-treatment must be investigated effectively by competent authorities. Those found guilty must be held responsible, and the alleged victims must themselves have effective remedies at their disposal, including the right to obtain compensation.'[311]

This comment indicates that a State's duty to investigate allegations of torture and to prosecute and punish the offender exists over and above its duty to provide an effective civil remedy. The Committee has repeatedly reaffirmed this position when examining amnesties passed by States Parties to the Covenant, in regards to the Chilean Amnesty Decree Law,[312] the French Amnesty Acts,[313] and amnesty laws passed in Lebanon,[314] El Salvador,[315] Haiti,[316] Peru,[317] Uruguay[318] and Yemen.[319] When examining the 1996 Amnesty Law of the Republic of Croatia which excludes 'war crimes,' but does not define them, the HRC expressed concern that this raised a danger that the law could be interpreted in such a way as to grant impunity for persons accused of serious human rights violations, and it urged Croatia to ensure that the amnesty law would not be applied to those accused of such crimes.[320] In his final report on the 'Question of impunity of perpetrators of human rights violations (civil and political),' Mr. Louis Joinet, the Special Rapporteur of the UN Sub-Commission on the Prevention of Discrimination and the Protection of Minorities, affirmed that '[a]mnesty cannot be accorded to perpetrators before the victims have obtained justice by means of an effective remedy.'[321]

It would appear from comments made by the Human Rights Committee that criminal punishment is necessary where serious forms of ill-treatment are involved,[322] while other disciplinary action may be appropriate for less grave

---

311 Report of the Human Rights Committee, 37 UN GAOR Suppl. (No. 40) Annex V, general comment 7(16), para. 1, UN Doc. E/CN.4/Sub.2/Add.1/963 (1992).

312 See HRC "Concluding Observations" to Chile in 1999, UN Doc. CCPR/C/79/Add.104, para. 7.

313 In its "Concluding Observations" to France in 1997, the HRC stated that 'the Amnesty Acts of November 1988 and January 1990 for New Caledonia are incompatible with the obligation of France to investigate alleged violations of human rights.' UN Doc. CCPR/C/79/Add.80, para. 13.

314 UN Doc. CCPR/C/79/Add.78, para. 12.

315 UN Doc. CCPR/C/79/Add. 34, para. 7.

316 UN Doc. A/50/40, paras. 224-241.

317 UN Doc. CCPR/C/79/Add.67, para. 9.

318 UN Doc. CCPR/C/79/Add.19, paras. 7 and 11; CCPR/C/79/Add.90, Part "C. Principal subjects of concern and recommendations"; and the Decision of 9 August 1994 in the case of Hugo Rodríguez (Uruguay), Communication No. 322/1988, CCPR/C/51/D/322/1988, para. 12.4.

319 UN Doc. A/50/40, paras. 242-265.

320 Concluding Observations of the Human Rights Committee: Republic of Croatia, 4 April 2001, UN Doc. CCPR/CO/71/HRV, para. 11.

321 Joinet Report, para. 32.

322 See, for example, in *Mutemba* v. *Zaire*, the Committee found that the government of Zaire had committed torture in violation of Art. 7, and concluded that the government was 'under an obligation to ... conduct an inquiry into the circumstances of [the victim's] torture, to punish those found guilty

infractions.[323] Although the terms used by the Committee such as 'bring to justice' and 'hold responsible' imply some flexibility in the exact measures used to achieve these ends, it would seem that a State Party's consistent failure to punish torture, extra-legal executions and disappearances would be a breach of the Covenant.[324] However, it should be recalled that the interpretations of the Committee are not judicial findings and States parties to the ICCPR are not bound to accept them, therefore while the Committee's interpretations may have some authority, these are not decisive. Moreover, the use of language by the Committee in its communications has been less than absolute with regard to the need to prosecute,[325] suggesting that alternative measures, such as lustration, or compensation, might fulfil the duty to punish.[326] By stating that amnesties are 'generally incompatible' in its 1992 General Comment, the Committee would seem to be suggesting that certain limited and conditional amnesties may not conflict with State's duties under the Covenant.[327]

A stronger argument with regard to the 'authoritative interpretation' argument can probably be made with regard to the jurisprudence of the Inter-American Commission and the Court of Human Rights with regard to their interpretation of the ACHR[328] as requiring States Parties to investigate and prosecute those accused of

---

of torture and to take steps to ensure that similar violations do not occur in the future.' Communication No. 124/1982, 39 GAOR Suppl. (No. 40) Annex XIII, UN Doc. A/39/40 (1984), para. 13.

[323] The Human Rights Committee has identified the duty to investigate, prosecute and punish those alleged of participating in extra-legal executions. See for example, *Baboeram* v. *Suriname*, a case involving the arrest and subsequent killing of 15 prominent persons including journalists, lawyers, professors and businessmen. The Committee found the Surinamese military police had intentionally deprived the victims of life in violation of Art. 6(1) of the Covenant, and urged the government 'to take effective steps (i) to investigate the killings …; (ii) to bring to justice any persons found to be responsible for the death of the victims; (iii) to pay compensation to the surviving families; and (iv) to ensure that the right to life is duly protected in Suriname.' Communication Nos. 146/1983, 40 UN GAOR Suppl. (No. 40) Annex X, para. 13.2, UN Doc. A/40/40 (1985). See also *Dermit* v. *Uruguay*, Communication No. 84/1981, 38 GAOR Suppl. (No. 40) Annex IX, para. 11a, UN Doc. A/38/40 (1980). See also cases involving enforced disappearances: *Bleier* v. *Uruguay*, Communication No. R.7/30, 37 UN GAOR Suppl. (No. 40) Annex X, UN Doc. A/37/40 (1982); *Quinteros* v. *Uruguay*, Communication No. 107/1981, 38 UN GAOR Suppl. (No. 40) Annex XXII, UN Doc. A/38/40 (1983).

[324] On the other hand, the Committee has stopped short of recognising a right by individuals to ensure that a particular person is prosecuted. In *H.C.M.A.* v. *The Netherlands*, the Committee rejected the claim that Art. 14(1) of the Covenant (the right to fair trial) establishes a right 'to see another person criminally prosecuted.' Communication No. 213/1986, 44 UN GAOR Suppl. (No. 40), UN Doc. A/44/40 (1989), para. 11.6.

[325] For example, the Committee 'urged' Suriname to prosecute acts of torture (Report of the Human Rights Committee, 39 UN GAOR, Suppl. (No. 40), Annex XIII, para. 13, at 188, UN Doc. A/39/40 (1984)) and stated that Uruguay 'should' bring those involved in enforced disappearances to justice (Report of the Human Rights Committee, 38 UN GAOR, Suppl. (No. 40), Annex XXII, para. 16, at 224, UN Doc. A/38/40 (1983).

[326] Scharf, "Swapping Amnesty for Peace", at 27.

[327] *Idem.*

[328] American Convention on Human Rights, adopted 7 January 1970, O.A.S. Official Records, OEA/ser.K./XVI/1.1, doc. 65, rev. 1, corr. 1 (1979).

serious violations of human rights. The Inter-American Court of Human Rights has decided on more than one occasion, that:

> 'a State has a legal duty to take reasonable steps to prevent human rights violations and to use the means as its disposal to carry out a serious investigation of violations committed within its jurisdiction, to identify those responsible, to impose the appropriate punishment and to ensure the victim adequate compensation.'[329]

This holding was first rendered in the *Velásquez Rodriguez* case, concerning the unresolved disappearance of student-activist Manfredo Velásquez in September 1981. Testimony before the Court indicated that he had been tortured and killed by the Honduran security forces. The Court held that the Honduran government was responsible for multiple violations of the American Convention, basing much of its judgment on the duty contained in Article 1(1):

> 'This obligation implies the duty of the States Parties to organize the governmental apparatus and, in general, all the structures through which public power is exercised, so that they are capable of juridically ensuring the free and full enjoyment of human rights. As a consequence of this obligation, the States must prevent, investigate, punish any violation of the rights recognized by the Convention and, moreover, if possible attempt to restore the right violated and provide compensation as warranted for damages resulting from the violation …'[330]

Although the judgment seemed to suggest that every violation of the American Convention entails a duty to prosecute and punish, the Court's reasoning should probably be confined to the serious violations raised in the case before it – disappearances, torture and extra-judicial execution.[331] In a subsequent judgment on compensation,[332] the Court discussed the measures that would constitute adequate reparation. It reiterated that such measures as investigation, the punishment of those responsible, public statements by the Honduran government condemning the practice of disappearances, and the Court's own judgment on the merits all con-

---

[329] Inter-American Court of Human Rights, Case *Velasquez Rodriguez*, Judgment of 29 July 1988 (ser. C), No. 4 (hereafter, *Velasquez Rodriguez* case), para. 174. See also Case *Neira Alegra and others*, Judgment of 19 January 1995 (ser. C), No. 20, para. 69; Case *Caballero Delgado and Santana*, Judgment of 8 December 1995 (ser. C), No. 22, para. 56; Case *Blake*, Preliminary Exceptions, Judgment of 2 July 1996 (ser. C), No. 27, para. 39 and Case *Castillo Paez*, Judgment of 3 November 1997 (ser. C), No. 34, para. 90.

[330] *Velasquez Rodriguez* case, para. 166.

[331] It should be noted, however, that the Court in the *Velasquez* case did not impose the remedy which seemed to be implied from the language of the judgment. The Court ordered only monetary compensation, despite lawyers for the victims families, the Inter-American Commission and a group of international law experts acting as *amici curiae* asking for an injunction requiring the Honduran government to prosecute criminally those responsible for disappearances, restructure the security apparatus, publicly condemn the practice of disappearances, and pay homage to the victims. This result is probably because this was the first contentious case before the Court and declarative relief was considered less invasive of sovereignty than injunctive measures.

[332] Compensation Judgment of July 21, 1989, IACtHR (ser. C), No. 7 (1989).

stituted part of the reparation.[333] Following these decisions, Honduras passed an amnesty law in 1991 which covered crimes such as killings, torture and unlawful arrests committed by police and military personnel, although it also explicitly recognised Honduras' international human rights obligations. The Court of Appeals of Honduras held on 5 January 1996 that military officers accused of human rights abuses were covered by the 1991 amnesty. However in January 1997, the Supreme Court overruled the decision, holding that the 1991 amnesty law did not prevent military and police officers from being charged with the attempted murder and unlawful detention of certain students.[334]

Amnesty laws have been held to be directly incompatible with obligations of the ACHR in the case of *Barrios Altos* v. *Peru*, in which the Court held in the judgment on the merits of 14 March 2001, that the laws 'run counter to the American Convention … and, consequently, have no legal effects.'[335] Two recent cases of the Inter-American Court have affirmed that self-granted amnesty laws covering crimes against humanity – in Chile and Peru respectively – have no legal effects and infringe a number of obligations under the ACHR, principally Articles 1(1) (Obligation to Respect Rights), 8 (Right to a Fair Trial) and 25 (Right to Judicial Protection).[336] In *Almonacid-Arellano* v. *Chile*, the Court held that '[t]he obligation that arises pursuant to international law to try, and, if found guilty, to punish the perpetrators of certain international crimes, among which are crimes against humanity, is derived from the duty of protection embodied in Article 1(1) of the American Convention.'[337] In general, the Court found that '[a]mnesty laws are overtly incompatible with the wording and the spirit of the American Convention, and undoubtedly affect rights embodied in such Convention' thereby generating international liability for the State.[338] In the case of *La Cantuta* v. *Peru*, the Court held that in cases of extra-legal executions, forced disappearances and other egregious human rights violations, 'the conduct of a prompt, serious, impartial and effective *ex officio* investigation is a fundamental and conditioning element for the protection of certain rights that are otherwise affected or annulled by those situations, such as the right to life, personal liberty and personal integrity. This duty to investigate becomes particularly intense and significant in cases of crimes against humanity.'[339]

The Inter-American Commission on Human Rights has also made decisions interpreting the American Declaration of the Rights and Duties of Man and the

---

[333] *Ibid.*, paras. 32-39.

[334] See US Delegation Draft, "State Practice Regarding Amnesties and Pardons", presented to PrepCom, 4th Sess., August 1997.

[335] *Barrios Altos* case, paras. 41-44.

[336] *Almonacid-Arellano, et al.*, v. *Chile*, IACtHR, Preliminary Objections, Merits, Reparations and Costs. Judgment of 26 September 2006 (ser. C), No. 154; *Case of La Cantuta* v. *Peru*, IACtHR, Merits, Reparations and Costs. Judgment of 29 November 2006 (ser. C), No. 162.

[337] *Almonacid-Arellano, et al.*, v. *Chile*, IACtHR, Preliminary Objections, Merits, Reparations and Costs. Judgment of 26 September 2006, para. 110.

[338] *Ibid.*, para. 119.

[339] *Case of La Cantuta* v. *Peru*, IACtHR, Merits, Reparations and Costs. Judgment of 29 November 2006 (ser. C), No. 162, para. 110.

American Convention. In cases involving violations of Article 1 of the Declaration concerning the right to life, liberty and personal security, the Commission has repeatedly recommended a 'thorough and impartial investigation' and the punishment of the individual or individuals responsible.[340] To States party to the American Convention, the Commission has recommended the investigation of serious violations of physical integrity and that States Parties 'try and punish those responsible for their occurrence,' as well as providing compensation.[341] The duty to punish has also been said to flow from a more general right to justice, which includes the right to an investigation that identifies those responsible for the violation; the right to prosecution of those identified as responsible; the right to punishment of those responsible; and the right to compensation for the wrong suffered.[342]

The Commission has in the past expressed the general view that it is up to national governments to determine the validity of amnesty laws enacted by previous governments, subject to the condition that the truth about past violations is made fully known.[343] More recent case law, however, has taken a stronger stand against amnesty laws and has ruled that laws restricting or prohibiting prosecutions of the military in Chile, El Salvador, Uruguay, and Argentina were incompatible with the Convention and that perpetrators had to be punished.[344] It should be noted, however, that all the amnesty laws considered by the Commission prevented both criminal and civil redress and were fairly blanket in scope. The Commission has observed that reparation, which most often takes the form of compensation, can also come in the form of truth,[345] accountability,[346] or punishment.[347] The right to compensatory reparations is violated by an amnesty that protects an individual

[340] See for example, Case 1870, Inter-Am. C.H.R; 52, OEA/ser.L./V/II.43, doc. 21 (1978); Case 2088, IACtHR 38, OEA/ser.L./V/II.0. doc. 13, rev. 1 (1980).

[341] See for example, Case 10.150, Informe 3/90 (Suriname), OEA/ser.L./V/II.77, doc. 23, at 14 (1990).

[342] *Espinoza* v. *Chile*, Case 11.725, IACtHR 133, OEA/ser.L/V./II.106, doc. 6 (1999), para. 75; *Velasquez Rodriguez*, No. 4 (1988), para. 174; *Hermonsilla*, Case 10.843, IACtHR 36 at para. 111.

[343] IACtHR OEA/ser.L./V/II.68. doc. 8, rev.1 (1986).

[344] Report No. 36/96, Case 10,843 (Chile), 15 October 1996; Report No. 26/92 (El Salvador), 82nd Sess., OEA/ser.L/V/II/82 (24 September 1992); Report No. 29/92 (Uruguay), 82nd Sess., OEA/ser.L/V/II.82, Doc. 25 (2 October 1992); Report No. 24/92 (Argentina), 82nd Sess., OEA/ser.L/V/II.82, Doc. 24 (2 October 1992). A speech by Ambassador Oliver H. Jackman before the First Committee of the XIX Regular Meeting of the General Assembly to Present the Annual Report of the IACTHR, November 1989 reflects the reasoning of this new line: 'A compact by which a whole nation is called upon to suspend its memory of torture, murder, forcible "disappearances" of loved ones, a compact which would have citizens pretend that the tragic losses and suffering which they have undergone never occurred, this … is no bargain. This is not amnesty; it is forcible amnesia. The "peace" that is bought at this price is supported by a thread slenderer even than the thread by which the sword of Damocles was suspended.'

[345] The Inter-American Commission has stated that truth can itself be a form of compensation, although not finding that truth is itself sufficient to satisfy the right to judicial protection. *Ellacuria*, para. 224; *Parada Cea*, para. 155; *Romero*, para. 148; *Myna Mack Chang* case, IACtHR, Vol. 101 (ser. C), paras. 274-275 (23 November 2003) (discussing the preventive and reparatory role that disclosure of the truth plays for family members and society as a whole).

[346] *Espinoza*, para. 153; *Blake* v. *Guatemala* case, IACtHR (ser. C) No. 36 (1998).

[347] *Blake* v. *Guatemala*, para. 97; *Ellacuria*, para. 195.

from civil liability, and thus access to damages by a civil judgment.[348] It may also be violated by an amnesty that only provides protection against criminal liability. Courts have also found that by foreclosing access to the civil courts, amnesties violate the right of a human rights victim to have her rights established by a tribunal previously established by law.[349]

The European Court of Human Rights has ruled that 'the notion of an "effective remedy" entails, in addition to the payment of compensation where appropriate, a thorough and effective investigation capable of leading to the identification and punishment of those responsible and including effective access for the complainant to the investigatory procedure.'[350] In the *Klass* case, the Court held that Article 13 which guarantees the right to a remedy[351] requires the State to ensure a remedy before a national authority in order both to have his claim (of a violation of a right provided by the Convention) decided and, if appropriate, to obtain redress.[352] The European Court has interpreted Article 1 which obliges the parties to 'secure to everyone within their jurisdiction the rights and freedoms defined' in the Convention as including an affirmative obligation to prevent or remedy breaches of the Convention.[353] The European Commission has interpreted this obligation as including criminal prosecution where appropriate.[354] Decisions of the European Court and Commission of Human Rights make it clear that prosecution and punishment play a part in the fulfilment of certain duties under the Convention.[355] In cases concerning serious crimes, the Court has considered the criminal law as the only adequate means to protect fundamental values.[356] The Commission and the Court

---

348 *Espinoza*, para. 84.

349 *Lincoleo* v. *Chile*, paras. 59-65.

350 European Court of Human Rights, Case *Zeki Aksoy* v. *Turkey*, Judgment of 18 December 1996, No. 100/1995/606/694, para. 98. The ECHR is the judicial mechanism of the European Convention for the Protection of Human Rights and Fundamental Freedoms, adopted 4 November 1950, 213 *UNTS* 221, ETS No. 5.

351 Art. 13 provides: 'Everyone whose rights and freedoms as set forth in this Convention are violated shall have an effective remedy before a national authority notwithstanding that the violation has been committed by persons acting in an official capacity.'

352 *Case of Klass and others* (F.R.G.), 28 ECtHR (ser. A) (1978).

353 'The Convention does not merely oblige the higher authorities of the Contracting States to respect for their own part the rights and freedoms it embodies; … the Convention also has the consequence that, in order to secure the enjoyment of those rights and freedoms, those authorities must prevent or remedy any breach at subordinate level.' *Ireland* v. *U.K.*, 25 ECtHR, para. 239 (ser. A) (1978).

354 In a complaint by the sister of a man killed by the IRA, the Commission found that Art. 2, protecting the right to life, gives rise to positive obligations on the part of the State. Those obligations do not extend to providing protection beyond criminal prosecution of offenders, implying that criminal prosecution is part of the obligations the State assumes by becoming party to the Convention. *Mrs. W.* v. *United Kingdom*, 32 *Collection of Decisions* 190 (28 February 1983), at 200.

355 However, the European Commission has repeatedly rejected claims that Art. 6 of the Convention, which guarantees the right to a fair trial, establishes a right to have criminal proceedings instituted against officials or other persons. See for example, *X* v. *Federal Republic of Germany*, 24 *Collection of Decisions* 50 (1967), at 61-62; *Kiss* v. *United Kingdom*, 7 *Decisions and Reports* 55 (1976), at 64.

356 In the case of *X and Y* v. *Netherlands*, concerning the inability of a mentally handicapped victim of rape to institute criminal proceedings against her attacker due to the fact that she was deemed incompetent, it was held that the Netherlands' failure to provide for prosecution of Miss Y's attacker

have also indirectly affirmed the principle that prosecution and punishment have a necessary role in securing certain rights in the Convention by insisting on the exhaustion of domestic remedies. Significantly, both bodies have found that claimants need not exhaust domestic remedies if their complaint concerns an 'administrative practice'[357] involving 'repetition of acts, and official tolerance.'[358] In recent case law, the ECHR has ruled that '[g]iven the fundamental importance of the rights guaranteed by Articles 2 [right to life] and 3 [right not to be subjected to torture] of the Convention, Article 13 requires, in addition to the payment of compensation where appropriate, a thorough and effective investigation capable of leading to the identification and punishment of those responsible for the deprivation of life and infliction of treatment contrary to Article 3, including effective access for the complainant to the investigation procedure leading to the identification and punishment of those responsible.'[359] Moreover, the requirements of Article 13 are broader than a Contracting State's obligation under Article 2 to conduct an effective investigation.[360]

Many of the cases dealing with the legality of amnesties have focused upon the degree to which the amnesty has prevented the 'truth' from being made public, or at least from being made available to the victim or the victim's family. Such a notion has been particularly prevalent in cases dealing with enforced disappearances whereby an amnesty law has prevented an investigation into the whereabouts of missing persons to be conducted and hence their families from knowing their fate. Courts, UN bodies and commentators have increasingly referred to a 'right to the truth' in international law, the origin of which may be traced to the

---

violated its affirmative duty to secure her enjoyment of the right to respect for private life, guaranteed by Art. 8 of the European Convention. The Court held that: '[T]he protection afforded by the civil law in the case of wrongdoing of the kind inflicted on Miss Y is insufficient. This is a case where fundamental values and essential aspects of private life are at stake. Effective deterrence is indispensable in this area and it can be achieved only by criminal-law provisions …' *X and Y and Z* v. *Netherlands*, 91 ECtHR (ser. A) (1985) (judgment), para. 27.

[357] 'Administrative practice' has been defined by the Court as 'an accumulation of identical or analogous breaches which are sufficiently numerous and inter-connected to amount not merely to isolated incidents or exceptions but to a pattern or system …' *Ireland* v. *United Kingdom*, 25 ECtHR (ser. A) (1978), at 64, para. 159. Where there is an administrative practice, an effective remedy cannot be had and the rule regarding exhaution of remedies does not apply.

[358] 'Official tolerance' means: 'that, though acts of torture or ill-treatment are plainly illegal, they are tolerated in the sense that the superiors of those immediately responsible though cognisant of such acts, *take no action to punish them or prevent their repetition*; or that higher authority, in fact of numerous allegations, manifests indifference by *refusing any adequate investigation of their truth or falsity*, or that in judicial proceedings, a *fair hearing of such complaints is denied.*' *The Greek* case, *Y.B. ECHR.* (1969), at196, paras. 29 (ECommHR). [Emphasis added]

[359] Case of *Bayasayeva* v. *Russia*, Appl. No. 74237/01, Judgment, 5 April 2007, para. 55. See also *Anguelova* v. *Bulgaria*, no. 38361/97, paras. 161-162, ECHR 2002-IV; *Assenov and Others* v. *Bulgaria,* Appl. No. 90/1997/874/1086, Judgment, 28 October 1998, para. 114 et seq.; and *Süheyla Aydın* v. *Turkey*, no. 25660/94, para. 208, 24 May 2005.

[360] *Bayasayeva* v. *Russia*, para. 55, citing *Orhan* v. *Turkey,* Appl. No. 25656/94, Judgment 18 June 2002, para. 384, and *Khashiyev and Akayeva*, nos. 57942/00 and 57945/00, 24 February 2005, para. 183.

right of families to know the fate of their missing relatives under Articles 32 and 33 of AP I as well as obligations incumbent on parties to armed conflicts to search for persons who have been reported missing. The inclusion of this provision in AP I was prompted by numerous resolutions of the UN GA since 1974 regarding the rights of families of missing persons or those subjected to enforced disappearances which referred to 'the desire to know' as a 'basic human need.'[361] This provision was then used by human rights mechanisms – namely, the *ad hoc* Working Group on the Situation of Human Rights in Chile, the UN Working Group on Enforced and Involuntary Disappearances and the Inter-American Commission on Human Rights – as the basis for developing a right to the truth in relation to the crime of enforced disappearances,[362] and later to other human rights violations.[363] The right to the truth has been inferred from a number of other rights guaranteed by human rights treaties. The Human Rights Committee (HRC), the monitoring body of the International Covenant on Civil and Political Rights of 1966 (ICCPR),[364] has recognised the right to know as a way to end or prevent the occurrence of psychological torture (Art. 7 ICCPR) of families of victims of enforced disappearances[365] or secret executions.[366] The HRC also found that in order to fulfil their obligation to provide an effective remedy, States parties to the ICCPR should provide information about the violation or, in cases of death of a missing person, the location of the burial site.[367]

---

361 See resolutions of the General Assembly: 3220 (XXIX) of 6 November 1974, 33/173 of 20 December 1978, 35/193 of 15 December 1980, 36/163 of 16 December 1981, 37/180 of 17 December 1982, 38/94 of 16 December 1983, 39/111 of 14 December 1984, 40/147 of 13 December 1985, 41/145 of 4 December 1986, 42/142 of 7 December 1987, 43/159 of 8 December 1988, 44/160 of 15 December 1989, 45/165 of 18 December 1990, 46/125 of 17 December 1991, 47/132 of 18 December 1992.

362 First report Working Group on Enforced or Involuntary Disappearances to the Commission on Human Rights, UN Doc. E/CN.4/1435, 22 January 1981, para. 187 and Annual Report of the Inter-American Commission of Human Rights, 1985-1986, OEA/Ser.L//V/II.68, Doc. 8, rev 1, 28 September 1986, at 205.

363 Inter-American Commission, Report No. 136/99, of 22 December 1999, *Case of Ignacio Ellacría, et al.*, para. 221.

364 International Covenant on Civil and Political Rights, 16 December 1966, 999 *UNTS* 171 (hereafter, ICCPR).

365 See the explanation by Mr. Bertil Wennergren, member of the Human Rights Committee, in his *Individual opinion* in the cases: *R.A.V.N., et al. (Argentina)*, communication Nos. 343, 344 and 345/1988, Decision of inadmissibility of 26 March 1990, UN Doc. CCPR/C/38/D/343/1988 (Appendix); S.E. *(Argentina)*, Communication No. 275/1988, Decision of inadmissibility of 26 March 1990, UN Doc. CCPR/C/38/D/275/1988 (Appendix); see, *inter alia*: Views of 16 July 2003, Case *Sarma, Sri Lanka* Communication No 950/2000, UN Doc. CCPR/C/77/D/887/1999, para. 9.5; "Concluding observations of the Human Rights Committee: Algeria", UN Doc. CCPR/C/79/Add.95, of 18 August 1998, para. 10, and "Concluding observations of the Human Rights Committee: Uruguay", UN Doc. CCPR/C/79/Add.90, of 8 April 1998, para. C.

366 Views of 3 April 2003, Case *Lyashkevich* v. *Belarus*, Communication No. 887/1999, UN Doc. CCPR/C/77/D/950/2000, para. 9.2.

367 *Ibid.*, para. 11; views adopted on 30 March 2005, Case *Khalilova* v. *Tajikistan*, Communication No 973/2001, UN Doc. CCPR/C/83/D/973/2001, and Views adopted on 16 November 2005, Case *Valichon Aliboev* v. *Tajikistan*, Communication No. 985/2001, UN Doc. CCPR/C/85/D/985/2001. The

The European Court of Human Rights has also inferred a right to the truth as part of the right to be free from torture or ill-treatment, the right to an effective remedy and the right to an effective investigation and to be informed of the results.[368] Similarly, the Court has held that a State's failure to conduct an effective investigation 'aimed at clarifying the whereabouts and fate' of 'missing persons who disappeared in life-threatening circumstances' constitutes a continuing violation of its procedural obligation to protect the right to life.[369] The Human Rights Chamber for Bosnia and Herzegovina also found a breach of the same treaty on the similar grounds in regards to the 1995 massacre in the Bosnian town of Srebrenica.[370] The African Commission on Human and Peoples' Rights has followed a similar approach to the European Court of Human Rights.[371] The Commission's 'Principles and Guidelines on the Right to a Fair Trial and Legal Assistance in Africa'[372] infers a right to the truth as a constitutive part of the right to an effective remedy.[373] The Inter-American Commission on Human Rights stands apart as having presented the right to know the truth as a direct remedy in itself, based on Article 9(1) of the Inter-American Convention providing that 'a State party is obligated to guarantee the full and free exercise of the rights recognized by the Convention.'[374] Its view is that ensuring rights for the future requires a society to learn from the abuses of the past. For this reason, this right to know the truth entails both an individual right applying to the victim and family members and a general societal right.[375] However, the Commission has also linked the right to truth to other obligations contained in the ACHR, such as the prohibitions of torture, extrajudicial

right to know the truth has also been invoked in relation to protection of the family guaranteed in Art. 23 of the ICCPR, as well as the right of the child to preserve his or her identity, including nationality, name and family relations as contained in Art. 8 of the Convention on the Rights of the Child of 1989 (CRC), the right of the child not to be separated from its parents provided in Art. 9 CRC, and other provisions of that Convention. UN Doc. E/CN.4/Sub.2/1991/20, Annex I, at 45.

368 See, *inter alia*, Judgment of 25 May 1998, *Kurt* v. *Turkey* case, Appl. No. 24276/94; Judgment of 14 November 2000, *Tas* v. *Turkey* case, Appl. No. 24396/94; and Judgment of 10 May 2001, *Cyprus* v. *Turkey* case, Appl. No. 25781/94.

369 ECHR, Art. 2. Judgment of 10 May 2001, *Cyprus* v. *Turkey* case, Appl. No. 25781/94, para. 136; see also, *inter alia*, Judgment of 18 December 1996, *Aksoy* v. *Turkey* case, Appl. No. 21987/93; and Judgment of 28 March 2000, *Kaya* v. *Turkey* case, Appl. No. 22535/93. This also applies where non-State actors may be involved: *Tanrikulu* v. *Turkey*, 1999-IV ECtHR 459 (1999).

370 The Chamber found that the failure of Republika Srpska authorities 'to inform the applicants about the truth of the fate and whereabouts of their missing loved ones,' including their failure to conduct a 'meaningful and effective investigation into the massacre,' violated Art. 3 and Art. 2 (right to life) of the ECHR. *Selimovic, et al.*, Case Nos. CH/01/8365, et al., Decision on Admissibility and Merits, para. 220 (4); see also para. 191 (7 March 2003).

371 *Amnesty International* v. *Sudan* case, Communication Nos. 48/90, 50/91, 52/91, 89/93 (1999), para. 54. See Art. 19(3) of the African Charter on the Rights and Welfare of the Child.

372 African Union Doc. DOC/OS(XXX)247.

373 Principle C) states that 'the right to an effective remedy includes: … 3. access to the factual information concerning the violations.'

374 Inter-American Commission, Report No. 136/99, of 22 December 1999, *Case of Ignacio Ellacría, et al.,* v. *El Salvador*, para. 221.

375 See also Annual Report of the Inter-American Court of Human Rights, 1985-1986, OEA/Ser.L//V/II.68, Doc. 8, rev 1, of 28 September 1986, at 205; Annual Report of the Inter-American

executions[376] and the right to simple and prompt recourse for the protection of the rights enshrined in the Convention (Art. 25).[377] The Inter-American Court of Human Rights has recognised the right of relatives of the victims of forced disappearance to know their fate and whereabouts.[378] The Court has recognised the right of the victim or his next of kin to obtain clarification of the facts relating to the violations and the corresponding responsibilities of the competent State organs, through investigation and prosecution established in Articles 8 (right to a hearing by a competent, independent and impartial tribunal) and 25 (right to an effective remedy and judicial protection) of the American Convention on Human Rights.[379] The Court has held that the right to the truth is not limited to cases of enforced disappearances but also applies to any kind of gross human rights violation.[380] The UN SC and GA have repeatedly stressed the importance of truth-telling in the aftermath of atrocities[381] and the CHR explicitly recognised the existence of a right to truth in a 2005 resolution.[382]

In his Final Report on impunity of 1997, the CHR appointed independent expert, Mr. Louis Joinet, identified an inalienable right to the truth to know about past events and about the circumstances which led to the perpetration of international crimes.[383] The updated version of these Principles by Professor Diane

Court of Human Rights, 1987-1988, OEA/Ser.L/V/II. 74, Doc. 10, rev 1, of 16 September 1988, at 359.

376 Inter-American Commission, Report No. 136/99, of 22 December 1999, *Case of Ignacio Ellacría, et al.,* v. *El Salvador*, para. 221.

377 The latter provision has been used as the basis for inferring the right to the truth both for the relatives of victims and for society as a whole. *Ibid.*, para. 255; Report 1/99 of 27 January 1999, *Lucio Parada, et al.,* v. *El Salvador*, para. 153.

378 Inter-American Court of Human Rights Judgment of 29 July 1988, *Velásquez Rodríguez* case, in Series C: Decisions and Judgments, No. 4, para. 181, at 75; Inter-American Court of Human Rights, Judgment of 20 January 1989, *Godínez Cruz* case, in Series C: Decisions and Judgments, No. 5; Judgment of 3 November 1997, *Castillo Páez* case; Judgment of 24 January 1998, *Blake* case; and Judgment of 25 November 2000, *Bamaca* case.

379 Inter-American Court of Human Rights, Judgment of 24 January 1998, *Blake* case, para. 97 and Judgment of 25 November 2000, *Bamaca* case, para. 201.

380 *Barrios Altos* case, para. 48.

381 See, e.g., SC Res. 1606 (2005) on Burundi, preambular paras. 2 and 7; SC Res. 1593 (2005) on Darfur, Sudan, para. 5, SC Res. 1468 (2003) on the Democratic Republic of the Congo, para. 5; SC Res. 1012 (1995) on Burundi, preambular para. 8; SC Res. 935 (1994) on Rwanda; and SC Res. 780 (1992) on the former Yugoslavia; See, e.g., GA Res. 57/105 (2003) on East Timor, para. 12; GA Res. 57/161 (2003) on Guatemala, para. 17; GA Res. 55/118 (2001) on Haiti, para. 7; GA Res. 53/187 (2000) on Haiti, para. 8, GA Res. 48/149 (1993) on El Salvador, para. 4; GA Res. 42/147 (1987) on Chile, para. 10; GA Res. 40/145 (1985) on Chile, para. 6; GA Res. 35/188 (1980) on Chile, paras. 6-8; GA Res. 34/179 (1979) on Chile, GA Res. 33/172 (1978) on Cyprus, para. 1; GA Res. 32/128 (1977) on Cyprus, para. 1; GA Res. 32/118 (1977) on Chile, para. 6; GA Res. 3450 (XXX) on Cyprus, preambular para. 5 and para. 1; GA Res. 3448 (XXX) on Chile, para. 2.

382 CHR Res. 2005/66, adopted at the 61st session '[r]ecognizes the importance of respecting and ensuring the right to the truth so as to contribute to ending impunity and to promote and protect human rights.'

383 Question of the impunity of perpetrators of human rights violations (civil and political), Final report prepared by Mr. Joinet pursuant to Sub Commission Decision 1996/119, UN Doc. E/CN.4/Sub.2/1997/20/Rev.1, Annex I, Principle 1.

Orentlicher affirm that '[e]very people has the inalienable right to know the truth about past events concerning the perpetration of heinous crimes ...'[384] and also recognise an imprescriptable right of victims and their families to know the truth about the circumstances in which violations took place and, in case of death or disappearance, the victim's fate.[385] The Principles do not require that the State guarantee the right to know by criminal proceedings, although they stress that the State 'must take appropriate action.' However, Principle 19 sets out the 'right to justice,' which states that States 'must undertake investigations of serious violations' and 'take appropriate measures in respect of the perpetrators, particularly in the area of criminal justice, by ensuring that those responsible for serious crimes under international law are prosecuted, tried and duly punished.' Principle 24 maintains that the perpetrators of serious crimes under international law may not benefit from amnesties 'until such time as the State has met the obligations to which principle 19 refers or the perpetrators have been prosecuted before a court with jurisdiction ... outside the State in question.'[386] This seems to suggest that a person may benefit from an amnesty *after* having been prosecuted for the crime. The principle would thus seem to be endorsing the use of pardons for international crimes, so long as these do not infringe the victim's right to reparation or right to know.[387]

None of the amnesties held to be incompatible with human rights guarantees incorporated any form of investigation or truth telling, although some were accompanied by other investigatory processes, such as truth commissions (e.g. Chile, Argentina, El Salvador). Although amnesties passed in Honduras and Guatemala were designed to hide the truth, they have been interpreted by their State's courts as requiring that the investigative phase of a prosecution be completed before the determination of whether or not an amnesty may be granted. President Alwyn of Chile also interpreted the 1978 Chilean amnesty as requiring a full judicial investigation before it could be applied, in order to know if the crimes fell within the scope of the amnesty.[388] In January 2004, the Santiago Court of Appeals ruled that the 1978 amnesty could not apply in respect of a kidnapping when the fate of the victim remained unclarified.[389]

The importance attached to the right to truth signifies that some amnesties, which facilitate the truth rather than hide it, might be considered legitimate. The South African amnesty provides the strongest claim since it creates a direct corre-

[384] Report of the independent expert to update the Set of principles to combat impunity, Diane Orentlicher, Addendum: Updated set of principles for the protection and promotion of human rights through action to combat impunity, UN Doc. E/CN.4/2005/102/Add.1, 8 February 2005 (hereafter Updated principles of impunity), Principle 2.

[385] *Ibid.*, Principle 4 'The victim's right to know.'

[386] The chapeau to this principle clarifies that such a principle applies even when the amnesty is intended to establish conditions conducive to a peace agreement or to foster national reconciliation. *Ibid.*, Principle 24.

[387] *Ibid.*, Principle 24(b).

[388] Hayner, *Unspeakable Truths*, at 98.

[389] *Sentencing of Fernando Laureani Maturana and Miguel Krassnoff Marchenko*, Santiago Court of Appeal (5 January 2004).

spondence between grants of amnesty and the revelation of truth.[390] In some States, courts have interpreted amnesty to require some amount of fact finding only when raised as a defence to a claim (such as in Honduras and Guatemala), so that truth telling will only take place if a prosecution is filed or civil claim against a person with an amnesty. In regards to States which enact truth commissions to compensate for an amnesty law, the Inter-American Commission, for its part, has stated that the quality of truth that derives from a trial is preferred to that derived from a truth commission,[391] and that a truth commission combined with an amnesty does not fulfil the obligations of the State under the American Convention.[392] In Argentina, during the period when domestic amnesties prevented prosecution for human rights violations, several Argentine courts allowed 'truth trials' to go forward to establish the fate of the disappeared. When the Argentinean Supreme Court ruled on 13 August 1998 that the courts lacked jurisdiction to hold proceedings due to the amnesty laws, a case was brought before the Inter-American Commission. In a friendly settlement, the Government of Argentina accepted and undertook to guarantee 'the right to the truth, which involves the exhaustion of all means to obtain information on the whereabouts of the disappeared persons.'[393] This ultimately resulted in the Argentinean courts continuance of truth trials and an *ad hoc* Prosecutor's Commission on truth proceedings was established to investigate cases.[394]

A right to the truth, if indeed, such a right exists in international law,[395] would intermesh strategically with the broader objectives of international criminal law, including, arguably, restoring and maintaining peace (because by exposing the 'truth,' societies are able to prevent similar occurrences from happening in the future), facilitating reconciliation processes (because, it has been argued, knowing the truth is essential to healing divides in communities),[396] contributing to the eradication of impunity (because knowing the truth about who was responsible for violations leads to accountability),[397] reconstructing national identities (by unify-

---

390 The Promotion of National Unity and Reconciliation Act 34 of 1995 sets up a mechanism to grant a broad amnesty for those who had committed politically motivated crimes during the *apartheid* regime.

391 *Ellacuria*, Case 10.488, para. 229; *Parada Cea y Otros* v. *El. Salvador*, Case 10.480, IACtHR 1, OEA/ser.L./V.II.02, doc. 6 (1999), para. 146.

392 *Lincoleo*, Case 11.711, Ch. 6; *Epinoza* v. *Chile*, Case 11.725, para. 102; *Romero*, Case 11.81, para. 144.

393 *Lapacó* v. *Argentina*, IACtHR (Case 12.059), Report No. 21/00, para. 17.1.

394 In July 2001, approximately 3,570 human rights cases were being investigated. See Report on Impunity, above, para. 16.

395 For a discussion of the strength of sources supporting a customary right to truth or the right to truth as a general principle of law, see generally, Naqvi, "The right to the truth in international law".

396 See, e.g., the *Supreme Decree No. 355* of the Chile National Commission on Truth and Reconciliation: 'Only upon a foundation of truth will it be possible to meet the basic demands of justice and create the necessary conditions for achieving true national reconciliation.'

397 See, e.g., Updated principles on impunity. Principle 2 declares that '[e]very people has the inalienable right to know the truth about past events concerning the perpetration of heinous crimes and about the circumstances and reasons that led, through massive or systematic violations, to the perpetration of those crimes.' Principle 4 articulates that '[i]rrespective of any legal proceedings, victims and their families have the imprescriptible right to know the truth about the circumstances in which viola-

ing countries through dialogue over a shared history)[398] and setting down a historical record (because the 'truth' of what happened can be debated openly and vigorously in court, adding credibility to the evidence accepted in a criminal judgment).

In summary, while the obligation to ensure basic rights and to provide an effective remedy for serious human rights violations may require States parties to properly investigate international crimes and to prosecute and punish offenders, this inferred obligation is not absolute where such rights may be guaranteed by alternative measures. So long as the victim or victim's family's right to know the truth is satisfied and that an effective remedy has been provided by appropriate measures, a limited and conditional amnesty might still be considered to be valid and accorded recognition. Moreover, any duty to investigate and prosecute human rights crimes is only binding on States parties to the relevant conventions and only relates to people in their territory or who are otherwise subject to their jurisdiction.[399]

2.4.3 Whether States are constrained not to amnesty international crimes due to the peremptory character of international crimes

The peremptory character of *jus cogens* crimes has also been argued to infer an obligation to prosecute. As noted in the previous Part, the *jus cogens* character of international crimes arguably entails a universal right to prosecute persons accused of such crimes. Those arguing for a duty to prosecute such crimes derive such

---

tions took place and, in the event of death or disappearance, the victims' fate.' Principle 1 states that it is an obligation of the State 'to ensure the inalienable right to know the truth about violations.' The first draft of these principles is contained in Annex II of the revised final report prepared by Mr. Joinet pursuant to Sub Commission Decision 1996/119, UN Doc. E/CN.4/Sub.2/1997/20/Rev.1.

[398] See, e.g., Act No. 12/2597 (14 May 1992) Germany: Law Creating the Commission of Inquiry on "Working Through the History and the Consequences of the SED Dictatorship", at I: 'To work through the history and consequences of the SED [East German Communist Party, known as the "German Socialist Union Party"] dictatorship in Germany is a joint task of all Germans. It is particularly important for the purpose of truly unifying Germany.'

[399] ICCPR, Art. 2(1). HRC General Comment No. 31, Nature of the General Legal Obligation Imposed on States Parties to the Covenant, CCPR/C/21/Rev.1/Add.13, 26 May 2004. See *Banković* v. *Belgium*, Appl. No. 52207/99, Admissibility Decision of 12 December 2001. The question of the jurisdictional scope of human rights obligations is still subject to some controversy. See Andrew Clapham, "Revisiting Human Rights in the Private Sphere: Using the European Convention on Human Rights to Protect the Right of Access to the Civil Courts", in C. Scott (ed.), *Torture as Tort: Comparative Perspectives on the Development of Transnational Human Rights Litigation* (Oxford: Hart Publishing, 2001), at 513. In *Al-Skeini and others* v. *the Secretary of State* [2008] 1 AC 153, arising from complaints against the UK about the deaths of six Iraqi civilians during the time when the UK was recognised as an Occupying Power in Basra, Iraq, the House of Lords held that under the UK's Human Rights Act 1998 (HRA) and the European Convention on Human Rights (ECHR), the family of Baha Mousa is entitled to an independent, impartial and thorough investigation into the circumstances surrounding his death in detention at a British military base in Basra, including his torture at the hands of British troops.

an obligation from the common interest in the repression of international crimes, combined with the universal right to prosecute.[400] It is commonly asserted that 'the implications of *jus cogens* are those of a duty and not of optional rights; otherwise, *jus cogens* would not constitute a peremptory norm of international law.'[401] In *Kallon and Kamara*, the SCSL inferred this line of reasoning in holding that 'the amnesty granted by Sierra Leone cannot cover crimes under international law that are the subject of universal jurisdiction' justified by the assertion that 'the obligation to protect human dignity is a peremptory norm and has assumed the nature of obligation *erga omnes*.'[402] This echoes the reasoning of the Inter-American Court of Human Rights in the 2001 *Barrios Altos* case, in which the Court stated that Peru's amnesty laws were inadmissible because, *inter alia*, they were intended to prevent the punishment of violations of non-derogable human rights.[403] A General Comment recently issued by the Committee against Torture maintained that 'amnesties or other impediments which preclude or indicate unwillingness to provide prompt and fair prosecution and punishment of perpetrators of torture or ill-treatment violate the principle of non-derogability.'[404] Invoking this declaration in its May 2008 concluding observations on Algeria's compliance with the Convention against Torture, the Committee observed that the Charter's provisions giving amnesties to armed groups and state forces 'do not conform to the obligation of every state party … to pursue the authors [of torture] …'[405]

While the above indicates a certain amount of practice in support of the *jus cogens* argument, there are some problems with this reasoning. First, as has been conceded by Bassiouni, a leading advocate of the 'duty to prosecute' position, such an argument rests on the assumption that the international society is a *civitas maxima*, which is still controversial.[406] Second, a distinction must be drawn, as the ICTY did in the *Furundžija* case, between the non-derogable nature of the *jus cogens* norm (the ban on the commission of the crime) and the *erga omnes* consequences (the method of enforcement) deriving from the breach of such a norm.[407] The latter obligation concerns the means of compliance with the peremp-

[400] Bassiouni, "International crimes", at 265: 'Legal obligations which arise from the higher status of such crimes include the duty to prosecute or extradite …'; See also Antonio Cassese, "On the current trends towards criminal prosecution and punishment of breaches of international humanitarian law", 9(1) *EJIL* 2-17 (1998); J. Paust, "Universality and the responsibility to enforce international criminal law: No sanctuary for alleged Nazi war criminals", 11 *Houston Journal of International Law* 337-40 (1989), reproduced in J. Paust, et al. (eds.), *International Criminal Law: Cases and Materials* (Durham: Carolina Academic Press, 1996), at 75.

[401] Bassiouni, "International Crimes", at 266.

[402] *Kallon and Kamara*, Decision on Amnesty case, para. 71.

[403] *Barrios Altos* case, para. 41.

[404] UN Comm. Against Torture, General Comment No. 2, Implementation of Article 2 by States Parties, para. 5, UN Doc. CAT/C/GC/2 (2008).

[405] UN Comm. Against Torture, Examen des Rapports Présentés par les États Parties en Application de l'Article 19 de la Convention, Observations finales du Comité contre la torture, Verson Non Editee, para. 11, UN Doc. CAT/C/DZA/CO/3 (2008).

[406] Bassiouni, "International Crimes", at 26-37.

[407] The ICTY identified the rationale behind these consequences as follows: 'While the *erga omnes* nature … appertains to the area of international enforcement (*lato sensu*), the *other* major fea-

tory norm.[408] Because *erga omnes* obligations are '[by] their very nature ... the concern of all States [and] all States can be held to have a legal interest in their protection ...'[409] under customary law, any State regardless of injury may invoke the responsibility of another State if the obligation breached is owed to the international community as a whole.[410] However, the fact that a State has a legal interest in ensuring that an obligation is complied with does not necessarily translate into a positive duty to prosecute every instance of *jus cogens* crimes. Moreover, there is no State practice assuming such a duty from the nature of the obligation.

The European Commission of Human Rights, in assessing an amnesty law passed in New Caledonia in the aftermath of the killing of four disarmed gendarmes by about 50 assailants, found that a 'State is justified in adopting, in the context of its criminal policy, any amnesty laws it might consider necessary, with the proviso, however, that a balance is maintained between the legitimate interests of the State and the interests of individual members of the public in having the right to life protected by law.'[411] While the act in question did not amount to a *jus cogens* crime, the fact that the Commission held that the protection of the right to life – a non-derogable right – could be balanced against other legitimate interests indicates that measures of enforcement of the non-derogable right do not translate into an absolute duty to prosecute.

A stronger argument that a duty to prosecute might emanate from the commission of *jus cogens* crimes relates to the duties of States under the law of State responsibility. Although all the consequences of *jus cogens* norms have not been clearly set out in any treaty, save for the Vienna Convention on the Law of

---

ture of the principle proscribing torture relates to the hierarchy of rules in the international normative order [*jus cogens*].' *Furundžija*, ICTY, Trial Chamber II, Judgment of 10 December 1998, Case No. IT-95-17/1-T; 39 *ILM* (1999), para. 153 [emphasis added]. This implies that the non-derogable nature applies only to the norm prohibiting torture.

[408] Examples of obligations *erga omnes* given by the ICJ are rules deriving from the outlawing of acts of aggression and genocide, and the rules and principles concerning the basic rights of the human person, including protection from slavery and racial discrimination. *Barcelona Traction* case (Second Phase), ICJ Reports 1970, 3 at 32; *East Timor* case *(Portugal* v. *Australia)*, ICJ Reports 1995, 90 at para. 29; *Legality of the Threat or Use of Nuclear Weapons*, Advisory Opinion of 8 July 1996, ICJ Reports 1996, at 258, para. 83; *Application of the Convention on the Prevention and Punishment of the Crime of Genocide (Bosnia Herzegovina* v. *Yugoslavia), Preliminary Objections*, ICJ Reports 1996, at 595, at 615-616, paras. 31-32. In the *Pinochet* litigation in the United Kingdom, Lord Hope made the point that the fact that an act has acquired the status of *jus cogens* under international law 'compels all states to refrain from such conduct under any circumstances and imposes an obligation *erga omnes* to punish such conduct.' *Pinochet No. 3*, House of Lords 24 March 1999, reproduced in R. Brody and M. Ratner (eds.), *The Pinochet Papers: The Case of Augusto Pinochet in Spain and Britain* (The Hague: Kluwer Law International, 2000), at 253-4.

[409] *Barcelona Traction, ibid.*

[410] Art. 48, Articles on Responsibility of States for Internationally Wrongful Acts, adopted by the International Law Commission on 29-31 August 2001, ILC, Report on the work of its fifty-third session, 23 April-1 June and 2 June-10 August 2001, GAOR 55th Sess., Suppl. (No. 10) (A/56/10).

[411] *Dujardin and Others* v. *France*, ECommHR, Admissibility Decision, 2 September 1991, Appl. No. 16734/90, 72 *D&R* 236 (1992), at 243-244.

Treaties,[412] which provides that any treaty conflicting with a *jus cogens* norm is void,[413] it is likely that the effects upon States' obligations are more extensive. Before turning to these other consequences, it may be useful to first outline how non-prosecution may generate State responsibility.

A State may be said to incur responsibility for an international crime, either because its agents carried out the crime or because a group acted under the instructions, directions or control of a State, or because it acknowledged and adopted the conduct as its own.[414] In terms of the latter possibility, it is possible to argue that the granting of amnesty over international crimes means that a State has officially endorsed such conduct, thereby acknowledging and adopting the conduct as its own.[415] Arguments along this line of thinking were adopted by a number of mixed commissions formed to arbitrate claims based on injuries to aliens in the late nineteenth and early twentieth century. In these cases, the failure to diligently investigate serious crimes and to prosecute and punish perpetrators was deemed sufficient to generate complicity and thereby incur liability.[416] The rationale is that the failure to prosecute may be deemed to be approval of the conduct and would give rise to a presumption of government complicity in the acts.[417] This presumption was especially applicable where the government had allowed the guilty parties to escape or had granted pardon or amnesty.[418] It has long been argued that State responsibility for internationally wrongful acts does not only consists in the failure of the violating State to observe its obligations, but also in the failure of the rest of the members of the international community to vindicate the law.[419] The *Restatement (Third) of the Foreign Relations Law of the United States* adopts the view that a complete failure to punish repeated or notorious violations of rights protected by customary

---

[412] Vienna Convention on the Law of Treaties, 23 May 1969, *UNTS* 1155 (hereafter, VCLT).

[413] VCLT, Art. 53: 'A treaty is void if, at the time of its conclusion, it conflicts with a peremptory norm of general international law. For the purposes of the present Convention, a peremptory norm of general international law is a norm accepted and recognized by the international community of States as a whole as a norm from which no derogation is permitted and which can be modified only by a subsequent norm of general international law having the same character.'

[414] ILC Draft Articles on State Responsibility, Articles 4, 8 and 11, respectively.

[415] Naturally, if the conduct was committed by State officials, State responsibility may already have arisen. The seminal case on this aspect of State Responsibility is the *United States Diplomatic and Consular Staff in Tehran*, ICJ Reports 1980, 3, in which the ICJ held that the Ayatolla Khomeini's repeated endorsement of the taking of the United State Embassy stage hostage by Iranian students as a means to exert pressure on the United States translated the continuing occupation of the Embassy and detention of hostages into acts of the State of Iran. *Ibid.*, at para. 74.

[416] In the *Neer* case, the United States-Mexican General Claims Commission held that: (1) international standards can obligate national authorities to take affirmative actions to investigate and apprehend; (2) failure to do so is a breach of a legal duty, giving rise to an international wrong; and (3) even if the laws are sound, the failure to provide effective execution constitutes a breach. *Neer* case (*U.S.* v. *Mexico*), 1927 U.S. and Mexico General Claims Commission 71, 4 *Reports International Arb. Awards* 60 (1926).

[417] *Janes* case (*U.S.* v. *Mexico*), 1927 U.S. and Mexico General Claims Commission 71, 4 *Reports International Arb. Awards* 82 (1926).

[418] *Ibid.*, at 86-87, 114.

[419] Glueck, *War Criminals*, at 89.

law renders a government sufficiently complicit to generate State responsibility.[420] This would appear to be in relation only to the territorial State. The responsibility of the State to prosecute these types of crimes, and not to prevent such investigations by the promulgation of amnesty laws, has been described as one side of the coin – the other face being individual penal responsibility – in the fight against 'atrocities, impunity, and injustice.'[421]

In the case of *jus cogens* crimes, there would appear to be an even higher threshold for required responses by third States. In the *Furundžija* case, the ICTY noted the effects of a peremptory norm at the inter-State level. According to the Tribunal:

> '... it serves to internationally de-legitimise any legislative, administrative or judicial act authorising torture. It would be senseless to argue, on the one hand, that on account of the *jus cogens* value of the prohibition against torture, treaties or customary rules providing for torture would be null and void *ab initio*, and then be unmindful of a State, say, taking national measures authorising or condoning torture or absolving its perpetrators through an amnesty law. If such a situation were to arise, the national measures, violating the general principle and any relevant treaty provision, would produce the legal effects discussed above and in addition would not be accorded international recognition.'[422]

One should be careful not to interpret the Tribunal's words as ruling out any possibility for the international recognition of amnesties for *jus cogens* crimes.[423] It is where the recognition of the amnesty law amounts to an authorisation, condoning or absolving of responsibility that the amnesty law loses all legal validity. The ILC has summed up the particular consequences of serious breaches of obligations under peremptory norms for third States in Article 41 of its Draft Articles. A serious breach involves a 'gross or systematic failure by the responsible State to fulfil the obligation.'[424] These consequences are that States shall co-operate to bring to an end through lawful means any serious breach and that no State shall recognize

---

[420] *Restatement (Third) of the Foreign Relations Law of the United States* (1987), para. 702. In *Henfield's* case and 1 *Op. Att'y Gen.* 68 (1797), at 69, the Court found that if a state did not initiate prosecution of one reasonably accused of an international crime, it was recognised that the state could become an 'accomplice' to illegality and be subject to various international sanctions.

[421] *Barrios Altos* case, Concurring Opinion of Judge Cançado Trindade, 14 March 2001, para. 13. He adds, 'It was necessary to wait many years to come to this conclusion, which, if it is possible today, is also due, - may I insist on a point which is very dear to me, – to the *awakening of the universal juridical conscience*, as the *material source par excellence* of International Law itself.' [Emphasis in original]

[422] *Furundžija* case, para. 155. [Citations omitted]

[423] As support for this statement, the Trial Chamber cites Human Rights Committee General Comment No. 20 on Article 7 of the ICCPR of 1994, in which the Committee noted that '[a]mnesties are *generally* incompatible with the duty of States to investigate such acts [torture]; to guarantee freedom from such acts within their jurisdiction; and to ensure that they do not occur in the future.' [Emphasis added]. *Compilation of General Comments and General Recommendations Adopted by Human Rights Treaty Bodies*, UN Doc. HRI\GEN\1\Rev. 1 at 30 (1994).

[424] ILC Articles on State Responsibility, Art. 40(2).

as lawful a situation created by a serious breach nor render aid or assistance in maintaining that situation.[425] Furthermore, Article 26 rules out the possibility of States invoking 'circumstances precluding wrongfulness' for any act of a State which is not in conformity with an obligation arising under a peremptory norm of general international law.

A duty to prosecute could possibly be inferred from these consequences since a criminal trial of the leaders of *jus cogens* crimes would be one way of bringing to an end the serious breach. However, this rule would seem to be referring more to political co-operation rather than to judicial measures.[426] With regard to the obligation not to recognise a situation created by a serious breach as lawful, this could be interpreted to rule out international recognition of certain blanket amnesties, although this may be a stretch given that virtually all examples refer to attempted acquisitions of sovereignty over territory.[427] However, while a third State's recognition of a blanket amnesty for international crimes self-proclaimed by an outgoing regime in another State would probably contravene the ILC principles, the international recognition of a principled and limited amnesty for the purposes of securing peace in a State or region, coupled with a truth commission would not amount to 'condoning,' 'authorisation,' 'absolving responsibility' nor indeed a recognition of the situation created by the breach of the *jus cogens* norm as legal. Allowing such an amnesty international recognition could also be considered as co-operating to bring to an end through lawful means any serious breach where the amnesty was granted as a way to negotiate an end to a brutal civil war.

---

[425] Art. 41, paras. 1 and 2, ILC Articles on State Responsibility. Art. 41 is without prejudice to the other consequences of a breach with may entail under international law (Art. 41(3)).

[426] James Crawford, *The International Law Commission's Articles on State Responsibility: Introduction, Text and Commentaries* (Cambridge: CUP, 2002), at 252 (citing examples of non-recognition of certain acts of Apartheid South Africa).

[427] This principle was enunciated in relation to any acquisition of territory brought about by force in the Declaration on Principles of International Law Concerning Friendly Relations and Co-operation Among States in Accordance with the Charter of the United Nations, General Assembly Res. 2625 (XXV), para. 10. The validity of the rule was affirmed by the ICJ in the *Nicargua* case, at 100, para. 188. The ICJ's advisory opinion in the *Namibia (South West Africa)* case also called for a non-recognition of the situation created by the denial by a State of the right to self-determination. *Legal Consequences for States in the Continuing Presence of South Africa in Namibia (South West Africa) notwithstanding Security Council Resolution 276 (1970)*, ICJ Reports 1971, 16 at 56, para. 126. The ICJ also held that all States were 'under an obligation not to recognize the illegal situation resulting from the construction of the wall in the Occupied Palestinian Territory, including in and around East Jerusalem' given the 'character and the importance of the rights and obligations involved.' *Legal Consequences of the Construction of a Wall in Occupied Palestinian Territory*, Advisory Opinion of 9 July 2004, ICJ Reports 2004, para. 159. See Stefan Talmon, "The Duty Not to 'Recognise as Lawful' a Situation Created by the Illegal Use of Force or Other Serious Breaches of a *Jus Cogens* Obligation: An Obligation without Real Substance?", in Christian Tomuschat and Jean-Marc Thouvenin (eds.), *The Fundamental Rules of the International Legal Order.* Jus Cogens *and Obligations* Erga Omnes (Leiden/Boston: Martinus Nijhoff Publishers, 2006), at 99.

2.5 Preliminary conclusions

International law neither completely prohibits nor completely authorises States to amnesty those accused of international crimes. However, it does provide some clear principles which assist in the evaluation of the legality of amnesties for international crimes. The first is that States' obligation to prosecute and punish those responsible for committing certain violations establishes a minimal requirement of accountability. This also ensures that States do not violate the principle of recognising a situation created by the unlawful act as lawful by measures which appear to condone, authorise or absolve responsibility for a serious violation. The second is that victims are entitled to some form of truth, reparations, and participation. It could be argued that amnesties which fulfil these principles should be considered consistent with international law, and should be given recognition by foreign and international courts.

A second way for international law to balance political contingency with the need for justice to be done and seen to be done in the aftermath of mass atrocities is through the principled use of prosecutorial discretion. Arguments based on the obligation to prosecute derive from the idea that prosecution tied to punishment is the best method in all circumstances for achieving the legitimate goals of a criminal justice system.[428] Those advocating against 'the absolutist claim of an obligation to prosecute' note that competing and compelling societal interests 'may conflict with a general policy of punishment – interests that are particularly important to a society undergoing a major transition.'[429] Thus, it is pointed out that an absolute obligation would not allow any discretion on the part of prosecutorial authorities, which would not only be an extremely difficult challenge for a post-conflict society which is normally lacking in prosecutorial resources,[430] but also may inter-

---

[428] International treaties and a number of decisions concerning State obligations speak of obligations to investigate and prosecute, and to punish (esp. Inter-American Court of Human Rights – e.g., *Barrios Altos* case, para. 13, *Velasquez Rodrigo* case, para. 166, *Lincoleo* v. *Chile*, Case 11.711, IACtHR 61, OEA/ser.L./V./II.111, doc. 20 (2001), paras. 55 and 79.) GA Resolutions also speak of the need to punish (e.g., GA Res. 3074, UN GAOR, 28th Sess., Suppl. (No. 30), at 79, UN Doc. A/9030 (1974), para. 1: 'War crimes and crimes against humanity, wherever they are committed, shall be subject to investigation and the persons against whom there is evidence that they have committed such crimes shall be subject to tracing, arrest, trial and, if found guilty, punishment.') Under international humanitarian law, a superior is under the obligation to punish a subordinate for the commission of a war crime. Failure to do so makes that superior criminally liable. (See Art. 6 of the Draft Code of Crimes Against the Peace and Security of Mankind; Statutes of ICTY and ICTR).

[429] Slye, "The Legitimacy of Amnesties under International Law and General Principles of Anglo-American Law ", at 173.

[430] But see *Romero*, at para. 143, noting the State's obligation to 'investigate *with the means at its disposal* the violations committed within its jurisdiction' [emphasis added]. *Monsignor Oscar Arnulfo Romero y Galdámez* v. *El Salvador* (Case 11.481), Report No. 37/00. In the *Čelebići* Appeals Decision, the ICTY noted that 'in many criminal justice systems, the entity responsible for prosecutions has finite financial and human resources and cannot realistically be expected to prosecute every offender which may fall within the strict terms of its jurisdiction.' *Delalić and others* (*Čelebići* case) *(appeal)*, ICTY Appeals Chamber, Judgment of 20 February 2001, Case No. IT-96-21-A, para. 602.

fere with the legitimate goals of a criminal justice system.[431] From this standpoint, prosecutorial discretion can arguably provide an important mechanism for a State to balance competing legitimate interests.[432] Robert Cryer, in his analysis of the use of selective enforcement of international criminal law by measuring it against the principle of the rule of law found that selective prosecution is 'not inherently wrong,' so long as the decisions made are not based upon arbitrariness, including by discrimination, and hence do not violate the right to equality before the law.[433] A carefully thought out use of prosecutorial discretion, which takes into account the public interest and balances the concerns of victims with societal expectations, and which is subject to review at the judicial level, may be an important way of accommodating the needs of transitional societies without violating the general obligation to prosecute international crimes.[434]

In this regard, the 'legitimating indicia' of amnesties provide a useful starting point to identify the 'legitimate' use of prosecutorial discretion. A number of factors have been identified by courts and commentators as being significant to the legitimacy of amnesty laws. The first relates to the purpose of the amnesty law. Only those amnesty laws which are promulgated for the purpose of ending or preventing a war or a protracted period of serious violence or otherwise to facili-

---

[431] For instance, no strategic decision-making about which criminals to prosecute and which crimes to pursue could be made under an absolute obligation which could result in a less efficient criminal justice system. Secondly, prosecution may undercut, or fail to advance, some legitimate goals of a criminal justice system and would exclude the use of other non-prosecutorial means. Professor Slye has noted that decisions not to prosecute may lead to further truth (when used to get additional testimony), accountability (when used to obtain a plea), and efficiency (when used to direct resources towards other more important social problems). Slye, "The Legitimacy of Amnesties under International Law", at 184.

[432] International law research has only just begun analysing the legal implications of prosecutorial discretion in international criminal law. See generally, Matthew R. Brubacher "The development of prosecutorial discretion in international criminal courts", in Edel Hughes, William A. Schabas and Ramesh Thakur (eds.), *Atrocities and International Accountability: Beyond Transitional Justice* (Tokyo/New York/Paris: United Nations University Press, 2007), at 142; Robert Cryer, *Prosecuting International Crimes: Selectivity and the International Criminal Law Regime* (Cambridge: CUP, 2005); Matthew R. Brubacher, "Prosecutorial Discretion within the International Criminal Court", 2 *JICJ* 71 (2004); Ntanda Nsereko, Daniel D., "Prosecutorial Discretion before National Courts and International Tribunals", 3 *JICJ* 124 (2005); Dan Sarooshi, "Prosecutorial Policy and the ICC: Prosecutor's *Proprio Motu* or Self-Denial?", 2 *JICJ* 940 (2004); Carla Del Ponte, "Prosecuting the Individuals Bearing the Highest Level of Responsibility", 2 *JICJ* 516 (2004).

[433] Cryer, *Prosecuting International Crimes*, at 193. He notes that general test for a plea of selective enforcement before the ICTY was enunciated as requiring the bringing of evidence '(i) establishing an unlawful or improper (including discriminatory) motive for the prosecution and (ii) establishing that other similarly situated persons were not prosecuted.' *Delalić and others* (*Čelebići* case) *(appeal)*, ICTY Appeals Chamber, Judgment of 20 February 2001, Case No. IT-96-21-A, para. 611.

[434] Legal theorists have rationalised the use of selective prosecution in transitional contexts on the basis that while in normal times the law maintains law and order, in periods of political upheaval, the legal responses create a '*sui generis* paradigm of transformative law.' Teitel, "Transitional Jurisprudence", at 2014. In the 'transitional domain,' the rule of law does not follow idealist conceptions. The rule of law is instead constructed in relation to past conceptions of injustice, and an extraordinary form of the rule of law emerges. In transitional criminal law, an extraordinary form of limited sanction emerges. *Ibid.*, at 2077.

tate social transition and reconciliation and not those granted in order merely to shield former leaders from criminal liability have been considered as legitimate.[435] Secondly, courts have indicated that those amnesties which have come into being through democratic processes[436] or which have resulted from multi-party negotiations have more legitimacy than those self-granted amnesties,[437] which violate the principle of self-judging.[438] Thirdly, amnesties which are designed to hide the truth and block investigations have been held to violate the victim's and society's right to the truth. Hence, only those amnesties which allows victims to know the truth about events which occurred, such as those which are tied to disclosure about politically-motivated crimes in a truth commission or co-operation with an investigation, have been deemed to be legitimate. Those amnesties which prevent the victim from claiming any type of reparation have also been regarded as invalid. It has also been argued that amnesties should be granted by a formal procedure that examines each individual candidate and imposes specific conditions for accepting the amnesty application based on the need for the truth to be told and to encourage rights-respecting behaviour.[439] Those laws which cover whole groups of people without any review process should not be considered legitimate. In this regard, a provisional amnesty that may be made permanent depending on the beneficiary fulfilling the conditions may be a regulated way to find the correct balance of restorative justice.

Finally, those considered 'most responsible' for the perpetration of international crimes, including leaders, should not escape the prosecutorial net. It may be recalled that the exclusion of the Emperor of Japan before the Tokyo Tribunal was criticised by Judges Bernard and Webb, the former stating that 'the Tribunal did not find itself in a position to control … that prosecution could be exercised in an equal and sufficiently justified manner regarding all justifiable [persons] … The consequences of this inequality are particularly apparent and regrettable in

---

[435] *AZAPO* case, para. 19.

[436] See for example *Garay Hermonsilla, et al.*, v. *Chile*, 'A *de facto* government lacks legal legitimacy … It is not juridically acceptable that such a regime should be able to restrict the actions of the constitutional government succeeding it as it tries to consolidate the democratic system, nor is it acceptable that the acts of a *de facto* power should enjoy all those attributes that accrue to the legitimate acts of a *de jure* power.' See also L. Joinet and E. Guisse, "Study on the Question of the Impunity of Perpetrators of Human Rights Violations", UN Sub-Commission on Prevention of Discrimination and Protection of Minorities, UN Doc. E/CN.4/Sub.2/1993/6, 19 July 1993; W. Burke-White, "Reframing Impunity", at 479.

[437] See Inter-American Commission on Human Rights, Report No. 133/99, Case 11,725 *Carmelo Soria Espinoza* (Chile), 19 November 1999, para. 76; Inter-American Court of Human Rights, Judgment of 14 March 2001, *Barrios Altos* case, para. 41: 'States parties to the Convention who adopt … self-amnesty laws, are in breach of articles 8 and 25 of the Convention. Self-amnesty laws leave victims defenceless and perpetuate impunity and are therefore clearly incompatible with the letter and spirit of the American Convention.'

[438] The Permanent Court of International Justice referred to the 'well-known rule that no one can be judge in his own suit' in the *1925 Frontier between Iraq and Turkey* case Art. 3, para. 2, Treaty of Leusenne (frontiers between Turkey and Iraq), 1925 PCIJ (ser. B), No. 12, at 32 (21 November 1925).

[439] Slye, "The Legitimacy of Amnesties under International Law".

regard to Emperor Hirohito.'[440] The omission of the members of Unit 731, Japan's chemical and biological weapons unit from the list of indictees before the Tokyo Tribunal as a result of the trade made with the US (immunity for chemical weapons expertise) has also been described as 'an illegitimate use of discretion' in view of the seriousness of the crimes and availability of evidence and suspects.[441]

[440] Dissenting Opinion of Judge Bernard, at 19. See also Separate Opinion of Judge Webb, at 19.
[441] Cryer, *Prosecuting International Crimes*, at 208.

Chapter 3
PARDONS

Pardons for international crimes have not attracted nearly as much attention or criticism as amnesties by courts or commentators in recent years. This is possibly because such measures have not been as common as amnesties in the aftermath of war or in political transitions in modern times and because when they have applied, they generally are directed towards certain specified individuals, and not to groups of people. Pardons are probably also arguably less offending to principles of justice given that an acceptance or finding of guilt accompanies such an act.[1] The fact that a pardon may be issued after a criminal trial means that there is no intention to hide the truth about past events, hinder investigations or revise a legal decision, as may be the case with amnesties. In addition, the sense of societal forgiveness inherent in the notion of pardon aligns with certain theories of punishment based upon the broader objectives of international criminal law.

It may also be that because States tend to be extremely jealous of their prerogative to issue pardons it is assumed that international law has little to say about it. More recent State practice, such as the establishment of judicial procedures to decide on the appropriateness of pardons to those convicted by the *ad hoc* ICTs and the binding nature of ICC sentences upon State parties would seem to counter this view.[2] However, contemporary State practice remains inconsistent with regard to issuing pardons for international crimes. While an Argentinean court in 2006 found the presidential pardons issued in 1989 and 1990 to members of the military involved in international crimes to be unconstitutional and invalid to the nature of the crimes at issue,[3] the Colombian Congress in 2005 passed the 'Law of Justice and Peace' offering 'judicial benefits' in the form of reduced sentences (a maximum of 5-8 years imprisonment) to those members of illegal armed groups

---

[1] Diane F. Orentlicher, "Settling Accounts: The Duty to Prosecute Human Rights Violations of a Prior Regime", 100 *Yale Law Journal* 9596-98 (1991); Luis Márquez Urtubey, "Non-Applicability for Statutes of Limitation for Crimes Committed in Argentina: Barrios Altos", 11 *Southwestern Journal of Law and Trade in the Americas* 128 (2005).

[2] Art. 28 ICTY and Art. 27 ICTR Statutes both provide that if the law in a State in which a convicted person is imprisoned provides that the person may become eligible for pardon or commutation of sentence, the State shall notify the International Tribunal. The matter will be decided by the President of the Tribunal, in consultation with the judges, on the basis of the interests of justice and the general principles of law. See also Art. 105 ICC Statute.

[3] Deborah Rey, "Another Setback for Ex-Junta Chief", *AP*, 6 September 2006, available at: <http://www.boston.com/news/world/latinamerica/articles/2006/09/06/another_legal_setback_for_ex_junta_chief/?p1=MEWell_Pos5> (last visited 25 March 2007).

willing to confess to their part in international crimes and who have demobilised and reintegrated.[4] The Constitutional Court of Colombia held in May 2006 that the Law is constitutional,[5] at the same time modifying certain component parts in order to ensure that a reduction of penalties for demobilised members of illegal groups only applies to those who co-operate fully with the clarification of crimes, contribute with all their property towards reparation policies and clearly contribute to dismantling illegal structures.[6] The decision also assures the rights of victims to participate actively in all stages of the criminal process. An analysis of the practice of States and the principles regulating the legality of pardons for international crimes reveals that international law does not render such exceptions to punishment illegal outright, but rather provides courts with a set of factors to be weighed against each other consistent with an interests-analysis approach.

3.1 Definition and historical background

A pardon may be defined as the 'act or instance of officially nullifying punishment.'[7] Although pardons are often treated as synonymous with amnesties, the legal effect of a pardon is substantially different. Pardons can be issued at any time after the commission of the act however, unlike amnesties, which prevent a prosecution from taking place, pardons are often issued after an individual has been found liable for a wrongful act. In such instances, the *exercise of jurisdiction* is not at issue, but the *expected legal consequence* of such an exercise of jurisdiction is central to the legality issue. The issue of pardons for international crimes is therefore symbiotically connected to the exercise of jurisdiction. For a person subject to a pardon subsequent to trial, the sentence imposed on them as a result of the finding of liability may be reduced or lifted, however *the finding of liability remains*.[8] In other countries, pardons may only be applied for after the sentence has been completed.[9] In some systems, a pardon need be accepted by the beneficiary, which indicates an admission of guilt.[10] Thus, while punishment for a wrongful act is removed or reduced in the case of a pardon, other objectives of criminal justice

---

[4] Law No. 975 of 25 July 2005, entitled "Law on Justice and Peace."

[5] Court Decision No. C-370/2006, Colombia, Constitutional Court, 25 May 2006.

[6] Those paramilitary members not co-operating fully or who re-engage in crime will lose the benefit of reduced penalties and will automatically receive substantial prison terms.

[7] Bryan A. Garner, *Black's Law Dictionary*, 8th edn. (St. Paul, Minn: West Group, 2004), at 1144.

[8] Ronald C. Slye, "The Legitimacy of Amnesties under International Law and General Principles of Anglo-American Law: Is Legitimate Amnesty Possible", 43 *VJIL* 235 (2002). For this reason, a pardon should be distinguished from mechanisms of corrective justice which are used to expunge a wrongful conviction, such as the writ of *coram nobis* in the US (codified in Fed. R. Civ. P. 60(b)). *Ibid.*

[9] This is the case in Canada, where pardons are considered by the National Parole Board under the Criminal Records Act, the Criminal Code and several other laws. However, a person's sentence may be reduced by virtue of clemency granted by the Governor-General of Canada or the Governor in Council (the federal cabinet) under the Royal Prerogative of Mercy.

[10] This is the case in the United States. See *Burdick* v. *United States,* 236 US 79 (1915).

are kept intact, namely the functions of accountability and truth.[11] Possibly for this reason, pardons have not been completely rejected in their possible application to persons found guilty of violations of international criminal law.[12]

As with amnesties, pardons have been used in almost every society throughout history. Except for China, every constitution in the world provides for the power of pardon.[13] The oldest known legal code – the Code of Hammurabi, dated around the eighteenth century B.C., noted specified circumstances allowing pardons for serious crimes (as considered at the time) such as adultery and limited punishment to the severity of the crime at issue.[14] The First Testament notes God's mercy with regard to Cain's banishment after he killed his brother Abel.[15] In ancient Athens, the people had the power of pardon. A person seeking pardon had to obtain the signatures of 6,000 citizens.[16] The Romans had a developed system of pardon, which could be granted by the will of the Emperor or by an 'accidental encounter with a vestal virgin.'[17] According to the four books of the Gospel, a Passover custom in Jerusalem allowed Pontius Pilate, the *praefectus* or governor of Judaea, to commute one prisoner's death sentence by popular vote, and the crowd, when offered a choice of whether to have Barabbas 'a notorious prisoner'[18] or Jesus Christ released from Roman custody, chose Barabbas.[19] The Romans also used pardons to quell mutinous soldiers and had the custom of pardoning prisoners on corona-

---

[11] Slye, "The Legitimacy of Amnesties under International Law", at 236.

[12] The ICTY, ICTR and SCSL Statutes all provide for the possibility of pardons, subject to judicial regulation. By contrast, Allied Control Council Law No. 10 and the Law Establishing the Extraordinary Chambers in Cambodia reject any pardons. The ICC Statute is silent about pardons, though a rejection may be implied. See *infra*, section 3.2.

[13] L. Sebba, "The Pardoning Power: A World Survey, " 78 *Journal of Criminal Law*, at 83.

[14] Art. 129. L. Sebba, "Clemency in Perspective", in *Essays in Honor of Israel Drapkin*, S. Landau and L. Sebba (eds.) (Lexington, Mass.: Lexington Books, 1977), at 221 (citing R. Driver and J. Mills, The *Babylonian Laws* (Oxford: Clarendon Press, 1952)).

[15] According to the Hebrew Bible at Genesis 4 and in the Qur'an at 5:27-32, God sentenced Cain to a lifetime of wandering the earth as punishment for the murder. When Cain protested that he would be killed by other men, God put a mark on Cain which signalled that he could not be killed until he had had seven generations of children. This has been interpreted as a kind of commutation of sentence: 'Merciful the Lord is, and just, and full of pity.' Ps. 116:5.

[16] Dean Moore, *Pardons*, at 16 (citing US Attorney General, 1929, 9 and E. Abramowitz and D. Paget, "Executive Clemency in Capital Cases", 39 *New York University Law Review* (January 1964), at 136).

[17] Dean Moore, *Pardons*, at 16 (citing Plutach, *Numa*, at 10, quoted in US Attorney General, 1939, at 13).

[18] It is not completely certain what crime Barabbas was said to have committed. John 18:40 refers to Barabbas as a *lēstēs*, 'bandit'; Mark and Luke further refer to Barabbas as one involved in a *stasis*, a riot. Mark 15:7; Luke 23:19. Matthew refers to Barabbas as a 'notorious prisoner.' Matthew 27:16. Various authors contend Barabbas's crime would translate today as terrorism. Stephen H. Travis, *The Bible in Time: An exploration of 130 passages providing an overview of the Bible as a whole* (Clements Publishing, 2004), at 200; James Montgomery Boice and Philip Graham Ryken, *Jesus on Trial* (Crossway Books, 2002) at 79. He is called a terrorist in the Contemporary English Version of the Bible. *Bible Gateway Contemporary English Version*, Matthew 27:16.

[19] Matthew (27:15-26), Mark (15:6-15), Luke (23:13–25), and the more divergent accounts in John (18:38-19:16) and the Gospel of Peter.

tion days and local holidays, evidently aware of their political appeal and power.[20] The practice of giving pardon for crimes in Europe and England from the Roman Empire until the Enlightenment was varied and prolific, and those vying for power often sought the exclusive right to pardon. In England, the right to pardon was assigned to the King since the seventh century, and remained so under the new code of laws of William the Conqueror. Pardon was used as a means of 'softening' the harsh criminal retributive system in place, allowing distinctions to be made in cases so that, for example, defences such as insanity, mistake or necessity in cases involving homicide might justify a pardon, before these were recognised as grounds for acquittal.[21] Although the Magna Carta forbade sales of justice, in practice pardons were exchanged for money by the church and the King. King James II would sell pardons for as little as two shillings.[22] The notion of conditional pardon became more entrenched in the seventeenth century, when it was used as a way to manage the chronic labour shortages in the colonies.[23] In the United Kingdom, pardons were granted to many in the 18th century on condition that the convicted felons accept transportation overseas, such as to Australia. The Founding Fathers of the United States of America gave the President an almost unlimited power to pardon.[24]

Because an issue of pardon emanates from sovereign authority, pardons generally lie with the Head of State,[25] although in constitutional monarchies, this power is essentially relegated to government[26] and in other systems may be subject to the approval of government ministers.[27] This is another essential difference to amnesties, which are generally passed by the legislature.[28] The power to grant pardon is usually written into the constitution.[29] Historically, pardons were deemed to be the

[20] Dean Moore, *Pardons*, at 16-17.

[21] *Ibid.*, at 17-18.

[22] C. Hewitt, *The Queen's Pardon* (London: Cassell, 1978), at 20.

[23] Sebba, *supra* n. 13, at 224.

[24] In the United States, the pardon power for Federal crimes is granted to the President by the United States Constitution, Art. II, Section 2, which states that the President: 'shall have power to grant reprieves and pardons for offenses against the United States, except in cases of impeachment.'

[25] As Gutto notes, 'in general constitutional law and practice, the exercise of mercy is reserved to the head of state, the Chief executive, be it monarch, an aristocrat, a popularly democratically elected ruler or any other head of state depending on the form of government.' S.B.O. Gutto, "Some Legal Comments on Hon. Waruru Kanja's Petition for Executive Clemency", *Verfassung und Recht in Ubersee: Law and Politics in Africa, Asia and Latin America* (1982), 289 at 292.

[26] For example, in the United Kingdom, the power to grant pardons and reprieves is a royal prerogative of mercy of the monarch of the United Kingdom. However, the monarch may only grant a pardon on the advice of the Home Secretary or the First Minister of Scotland.

[27] This is the case in Ireland and in France.

[28] For example, in France, while pardons and acts of clemency (*grâces*) are granted by the President of France, who, ultimately, is the sole judge of the propriety of the measure, although it is also signed by the Prime Minister, the Minister of Justice and possibly other ministers involved in the consideration of the case. By contrast, it is the Parliament of France which, on occasion, grants amnesty, for which there is a different procedure.

[29] For example, in the Islamic Republic of Iran, the Supreme Leader has the power to pardon and offer clemency under Art. 110, § 1, §§ 11 of the Constitution of Islamic Republic of Iran (adopted

prerogative of the king due to the logic that a criminal act was an offence against the person of the king. As monarchies moved towards democracies, this legal fiction became severely strained. The power to pardon in a democracy instead was thought to lie with 'the people' since a criminal act is an offence against the laws enacted by their elected representatives. Because a pardon would negate the will of the people as reflected in the criminal law, Montesquieu and Blackstone were sceptical of their role in a republic, although they felt that pardons in principle might be defended.[30] The French Revolution saw the power of pardon wiped out completely. However, this only lasted a decade and would appear to be the only time in history that a society has governed without some form of pardon.[31]

Pardons have also been used to end wars. While pardons have traditionally been viewed as an institution of national law, they have sometimes been incorporated in inter-State peace treaties.[32] Pardons have also been issued as a way to win or bring civil wars to a close.[33] In the United States, President John Adam pardoned the rebels of Fries' Rebellion, President Thomas Jefferson pardoned deserters from the Continental Army, President James Madison pardoned deserters of the War of 1812, and after the war, pardoned Lafitte's pirates and President Andrew Jackson pardoned deserters. During the Civil War, presidential clemency was extended to deserters on condition they return to their units and to supporters of the Confederacy as a means to undermine the rebellion. After the Civil War, the leaders of the Confereracy were pardoned by President Andrew Johnson and many others by President Ulysses S. Grant.[34]

on 24 October 1979); under the Constitution of Ireland Art. 13 Section 6 the President of Ireland can pardon convicted criminals (though this requires the approval of government); in Italy the President of the Republic can '... grant pardons, or commute punishments ...' by virtue of Art. 87 of the Italian Constitution; the President of the Russian Federation is granted the right of pardon by Art. 89 of the Constitution of the Russian Federation; in the United States, the pardon power for Federal crimes is granted to the President by the United States Constitution, Art. II, Section 2; section 84(2)(j) of the Constitution of the Republic of South Africa, 1996 (Act 108 of 1996) gives the President the authority to pardon or reprieve offenders.

[30] Dean Moore, *Pardons*, at 23-49.

[31] *Ibid.*, at 24-25. Eventually, a pardoning power was formally granted to the First Consul in 1802.

[32] For example, Art. II of the Treaty of Westphalia of 1648 provided: 'That there shall be on the one side and the other a perpetual Oblivion, Amnesty, or Pardon of all that has been committed since the beginning of these Troubles ...' The Treaty of Vienna of 1809 included a clause of pardon for those involved in the insurrection of the inhabitants of Tyrol and Vorarlburg. The 1829 Treaty of Adrianople which put an end to the Russo-Turkish War of 1828-29, contained a general pardon and a full and entire amnesty for all those involved in military operations.

[33] For example, the Ugandan Amnesty Act of 2000, Section 2, defines amnesty as 'a pardon, forgiveness, exemption or discharge from criminal prosecution or any other form of punishment by the State.' The legislation was enacted with the aim of ending the hostilities in Northern Uganda, in particular, by trying to persuade the Lord's Resistance Army rebel group to disarm. The 1999 Lomé Accord between the Kabbah Government and the RUF, which strove to end the civil war in Sierra Leone provided in Art. 9(1): 'In order to bring lasting peace to Sierra Leone, the Government of Sierra Leone shall take appropriate legal steps to grant Corporal Foday Sankoh absolute and free pardon.'

[34] Dean Moore, *Pardons*, at 51.

Clemency is an associated term, meaning the lessening of the penalty of the crime without forgiving the crime itself. The act of clemency is a reprieve. The function of clemency functions as an extra-judicial check on the discretion of courts and has been justified partly because the 'administration of justice by the courts is not necessarily always wise or certainly considerate of circumstances which may properly mitigate guilt.'[35] The two main goals of clemency are enhanced fairness of criminal justice and correction of error.[36] Clemency programs during which sentences for specific crimes or groups of people are commuted or lifted have also been used throughout history often as a means to smooth political transitions.

3.2 Pardons and international and hybrid criminal courts and tribunals

Unlike amnesty, pardon has featured more prominently in the statutes setting up both international and hybrid courts. Pardon was not contemplated in either the constitutive instruments of the IMT or the IMTFE, although there was the possibility for a reduction in sentence at any time issued by the 'Control Council' or the 'Supreme Commander for the Allied Powers' respectively.[37] Control Council Law No. 10,[38] which established the courts of the four Allied nations in the occupied German territory in order to prosecute the lesser war criminals,[39] in Article 5 stated that any pardon granted under the Nazi regime would not be admitted as a bar to punishment. The possibility for pardons is foreseen in both the ICTY and ICTR Statutes, the authority for which ultimately lies with the President of the Tribunals in consultation with the judges, who is obliged to decide the matter 'on the basis of the interests of justice and the general principles of law.'[40] Unlike the ICTY and ICTR, there is no explicit provision on pardons in the ICC Statute. Article 105 of the ICC Statute, which provides that 'the sentence of the imprisonment shall be binding on the States Parties, which shall in no case modify it,' seems to suggest that pardons are not an option for those convicted by the ICC.[41]

---

[35] *Ex parte Grossman*, 267 US 87 (1925), at 120-121.

[36] Michael Heise, "Mercy by the Numbers: An Empirical Analysis of Clemency and its Structure", 89(2) *Virginia Law Review* 240 (April 2003).

[37] IMT Charter, Art. 29; IMTFE Charter, Art. 17.

[38] Allied Control Council Law No. 10, Punishment of Persons Guilty of War Crimes, Crimes Against Peace and Against Humanity, 20 December 1945, *Official Gazette of the Control Council for Germany*, No. 3, Berlin, 31 January 1946.

[39] Allied Control Council Law No. 10, preamble (stating that these trials sought 'to give effect to the terms of the Moscow Declaration of 30 October 1943 and the London Agreement of 8 August 1945, and the Charter issued pursuant thereto … in order to establish a uniform legal basis in Germany for the prosecution of war criminals and other similar offenders, other than those dealt with by the International Military Tribunal …').

[40] Art. 28 ICTY Statute; Art. 27 ICTR Statute.

[41] In this respect, it is worth noting that in their implementing legislation for the ICC Statute, the Dutch government stated that a pardon was not considered as a sovereign prerogative, but as a discretionary power that can be transferred to an international organisation. Explanatory memorandum to the Ratification Act, *TK, vergaderjaar 2000-2001*, 27 484 (R 1699), No. 3, at 9, 10.

As noted in the previous chapter, the Law establishing the Extraordinary Chambers in Cambodia obliges the Government of Cambodia to refrain from enacting any amnesty or pardon for the international crimes in the subject-matter jurisdiction and gives the Chambers the power to review the scope of any amnesty or pardon promulgated before the enactment of the Law.[42] This suggests that the Chambers would be able to either override or at least reduce the scope of the royal pardon granted in 1996 to Ieng Sary, Brother No. 3 – Deputy Prime Minister and Minister for Foreign Affairs and Central and Standing Committee member of the Khmer Rouge regime, for a conviction of genocide that had been handed down in Phnom Penh in 1979 by a Vietnamese-sponsored court.[43] With regard to the 1996 pardon, the Chambers may well decide that a pardon may not be given for the crime of genocide and is thus invalid.[44]

Pardons are dealt with in Article 23 of the SCSL Statute, which again mirrors the provisions in the ICTY and ICTR Statutes. However, unlike those tribunals, it is likely that it will be the law of Sierra Leone, rather than any other host State, that will apply to those serving prison terms. In this regard, the power of issuing pardons being vested in the Special Court serves as an international check against any future national policy of pardons by Sierra Leone and constitutes quite a significant delegation of sovereignty in this regard. Pardons are not overtly dealt with in the regulations setting up the Special Panels for Serious Crimes in East Timor.

3.3 Contextual and policy considerations

In modern democracies, pardons are generally not 'a simple matter of personal whims of a head of state but rather a necessary public and legal power that enables a ruler to do justice beyond what the ordinary laws of the land may offer.'[45] In particular, 'pardon and reprieve by the Head of State are normally made in sensitive

---

[42] Law on the Establishment of the Extraordinary Chambers in the Court of Cambodia for the Prosecution of Crimes Committed During the Period of Democratic Kampuchea, with inclusion of amendments as promulgated on 27 October 2004 (NS/RKM/1004/006) (hereafter, Law Establishing ECCC, as amended), Chapter XII, Art. 40.

[43] The decree read: 'Amnesty is granted to Mr. Ieng Sary, former Deputy Prime Minister responsible for Foreign Affairs in the Government of Democratic Kampuchea, who was sentenced to death and confiscation of all property by order of the People's Revolutionary Court of Phnom Penh date 19 August 1979 and with regard to penalties stipulated by the Law on the Outlawing of the Democratic Kampuchea Group which was promulgated by Royal Proclamation No. 01 BM 94 dated 15 July 1994.' For a legal analysis, see Ronald C. Slye, "The Cambodian Amnesties: Beneficiaries and the Temporal Reach of Amnesties for Gross Violations of Human Rights", *ExpressO Preprint Service – Working Paper* 33 (available at: <http://law.bepress.com/cgi/viewcontent.cgi?article=1063&context=expresso>) (2003). For an overview of the trial which convicted Ieng Sary and Pol Pot and its primary documents, see Howard J. De Nike, John Quigley and Kenneth J. Robinson (eds.), *Genocide in Cambodia: Documents from the Trial of Pol Pot and Ieng Sary* (Philadelphia: University of Pennsylvania Press, 2000).

[44] The Genocide Conventions obliges States parties to ensure that those convicted of genocide receive 'an effective penalty,' which a pardon would seem to violate. Genocide Convention, Arts. 1 and 5. Cambodia has been a party to the Genocide Convention since 1950. See *infra*, section 3.4.1.

[45] Gutto, *supra* n. 25, at 292.

cases that have strong public appeals.'[46] There are several justifications for pardons, some of which are similar to those governing the decision to issue amnesties.

First, a pardon may be an expression of the official grace and wisdom of a leader or government. Examples of these are the 'amnesties' issued by many countries to commemorate an important event.[47] Second, a pardon may be the expression of societal forgiveness for an offence against the law. The South African amnesty was characterised by Archbishop Desmond Tutu in a sense as an act of forgiveness, which gave the amnesty the quality of a pardon, although no criminal liability attached to amnesty beneficiaries.[48] Arguably, however, those who testified before the Amnesty Commission and the TRC were made accountable in a non-judicial sense by having to make public admissions.[49] Third, a pardon may be granted where a person has been recognised as rehabilitated.[50] Although it might be argued that amnesties do not allow for the same judgments to be made about the rehabilitation of beneficiaries,[51] it is possible that the concept of provisional amnesty could be one way of allowing such an assessment to be made, with permanent amnesty made possible only where the beneficiary has proved to be displaying rights-respecting behaviour.[52]

Pardons have been justified as a contribution towards social stability. This utilitarian justification of pardons is often used in transitional contexts, such as those issued at the end of the US Civil War[53] and more recently, those in Argentina,[54]

---

[46] *Ibid.*, at 294.

[47] The first General Pardon in England was issued in celebration of the coronation of Edward III in 1327. In China in ancient and medieval times, amnesties were granted with the accession of a new emperor as a signal of rebirth and renewal. See Brian McKnight, *The Quality of Mercy: Amnesties and Traditional Chinese Justice* (1981). Vietnam released almost 2,000 prisoners and reduced the sentences of 4,000 others in celebration of the 54th anniversary of its independence in 1999. *BBC World Online* (1 September 1999).

[48] Desmond Tutu, *No Future Without Forgiveness* (New York: Random House, 1999), at 257-82.

[49] Susan de Villiers (ed.), *Truth and Reconciliation Commission of South Africa, Report*, Vol. 1 (1998), at 50, Foreword by Chairperson, Desmond Tutu: 'The amnesty applicant has to admit responsibility for the act for which amnesty is being sought, thus dealing with the matter of impunity. Furthermore, apart from the most exceptional circumstances, the application is dealt with in a public hearing. The applicant must therefore make his admissions in the full glare of publicity. Often this is the first time that an applicant's family and community learn that an apparently decent man was, for instance, a callous torturer or a member of a ruthless death squad that assassinated many opponents of the previous regime. There is, therefore, a price to be paid.'

[50] The General Standards for Granting Pardon or Commutation contained in Rules 124-6 of the ICTR and ICTY RPE allow for a prisoner's demonstration of rehabilitation to be considered as one of the reasons to grant a pardon or commutation of sentence.

[51] Slye, "The Legitimacy of Amnesties under International Law", at 237.

[52] See the discussion of this option, *infra* section 3.4.2. See also Slye, "The Cambodian Amnesties".

[53] See generally Jonathan Truman Dorris, *Pardon and Amnesty under Lincoln and Johnson*; *The Restoration of the Confederates to Their Rights and Privileges, 1861-1898* (Westport: Greenwood Press, 1953).

[54] In October 1989 President Carlos Menem of Argentina issued two sweeping pardons for officials of the former military regime who had been found guilty of crimes committed during the 'Dirty

Cambodia,[55] and Sierra Leone.[56] The American Civil War left behind a country bitterly divided. During the war, Lincoln proclaimed a pardon/amnesty for all participants in the rebellion.[57] After Lincoln's assassination in 1865, President Andrew Johnson adopted a policy of leniency, and offered amnesties to all former rebels who would take the oath of allegiance, while those with a post-war wealth of more than US $20,000 would have to apply to him personally for pardon, which he normally gave.[58]

In Argentina, the presidential pardons issued in 1989 and 1990 were aimed at quelling military riots and severe military discontent that was threatening to upset the transition to democratic civilian rule. It is worth recalling briefly the events that led to the issuing of the pardons.[59] Thousands of people had been secretly kidnapped, tortured and killed between 1976 and 1983 at the hands of a military regime led by Jorge Raphael Videla trying to stamp out opposition.[60] When civilian government was restored under Raúl Alfonsín, a truth commission was established as a means to provide information about the period of repression. Its shocking findings, including documenting 8,960 disappearances, forced judges to react. Alfonsín had also repealed the national security doctrine and the military's self-amnesty law of September 1983, paving the way for prosecutions.[61] After the military tribunal declared its inability and unwillingness to complete proceedings against the junta leaders,[62] public trials of military officials were held in 1985 and

War' in a bid to quell military opposition and to smooth the transition to democracy. See Decree 1002/89 of 6 October 1989 and Decree 2741/90 of 29 December 1990.

[55] A royal pardon was issued to Ieng Sary, Deputy Prime Minister of the Khmer Rouge regime in 1996 in return for his defection, along with hundreds of Khmer Rouge affiliates, to the government.

[56] The 1999 Lomé Accord between the Kabbah Government and the RUF, which strove to end the civil war in Sierra Leone provided in Art. 9(1): 'In order to bring lasting peace to Sierra Leone, the Government of Sierra Leone shall take appropriate legal steps to grant Corporal Foday Sankoh absolute and free pardon.'

[57] The Proclamation of Amnesty and Reconstruction of 8 December 1863 offered pardon and restoration of property – except slaves – to Confederates who swore allegiance to the Union and agreed to accept emancipation.

[58] This was called the plan of Presidential Reconstruction adopted on 29 May 1865. J.G. Randall, *The Civil War and Reconstruction* (1937), at 689.

[59] For a detailed analysis, see Jose Sebastian Elias, "Constitutional Changes, Transitional Justice, and Legitimacy: The Life and Death of Argentina's 'Amnesty Laws'", 31 *Hastings International and Comparative Law Review* 587 (2008).

[60] The Argentine National Commission on Disappeared Persons (CONADEP) estimates that more than 10,000 people were killed by the military regime. *Nunca Más: Informe de la Comisión Nacional sobre la Desaporaición de Personas* (Buenos Aires: Eudeba, 1984), at 54.

[61] See "Law of National Pacification", Law No. 22.924 (22 September 1983) and "Amnesty Nullification", Law No. 23.040 (27 December 1983), reprinted in Neil J. Kritz, *Transitional Justice: How Emerging Democracies Reckon with Former Regimes*, Vol. III, *Laws, Rulings and Reports* (Washington, D.C: United States Instiute of Peace Press, 1995), at 477-480.

[62] Alfonsín, in a bid to appear 'fair' to the military, had offered them the chance to try their own people for the crimes before military courts, headed by the Supreme Council of the Armed Forces (SCAF). An initial six months to complete the process expired with no results. After the expiry of another six months with no progress, public pressure was brought to bear on the government to try the military in civilian courts.

1986, as a result of which 481 military and police officials were indicted; 16 were tried and 11 were convicted.[63] Nonetheless, the selective prosecutions resulted in new demands for justice and four armed rebellions were provoked, which underlined the continuing threat of the military in Argentinean politics.[64] As a result, two laws were passed by Congress which tried to restrict the trials of military personnel. The first was the *Ley de Punto Final* (Full Stop Law),[65] which established a 60 day deadline for bringing criminal complaints against the military.[66] The second was the *Ley de Obedienca Debida* (Law of Due Obedience),[67] which provided an irrefutable presumption that all military officers beneath the status of colonel, were acting on superior orders.[68] The Supreme Court found that the Due Obedience argument was unacceptable and the majority stated that in order to be valid, the law had to be considered as a form of amnesty.[69] Two military uprisings followed and Alfonsín was forced to step down.[70] Carlos Menem took over in June 1989. While he forcefully suppressed the military uprising, he also issued two pardons that ended the prosecutions against the military. The first pardon, issued on 8 October 1989, applied to 277 people – those generals awaiting trial, low-ranking officers involved in military rebellions, former guerrilla leaders and the former minister of the economy.[71] A second pardon, issued on 28 December 1990, applied to those generals who had been found guilty and were imprisoned, including Videla, Massera and others.[72] The two pardons were justified as a way to achieve national reconciliation and called upon Argentineans to show a 'loftiness of spirit that can overcome rancor – however understandable it may be – and replace it with magnanimity.' Decree 1002/89 described the pardon as 'a political mechanism, provided for by the constitution in order to create the conditions necessary for national pacification.'

With regard to Cambodia, King Sihanouk granted a royal pardon to Ieng Sary in 1996, at the request of the government, in return for his defection, along with thousands of Khmer Rouge members, to the government. Sary had been convicted in 1979 for genocide in an *in absentia* trial.[73] As it turned out, the pardon deal did succeed in splitting the Khmer Rouge and significantly reducing the anti-governmen-

---

[63] Luis Moreno Ocampo, "Beyond Punishment: Justice in the Wake of Massive Crimes in Argentina", 52(2) *Journal of International Affairs* 599 (Spring 1999).

[64] Elin Skaar, "Argentina: Truth, Justice, and Reconciliation", in Elin Skaar, Siri Gloppen and Astri Suhrke (eds.), *Roads to Reconciliation* (Lanham: Lexington Books, 2005), at 162.

[65] Law No. 23492 (23 December 1986), reprinted in Kritz (ed.), *Transitional Justice*, at 505.

[66] Lower court judges still managed to indict 450 officers before the expiry of the deadline.

[67] Law No. 23521 (4 June 1987), reprinted in Kritz (ed.), *Transitional Justice*, at 507.

[68] An exception was made for the crimes of kidnapping, child theft and falsification of public documents intended to change the children's identity.

[69] *Fallos de la Corte Suprema de Justicia de la Nación,* Argentina, Supreme Court, Buenos Aires, no. 310, 1984.

[70] Economic deterioration and hyperinflation also led to his presidential downfall.

[71] Decree 1002/89, 6 October 1989.

[72] Decree 2741/90, 29 December 1990.

[73] See De Nike, Quigley and Robinson (eds.), *Genocide in Cambodia.*

tal forces.[74] Only a few hardliners, including Pol Pot, Nuon Chea, Ta Mok, Khieu Samphan, Son Sen and his wife Yun Yat, remained in the north of the country.[75] Factional fighting in 1997 led to Pol Pot's trial and imprisonment by the Khmer Rouge.[76] Pol Pot died in April 1998. Khieu Samphan surrendered in December. On 29 December 1998, the remaining leaders of the Khmer Rouge apologised for the 1970s genocide.[77] By 1999, most members had surrendered or been captured. In December 1999, Ta Mok and the remaining leaders surrendered, and the Khmer Rouge effectively ceased to exist. Although the Extraordinary Chambers in Cambodia, established to try the senior leaders of Khmer Rouge for international crimes committed during the Khmer Rouge regime, have the power to review the scope of any pardon granted in the past,[78] an official of the Court has suggested that instead of overturning the pardon, charges apart from genocide, which were not covered by the 1996 pardon, may be laid against Sary.[79] This is what occured; Sary was charged with crimes against humanity and grave breaches of the Geneva Conventions of 1949.[80]

While the scope and authority of presidential pardons would appear to be extremely broad,[81] laws setting out the scope of pardons particularly in transitional contexts have sometimes excluded certain serious crimes.[82] Pardons have also been issued when community attitudes regarding certain crimes have shifted because of changing values or information. For instance, in 2006 hundreds of British soldiers executed for cowardice during World War I were officially pardoned, mainly in the

---

74 An estimated 4,000 Khmer Rouge members defected as a result of the 1996 deal.

75 Dominic Faulder, "Trying Times in Cambodia", *The Irrawaddy,* Vol 9, No. 6, July 2001, available at: <http://www.crimesofwar.org/resources/links/irrawaddy1.html>.

76 Pol Pot was tried by the Khmer Rouge for the murder of his life-long right hand man Son Sen and 11 members of his family, whose execution he ordered because of his attempt to make a settlement with the government.

77 Seth Mydans, "Under Prodding, 2 Apologize for Cambodian Anguish", *New York Times*, 30 December 1998, A3.

78 Law Establishing ECCC, as amended, Art. 40 new.

79 "Official: Former Khmer Rouge foreign minister not immune from prosecution", *International Herald Tribune*, AP, 26 October 2006 (quoting Reach Sambath, a spokesman for the Extraordinary Chambers in the Courts of Cambodia).

80 Extraordinary Chambers in the Courts of Cambodia, Office of the Co-Investigating Judges, Criminal Case File No. 002/14-08-2006, Investigation No. 002/14-08-2006, Instruction No. 002/19-09-2007-ECCC/OJIC, Provisional Detention Order, 14 November 2007, C23, at 1.

81 For example, the Constitution of the United States grants the President the 'Power to Grant Reprieves and Pardons for Offenses against the United States, except in Cases of Impeachment.' Art. II, Section 2.

82 For example, in Romania a law described as a pardon was passed in 1990 that dealt with politically motivated crimes committed between 30 December 1947 and 22 December 1989 (i.e., during the period of communist rule), but which excluded murder, severe bodily injury, rape, theft, prison escape, abuse of power contrary to the public interest, bribery, intercession, illegal arrest and abusive investigation, ill-treatment and unfair repression. Edwin Rekosh, "Romania: A Persistent Culture of Impunity", in Naomi Roht-Arriaza (ed.), *Impunity and Human Rights in International Law and Practice* (Oxford: OUP, 1995), at 134-5.

light of the probability that many of them would have been suffering from post-traumatic stress disorder brought on by their experience of trench warfare.[83]

Pardons of specific people are also issued for reasons closely tied to the political contingencies of a particular government, though they are usually publicly justified on different grounds, such as the need to restore the tranquillity of the nation.[84] In the United States, pardons in transitional contexts have sometimes been justified on the doctrine espoused in the 1926 case of *Biddle* v. *Perovich*, which recognised pardon as a tool for the public good. In that case, Justice Holmes stated that a pardon is not an act of grace, but a 'determination of the ultimate authority that the public welfare will be better served' by a pardon.[85] A number of highly controversial pardons have been issued by US Presidents, all prior to any trial or conviction. These include President Ford's pardon of Richard Nixon,[86] President George H.W. Bush's pardon of Casper Weinberger[87] and five other Reagan administration officials accused and/or convicted in connection with the Iran-Contra affair and President Clinton's pardon of convicted FALN terrorists and billionaire fugitive Marc Rich.[88]

Clemency programs also have a variety of purposes, particularly in the aftermath of war crimes trials. The American war crimes operation in occupied Germany had a clemency program, divided into two phases – the first from 1946 to 1951 and the second from 1951 to 1955. In the first phase, the clemency program was thought to serve as an 'educational device' in addition to the trials of Nazis themselves as part of the US effort to reform and re-educate the German people. The trials themselves were intended to demonstrate to the Germans the horrendous crimes Nazism had inflicted upon its victims. By contrast, the sentence review and

[83] Lucy Bannerman and David Sanderson, "Pardon at last for shell-shocked soldier shot for war cowardice", *Times Online*, 16 August 2006.

[84] For example, Ford's pardon of Nixon strongly reflected the language of Alexander Hamilton: A pardon 'may restore the tranquillity of the commonwealth … which, if suffered to pass unimproved, it may never be possible afterwards to recall.' Alexander Hamilton, "The Command of the Military and Naval Forces, and the Pardoning Power of the Executive", *The Federalist* (New York: Random House, 1937), at 481. Ford's proclamation reads, in part, 'It is believed that a trial of Richard Nixon, if it became necessary, could not fairly begin until a year or more has elapsed. In the meantime, the tranquillity to which this nation has been restored by the events of recent weeks could be irreparably lost by the prospects of bringing to trial a former President of the United States. The prospects of such a trial will cause prolonged and divisive debate over the propriety of exposing to further punishment and degradation a man who has already paid the unprecedented penalty of relinquishing the highest elective office in the United States.' Proclamation 4311, 39 *Fed. Reg.* 32601 (1974).

[85] *Biddle* v. *Perovich*, 274 US 480 (1926), 47 Sup. Ct. 665.

[86] *Murphy* v. *Ford*, 390 F. Suppl. 1372 (W.E. Mich. 1975) (upholding the pardon).

[87] "The Pardons: Text of President Bush's Statement on the Pardon of Weinberger and Others", *New York Times*, 24 December 1992, A22.

[88] Michael Powell, "Pardons with a Precedent: Marc Rich Drama is Latest in a Long Line of Last Acts", *Washington Post*, 26 February 2001, C1. Marc Rich, a fugitive, was pardoned of tax evasion, after clemency pleas from Israeli prime minister Ehud Barak, among others. According to Paul Volcker's independent investigation of Iraqi Oil-for-Food kickback schemes, Marc Rich was a middleman for several suspect Iraqi oil deals involving over 4 million barrels of oil.

clemency were meant to promote the 'superior values of democratic society, which entitled even the perpetrators of mass murder to fair treatment.'[89]

The second phase of the clemency program was much more utilitarian in motive. It was designed principally to end the war crimes program as quickly as possible without causing too much protest from Allied countries.[90] The perceived need for a German contribution to the defence of the West led to the view that a continuation of thc trials, which were highly unpopular among the German population, might harm this co-operation. Many Germans felt the trials implied the collective guilt of the German people. '*Schlußstrich ziehen*' (drawing the final line) became the motto of the post-war years, calling for complete discontinuity of the war crimes trials, culminating in the demand for a general amnesty for war criminals in the 1950s. On the other hand, the Americans had to consider how best to accommodate American public opinion, which favoured prosecution as well as conveying the impression that the integrity and the credibility of the war crimes program had been preserved and that the US had not traded the Landsberg prisoners for German rearmament. Thus occupation officials ruled out a general amnesty as well as any re-examination of the original verdicts and judgments.[91] Instead, it was agreed to set up a mixed Commission consisting of six members – three Germans and one from each major Allied government, which would act independently of the appointing government. The commission was established pursuant to Article 6 of the Convention on the Settlement of Matters Arising out of the War and the Occupation. The Article reserved the Allies the exclusive right to grant pardons.

The United States has also used presidential clemency as a means to shorten the sentence of convicted US servicemen for domestically unpopular war crimes trials. For instance, in the case concerning Lieutenant William Calley, a platoon leader accused of war crimes for the mass murder and rape of civilians in the village of My Lai in Vietnam during the war, President Nixon intervened personally to review the record and effectively ended Calley's sentence.[92] This intervention has been described as 'unquestionably a miscarriage of justice and one which will return to haunt the United States.'[93]

3.4 Legal rationales with regard to the use of pardons covering international crimes

Where pardons are issued prior to the prosecution and conviction of those accused of international crimes, the same legal rationales as for rejecting amnesties are per-

[89] Frank M. Buscher, *The U.S. War Crimes Trial Program in Germany, 1946-1955* (New York: Greenwood Press, 1989), at 69. Many US officials believed that Germany's perceived preference for militarism and authoritarianism over democracy and pluralism had greatly facilitated the commission of the international crimes committed during the war.

[90] *Ibid.*, at 69-70.

[91] *Ibid.*, at 162.

[92] 46 CMR 1131 (1973); *US* v. *Medina* (1971) 43 CMR 243.

[93] Howard Levie, *Terrorism in War: The Law of War Crimes* (New York: Oceana, 1992), at 207.

tinent, i.e., that an obligation to prosecute certain international crimes may prevent States from pardoning such offences prior to trial, that the fundamental rights of victims (to ensure rights, to provide an effective remedy, and to guarantee the right to truth) vitiate the possibility of pardons for international crimes,[94] and that the *jus cogens* nature of international crimes gives rise to obligations not to condone, authorise or absolve from responsibility a person accused of an international crime, which might rule out certain types of pardon. However, because a pardon is accompanied by an acceptance of guilt – even where there is no trial – it is unlikely that a pardon for international crimes could be held to violate a State's duty not to condone, authorise or absolve from responsibility a person accused of an international crime. Neither would a third State's recognising a pardon for international crimes amount to a failure to co-operate to bring to an end serious breaches of *jus cogens* norms, or recognising a situation created by the commission of the serious breach as lawful. In general, the arguments used to reject amnesties for international crimes are weaker when used in relation to pardons due to the fact that pardons satisfy to some degree the need for accountability and for truth in a way that amnesties – at least those of the amnesiac variety[95] – do not.

For those pardons issued subsequent to the conviction of a person accused of an international crime, different reasoning for rejecting such pardons becomes applicable. Because these pardons do not actually prevent the exercise of jurisdiction, but rather impact upon the proper consequences of conviction, the focus becomes the obligation of States 'to punish' a person convicted of such a crime. Such a rationale also takes into account the rights of victims to justice in the form of appropriate sentencing of the offender. Can a victim's right to justice really be said to be satisfied where the perpetrator is convicted as guilty but does not serve a sentence commensurate with the gravity of the crime? The application of an interests-analysis approach puts a different spin on this question. Instead of attempting to answer the question by analysing the normative scope of the concept of 'the right to justice,' one should ask how a victim's right to justice may be attained while ensuring that the decision on pardon does not ignore other valid policy considerations, such as the need to ease political tensions, the symbolic effect of an act of forgiveness

[94] In *Consuelo, et al.,* v. *Argentina*, Cases 10.147, 10.181, 10.240, 10.262, 10.309, 10.311 Report No. 28/92, IACtHR, OEA/Ser.L/V/II.83 Doc. 14, at 41 (1993), the Inter-American Commission of Human Rights held that the Presidential Decree of Pardon No. 1002, of October 7, 1989, which ordered that any proceedings against persons indicted for human rights violations who had not benefited from the earlier amnesty laws be discontinued, violated Art. XVIII (right to a fair trial) of the American Declaration of the Rights and Duties of Man and Arts. 1 (to ensure rights), 8 (right to fair trial) and 15 (right of assembly) of the American Convention on Human Rights.

[95] Professor Ronald Slye identifies 'amnesiac amnesties' as those blanket amnesties, typically granted by a regime that has been involved in human rights abuses, which are characterised by concealment and anonymity and provide little or no information about past crimes. Such amnesties are granted to certain groups and are not remedial, nor designed to further any sort of inquiry. Examples include the 1978 Chilean amnesty, the 1986 Argentinean Full Stop Law and the 1993 El Salvadorian amnesty. Slye, "The Legitimacy of Amnesties under International Law", at 239.

upon a divided community, and the utilitarian benefits which might attach to a conditional pardon that furthers the overall goal to secure and maintain the peace.

3.4.1 The scope of the obligation to punish those convicted of international crimes

Where jurisdiction over international crimes is exercised, there is also an obligation to punish a person convicted as guilty as a result of the prosecution. The manifest intent of both the Genocide Convention and the Torture Convention were to ensure that persons convicted of genocide or torture serve harsh sentences. States parties to the Genocide Convention are obliged to 'prevent and punish' acts of genocide and to legislate so that 'effective penalties for persons guilty of genocide' are ensured.[96] The Torture Convention similarly requires States parties to 'make these offences punishable by appropriate penalties which take into account their grave nature.'[97] In the view of the Torture Convention's drafters: 'In applying Article 4 … it seems reasonable to require that the punishment for torture should be close to the penalties applied to the most serious offenses under the domestic legal system.'[98] According to Scharf, 'this wording of the Torture Convention should not be construed to suggest the permissibility of amnesties or pardons.'[99] While an amnesty would seem to violate the obligation to prosecute those accused of such crimes, Scharf's conclusion may be slightly stretching the implications of the obligations to ensure effective penalties so as to rule out pardons. A penalty may still be 'effective' and 'appropriate' in the sense of achieving the goals of deterrence, stigmatisation and reprobation, without necessarily being harsh.[100] A policy of leniency would only appear to contradict the obligations under the Conventions where the overall goals to prevent and punish acts of genocide or torture is not intended to be achieved.

The question of the legality of pardon thus looks both to the sentence's preventive effect and to its reprobative effect. With regard to any preventive or deterrent effect of punishment, traditional criminological theory posits that the more severe and certain the penalty, the greater the deterrent effect,[101] suggesting that a policy of leniency would directly counter this goal. However, two arguments may be made in response to this contention. First, one may recall the significant doubts expressed in the previous chapter about the deterrent impact of criminal punishment of those found guilty of international crimes upon the future behaviour of

---

[96] Genocide Convention, Arts. 1 and 5, respectively.

[97] Convention against Torture, Art. 4(2).

[98] Herman J. Burgers & Hans Danelius, *The United Nations Convention Against Torture: A Handbook on the Convention against Torture and Other Cruel, Inhuman or Degrading Treatment or Punishment* (Dordrecht: Martinus Nijhoff, 1988), at 129.

[99] Michael P. Scharf, "Swapping Amnesty for Peace: Was there a duty to prosecute international crimes in Haiti?", 31(1) *Texas International Law Journal* 24 (1996).

[100] See the discussion on the objectives of punishment, *supra* section 3.3.

[101] Classical deterrence theory was first postulated by Beccaria and Bentham. See Henry N. Pontell, "Deterrence: Theory vs. Practice", 16(1) *Criminology* 3 (May 1978).

persons likely to commit similar crimes based on studies analysing the root causes of serious violations.[102] Even if deterrence theory may be empirically proven to work in the penal systems of States during periods of relative peace – something that is still contested[103] – there are no empirical studies showing its effect in periods of war or internal strife when most international crimes are committed. Second, the obligation 'to prevent' international crimes from occurring may be interpreted not merely in the narrow sense of locking away known torturers or genocidaires, or even in the broader sense of deterrence theory, but also in the sense that States should strive to create the politico-social conditions likely to minimise the occurrence of such crimes in the future. While criminal prosecution of alleged perpetrators undoubtedly forms part of this enterprise, a policy of leniency might be equally valid and effective to the overall goal. With regard to the retributive effect of punishment, the victim's perspective is surely the most important of the factors to be taken into account.[104] This does not necessarily entail a subjective reading of each individual victim's particular feelings – whether antagonistic or empathetic – towards the perpetrator, but makes reference to the communal values shared by victims, most notably the desire for the truth, the need for the public acknowledgment of suffering, and the requirement of reparation. If these are satisfied, one may reasonably argue that a policy of leniency would not be incompatible with the obligation to punish offenders.

The grave breaches regime set up under the Geneva Conventions of 1949 only refers to the obligation of States parties to search for and bring persons alleged to have committed grave breaches to their own courts (or otherwise to extradite).[105] It does not mention an obligation 'to punish' those found guilty. Logic dictates that the obligation to search for and prosecute those accused of grave breaches implies the requirement to mete out due punishment following a conviction, however there is nothing in the wording of the GCs to suggest that pardons must always be ruled out. The official ICRC Commentary to the Geneva Conventions does not comment on the issue of pardons for grave breaches, although it makes clear that the objective of the grave breaches regime is to ensure 'the universality of punishment,'[106] which suggests that a pardon would negate the main purpose of the grave breaches system. With regard to crimes against humanity and other serious violations of IHL, the preamble of the Convention on the Non-Applicability of Statutory Limitations to War Crimes and Crimes Against Humanity notes that 'effective punishment of war crimes and crimes against humanity is an important element in the prevention

---

[102] Daniel Muñoz-Rojas and Jean-Jacques Frésard, ICRC, *The Roots of Behaviour in War: Understanding and Preventing IHL Violations* (Geneva: ICRC, October 2004), at 6-10.

[103] Pontell, *supra* n. 101, at 4 (expressing doubt as to whether studies on deterrence really prove the theory works because of the myriad factors that impact upon a person's decision to commit a crime, including unemployment, drug abuse, social class, and others).

[104] See Tatjana Hörnle, "Distribution of Punishment: The Role of a Victim's Perspective", 3 *Buffalo Criminal Law Review* 175 (1999-2000).

[105] GC I, Art. 49; GC II, Art. 50; GC III, Art. 129; GC IV, Art. 146.

[106] Jean S. Pictet, *Commentary to IV Geneva Convention Relative to the Protection of Civilian Persons in Time of War* (Geneva: ICRC, 1958), at 587.

of such crimes [and] the protection of human rights and fundamental freedoms …' Moreover, the obligation of States parties to abrogate legislative or other limitations apply to both to the prosecution and punishment of such crimes.[107] A pardon would arguably constitute a limitation to the punishment of such crimes.[108] The GA's Principles of International Co-operation in the Detection, Arrest, Extradition and Punishment of Persons guilty of War Crimes and Crimes against Humanity maintain that war crimes and crimes against humanity shall not only be subject to investigation and the persons against whom there is evidence that they have committed such crimes subject to tracing, arrest and trial, but also, if found guilty, 'shall be subject' to punishment.[109]

The general principle of punishment for international crimes is set out in Article 3 of the ILC's Draft Code of Crimes Against the Peace and Security of Mankind of 1996, which provides that: 'An individual who is responsible for a crime against the peace and security of mankind shall be liable to punishment. The punishment shall be commensurate with the character and gravity of the crime.'[110] The imperative character of the words 'punishment shall be commensurate' suggests that pardons would not be compatible with this principle. However, the Draft Code is not a binding legal instrument and cannot be taken to be evidence *per se* of a general rule of customary law precluding the use of pardons for international crimes. Nonetheless it seems clear that there is a general obligation to punish those found guilty of international crimes. However, the question is whether a pardon is always incompatible with the need to punish. According to Grotius, the essential objective of sentencing is 'Equality between the Offence and the Punishment'[111] which would appear to articulate the same principle as stated by the ILC. However, this does not necessarily rule out pardons in Grotius' view:

> '… [I]t doth not follow from hence, that he must necessarily be punished. Nor is it true, for both GOD and Men do pardon many Offenders, many Offences, and are commonly praised for it. For as Plato first, and after him Seneca, well observed, No wise Man punishes an Offender, because he hath offended, but that he may not offend again. For what is once done cannot be recalled, but what is to come may be prevented. Therefore all Punishments have regard to the future, and he that punisheth should not be angry, but provident.'[112]

[107] Convention on the Non-Applicability of Statutory Limitations to War Crimes and Crimes Against Humanity, Art. IV. States are also obliged to assist each other in punishing convicted criminals. See Principle 4.

[108] This is probably stretching the meaning of 'limitation' as used under the Convention, the main purpose of which was designed to counter the effects of *temporal* limitations on the prosecution of those accused of war crimes and crimes against humanity, not limitations of any sort.

[109] GA Res. 3074 (XXVIII) of 3 December 1973, Principle 1.

[110] Draft Code of Crimes Against the Peace and Security of Mankind, adopted by the ILC at its forty-eighth session in 1996, *Yearbook of the International Law Commission 1996*, Vol. II (Part Two).

[111] Grotius, *The Rights of War and Peace*, Book II, Ch. XX, at 951.

[112] *Ibid.*, at 956.

Apart from the need to prevent further crimes, Grotius also recognised that punishment related to both to the need to rehabilitate the offender and the needs of the victim.[113] He was concerned that punishment should only be done for the purposes of achieving the objective of punishment, that of setting an example.[114] He criticised the argument of the Stoicks that 'Pardon … is the Remission of a Punishment that is due, but a wise Man will always do what he ought to do' on the basis that a wise man is not 'indispensably obliged' to exact punishment, but is permitted only.[115] It follows from this that punishment is not absolutely required, and need only be instituted if required to satisfy moral needs and its other objectives.[116] Other philosophers have struggled with the acceptable parameters of pardon, however, rarely have pardons been ruled out completely. Even Jeremy Bentham, who felt that from 'pardon power unrestricted, comes impunity to delinquency in all shapes: from impunity to delinquency in all shapes: from impunity to maleficence in all shapes, dissolution of government: from dissolution of government, dissolution of political society,' noted that, in line with the 'principle of utility,'[117] punishment should not be exacted (1) where it would be inefficacious; (2) where it would be groundless; (3) where it is needless; and (4) where it is too expensive.[118] Kant, who recognised that '[t]he right to pardon a criminal, either by mitigating or by entirely remitting the punishment, is certainly one of the most slippery of

[113] '… Punishment may have Regard either to the Good of the Offender, or of him who suffers by the Offence, or of any Persons indiscriminately.' *Ibid.*, at 963.

[114] 'To prevent the injured Persons being injured by others, all Kinds of Punishments are not to be inflicted, but only such as are open and publick, which appertains to that End of Punishment, that is for Example.' *Ibid.*

[115] 'It remains now that we enquire, whether we may not sometimes forgive or pardon Offences. For the Stoicks deny it … but their argument is very weak. *Pardon*, say they, *is the Remission of a Punishment that is due, but a wise Man will always do what he ought to do*. Here the Fallacy lies in the Word *due*. For if by *due* be meant, that he, who has offended, deserves to be punished, that is, may be punished without Injustice, it will not follow from hence, that he, who forbears to punish him, does what he ought not to do. But if it be meant, that Punishment is in such a Manner due from a wise Man, that he is indispensably obliged to exact it, we say, that that doth not always happen, and therefore this Sense Punishment is not always due, but permitted only. And that may be true, as well before the penal Law as afterwards.' *Ibid.*, at 996.

[116] 'But it does not follow from hence, that Punishment must needs be exacted; because this depends upon the Connection of the Ends, for which Punishment was instituted, with the Punishment itself. Wherefore if those Ends be not in a Moral sense necessary, or if quite contrary Ends do occur no less Profitable or Necessary, or the Ends proposed by Punishment can be obtained another Way, then it plainly appears, that there is nothing, which can strictly oblige us to exact Punishment.' *Ibid.*

[117] 'By the principle of utility is meant that principle which approves or disapproves of every action whatsoever, according to the tendency which it appears to have to augment or diminish the happiness of the party whose interest is in question … A measure of government … may be said to be conformable to … the principle of utility, when in like manner the tendency which it has to augment the happiness of the community is greater than any which it has to diminish it.' Jeremy Bentham, *The Principles of Morals and Legislation* (Darien, Conn.: Hafner Publishing Company, 1948), at 2-3.

[118] *Ibid.*, at 171-177.

all the rights of the sovereign'[119] and who viewed punishment as a 'categorical imperative,'[120] nonetheless excused pardon 'in case of necessity.'[121]

In order to weigh the competing interests of punishment and pardon, it is necessary to also identify the key purposes of punishment for international crimes. The jurisprudence of the ICTY suggests that retribution and deterrence are the main guiding principles in sentencing for international crimes.[122] Interestingly, the current Prosecutor of the ICC, Luis Moreno Ocampo, commenting in 1999 upon the lessons learned from prosecuting military officials accused of kidnapping, torture and murder in Argentina, expressed his belief that 'mere retribution is not productive' and that 'information revealed about past crimes in public trials may be as important as the punishment.'[123] Reprobation and stigmatisation have also been considered among the main purposes of sentencing.[124] In addition, a Trial Chamber of the ICTY was guided in its determination of the sentence by the principle proclaimed by Cesare Beccaria in 1764 that 'punishment should not be harsh, but must be inevitable.'[125] On this basis, the Trial Chamber asserted that '[i]t is the infallibility of punishment, rather than the severity of the sanction, which is the tool for retribution, stigmatisation and deterrence. This is particularly the case for the international tribunal; penalties are made more onerous by its international stature, moral authority and impact upon world public opinion, and this punitive effect must be borne in mind when assessing the suitable length of sentence.'[126] This statement suggests that a pardon for an international crime can never be a given because this would create an impression that punishment is not inevitable. Howe-

119 Immanuel Kant, *The Metaphysical Elements of Justice* (NewYork: Bobbs-Merrill, 1965), at 107-108.

120 'The law concerning punishment is a categorical imperative, and woe to him who rummages around in the winding paths of a theory of happiness looking for some advantage to be gained by releasing the criminal from punishment or by reducing the amount of it …' *Ibid.*, at 100.

121 He noted that if murder was committed by an enormous number of people, then, 'the state would soon approach the condition of having no more subjects if it were to rid itself of these criminals, and this would lead to its dissolution and a return to the state of nature … Since a sovereign will want to avoid such consequences and, above all, will want to avoid adversely affecting the feelings of the people by the spectacle of such butchery, he must have it within his power in case of necessity … to assume the role of judge and to pronounce a judgment that, instead of imposing the death penalty on the criminals, assigns some other punishment that will make the preservation of the mass of the people possible, such as, for example, deportation.' *Ibid.*, at 337.

122 *Delalić and others* (*Čelebići* case), ICTY Appeals Chamber, Judgment of 20 February 2001, Case No. IT-96-21-A, para. 806; *Aleksovski*, ICTY, Appeals Chamber, Judgment of 24 March 2000, Case No. IT-95-14/1-A, para. 185; *Furundžija*, ICTY, Trial Chamber II, Judgment of 10 December 1998, Case No. IT-95-17/1-T; 39 *ILM* (1999), para. 288.

123 Moreno Ocampo, "Beyond Punishment", at 600-601.

124 *Erdemović (sentencing judgment),* ICTY, Trial Chamber I, Judgment of 29 November 1996, Case No. IT-96-22-T, para. 65; *Furundžija*, ICTY, Trial Chamber II, Judgment of 10 December 1998, Case No. IT-95-17/1-T; 39 *ILM* (1999), para. 289; *Blaškić,* ICTY, Trial Chamber I, Judgment of 3 March 2000, Case No. IT-95-14-T, para. 763-4.

125 Cesare Beccaria, *An Essay on Crimes and Punishments* (1775), reprinted (Brookline Village, MA: Brandon Press Inc., 1983).

126 *Furundžija*, ICTY, Trial Chamber II, Judgment of 10 December 1998, Case No. IT-95-17/1-T; 39 *ILM* (1999), at 290.

ver, given the particular stigma that attaches to such crimes, particularly when judged by an international tribunal, a reduced sentence would not necessarily be inconsistent with the notion of just punishment.

There are few cases at the national or international level which have dealt with the legality of pardons for international crimes. The Argentine pardons are the exception to this generality. The Inter-American Commission on Human Rights issued a decision in 1992 with regard to the Presidential Decree of Pardon No. 1002, of 7 October 1989, which ordered that any proceedings against persons indicted for human right violations who had not benefited from the two amnesty laws of 1986 and 1987 to be discontinued. The Commission found that the Decree (as well as the two amnesty laws) was incompatible with Article XVIII (right to fair trial) of the American Declaration of the Rights and Duties of Man and Articles 1 (obligation to ensure and respect rights), 8 (right to fair trial), and 15 (right to judicial protection) of the ACHR.[127] The Commission relied in part on the holding of the Inter-American Court of Human Rights in the *Velásquez Rodriguez* case that '[a]s a consequence of this obligation [in Article 1.1], the States must prevent, investigate and *punish* any violation of the rights recognized by the Commission ...'[128] The Commission pays particular attention to the statements that 'The State has a legal duty to ... identify those responsible, to impose the *appropriate punishment* ...'[129] and '... If the State apparatus acts in such a way that the *violation goes unpunished* and the victim's full enjoyment of such rights is not restored as soon as possible, the State has failed to comply with its duty to ensure the free and full exercise of those rights to the persons within its jurisdiction.'[130] However, the *Velásquez Rodriguez* case dealt with a situation involving an unresolved disappearance of a student in which the Honduran authorities had done nothing to investigate the incident or find the culprits. Decree No. 1002 prevented the continuation of criminal proceedings and any possible convictions and therefore was similar to the *Velásquez Rodriguez* case in that such actions arguably violated the implied duty to prosecute those accused of serious human rights crimes by reason of the obligation to ensure protected rights. The pardon may thus be distinguished from subsequent Decree 2741 issued on 29 December 1990, which granted freedom to those military officers who had already been convicted and were imprisoned. One could argue that the latter pardon did not impugn protected rights under the ACHR, including the implied duty to investigate and punish those accused of serious violations because investigations had been carried out, those arrested had been subjected to a criminal trial and those found guilty sentenced for appropriate periods of imprisonment (even if these sentences were not fully carried out). In 2004,

---

[127] Report No. 28/92 (Argentina), Cases 10.147, 10.181, 10.240, 10.262, 10.309, 10.311, 82nd Sess., OEA/ser.L/V/II.82, Doc. 24 (2 October 1992).

[128] *Velàsquez Rodriguez*, IACtHR (ser. C) No. 4 (1988), para. 166. [Emphasis added]

[129] *Ibid.*, at para. 174. [Emphasis added]

[130] *Ibid.*, at para. 176. [Emphasis added]

the Argentine Supreme Court found that the pardons issued by President Menem exempting senior officers from trial were unconstitutional.[131]

However, the validity of Decree 2741 has recently come under the scrutiny of Argentinean courts. On 5 September 2006, in a case concerning charges against Jorge Raphael Videla, an Argentine judge declared that the Presidential pardon issued in 1990 was unconstitutional and invalid.[132] The previous day, the same judge had also declared invalid thc 1989 pardon of former economy minister Jose Alfredo Martinez de Hoz and former interior minister Albano Harguindeguy in connection with an investigation of two dictatorship-era abductions. The case follows closely in the footsteps of the Supreme Court's 2005 ruling that the Full Stop Law and the Due Obedience Law were unconstitutional and had no legal effect.[133] Under the Argentine Constitution, as reformed in 1994, a number of international conventions are given constitutional hierarchy, including the Genocide Convention, the Torture Convention, the ICCPR and the ACHR.[134] These conventions do not repeal any section of the First Part of the Constitution (setting out basic rights and guarantees of Argentine citizens) and are to be understood as complementing the rights and guarantees contained therein.[135] The power of the Executive to grant pardons 'for crimes subject to federal jurisdiction, after the report of the corresponding court' is contained in Section 95(5) of the Constitution.[136] It would appear that the Court interpreted the Constitution as barring any executive pardon over the crimes set out under the international conventions or where such a pardon would violate victims' rights guaranteed under the treaties.

As noted earlier, in May 2006 the Constitutional Court of Colombia upheld the constitutionality of the 'Law on Justice of Peace' which offers reduced sentences to those members of illegal armed groups found guilty of serious human rights violations in exchange for their full disclosure of their knowledge of the perpetration of international crimes by themselves or by their cohorts. The Constitutional Court held that those reduced sentences must be 'effective sanctions … that do not cover up phenomena of impunity, in the sense that they constitute just and adequate state reactions to the crimes perpetrated.'[137] It would seem that for the Court, so long as victims' rights to truth, justice and reparations were ensured to a minimal degree, a reduced sentence could be justified.

---

131 *Suarez Mason*, P Inst. [Sup. Const.] L.L. 4 (2004).

132 Deborah Rey, "Another Setback for Ex-Junta Chief", *AP*, 6 September 2006, available at: <http://www.boston.com/news/world/latinamerica/articles/2006/09/06/another_legal_setback_for_ex_junta_chief/?p1=MEWell_Pos5>.

133 *Simón, Julio Héctor y otros s/privación ilegítima de la libertad*, Argentina, Case S. 1767. XXXVIII (14 June 2005).

134 Section 75(22) Constitution of Argentina 1994.

135 For a thorough discussion on how international law is incorporated in Argentinean law, see Rodolfo Mattarollo, "Recent Argentine Jurisprudence in the Matter of Crimes Against Humanity", 62-63 *The Review: International Commission of Jurists* (September 2001), at 11.

136 The only exception to the power of pardon is cases of impeachment by the House of Deputies.

137 See Court Decision No. C-370/2006, section 6.2.3.3.4.3.

The pardon issued to Foday Sankoh in the Lomé Accord undoubtedly would have become the subject of a defence submission regarding the legitimacy of the SCSL to exercise its jurisdiction over Sankoh had the case gone to trial.[138] Interestingly, the Statute of the SCSL only explicitly rejects 'amnesty' in respect of international crimes in the jurisdiction of the Court as a bar to prosecution.[139] The only mention of pardon is in Article 23, which obliges States in which convicted persons are imprisoned to notify the Tribunal if the person qualifies for pardon or commutation of sentence and provides that any decision about pardon shall be made by the judges of the Special Court. This is somewhat surprising drafting considering that Sankoh was a prime target of the Court and, according to the terms of the Lomé Accord, he was specifically given an 'absolute and free pardon,' separate from the pardon provided to all combatants and collaborators and from the amnesty accorded to members of the rebel groups under the Accord.[140] It is true that this 'pardon' is more properly characterised as an amnesty due to the fact that no guilt was ascribed to Sankoh in his signing of the Accord, which is generally the case for pardons issued prior to trial. However, it might have been prudent for the Statute to explicitly state that pardons issued in respect of international crimes would be no bar to the jurisdiction of the Court.

Had Ieng Sary been indicted for genocide before the Extraordinary Chambers in Cambodia, it is likely that the legality of the royal pardon of Ieng Sary for the crime of genocide would have been raised in the proceedings brought against him. Given that the Chambers have the right to review the scope of the pardon,[141] it would appear that the Law at least contemplates the possibility that the pardon could be revoked. No doubt an abuse of process complaint could have been lodged by Sary against the Chambers ruling in this way given that his defection in 1996 was tied to the belief that he would not be punished in relation to the 1979 conviction for genocide. While this doctrine was dismissed by the SCSL in the *Kallon and Kamara* case concerning the Lomé amnesty due to the fact that the Court, as an international criminal court, was 'not tainted' by any undertakings made by the

[138] Sankoh was indicted by the Court on 7 March 2003, but died while in custody awaiting trial on 8 December 2003.

[139] SCSL Statute, Art. 10.

[140] Art. IX of the Lome Accord provided: '1. In order to bring lasting peace to Sierra Leone, the Government of Sierra Leone shall take appropriate legal steps to grant Corporal Foday Sankoh absolute and free pardon. 2. After the signing of the present Agreement, the Government of Sierra Leone shall also grant absolute and free pardon and reprieve to all combatants and collaborators in respect of anything done by them in pursuit of their objectives, up to the time of the signing of the present Agreement. 3. To consolidate the peace and promote the cause of national reconciliation, the Government of Sierra Leone shall ensure that no official or judicial action is taken against any member of the RUF/SL, ex-AFRC, ex-SLA or CDF in respect of anything done by them in pursuit of their objectives as members of those organisations, since March 1991, up to the time of the signing of the present Agreement. In addition, legislative and other measures necessary to guarantee immunity to former combatants, exiles and other persons, currently outside the country for reasons related to the armed conflict shall be adopted ensuring the full exercise of their civil and political rights, with a view to their reintegration within a framework of full legality.'

[141] Law Establishing ECCC, as amended, Art. 40 new.

Sierra Leone government and because the 'crystallising norm' that amnesties for international crimes are illegal reduced the strength of an abuse of process claim,[142] the same arguments could not be made in relation to the Extraordinary Chambers. These Chambers are part of the Cambodian judicial system, and the jurisdiction is clearly based on territoriality, notwithstanding the fact that international crimes form part of the subject matter. Thus, the pardon issued to Ieng Sary would normally be binding upon the judicial organs of Cambodia. Moreover, there is no clear rule that pardons for acts of genocide are invalid under general international law[143] (though a textual argument based on the Genocide Convention can certainly be made) and hence Sary could reasonably have expected to rely on the promise of non-punishment in return for his defection. In any case, the issue is now moot since the Indictment against Sary omitted any charges of genocide, possibly to avoid precisely these types of legal problems.

3.4.2 The possibility of pardons or commutation of sentence by international criminal courts

As noted, the ICTR and ICTY Statutes, as well as the Statute of the SCSL, all of which provide international jurisdiction over the most serious crimes in the international legal order, contemplate the possibility of pardons or commutation of sentence.[144] This may well be an indicator in itself that pardons for international crimes are legally permissible. By contrast, pardons issued under the Nazi regime were explicitly rejected as a jurisdictional bar in Allied Control Council Law No. 10,[145] although the clemency program instituted in the aftermath of the trials in the American sector suggest that a form of pardon decided upon by the Allies was acceptable.[146] Under the Law establishing the Extraordinary Chambers in Cambodia, the Government has undertaken not to pardon anyone subject to the international crimes under the Chambers' jurisdiction and those pardons issued in the past for such crimes may be subject to judicial review by the Chambers.[147]

---

[142] *Kallon and Kamara*, Decision on Amnesty case, para. 84.

[143] State practice and *opinio juris* on the matter are scarce and contrary. While the Genocide Convention, the obligations of which are *erga omnes*, could be construed as rejecting pardons for genocide, the text of the Convention is not decisive on this point. Moreover, the practice of States showing leniency to those accused of acts of genocide, such as in the case of the American clemency program in Germany post WW II which indicates that States do not consider pardons completely incompatible with the terms of the Genocide Convention.

[144] ICTY Statute, Art. 28, ICTR Statute, Art. 27, SCSL Statute, Art. 23.

[145] Allied Control Council Law No. 10, Art. II(5): 'In any trial or prosecution for a crime herein referred to, the accused shall not be entitled to the benefits of any statute of limitation in respect to the period from 30 January 1933 to 1 July 1945, nor shall any immunity, pardon or amnesty granted under the Nazi regime be admitted as a bar to trial or punishment.'

[146] See the discussion of the American War Crimes Clemency program, *supra* notes 89-91 and accompanying text.

[147] Law on the Establishment of the Extraordinary Chambers in the Court of Cambodia for the Prosecution of Crimes Committed During the Period of Democratic Kampuchea, with inclusion of amendments as promulgated on 27 October 2004 (NS/RKM/1004/006), Chapter XII, Art. 40 new.

The ICC Statute, for its part, does not explicitly deal with pardons, but it does strictly regulate sentence reduction for those convicted by the Court, which implies that national pardons of State parties may not be applied to ICC-convicted prisoners. Under the Statute, States parties are bound by the sentence proscribed by the Court and the State where the convicted person serves his sentence is not allowed to reduce or change the penalty or release the person before expiry of the sentence pronounced by the ICC.[148] Only the ICC can decide upon a change in sentence.[149] The Court is required to review a sentence once two thirds of it has been carried out (or 25 years of a life sentence), though this would not preclude the Court reviewing a sentence before this time. The sentence may be reduced only if one or more of three factors are present: (a) the person has shown an early willingness to co-operate with the Court in its investigations and prosecutions; (2) the person has voluntarily assisted the Court in enabling the enforcement of judgment in other cases, in particular by locating assets subject to orders of fine, forfeiture or reparation which may be used for the benefit of victims; and (3) where there has been a clear and significant change of circumstances sufficient to justify the reduction of sentence, as provided in the RPE.[150] Rule 223 of the ICC RPE sets out the criteria for review concerning reduction of sentence, which provide additional factors that the ICC is required to take into account in deciding whether a sentence should be reviewed:

(a) The conduct of the sentenced person while in detention, which shows a genuine dissociation from his or her crime;
(b) The prospect of the re-socialisation and successful resettlement of the sentenced person;
(c) Whether the early release of the sentenced person would give rise to significant social instability;
(d) Any significant action taken by the sentenced person for the benefit of the victims as well as any impact on the victims and their families as a result of the early release;
(e) Individual circumstances of the sentenced person, including a worsening state of physical or mental health or advanced age.

It is unlikely that a State party where a sentenced person is residing could claim that its right to pardon lies unaffected by the Rome Statute in light of the binding nature of the ICC sentence.[151] With regard to the ICTY and ICTR, the power of States to pardon the crimes in the jurisdiction of the respective Statutes is subject to the determination of its appropriateness by the *ad hoc* Tribunals. Article 28 of the ICTY Statute and Article 27 of the ICTR Statute provide that:

---

[148] ICC Statute, Art. 110(1) and (2).

[149] ICC Statute, Art. 105(1).

[150] ICC Statute, Art. 110(3) and (4).

[151] A State may not rely on the provisions of its internal law, even constitutional law, as justification for failure to comply with its obligations under international law. See Art. 32 ILC Draft Articles on State Responsibility.

> 'If, pursuant to the applicable law of the State in which the convicted person is imprisoned, he or she is eligible for parole or commutation of sentence, the State concerned shall notify the International Tribunal accordingly. The President of the Tribunal, in consultation with the judges, shall decide the matter on the basis of the interests of justice and the general principles of law.'

The procedure and principles governing this possibility are governed by Rules 124-126 of the ICTR RPE and Rules 123-125 of the ICTY RPE, which are identical in content. They provide that if a person becomes eligible for pardon in the country in which they are imprisoned, the State shall notify the Tribunal. It is up to the President of the Tribunal, in consultation with the members of the Bureau and any permanent judges of the sentencing Chamber who remain judges of the Tribunal, to determine if a pardon or commutation of sentence would be appropriate. The General Standards for Granting Pardons or Commutation are set out in Rule 126, which provides that:

> 'In determining whether pardon or commutation of sentence is appropriate, the President shall take into account, *inter alia*, the gravity of the crime or crimes for which the prisoner was convicted, the treatment of similarly-situated prisoners, the prisoner's demonstration of rehabilitation, as well as any substantial cooperation of the prisoner with the Prosecutor.'

Although these standards are fairly consistent with principles governing pardons at the national level, they take on a new significance in the light of the crimes at issue before the *ad hoc* ICTs and are therefore important in identifying the parameters of a legitimate pardon for an international crime.

First, the fact that the gravity of the crime need be taken into account signifies that it is possible that some forms of liability could be considered more forgivable than others, depending on the circumstances of a case.[152] The standard of 'treatment of similarly-situated prisoners' ensures that like crimes are treated alike, gives guidance as to the acceptability of giving pardons for certain crimes, and protects against arbitrariness, particularly on the basis of discrimination. In the case of the ICTR, the fact that 'similarly-situated prisoners' convicted in Rwanda may have received the death penalty would weigh heavily against any pardon.[153]

---

[152] For instance, while the direct perpetration of, or ordering to be committed, an international crime (e.g. murder or rape as a war crime) might be considered to be of such gravity as to be unpardonable, it is possible that participating in a common criminal design, where such crimes had not been expressly agreed upon but were foreseeable as a risk, might be considered more pardonable in some circumstances. See *Tadić*, ICTY, Appeals Chamber, Judgment of 15 July 1999, Case No. IT-94-1-A, para. 228.

[153] The fact that the most severe punishment that may be imposed by the ICTR is life imprisonment has been the source of some ire in Rwanda where serious crimes warranted the death penalty under the criminal code. Prior to August 2007, when Rwanda abolished the death penalty, this led to the unfortunate result that those convicted by the ICTR (i.e., those considered most responsible) received life sentences or less for their participation in the genocide while those convicted by Rwandan courts (i.e., those less responsible) got the death penalty.

The third consideration of whether the person has demonstrated any rehabilitation suggests that the purpose of punishment of war criminals is not merely retribution, but also to rehabilitate offenders. An ICTY Trial Chamber in *Furundžija* stated that none of the various purposes of punishment such as retribution, deterrence, and stigmatisation was to detract 'from the Trial Chamber's support for rehabilitative programmes in which the accused may participate while serving his sentence; the Trial Chamber is especially mindful of the age of the accused in this case.'[154] Such considerations arguably would have particular significance for those offenders who have been indoctrinated into committing atrocities through harmful propaganda, dehumanising experiences and military pressure. It would seem less relevant for those leaders who have orchestrated the perpetuation of mass crimes. The ICC RPE directs the Court to consider whether a prisoner has demonstrated a 'genuine dissociation from his or her crime,' which has a rehabilitative element to it. The latter also puts emphasis on any action the prisoner has taken for the benefit of the victims, which might also be a sign of rehabilitation.

Finally, the consideration of how co-operative the prisoner has been with the Prosecutor suggests that those persons who contribute to ongoing investigations into atrocities may benefit from a pardon. Such a consideration can be justified on two levels. First, such a possibility is clearly a useful bargaining tool to induce prisoners to supply more information about past events which would help to illuminate the truth about what happened and would also broaden accountability. Second, a prisoner can demonstrate that he or she has renounced past affiliations with groups which committed human rights crimes. The degree of co-operation of the prisoner with investigations or prosecutions figures prominently in the factors to be taken into account by the ICC in sentence review. In addition, any contribution the prisoner makes to help the ICC enforce the sentence in *other* judgments is also to be taken into account – a factor justified by utilitarian objectives, but also to help bring reparation to victims and to break any continuing group loyalties of the prisoner.

Unlike the ICC RPE, the RPEs of the ICTY and ICTR do not require that the judges take into account the effect of the early release of the prisoner upon the victim or victim's family. Although the ICTR is required to notify the Government of Rwanda when it has been alerted about a possible pardon for a convicted person, there does not appear to be any obligation to take the Governments' or the victims' views into account when deciding upon the appropriateness of the pardon.[155] This difference is probably because the ICC Statute is generally more cognisant of victims' rights than is the case for the ICTY and ICTR. The wording of the Rule in the ICC RPE seems to indicate that the Court should consider any *negative* or *positive* impact the early release might have on the victim (i.e., whether they are likely to suffer harm or mental anguish or, conversely, a feeling of closure). It does

---

[154] *Furundžija*, ICTY, Trial Chamber II, Judgment of 10 December 1998, Case No. IT-95-17/1-T; 39 *ILM* (1999), para. 291.

[155] ICTR RPE Rule 125. The ICTY RPE does not contain the same obligation to notify a particular government before making a decision about pardon.

not appear to suggest that a victim's right to justice might be violated by a sentence reduction or pardon.

Another factor to be taken into account by the ICC, but not mentioned in the RPE of the *ad hoc* Tribunals is whether the early release of the sentenced person would provoke significant social instability. This factor would seem to be concerned with preventing the outbreak of social violence by the release of a convicted person. However, by using the word 'instability,' it would appear that the Court is not meant to consider if the issuing of a pardon or commutation of sentence might contribute positively to 'stability.' Such an interpretation would rule out, for example, those uses of pardon in Argentina and Cambodia which were used to quell social instability caused by the trials of military officers in the former case, and ongoing hostilities with the Khmer Rouge in the latter case. However, concerns to stabilise a society could possibly be considered by the Court if an early release of a sentenced person was deemed likely to have a positive and stabilising impact upon victims and their families.[156]

3.4.3 Clemency by way of the guilty plea

Another means of clemency for those accused of international crimes is through the operation of a guilty plea, in return for a reduced sentence or a change or reduction in charges. Despite an initial reluctance to enter into this type of arrangement, given the nature of the crimes under their mandates, the *ad hoc* international criminal tribunals have gradually come to accept the use of plea bargaining as a means to make international criminal processes more efficient.[157] This began with sentence bargaining, but has now come to include charge bargaining.[158] While the need for efficiency in the work of the ICTs was the original motivation behind the move to institute guilty pleas, the conditions attaching to a guilty plea may be an important means of attuning the criminal justice system to the wider goals of the international public order. For instance, a guilty plea may be important for establishing the truth because it removes the source of conflict over responsibility and evidence and provides an incentive to defendants to provide information that may otherwise remain unknown. The best example of this is the plea agreement of Momir Nikolić before the ICTY. In his Statement of Facts and Acceptance of Responsibility attached to the plea agreement, Nikolić stated that the executions of thousands of Muslim men and boys at Srebrenica were planned and known about at the highest levels in the Bosnian Serb Army (VRS), thereby countering the deni-

[156] See ICC RPE, Rule 223(d). If victims or victim groups have suffered discrimination or violence as a result of ICC prosecutions and convictions of perpetrators, it might be that early release of some perpetrators would satisfy those in society who were opposed to such trials and the victims would cease being harassed. Another possibility would be if the release of the convicted person meant that reconciliation between groups had more likelihood of success. This would also impact positively upon the victims.

[157] On 12 July 2001, the ICTY and ICTR added Rule 62*ter* of the Rules of Procedure and Evidence, which sets forth the procedure for accepting a plea arrangement.

[158] Sentencing Judgment, *Plavšić* (IT-00-39&40/1-S), Trial Chamber III, 27 February 2003.

als that has been issued regarding responsibility at the individual and State level for the massacre.[159]

The Trial Chamber is not, however, bound to accept any plea agreement[160] and in practice before the ICTR, besides pleading guilty, the suspect has to explain the reasons for his voluntary participation in genocide and express contrition, regret, or sympathy for the victims in Rwanda. For this reason, although Kambanda entered a guilty plea, he was still subjected to the highest sentence allowed because he did not express contrition, regret or sympathy to the victims of the Rwandan genocide 'even when given the opportunity to do so by the Chamber, during the hearing of 3 September 1998.'[161] By contrast, in the case of *Serushago*, the Tribunal held that 'having reviewed all the circumstances of the case, the Trial Chamber is of the opinion that exceptional circumstances in mitigation surrounding the crimes committed by Omar Serushago may afford him some clemency.'[162] One of the most significant of these circumstances was that 'during the pre-sentencing hearing, Omar Serushago expressed his remorse at length and openly. He asked for forgiveness from the victims of his crimes and the entire people of Rwanda. In addition to this act of contrition, he appealed for national reconciliation in Rwanda.'[163]

It is possible that 'charge bargaining,' where more serious charges are dropped in return for a defendant's guilty plea, also has the potential to distort the historical record. In this sense, one could well ask whether charge bargaining is compatible with the right to the truth of society and of victims. In the case of *Plavšić* at the ICTY, the accused admitted the facts supporting the charge in a five-page document appended to the plea agreement, which may serve to develop a generally accepted historical record. But Plavšić only had to admit to facts relevant to the

[159] As Assistant Commander for Security and Intelligence of the Bratunac Brigade of the VRS, Nikolić was ordered to co-ordinate and supervise 'the transportation of the women and children to Kladanj and the separation and detention of able-bodied Muslim men,' which he did. He was asked to help identify sites for detention where the men and boys were to be detained pending their execution. Nikolić passed this information on to his commander and co-accused, Vidoje Blagojevic, who appeared to be 'fully informed of the transportation and killing operation.' He also admits his involvement in exhumation of mass graves and reburial – and names those who ordered him to do it. In addition, he relates the intentional destruction of compromising evidence by officers of the VRS Drina Corps, as well as meetings with VRS officers and a visit from the State Security Service to encourage his silence after he was summoned for questioning by the ICTY.

[160] ICTY RPE, Rule 62*ter*(B) and ICTR RPE, Rule 62*bis*(B).

[161] *Kambanda, Jean*, ICTR, Case No. ICTR-97-23SII, para. 51.

[162] *Serushago, Omar*, ICTR, Case No. ICTR-98-39S, para. 42.

[163] *Ibid.*, para. 40. Commentators have observed that while such actions are no doubt important to reconciliation, it is regretful that his declaration was made in the ICTR courtroom in Arusha and not in Gisenyi where the crimes were committed. Kamatali, "The Challenge of Linking International Criminal Justice and National Reconciliation", at 131 ('What is the significance of expressing remorse and sympathy with the victims if the latter cannot know that the criminal ever expressed them?'). A real act of clemency arguably would involve the victims hearing the perpetrator apologise for his deeds and to ask for forgiveness which only the victims have the right and power to bestow. The framework of retributive justice for deciding upon clemency means that such measures may have little impact upon reconciliation, notably because of the missing role of the victim and restoring the relationship between him and the perpetrator, in such assessments.

remaining charge of persecution, so that her involvement in any acts of genocide (the original charge) remain unknown. In fact, many Serbs did not see the plea bargain as an act of truth-telling, but as a self-interested compromise in return for judicial benefits.[164]

Negotiated justice has been justified on the basis of post-modern philosophical thought which sees the most appropriate concept of truth as one that defines 'truth' as that version of facts which is acceptable to all concerned.[165] A general principle of a 'right to the truth' might help courts to attune their use of plea-bargaining and other measures of negotiated justice better to the overriding objectives of international criminal justice. It's a delicate balance to achieve: while agreement and compromise may not be most reliable path to accurate fact-finding, a defendant may be induced to provide important evidence, which might otherwise not come to light.[166] In this sense, applying an interests-analysis approach may clarify how to weigh competing policy considerations: on the one hand the need to offer an inducement to truth-telling about the circumstances surrounding serious violations, and on the other the need to ensure that any negotiated agreement does not distort the historical record. One way to accommodate both goals in the case of charge bargaining would be to require defendants to append a document to the plea agreement detailing their involvement in all the facts in the original indictment, not merely pertaining to the remaining charge. Another way would be to remove the possibility of charge bargaining at all, but to allow sentence bargaining in exchange for full disclosure and, possibly, genuine signs of remorse as in the practice of the ICTR.

3.4.4 The possible *ne bis in idem* effect of pardon

Many States are precluded from exercising jurisdiction over a crime which has been pardoned in a foreign jurisdiction. In the *Finta* case in Canada, the Canadian

---

164 Michael P. Scharf, "Trading Justice for Efficiency", 2 *JICJ* 1080 (2004).

165 Mirjan Damaška, "Negotiated Justice in International Criminal Courts", 2 *JICJ* 1018-1039 (2004), at 1029. The relativism of truth is a concept that becomes important in the legal formulation of the right to the truth because we can work out what information needs to be provided according to the needs of the right-holder. Further, the pragmatic theory of truth looks mainly to extrinsic signs – not to some feature of the idea or thought itself, but to its consequences and its *usefulness*. This theory is clearly represented in some of the implementing mechanisms of the right to the truth, such as truth and reconciliation commissions, which by virtue of their mandate often formulate their inquiries into the 'truth' of past events with an eye to how the truth-seeking process will contribute to reconciliation. For example, the stated objective of the Commission of Truth and Friendship established by Indonesia and Timor-Leste in March 2005 is '[t]o establish the *conclusive truth* in regard to the events prior to and immediately after the popular consultation in 1999, *with a view to further promoting reconciliation and friendship*, and ensuring the non-recurrence of similar events.' Terms of Reference for the Commission of Truth and Friendship Established by the Republic of Indonesia and The Democratic Republic of Timor-Leste, 10 March 2005. [Emphasis added]

166 For its part, the ICC Statute allows 'admissions,' which have to follow the strict conditions required for admission statements. They must be supported, *inter alia*, by materials supplementing the prosecution's charges as well as any other evidence presented by the parties. A judge can request that the prosecution present additional evidence, including the testimony of witnesses (Art. 65 ICC Statute).

Supreme Court found that the general amnesty issued by Hungary on 27 January 1958 subsequent to Finta's *in absentia* trial for 'crimes against the people' in Hungary in 1948-49 did not amount to a pardon and therefore would not bar the exercise of jurisdiction.[167] This suggests that had the amnesty been considered as a pardon, the Canadian court would have declined to exercise jurisdiction. Spanish courts similarly do not have jurisdiction in cases where the accused 'has been exonerated, pardoned or punished abroad.' In the case before the Spanish National Court (*Audiencia Nacional*) concerning whether the courts had jurisdiction over the crimes of genocide and terrorism committed in Argentina during the dirty war, the Court noted that the two amnesty laws – the Full Stop Law and the Due Obedience Law – could not preclude prosecution in Spain because, *inter alia*, they did not amount to an acquittal or a pardon.[168] The Argentine defendant in the case, Scilingo, was not among those to receive the Presidential Pardon in 1990, having never been tried due to the operation of the two amnesty laws prevailing at the time. It is possible that since the 5 September 2006 ruling of a judge in Argentina declaring the 1990 pardons as unconstitutional, Spain would not feel bound by the pardons either, despite the rule precluding exercise of jurisdiction in case of pardons.

Although he has not been indicted for genocide, it could be theorised that the 1996 pardon granted to Ieng Sary for the 1979 genocide conviction would also preclude the Extraordinary Chambers in Cambodia from re-trying Sary for genocide based on the *ne bis in idem* rule, which clearly applies in a purely internal setting.[169] However, the Chambers have the power to review the scope of any pardons and may decide that it does not block a re-trial of Sary for genocide. It may also rule that the pardon itself was invalid due to the fact that Cambodia, as a party to the Genocide Convention,[170] was obliged to prevent and punish acts of genocide by ensuring that convicted genocidaires received effective penalties.[171] Even if a pardon for genocide could be contemplated under international law, it may be argued that the conviction for genocide was not valid due to the major procedural and substantive shortcomings of the 1979 trial.[172] This would mean that the 1996 pardon was meaningless, having no *res judicata* effect, and would be no impediment to the jurisdiction of the Extraordinary Chambers.[173]

---

[167] *Regina* v. *Finta*, Canada [1994] 1 SCR 701, Supreme Court of Canada, 24 March 1994; case note by Cotler in the 90 *AJIL* 460 (1996).

[168] *Scilingo, Adolfo*, Spain, Central Criminal Court (*Audiencia Nacional*), Order (auto) of 5 November 1998, no. 1998/22605, rec. 173/1998, Case 19/97, in EL DERECHO, at 8. The Spanish courts have made it clear that they are also not bound by these amnesties due to the fact that they violate international conventions to which Argentina is party and *jus cogens*.

[169] ICCPR, Art. 14(7).

[170] Cambodia acceded to the Genocide Convention on 14 October 1950.

[171] Arts. 1 and 5, Genocide Convention.

[172] See John Quigley, "Introduction", in Howard J. De Nike, John Quigley and Kenneth J. Robinson (eds.), *Genocide in Cambodia: Documents from the Trial of Pol Pot and Ieng Sary* (Philadelphia: University of Pennsylvania Press, 2000), at 1.

[173] This argument is explained in more detail in the Chapter 6, *infra*.

The question of pardon in the context of the principle *ne bis in idem* was also raised in the case against Argentinean former general Videla, who was pardoned in 1990 by Carlos Menem for international crimes committed during the military dictatorship, and who is now again under indictment before the courts in Argentina on charges relating to the theft of children (a crime for which he was not judged in 1985 and is therefore not covered by the pardon and which was excluded from the amnesty laws),[174] and later for his part in Operation Condor.[175] In May 2002, the Buenos Aires Court of Appeal rejected Videla's claim that the prosecution was barred on double jeopardy grounds due the fact that the Condor-related charges had not been part of his 1985 trial.[176] The Court found that the 700 cases included in the accusation in 1985 (commonly referred to as Case 13) did not amount to an implied pardon for all the other crimes that were not chosen to be prosecuted in the case.[177] For this reason, the new proceedings did not violate the constitution's guarantee against double jeopardy.

However, pardon may only be relevant to the *ne bis in idem* principle where a trial has actually taken place. In the case of former Argentinean general Guillermo Suárez-Mason, who was covered by the terms of Argentine President Menem's pardon, the German government, following investigations into murders and disappearances of its citizens during the military dictatorship, disputed the Argentinean governmental view that such a pardon violated the *ne bis in idem* principle because there had been no prior trial or conviction. Up to this point, the 'official doctrine' of Argentina was to deny all extradition requests with regard to 'dirty war'-related crimes on national sovereignty grounds.[178] For the first time, another friendly government was asking Argentina to re-open extradition proceedings and was questioning Argentina's respect for its international obligations.[179] The Buenos Aires Federal Court, in June 2002, accepted the complaint. The 'official doctrine' was repealed in 2003 when the Kirschner government came to power, with the declaration that extradition will be allowed to European countries in these cases.

---

[174] This indictment was issued by Judge Roberto Marquevich in June 1998. The charges were child kidnapping, concealment, forgery of birth certificates, and suppression of the civil status of a minor.

[175] In 2001, a federal judge indicted and called for the arrest of a number of members of the armed forces of Argentina, Chile, Uruguay and Paraguay for their part in Operation Condor, responsible for orchestrating a violent region-wide repression of those considered politically subversive to the right wing governments. The charges include illegal association (conspiracy), unlawful deprivation of liberty, aggravated kidnapping, torture, homicide, and forced disappearance.

[176] *Videla, Jorge R. s/procesamiento*, Cámera Federal de Buenos Aires, Causa 33714, Sala I, 23 May 2002 (appeals court).

[177] *Videla*, CSJN [2003-F] 87 (2003), discussed in Luis Márquez Urtubey, "Non-Applicability for Statutes of Limitation for Crimes Committed in Argentina: Barrios Altos", 11 *Southwestern Journal of Law and Trade in the Americas* 114 (2005).

[178] Decree 1581/2001, *Cooperación Internacional en Materia Penal*, 5 December 2001, denied judicial assistance or extradition in any inquiry into the 1976-83 period crimes covered by the amnesty laws. Decree 111/98 was specific to the Spanish investigation and prohibited all judicial co-operation as well as extradition. See <www.u-j.info/index/134018>.

[179] Naomi Roht-Arriaza, *The Pinochet Effect: Transnational Justice in the Age of Human Rights* (Philadelphia: University of Pennsylvania Press, 2005), at 138.

As noted, pardons and amnesties were rejected in the context of the rule of *ne bis in idem* in the Rome Statute.[180] A proposal to include a provision which would have allowed the ICC to re-try a person 'if a manifestly unfounded decision on the suspension of the enforcement of a sentence or on a pardon, a parole or a commutation of the sentence' had been made by a State,[181] was rejected.[182] Thus, it would appear that the 'sham prosecution' principle in the Rome Statute does not apply to a pardon issued subsequent to a prosecution. This means that pardons at the national level for international crimes, if issued after a prosecution which was conducted impartially and independently and with genuine intent to bring the person to justice, would bar any re-trial before the ICC.

The failure of the Rome Statute to deal with this possibility has been described as a 'serious lacuna' in the instrument.[183] On the other hand, the absence of a rule on this issue may allow for some 'restorative' justice mechanisms to apply on the national level. As noted, States often choose to qualify or limit the sentences handed down to those convicted of politically-motivated offences in a bid to ease the transition from war to peace. For instance, the Northern Ireland Good Friday Peace Agreement laid down a maximum of two years imprisonment for prisoners affiliated with the organisations committed to the cease-fire even for those convicted of serious crimes.[184] The 2005 Law of Peace and Justice in Colombia provides another example of negotiated sentencing.[185] If, hypothetically-speaking, the ICC had jurisdiction over these crimes, could it find that these reduced sentences amounted to conducting proceedings in a manner that was *without* intent to bring the persons to justice, and thus be able to re-try the people? More importantly, should the ICC make such a finding? One may note that the notion of 'justice' as used in the Rome Statute is not a vague concept related to socio-political justice or even to the interests of peace.[186] It is very much a notion grounded in criminal justice, and therefore it is likely that a sentence that is manifestly disproportionate to the gravity of the crime would be considered as contrary to the criminal notion of justice, as contained in the Rome Statute. In any case, the Rome Statute does not give the ICC the option to make such a finding. Therefore, the 'serious lacuna' of

---

[180] Arts. 17 and 20 ICC Statute govern the principle of *ne bis in idem* before the ICC.

[181] This was Draft Art. 19. The draft article was also included in the Report of the Inter-Sessional Meeting from 19 to 30 January 1998 in Zutphen, The Netherlands, UN Doc. A/AC.249/1998/L.3. See also the proposal of Amnesty International in Draft Statute of the International Criminal Court, UN Doc. A/CONF.183/2/Add.1, at 46.

[182] Immi Tallgren, "Article 20: Ne bis in idem", in Otto Triffterer (ed.), *Commentary on the Rome Statute of the International Criminal Court: Observers' Notes, Article by Article* (Baden-Baden: Nomos Verlagsgesellschaft, 1999), at 434.

[183] Van den Wyngaert and Ongena, "*Ne bis in idem* Principle", at 727.

[184] Agreement between the Government of the United Kingdom of Great Britain and Northern Ireland and the Government of Ireland, 10 April 1998, Art. 10(3), available at: <http://www.nio.gov.uk/agreement.pdf>. The provision does allow for some consideration of the gravity of the crime.

[185] Law No. 975 of 25 July 2005, entitled "Law on Justice and Peace" (Colombia).

[186] Comments of Paul Seils, Senior Analyst in the Jurisdiction, Cooperation and Complementarity Division, Office of the Prosecutor of the ICC, speaking in his personal capacity at the T.M.C. Asser Institute, The Hague, on 15 November 2006.

the Rome Statute may in fact represent a significant means for States to achieve a negotiated justice settlement to protracted disputes through the use of conditional pardons.

3.5 Preliminary conclusions

Pardon is a political mechanism that allows some manoeuvrability of the legal consequences of crime in order to attune such measures to the overall desired outcomes of the criminal justice system. The possibility of issuing pardons for international crimes reduces the risk of an overly rigid and legalistic application of international criminal law to situations which might call for a more nuanced approach. In the absence of an international executive body with the authority to issue a pardon to those convicted by the international criminal tribunals and courts, the decision about the appropriateness of a pardon or early release has been placed in the hands of judges, who have also been issued (at least in the case of the ICC) with a determined set of factors to be taken into account when reviewing sentences. On the one hand, this is a welcome development, as decisions about pardons are likely to be more predictable, influenced by considerations of international law, and less politically-motivated than those of the executive functions in States. However, this discounts the fact that pardons are *supposed* to be political in nature precisely in order to override or to adjust legal formulations when these appear to stretch the limits of political feasibility. At the same time, the factors identified under the ICC RPE are arguably broad enough for judges to incorporate a semblance of political consideration into their sentence reviewing.

The analysis of the law and practice of pardon for international crimes suggests that while international law requires that international crimes be punished and those convicted subjected to appropriately harsh sentences, this does not preclude the possibility of pardons in certain limited situations where the issuing of the pardon is consistent with the objectives of international criminal law of ensuring victims their rights to truth, accountability and reparation. In addition, a pardon for an international crime should not be inconsistent with the main purposes of punishment – deterrence, stigmatisation, rehabilitation, and retribution. It would also appear important that a pardon is an exceptional measure and cannot ever be expected of a person facing prosecution in order to counter any perception of impunity. The Statute and RPE of the ICC suggest that a pardon may only be issued where it would have a beneficial impact upon victims or victims groups and would not cause social instability. In this sense, a pardon issued in order to further reconciliation or peace processes does not appear to be ruled out. Pardons may also be used for the important utilitarian purpose of inducing prisoners to contribute to ongoing investigations and prosecutions.

Such factors will undoubtedly become increasingly important as States grapple with the issue of sentence review of those convicted of international crimes. The usually unlimited sovereign right of pardon of States cannot but be affected by their obligations to prevent and punish international crimes. Where a State party to the ICC is hosting an ICC-convicted person, the right to pardon is completely overridden by the binding nature of the ICC sentence and any review must be made by the ICC. One obvious problem with the system of pardon review under the ICTY and ICTR is that these tribunals are non-permanent bodies and will disband in a few years in accordance with their exit strategies. It is well worth considering who then will make decisions about possible pardons and what factors will be taken into account in so doing. It is likely that the decision would fall to those States where the sentenced persons are imprisoned. Although there will not be any obligation to comply with the directions of the ICTR and ICTY as set out in the RPE (unless the Security Council passes a resolution to that effect), it is suggested that States should, either through their judicial organs or by having the judicial branch check presidential discretion,[187] apply those 'general principles of international law' and 'interests of justice' which govern the decisions of the *ad hoc* Tribunals in relation to pardons. In addition, the impact of any pardon upon victims and upon social stability should be taken into account by those courts.

[187] Judicial checks on presidential pardons have been commonly advocated as a check upon abuse of pardon or any conditions attached thereto that might shock the public conscience. See Harold K. Krent, "Conditioning the President's Conditional Pardon Power", 89(6) *California Law Review* 1665 (December 2001).

Chapter 4
STATUTES OF LIMITATION

Statutes of limitation are designed to protect individuals from having to defend themselves from trials based upon 'stale' evidence, as well as to create stability and certainty in the law. The question of whether statutes of limitation may apply to international crimes has generated considerable controversy due to the fact that no overriding consensus on the matter can be found in State practice,[1] despite the existence of one international convention and one regional convention (neither of which are widely ratified) specifically precluding the operation of such limitations to international crimes prosecution[2] and numerous court decisions rejecting such barriers to the exercise of adjudicatory jurisdiction over international crimes.[3]

In addition, strong arguments for rejecting the application of time limitations can be drawn from the nature of international crimes and obligations to prosecute them arising under treaty and custom, as well as victims' fundamental human rights. Those opposing the applicability of statutes of limitation to international crimes also note that the basic rationales justifying statutes of limitation at the national level do not appear to account for the specificities of cases involving international crimes.[4] Furthermore, the general principle in some national criminal systems that the more serious the crime, the longer the period of limitation suggests that those crimes of the gravest character should not be subject to any time limitation at all.

---

[1] Mireille Delmas-Marty, "La responsibilité pénale en échec (prescription, amnistie, immunités)", in Antonio Cassese & Mireille Delmas-Marty (eds.), *Jurisdictions nationales et crimes internationaux* (Paris: PUF, 2002), at 618; J. Graven, "Les crimes contre l'humanité peuvent-ils bénéficier de la prescription?" 81 *Revue Pénale Suisse* 113 (1965) (hereafter, Les crimes contre l'humanité); J.-B. Herzog, "Etude des lois concernant la prescription des crimes contre l'humanité", 20 *Revue de Science Criminelle et de Droit Pénal Comparé* 337 (1965); S. Glaser, "Quelques observations sur la prescription en matière de la criminalié de guerre", 45 *Revue de Droit Pénal et de Criminologie* 511 (1964-65).

[2] Convention on the Non-Applicability of Statutory Limitations to War Crimes and Crimes Against Humanity, 26 November 1968, GA Res. 2391 (XXIII, annex 23 UN GAOR Suppl. (No. 18) at 40, UN Doc. A/7218 (1968), 754 *UNTS* 73, entered into force 11 November 1970. As of July 2009, there are 53 States parties. European Convention on the Non-Applicability of Statutory Limitations to Crimes against Humanity and War Crimes, *ETS* 82, 13 *ILM* 540, 25 January 1974, entered into force 26 June 2003. As of July 2009 there are 5 ratifications (Belgium, Bosnia and Herzegovina, the Netherlands and Romania, Ukraine).

[3] See the discussion, *infra* notes 174-188 and accompanying text.

[4] Delmas-Marty, "La responsibilité pénale en échec", at 617.

4.1 Definition and historical background

A statute of limitation, or prescription, is a municipal law concept which prescribes the periods within which proceedings to prosecute a crime must be taken or the act is barred.[5] In some States, if a sentence pronounced for a crime has not been served after a number of years, it is no longer applicable.[6]

Statutes of limitation in criminal law is not a universal concept, and may be distinguished from the practice in common law countries where the principle of setting a time limit for the prosecution of crime is generally not recognised.[7] In the common law system, such practices find their historical origins[8] in the well known and ancient maxim *nullum tempus occurrit regi*, which holds that in the absence of some statutory bar, a prosecution can be brought no matter how long the time which has elapsed since the crime charged was committed.[9] Although in the common law system there was no general statute of limitations in personal actions until the seventeenth century limitations of time in criminal and real actions have existed for centuries.[10] The early English common law was based on a rough *lex talionis* and did not apply such limitations. For some time after their introduction they were viewed as mere acts of process, to be construed in doubtful cases against the defendant, and not as acts of grace.[11] However, in the last century, the views of common law courts regarding statutes of limitations have changed. In 1830 Justice McLean of the Supreme Court of the United States noted that '[o]f late years, the courts in England and this country have considered statutes of limitations more favorably than formerly. They rest upon sound policy, and tend to the peace and welfare of society.'[12] Justice Story also defended such limitations, stating that '[a] statute of limitations instead of being viewed in an unfavorable light as an unjust and discreditable defense, should have received such support from courts of justice as would have made it, what it was intended emphatically to be, a statute of repose.'[13] Despite judicial warming up to the notion of time bars, the situation

[5] Bryan A. Garner, *Black's Law Dictionary*, 8th edn. (St. Paul, Minn: West Group, 2004), at 1423: 'A law that bars claims after a specified period.'

[6] E.g., France, under Art. 7 of the Code of Criminal Procedure, the right to prosecute a crime is forfeited within 10 years of the perpetration of the crime, while Arts. 132-3 of the Criminal Code provides that a penalty is no longer applicable 20 years after the issuance of a final sentence. Similar provisions exist in Austria, Germany, Switzerland, Portugal and Denmark.

[7] Robert H. Miller, "The Convention on the Non-Applicability of Statutory Limitations to War Crimes and Crimes against Humanity", 65 *AJIL* 475 (1971), fn. 3.

[8] See Ruth Kok, *Statutory Limitations in International Criminal Law* (The Hague: TMC Asser Press, 2007), at 14-17 on the origins of statutory limitations in the civil law, common law and Shariah law systems.

[9] Forrest Revere Black, "Statutes of Limitation and the Ex-Post Facto Clauses", 26 *Kentucky Law Journal* 41 (1937-1938).

[10] E. Atkinson, "Some Procedural Aspects of the Statute of Limitations", 27 *Col. L. Rev.* 157.

[11] F. Wharton, *Criminal Pleading and Practice*, 8th edn. (1880) at 211.

[12] *M'Cluny* v. *Silliman*, 3 Peters (U.S.) 270 (1830).

[13] *Bell* v. *Morrison*, 1 Peters (U.S.) 349, 360 (1828).

remains that in the common law system, in the absence of a specific rule mandating a time bar on a particular offence, there is no limitation to bringing a prosecution.

Having said this, the judicially-made doctrine of 'abuse of process'[14] in the Anglo-American common law system, does allow judges a discretionary power to stay proceedings where a long delay in the bringing of a case causes an unjust trial for the accused. While the running of time does not in itself suffice to demonstrate an abuse of process,[15] it may be considered as an element leading to such an outcome.[16] There does not appear to be any rule precluding judges from applying the abuse of process doctrine to international crimes. In the Australian case of *DPP* v. *Polyukhovich*,[17] concerning war crimes involving the alleged murder of 850 Jews in the Ukraine between 1941 and 1943, Justice Cox did not rule out the application of the abuse of process doctrine in spite of the nature of the crimes at issue. Instead, the judge adopted the balancing test in *Jago* v. *The District Court of NSW*[18] to determine if fairness could be achieved – and if it could not be, to exercise the inherent right to stay the prosecution. In the case at issue, essentially the defence arguments for a stay of proceedings were based on mistaken identity.[19] Justice Cox did not stay proceedings where he felt that the question of identification could properly be left to the jury. Gillian Triggs has noted that '[i]ndeed, had there not been legislation specifically permitting these prosecutions, it would have been strongly

---

[14] Abuse of process may be defined as the 'improper and tortuous use of a legitimately issued court process to obtain a result that is either unlawful or beyond the process' scope.' Garner (ed.), *Black's Law Dictionary*, at 11.

[15] See *R.* v. *Sawoniuk*, United Kingdom, Court of Appeal (Criminal Division) Judgment of 10 February 2000 [2000] 2 *Cr App R* 220 (in which 56 years had elapsed since the commission of the crimes, constituting 2 counts of murder as violations of the laws and customs of war). In this case, the judge applied the principles laid down in Attorney-General's Reference (No.1 of 1990) [1992] QB 630 (1992) 95 *Cr App R* 296: '(1) that generally speaking a prosecutor has as much right as a defendant to demand a verdict of a jury on an outstanding indictment and, where either demands a verdict, a judge has no jurisdiction to stand in the way of it and therefore the jurisdiction to stay proceedings is exceptional; (2) a stay should never be imposed where the delay has been caused by the complexity of the proceedings; (3) it would be rare for a stay to be imposed in the absence of fault on the part of the prosecutor or complainant; (4) delay contributed to by the actions of the defendant should not found the basis of a stay; (5) the defendant needs to show on a balance of probabilities that owing to the delay he will suffer serious prejudice to the extent that no fair trial can be held. In other words, the continuance of the proceedings amounts to an abuse of the process of the court.' The judge went on to cite the passage in the judgment of the court (at 644 and 303) in which it was made plain that the prejudice which a defendant would have to show to justify the grant of a stay is prejudice which could not be cured by an appropriate ruling in the course of a trial, or by a judicial exclusion of evidence, or by an appropriate direction to the jury. Judgment available at: <http://www.icrc.org/ihl-nat.nsf>.

[16] In *Polyukhovich* v. *Commonwealth*, 172 *CLR* 501 (Austl. 1991), Justice Cox reasoned that although it would be a 'rare case' in which mere delay will justify a stay of proceedings unless there is evidence of actual prejudice, 'the longer the delay, the more readily will the court infer prejudice to the accused by reason of that delay.'

[17] *Ivan Timofeyevich Polyukhovich*, No. S3782 (Sup. Ct. of South Australia, 22 December 1992) (Cox J.) (unreported ruling Sup. Ct. S.A.).

[18] 168 *CLR* 23 (Austl. 1989).

[19] Indeed, the defence did not rely on section 13(5) of the Act which provides a legislative response in cases of abuse of process, because it did not want to set out its case at this point in the proceedings.

arguable that war crimes trials more than fifty years after the offences occurred are *ipso facto* an abuse of process.'[20] The proceedings against *Polyukhovich* before the Supreme Court were ultimately ended when the indictments were quashed for lack of evidence, apparently due to doubts about the credibility of the witnesses.[21] In another prosecution under the Australian War Crimes Act, the accused, Michael Berezowsky, was charged with having been involved in the murder of 102 Jews near the Ukrainian village of Gnivan. After a five week committal hearing during which twenty-two prosecution witnesses from overseas were called, the Magistrate found Berezowsky had no case to answer because of identification difficulties.[22] These cases indicate that the question of whether a long delay will prejudice the fair trial of the accused may be decided on a case by case basis, depending on the reliability of witnesses and the strength of evidence at hand. These judges chose to proceed to exercise jurisdiction notwithstanding the significant passing of time until the evidence proved too weak to support the cases.[23]

In the United Kingdom, the same argument was used with more success in *R.* v. *Sawoniuk*, concerning a conviction of murder on two counts of two civilian members of the Jewish population in Domachevo, Belorussia in 1942, based on two eyewitnesses who at the time were aged 13 and 20 respectively. The Court of Appeals rejected a plea of abuse of process, finding that 'the conclusion reached by the judge, despite the unprecedented passage of time since 1942, was correct.'[24]

By contrast, in civil law systems, countries generally impose a time limitation on the prosecution of crimes.[25] Nonetheless, statutory limitation for a criminal offence is 'neither a general rule nor an absolute rule.'[26] Many countries provide a period of prescription commensurate with the gravity of the crime and the expected sentence; the heavier the sentence, the longer the period of prescription, which might mean that at least certain classes of international crime would be covered.[27]

---

[20] Gillian Triggs, "Australia's War Crimes Trials: All Pity Choked", in Timothy L.H. McCormack & Gerry J. Simpson (eds.), *The Law of War Crimes: National and International Approaches*, (The Hague: Kluwer Law International, 1997), at 132.

[21] *DPP* v. *Polyukhovich* [No. 2], No. S4067 (Sup. Ct. of South Australia, judgment of Cox, J., delivered 4 March 1993); *DPP* v. *Polyukhovich* [No. 3], No. S4068 (Sup. Ct. of South Australia, judgment of Cox, J., 9 March 1993).

[22] *Mikolay Berezowsky*, File No. 91/25241 (Adelaide Magis. Ct., 16 July 1992) 9 (D.C. Gurry S.M.). All charges were dismissed on 29 July 1992.

[23] Arguably, a judge would equally be able to dismiss such an abuse of process motion taking into account the specificities of international crimes. Delmas-Marty, "La responsibilité pénale en échec", at 619.

[24] *R.* v. *Anthony Sawoniuk*, United Kingdom, Decision of 10 February 2000 [2000] 2 *Cr App R* 220.

[25] See Report of the Secretary-General on measures taken by governments to prevent the application of statutory limitation to war crimes and crimes against humanity, UN Doc. E.CN.4/927 and Add. 1-6 (1967).

[26] UN Doc. E/CN.4/SR/943 (1967), statement of Professor Jean Graven, representing the International Penal Association.

[27] E.g., Art. 113 of the Spanish Criminal Code sets a statutory limit of 20 years for *reclusion mayor* (imprisonment of 26-30 years) and 15 years for *reclusion menor* (imprisonment of 12-20 years). In Italy, a 20 year statutory limit applies to international crimes unless they require a sentence of life

In other States, special rules regulate any limitations on prosecutions for international crimes.[28] A large and growing number of States have statutes that remove any limitation to prosecutions in case of war crimes, genocide and crimes against humanity.[29] However, statutory limitations still apply in several States.[30] In the States which have not adopted any particular provision about prescription over international crimes, the general rules of prescription apply. Thus, in France, war crimes are subject to the statute of limitation in the general criminal rules (20 years). This is also the case for Germany for the crime of torture and for all international crimes in China and Senegal.[31]

While the civil law approach might suggest that prescription is necessary to fulfil an element of the criminal justice system, it has been strongly argued that:

> 'Statutory limitation with respect to criminal offenses is not an essential right of the individual, much less of the accused, or even convicted criminal. It is not an requirement of justice itself, generally recognized in the institutions of civilized peoples, it is a practice of expediency which has only quite recently become a rule which, furthermore, has not been accepted in some important legal systems, and which is still disputed or criticized in those systems which have adopted it.'[32]

Because of the fact that the concept of prescription is absent from some legal systems[33] and given that those States which utilise the principle hedge it with various

imprisonment. Germany also has a similar rule, where murder is not subject to a statute of limitations. In Japan, Art. 250 of the Code of Criminal Procedure provides a statutory limitation of 50 years if a crime involves the death penalty, 10 years if the crime involves life imprisonment, and 7 years if the crime involves imprisonment for more than 10 years. Antonio Cassese, *International Criminal Law* (Oxford: OUP, 2003), at 316-317. Israel's Criminal Procedure Law sets the period of limitation for the most serious crimes at 20 years and for other crimes at 10 years. Art. 17(3) of the Declaration on the Protection of All Persons from Enforced Disappearances, GA Res. 47/133, 47 UN GAOR Suppl. (No. 49) at 207, UN Doc. A/47/49 (1992), of 18 December 1992, provides that '[s]tatutes of limitations, where they exist, relating to acts of enforced disappearance shall be substantial and commensurate with the extreme seriousness of the offence.'

[28] Colombia has a statute of limitation of 30 years for torture, genocide, and forced disappearances. Spain sets a 20 year limit for torture and terrorism. France sets a 20 year limit (for a misdemeanour or *délit*) or 30 years (for a serious offence or *crime*) for terrorism. War crimes are subject to a 20 year statute of limitations, while a law of 26 December 1964 removes any statute of limitations over crimes against humanity.

[29] See the law listed below. Israel's Nazis and Nazi Collaborators (Punishment) Law (1950) provides that there shall be no statute of limitation for the crimes against the Jewish people, crimes against humanity and war crimes (Section 12). Israel's Crime of Genocide (Prevention and Punishment) Law (1950), Section 6, excludes the applicability of the provision of the Penal Code dealing with limitations. See UN Doc. E/CN.4/906, at 53-82 (citing the laws of Austria, Bulgaria, China, the Czech Republic, Denmark, France, Hungary, Israel, Ireland, Italy, Leichtenstein, the Netherlands, Poland and the Russian Federation, United Kingdom).

[30] E.g., Greece, Malta, Norway, Portugal, Sweden, Switzerland and Turkey. See Parliamentary Assembly of the Council of Europe, 31 January 1979, Doc. 4275.

[31] Delmas-Marty, "La responsibilité pénale en échec", at 20.

[32] Graven, "Les crimes contre l'humanité", at 132.

[33] E.g., the United Kingdom, and most Commonwealth countries. It has also been noted that Islamic law militates towards imprescriptibility. In Iran, prescription was totally deleted from the books following the Islamic revolution of 1979 and has not been re-established in the Code of Criminal

restrictions and limitations, it is unlikely that prescription is a general principle of international law recognised by civilized nations.[34]

4.2 Statutes of limitation and international and hybrid criminal courts and tribunals

The constitutive instruments of international and hybrid courts tend to be mixed with regard to their treatment of statutes of limitation. The IMT and IMTFE are both silent on the issue of statutes of limitation.[35] On the other hand, Control Council Law No. 10,[36] which established the courts of the four Allied nations in the occupied German territory in order to prosecute the lesser war criminals,[37] stated in Article 5 that an accused would not be entitled to the benefits of any statute of limitation in respect to the period from 30 January 1933 to 1 July 1945.

Like the IMT and IMTFE, the Statutes of the ICTR and ICTY are also silent on statutes of limitation. This might be explained the fact that they were all temporary *ad hoc* tribunals which were designed to run for a finite period of time, fairly soon after the respective wars ended, and hence there was no need to institute a provision barring the application of statutes of limitation.[38] By contrast, statutes of limitation are expressly declared to be inapplicable to the crimes in the subject-matter jurisdiction of the ICC in Article 29 of the Statute.[39] Article 29 thus allows the Prosecutor to hold off on the institution of criminal proceedings possibly because of the need to allow for the restoration of peace and stability in complex political

---

Procedure of 1999 except for some infractions and subject to the rights of victims. If the offence is one of physical violence and murder (*Quesas*), punishment is a right of the victim and his family. Such a right can allow for pardon to be bestowed but not prescription. If, however, the offence is one against divine law (*Hudud*), for which the sanction is provided in the Koran, then both pardon and prescription are excluded. Delmas-Marty, "La responsibilité pénale en échec", at 619.

[34] The delegates of Austria and the Philippines made this point during the negotiations of the 1968 Convention. See UN Doc. E/CN.4/SR/873, at 8 and 17.

[35] There may have been an assumption that such an impediment was *ipso facto* contrary to the object and purpose of the Charters, and therefore invalid. However, the assumption may also have been that as international criminal tribunals, such an impediment does not pose any obstacle to jurisdiction and therefore it was unnecessary to mention it.

[36] Allied Control Council Law No. 10, Punishment of Persons Guilty of War Crimes, Crimes Against Peace and Against Humanity, 20 December 1945, *Official Gazette of the Control Council for Germany*, No. 3, Berlin, 31 January 1946.

[37] Allied Control Council Law No. 10, preamble (stating that these trials sought 'to give effect to the terms of the Moscow Declaration of 30 October 1943 and the London Agreement of 8 August 1945, and the Charter issued pursuant thereto … in order to establish a uniform legal basis in Germany for the prosecution of war criminals and other similar offenders, other than those dealt with by the International Military Tribunal …').

[38] The logical implication from the silence of these instruments on the subject was that no statute of limitations would bar the exercise of jurisdiction of these courts. Schabas, "Article 29", at 523.

[39] ICC Statute, Art. 29: 'The crimes within the jurisdiction of the Court shall not be subject to any statute of limitations.' See "Article 29, Non-applicability of statute of limitations", in Roy S. Lee (ed.), *The International Criminal Court: The Making of the Rome Statute* (The Hague: Kluwer Law International, 1999), at 204.

environments without the fear of losing the window of opportunity to institute criminal charges. Despite some concerns raised during the preparatory stages[40] and at Rome about the unfairness that could arise from trials based on 'stale' evidence or that war crimes should be able to be time-barred,[41] all dissenting delegations implicitly accepted the provision as it now stands.

The Law on the Establishment of the Extraordinary Chambers in the Courts of Cambodia bars any statute of limitation for genocide and crimes against humanity[42] but is silent as to whether a statute of limitation may bar proceedings for grave breaches of the 1949 Geneva Conventions, violations of the 1954 Cultural Property Convention or the 1961 Vienna Convention on Diplomatic Relations. In order to interpret the Law to give effect to its intent, i.e., to try the senior leaders for international crimes recognised in Cambodia 'committed during the period from 17 April 1975 to 6 January 1979,' one would have to assume that no statute of limitation applies to all the international crimes in the subject-matter jurisdiction. By contrast, the Law states that the statute of limitations in the 1956 Penal Code shall be extended for 30 years for the (domestic law) crimes specified in Article 3.[43]

Like the ICTR and ICTY, the Statute of the Special Court for Sierra Leone is silent on the question of statutes of limitation. By contrast, Section 17.1 of Regulation No. 2000/15 of the Special Crimes Unit for East Timor removes any impediment regarding a statute of limitations for the criminal offences of war crimes, acts of genocide, crimes against humanity and torture.[44]

---

[40] Concerns about the fairness and usefulness of trials concerning crimes committed a significant period of time before the institution of criminal proceedings began to be voiced during the Ad Hoc Committee session of 1995. Several delegations underscored the importance of the principle, 'which reflected the decreasing social importance of bringing culprits to justice and the increasing difficulties in ensuring a fair trial as time elapsed.' Report of the Ad Hoc Committee on the Establishment of an International Criminal Court, UN Doc. A/50/52, para. 127, at 29. See also Report of the Preparatory Committee on the Establishment of an International Criminal Court, UN Doc. A/51/10, Vol. I, paras. 195-196, at 45.

[41] China and France assented to have their differing positions set out in a footnote to the Committee of the Whole. This footnote reads: 'Two delegations were of the view that there should be statute of limitations for war crimes. One delegation agreed to the above text in a show of flexibility, but stressed that there should be a possibility not to proceed if, due to the time that has passed, a fair trial cannot be guaranteed. There must also be a special regime for crimes against the integrity of the Court. The absence of a statute of limitations for the Court raises an issue regarding the principle of complementarity given the possibility that a statute of limitations under national law may bar action by the national courts after the expiration of a certain time period, whereas the ICC would still be able to exercise jurisdiction.' UN Doc. A/CONF.183/C.1/WGGP/L.4, at 4, fn. 7; UN Doc. A/CONF.183.C.1/WGGP/L.4/Corr.1, fn. 7. Japan eventually changed its position on the principle, although it maintained that a long lapse of time could be a mitigating factor.

[42] Law Establishing ECCC, as amended, Arts. 4 and 5, respectively.

[43] 2001 Law (as amended), Art. 3, para. 2.

[44] UNTAET Regulation 2000/15, Section 17.2. The remaining 'serious criminal offences' (murder and sexual offences) in the subject-matter jurisdiction of the special panels are 'subject to applicable law' in this regard. This could mean that a statute of limitations in the domestic law could prevent a prosecution for these crimes should the case open after the expiry of the period.

4.3 Contextual and Policy Considerations

Statutes of limitation have been justified on numerous grounds.[45] The main reasons relate to the fact that the passage of time makes the collection of evidence to properly prosecute the crime very difficult and less reliable, especially with regard to finding credible witnesses.[46] Having proceedings brought promptly minimises the risk that facts will get distorted. Thus, statutes of limitation are important ways to safeguard the fair trial rights of accused persons.[47] As stated by one court,

> 'Statutes of limitation, like the equitable doctrine of laches, in their conclusive effects are designed to promote justice by preventing surprises though the revival of claims that have been allowed to slumber until evidence has been lost, memories have faded, and witnesses have disappeared.'[48]

A striking example of the problem of reliance upon eye witness evidence after the passing of long periods of time was the inability of the Supreme Court of Israel to convict Demjanjuk, who was accused of being Ivan the Terrible, the operator of the gas chambers in the Extermination Camp at Treblinka. The question of his identity was crucial to his conviction, but it was dependent on the tenuous probative value of forty year old identification evidence. The District Court reached the conclusion that:

> 'anyone who underwent this shock, and experienced the terrible reality of the Treblinka extermination camp, cannot forget what his eyes have seen … All the identifying witnesses, from among the Holocaust survivors who have testified that they identify Ivan the Terrible from Treblinka, were near him, day after day, month after month … the powerful store of impressions which these people kept within themselves relating to the image of Ivan the Terrible, is strong, and has been preserved through the course of time.'[49]

---

[45] See Kok, *Statutory Limitations in International Criminal Law*, at 239-288 (discussing the pros and cons of statutes of limitations).

[46] Cassese, *International Criminal Law*, at 316.

[47] Miller, "The Convention on the Non-Applicability of Statutory Limitations", at 483.

[48] *Order of R.R. Telegraphers* v. *Railway Express Agency*, 321 US 342, at 348-49, 64 S.Ct. 582, 586 (1944). See also *Toussie* v. *United States*, 397 US 112, 90 S.Ct. 858 (1970): 'Such a limitation is designed to protect individuals from having to defend themselves against charges when the basic facts have become obscured by the passage of time and to minimize the danger of official punishment because of acts in the far-distant past.'

[49] Quoted in Jonathan M. Wenig, "Enforcing the Lessons of History: Israel Judges the Holocaust", in Timothy L.H. McCormack & Gerry J. Simpson (eds.), *The Law of War Crimes: National and International Approaches* (The Hague: Kluwer Law International, 1997), at 116. The District Court ultimately concluded that 'We are aware of human weakness and the failings of the human memory. But we have also learned how powerful are the torments imprinted on the souls of survivors who were snatched like burning brands from that inferno … their memory is a living memory; their testimony – is truthful testimony.'

However, when the matter reached the Supreme Court of Israel, the defence presented a range of evidence, including documents and witness testimonies, showing that another individual – Ivan Marchenko – was in fact the infamous Ivan the Terrible of Treblinka.[50] This evidence was sufficient to raise a reasonable doubt as to whether Demjanjuk was Ivan the Terrible. Hence, the Court was compelled to acquit the accused, concluding that '[t]he matter is closed – but not complete. The complete truth is not the prerogative of the human judge.'[51] One commentator noted that '[t]he lesson of the trial is that even compelling eyewitness testimony (a number of individuals identified Demjanjuk as Ivan the Terrible without hesitation) may be defeated by weak documentary evidence. It simply becomes too difficult for the system of justice to extract the truth.'[52]

Statutes of limitation have also been justified by the importance of 'quieting title' or settling expectations.[53] It has equally been argued that the degree of deterrence decreases over time, reducing the appropriateness and need for prosecution. In addition, there may be a reduced need for institutional reformation of persons whose only provable crime occurred in the distant past, which lessens the objective of rehabilitation. A positive effect of statutes of limitation is the encouraging of law enforcement officials to promptly investigate suspected criminal activity.[54] Finally, there is said to be diminished public clamour for retribution when an offender is not apprehended until long after the crime.[55] A further reason is that it is deemed preferable for society to forget certain crimes, particularly where time has helped to reconcile victims and perpetrators within a certain political transitional context.[56]

Argentina's 'Full Stop Law,' which precluded the initiation of criminal complaints against military officials of the former regime after a 60 day deadline provides an interesting example of an amnesty law in the guise of a statute of limitation. In general, justifications based upon stale evidence, protection of innocent defendants, cost of record keeping, secondary deterrence, rehabilitation, and retribution, do not apply to amnesties.[57] It was precisely due to these differences that the Argentine Supreme Court found the Full Stop Law to be invalid. Although the Full Stop Law allowed a small window of opportunity for launching com-

[50] *Demjanjuk* (Israel Supreme Court), Crim. App. No. 347/88 (Sup. Ct. of Israel, 29 July 1993), at paras. 453-5 of the Unofficial English Transcript.

[51] *Ibid.*, at para. 471.

[52] Wenig, "Enforcing the Lessons of History", at 118.

[53] Slye, "The Legitimacy of Amnesties under International Law", citing Christopher D. Stone, "Conspiracy, Concealment and the Statute of Limitations", 70 *Yale Law Journal* 1311 (1961).

[54] *Toussie* v. *United States*, 397 US 112, 90 S.Ct. 858 (1970).

[55] William D. Ferguson, *The Statutes of Limitation Savings Statute* (Charlottesville, VA.: Michie Co., 1978), at 7-47 (concluding that the purposes of statutes of limitation include the protection of defendants against loss of witnesses and evidence, and defendant's acts taken in reasonable reliance on plaintiff's inaction).

[56] Cassese, *International Criminal Law*, at 316. French courts have justified the applicability of statutes of limitations to war crimes, but not to crimes against humanity, on these grounds. See *Barbie*, France, *Cour de cassation*, decision of 20 December 1985, JCP 1986, II, no. 20655; *Bull. crim.* 1985, 1038-55. English translation in 78 *ILR* 136-47.

[57] Slye, "The Legitimacy of Amnesties under International Law", at 223.

plaints, the purposes and policies underlying statutes of limitation did not apply to the Full Stop Law due to the very short time period in question and the Court ultimately held that the Law was an amnesty and not a statute of limitation.[58] One may note that statutes of limitation and amnesties share some policy justifications. Both obstacles to prosecution in general have the goal of contributing to social reconciliation, the former by avoiding reviving a spirit of vengeance and the latter by appeasing conflicts.[59] However, there are also important differences. While statutes of limitation initially allow for a complaint to be made and then block this possibility after a set amount of time has passed, amnesties generally prevent the initial complaint from being made.[60] While the policy reasons for amnesties are tied to political compromise to facilitate power transition and post-conflict reconciliation, statutes of limitation are justified by the need for stability and certainty of the law. This suggests that the overturning of amnesty laws once a stable peace has been achieved negates the very policy foundations underlying statutes of limitation.

4.4 Legal rationales with regard to statutes of limitation covering international crimes

Courts have rejected statutes of limitation as a bar to the prosecution of international crimes primarily based on the rationale that customary international law precludes such time bars because of the nature of the crimes at issue. A second rationale for the non-applicability of statutes of limitation to international crimes pertains to the obligations under treaty and custom to prosecute persons accused of such crimes or to ensure the enjoyment of fundamental protections, which renders statutes of limitation incompatible with these obligations. Thirdly, it has been argued that the justifications for such limitations do not account for the specificities of international crimes. Finally, courts have found ways to circumvent statutes of limitation by identifying factors that show that time has been tolled, or by characterising the offence as a continuous or permanent crime.

4.4.1 International customary law precludes the use of statutes of limitation over international crimes

The argument that there is a customary rule providing that statutes of limitation may not apply to international crimes is largely the product of judicial activity, rather than any overwhelming State practice and *opinio juris* on the matter, though

[58] *Resolución del Cavallo*, Argentina, Decision of 6 March 2001 Case 8686/2000, *Juzgado Nacional en lo Criminal y Correccional Federal*, No. 4 (6 March 2001), available at: <http://www.derechos.org/nizkor/arg/ley/juezcavallo03mar.html>, at para. v(A).

[59] Juliette Lelieur-Fischer, "Prosecuting the Crimes against Humanity Committed during the Algerian War: an Impossible Endeavour? The 2003 Decision of the French Court of Cassation in *Aussaresses*", 2 *JICJ* 241 (2004).

[60] Fannie Lafontaine, "No Amnesty or Statute of Limitation for Enforced Disappearances: The *Sandoval* Case before the Supreme Court of Chile", 3 *JICJ* 480 (2005).

recent years have seen an increase in both.[61] As may be gleaned from the above, State practice regarding statutes of limitation in regard to international crimes is by no means uniform or consistent. This is largely due to the fact that States deal with such principles in heterogeneous ways. While some States reject prescription by way of their national law for certain serious crimes not defined in international law but by reference to their nature (e.g. Germany[62] and Zimbabwe[63] with regard to murder) or by the punishment expected (e.g. Italy and Austria[64] with regard to life imprisonment), other States have adapted their national systems to international law, by adopting a specific law with a general character (e.g. Belgium, which rejects prescription for all international crimes proscribed under its legislation, and Venezuela, which establishes in its Constitution (Art. 271) the imprescriptibility of offences against fundamental human rights).

Most legal systems,[65] however, have a mixed model with selective adaptation.[66] Thus, *crimes against humanity* have been the subject of specific legislation making statutes of limitation inapplicable in Albania,[67] Argentina,[68] Belgium,[69] Cuba,[70] Ethiopia,[71] France,[72] Germany,[73] Hungary,[74] Israel,[75] Mali,[76] the Nether-

[61] The study by Kok shows that as of 2007, 88 countries, including 11 common law countries had adopted legislation excluding the applicability of statutory limitations to international crimes, while 52 countries did not have legislation excluding the application of statutory limitations to international crimes. Kok, *Statutory Limitations in International Criminal Law*, at 84.

[62] Germany, Act Repealing the Statute of Limitations for the Crimes of Genocide and Murder, Sixteenth Act for the Amendment of Criminal Law (16 July 1979), Art. 1 (amending section 78 of the Criminal Code), reprinted in Kritz (ed.), *Transitional Justice*, at 628.

[63] Zimbabwe, *Criminal Procedure and Evidence Act as amended* (1927), Section 23.

[64] Austria, *Penal Code* (1974), Art. 57(1). Those crimes subject to imprisonment of 10-20 years are also not subject to statutory limitation.

[65] Most of the following information regarding national military manuals and legislation derives from Jean-Marie Henckearts and Louise Doswald-Beck (eds.), *Customary International Humanitarian Law*, Vol. II, Part 2, *Practice* (Cambridge: CUP, 2005), at 4044-4073.

[66] Delmas-Marty, "La responsibilité pénale en échec", at 625.

[67] Albania, *Law concerning the Imprescriptibility of War Crimes and Crimes against Humanity* (1995).

[68] Argentina, *Law concerning the Imprescriptibility of War Crimes and Crimes against Humanity* (1995).

[69] Belgium, *Law concerning the Repression of Grave Breaches of the Geneva Conventions and their Additional Protocols as amended* (1993), Arts. 1(1), (2), (3) and 8.

[70] Cuba, *Penal Code* (1987), Art. 65(5).

[71] See Ethiopia, *Constitution* (1994), Art. 28(1); Ethiopia, *Special Public Prosecutor's Office Establishment Proclamation* (1992), Art. 7(2).

[72] However, it should be noted that the French 1964 law restricts the definition of crimes against humanity to crimes committed during the Second World War. However, the new criminal code recognises a wider definition of crimes against humanity. See France, *Penal Code* (1994), Art. 213(5).

[73] Germany, *Penal Code* (1998), Section 78(2); *Law Introducing the International Crimes Code* (2002), Art. 1(5).

[74] Hungary, *Criminal Code as amended* (1982), Art. 9.

[75] Israel's Nazis and Nazi Collaborators (Punishment) Law (1950) provides that there shall be no statute of limitation for the crimes against the Jewish people, crimes against humanity and war crimes (Section 12).

[76] Mali, *Penal Code* (2001), Art. 32.

lands,[77] Niger,[78] Poland,[79] the Russian Federation,[80] Rwanda,[81] and Tajikistan,[82] while other countries indirectly recognise this principle by reason of a wide interpretation of genocide.[83] Imprescriptibility of *genocide* is recognised in Armenia,[84] Belgium,[85] Croatia,[86] Ethiopia, France,[87] Germany,[88] Israel,[89] Lithuania,[90] Mali,[91] the Netherlands,[92] Niger,[93] the Russian Federation,[94] Rwanda,[95] Slovenia,[96] Spain,[97] Switzerland,[98] Tajikistan[99] and Uzbekistan.[100] *War crimes* are recognised as not subject to statutes of limitation if of a particular gravity in Albania,[101] Argentina,[102] Armenia,[103] Australia,[104] Azerbaijan,[105] Belarus,[106] Belgium,[107]

---

[77] Netherlands, *International Crimes Act* (2003), Art. 13.

[78] Niger, *Penal Code as amended* (1961), Art. 208.8.

[79] Poland, *Penal Code* (1997), Art. 109.

[80] Russian Federation, *Criminal Code* (1996), Arts. 78(5) and 83(4).

[81] Rwanda, *Law on the Prosecution of the Crime of Genocide and Crimes against Humanity* (1996), Art. 37; *Law Setting up Gacaca Jurisdictions* (2001), Art. 92.

[82] Tajikistan, *Criminal Code* (1998), Arts. 75 and 81.

[83] This is the case, e.g., for the Russian Federation and Spain.

[84] Armenia, *Penal Code* (2003), Art. 75(6).

[85] Belgium, *Law concerning the Repression of Grave Breaches of the Geneva Conventions and their Additional Protocols as amended* (1993), Arts. 1(1), (2), (3) and 8.

[86] Croatia, *Criminal Code* (1997), Art. 18(2).

[87] France, *Penal Code* (1994), Art. 213(5).

[88] Germany, *Penal Code* (1998), Section 78(2); *Law Introducing the International Crimes Code* (2002), Art. 1(5).

[89] Israel's Crime of Genocide (Prevention and Punishment) Law (1950), Section 6, excludes the applicability of the provision of the Penal Code dealing with limitations.

[90] Lithuania, *Criminal Code as amended* (1961), Art. 49.

[91] Mali, *Penal Code* (2001), Art. 32.

[92] Netherlands, *International Crimes Act* (2003), Art. 13.

[93] Niger, *Penal Code as amended* (1961), Art. 208.8.

[94] Russian Federation, *Criminal Code* (1996), Arts. 78(5) and 83(4).

[95] Rwanda, *Law on the Prosecution of the Crime of Genocide and Crimes against Humanity* (1996), Art. 37; *Law Setting up Gacaca Jurisdictions* (2001), Art. 92.

[96] Slovenia, *Penal Code* (1994), Art. 116.

[97] Spain, *Penal Code* (1995), Arts. 131(4) and 133(2).

[98] Switzerland, *Military Criminal Code as amended* (1927), Art. 56*bis*; *Penal Code* as amended (1937), Art. 75*bis*.

[99] Tajikistan, *Criminal Code* (1998), Arts. 75 and 81.

[100] Uzbekistan, *Criminal Code* (1994), Arts. 64 and 69.

[101] Albania, *Law concerning the Imprescriptibility of War Crimes and Crimes against Humanity* (1995).

[102] Argentina, *Law concerning the Imprescriptibility of War Crimes and Crimes against Humanity* (1995).

[103] Armenia, *Penal Code* (2003), Art. 75(6).

[104] Australia, Commander's Guide (1994), para. 1307 (stating that no statute of limitation will apply to 'a major war crime').

[105] Azerbaijan, *Criminal Code* (1999), Art. 75.

[106] Belarus, Criminal Code (1999), Art. 85. Statutory limitation equally does not apply to crimes against peace or crimes against the security of mankind.

[107] Belgium, *Law concerning the Repression of Grave Breaches of the Geneva Conventions and their Additional Protocols as amended* (1993), Arts. 1(1), (2), (3) and 8.

Congo,[108] Croatia,[109] Estonia,[110] Germany,[111] Hungary,[112] Israel,[113] Italy,[114] Lithuania,[115] Luxembourg,[116] Mali,[117] the Netherlands,[118] Niger,[119] Poland,[120] the Russian Federation,[121] Slovenia,[122] Switzerland,[123] Tajikistan,[124] Uzbekistan,[125] the United States[126] and Yemen.[127] The ICRC Customary Law Study, on the basis of this practice, found as a rule of customary international law that '[s]tatutes of limitation may not apply to war crimes.'[128] However, despite the high number of States which have legislation to this effect, there is arguably no clear consensus that war crimes must not be subject to a statute of limitations. France has in the past stringently defended its 20 year time limitation on war crimes prosecutions, so long as these do not amount to crimes against humanity.[129] At the same time, France was a member of ECOSOC when it adopted Resolution 1158 (XLI) in

---

108 Congo, *Genocide, War Crimes and Crimes against Humanity Act* (1998), Art. 14.

109 Croatia, *Criminal Code* (1997), Art. 18(2).

110 Estonia, *Criminal Code, as amended* (1992), Section 53.

111 Germany, *Penal Code* (1998), Section 78(2); *Law Introducing the International Crimes Code* (2002), Art. 1(5).

112 Hungary, *Criminal Code as amended* (1982), Art. 9.

113 Israel's Nazis and Nazi Collaborators (Punishment) Law (1950) provides that there shall be no statute of limitation for the crimes against the Jewish people, crimes against humanity and war crimes (Section 12).

114 Italy, *IHL Manual*, Vol. I (1991), para. 86.

115 Lithuania, *Criminal Code as amended* (1961), Art. 49.

116 Luxembourg, *Law on the Non-Applicability of Statutory Limitations to War Crimes* (1974).

117 Mali, *Penal Code* (2001), Art. 32.

118 Netherlands, *International Crimes Act* (2003), Art. 13.

119 Niger, *Penal Code as amended* (1961), Art. 208.8.

120 Poland, *Penal Code* (1997), Art. 109.

121 Russian Federation, *Criminal Code* (1996), Arts. 78(5) and 83(4).

122 Slovenia, *Penal Code* (1994), Art. 116.

123 Switzerland, *Military Criminal Code as amended* (1927), Art. 56*bis*; *Penal Code* as amended (1937), Art. 75*bis*.

124 Tajikistan, *Criminal Code* (1998), Arts. 75 and 81.

125 Uzbekistan, *Criminal Code* (1994), Arts. 64 and 69.

126 United States, *Instructor's Guide* (1985), at 13 (stating that 'there is no statute of limitations on the prosecution of a war crime'). See also United States, *Naval Handbook* (1995), para. 6.2.5.3. In a diplomatic note to Iraq in 1991, the US stated that 'under International Law, violations of the Geneva Conventions, the Geneva Protocol of 1925, or related International Laws of armed conflict are war crimes, and individuals guilty of such violations may be subject to prosecution at any time, without any statute of limitations.' US, Department of State, Diplomatic Note to Iraq, Washington, 19 January 1991, annexed to Letter dated 21 January 1991 to the President of the UN Security Council, UN Doc. S/22122, 21 January 1991, Annex I, at 2.

127 Yemen, *Military Criminal Code* (1998), Art. 22.

128 Jean-Marie Henckaerts and Louise Doswald-Beck, *Customary International Humanitarian Law*, Vol. I. (Cambridge: CUP, 2005), Rule 160, at 614.

129 In the *Barbie* case in 1985, the French court suggested that limitation statutes *should* be applicable to war crimes: 'Following the termination of hostilities, it is necessary that the passage of time should be allowed to blur acts of brutality which may have been committed in the course of armed conflict, even if those acts constituted violations of the laws and customs of war or were not justified by military necessity, provided that those acts were not of such a nature as to deserve the qualification of crimes against humanity. There is no principle of law with an authority superior to that of French law which would allow war crimes … to be declared not subject to statutory limitation.' *Barbie*, France,

1966, which affirmed 'the principle that there is no period of limitation for war crimes and crimes against humanity,' and was supportive of the principle of non-applicability of statutes of limitation to war crimes in debates leading to the adoption of the UN Convention on the Non-Applicability of Statutory Limitations to War Crimes and Crimes Against Humanity, although it never became a party. It also signed the European Convention on Non-Applicability of Statutory Limitations to War Crimes and Crimes Against Humanity (although it did not ratify it) and has ratified the ICC Statute, which could suggest a shift in its position.[130]

The United Kingdom has also shown some sympathy for the applicability of statues of limitations to war crimes in the past; its Military Manual of 1958 stated that it is 'open to two or more belligerents to agree in a peace treaty, or even in a general armistice, that no further war crimes trials will be instituted by them after a certain agreed date or as from the date of the treaty of the armistice,'[131] though more recent manuals are silent on this aspect.[132] The ICRC Study on Customary Law notes that although the Manual 'can be interpreted as contrary practice,' it should be borne in mind that the 1958 Manual was issued prior to the adoption of the UN and European Conventions on Non-Applicability of Statutory Limitations to War Crimes and Crimes Against Humanity (neither of which the UK ratified) and that the UK is now a party to the ICC Statute, suggesting that it now 'recognises that statutes of limitation do not apply to war crimes, at least not those war crimes recognised in the Statute.'[133]

During a debate in the Third Committee of the UN General Assembly on the question of the punishment of war criminals in 1967, Honduras stated that: 'War criminals should have the benefit of statutory limitation for humanitarian reasons. Many countries' constitutions established the principle and made it part of their law … It was … reasonable that when the period of statutory limitation expired [a war criminal] should gain a certain degree of relief.'[134]

For its part, the crime of torture is considered imprescriptible in Argentina, Egypt, Ethiopia, and, only when committed in time of war, the Netherlands.[135] Several draft regional conventions of Arab countries also provide that torture may not be prescribed.[136]

Most instruments dealing with the prosecution of international crimes are silent with regard to statutes of limitation. As noted, neither the Charter of the IMT, nor that of Tokyo made any mention of statutes of limitation. By contrast, Allied

Cour de cassation, decision of 20 December 1985, JCP 1986, II, no. 20655; *Bull. crim.* 1985, 1038-55. English translation in 78 *ILR* 136-47.

[130] Henckaerts and Doswald-Beck, *Customary International Humanitarian Law*, Vol. I., at 617.

[131] UK, *Military Manual* (1958), para. 641, fn. 1.

[132] UK Ministry of Defence, *The Manual of the Law of Armed Conflict* (Oxford: OUP, 2004).

[133] Henckaerts and Doswald-Beck, *Customary International Humanitarian Law*, Vol. I., at 618, fn. 275.

[134] Honduras, Statement before the Third Committee of the UN General Assembly, UN Doc. A/CN.4.SR.1547, 12 December 1967, para. 7.

[135] Netherlands, *International Crimes Act* (2003), Art. 13.

[136] E.g., the Draft Arab Convention against Torture, the Draft Arab Charter of Human Rights and Peoples Rights and Art. 33 of the Constitutional Model of *Azhar*.

Control Council Law No. 10 explicitly rejected statutes of limitation to crimes committed in the period 30 January 1933 and 1 July 1945. The reason for this is that since the subsequent prosecutions were within Germany, any time bars to trials for Nazi-era crimes needed to be neutralised.[137] The Genocide Conventions of 1948, the ILC Principles of Nuremberg adopted in 1950 and the four Geneva Conventions of 1949 do not contain any mention of statutes of limitation. Twenty years later, the issue of statutes of limitation was brought to bear on the international stage when it appeared that a certain number of crimes committed during the Second World War would soon be time-barred in Germany and hence there was a serious risk that further prosecutions would be made impossible.[138] In 1968, the United Nations General Assembly responded by adopting a convention providing that no statutory limitation 'shall apply' to war crimes or crimes against humanity (including the crime of genocide) as defined in the Convention, irrespective of the date of their commission.[139] While a number of States viewed the Convention as having a declaratory character which simply restated a principle of international law which had existed since the adoption of international instruments to punish war criminals,[140] other States considered it a new principle which was yet to be established in international law.[141]

The most controversial aspect of the Convention was the fact that the principle of imprescriptibility is to apply retroactively, so that crimes committed before the entry into force of the Convention are no longer time-barred.[142] Most

---

[137] William A. Schabas, "Article 29: Non-applicability of statute of limitations", in Otto Triffterer (ed.), *Commentary on the Rome Statute of the International Criminal Court: Observers' Notes, Article by Article* (Baden-Baden: Nomos Verlagsgesellschaft, 1999).

[138] The Bundstag of the Federal Republic of Germany adopted legislation on 13 April 1965, which extended the period of limitations for prosecution of the most serious crimes from 8 May 1945 until 31 December 1969. The Law concerning the Calculation of Periods for Criminal Prosecution, *Federal Law Gazette*, Part I, at 315, passed on 13 April 1965.

[139] Convention on the Non-Applicability of Statutory Limitations to War Crimes and Crimes against Humanity, General Assembly Res. 2391, 26 November 1968, Art. I. One commentator observed in 1971 that '[i]n the absence of an international tribunal which would apply the convention's substantive and adjective law, the convention accords with the realities of international penal law by leaving the mechanics of prosecution and punishment of persons charged with those crimes to national legal systems.' Miller, "The Convention on the Non-Applicability of Statutory Limitations", at 477.

[140] Mainly those States in Eastern Europe and the USSR. See, e.g., comments of the Polish delegate in UN Doc. E/CN.4.SR/873, at 5, those of the USSR (UN Doc. E/CN.4.SR/931, at 6), and those of the Ukrainian S.S.R. (UN Doc. E/CN.4/873, at 10). These States interpreted the silence as to statutes of limitation in the existing international instruments relating to the prosecution of Nazi war criminals as implying the prohibition of such limitations.

[141] These States included Austria, France, the Netherlands, Philippines and Sweden. UN Doc. E/CN.4.SR/873 and UN Doc. E/CN.4.SR/875. For these States, the conclusion that there exists a principle in international law barring statutes of limitation for international crimes could not be based solely on the silence in the existing international instruments on the matter. It was pointed out that limitations on State sovereignty could not be presumed but should be expressly stated in international law. In this light, the silence in these instruments should be regarded as leaving each State free to decide to adopt any law or policy it deems to be equitable in the matter. Miller, "The Convention on the Non-Applicability of Statutory Limitations", at 483.

[142] Greece was the only country to raise concerns about unlimited prosecutions during the drafting of the Convention. UN GA, Third Committee, 1515th Meeting, 15 November 1967, UN Doc. A/C.3/SR.1515, 265, para. 117.

countries remained very critical of this aspect of the Convention resulting in only half the members of the UN GA voting for the Convention[143] and subsequently a low number of ratifications.[144] The notion of *ex post facto* imprescriptibility has remained controversial. In 1992, the Hungarian Constitutional Court struck down the laws introducing imprescriptibility for certain categories of crimes committed between 21 December 1944 and 2 May 1990 based on the view that re-imposition of criminal liability for offences for which the statute of limitation had run is unconstitutional, mainly on the basis that it violates security of the law.[145] The Swiss Federal Court has also refused to apply Article 75(1)*bis* of the Swiss Penal Law and Article 56*bis* of the Military Criminal Code invalidating prescription to genocide and grave breaches to crimes that had already been time barred by the time the provisions entered into force.[146] Given these criticisms, the Council of Europe in 1974 adopted a convention barring statutes of limitation from applying to war crimes and crimes against humanity, but which would apply only to crimes committed after the treaty entered into force.[147] Entry into force occurred on 26 June 2003 with the third ratification by Belgium (in addition to Romania and the Netherlands).[148] International instruments adopted since the two Conventions have been silent on the matter, such as the 1973 Convention against Apartheid, the two Additional Protocols to the GCs of 1977, the 1984 Convention against Torture, and the host of anti-terrorist conventions providing for the duty to prosecute or extradite the crimes defined therein.[149] The one exception is the 1994 Inter-American Convention on Forced Disappearances of Persons,[150] which provides that:

---

[143] The Convention was approved by 58 votes in favour and 7 against, with 36 abstentions. No Western States voted for the Convention and only three Latin American States – Chile, Cuba and Mexico – cast affirmative votes.

[144] As of July 2009, only 53 States are parties to the 1968 Convention.

[145] Decision No. 2086/a/1991/14, 5 March 1992, translated in English in N. Kritz (ed.), *Transitional Justice*, Vol. III, at 629. The Court also found that extension of the statutes of limitation for criminal offences for which the statutes have not yet run is unconstitutional.

[146] *Spring*, Switzerland, Federal Court, Judgment of 21 January 2001. The claim to compensation was initiated by an Auschwitz survivor who was handed over to German troops by Swiss border guards in November 1943.

[147] European Convention on the Non-Applicability of Statutory Limitations to Crimes against Humanity and War Crimes, *ETS* 82, 13 *ILM* 540, 25 January 1974.

[148] France has also signed the treaty.

[149] One commentator notes that it is improbable that acts of terrorism would be subject to a statute of limitation given that it is clearly in the interests of States to prosecute those accused of such crimes. Micaela Frulli, "Le droit international et les obstacles à la mise en oevre de la responsibilité pénale pour crimes internationaux", in Antonio Cassese & Mireille Delmas-Marty (eds.), *Crimes internationaux et jurisdictions internationales* (Paris: PUF, 2002), at 239. However, because decisions to prosecute terrorist acts are usually tied to political contingencies, this assumption is not always a given in a changing political environment where a prosecution for a terrorist act committed many years prior may risk causing socio-political friction.

[150] Inter-American Convention on the Forced Disappearance of Persons, signed 9 June 1994, OAS Doc. OEA/Ser.P/AG/doc.3114/94 (1994).

'Criminal prosecution for the forced disappearance of persons and the penalty judicially imposed on its perpetrators shall not be subject to statutes of limitations. However, if there should be a norm of a fundamental character preventing application of the stipulation contained in the previous paragraph, the period of limitation shall be equal to that which applies to the gravest crime in the domestic laws of the corresponding party.'[151]

The Code of Crimes against the Peace and Security of Mankind adopted by the ILC in 1996 is silent as to the validity of statutes of limitation. An earlier text of the Code adopted at its first reading in 1991 had contained a rule on the imprescriptibility of international crimes. However, it was deleted at the second reading because the ILC reasoned that the rule was not applicable to all the categories of crimes under the Code.[152] Some have interpreted the omission in the 1996 Code as demonstrating that the principle of imprescriptibility was not considered to be a customary norm applicable to all serious international crimes in 1996.[153]

As noted, the Statutes of the ICTY and ICTR also omit any reference to statutes of limitation.[154] More recent regulations establishing international or hybrid criminal courts have rejected statutes of limitation as a bar to the prosecution of international crimes. In addition to Article 29 of the ICC Statute, which states that 'the crimes within the jurisdiction of the Court shall not be subject to any statute of limitations,' the 2001 Law establishing the Extraordinary Chambers in Cambodia provides that there shall be no statute of limitation for genocide or crimes against humanity.[155] Article 3 of the Law extends by 20 years the statute of limitation set out in the 1956 Penal Code for homicide, torture and religious persecution. The Law is curiously silent about any statute of limitation for war crimes.[156] The UNTAET Regulation establishing the Special Panels in East Timor rejects statutes of limitation for genocide, war crimes, crimes against humanity and torture, but subjects the other crimes under the Panels' jurisdiction (murder and sexual offences) to the 'applicable law.'[157] The Statute of the Iraqi Special Tribunal, which

[151] Art. VII, Inter-American Convention on Forced Disappearances of Persons (1994).

[152] *YILC* (1994), Vol. I, para. 125 and 130; Vol. II, part. II, para. 80.

[153] Frulli, "Le droit international et les obstacles à la mise", at 238.

[154] However, a Trial Chamber of the ICTY in a significant *obiter* suggested that statutes of limitation might not apply to torture due to its nature as a norm of *jus cogens*. *Furundžija*, ICTY, Trial Chamber II, Judgment of 10 December 1998, Case No. IT-95-17/1-T; 39 *ILM* (1999), para. 157: 'It would seem that other consequences include the fact that torture may not be covered by a statute of limitations, and must not be excluded from extradition under any political offence exemption.'

[155] Arts. 4 and 5, 2001 Law Establishing the Extraordinary Chambers in the Courts of Cambodia for the Prosecution of the Crimes committing During the Period of Democratic Kampuchea.

[156] Given that the Cambodian legal system is largely based upon the French legal system, it is possible that the French attitude to statutes of limitation and war crimes (i.e., that normal rules of prescription should apply) influenced the drafters' decision to remain silent in this regard. However, if a 20 year time limitation did apply to war crimes in Cambodia, this would defeat the object of the 2001 Law with regard to including war crimes within its jurisdiction as this would mean that the statute of limitation had expired (as of 1999). Hence, such an interpretation is likely to produce an absurd result.

[157] Section 17, UNTAET Regulation No. 2000/15, on the Establishment of Panels with Exclusive Jurisdiction over Serious Criminal Offences.

has jurisdiction over crimes committed since 17 July 1968 and up until and including 1 May 2003 also provides that '[t]he crimes stipulated in Articles 11 to 14 [i.e. genocide, crimes against humanity, war crimes, and violations of stipulated Iraqi law] shall not be subject to any statute of limitations' under the section 'General Principles of Criminal Law.'[158]

Although Article 29 of the ICC Statute is placed among the articles dealing with general principles of substantive criminal law, it remains unclear whether the provision reflects a customary rule of international criminal law given the lack of unanimity on the subject. It does not necessarily follow that States parties must also abrogate national legislation providing for time limitations on prosecutions involving international crimes,[159] though some States have chosen to do so.[160] Some have argued that the provision confirms the development of such a norm.[161] One commentator has described the provision as 'a clear demonstration of the Statute's contribution to the *progressive development* of international law.'[162] Others have found that within the context of recent case law rejecting statutes of limitation for serious international crimes that have a *jus cogens* prohibition,[163] 'it is arguable that Article 29 of the Rome Statute reflects customary international law.'[164] Either way, the effect of Article 29 upon national jurisdictions and hence upon the development or affirmation of customary law may be profound given the operation of the principle of complementarity in Article 17. As national statutes of limitation work to bar prosecutions at the national level, the ICC may make the finding that a State with such a law is 'unable or unwilling' to prosecute the person concerned and thereby assert jurisdiction over the person.[165] This possibility will undoubtedly

[158] Section 6, Art. 17(d) Statute of the Iraqi Special Tribunal, available at: <http://www.cpa-iraq.org/human_rights/Statute.htm>.

[159] E.g., Canada's Crimes against Humanity and War Crimes Act (2000, c.24) is silent as to the issue of statutes of limitation over the crimes under ICC jurisdiction, as is Colombia's Decree Number 2764 of 2002, *Diario Oficial* Year CXXXVIII, No. 45015, 30 November 2002, at 1, and Costa Rica's Criminal Prosecution to Punish War Crimes and Crimes against Humanity, No. 8272. Some States have promulgated laws which stop the national statute of limitation from running in the event that proceedings were interrupted by a request to transfer the suspect to the ICC for proceedings there. This is the case for Croatia. See Art. 21(5) 175 4 November 2003 Law on the Application of the Statute of the International Criminal Court and on the Prosecution of Criminal Acts against the International Law on War and Humanitarian Law (Croatia).

[160] See, e.g., Art. 29, International Criminal Court Act 2002, No. 41 (Australia) ('The crimes within the jurisdiction of the Court shall not be subject to any statute of limitation'); Art. 29, Implementation of the Rome Statute of the International Criminal Court Act, 2002, No. 27 (South Africa).

[161] Frulli, "Le droit international et les obstacles à la mise", at 239.

[162] Schabas, "Article 29", at 524. [Emphasis added]

[163] Cases cited are *Hass and Priebke*, Italy, Supreme Court of Cassation, Judgment of 16 November 1998 and *Furundžija*, ICTY, Trial Chamber II, Judgment of 10 December 1998, Case No. IT-95-17/1-T; 39 *ILM* (1999).

[164] Christine Van den Wyngaert and John Dugard, "Non-Applicability of Statute of Limitations", in Antonio Cassese, Paola Gaeta and John R.W.D. Jones (eds.), *The Rome Statute of the International Criminal Court: A Commentary*, Vol. I (Oxford: OUP, 2002), at 887.

[165] Schabas, "Article 29", at 526: 'Certainly on a practical level, statutory limitations in national law will be unable to shelter offenders. Should the national courts grant exceptions based on statutory limitation, the complementarity provisions of the *Statute* will grant the ICC jurisdiction.'

have the effect of obliging States to change any such laws so as to allow prosecution of persons accused of Article 5 crimes, unless they are willing to have the ICC exercise jurisdiction in their place. However, it has also been pointed out that if national limitation statutes are considered as 'fundamental principles' in the sense of Article 93(3),[166] then the ICC may have to modify its request for assistance from a country with such a statute.[167]

Article 29 also serves another important purpose. States parties will not be able to rely on domestic statutes of limitation to refuse extradition to the ICC of persons in their jurisdiction.[168] However, it is less clear whether States parties would be obliged to extradite to *other States* regardless of the existence of a domestic statute of limitations for serious international crimes. In the absence of a clear customary rule on the matter, this question has still to be resolved. But the trend towards an affirmative answer is undeniable.

The latest international treaty adopted which mentions statutes of limitation is the International Convention for the Protection of All Persons from Enforced Disappearance adopted by consensus by the UN General Assembly on 20 December 2006.[169] Like its regional predecessor, States parties are not required to abrogate statutes of limitation for this crime. Rather, Article 8 provides that States Parties which apply a statute of limitations in respect of enforced disappearance must take the necessary measures to ensure that the term of limitation for criminal proceedings is of a long duration and proportionate to the extreme seriousness of this offence. The institution of a statute of limitation is further restricted by the rule that any such time period only commences 'from the moment when the offence of enforced disappearance ceases, taking into account its continuing nature.' While the 'continuing nature' of enforced disappearances is otherwise not mentioned in the Convention, one may refer to Article III of the Inter-American Convention which provides: 'This offense shall be deemed continuous or permanent as long as the fate or whereabouts of the victim has not been determined.' Thus, so long as the fate of the disappeared person is not clarified whether by the production of a body or the person being released from custody, the offence is considered ongoing and no statute of limitations may apply. Victims of enforced disappearance are also guaranteed an effective remedy during the term of limitation.[170] Interestin-

---

[166] Art. 93(3) of the ICC Statute provides: 'Where execution of a particular measure of assistance detailed in a request presented under paragraph 1, is prohibited in the requested State on the basis of an existing fundamental legal principle of general application, the requested State shall promptly consult with the Court to try to resolve the matter. In the consultations, consideration should be given to whether the assistance can be rendered in another manner or subject to conditions. If after consultations the matter cannot be resolved, the Court shall modify the request as necessary.'

[167] Van den Wyngaert and Dugard, "Non-Applicability of Statute of Limitations", at 876. In the light of Article 29, it is unlikely that national statutes of limitation will be given this status.

[168] Schabas, "Article 29", at 525.

[169] The Convention will enter into force 30 days after the 20th instrument of ratification. Art. 40, International Convention for the Protection of All Persons from Enforced Disappearance. Text available at: <http://www.ohchr.org/english/law/disappearance-convention.htm>.

[170] Victims are defined in extremely broad terms under the Convention, as the disappeared person 'and any individual who has suffered harm as a direct result of an enforced disappearance.' Art. 24, International Convention for the Protection of All Persons from Enforced Disappearance.

gly, in the *Menéndez, et al.,* case, an Argentinean Federal Tribunal extended the 'continuing crime' reasoning to crimes against humanity in general, quoting the following passage from the Supreme Court's *Mirás* case: 'an exception to statutes of limitations is found in crimes against humanity, as they are acts that society as a whole continue to experience due to their magnitude and significance. Thus the crime maintains its continuous character not only for national societies but also for the international community as a whole.'[171]

The chapeau of Article 8 of the Convention states that the provision is 'without prejudice to article 5,' which provides that enforced disappearances committed on a widespread or systematic scale amount to crimes against humanity, and as such 'shall attract the consequences provided for under such applicable international law.' Although Article 5 may be viewed as simply a reference to the ICC Statute, which includes enforced disappearances within the list of acts which may constitute a crime against humanity if committed on a widespread or systematic scale,[172] given the clear reference to the provision in Article 8, one could also argue that this strongly suggests that another such 'consequence' provided for under applicable international law is that no statute of limitations may apply to enforced disappearances amounting to crimes against humanity.

In terms of 'soft law' instruments, one may note that the UN Basic Principles and Guidelines on the Right to a Remedy and Reparation for Victims of Gross Violations of International Human Rights Law and Serious Violations of International Humanitarian Law, adopted by the General Assembly on 16 December 2005, provides that: 'Where so provided for in an applicable treaty or contained in other international legal obligations, statutes of limitations shall not apply to gross violations of international human rights law and serious violations of international humanitarian law which constitute crimes under international law.'[173] While such statements might be indicative of the trend towards outlawing statutes of limitation for international crimes, given the proviso 'Where so provided for in an applicable treaty or contained in other international legal obligations,' it is unclear how this adds to practice evidencing a customary rule on the matter of statutes of limitation for international crimes.

A string of decisions by national and international courts have identified a customary rule precluding statutes of limitation over certain international crimes. In the *Bohne* extradition case in 1966, the Argentine Supreme Court rejected the argument that the prescription of 15 years applied to the offence of participation in a simple homicide given that the accused was indicted for the widespread and sys-

[171] *Menéndez, et al.,* case, at 351, unofficial translation in Gabriel ChavezTafur, "Using International Law to By-pass Domestic Legal Hurdles: On the Applicability of the Statute of Limitations in the *Menéndez et al.* Case", at 1070.

[172] See Susan McCrory, "The International Convention for the Protection of all Persons from Enforced Disappearances", 7 *Human Rights Law Review* 545 (2007).

[173] Basic Principles and Guidelines on the Right to a Remedy and Reparation for Victims of Gross Violations of International Human Rights Law and Serious Violations of International Humanitarian Law, Adopted by GA Res. 60/147 of16 December 2005, para. IV(6).

tematic execution of mentally ill persons in 1939 and 1940.[174] In France, the *Cour de Cassation* held in the 1985 trial of Barbie that the inapplicability of statutes of limitation to crimes against humanity, as provided for in French legislation, derives from principles recognised by all civilised nations.[175] Crimes against humanity, as defined in Article 6(c) of the Nuremberg Charter were 'by nature' not subject to prescription. In 1995, the Argentine Supreme Court held in the *Preibke* case that a German national who had subsequently acquired Argentinean nationality could be extradited to Italy to face war crimes charges (related to the Ardeatine Caves massacre near Rome in 1944) despite a statute of limitation of 15 years for murder because the crimes amounted to crimes against humanity.[176] In the subsequent proceedings in Italy, the first trial of the Military Court in Rome ended on 1 May 1994 with a finding that prosecution was blocked by reason of the expiry of the Italian statute of limitations. The Court held that that there were mitigating circumstances (the accused had acted on orders and failure to obey them might have entailed serious consequences for him and his family) warranting the reduction of his sentence to thirty years; accordingly, prosecution for the offence he had committed had been statute-barred since 1966. Since crimes against humanity – which were not subject to limitation – had not existed in Italian legislation until 1967, the Court reasoned that the applicant could not have been convicted of an offence not defined by law at the time when it had been committed. The Supreme Court of Cassation in 1996 quashed the first decision. At the second trial, the statute of limitations argument was rejected and the judgment handed down on 22 July 1997 clearly defined the acts committed as war crimes and crimes against humanity, a decision upheld by the Military Court of Appeal[177] and the Supreme Court of Cassation.[178] The case is significant because Italy is not a party to the Convention on the Non-Applicability of Statutory Limitations to War Crimes and Crimes Against Humanity.[179] The Military Court of Rome, however, stated that the 'imprescriptibility of war crimes and crimes against humanity' is a principle of international law which enjoys the objective character of *jus cogens*.[180] A decision of the European Court of Human Rights found no irregularities in the way the trial had been conducted, though it did not pronounce on the issue of statute of limitations.[181]

---

174 *Bohne*, Argentina, Supreme Court of Justice, 24 August 1966.

175 *Barbie*, France, *Cour de cassation*, decision of 20 December 1985, JCP 1986, II, no. 20655; *Bull. crim.* 1985, at 1038-55. English translation in 78 *ILR* 136-47.

176 *Priebke, Erich (extradition)*, Argentina, Supreme Court of Argentina, Decision of 2 November 1995, in Fallos de la Corte Supreme de Justicia. Tomo 318/3 at 2148-228. English translation in *YIHL* 1998 (Priebke, Erich's extradition request, Case 16.063/94, 2 November 1995).

177 *Hass and Priebke (Appeal)*, Italy, Military Court of Appeal of Rome, Judgment of 7 March 1998, in *L'Indice Penale* (1998), at 959-1000.

178 *Hass and Priebke*, Italy, Supreme Court of Cassation, Judgment of 16 November 1998.

179 Argentina, the country which extradited the accused to Italy was similarly not a party to the 1968 Convention.

180 *Hass and Priebke*, Italy, Supreme Court of Cassation, Judgment of 16 November 1998, at 49, para. 1.1.14(d).

181 See "Preibke v. Italy", 12 *Human Rights Case Digest* 413 (2001).

The Special Prosecutor of Ethiopia, charged with conducting the trial against Colonel Mengistu Haile Mariam and former members of the Derg for allegedly committing genocide, crimes against humanity and war crimes between 1974 and 1991 referred in his conclusions in 1995 to the 'the well established custom and belief that war crimes and crimes against humanity are not … barred by limitation.'[182] In Belgium in 1998, a magistrate deciding whether a case against Pinochet brought by six Chilean exiles living in Belgium would be time barred in view of the Belgian statute of limitation,[183] which sets the prescription of felonies at 10 years,[184] relied on customary law, finding that:

> 'Prescription does not seem to be a principle of international criminal law and appears to be irreconcilable with the character of the offenses … Their imprescibtibility is inherent in their nature. Therefore, we find that, as a matter of customary international law, crimes against humanity cannot prescribe and that this principle is directly applicable in the domestic legal order.'[185]

A similar decision was reached in Spain on 18 December 1998 in the *Pinochet* case, which held that no statute of limitations could prevent prosecutions for genocide, torture or terrorism, given that these constituted crimes against humanity and that even if a statute of limitation existed, the period of limitation only applies from the moment there is an effective possibility to initiate proceedings.[186] The judge reasoned that crimes against humanity are imprescriptible 'by nature' independently of their incorporation in domestic law.[187] In the same year (1998), however, the Supreme Court in Chile threw out cases against military officials for similar crimes on the basis that the statute of limitation had run.[188]

International courts have also made similar findings as to the imprescriptible nature of international crimes. As noted, in the *Furundžija* case, the ICTY stated in *obiter dictum* that '[i]t would seem that other consequences [of torture's

[182] Ethiopia, Special Prosecutor's Office, *Mengistu and Others* case, Reply submitted in response to the objection filed by counsels for defendants, 23 May 1995, Conclusion.

[183] At the time of the case, Belgium was not a party to any convention barring statutes of limitation over war crimes or crimes against humanity. Belgium has since ratified the 1974 European Convention on the Non-Applicability of Statutory Limitations to Crimes against Humanity and War Crimes (on 26 March 2003).

[184] Arts. 21 and 22 of the preliminary title of the code of criminal procedure (Belgium).

[185] Pinochet, Belgium, Belgian Tribunal of First Instance of Brussels (investigating magistrate), 8 November 1998. Luc Reydams, "Case note: Belgian Tribunal of First Instance of Brussels (investigating magistrate), 8 November 1998", 93 *AJIL* 703 (1999).

[186] *Auto por el que se informe a la Fiscalía de la Corona sobre la imprescriptinilidad de las conductas imputas a Augusto Pinochet, Juzgado Central de Instrucción Número Cinco,* 18 December 1998, cited in Redress/FIDH, "Legal Remedies for Victims of International Crimes: Fostering an EU Approach to Extraterritorial Jurisdiction", *Background Paper*, July 2003, available at: <http://www.redress.org/conferences/Background%20paper%20-%20final%2015%20July%202003.pdf>.

[187] Delmas-Marty, "La responsibilité pénale en échec", at 624.

[188] E.g., *Caso Uribe Tamblay, et al.,* Chile, Supreme Court, 19 August 1998; *Caso Quinones Lembach*, Chile, Supreme Court, 6 October 1998; *Caso Eugenia Martinez*, Chile, Supreme Court, 11 November 1998.

jus cogens nature] include the fact that torture may not be covered by a statute of limitations.'[189] The Committee of Eminent African Jurists on the Case of Hissene Habré also stated that no statute of limitations should apply to the crimes of which he is accused (i.e., torture).[190] The Inter-American Court of Human Rights adopted similar reasoning in the *Barrios Altos* case, which concerned the repeated failure of Peru to investigate or prosecute those involved in the murder of 15 persons and serious injury of four by the Peruvian Army in a neighborhood gathering on 3 November 1991. The Court held that 'all amnesty provisions, provisions on prescription and the establishment of measures designed to eliminate responsibility are inadmissible, because they are intended to prevent the investigation and punishment of those responsible for serious human rights violations such as torture, extrajudicial, summary or arbitrary execution and forced disappearance, all of them prohibited because they violate non-derogable rights recognized by international human rights law.'[191] Although the case did not factually involve a statute of limitations, but rather two amnesty laws which sought to block prosecutions of the military, the implication was that laws of prescription would be subject to the same legal rationales as those invalidating amnesties for international crimes. The reasoning was that since certain human rights have a non-derogable character (such as the right to life in this case), there is an absolute duty to investigate violations of these rights and to prosecute any person suspected to have committed such crimes. This obligation cannot be derogated from by reason of an amnesty law or by reason of a statute of limitations. The same conclusion was adopted by an Argentinean federal judge on 6 March 2001 in *Simon, Julio, Del Carro, Juan Antonio*.[192]

In the 2006 case of *Almonacid Arellano* v. *Chile*, the Inter-American Court of Human Rights held that 'the non-applicability of statutes of limitations to crimes against humanity is a norm of General International Law (*ius cogens*).'[193] On 24 July 2008, an Argentinian Federal Tribunal classified the deprivation of liberty, torture and aggravated murder of four political dissidents by the State's security forces as crimes against humanity and on that basis found that no statute of limitations could prevent prosecution.[194] It bolstered its reasoning by relying on the *jus*

189 *Furundžija*, ICTY, Trial Chamber II, Judgment of 10 December 1998, Case No. IT-95-17/1-T; 39 *ILM* (1999), para. 157.

190 *Report of the Committee of Eminent African Jurists on the Case of Hissene Habré*, available at: <http://www.hrw.org/justice/habre/CEJA_Repor0506.pdf>, paras. 14 and 15.

191 *Barrios Altos (Chumbipuma Aguirre and others* v. *Peru)*, IACtHR (ser. C) (2001), para. 41. For commentary, see Urtubey, "Non-Applicability for Statutes of Limitation".

192 *Simon, Julio, Del Cerro, Juan Antonio s/sustracción de menores de 10 años,* Juzgado Nacional en lo Criminal y Correccional Federal No. 4, Dr. Gabriel Cavallo, 6 March 2001, available at: <www.derechos.org/nizkor/arg/ley/juezcavallo03mar.htm>, at 78-84. For commentary, see Santiago Legarre, "Crimes Against Humanity, Reasonableness and the Law: the *Simon* case in the Supreme Court of Argentina", 5(3) *Chinese JIL* 723 (2006).

193 *Almonacid-Arellano, et al.,* v. *Chile*, IACtHR, Preliminary Objections, Merits, Reparations and Costs. Judgment of 26 September 2006 (ser. C), No. 154, para. 153.

194 *Menéndez Luciano Benjamín, et al., p.ss.a autores de privación ilegítima de la libertad, imposición de tormentos agravado y homicidio agravado*, Oral Tribunal for Federal Crimes No. 1, File 40/M/2008, 24 July 2008. For a critical analysis of the case, see Gabriel ChavezTafur, "Using Interna-

cogens nature of statute of limitations, which had the consequence, according to the Tribunal, of allowing it to retroactively apply its obligations under the Convention on the Non-applicability of Statutory Limitations to War Crimes and Crimes against Humanity, which it acceded to in 2003.[195]

A similar view was held by a Mexican federal judge in deciding to extradite Cavallo, an Argentinean officer, to Spain.[196] In this case, the judge held that the accused could only be extradited for the charges of genocide and terrorism due to the fact that torture was covered by a statute of limitation in Argentinean law. However, the Minister of Foreign Affairs of Argentina, who was charged with making the final decision, decided that Cavallo could also be extradited for torture because such a crime could not be subject to any statute of limitation.[197] In Argentina, in a case concerning the murder of Chile's Army Commander-in-Chief and his wife during the government of Salvador Allende in the city of Buenos Aires in 1974, the court rejected the plea that the statute of limitations had run due to the fact that the crime amounted to a crime against humanity, which may not be subject to such time bars.[198] The same holding has been recently confirmed by the Argentine Federal Supreme Court concerning crimes committed within the framework of Operation Condor.[199]

Contrary to this trend is the French Court of Cassation's 2003 decision in *Aussaresses*, in which it found that prosecution of the former general for the crimes against humanity committed against civilians in Algeria between 1955 and 1957 was barred due to the fact that Article 212-1 of the penal code could not be retroactively applied to acts committed before its adoption.[200] Since the penal code in force at the time the crimes were committed did not contain a provision for crimes against humanity, the acts would have to be prosecuted as murder, killing or aggravated assault and battery, all of which fall under a 10 year statute of

tional Law to By-pass Domestic Legal Hurdles: On the Applicability of the Statute of Limitations in the *Menéndez et al.* Case", 6 *JICJ* 1061 (2008).

[195] *Ibid.*, at 352: 'if Argentina could not legally enter international treaties that violated the jus cogens norms contained in the principle of the non-applicability of statutes of limitations for crimes against humanity found in the Convention on Statutory Limitations, then it follows that one of the branches of a state, namely the Judiciary, would also not be able to accept that such crimes have indeed fallen under the statute of limitations, as that would mean a clear and flagrant violation of the jus cogens norm. In sum, to not accept that crimes against humanity do not fall under statutes of limitations would go against Art. 53 of the Vienna Convention, part of our domestic law before the offences were committed.' Unofficial translation in ChavezTafur, "Using International Law to By-pass Domestic Legal Hurdles", at 1070.

[196] *Cavallo, Ricardo Miguel*, Mexico, Extradición Ricardo Miguel Cavallo, Suprema Corte de Justicia de la Nación, Amparo en Revisión 140/2002, 10 June 2003, <http://www.scjn.gob.mx/Asuntos/2003/CAVALLOENGROSE(X)2.pdf>.

[197] *Ibid.*, at 58-9.

[198] *Videla*, CSJN [2003-F] L.L. 87 (2003).

[199] See Corte Suprema de Justicia [CSJN], 24 December 2004, *Arancibia Clavel, Enrique Lautaro y otros*, Colección Oficial de Fallos de la Corte Suprema de Justicia de la Naćion [Fallos] (2004-327-3294) (Arg.).

[200] *Aussaresses*, France, Criminal Chamber of the Court of Cassation, Judgment of 17 June 2003, *Bull. crim.* (2003) 122, at 465-469.

limitations, which had long since run out.[201] In adopting this decision, the Court appeared to have changed its position *vis-à-vis* the issue of non-retroactivity of a more severe criminal law. Klaus Barbie, Paul Touvier[202] and Maurice Papon had all been convicted by French courts for crimes against humanity despite the fact that this offence did not exist at the time the crimes were committed.[203] The law of 26 December 1964[204] which made statutes of limitation inapplicable to crimes against humanity was relied on by the courts to assert that crimes against humanity 'as defined by UN Resolution of 13 February 1946, taking notice of the definition of crimes against humanity laid down in the Charter of the International Tribunal established on 8 August 1945 …' were 'by nature,' not subject to a statute of limitations. In the case at hand, the argument that a customary law prohibition of crimes against humanity existing at the time the crimes were committed could be applied directly was rejected by the Court on the basis that Article 6(c) of the Charter of the Nuremberg Tribunal, which constitutes the foundation of the international customary prohibition of crimes against humanity, only relates to crimes committed by the Axis forces during WW II.

Such a conclusion has been strongly criticised by commentators, who rightly note that the contextual factors limiting the jurisdiction of the IMT do not necessarily restrict the material scope of crimes against humanity, save that Article 6(c) requires that such crime be in connection with a war crime or a crime against peace (a nexus which no longer is required).[205] Moreover, if certain crimes are 'by their nature' imprescriptible, it is nonsensical to limit the definition of such a crime to one particular historical context.

Commentators have largely supported the conclusions of the courts that statutes of limitation may not apply to international crimes. Cassese has argued that '[t]he application of statutes of limitation to the most serious international crimes proves contrary to the very nature of international rules prohibiting such crimes. These are so abhorrent that their authors must be punished, even after the lapse of much time.'[206] Others agree that '[e]xceptional treatment should be accorded to war crimes and crimes against humanity because of their nature and gravity.'[207]

---

[201] See Juliette Lelieur-Fischer, "Prosecuting the Crimes against Humanity Committed during the Algerian War: an Impossible Endeavour? The 2003 Decision of the French Court of Cassation in *Aussaresses*", 2 *JICJ* 232 (2004).

[202] It is worth recalling that Touvier had been tried and sentenced to death twice (in 1945 and 1947) *in absentia* for 'treason and intelligence with the enemy,' but had evaded capture during the period of the statute of limitations, waiting for it to run its course. President Pompidou had officially pardoned him in 1971, however, new charges were laid.

[203] *Barbie*, France, *Cour de cassation*, decision of 20 December 1985, JCP 1986, II, no. 20655; *Bull. crim.* 1985, 1038-55. English translation in 78 *ILR* 136-47; *Touvier*, France, *Cour de cassation*, decision of 21 October 1993, *Bull. crim.* 1993, at 770-4; *Papon*, France, Court de Cassation, decision of 23 January 1997, no. 502, at 15.

[204] Law No. 64-1324 of 26 December 1964, *Journal Officiel*, 28/29 December 1964, 11788.

[205] Lelieur-Fischer, "Prosecuting the Crimes against Humanity Committed during the Algerian War", at 239.

[206] Cassese, *International Criminal Law*, at 318.

[207] Miller, "The Convention on the Non-Applicability of Statutory Limitations", at 500.

In addition, given that all States have a universal interest in the repression of such crime, it may be anomalous for one State's law to be able to set aside the consequences of perpetrating international crimes.[208] In this vein, Chile's Court of Santiago in a 1994 case dealing with alleged war crimes committed in 1974 held that '[a]ny attempt by a State to tamper with the criminality of and consequent liability for acts which infringe the laws of war and the rights of persons in wartime is beyond the State's competence while it is a Party to the Geneva Conventions on humanitarian law.'[209] Kok, in her detailed study of State practice and *opinio juris* on statutes of limitations and international crimes concluded that while there is insufficient evidence to show that a customary rule prohibiting statutes of limitations over international crimes already existed before the end of the 1990s, since then there has been an unprecedented development in the area of legislative reform towards making such crimes imprescribable.[210] In her view, 1 July 2002, the date of the entering into force of the ICC Statute, constitutes a decisive moment for determining the start date of a possible customary rule on statutes of limitation over international crimes since from that time 'a significant number of states traditionally applying statutes of limitation to international crimes assumed the obligation to abolish them.'[211]

The ICTY Trial Chamber's tentative add-on to its *obiter dictum* about the inter-State consequences of *jus cogens* crimes that statutes of limitation would be inapplicable to torture deserves some scrutiny. As previously noted,[212] the claim that the *jus cogens* nature of international crimes entails an equally non-derogable obligation to prosecute is highly doubtful. The best case for such an argument would relate to the duties of the territorial State, which may be obliged to guarantee certain fundamental human rights to victims of *jus cogens* crimes by way of prosecution. However, simply because the *jus cogens* norm itself has a non-derogable character does not immediately entail that the method of enforcement of such a norm (*erga omnes* obligations) are also absolute. Only where a State's behaviour in regard to having a statute of limitations could be deemed to make the State complicit in the crime, or where such a law could be considered as evidence of the State authorising, condoning or absolving the perpetrator of responsibility, would a statute of limitations violate the expected consequences of a *jus cogens* crime. However, because a statute of limitations does not affect the recognised criminality of the offence even after the time has run, it is unlikely that a State could be accused of having authorised, condoned or absolved the person from responsibility simply by virtue of having a law ruling out prosecutions not brought in a timely manner.[213]

---

[208] Cassese, *International Criminal Law*, at 318.

[209] *Videla*, Chile, Appeal Court of Santiago, Third Criminal Chamber, Judgment of 26 September 1994.

[210] Kok, *Statutory Limitations in International Criminal Law*, at 375 ('a total of 146 of the 192 Member States of the United Nations exclude the applicability of statutory limitations either generally to serious crimes, or specifically to international crimes, or both').

[211] *Ibid.*, at 380.

[212] See Chapter 2, at 2.4.3, *supra*.

[213] But see *infra* section 4.4.4 the possibilities for 'equitable tolling.'

Furthermore, bearing in mind that judicial decisions and the writings of publicists are a subsidiary means for the determination of customary rules,[214] one cannot base a conclusion on the existence of such a customary rule on these sources alone. Noting that in a number of States some categories of international crimes may be subject to statutory limitations and that no State has ever protested against such limitations, Cassese concludes that 'no customary rule endowed with a far-reaching content has yet evolved on this matter. In other words, no rule has come into being prohibiting the application of statutes of limitations to all international crimes.'[215] It may be, however, that specific customary rules reject statutes of limitation as a bar to prosecution for some crimes, such as genocide, crimes against humanity, war crimes and torture. The large amount of legislation providing such an exception to the normal rules of prescription, combined with the *opinio juris* gleaned from court decisions and widespread support of Article 29 of the Rome Statute[216] and other recent instruments establishing hybrid courts are strong evidence of the development of such a customary rule.

4.4.2 Obligations to prosecute international crimes or to ensure fundamental human rights are incompatible with statutes of limitation

One could also argue that treaty or customary rules imposing a duty to prosecute the authors of international crimes mean that any statute of limitation precluding such action would be a violation of these obligations.[217] As noted above, the Inter-American Court's reasoning in the *Barrios Altos* case to reject statutes of limitation covering *jus cogens* norms ran along these lines. National courts have not relied as often upon this argumentation. In 1996, the Constitutional Court of Hungary held that the rule concerning the imprescriptibility of war crimes and crimes against humanity as contained in the Penal Code could only be applied to grave breaches and serious violations of Article 3 common to the Geneva Conventions.[218] The Supreme Court of Chile in 2004 upheld the conviction and sentence of Miguel Krassnoff Martchenko, Juan Manuel Contreras Sepúlveda and others in a case of forced disappearance that occurred in 1975 on a similar basis.[219] Finding that com-

[214] Art. 38(1)(d) Statute of the International Court of Justice.

[215] Cassese, *International Criminal Law*, at 319.

[216] Upon signature of the ICC Statute, Egypt declared that 'The Arab Republic of Egypt declares that the principle of the non-retroactivity of the jurisdiction of the Court, pursuant to articles 11 and 24 of the Statute, shall not invalidate the well established principle that no war crime shall be barred from prosecution due to the statute of limitations. Egypt, Declaration made upon signature of the ICC Statute, 26 December 2000, para. 5, quoted in Henckearts and Doswald-Beck (eds.), *Customary International Humanitarian Law*, at 4045.

[217] Cassese, *International Criminal Law*, at 317; Lafontaine, "No Amnesty or Statute of Limitation for Enforced Disappearances", at 481.

[218] Hungary, Constitutional Court of Hungary, Judgment No. 36/1996, 4 September 1996.

[219] *Contreras Sepúlveda, Juan y otros (crimen) cascación fondo y forma*, Chile, Corte Suprema, 517/2004, Resolución 22267, available at: <www.derechos.org/nizkor/chile/doc/krassnoff.html>.

mon Article 3 of the Geneva Conventions applied to the situation in Chile at the time of the crime, it held that the 1949 Geneva Conventions enjoyed supremacy in the Chilean constitution so that the obligation to ensure the rights contained therein overrode any incompatible domestic legislation.[220] The implication was that the obligation to guarantee the protection of persons under common Article 3 entailed the illegality of any measure that would shield persons from criminal liability arising from a violation of those protections. Thus, the 1978 amnesty and any statute of limitation would be a violation of the obligations arising under common Article 3 of the GCs.[221]

As noted with regard to amnesties, while such obligations may be said to exist with regard to grave breaches of the GCs and torture (where the alleged offender is on the territory of the State) and genocide (for the territorial State), it is doubtful whether a customary rule obliges States to prosecute persons suspected of crimes against humanity. Moreover, the obligation to prosecute may arguably still be said to be fulfilled in the case of a statute of limitation (as opposed to an amnesty law) given that ample opportunity for a complaint to be brought was provided by the time period. Such an argument could be refuted, however, where circumstances precluded the ability of bringing prosecutions.[222] Furthermore, at least one international body has implied that the obligation to prosecute is not fulfilled where a statute of limitations has expired. The European Commission on Human Rights, in an admissibility decision of 1976 concerning an application relative to the right to be tried within a reasonable time in criminal matters, stated that:

> 'The Commission had regard to the fact that the rules of prescription do not apply to war crimes and that the international community requires the competent authorities of the Federal Republic of Germany to investigate and prosecute these crimes despite the difficulties encountered by reason of the long time that has elapsed since the commission of the acts concerned. In this situation the Commission considers that the criteria determining reasonableness of the length of ordinary criminal proceedings are not applicable to proceedings concerning war crimes.'[223]

[220] *Ibid.*, at para. 35: 'Through these Conventions, the State of Chile imposed on itself the obligation to guarantee the security of persons who may have participated in armed conflicts within its territory, particularly detainees. This leaves out of the bounds of law all measures that shield offenses committed against certain persons or that achieve the impunity of those responsible for such acts, considering especially that international agreements must be complied with in good faith. As the Pact [*sic*] seeks to ensure protection of basic rights that stem from human nature, its application takes preeminence considering that the Supreme Court, in various sentences, has recognized that the internal sovereignty of Chile acknowledges its limits in those rights that derive from human nature. These are values above any law that the authorities may enact, and they may not be disavowed.' See Lafontaine, "No Amnesty or Statute of Limitation for Enforced Disappearances", at 471-476.

[221] Cassese has argued along similar lines that, '[a]s already stated above with regard to amnesties, whenever international treaties, or such customary rules as those on grave breaches of the Geneva Conventions, impose upon States the obligation to take proceedings against the alleged authors of international crimes they envisage, the establishment or application of a statute of limitation may prove contrary to such treaties or rules.' Cassese, *International Criminal Law*, at 317.

[222] See the discussion below on tolling time, in section 4.4.4.

[223] *X* v. *FRG*, ECommHR, Decision, 6 July 1976, para. 1.

Nonetheless, States in general would not seem to construe such obligations as ruling out statutes of limitation for such crimes, given the number of States which apply a time limitation on such prosecutions.

4.4.3 The purposes and principles underlying the use of statutes of limitation do not account for the specificities of cases dealing with international crimes

There are valid arguments to support the view that the passage of time does not have the effects predicted by the justifications underlying the use of statutory limitations when applied to war crimes trials. History has shown that immediate prosecution of international crimes is often a risky business in the aftermath of serious violence where a resumption of hostilities may be easily provoked or may be obstructed by the institution of amnesty laws. Victims may also decline to appear as witnesses in criminal cases in the immediate aftermath of the commission of crimes due to serious misgivings about their personal safety or because of the traumatising effect of confronting their aggressors so soon after the fact.[224] In such circumstances, initiating such proceedings may be 'psychologically painful, or politically dangerous, or legally impossible.'[225] On the other hand, it is possible that descendants of victims, either individually or through victims' associations, might attempt to later launch a complaint on behalf of their relatives.[226]

Countries racked by civil war are also often more concerned with directing resources towards rebuilding key infrastructure and providing shelter, food and security to civilians, rather than punishing offenders of international crimes. Perpetrators may flee the country, assume different identities and destroy key evidence, all making prompt prosecution a virtual impossibility. For example, criminal investigations of Klaus Konrad, a lieutenant in the German army in 1944 accused of war crimes in Occupied Italy,[227] only began in 2004 after 700 files concerning war crimes carried out by the Nazis had been found by chance in a box in the building of the military court in Rome and subsequently analysed.[228] In the light of such factors, a time bar on the prosecutions of persons suspected of involvement in international crimes loses much of its appropriateness.

---

[224] Similar arguments have been made about statutes of limitation for victims of sexual violence, coupled with the fact that DNA samples may provide evidence that does not go 'stale' after the passing of time. See Amy Dunn, "Criminal Law – Statutes of Limitation on Sexual Assault Crimes: Has the Availability of DNA Evidence Rendered Them Obsolete", 23 *University of Arkansas at Little Rock University Law Review* 839 (2000-2001).

[225] Delmas-Marty, "La responsibilité pénale en échec", at 617-18.

[226] *Ibid.*, 617.

[227] He was accused of taking part in the torture and killing of at least 54 civilians.

[228] For a description of the facts leading to the investigations against Konrad, see his profile on Trial Watch: <http://www.trial-ch.org/en/trial-watch/profile/db/legal-procedures/klaus_konrad_460.html>.

Justification of statutes of limitation based on the need for certainty in the law has also been negated in cases of international crimes. The Czech Constitutional Court pointedly stated that '[t]his "legal certainty" of offenders is, however, a source of legal uncertainty to citizens (and vice versa). In a contest of these two types of certainty, the Constitutional Court gives priority to the certainty of civil society, which is in keeping with the idea of a law-based State.'[229] Furthermore, most countries that use statutes of limitation preclude their application to murder. Historically, the reasons cited for this are 1) because it is assumed that the discovery and collection of evidence for acts of murder would be time-consuming and present obstacles and 2) because of concern for the 'long continued impact on the sense of general security of the community.'[230] The same reasons could well be said of international crimes. In fact, the complex nature of international crimes, often involving large numbers of murders and other ill-treatment the evidence of which is often hidden or destroyed by implicated State officials, gives even greater force to the reasoning. Considering the potential impact of international crimes upon peaceful international relations, as well as the international legal order, the lack of any time limitation to prosecution may well be important to ensuring the general security of the international community.[231]

The fact that Nazi war criminals are still being pursued when identified in various countries suggests that the international community's desire for retribution for these types of crimes is undiminished by the course of time.[232] Current trials underway in Argentina and other countries against former military officials accused of being involved in international crimes during the military dictatorship

---

[229] Decision relating to Law No. 198/1993, 21 December 1993, translated in English in Kritz (ed.), *Transitional Justice*, Vol. III, at 623. The law at issue was Act No. 198/1993, Art. 5 of which provides that 'the period of time from 25 February 1948 until 29 December 1989 shall not be counted as part of the limitation period for criminal acts if, due to political reasons incompatible with the basic principles of the legal order of a democratic State, [a person] was not finally and validly convicted or the charges [against him] were dismissed.'

[230] Model Penal Code, para. 1.07 (Tentative Draft No. 5, 1956), cited in Slye, "The Legitimacy of Amnesties under International Law", at 234.

[231] Slye, "The Legitimacy of Amnesties under International Law", at 234.

[232] Trials of Nazi war criminals have continued into the 1990s and the 21st century. In 1992, Josef Schwammberger was sentenced to life in prison by a German court on multiple counts of murder and accessory to murder. The criminal trial of René Bousquet in France ended in 1993 with his assassination. Although on 1 August 1996, an Italian military tribunal acquitted Erich Priebke of crimes against humanity due to the lapse of time this decision was later overturned and on 9 March 1998, Priebke and Hass were condemned to life imprisonment for crimes against humanity. The European Court of Human Rights, by a judgment of 5 April 2001, decided that the procedure in the case of Priebke did not exhibit any irregularities. On 2 March 2001, Alois Brunner, an SS officer, was condemned, *in absentia*, in France for war crimes and crimes against humanity, to life imprisonment. Alfred Schönenberg and seven other co-defendants were sentenced by the Italian Military Tribunal of La Spezia on 22 June 2005 to life imprisonment and to payment of compensation for his participation in several murders committed with particular brutality. A trial against Klaus Konrad in Italy which began in March 2006 ended in August 2006 with his death. A Munich court is currently trying John Demjanjuk, accused of being an accessory to 27,900 counts of murder at Nazi death camps. This has been widely reported as the last Nazi trial.

in 1976-1983, i.e., more than 20 years ago, also support this conclusion. Similarly, present day efforts to prosecute leaders of the Khmer Rouge for the atrocities committed during its reign in Cambodia from 1975 to 1979 underscore the desire for justice even when most of the possible candidates for trial are dead or far and few in between.[233]

It is a matter of speculation as to whether trials of international criminals held significant periods of time after the commission of the offence have any deterrent value.[234] Obviously, there would not be any deterrent effect upon behaviour during the specific conflict or political context in which the offence was committed. However, it is not beyond reasoned contemplation that a person in a current conflict may hesitate to commit such crimes if he knows that punishment for this crime may be enforced by any country or by the ICC or another relevant tribunal at any time in the future. Such a deterrent value is probably most effective in regard to the leaders and major players responsible for creating a context in which international crimes are committed (e.g. a war of ethnic cleansing).

With regard to the justification of statutes of limitation based upon the reduced need for rehabilitation of alleged offenders after the passing of time, this aspect of punishment would need to be assessed against the other objectives of punishment of international crimes – i.e., deterrence, retribution and stigmatisation.[235] Arguably, the trend of international law is to emphasise the importance of the example of the punishment of international criminals rather than to focus on the actual rehabilitative possibilities of the particular offender by way of punishment. Such an emphasis is justified by the exceptional gravity of the crimes committed, which threaten the very foundation of the international system. Thus, the individual rehabilitative aspect of the single offender becomes relegated to the importance of the trial as a means to safeguard a collective fundamental value of the international community as a whole.

The question of whether trials initiated a significant period of time after the commission of the crime pose a risk to reconciliation processes is also difficult to answer in the absence of more anecdotal evidence. One may note that the trials of Nazis more than half a century after the offences committed during WW II occurred have not resulted in any significant provocation of pro-Nazi elements in German society. Argentinean society appears to more and more openly welcome the trials of military officials accused of committing serious crimes during the reign of the military regime and the judgments of its courts have contributed more significantly than any other States' to the development of the principle of non-applicability of statutes of limitation to international crimes. Contrary to the risks posed by prosecution in the immediate aftermath of war or political transition, trials for

---

[233] As of July 2009, 1 person (Guek Eav Kaing, alias Duch) has been indicted, while four others (Nuon Chea, Ieng Sary, Ieng Thirith and Khieu Samphan) have been charged with crimes still under investigation.

[234] See *supra* Chapter 2, at 2.3.4 for the discussion of the deterrent effect of international criminal trials.

[235] On the objectives of punishment for international crimes, see *supra* Chapter 3.

international crimes held years after their commission do not appear to *revive* any sense of vengeance on the part of victim communities – it is possibly more accurate to postulate that that sense of requiring justice was never dormant.

4.4.4 Time may be tolled in many cases where international crimes have been committed

In those States which provide for prescription over international crimes, a number of national courts have found ways to circumvent statutes of limitation by arguing that time has been tolled, thus delaying the expiry of the limitation period. It is commonly accepted that the date from which time begins to run may be postponed for disability, fraudulent concealment or mistake.[236] However, in cases dealing with international crimes, other reasons for tolling time have also been cited. Crimes such as terrorism and forced disappearances have been considered as continuing crimes or permanent crimes.[237] The Inter-American Convention on the Forced Disappearances of Persons provides that such crimes 'shall be deemed continuous or permanent as long as the fate or whereabouts of the victim has not been determined.'[238] The recently adopted International Convention for the Protection of All Persons from Enforced Disappearance also provides that a statute of limitations over such a crime '[c]ommences from the moment when the offence of enforced disappearance ceases, taking into account its continuous nature.'[239] In Chile, where the Supreme Court has dismissed cases dealing with international crimes on the basis that time limitations have expired,[240] the Court has allowed the reopening of disappearances on the basis that these are a continuing crime; until a body is found, no statute of limitations can apply.[241] This reasoning was adopted by the Supreme Court of Chile in its judgment of 17 November 2004 in which it upheld the conviction and sentence of Miguel Krassnoff Martchenko, Juan Manuel Contreras Sepúlveda and others in a case of forced disappearance that occurred in 1975.[242] The Court found that the crime of aggravated abduction was continuous in

---

[236] See, e.g., Limitation Act 1980, Part II (UK).

[237] The Declaration on the Protection of All Persons from Enforced Disappearances, GA Res. 47/133, 47 UN GAOR Suppl. (No. 49) at 207, UN Doc. A/47/49 (1992), of 18 December 1992 provides in Art. 17(1) that '[a]cts constituting enforced disappearance shall be considered a continuing offence as long as the perpetrators continue to conceal the fate and the whereabouts of persons who have disappeared and these facts remain unclarified.' The second paragraph states that when the remedies provided for in article 2 of the International Covenant on Civil and Political Rights are no longer effective, the statute of limitations relating to acts of enforced disappearance shall be suspended until these remedies are re-established.

[238] Art. III.

[239] Art. 8(b) International Convention for the Protection of All Persons from Enforced Disappearance (2006).

[240] E.g., *Caso Uribe Tamblay, et al.*, Chile, Supreme Court, 19 August 1998; *Caso Quinones Lembach*, Chile, Supreme Court, 6 October 1998; *Caso Eugenia Martinez*, Chile, Supreme Court, 11 November 1998.

[241] E.g., *Caso Contreras Maluje*, Chile, Supreme Court, 26 October 1998.

[242] *Contreras Sepúlveda, Juan y otros (crimen) cascación fondo y forma*, Chile, Corte Suprema, 517/2004, Resolución 22267, available at: <www.derechos.org/nizkor/chile/doc/krassnoff.html>.

nature and was not completed within the period covered by the amnesty law. Given that prescription for a criminal act begins to run upon the cessation of that act, the Court held that this principle could not be applied to the case at issue because the criminal act was ongoing.[243] In the *Videla* case, the Supreme Court of Argentina held that the crime of baby-snatching and denial of identity were also continuing crimes until the children were found and their original identity was restored, so that the statute of limitations would only begin to run at that point.[244]

However, legal theories about statutes of limitations have varied drastically because of differences in domestic law. Thus, while Spanish and French courts have held that while a body has not been found, the statute of limitations for murder cannot run and the kidnapping should be treated as a continuing offence, German prosecutors have argued that where the body is never found, the case should be treated like a murder case (which in German law has no statute of limitation).[245] The recently adopted International Convention on Enforced Disappearances may help to harmonise domestic laws on this subject.[246] However, the 'continuing crime' theory in the case of disappearances until a body is found is by no means foolproof. When Argentinean major Jorge Olivera was arrested in Italy in July 2000 by reason of a French arrest warrant pertaining to the alleged torture and disappearance of a 22 year French woman in 1976 in Argentina, he managed to arrange a forged death certificate to be faxed to Italy, where the Appeals Court accepted it as proof that the victim had died on 11 November 1976 and that therefore the 22 year statute of limitations for kidnapping had since expired. This meant that the double criminality requirement for extradition was not fulfilled and Olivera was released from custody. Eight months later, the Italian Supreme Court of Cassation overturned the decision, noting that even if the certificate had been authentic, the crime could be characterised as 'the kidnapping of a person in order to interrupt the democratic order' – a crime subject to a 30 year statute of limitation, which meant Olivera could have been extradited to France.[247]

Time has also been deemed to have stopped in the case of crimes which form a whole from various difference offences.[248] Judges may also have to consider if time has tolled where legal proceedings have been brought in a different jurisdiction.[249] Where effective penal action has not been possible to initiate, courts have

[243] *Ibid.*, at paras. 37-39.

[244] *Videla, Jorge Rafael, s/recursos de apelacíon y nulidad*, Argentina, Resolution of the Cámera Federal de Apelaciones en lo Criminal y Correccional, Sala I, 9 September 1999.

[245] Under German law dating from the 1960s and 1970s prosecution of ex-Nazis, murder has no statute of limitations, while kidnapping is subject to such a limitation. Naomi Roht-Arriaza, *The Pinochet Effect: Transnational Justice in the Age of Human Rights* (Philadelphia: University of Pennsylvania Press, 2005), at 137.

[246] Art. 8, International Convention for the Protection of All Persons from Enforced Disappearances.

[247] Roht-Arriaza, *The Pinochet Effect*, at 129.

[248] Delmas-Marty, "La responsibilité pénale en échec", at 642.

[249] For example, in France, in proceedings concerning crimes of disappearances committee in Argentina – equated to kidnappings with torture in French law – the judge initially held that in two cases where the bodies of prisoners had been recovered the prescription period had expired. The Paris

found that time may be tolled. For instance, war has sometimes been argued to have prevented timely prosecution.[250] Courts have also recognised that time may be suspended when the actions of the accused have frustrated the inquiry or judgment[251] or where the prosecutor has not begun an investigation until the victims bring a complaint.[252]

Significantly in the case of international crimes, courts have taken into account the equitable consideration that criminal prosecutions may be virtually impossible to initiate during certain political regimes. A decision of the Czech Constitutional Court in 1993 confirmed the legitimacy of a law which sought to toll the limitation period from 25 February 1948 to 29 December 1989 for criminal acts for which people were not convicted due to 'political reasons incompatible with the basic principles of the legal order of a democratic State.'[253] The Court described its task as assessing 'whether the institution of the limitation of actions should be viewed as real or as fictional for a period when the infringement of legality in the entire sphere of legal life became component of the politically as well as governmentally protected regime of illegality.'[254] The Court held that '[i]f the State does not want to prosecute certain criminal acts or certain offenders, then the limitation of actions is pointless: in such cases, the running of the limitation period does not take place in reality and the limitation of actions, in and of itself, is fictitious.'[255]

Similarly, on 1 December 2005, the 11th Circuit Court of Appeals of the United States overturned a decision of the Federal Court which had found that a complaint against Colonel Carl Dorélien, a former member of Haiti's High Command during the period the military regime held power accused of serious human rights abuses was blocked by reason of the expiry of the 10 year statute of limitation. The Appeals Court found that the requirement that plaintiffs file within 10 years after abuses occurred can be suspended until a defendant enters the United States and personal jurisdiction can be obtained over him. Although the complainant filed his claims 10 years and five months after his torture, Dorélien did not come to the United States until 1995, so the filing of the complaint in October 2003 was timely. The court also held that the statute of limitations may be tolled until a defendant's regime is removed from power, based on the reasoning that:

Appeals Court reversed on 15 March 2000 on the grounds that the investigating magistrate had to consider if the statute of limitations had been tolled or interrupted on the basis of legal proceedings outside of France. Roht-Arriaza, *The Pinochet Effect*, at 124.

[250] Charles Noble Gregory, "The Effect of War on the Operation of Statutes of Limitation", 28 *Harvard Law Review* 673 (1914-1915).

[251] E.g., Art. 88 of the Chinese Penal Code.

[252] E.g., Art. 88(2) of the Chinese Penal Code.

[253] Decision relating to Law No. 198/1993, 21 December 1993, translated in English in Kritz (ed.), *Transitional Justice*, Vol. III, at 620. The law at issue was Act No. 198/1993, Art. 5 of which provides that 'the period of time from 25 February 1948 until 29 December 1989 shall not be counted as part of the limitation period for criminal acts if, due to political reasons incompatible with the basic principles of the legal order of a democratic State, [a person] was not finally and validly convicted or the charges [against him] were dismissed.'

[254] *Ibid.*, at 622.

[255] *Ibid.*, at 623.

> 'Congress acknowledged that plaintiffs face unique impediments such as reprisals from death squads and immunity of high-ranking government officials in bringing human rights litigation. Litigation will often not be possible until there has been a regime change in the plaintiff's country of origin, after which the plaintiff can investigate and compile evidence without fear of reprisals against him, his family and witnesses.'[256]

This reasoning is a powerful way of circumventing the expiry of a statute of limitations. If, hypothetically-speaking, an existing statute of limitation in Iraq had run for the crimes being prosecuted before the Iraqi Special Tribunal, one could imagine that a defendant before this tribunal could argue that Article 17(d) of the Statute (precluding statutes of limitations to international crimes and other crimes under Iraqi law committed in the period 17 July 1968 to 1 May 2003) violates the guarantee against *ex post facto* criminal liability. However, the principle of 'equitable tolling' could be argued to apply given that it was probably unimaginable that a victim of such crimes could have brought an action against the defendants during the reign of Saddam Hussein.

On the one hand, judicial reasoning based on the tolling of statutes of limitation could be considered to constitute contrary evidence of a customary rule prohibiting prescription for international crimes given that the objective of such argumentation is not to defeat the principle of prescription for such crimes but to prove that time has not yet run. On the other hand, all these considerations underscore the myriad of political and practical factors impacting upon the ability to begin politically-charged trials involving international crimes in good time and thereby support the idea that time should be no bar to the prosecution of the most serious crimes of the international legal order.

4.5 Preliminary conclusions

The analysis of international instruments and State practice pertinent to statutes of limitation reveals a general progression towards a customary rule banning their applicability to international crimes. Evidence of such a development is strongest for genocide and crimes against humanity, while the applicability of time limitations to war crimes would seem to be still contested by a significant vocal minority and only a handful of States would appear to explicitly rule out statutes of limitations for torture *per se*. The arguments relied on by a host of courts to reject statutes of limitation based upon the *nature* of such crimes, i.e., their non-derogable character, is supported by practice in the sense that more serious crimes have generally either not been subject to limitation periods or are subject to longer ones. However, the reasoning that the enforcement obligations flowing from the violation of a peremptory norm are also absolute does not appear to be founded upon consistent or uniform State practice or by the obligations deriving from the

---

[256] *Jean* v. *Dorélien*, United States, Judgment of the 11th Circuit of the Court of Appeals, 1 December 2005.

international law of State responsibility, particularly with regard to States other than the territorial one.

It should be kept in mind that the notion of prescription is a municipal law concept not universally recognised and does not amount to a general principle of law. Hence, the 'problem' of making statutes of limitation inapplicable to international crimes only arises in those (mainly civil law) States where general or specific rules of prescription are laid down in legislation. For those States that do not recognise general rules of prescription (mainly common law countries), the interests justifying statutes of limitation are protected by the judicially-made abuse of process doctrine which provides judges with discretionary power to stay proceedings where it appears that the long delay in initiating proceedings has caused such prejudice to the extent that a fair trial cannot be held. A number of unsuccessful cases by reason of poor or inconsistent witness testimony brought against persons for international crimes allegedly committed during WW II attests to the real problem of relying on this type of evidence so long after the fact. Instead of simply resting on the assumption (largely justifying in part statutes of limitation) that all criminal trials of persons accused of offences a significant number of years ago are *ipso facto* violative of fair trial guarantees, application of the abuse of process doctrine allows a judge to assess the strength of evidence according to the case at issue. This process is fairly close to an interests-analysis approach, which encourages the judge to balance competing interests in order to reach a reasonable and equitable solution to a legal problem – in this case, the interest of ensuring that defendants are not convicted upon 'stale' evidence *versus* the interest of punishing a crime of exceptional gravity despite the long delay in bringing a criminal complaint. The Australian cases suggest that decisions based on the need to balance competing policy considerations may validly be made on a case by case basis, dependent upon contextual specificities (e.g. the existence of probative evidence, reliable witnesses, etc.) rather than requiring a blanket rule outlawing statutes of limitations for international crimes.

The second main justification for statutes of limitation – that such laws ensure certainty and stability in the legal system – also needs to be balanced against the need for victims of international crimes to be certain that their tormentors will be brought to justice, notwithstanding how long it may take to bring the case to court. The myriad of obstacles to speedy trial of those accused of international crimes – political, practical and legal – militate against the concept of a time bar for these types of crimes. Nonetheless, it is true that if a person has committed a crime which is subject to a statute of limitation that has run, it would constitute a violation of the general principle of non-retroactivity for that person to then have to face charges for a crime committed at a time when charges could only be brought for a set period of time.[257] The major caveat to this statement is that time may be said to have tolled where the charges could not have been brought in an earlier period due to the political or legal circumstances of the time (e.g. a particular regime responsible

[257] See Miller, "The Convention on the Non-Applicability of Statutory Limitations", at 501.

for the atrocities committed holding power or amnesty laws upheld by the courts), or because of the acts of the accused (e.g. destroying evidence, going into hiding, assuming a different identity). Such reasoning based upon the principle of 'equitable tolling' aligns well with the practical realities of the problems facing victims or prosecutors in seeking timely justice for international crimes while at the same time not violating the fundamental human right not to be subject to retroactive law.

Chapter 5
IMMUNITIES

One type of impediment to the exercise of adjudicatory jurisdiction that has attracted enormous controversy historically and in recent years is immunities from prosecution. Jurisdictional immunity is an area of international law that has been the subject of extensive case-law and has attracted a large amount of scholarship and analysis. This chapter will attempt to confine the analysis to the parameters of our specific inquiry, i.e., what arguments have courts used to either uphold or reject immunity of individuals accused of international crimes, the relative strengths of these, and whether an interests-analysis approach would help to resolve any clashes between the rule of immunity and the imperative of prosecuting persons accused of international crimes.

First, it may be helpful to recall that that there are at least four different types of immunity which need to be distinguished from each other and which operate in different ways upon the exercise of jurisdiction. These are: (1) State immunity; (2) Functional immunity; (3) Personal immunity; and (4) national immunity. Only the latter three types of immunity attach to the State's organs as individuals and hence are directly the subject of international criminal processes. Nonetheless, although the first type – State immunity – is concerned with suing a foreign State in civil or administrative proceedings, there exists a close/analogous relation to the other two types of immunity in international law (functional and personal) and hence the case law and commentary relating to issues of State immunity remains extremely relevant to our topic. In addition to these immunities, the Act of State doctrine – a mechanism of judicial self-restraint applied in some legal systems – which does not strictly amount to immunity, but which has similar consequences and is related in some aspects, particularly to functional immunity, needs to be considered.

Rules of immunity, founded upon the inviolability of the State and its agents as a means to promote peaceful inter-State relations, have increasingly become subject to doubt as to their applicability, consistency or legitimacy *vis-à-vis* international crimes because of the serious nature of the offences at issue which suggests that individuals should not be immune from prosecution for these types of violations which offend the international legal order and which all States have an interest in repressing. A variety of legal theories have been advanced in litigation, with varying degrees of success, to defeat all types of immunity. The opinions of the majority judges in the seminal *Pinochet* case in the United Kingdom House of Lords reflect strains of these legal theories in a judgment that ultimately does not

Y.Q. Naqvi, Impediments to Exercising Jurisdiction over International Crimes

recognise the immunity of the former Head of State of Chile (functional immunity) for the crime of torture.[1]

With regard to personal immunity, in an important judgment the International Court of Justice (ICJ) upheld the absolute personal immunity of an incumbent minister of foreign affairs in regard to other national jurisdictions notwithstanding whether he or she was accused of international crimes.[2] In *obiter*, the Court listed a number of so-called 'exceptions' to this immunity as a way to underline that immunity does not lead to (or mean the same thing as) impunity. In coming to its judgment in the *Arrest Warrant* case, the ICJ ostensibly sought to balance two competing interests – the interest of preserving peaceful inter-State relations by ensuring that foreign ministers could effectively perform their role without outside interference with the interest of repressing the most serious crimes of international concern. Some commentators have questioned how much weight the Court accorded to competing values 'such as the struggle to prevent and punish attacks upon individual human dignity,' which, it is claimed, 'were not given any priority or recognition by the Court.'[3] The question of the legality of immunities, both personal and functional, under international law for international crimes is therefore unquestionably one amenable to an interests-analysis approach, and in this sense, cannot be said to be a settled matter.[4]

5.1 Definition and historical background

Immunity may be broadly defined as '[a]ny exemption from a duty, liability, or service of process; esp. such an exemption granted to a public official.'[5] It should be clarified at the outset that the question of immunity arises only once jurisdiction has been established. If there is no jurisdiction over a case, then a court need not consider any further pleas based on immunity.[6] This impediment is therefore more accurately characterised as a preliminary exception to jurisdiction. As noted

---

[1] *R* v. *Bow Street Metropolitan Stipendiary Magistrate*, ex parte *Pinochet Ugarte*, United Kingdom, House of Lords Judgment of 24 March 1999 [1999] 2 *All ER* 97 (referred to as '*Pinochet III*' in the text).

[2] *Arrest Warrant of April 11th 2000 (Democratic Republic of the Congo* v. *Belgium)*, Judgment, Merits, 41 *ILM* 536 (2002) (hereafter, *Arrest Warrant* case).

[3] Andrew Clapham, "National Action Challenged: Sovereignty, Immunity and Universal Jurisdiction before the International Court of Justice", in Mark Lattimer and Philippe Sands QC (eds.), *Justice for Crimes Against Humanity* (Oxford and Portland, Oregon: Hart Publishing, 2003), at 312.

[4] See Sir Arthur Watts, "The Legal Position in International Law of Heads of States, Heads of Governments and Foreign Ministers", 247 *RdC-III* 52 (1994), noting that this is an area of law 'which is in many respects still unsettled, and on which limited state practice casts an uneven light.'

[5] Bryan A. Garner, *Black's Law Dictionary*, 8th edn. (St. Paul, Minn: West Group, 2004), at 765.

[6] The judgment of the majority in the *Arrest Warrant* case has been criticised for failing to assess whether Belgium's exercise of universal jurisdiction over war crimes and crimes against humanity allegedly committed in the DRC was lawful prior to examining the question of whether Mr. Yerodia enjoyed personal immunity thereof. See *Arrest Warrant* case, President Guillaume's Separate Opinion, paras. 1-17; Judge Ranjeva's Opinion, paras. 1-12; Judges Higgings, Kooijmans, Buergenthal's Joint

above, there are four types of immunity which need to be distinguished from each other, though the thrust of this chapter and study is concerned with only two of these – functional and personal immunity – which relate to criminal proceedings against individuals accused of international crimes. For this reason, these two will be defined first. The Act of State doctrine is briefly examined in connection with functional immunity.

5.1.1 Functional immunity

Functional immunity (immunity *ratione materiae*) essentially means that 'State officials cannot suffer the consequences of wrongful acts which are not attributable to them personally but to the State on whose behalf they act …'[7] This type of immunity is thus a *substantive defence* to a violation of a national or international rule. Any responsibility for an internationally unlawful act is deemed to be imputable to the State and not to the individual. Hence, to benefit from this immunity, a person must be either a *de jure* or *de facto* State official.[8] The acts of an official that are performed within the context of the exercise of State authority under international law are presumptively committed on behalf of the State.[9] This means that this type of immunity continues even after the person has left office.[10]

It is generally accepted that functional immunity is a creature of customary international law,[11] which 'stems from the concept of sovereignty.'[12] As sovereignty protects States from undue inference in their internal affairs, this type of immunity entails that a person acting on behalf of a sovereign State is not individually accountable for any acts committed while acting in an official function. Moreover, sovereignty means that States may not sit in judgment upon each other for acts performed in a 'sovereign capacity.' The practice of conferring such immunity dates back to the eighteenth and nineteenth centuries.[13] The classic articulation of

---

Separate Opinion, paras. 2-18; Judge Rezek's Opinion, paras. 3-11; *Ad hoc* Judge van den Wyngaert's Dissenting Opinion, paras. 4 and 7.

[7] *Blaškić (judgment on the request of Croatia)*, ICTY, Appeals Chamber, Judgment of 29 October 1997, Case No. IT-95-14-AR108*bis*, para. 38.

[8] See Arts. 4-11, ILC Articles on State Responsibility (2001).

[9] On the presumption of authority in functional immunity, see Rosanne Van Alebeek, *The Immunity of States and their Officials in the Light of International Criminal Law and International Human Rights Law* (Oxford: OUP, 2008), at 112-135.

[10] An example of State practice in this regard may be found in the *travaux préparatoires* on Art. 39(2) of the Vienna Convention on Diplomatic Relations, which provides that 'with respect to acts performed by such a person in the exercise of his functions as a member of the mission, immunity shall continue to subsist.' The ILC, in their discussions on the Article, considered that such acts were 'not really private acts at all but acts of the sending State.' Chairman J. Zourak on the rationale of Art. 30.2 of its Draft Report on the Law Relating to Diplomatic Intercourse and Immunities (now Art. 39.2 VCDR), 1 *YBILC* 217 (1957), para. 22.

[11] Antonio Cassese, *International Criminal Law* (Oxford: OUP, 2003), at 264.

[12] Clapham, "National Action Challenged", at 313.

[13] *Blaškić (judgment on the request of Croatia)*, ICTY, Appeals Chamber, Judgment of 29 October 1997, Case No. IT-95-14-AR108*bis*, para. 38, fn. 5: '*See, e.g.,* the statement made as early as 1797 by

functional immunity is found in the famous *McLeod* (or *Caroline*) case.[14] During the Canadian rebellion of 1837 against the British authorities (Canada being at the time under British sovereignty), British troops, led by Captain McLeod, violently captured the ship *Caroline*, which the British government claimed was being used to transport the rebels and carry supplies to them. The ship was set on fire and cast down Niagara Falls, killing two Americans in the process. In 1840, McLeod was arrested in Lewiston (New York State) on charges of murder and arson. An exchange of diplomatic notes between the two Governments ensued. United States Secretary of State Webster enunciated the official position of the United States,

> '[t]hat an individual forming part of a public force, and acting under the authority of his Government, is not to be held answerable, as a private trespasser or malefactor, is a principle of public law sanctioned by the usages of all civilised nations, and which the Government of the United States has no inclination to dispute … [W]hether the process be criminal or civil, the fact of having acted under public authority, and in obedience to the orders of lawful superiors, must be regarded as a valid defence; otherwise individuals would be holden responsible for injuries resulting from the acts of Government, and even from the operations of public war.'[15]

More recent practice confirming the rule of functional immunity includes statements made by France in the *Rainbow Warrior* case,[16] and the Supreme Court of

---

the United States Attorney-General in the *Governor Collot* case. A civil suit had been brought against Mr. Collot, Governor of the French island of Guadeloupe. The United States Attorney-General wrote: "I am inclined to think, if the seizure of the vessel is admitted to have been an official act, done by the defendant by virtue, or under colour, of the powers vested in him as governor, that it will of itself be a sufficient answer to the plaintiff's action; that the defendant ought not to answer in our courts for any mere *irregularity* in the exercise of his powers; and that the *extent* of his authority can, with propriety or convenience, be determined only by the constituted authorities of his own nation." J.B. Moore, *A Digest of International Law*, 1906, vol. II, at 23.'

[14] Robert Y. Jennings, "The *Caroline* and *McLeod* cases", 32 *AJIL* 82 (1938).

[15] *British and Foreign State Papers*, Vol. 29, at 1139, cited in Jennings, *ibid.*, at 94. Although McLeod was not immediately released due to lack of appropriate legal instruments to allow the federal government to compel the State of New York to release him, Webster, in further communications to the British Foreign Secretary Lord Ashburton, acknowledged that, 'for an act committed by the command of his sovereign … an individual cannot be responsible, in the ordinary courts of another State. It would regard it as a high indignity if a citizen of its own, acting under its authority, and by its special command, in such cases, were held to answer in a municipal tribunal, and to undergo punishment, as if the behest of his Government were no defense or protection to him.' Report Law Officers (1854), F.O. 83.2209, cited in Jennings, *ibid.*, at 97.

[16] When the two French agents who had sunk the *Rainbow Warrior* in New Zealand were arrested by the local police, France stated that their imprisonment in New Zealand was not justified 'taking into account in particular the fact that they acted under military orders and that France [was] ready to give an apology and to pay compensation to New Zealand for the damage suffered' (see the Ruling of 6 July 1986 of the United Nations Secretary-General, in United Nations Reports of International Arbitral Awards, Vol. XIX, at 213).

Israel in the *Eichmann* case,[17] as well as the judgment of the German Supreme Court in the *Scotland Yard* case.[18]

However, not all commentators view functional immunity as an autonomous rule, but rather rationalise functional immunity as a corollary of State immunity. For instance, Kelsen explained functional immunity in the following way:

> 'No state is allowed to exercise through its own courts jurisdiction over another state unless the other state expressly consents ... Since a state manifests its legal existence only through acts performed by human beings in their capacity as organs of the state, that is to say, through acts of state, the principle that no state has jurisdiction over another state must mean that a state must not exercise jurisdiction through its own courts over acts of another state unless the other state consents. Hence the principle applies not only in case a state as such is sued in a court of another state but also in case an individual is the defendant or the accused and the civil or criminal delict for which the individual is prosecuted has the character of an act of state.'[19]

For Kelsen, the absence of personal responsibility is the consequence of State immunity. His argument stems from a much broader notion of act of State immunity, which protects the governmental acts themselves, not merely the State from the exercise of jurisdiction by foreign State.[20] However, there are strong arguments supporting the alternative view that functional immunity is an autonomous rule. First, there is the fact that State officials may be immune in cases where the State is not. This is most apparent in cases where the restrictive approach to State immunity is applied.[21] Thus, while a State may be sued for *acta jure gestionis*, the State official who performed or authorised the act is not individually responsible for pay-

[17] The Court stated that: 'The theory of "Act of State" means that the act performed by a person as an organ of the State – whether he was head of the State or a responsible official acting on the Government's orders – must be regarded as an act of the State alone. It follows that only the latter bears responsibility therefor, and it also follows that another State has no right to punish the person who committed the act, save with the consent of the State whose mission he performed. Were it not so, the first State would be interfering in the internal affairs of the second, which is contrary to the conception of the equality of States based on their sovereignty,' 36 *ILR* 308-09. The Court went on to argue, however, that this type of immunity did not apply to war crimes and crimes against humanity.

[18] *Scotland Yard*, Germany, Federal High Court [*Bundesgerichtshof*], Decision of 26 September 1978, in 32 *Neue Juristische Wochenschrift* 1101-2 (1979) (finding that the Director of Scotland Yard could not face German civil jurisdiction because he had acted as a State agent in issuing a report on the criminal activities of the Church of Scientology). In a similar case, a Dutch court considered that a report of the German Police on the Church of Scientology 'can only be regarded as an act done in his official capacity and not as a private person.' *Church of Scientology in the Netherlands Foundation and Others* v. *(1) Herold and (2) Heinrich Bauer Verlag,* The Netherlands (1980), 65 *ILR* 380, at 381-382.

[19] Hans Kelsen, *Principles of International Law*, 2nd edn. (New York: Holt, Rinehart & Winston, 1966), at 358.

[20] As Kelsen puts it, 'The immunity from the jurisdiction of another State is not, as this principle is usually formulated, attached to the very "person" of the State ... but to the acts of the State as the acts performed by the government, at its command, or with its authorization.' Hans Kelsen, *Peace through Law* (Chapel Hill: University of North Carolina Press, 1944), at 82-83.

[21] See notes 109-116 *infra*, for an explanation of the development of the restrictive approach to State immunity.

ing any damages. As explained by one commentator, '[w]hile under the reasoning proposed by Kelsen the individual state official cannot be held personally responsible; in the autonomous variant the individual state official bears no responsibility in his personal capacity.'[22] This is why Anzilotti described the acts performed by diplomatic agents in the exercise of official functions as 'facts legally imputable not to him but to another subject.'[23] Similarly, Conforti has explained that 'the agent cannot be summoned to appear in court to account for them civilly or criminally, not because he is accorded immunity, but because they are not his acts.'[24] In this sense, the term 'immunity' is probably the wrong term to describe this impediment to prosecution, which is really a defence by reason of lack of legal liability.

5.1.2 **Act of State doctrine**

While functional immunity is a rule of customary law, the Act of State doctrine is a domestic doctrine of judicial self-restraint whereby domestic courts will refrain from judging the acts of a foreign sovereign done in his own territory.[25] In other words, it is a form of non-justiciability. The doctrine applies to the merits of the case and may be pleaded by any person regardless of their status. The act of State doctrine precludes a claim or defence that relies upon an assertion that a foreign official act was illegal under foreign law. The doctrine is not a rule of international law,[26] although there are similar considerations to the principle of immunity due to the fact that 'the doctrine is probably a derivative of foreign sovereign immunity in its early absolute version.'[27] The doctrine has mainly developed in common law jurisdictions,[28] though with some variations.[29] In the United States, while the doctrine was fairly widely conceived in early jurisprudence,[30] its scope has gradually been narrowed over time and restricted to cases requiring courts to ascertain the

---

[22] Van Alebeek, *The Immunity of States and their Officials*, at 107.

[23] D. Anzilotti, "Case Comment", 9 *RDI* 217 (1915), at 219, transl. by van Alebeek, *The Immunity of States and their Officials*, at 107.

[24] B. Conforti, *Diretto internazionale*, 3rd edn. (1987), at 220, transl. by van Alebeek, *The Immunity of States and their Officials*, at 107.

[25] Brigitte Stern, "Immunities for Heads of State: Where Do We Stand?", in Mark Lattimer and Philippe Sands QC (eds.), *Justice for Crimes Against Humanity* (Oxford and Portland, Oregon: Hart Publishing, 2003), at 77, fn. 18 (noting that the Executive can ask the courts to set aside the doctrine of Act of State).

[26] See A. Watts and R. Jennings (eds.), *Oppenheim's International Law* 9th edn. (1992), at 369. See also *Border Guards* case, 100 *ILM* 364, at 372 (in which the German *Bundesverfassungsgericht* stated that the act of state doctrine is not a general rule of international law).

[27] Andrea Bianchi, "Immunity v Human Rights: The Pinochet Case", 2 *EJIL* 268 (1999).

[28] Some civil law countries do apply the same doctrine. See Benedetto Conforti, *International Law and the Role of Domestic Legal Systems* (1993), at 20 et seq.; Prosper Weil, "Le contrôle par les tribuneaux nationaux de la liceité internationale des actes des Etats étrangers", *Annuaire Français de Droit International* (1971), at 9 et seq.

[29] See M. Singer, "The Act of State of the United Kingdom: An Analysis with Comparison to the United States", 75 *AJIL* 283 (1981).

[30] The classic statement of the Act of State doctrine is said to derive from *Underhill* v. *Hernandez*, 168 US 250 (1897), at 253: 'Every sovereign is bound to respect the independence of every other

validity of the sovereign acts of foreign States.[31] A number of exceptions, arguably including in the case of human rights violations, have emerged in jurisprudence.[32] In the United Kingdom, the early articulation of the doctrine by the House of Lords in *Duke of Brunswick* v. *King of Hanover* gave a similarly wide scope of judicial restraint.[33] The modern version of the doctrine has been asserted by Lord Wilberforce in the *Buttes Gas* case, to the effect that there is in English law a general principle of judicial restraint which prevents courts from judging any case involving transactions of foreign States.[34] In *Pinochet I*, the Law Lords confirmed that this is the controlling precedent in the United Kingdom. However, the majority judges held that any plea of Act of State would be overridden by clear contrary parliamentary intent as reflected in legislation.[35] A public policy exception to the doctrine also appears to be fairly well accepted.[36]

---

sovereign State, and the courts of one country will not sit in judgment on the acts of the government of another, done within its own territory.'

[31] See, e.g., *Alfred Dunhill* v. *Republic of Cuba*, United States, 425 US 682 (1976), 15 *ILM* 735, 66 *ILR* 212 (refusing to recognise a repudiation by the state of Cuba of commercial obligations as an act of State).

[32] See *Trajano* v. *Marcos*, 878 F.2d 1439 (9th Cir. 1989); *Filartiga* v. *Pena-Irala*, 630 F.2d 876, 889-90 (2d Cir. 1980); *Forti* v. *Suarez-Mason*, 672 F. Suppl. 1531, 1545 (N.D. Cal. 1987); *Kadić, et al.*, v. *Karadžić*, 70 F. 3rd 232 (2nd Cir. 1995). See also *Restatement (Third) of the Foreign Relations Law of the United States*, 1987, § 443.

[33] *Duke of Brunswick* v. *King of Hanover* (1848) 2 HL Cas. 1, at 17 (*per* Lord Cottenham).

[34] *Buttes Gas* v. *Hammer (Nos. 2 &3)* [1981] 3 *All ER* 616, at 628; *(no. 3)* [1982] AC 888, at 931 et seq.

[35] *Pinochet I*, at 1332 and 1338. Lord Nicholls described the doctrine as 'a common law principle of uncertain application which prevents the English courts from examining the legality of certain acts which formed in the exercise of sovereign authority within a foreign country, or occasionally yields to it.' The Court found that the legislation enacting the Torture Convention and the Convention on the Taking of Hostages clearly indicated that the British Parliament intended UK courts to exercise jurisdiction over such offences when committed extra-territorially. Criminal Justice Act 1988 (UK).

[36] In *Pinochet III*, the Law Lords did not discuss Act of State in detail, however Lord Saville was of the view that any such plea based on non-justiciability would be defeated by reason of the fact that parties to the Torture Convention must have accepted that foreign domestic courts could exercise jurisdiction over their own officials should they commit torture. Lord Millet also noted that immunity *ratione materiae* is almost indistinguishable from the Act of State doctrine, and so by rejecting the former, also indirectly rejected the latter as applied to acts of torture. It may also be recalled that in an earlier case, the House of Lords refused to recognise a Nazi decree depriving German Jews residing abroad of their citizenship and taking their properties as being a law. *Oppenheimer* v. *Cattermole*, United Kingdom, 1976 AC 249. The Court held that 'so grave an infringement of human rights' should lead to the refusal of recognition of the decree as law. In the more recent case of *Kuwait Airways Corporation (KAC)* v. *Iraqi Airways Company (IAC) and others*, it was held for the first time that the acts of a foreign State within its territory may be refused recognition because they constitute flagrant breaches of public international law. *Kuwait Airways Corporation (KAC)* v. *Iraqi Airways Company (IAC) and others*, United Kingdom, Court of Appeal, November 2000, 3 *WLR* 1117, at 1127H-1128E; confirmed by the House of Lords, 16 May 2002 [2002] UKHL 19, available at: <www.parliament.the-stationary-office.co.uk/pa/ld200102/ldjudgmt>. Thus, because Resolution 369 of 9 September 1990, which transferred all property of KAC worldwide to IAC, was linked to the illegal aggression towards Kuwait by Iraq on 2 August 1990, it was given no recognition. Lord Steyn commented that in his opinion, 'the Court of Appeal was right to extend the public policy exception beyond human rights to flagrant breaches of public international law.' *Ibid.*, HL, at para. 114.

5.1.3 **Personal immunity**

Personal immunity refers to the comprehensive immunity from the jurisdiction of foreign national courts enjoyed by a limited group of State officials during their tenure. This immunity relates to procedural law meaning that the person enjoys inviolability from civil or criminal jurisdiction.[37] As stated by the IMTFE, in the case of *Oshima*, Ambassador of Japan in Germany:

> 'Oshima's special defence is that in connection with his activities in Germany he is protected by diplomatic immunity and is exempt from prosecution. Diplomatic privilege does not import immunity from legal liability, but only exemption from trials by the Courts of the state to which an Ambassador is accredited. In any event this immunity has no relation to crimes against international law charged before a tribunal having jurisdiction.'[38]

Such immunity attaches to the status of the person and immunises the person for all acts – both private and public – from prosecution before the courts of certain other States while they are in office. This means that such officials are immune from proceedings in other States even when on a private visit or acting in a private capacity while holding office, because as one court put it, private acts 'constitute the necessary basis for the exercise of public activities.'[39] Personal immunity is not a right of the individual and it can be waived by the State. The immunity ends when the person leaves office. However, those persons benefiting from personal immunity also enjoy functional immunity, which will continue once the person has left office. Some distinctions, however, need to be made between various types of personal immunities. Apart from heads of State, persons who may benefit from such immunity include senior members of cabinet, diplomatic agents and high-ranking agents of international organisations.[40] The scope of the immunities granted to these varies dependant on the customary rule and the functionality of the office and should therefore be examined separately.

---

[37] Cassese, *International Criminal Law*, at 266.

[38] B.V.A. Röling and C.F. Rüter (eds.), *The Tokyo Judgment. The International Military Tribunal for the Far East, 29 April 1946-12 November 1949*, Vol. 1 (Amsterdam, UP Amsterdam BBV, 1977), at 456.

[39] *De Meeüs* v. *Forzano*, Italy, Corte di Cassazione (1940), 32 *RDI* (1940), 93 at 94, transl. van Alebeek, *The Immunity of States and their Officials*, at 161.

[40] *Arrest Warrant* case, para. 51: 'in international law it is firmly established that, as also diplomatic and consular agents, certain holders of high-ranking office in a State, such as the Head of State, Head of Government and Minister of Foreign Affairs, enjoy immunities from jurisdiction in other States, both civil and criminal.' The immunity of high-ranking agents of international organisations does not form part of this chapter. On this subject, see *Difference Relating to Immunity from Legal Process of a Special Rapporteur of the Commission on Human Rights*, ICJ Advisory Opinion of 29 April 1999, ICJ Reports 1999; and *Applicability of Article VI, Section 22, of the Convention on the Privileges and Immunities of the United Nations*, ICJ Advisory Opinion of 15 December 1989, ICJ Reports 1990.

5.1.3.1 *Diplomatic immunity*

The inviolability of diplomatic agents is a well established customary rule, having a long history dating back to the practice of the Hittites, Babylonians, Egyptians, Greeks and Romans.[41] Although there was some early practice of a restrictive immunity for diplomatic agents during the Renaissance based upon a reading of Roman law, this eventually passed out of practice.[42] It was accepted at an early stage that ambassadors enjoyed immunity from criminal proceedings, even when crimes had been committed against the receiving State.[43] In the present time, diplomatic agents enjoy almost absolute immunity from civil suit in the receiving suit as well.[44] This does not mean that diplomatic agents are exempted from liability; they are merely immune from suit.[45] While a court considering the existence of functional immunity must look into the nature of the acts, diplomatic immunity prevents *any* finding on the merits.[46] This entails that courts would first look to the personal immunity before deciding if functional immunity exists.[47] The 1961 Vienna Convention on Diplomatic Relations authoritatively codifies the rules of diplomatic immunity and is widely accepted to reflect customary law.[48] Article 31(1) of the Convention lays down the rule on immunity. While inviolability of diplomatic agents is absolute with regard to criminal proceedings,[49] the Article

---

[41] See, e.g., Linda Frey and Marsha Frey, *The History of Diplomatic Immunity* (Columbus, OH: Ohio State University Press, 1999); F. Przetacznik, "The history of the jurisdictional immunity of the diplomatic agents in English law", 7 *The Anglo-American law review* 348-395 (1978). Art. 29 of the Vienna Convention on Diplomatic Relations, 500 *UNTS* 95 lays the principle that: 'The person of a diplomatic agent shall be inviolable. He shall not be liable to any form of arrest or detention. The receiving state shall treat him with due respect and shall take all appropriate steps to prevent any attack on his person, freedom and dignity.'

[42] George Jn., B.J., "Immunities and Exceptions", in M. Cherif Bassiouni (ed.), *International and Criminal Law*, 2nd edn., Vol. II (Ardsley, New York: Transnational Publishers, Inc., 1999), at 107.

[43] See Eileen Denza, *Diplomatic Law, A Commentary on the Vienna Convention on Diplomatic Relations,* 2nd edn. (Oxford: Clarendon Press, 1998), at 229 for an overview of developments.

[44] This was established in English law as early as 1708 (see The English Diplomatic Privileges Act 1708 (Anne's Law)). See also *Taylor* v. *Best*, United Kingdom, 14 CB 487, at 519. Italy was one of the last countries to recognise this almost absolute immunity. See *De Meeüs* v. *Forzana*, Italy 93 *RDI* (1940).

[45] *Empson* v. *Smith*, United Kingdom (1965), [1965] 2 *All ER* 881, at 886 (*per* Lord Diplock); 41 *ILR* 407, at 514.

[46] Van Alebeek, *The Immunity of States and their Officials*, at 162.

[47] As Dinstein put it, functional immunity 'is eclipsed by the shadow of the personal immunity.' Yoram Dinstein, "Diplomatic Immunity from Jurisdiction *Ratione Materiae*", 15 *ICLQ* 76 (1966), at 79.

[48] As of July 2009, 186 States are party to the 1961 Convention. In 1969, the Supreme Court of China held that '[t]he fact that the Republic of China has not yet ratified the Vienna Convention does not prevent the application of Article 31 in our country because it is a principle of international law, common and customary, that this provision has crystallized, being on an expression of it.' *M.H.* v. *Embassy of the Republic of China* (1969), 70 *ILR* 394. See also *Case Concerning United States Diplomatic and Consular Staff in Tehran (United States of America* v. *Iran)*, Judgment, ICJ Reports 1980, 3, at 40, para. 86.

[49] The only recourse for the receiving State would be to declare the agent *persona non grata* in accordance with Art. 9 of the Convention. The sending State would then need to recall the person or

lists three exceptions to the rule of immunity for civil or administrative jurisdiction.[50] Diplomatic immunity is not a right and the sending State is able to waive the personal immunity of a diplomatic agent.[51] Moreover, unlike the other types of immunity, diplomatic immunity is very much tied to the notion of consent of the forum State.

5.1.3.2 *Head of State Immunity*

Personal immunity for heads of State is a rule of customary international law and is historically based on the assumption that the head of State and sovereign are one.[52] Justice Robert H. Jackson, in his Report to the US President on the works for the prosecution of major German war criminals, described head of state immunity as an 'obsolete doctrine' which was probably 'a relic of the doctrine of the divine right of kings.'[53] Arguably, since the formation of the modern State, the position of head of State has changed to a remarkable degree and may in fact be dependent upon the constitutional organization of the State.[54] Heads of State enjoy absolute immunity from the criminal jurisdiction of foreign States.[55] As for diplomatic immunity, such immunity may however be waived.[56] According to the Institut de Droit International (IDI), such a waiver may be explicit or implicit but it must be certain.[57] In its 2001 resolution on the matter of immunities, the IDI stated that '[s]uch a waiver *should* be made when the Head of State is suspected of having committed crimes of a particularly serious nature, or when the exercise of his or her

terminate his functions within the mission.

[50] These exceptions are (a) A real action relating to private immovable property situated in the territory of the receiving State, unless he holds it on behalf of the sending State for the purposes of the mission; (b) An action relating to succession in which the diplomatic agent is involved as executor, administrator, heir or legatee as a private person and not on behalf of the sending State; (c) An action relating to any professional or commercial activity exercised by the diplomatic agent in the receiving State outside his official functions. Art. 31(1) Vienna Convention on Diplomatic Relations.

[51] Art. 32(1) of the Convention provides that 'immunity from jurisdiction of diplomatic agents … may be waived by the sending State.'

[52] See, e.g., *Lafontant* v. *Aristide*, 844 F. Suppl. 128, 132 (EDNY 1994): 'Head of state immunity, like foreign sovereign immunity, is premised on the concept that a state and its ruler are one for purposes of immunity.'

[53] Justice Robert H. Jackson, Report to the US President on 6 June 1945, in *International Conference on Military Trials*, at 47.

[54] Sir Arthur Watts, "The Legal Position in International Law of Heads of States, Heads of Governments and Foreign Ministers", 247 *RdC-III* 21 (1994).

[55] See, e.g., *ibid.*, at 13; Hazel Fox, *The Law of State Immunity* (2002), at 441; J. Salmon, *Manuel de droit diplomatique* (1994), at 599; *Pinochet III*; Institut de Droit International, Resolution on the Immunities from Jurisdiction and Execution of Heads of State and of Government in International Law (2001), 69 *AIDI* 743 (2000-2001) (hereafter, IDI Resolution on Immunities), Art. 2.

[56] See In re *Doe*, United States, 860 F.2d 40, 45 (2d Cir. 1988): 'Because it is the state that gives the power to lead and the ensuing trappings of power – including immunity – the state may therefore take back that which it bestowed upon its erstwhile leaders … [B]y issuing the waiver, the Philippine government has declared its decision to revoke an attribute of [the Marcos'] former political positions; namely, head-of-state immunity.'

[57] IDI Resolution on Immunities, Art. 7.

functions is not likely be impeded by the measures that the authorities of the forum may be called upon to take.'[58] However, this would appear to be an exhortation based on policy considerations rather than on obligations under international law.[59] There is certainly no State practice supporting this statement.

In the *Arrest Warrant* case, the ICJ noted that 'certain international courts' are not bound by immunities, whether personal or functional, citing as examples the two *ad hoc* international criminal tribunals, both of which had indicted incumbent heads of State and Government[60] and the Statute of the ICC.[61] On this basis, the Special Court for Sierra Leone held that Charles Taylor – the incumbent President of Liberia when the indictment was issued by the Court – could be subject to its jurisdiction as an international court.[62] The ICJ also noted that States could lift the immunity of their own officials to prosecute them for international crimes. This paved the way for Saddam Hussein to be prosecuted before the Iraqi Special Tribunal and also for Pinochet to be stripped a number of times of his parliamentary immunity in order to be prosecuted in Chile. However, these examples are not strictly speaking 'exceptions' to the general rule of immunity,[63] although they are framed in this way by the ICJ as a way to soften its absolute stance on personal immunity. By reason of its definition and logic, the operation of immunity only arises in cases involving two sovereign States. It is questionable then whether these cases may be used as evidence of the 'defeat' of the sovereign immunity preliminary exception to jurisdiction as has been claimed by some commentators.[64] In every case before a *national* court – where the personal immunity principle is most certainly relevant – proceedings have been stayed by reason of the head of State immunity enjoyed by the defendant.[65]

---

[58] *Ibid.*, Art. 7(2). [Emphasis added]

[59] See also Institut de Droit International, Resolution on International Crimes and Immunities from Jurisdiction of States and their Agents, adopted 10 September 2009, at Naples (on file with author) (hereafter, IDI Resolution on International Crimes and Immunities), Art. II(3): 'States *should* consider waiving immunity where international crimes are allegedly committed by their agents'. [Emphasis added]

[60] See *Milošević*, ICTY, Decision on Preliminary Motions, 8 November 2001, Case. No. IT-02-54-PT, at paras. 26-34; *Kambanda,* ICTR, Judgment of 4 September 1998, Case No. ICTR-97-23-S, para. 44.

[61] *Arrest Warrant* case, para. 61.

[62] *Taylor, Charles Ghankay*, SCSL, Case No. SCSL-2003-01-I, Decision on Immunity from Jurisdiction, 31 May 2004 (hereafter, *Taylor* Decision on Immunity).

[63] See, e.g., Christian Dominicé, "Quelques observations sur l'immunité pénale de l'ancien chef d'Etat", 2 *RGDIP* (1999), at 307: 'The notion of immunity from jurisdiction is irrelevant before an international tribunal.' Author's translation.

[64] See, e.g., Michael J. Kelly, *Nowhere to Hide: Defeat of the Sovereign Immunity Defense for Crimes of Genocide and the Trials of Slobodan Milosevic and Saddam Hussein* (New York: Peter Lang, Inc., 2005).

[65] See, e.g., *Castro, Fidel*, Spain (*Audiencia nacional*), Order (auto) of 4 March 1999, no. 1999/2723, in CD Rom, EL DERECHO, 2002, Criminal case law; *Sharon Ariel and others*, Belgium, Court of Cassation, Judgment of 12 February 2003, available at: <www.cass.be/cgi-juris/juris-cass-a1.pl> (hereafter, *Sharon* case). In *Mugabe*, reported in 53 *ICLQ* 789 (2004), an English court held that a warrant could not be issued for the arrest of Robert Mugabe on charges of international crimes on

On the other hand, the scope of Head of State immunity in respect of civil proceedings is subject to some controversy.[66] Early cases rejected personal immunity from civil jurisdiction for acts of a private nature.[67] However, in the nineteenth century common law countries came to extend immunity to private acts of Heads of State from civil proceedings.[68] The 1978 State Immunity Act (UK) (SIA) grants a wide immunity to foreign Heads of State from civil suit, by reference to the Diplomatic Privileges Act 1964 (subject to necessary modifications) which gives effect to the 1961 Vienna Convention on Diplomatic Relations.[69] This rule applies whether or not the Head of State is visiting for private or official reasons and indeed whether they are in the UK or not.[70] Similar rules apply in the relevant legislation in Australia.[71] Legislation in South Africa, India, and Malaysia does not allow for any exceptions to immunity.[72] In the United States, the question of civil suits against Heads of State has generated considerable academic and judicial debate, leading one scholar to comment that Head of State immunity is 'at best [an] amorphous legal doctrine whose very existence is not entirely settled in U.S. law and whose reach is almost completely uncertain.'[73] The 1976 Foreign State Immunity Act (FSIA) does not codify the rule, which means that courts rely on conclusive executive suggestions of immunity. The State Department has consistently held the view that foreign Heads of State enjoy absolute immunity from civil jurisdiction in the US, a position that courts have tended to accept.[74] For its part, the IDI resolution rejects inviolability of Heads of State from civil and administrative jurisdiction except in relation to acts performed in the exercise of his or her official function.[75]

---

the basis that he was a presently serving Head of State of Zimbabwe at the time the proceedings were brought. But see *Kadhafi*, France, *Cour de Cassation*, decision of 13 March 2001, no. 1414, in Bulletin des arrêts de la Court de Cassation, Chambre criminelle, March 2001, no. 64, at 218-19.

[66] See S.V. George, "Head of State Immunity in the United States Courts: Still Confused After All These Years", 64 *Fordham Law Review* 1051 (December 1995).

[67] E.g., *The Schooner Exchange,* v. *M'Faddon*, United States, 11 US 116 (1812), at 144-145.

[68] E.g., *Mighell* v. *Sultan of Johore*, UK, Court of Appeal [1894] 1 QB 149.

[69] Art. 20(1) State Immunity Act of 1978 (UK).

[70] *Pinochet III*, at 97 (*per* Lord Wilberforce).

[71] Australian Foreign States Immunities Act of 1985, Section 36.

[72] See Section 4.1 Diplomatic Immunities and Privileges Act 37 of 2001 (South Africa); Section 86 Code of Civil Procedure (India); Art. 181.2 Constitution (Malaysia).

[73] K. Highet, et al., "*Lafontant* v. *Aristide*", 88 *AJIL* 528 (1994), at 531.

[74] See, e.g., Letter dated 14 September 1965, partly reproduced in 60 *AJIL* 100 (1966), at 101 (upholding the immunity of King Faisal Bin Abdull Aziz Al-Saud of Saudi Arabia); *Lafontant* v. *Aristide*, US, District Court for the Eastern District of New York, 844 F. Suppl. 128 (1994) (in which the US Justice Department supported the immunity of Jean-Bertrand Aristide of Haiti in a case concerning the alleged extra-judicial execution of the plaintiff's husband).

[75] IDI Resolution on Immunities, Art. 3. The Resolution goes on to state that even where the civil suit does involve acts performed in the exercise of official functions, no immunity arises in respect of a counterclaim. Nonetheless, court proceedings may not commence while a Head of State is in the forum territory in the exercise of official functions.

5.1.3.3 *Head of government and foreign minister immunity*

The question of the immunity of heads of government and ministers of foreign affairs was dealt with by the Institut de Droit International in Article 15 of its *Resolution on Immunities from Jurisdiction and Execution of Heads of State and of Government in International Law* (2001), which provided, in paragraph 1, that the Head of Government of a foreign State enjoys the same inviolability, and immunity from jurisdiction, recognised to the head of State. Paragraph 2 stated that this rule was without prejudice to such immunities to which other members of the government may be entitled to on account of their official functions.[76] Some six months after the Resolution was adopted, the ICJ issued its decision in the *Arrest Warrant* case.[77] The judgment found that the issuance of an international arrest warrant by a Belgian investigating judge against the incumbent minister of foreign affairs of the Democratic Republic of the Congo for charges of war crimes and crimes against humanity allegedly committed on the territory of the Congo, had violated the immunity from criminal jurisdiction and the inviolability enjoyed by ministers of foreign affairs in international law. Although it does not do so explicitly, the judgment appears to equate the position of ministers of foreign affairs to that of heads of State under international law, who enjoy absolute immunity from jurisdiction regardless of the nature of the act or the nature of the visit abroad. This is a fairly controversial position. It differs from the view of Watts, who argued that '[a] lthough it may well be that a Head of State, when on a private visit to another State, still enjoys certain privileges and immunities, it is much less likely that the same is true of heads of governments and foreign ministers.'[78] Although the latter 'may be accorded certain special treatment by the host State, this is more likely to be a matter of courtesy and respect for the seniority of the visitor, than a reflection of any belief that such treatment is required by international law.'[79] Most commentators agree that personal immunity of heads of government and ministers of foreign affairs only applies when such persons are on official visits abroad.[80]

The 1973 Convention on the Prevention and Punishment of Crimes against Internationally Protected Persons, including Diplomats does distinguish between the position of heads of state and that of heads of government and ministers of foreign affairs.[81] Article 21 of the 1969 Convention on Special Missions also seems to suggest a difference between the position of heads of state from heads of govern-

---

[76] IDI Resolution on Immunities, Art. 15.

[77] *Arrest Warrant* case.

[78] Watts, "The Legal Position in International Law of Heads of States", at 109.

[79] *Idem.*

[80] See, e.g., Philippe Cahier, *Le droit diplomatique contemporain* (Geneva: Librairie E. Droz; Paris: Librairie Minard, 1962), 346; Robert Jennings and Arthur Watts (eds.), *Oppenheim's International Law*, 9th edn., Vol. 1 (London: Longman, 1992), 1046, para. 459; Jean Salmon, *Manuel de droit diplomatique* (Brussels: Bruyant, 1994), at 539.

[81] See Art. 1 1973 Convention on the Prevention and Punishment of Crimes against Internationally Protected Persons, including Diplomats, providing for the definition of 'protected person' for the purposes of the Convention.

ment and ministers of foreign affairs. It may also be noted that the UN Convention on Jurisdictional Immunities of States and Their Property of 2004[82] (not in force) only provides in respect of heads of State.[83] A previous report of the ILC had stated that privileges and immunities granted to foreign ministers were only on the basis of comity rather than on the basis of customary international law rules.[84] There is little case law on the subject, although the relevant few cases have tended to support the contention that foreign ministers would enjoy immunity, though these are mostly confined to cases where the minister was on an official visit.[85]

Despite this paucity of sources and practice, the ICJ held in the *Arrest Warrant* case that 'in international law it is firmly established that … certain holders of high-ranking office in a State, such as the Head of State, the Head of Government and Ministers of Foreign Affairs, enjoy immunities from jurisdiction in other States, both civil and criminal.'[86] The Court's argumentation was that since the Vienna Convention on Diplomatic and Consular Relations and the Convention on Special Missions did not specifically define the immunities enjoyed by ministers of foreign affairs, the extent of such immunities would need to be determined according to 'the nature of the functions exercised by a Minister of Foreign Affairs.'[87] As a minister of foreign affairs is in charge of a country's diplomatic affairs and represents the State in international negotiations, he is presumed to have full powers to act on behalf of the State, and to fulfil such duties he is required to travel abroad frequently and hence 'must be in a position freely to do so whenever the need should arise.'[88] This means that 'the functions of a Minister for Foreign Affairs are such that, throughout the duration of his or her office, he or she when abroad enjoys full immunity from criminal jurisdiction and inviolability. That immunity and inviolability protect the individual concerned against any act of authority of another State which would hinder him or her in the performance of his or her duties.'[89] Thus, it

[82] UN GA Res. A/59/38 (2004), 2 December 2004.

[83] Art. 3(2) UN Convention on Jurisdictional Immunities of States and Their Property 2004.

[84] 2 *YILC* (1989), at 102-103 (Commentary on Art. 4).

[85] See *Ali Ali Reza* v. *Grimpell*, France, Court of Appeal of Paris (1961), 47 *ILR* 275 (denying immunity to a minister of state of Saudi Arabia who was in Paris attending a UN conference and was sued in respect of a lease of a flat in Paris. The Court implied that had he been a minister of foreign affairs, he would have been able to plead personal immunity); *Tachiona* v. *Mugabe*, US, District Court for the Southern District of New York, 169 F. Suppl. 2d 259 (2001) (affirming diplomatic immunity for a minister of foreign affairs); US, Court of Appeals 2nd Circuit, *Tachiona* v. *United States*, 386 F. 3d 205 (2004); *Chong Boon Kim* v. *Kim Yong Shik and David Kim*, US, Court of Appeal 1st Circuit (1963), 81 *ILR* 604, 58 *AJIL* 186 (1964); *Saltany and Others* v. *Reagan and Others*, US, District Court for the District of Columbia, 702 F. Suppl. 319 (1988), 87 *ILR* 680 (upholding personal immunity of a head of government).

[86] *Arrest Warrant* case, para. 51.

[87] *Ibid.*, para. 53.

[88] *Idem.* The Court further reasoned that 'the mere risk that, by travelling to or transiting another State a Minister for Foreign Affairs might be exposing himself or herself to legal proceedings could deter the Minister from travelling internationally when required to do so for the purposes of the performance of his or her official functions.' *Ibid.,* para. 55.

[89] *Ibid.*, para. 54.

would appear that the Court 'derived the scope of immunity from an assessment of what is necessary to protect the functions of a minister of foreign affairs.'[90]

Ad hoc Judge Van den Wyngaert, in her dissenting opinion, was particularly critical of this form of argumentation by the Court. In her view, the ICJ should have relied on evidence of State practice and *opinio juris* to prove the existence of the rule.[91] It is true that the Court made almost no attempt to ground its finding that ministers of foreign affairs enjoy absolute immunities in the national courts of third States on any State practice, not even recalling the cases cited above, which could have perhaps supported the finding to some extent. By finding that the functions of ministers of foreign affairs require full immunity from foreign criminal jurisdiction whenever ministers are abroad, whether on private or official visits,[92] the Court seems to have over-stretched the functionality rationale as well as the more commonly accepted parameters of the scope of immunity of ministers of foreign affairs under international law. One may recall that the Belgian arrest warrant was explicitly qualified in respect of official visits.[93] Hence, the Court clearly (if not overtly) equated the functions of a minister of foreign affairs to those of a head of State. The IDI Rapporteur on Immunities, Joe Verhoeven, was of this mind when drafting the IDI resolution. After a discussion of these two functions, he concluded that it

[90] Van Alebeek, *The Immunity of States and their Officials*, at 191.

[91] *Arrest Warrant* case, Dissenting Opinion of Judge Van den Wyngaert, at 143, para. 11 and para. 12: 'It is not sufficient to compare the rationale for the protection from suit in the case of diplomats, Heads of State and Foreign Minister to draw the conclusion that there is a rule of customary international law protecting Foreign Ministers: identifying a common raison d'être for a protective rule is one thing, elevating this protective rule to the status of customary international law is quite another thing. The Court should have first examined whether the conditions for the formation of a rule of customary law were fulfilled in the case of incumbent Foreign Ministers … In the brevity of its reasoning, the Court disregards its own case law on the subject on the formation of customary international law. In order to constitute a rule of customary international law, there must be evidence of state practice (*usus*) and *opinio juris* to the effect that this rule exists.'

[92] *Arrest Warrant* case, para. 55: 'no distinction can be drawn between acts performed by a Minister for Foreign Affairs in an "official" capacity, and those claimed to have been performed in a "private capacity", or, for that matter, between acts performed before the person concerned assumed office as Minister for Foreign Affairs and acts committed during the period of office. Thus, if a Minister for Foreign Affairs is arrested in another State on a criminal charge, he or she is clearly thereby prevented from exercising the functions of his or her office. The consequences of such impediment to the exercise of those official functions are equally serious, regardless whether the Minister for Foreign Affairs was, at the time of arrest, present in the territory of the arresting State on an "official" visit or a "private" visit.'

[93] *Ibid.*, at 28-29, paras. 68-70. The Belgian investigating judge issuing the warrant stated that 'Pursuant to the general principle of fairness in judicial proceedings, immunity from enforcement must, in our view, be accorded to all State representatives welcomed as such on to the territory of Belgium (on "official visits"). Welcoming such foreign dignitaries as official representatives of sovereign States involves not only relations between individuals but also relations between States. This implies that such welcome includes an undertaking by the host State and its various components to refrain from taking any coercive measures against its guest and the invitation cannot become a pretext for ensnaring the individual concerned in what would be labelled a trap. In the contrary case, failure to respect this undertaking could give rise to the host State's international responsibility.'

was hard to see how 'une distinction puisse sérieusement être établi entre eux.'[94] However, this reasoning, based upon the consideration that head of State immunity in the present day is justified upon 'des besoins strictement fonctionnels,'[95] does not take into account the fact that the scope of head of State immunity is not based solely upon functionality, but upon the archaic notions of the dignity of kings and princes and the personification of the State in the person of its ruler.[96] The same rationale does not extend to heads of government or ministers of foreign affairs.[97] It is argued therefore that the scope of the personal immunity enjoyed by the latter extends only to official visits.[98]

5.1.4 **State immunity**

State immunity, which acts as a bar to the civil and administrative jurisdiction of States when faced with claims against foreign States, has uncertain legal origins. It is often contended that State immunity arose out of the principles of independence, equality and dignity of States.[99] However, this assertion has been authoritatively challenged[100] and the alternative explanation put forward that State immunity may be traced to foreign head of State immunity.[101] With the emergence of the modern State, this immunity was transferred to the sovereign State. Another explanation is that it arose out of tension between two fundamental international law norms – sovereign equality and exclusive territorial jurisdiction.[102] The United States Supreme

---

[94] Joe Verhoeven (Rapporteur IDI), *Les immunités de juridiction et d'exécution du chef d'Etat et de gouvernement en droit intenational*, Rapport provisoire (2000), 69 *AIDI* 482 (2000-2001), at 543, para. 42.

[95] *Ibid.*, at 250.

[96] Van Alebeek, *The Immunity of States and their Officials*, at 194.

[97] See, e.g., Watts, "The Legal Position in International Law of Heads of States", at 102: 'heads of government and foreign ministers … do not symbolize or personify their States in the way that Heads of States do. Accordingly, they do not enjoy in international law any entitlement to special treatment by virtue of qualities of sovereignty or majesty attaching to them personally.' See also R. Jennings and A. Watts (eds.), *Oppenheim's International Law*, 9th edn., Vol. 1 (1992), at 1033, para. 445: '[The head of government] does not represent the international *persona* of the state in the same way in which the Head of State does.'

[98] This means that so long as Belgium's arrest warrant was not exercised during an official visit, it would not have violated international law. Van Alebeek, *The Immunity of States and their Officials*, at 195.

[99] For an overview of the subject, see Hazel Fox QC, *The Law of State Immunity* (Oxford: OUP, 2004).

[100] Hersch Lauterpacht, "The Problems of Jurisdictional Immunities of Foreign States", 28 *BYIL* (1951), at 228: 'It is submitted that the view, so often expressed in textbooks and elsewhere, that the immunity of foreign states and their property from the jurisdiction of courts of foreign states follows from a clear principle of international law, namely, the principle of equality and independence of states needs re-examination. It finds no support in classical international law.'

[101] Lauterpacht, "The Problems of Jurisdictional Immunities of Foreign States", at 228: 'It [State immunity] is rooted, to some extent, in the doctrine of the personal immunity of heads of states.'

[102] See Lee M. Caplan, "State Immunity, Human Rights and Jus Cogens: A Critique of the Normative Hierarchy Theory", 97 *AJIL* 741 (2003).

Court decision *The Schooner Exchange* v. *McFaddon*[103] is widely regarded as the first definitive statement of the doctrine of foreign State immunity.[104] On appeal to the Supreme Court, Chief Justice John Marshall observed that on the one hand, international law dictated that '[t]he jurisdiction of the nation within its own territory is necessarily exclusive and absolute' and on the other hand, the principle of sovereign equality discouraged one sovereign from standing in judgment of another.[105] In the end, Justice Marshall found that US courts were barred from inquiring into the validity of title to the *Exchange* because the schooner was 'a national armed vessel, commissioned by, and in the service of the emperor of France.'[106] Essentially, it was held that the territorial State has exclusive jurisdiction on its territory unless it waives it to the benefit of a foreign State.[107] For this reason, State immunity may be characterised as 'a privilege granted by international law to States to prevent abuses from being perpetrated against them.'[108]

Domestic courts have tended to adapt the way they interpret the rule of State immunity according to the changing demands of international relations and community. This explains the development of the commercial activity exception (to ensure equality and fairness in the economic sphere) and also the torts exception (to protect individuals from damage to person or injury arising from a foreign State's misconduct).[109] Mainstream legal commentary asserts that State immunity before foreign courts was absolute.[110] This position changed when States became

---

103 11 US (7 Cranch) 116 (1812).

104 In 1812, while sailing off the American coast, a commercial schooner, the *Exchange*, owned by two citizens of Maryland, was seized by the French navy. By general order of the emperor Napoleon Bonaparte, the French navy converted the schooner into a ship of war. The original owners brought an *in rem* libel action against the ship for recovery of their property. The French government resisted the action, arguing that, as a ship of war, the *Exchange* was an arm of the emperor and was thus entitled to the same immunity privileges as the emperor himself. *Ibid.*, at 126-127.

105 *Ibid.,* at 136-137.

106 *Ibid.*, at 146.

107 'The jurisdiction of the nation within its own territory is necessarily exclusive and absolute. It is susceptible of no limitation not imposed by itself ... All exceptions, therefore, to the full and complete power of a nation within its own territories must be traced up to the consent of the nation itself.' *Ibid.*, at 136. See Gamal Moursi Badr, *State Immunity: An Analytical and Prognostic View* (The Hague: Nijhoff, 1984), at10 et seq.

108 Andrea Bianchi, "Denying State Immunity to Violators of Human Rights", 46 *Austrian Journal of Public and International Law* 200 (1994).

109 *Ibid.*, at 202.

110 However, other commentators have pointed out that the title of 'absolute immunity' has more historical than legal significance and should not be interpreted as meaning that States were exempt at that time from foreign jurisdiction in all circumstances. For example, after examining *The Schooner Exchange*, Gamal Badr argued that: 'For [Chief Justice] Marshall ... the starting point [of the case] was the local state's exclusive territorial jurisdiction to which immunity was an exception emanating from the will of the local state itself. He did not envisage a blanket immunity for the foreign state as a general rule, to which exceptions would be made to permit the exercise of the local state's territorial jurisdiction.' Badr, at 11. This observation led Badr to conclude that *The Schooner Exchange* 'does not uphold the proposition that there exists a peremptory rule of international law requiring that an absolute immunity from the territorial jurisdiction be recognized in favour of foreign states.' Badr, *State Immunity: An Analytical and Prognostic View*, at 13.

involved in international trade and finance.[111] Municipal courts began to challenge State immunity in cases dealing with the commercial activity of States. Hence, a distinction arose between acts of the State which were *jure imperii* (acts undertaken in a sovereign capacity) and those *jure gestionis* (acts undertaken in a private or commercial capacity). Only the former acts were considered immune from foreign State's jurisdiction.

Due to the difficulties courts were experiencing in distinguishing between those acts which would be immune and those which would not, some States passed legislation which codified the general principle of State immunity and listed the exceptions to it.[112] A general human rights exception does not form part of these exceptions, although the UK's State Immunity Act (SIA) does provide an exception to immunity in case of death or injury caused by an act performed in the territory of the United Kingdom[113] and the US Foreign Sovereign Immunities Act (FSIA) provides a restricted human rights exception which applies in respect of a claim for damages for personal injury or death caused by an act of torture, extra-judicial killing, aircraft sabotage or hostage-taking, against a State designated by the US as a sponsor of terrorism, where the claimant or victim was a national of the US at the time of the facts.[114] Commentators have noted that these exceptions sit uneasily with the *jure imperii* and *jure gestionis* framework given that such acts do not appear to be private or commercial acts.[115] Moreover, the markedly political treatment of the immunity question as illustrated by the US Anti-Terrorism and Effective Death Penalty Act of 1996, which assigns or removes immunity according to the ever-changing US list of State sponsors of terrorism, strongly suggests that State immunity is more a question of comity based on good inter-State relations rather than a rule of international law.[116]

---

[111] For a detailed account of the development of the international law of State immunity, see Christoph Schreuer, *State Immunity: Some Recent Developments* (Cambridge: Grotius, 1988).

[112] E.g., State Immunity Act (UK) of 20 July 1978, Part I; Foreign Sovereign Immunities Act (US) of 1976, amended in 1988 and 1996.

[113] State Immunity Act (UK) of 20 July 1978, Part I, s. 5.

[114] This exception was brought in by s. 221 of the Anti-Terrorism and Effective Death Penalty Act of 1996. See Naomi Roht-Arriaza, "The Foreign Sovereign Immunities Act and Human Rights Violations: One Step forward, Two Steps Back?", 16(1) *Berkeley Journal of International Law* 81-82 (1998).

[115] See Bianchi, "Denying State Immunity to Violators of Human Rights", at 216; Schreuer, *State Immunity: Some Recent Developments* (Cambridge, 1988), at 47 et seq. Caplan takes this observation further, noting that '[t]he emergence of a restrictive approach to immunity is itself antithetical to the "fundamental right" approach. If State immunity were a fundamental State right, it would never be susceptible to theoretical division along public/private lines.' Caplan, "State Immunity, Human Rights and Jus Cogens: A Critique of the Normative Hierarchy Theory", at 741.

[116] One of the original reasons for the amendment was to facilitate suits against Libya in the aftermath of the Lockerbie bombing. The case that prompted the amendment was *Smith* v. *Socialist People's Libyan Arab Jamahiriya*, 886 F. Suppl. 306 (EDNY 1996), *aff'd* 101 F. 3d 239 (2d Cir. 1996). The original list, established on 29 December 1979, listed Libya, Iraq, South Yemen, and Syria. As of December 2004, the countries currently on the list are: Cuba, Iran, Sudan and Syria. The list is available at: <http://www.state.gov/s/ct/c14151.htm>. Iraq was removed from the list in 1982 to make it eligible for US military technology while it was fighting Iran in the Iran-Iraq War; it was put back

The cross-linkage between State immunity and the immunity of State officials has been relied upon by courts in their considerations of both types of immunity. In the Divisional Court decision in *Pinochet*, Lord Bingham relied on *Al Adsani* to argue that '[i]f the Government there could claim immunity in relation to alleged acts of torture, it would not seem surprising that if the same immunity could be claimed by a defendant who had at the relevant time been the ruler of that country.'[117] In the House of Lords, most judges regarded *Al Adsani* to be irrelevant given that it concerned exclusively civil proceedings.[118] However, some acknowledged that in the field of civil litigation, there was some authority for the proposition that a plea of immunity could be successful in the face of allegations of serious violations of human rights.[119] Since the *Pinochet* case, this suggests that while a former State official does not enjoy functional immunity with regard to the act of torture in criminal proceedings, they and their State might still be immune from civil proceedings.[120] Some commentators have viewed this incongruence as indicating a 'manifest inconsistency which ought to be remedied by denying immunity also to state and state officials in civil proceedings.'[121] However, national courts have not so far been persuaded by these arguments. In the recent case of *Jones*, concerning a civil suit in relation to acts of torture allegedly perpetrated in Saudi Arabia, the UK House of Lords, in upholding the immunity of Saudi Arabia, underlined that criminal proceedings were 'categorically different' for immunity purposes.[122]

In the United States, since the decision of the Ninth Circuit in *Chuidan* v. *Philippine National Bank*,[123] a number of courts have analysed the immunity of individu-

---

on in 1990 following its invasion of Kuwait. It has since been removed following the 2003 invasion, on 23 September 2004. Libya was removed from the list 45 days following the announcement on 15 May 2006. Notably, neither Afghanistan nor Saudi Arabia were ever on the list. Litigation arising out of the list includes: *Alejandre* v. *Republic of Cuba*, 996 F. Suppl. 1239 (S.D. Fla. 1997); *Cicippio* v. *Iran*, 18 F. Suppl. 2d 62, 68 (D.D.C. 1998); In re *Estate of Weinstein*, 712 N.Y.S. 2d. 300 (Sup. Ct. 2000). See also Keith Sealing, "Cuba is no Longer a 'State Sponsor of Terrorism': Why the Foreign Sovereign Immunities Act Sanction Failed", 14 *Transnational Law and Contemporary Problems* 143 (2004-2005).

[117] *Augusto Pinochet Ugarte*, United Kingdom, Judgment of 28 October 1998, Divisional Court Judgment of the Queen's Bench Division, 38 *ILM* 68 (1999) (Q.B. Div'l Ct. 1998) (referred to as *Divisional Court* in the text), para. 73.

[118] Lord Lloyd in *Pinochet I* (at 1324), relied on *Al Adsani* and *Siderman* to hold that allegations of torture may not override a plea of immunity.

[119] See, e.g., Lord Phillips in *Pinochet III*, at 187, citing cases where State immunity had been upheld.

[120] Such a position was held by the UK Court of Appeal in *Jones* v. *Ministry of Interior Al-Mamlaka Al-Arabiya AS Saudiya (the Kingdom of Saudi Arabia) and others*, United Kingdom, EWCA Civ 1394 (2004).

[121] Bianchi, "Immunity versus Human Rights", at 264.

[122] *Jones* v. *Ministry of Interior Al-Mamlaka Al-Arabiya AS Saudiya (the Kingdom of Saudi Arabia) and others*, United Kingdom [2006] UKHL 26; [2007] 1 AC 270, para. 31 (hereafter, *Jones* case).

[123] *Chuidan* v. *Philippine National Bank*, United States, 912 F.2d 1095 (9th Cir. 1990).

al foreign officials under the rubric of the FSIA.[124] The reasoning for this is based on the consideration that 'a suit against an individual acting his official capacity is the practical equivalent of a suit against the sovereign directly.'[125] Hence, unless sovereign immunity extends to individual foreign officials, litigants could easily circumvent the immunity provided to foreign States under the FSIA.[126] The statutory interpretation is not really convincing. The Ninth Circuit based its reasoning upon the notion that 'a bifurcated approach to sovereign immunity was not intended by the Act' (at 1102), meaning that the Act was supposed to be comprehensive. However, this reading is not only inconsistent with the statute's text and legislative history, but also ignores the fact that courts have applied a 'bifurcated approach to sovereign immunity' in cases involving heads of State, which the FSIA clearly does not regulate.[127] The same reasoning applies to officials other than heads of State. Moreover, it makes no sense when considering that foreign officials would also be subject to the same exceptions to immunity as listed in the FSIA. As noted previously, functional immunity exceeds State immunity in these areas. A State official does not become personally liable to pay damages in respect of commercial acts undertaken on behalf of the State.

5.1.5 **National immunity**

National legislation may also provide for immunity to certain State officials such as parliamentarians, members of cabinet and the head of State. The scope of such immunity depends on the national law in question. Some countries include such immunities in their constitutions.[128] In order to ensure that impunity does not result, these immunities are sometimes accompanied by some privileges of jurisdiction, meaning that special courts may be used to try such persons.[129] In addition, the legislative body may be authorised to lift immunity in certain cases. For instance, the court of Santiago on 5 June 2000, and then the Chilean Supreme Court on 11 August 2000, lifted the parliamentary immunity which had been (self)granted to

[124] See, e.g., *Velasco*, 370 F.3d at 399; In re *Terrorist Attacks*, 349 F. Suppl. 2d at 788; *Doe I* v. *Israel*, 400 F. Suppl. 2d 86, 104 (D.D.C. 2005); *Herbage* v. *Meese*, 747 F. Suppl. 60, 66 (D.D.C. 1990).

[125] *Chuidian*, *supra* n. 123, at 1101.

[126] *Ibid.*, at 1102: 'Such a result would amount to a blanket abrogation of foreign sovereign immunity by allowing litigants to accomplish indirectly what the Act barred them from doing directly.' A similar holding was reached by the UK House of Lords in the *Jones* case, para. 10 (2006): 'the foreign state's right to immunity cannot be circumscribed by suing its servants or agents.'

[127] See, e.g., *Tachiona* v. *United States*, Untied States, 386 F. 3d 205 (2d Cir. 2004), at 220-21: 'We have some doubt as to whether the FSIA was meant to supplant the "common law" of head-of-state immunity, which generally entailed deference to the executive branch's suggestions of immunity. For one thing, the FSIA applies only to foreign states, which are defined as including "political subdivision[s]," and "agenc[ies] or instrumentalit[ies] thereof." "[A]genc[ies] [and] instrumentalit[ies]" in turn are defined in terms not usually used to describe natural persons. Moreover, the only references to heads of state or other foreign officials in the FSIA's legislative history suggest that their immunity is not governed by the Act.'

[128] E.g, Arts. 26 and 68 of the French Constitution of 4 October 1958.

[129] *Ibid.*, Art. 68(2).

Pinochet in 1980, making him a 'senator for life' in order to prosecute him in cases dealing with the killing of political prisoners in 1973[130] and again more recently in relation to disappearances in connection with Operation Condor.[131] Notably, some countries, after having signed or ratified the ICC Statute, have needed to change their national immunity laws. France for example was required to adopt a modification to its Constitution subsequent to its ratification of the Rome Statute.[132]

Finally, it should be pointed out that just as the Act of State doctrine serves to restrain judicial activity with regard to the acts of foreign States in their territory, there are equally domestic doctrines of self-restraint which apply in respect of acts performed by a State's own government. In the United States, the 'political acts' or 'political question' doctrine has served this purpose,[133] while in France, the doctrine of acts of government (*actes de gouvernement*) has the same effect.[134] The issuing of amnesty laws has on occasion been ruled to fall into the scope of this doctrine. For instance, when Salvadoran citizens brought suit before domestic courts in an attempt to have the El Salvador amnesty law declared invalid, the Supreme Court of Justice in El Salvador ruled that the granting of amnesty in these circumstances constituted a political question that the courts lacked competence to address.[135] Even international bodies have sometimes shown a reticence to get involved in the political decisions of States with regard to how they choose to end conflicts. In its admissibility decision in *Dujardin and others* v. *France* in 1991, the European Commission of Human Rights considered that, '... the amnesty law, which is entirely exceptional in character, was adopted in the context of a process designed to resolve conflicts between the various communities of the islands. It is not for the Commission to assess the advisability of the measures taken by France to that end.'[136]

---

130 The Santiago Court of Appeals stripped Pinochet of his parliamentary immunity in relation to the killings (*Pinochet*, Chile, Santiago Court of Appeal, Decision of 5 June 2000, available at: <www.tercera.cl/casos/pinochet/documentos/desafuero/fallo1.html>) and this decision was upheld by the Chilean Supreme Court (see, e.g., "Pinochet Isn't Immune", *International Herald Tribune*, 11 August 2000).

131 *Pinochet*, Chile, Supreme Court of Chile, Decision of August 2004, available at: <www.emol.com/noticiaas/documentos/desafuero_pinochet.asp>. Three conditions are required for parliamentary immunity to be lifted under the Chilean Code: the judge must have jurisdiction, the crime must be defined by law and there must be prima facie responsibility of the accused.

132 Stern, "Immunities for Heads of State", at 89. See Decision Nos. 98-408, 22 January 1999.

133 This doctrine has been applied mainly to cases dealing with the relation between the executive and the legislature, foreign relations and the conduct of war, as well as federal-state relations.

134 Stern, "Immunities for Heads of State", at 90.

135 El Salvador: Supreme Court of Justice Decision on the Amnesty Law, Proceedings No. 10-93 (20 May 1993), reprinted in: Kritz (ed.), *Transitional Justice*, Vol. III, at 549. However, in this case, it should be pointed out that the issue before the Court was the constitutionality of the amnesty law in relation to the powers of the legislature, not whether the amnesty law was invalid as a violation of international law. Indeed the Court made clear that 'there are cases where there is constitutional jurisdictional control over amnesty, and it is the competence of the Constitutional Chamber to pronounce itself over its [merits or lack of merits] *ab initio*, or to initiate proceedings, in accordance [with] the case, inasmuch as they are filed before the Chamber.' *Ibid.*

136 *Dujardin and Others* v. *France*, ECommHR, Admissibility Decision, 2 September 1991, Appl. No. 16734/90, 72 *D&R* 236 (1992), at 243-244.

In the United States, however, the political question doctrine has been held not to apply to cases involving serious human rights violations, at least those committed on foreign territory. For example, in *Linder* v. *Portocarrero*, the Court of Appeals for the 11th Circuit held that the political question doctrine does not apply to an action against the Contras in Nicaragua for alleged acts of torture, summary execution and the violation of common Article 3 of the Geneva Conventions of 1949.[137] While the political question doctrine is meant to shield the executive from judicial interference in its conduct of foreign affairs, this does not amount to a blanket rule of judicial abstention on all questions that have a bearing on judicial affairs.[138] It is arguable that in the light of the current state of general international law with its emphasis on the scrutiny of governments' human rights records that judicial activity in this area would not be considered as infringing upon the executive's prerogatives in the area of foreign affairs. One could also argue that just as international crimes are deemed not to be 'political offences' for the purposes of extradition,[139] cases dealing with international crimes are not 'political questions.' In both scenarios, the seriousness of the crimes overrides the political aspects of the issue, making enforcement more important than judicial abstention on political or other grounds.[140] Such considerations might indicate to a court applying an interests-analysis approach that the imperative to prosecute holds more weight in

---

[137] *Linder* v. *Carrero-Portocarrero*, 963 F.2d 332 (11th Cir. 1992), reprinted in 99 *ILR* 55.

[138] This was acknowledged in the seminal case on the political question doctrine of *Baker* v. *Carr*, 369 US 186 (1962), which stated the requirements of the doctrine as follows: 'Prominent on the surface of any case held to involve a political question is found a textually demonstrable constitutional commitment of the issue to a coordinate political department; or a lack of judicially discoverable and manageable standards for resolving it, or the impossibility of deciding without an initial policy determination of a kind clearly for nonjudicial discretion; or the impossibility of a court's undertaking independent resolution without expressing lack of the respect due to coordinate branches of government; or an unusual need for unquestioning adherence to a political decision already made or the potentiality of embarrassment from multifarious pronouncements by various departments on one question.' *Ibid.*, at 217.

[139] The few courts that have prosecuted individuals accused of violations of international criminal law have suggested that acts for which the accused is charged are beyond the scope of doctrines like the political offence exception. See, e.g., *Barbie*, in which the *Chambre d'accusation* regarding the claim that it did not have jurisdiction over Klaus Barbie since the latter had been kidnapped and brought to France for trial, stated that 'by reason of their nature, the crimes against humanity with which Klaus Barbie, who claims German nationality, is charged in France where those crimes were committed, do not simply fall within the scope of French municipal law but are subject to an international criminal order to which notions of frontiers and extradition rules arising therefrom are completely foreign.' Cass. Crim. [Criminal Chamber], 20 December 1985, translated in 78 *ILR* 125, at 130.

[140] The ICTY Rules of Procedure provides that States are to surrender an accused person to its jurisdiction regardless of 'any legal impediment to the surrender or transfer of the accused to the Tribunal which may exist under the national law or extradition treaties of the State concerned.' Rule 58, Rules of Procedure and Evidence for the ICTY. The ICTR has a similar rule. Most States have cooperated, passing legislation for surrender of suspects without any of the normal conditions attached to extradition proceedings. The provisions in the Statute for the ICC providing for surrender also do not include a political offence exception.

a case dealing with international crimes than the foreign policy objections of the national government to a particular prosecution.[141]

5.2 Immunities and international and hybrid criminal courts and tribunals

Of all the impediments discussed in this book, functional immunity stands alone as the only impediment to be regulated by every international and hybrid criminal court or tribunal, while personal immunity has often either been regulated or impliedly covered. Both the IMT and IMTFE rejected the defence of official position, including as Head of State, although the IMTFE did allow this to be argued as a mitigating factor.[142] Some have interpreted the rejection of official position defence as also including the rejection of personal immunities.[143] However, this interpretation confuses the two issues, and makes no sense in light of the fact that the IMTFE allowed official position to be a mitigating factor.[144] Control Council Law No. 10,[145] which established the courts of the four Allied nations in the occupied German territory in order to prosecute the lesser war criminals,[146] also stated in Article 4(a) that the official position of an accused person, including Head of State, would not free him of responsibility or mitigate punishment. Article 5 further provided that in any trial or prosecution, the accused would not be entitled to the benefits of any immunity granted under the Nazi regime as a bar to trial or punishment.

In the ICTR and ICTY Statutes, the defence of official position is rejected in a provision that mirrors Article 7 of the IMT Charter. Although there is no mention of procedural immunity in the Statutes, the ICJ in the *Arrest Warrant* case mentioned the ICTY and the ICTR as examples of 'certain international criminal courts' which could prosecute a former or incumbent Minister of Foreign Affairs, suggesting that neither substantive nor procedural immunities would preclude the

---

141 See Christine van den Wyngaert, *The Political Offence Exception to Extradition: The Delicate Problem of Balancing the Rights of the Individual and the International Public Order* (The Hague: Kluwer, 1980).

142 IMT Charter, Art. 7; IMTFE Charter, Art. 6.

143 E.g., *Milošević*, ICTY, Decision on Preliminary Motions, 8 November 2001, Case No. IT-02-54-PT, at paras. 26-34.

144 William A. Schabas, *The UN International Criminal Tribunals: The Former Yugoslavia, Rwanda and Sierra Leone* (Cambridge: CUP, 2006), at 328.

145 Allied Control Council Law No. 10, Punishment of Persons Guilty of War Crimes, Crimes Against Peace and Against Humanity, 20 December 1945, *Official Gazette of the Control Council for Germany*, No. 3, Berlin, 31 January 1946.

146 Allied Control Council Law No. 10, preamble (stating that these trials sought 'to give effect to the terms of the Moscow Declaration of 30 October 1943 and the London Agreement of 8 August 1945, and the Charter issued pursuant thereto … in order to establish a uniform legal basis in Germany for the prosecution of war criminals and other similar offenders, other than those dealt with by the International Military Tribunal …').

exercise of their jurisdiction.[147] Moreover, given that all member States of the UN are obliged to co-operate with the Tribunals under Chapter VII of the Charter by, for instance, arresting and surrendering individuals to the Tribunals, an exception to procedural immunity could also be implied.[148] In contrast to the IMTFE, the ICTR has treated official position as an aggravating factor,[149] while the ICTY has rejected any challenge to the provision.[150]

Article 27 of the ICC Statute rejects both substantive immunity and procedural immunity as bars to the exercise of its jurisdiction.[151] This sets the ICC Statute apart from the Statutes of the previous international criminal courts, which only explicitly dealt with substantive immunity.[152] In practice, however, it may be difficult for the ICC to gain custody over such officials given that States are still required to respect procedural immunities,[153] a fact recognised in Article 98(1) of the Statute, which states that the ICC may not proceed with a request for surrender or assistance from a State which would be acting in contravention to its obligations under international law with respect to the State or the diplomatic immunity of a person or property of a third State, without first having sought the co-operation of the third State for the waiver of the immunity. As one commentator notes, 'a failure to proceed successfully according to article 98 may *in practice* and contrary to the wording of article 27, "bar the Court from exercising its jurisdiction over such a

[147] *Arrest Warrant* case, para. 61.

[148] However, it should be noted that Rwanda and Yugoslavia, the two countries most concerned by the obligation to co-operate would not be bound by procedural immunity of their own officials and would be thus free to arrest and surrender them to the Tribunals.

[149] *Kambanda,* ICTR, Judgment of 4 September 1998, Case No. ICTR-97-23-S, para. 44: 'The crimes were committed during the time when Jean Kambanda was Prime Minister and he and his government were responsible for maintenance of peace and security. Jean Kambanda abused his authority and the trust of the civilian population. He personally participated in the genocide by distributing arms, making incendiary speeches and presiding over cabinet and other meetings where the massacres were planned and discussed. He failed to take necessary and reasonable measures to prevent his subordinates from committing crimes against the population. Abuse of positions of authority or trust is generally considered an aggravating factor.'

[150] *Milošević*, ICTY, Trial Chamber, Decision on Preliminary Motions, 8 November 2001, Case No. IT-02-54-PT, paras. 26-34: '[t]here is absolutely no basis for challenging the validity of Article 7, paragraph 2, which at this time reflects a rule of customary international law.'

[151] Art. 27 ICC Statute, para. 1 provides that official capacity, including as Head of State, shall in no case exempt a person from criminal liability nor mitigate punishment. The second paragraph states: 'Immunities and special procedural rules which may attach to the official capacity of a person, whether under national or international law, shall not bar the Court from exercising its jurisdiction over such a person.'

[152] The ICJ in the *Arrest Warrant* case drew attention to the second paragraph of Article 27 of the Rome Statute to support its statement that 'certain international criminal courts,' such as the ICC, could exercise jurisdiction over an incumbent and/or former Minister of Foreign Affairs, as an exception to the general rule on immunities. *Arrest Warrant* case, para. 61.

[153] The ICJ in the *Arrest Warrant* case stated that such rules in the Statutes of international criminal courts did not mean that a customary rule exists to the effect of an exception to functional immunity in case of grave international crimes in proceedings before national courts. *Arrest Warrant* case, para. 58.

person," if the Court cannot secure the attendance of the person in any other way because the Rome Statute does not provide a trial *in absentia*.'[154]

Article 29 of the Law establishing the Extraordinary Chambers in the Courts of Cambodia specifies that position or rank of any suspect shall not relieve the person of criminal responsibility or mitigate punishment, thereby rejecting functional immunity. As for the Special Court for Sierra Leone, the defence of functional immunity is removed in Article 6(2), while procedural immunities are not regulated. However, while the SCSL's indictment of sitting head of State of Liberia Charles Taylor indicates that the Special Court did not consider itself bound by personal immunities,[155] the refusal of Ghana to arrest Taylor when he was on its territory in conformity with the principle of immunities suggests that it would have been nigh impossible to have had Taylor arrested and transferred during his tenure.[156] The Special Court relied on its proclaimed status as 'an international court' in order to deny a challenge to its jurisdiction based upon the immunity of Charles Taylor as a former Head of State,[157] relying on the ICJ's *obiter dictum* in the *Arrest Warrant* case that 'certain international criminal courts' are not barred by the principle of procedural immunity.[158] Commentators have noted that it is somewhat strange that while Sierra Leone as a sovereign State must respect the immunities of foreign State officials, it is able to enter into a treaty with an international organisation to create a court that is not bound by immunities of the officials of third States; as put by Professor Schabas, '[t]hey would be doing jointly what they cannot do individually.'[159]

In terms of the Special Panels with Exclusive Jurisdiction Over Serious Criminal Offences in East Timor, Section 15 of Regulation 2000/15 mirrors Article 27 of the ICC Statute. Thus, the defence of official position (and hence functional immunity) is rejected as a possible bar to the exercise of jurisdiction, as are immunities or special procedural rules which may attach to the official capacity of a person, whether under national or international law (i.e., procedural immunity).[160] This is a significant distinction of the Special Panels in comparison with the other hybrid courts and indeed the ICTY and ICTR, and would appear to be somewhat of a departure from the ICJ's contention in the *Arrest Warrant* case that only 'certain international criminal courts' are exempted from the principle of procedural immunity. While the Panels were set up by the UN Transitional Authority in East Timor

---

[154] Otto Triffterer, "Article 27: Irrelevance of official capacity", in Otto Triffterer (ed.), *Commentary on the Rome Statute of the International Criminal Court: Observers' Notes, Article by Article* (Baden-Baden: Nomos Verlagsgesellschaft, 1999), at 513. [Emphasis in original]

[155] The Indictment and arrest warrant were approved by Judge Bankoke Thompson on 7 March 2003. *The Prosecutor* v. *Charles Ghankay Taylor*, Indictment, Case No. SCSL-03-I, 3 March 2003. Charles Taylor remained Head of State in Liberia until August 2003.

[156] Schabas, *The UN International Criminal Tribunals*, at 59.

[157] *Taylor* Decision on Immunity.

[158] *Arrest Warrant* case, para. 61.

[159] Schabas, *The UN International Criminal Tribunals*, at 329.

[160] UNTAET Regulation 2000/15, Section 15.2. See also Section 15.1 ('The present regulation shall apply equally to all persons without any distinction based on official capacity …').

and in this sense reflected a similar basis of jurisdiction as the ICTY and ICTR, they differed significantly in that they formed part of the domestic court system of Timor Leste and also had jurisdiction over some domestic offences, suggesting that (quasi)domestic courts with clear jurisdiction over international crimes need not uphold procedural immunities.

5.3 Contextual and policy considerations

Essentially immunity is conferred to an entire group or class of persons 'under circumstances where considerations of public policy are thought to require special protection for the person, activity or entity in question at the expense of those injured by its tortuous act.'[161] The rationales for functional and personal immunity differ somewhat, but are also related. The Institut de Droit International (IDI) has opined that immunities (in general) 'are conferred to ensure an orderly allocation and exercise of jurisdiction in accordance with international law in proceedings concerning States, to respect the sovereign equality of States and to permit the effective performance of the functions of persons who act on behalf of States.'[162] Immunity from prosecution has been justified on a number of grounds, including the nature and dignity of the office, comity, mutual respect among nations, and the stability of international relations and diplomacy.[163] Notably, such considerations stand in contrast to the policy reasons advanced in support of international criminal trials.[164] This clash of principles strongly suggests that absent a controlling rule of international law, an interests-analysis approach would provide a workable framework for resolving disputes.

5.3.1 **Functional immunity**

The rationale for functional immunity was outlined by the Appeals Chamber of the ICTY in *Prosecutor* v. *Blaškić*, in which it held that

> 'customary international law protects the internal organization of each sovereign State: it leaves it to each sovereign State to determine its internal structure and in particular to designate the individuals acting as State agents or organs. Each sovereign State has the right to issue instructions to its organs, both those operating at the internal level and those operating in the field of international relations, and also to provide for sanctions or other remedies in case of non-compliance with those instructions. The corollary of this exclusive power is that each State is entitled to claim that acts

---

[161] Edward J. Kionka, *Torts in a Nutshell*, 2nd edn. (1992), at 341.

[162] IDI Resolution on International Crimes and Immunities, Art. II(1).

[163] See *Lafontant*, at 132 (mentioning each of these justifications); The *Schooner Exchange* v. *McFaddon*, 11 US 116 (1812), at 137-38 (state immunity based on the dignity of the office and nation and on the common interest in mutual intercourse among nations); In re *Doe*, 860 F.2d 40, 45 (2d Cir. 1988) (head of state immunity based on mutual respect and comity).

[164] See the policy considerations discussed in Chapter 2, *supra*.

or transactions performed by one of its organs in its official capacity be attributed to the State, so that the individual organ may not be held accountable for those acts or transactions.'[165]

The rationale is thus intimately connected to notions of sovereignty. However, the development of human rights law has had a considerable impact upon the traditional notion of sovereignty. For instance, the International Commission on Intervention and State Sovereignty in their report of 2001 viewed sovereignty in terms of responsibility to protect the safety and lives of people and to promote their welfare.[166] This entailed assuming accountability for acts of commission and omission.[167] It has also been pointed out that if sovereignty is regarded as a normative concept, then it does not make much sense that conduct that violates the most cardinal values of the international legal system should be protected by the rules of that system.[168] Moreover, the principle of sovereign equality may be equally satisfied by a rule of non-immunity in cases of international crimes, given that this principle merely requires the conduct of all States to be treated alike.[169] Such interpretations of the notion of sovereignty have not yet been adopted, but it is possible that cases such as *Pinochet* signal a movement in this direction.

However, policy reasons have also had considerable influence on the upholding of functional immunity. For example, Lord Goff in the *Pinochet* case noted with some alarm that lifting functional immunity of former heads of State for acts of torture opened the possibility of prosecuting agents of Great Britain in regard to its actions in Northern Ireland.[170] In its statement of interest in the *Dichter* case, the US government also set out some practical reasons for upholding his immunity: 'any refusal by U.S. courts to grant immunity to foreign officials for their

[165] *Blaškić (judgment on the request of Croatia)*, ICTY, Appeals Chamber, Judgment of 29 October 1997, Case No. IT-95-14-AR108*bis*, para. 41.

[166] The International Commission on Intervention and State Sovereignty proposed that 'Thinking of sovereignty as responsibility, in a way that is increasingly recognised in state practice, has a threefold significance. First, it implies that the state authorities are responsible for the functions of protecting the safety and lives of citizens and promotion of their welfare. Secondly, it suggests that the national political authorities are responsible to the citizens internally and to the international community through the U.N. And thirdly, it means that the *agents of state are responsible for their actions*; that is to say, they are accountable for their acts of commission and omission. The case for thinking of sovereignty in these terms is strengthened by the ever-increasing impact of international human rights norms, and the increasing impact in international discourse of the concept of human security.' [Emphasis added]. *The Responsibility to Protect: Report of the International Commission on Intervention and State Sovereignty*, December 2001, at 12. See also the comment by former UN Secretary-General Kofi Annan that 'National sovereignty offers vital protection to small and weak States, but it should not be a shield for crimes against humanity.' Secretary-General Statement to the General Assembly on the presentation of the Millennium Report, New York, 3 April 2000, SG/SM/7343, GA/9705.

[167] *Idem.*

[168] Andrea Bianchi, "Serious Violations of Human Rights and Foreign States' Accountability before Municipal Courts", in Lal Chand Vohrah, et al. (eds.), *Man's Inhumanity to Man. Essays on International Law in Honour of Antonio Cassese* (The Hague: Kluwer Law International, 2003), at 154.

[169] *Idem.*

[170] *Pinochet III*, at 128-9, *per* Lord Goff.

official acts could seriously harm U.S. interests, by straining diplomatic relations and possibly leading foreign nations to refuse to recognize the same immunity for American officials.'[171] This was a particular concern '[g]iven the global leadership responsibilities of the United States, [which put] its officials are at special risk of being made the targets of politically driven lawsuits abroad – including damages suits arising from alleged war crimes.'[172]

5.3.2 Act of State doctrine

The Act of State doctrine has been justified on three grounds: (1) the inherent powers of sovereign equality and comity among sovereigns; (2) the political, in particular foreign policy, ramifications of such a judgment; and (3) particularly in the United States, domestic separation of power concerns (or political question doctrine – focused on the political, rather than legal, nature of the judgment at issue). The classic statement of the first justification for the act of State doctrine – sovereign equality and comity – is found in the first two sentences of *Underhill*.[173] The political ramification concern is reflected in the opinions of numerous federal circuits. For example, the Ninth Circuit in *Siderman* noted that the act of State doctrine 'reflects the prudential concern that the courts, if they question the validity of sovereign acts taken by foreign states, may be interfering with the conduct of American foreign policy by the Executive and Congress.'[174] The separation of powers concern is also reflected in the opinions of numerous federal courts, most notably, the US Supreme Court in *Banco Nacional de Cuba* v. *Sabbatino*.[175] The Court noted that absent a clear rule of controlling international law, the determination of the validity of a foreign official act is a political, rather than a legal, inquiry for which courts are ill-suited.[176] The concern is that courts, by ruling on a case which has foreign policy issues, might embarrass the executive branch in its conduct of foreign relations and infringe upon its prerogatives in this area.[177]

---

[171] *Ra'ed Mohamed Ibrahim Matar* v. *Avraham Dichter*, 05 Civ.10270 (WHP), ECF Case, Statement of Interest of the United States of America, United States District Court, Southern District of New York, 17 November 2006, available at: <http://www.ccr-ny.org/v2/legal/human_rights/docs/Statement_of_Interest_Dichter.pdf> (last visited 15 May 2007).

[172] *Ibid.*, at 22.

[173] *Underhill* v. *Hernandez*, United States, 168 US 250 (1897), at 253: 'Every sovereign is bound to respect the independence of every other sovereign State, and the courts of one country will not sit in judgment on the acts of the government of another, done within its own territory.'

[174] *Susana Siderman De Blake, et al.,* v. *The Republic of Argentina*, United States, 965 F 2d 699 (1992) (US Court of Appeals, 9th Cir.)

[175] *Banco Nacional de Cuba* v. *Sabbatino*, 376 US 398 (1964).

[176] *Sabbatino*, 376 US 432-33 (noting that the act of state doctrine appropriately restricts courts to their traditional role as law interpreters rather than law makers, the latter being appropriately reserved to the executive and legislative branches). See also *W.S. Kirkpatrick* v. *Environmental Tectonics* 493 US 400 (1990) (*per* Scalia J).

[177] This is similar to the US 'political question doctrine,' which imposes judicial self-restraint when required to review congressional or executive acts related to the conduct of foreign affairs. Some courts have refused to apply the doctrine in cases dealing with human rights violations. See, e.g., *Linder* v. *Portocarrero*, 963 F.2d 332 (11th Cir. 1992).

Courts have also applied the doctrine where international law norms are unclear.[178] Some commentators have noted that neither of these concerns arises in the case of international crimes, which are universally condemned and are unlikely therefore to cause any embarrassment on the part of the executive.[179] Courts have also noted that to uphold Act of State after having refused to recognise either functional or personal immunities at the jurisdictional stage would amount to reintroducing in the guise of non-justiciability the immunity which had been removed.[180]

5.3.3 **Personal immunity**

The rationale for personal immunity, as for the scope of the immunity, differs somewhat between the different types of personal immunity, i.e., diplomatic immunity, head of State immunity, and immunity for heads of government and foreign ministers.

5.3.3.1 *Diplomatic immunity*

Although the personal immunity of certain state officials such as ambassadors were more and more viewed as the direct representative of the monarch that sent him, this theory of representation (which aligns this type of immunity with State immunity) is not the current understanding of the principle underlying diplomatic immunity. Rather, such immunity is deemed necessary to ensure the free and independent performance of diplomatic functions (*ne impediatur legatio*).[181] Diplomatic immunities are justified on the basis that the persons enjoying them are able to discharge their official mission free from interference or impairment.[182]

5.3.3.2 *Head of State immunity*

Head of State immunity is based on a different rationale. This type of immunity is historically based on the assumption that the head of State and sovereign are

---

[178] See *Banco Nacional de Cuba* v. *Sabbatino*, 376 US 398 (1964) (setting out these concerns).

[179] Bianchi, "Immunity v Human Rights", at 269-70. See also Peter Malanczuk, *Akehurst's Modern Introduction to International Law*, 7th edn. (New York: Routledge, 1997), at 122.

[180] See *A Limited Bank* v. *B. Bank and Bank of X, England*, Court of Appeal, Judgment of 31 July 1996 (11 *ILR* 591), quoting Kerr LJ in Maclaine in *Watson & Co.* v. *International Tin Council* [1988] 3 *WLR* 1169, at 1188.

[181] Vattel expressed the rationale in the following way: 'ambassadors and other public ministers are necessary instruments in the maintenance of that general society of Nations and of that mutual intercourse between them. But they can not accomplish the object of their appointment unless they are endowed with all the prerogatives necessary to perform the duties of their charge safely, freely, faithfully and successfully. Consequently, [nations are obliged] to accord them all the rights they require and all the privileges necessary for the performance of their duties.' E. De Vattel, *Le droit de gens ou principes de la loi naturelle, appliqués à la conduite & aux affaires des nations & des soverains*, Vol. 3 (1758), transl. by C.G. Fenwick, *The Law of Nations* (1983), at 376.

[182] Cassese, *International Criminal Law*, at 264.

one.[183] In addition, it is clear that the functions of Heads of State are different to the functions of diplomats and of government ministers. Heads of State may act on behalf of the State in all international intercourse. Therefore, as Watts put it, the Head of State is 'the representative *par excellence* of his State' and is therefore 'an *a fortiori* case.'[184] Moreover, 'the exposure of a head of state to media attention and the related risk of frivolous claims may justify a more extensive protection of the head of state compared to the state's diplomatic agents.'[185] It therefore appears that something more than the functionality rationale underlying diplomatic and ministerial immunity is required in the case of heads of State. It would appear that the head of State immunity rule does in fact reflect the remnants of the archaic notion of the majestic dignity of kings and princes as well as the idea that the head of State is the personification of the State. As Watts noted,

> 'the mystique of sovereignty, whether of States or their Heads, is much diminished. Nevertheless, the earlier close identity of the law governing the position of States with that of Heads of States, with both aspects being informed by notions of "sovereignty," has left its mark on current legal ideas relating to the position of Heads of States … Heads of States are still in a special position as the supreme representatives of, and in some respects the personal manifestations of, their States.'[186]

This rationale was recognised in the Swiss case of *Marcos* v. *Federal Department of Police*, in which the court considered that '[c]ustomary international law grants such privileges *ratione personae* to Heads of State as much to take account of their functions and symbolic embodiment of sovereignty as by reason of their representative character in inter-State relations.'[187] Similar contentions were made in the *Pinochet* case in the UK[188] and in the *Fidel Castro* case in Spain.[189]

5.3.3.3 *Head of Government and Foreign Minister immunity*

The rationale of extending personal immunity to heads of government and foreign ministers is directly related to their functions of office. In the *Arrest Warrant* case, the ICJ upheld the immunity of an incumbent minister of foreign affairs on the basis that such immunities are necessary to prevent any prejudice to the 'effective

[183] See, e.g., *Lafontant* v. *Aristide*, 844 F. Suppl. 128, 132 (EDNY 1994): 'Head of state immunity, like foreign sovereign immunity, is premised on the concept that a state and its ruler are one for purposes of immunity.'

[184] Watts, "The Legal Position in International Law of Heads of States", at 40.

[185] Van Alebeek, *The Immunity of States and their Officials*, at 179.

[186] Watts, "The Legal Position in International Law of Heads of States", at 36.

[187] *Marcos and Marcos* v. *Federal Department of Police*, Switzerland, Federal Tribunal (1989), 102 *ILR* 201.

[188] *Pinochet III* (*per* Lord Browne-Wilkinson, at 112-15, Lord Hope of Criaghead, at 145-52, Lord Saville of Newdigate, at 169-70, Lord Millett, at 171-91 and Lord Phillips of Worth Matravers, at 181-90).

[189] *Castro, Fidel*, Spain (*Audiencia nacional*), Order (auto) of 4 March 1999, no. 1999/2723, in CD Rom, EL DERECHO, 2002, Criminal case law.

performance' of his functions.[190] According to the Court, even the issuing of an arrest warrant may seriously jeopardise the conduct of international affairs of the State for which that person acts:

> 'if a Minister for Foreign Affairs is arrested in another State on a criminal charge, he or she is clearly thereby prevented from exercising the functions of his or her office. The consequences of such impediment to the exercise of those official functions are equally serious, regardless whether the Minister for Foreign Affairs was, at the time of arrest, present in the territory of the arresting State on an "official" visit or a "private" visit …'[191]

By putting so much emphasis on the functionality rationale, the ICJ effectively expanded the scope of the immunity afforded to ministers of foreign affairs.

5.3.4 State immunity

Two leading rationales explain the legal source of State immunity. Each of these rationales gives rise to vastly different implications for the nature and operation of the doctrine of foreign State immunity. One asserts that State immunity is a fundamental State right by virtue of the principle of sovereign equality. The view that foreign State immunity is a fundamental State right derives from the maxim *par in parem non habet imperium* (an equal has no power over an equal).[192] According to the 'fundamental right' rationale, *par in parem non habet imperium* is simply a specific application of the general principle of sovereign equality. Applying this logic, Sucharitkul argues that the principle of State jurisdiction must give way to the principle of sovereign equality to effectuate a State's right of immunity.[193]

The second theory is that State immunity arises as an exception to the principle of State jurisdiction. The reasoning is that when the forum State suspends its right of adjudicatory jurisdiction as a practical courtesy to facilitate inter-State relations State immunity is justified by 'practical necessity or convenience and particularly the desire to promote good will and reciprocal courtesies among nations.'[194] Justice Marshall applied this reasoning in *The Schooner Exchange*, where he recognised that 'intercourse' between nations and 'an interchange of those good offices which humanity dictates and its wants require and foster "mutual benefit."'[195] He noted

[190] *Arrest Warrant* case.

[191] *Ibid.*, at para. 55.

[192] *Black's Law Dictionary* 1673, 7th edn. (1999). The maxim has been traced back to the fourteenth century Italian jurist, Bartolus, who wrote "*Non enim una civitas potest facere legem super alteram, quia par in parem non habet imperium*" Gamal Moursi Badr, *State Immunity: An Analytical and Prognostic View* (1984), at 89, quoting Bartolus, *Tractatus Repressalium*, Questio I/3, para. 10 (1354).

[193] Sompong Sucharitkul, "Immunities of Foreign States Before National Authorities", 149 *RdC* 87 (1976 I), at 117-119.

[194] Theodore R. Giuttari, *The American Law of Sovereign Immunity: An Analysis of Legal Interpretation* (1970), at 6.

[195] *The Schooner Exchange*, at 136.

that 'all sovereigns have consented to a relaxation in practice ... of that absolute and complete jurisdiction within their respective territories which sovereignty confers' and that that the forum State could advance international affairs by granting a foreign sovereign 'licence' to conduct its affairs in the forum State. The effect of this 'relaxation' of jurisdictional authority was to permit a foreign sovereign to enter and operate within the forum State without fear of arrest, detention, or adverse legal proceedings.

The notion of comity has also been prevalent in justifications given by courts to uphold this type of immunity (as well other the other types of immunity examined). It is worth recalling that international comity, *comitas gentium*, is essentially a doctrine for resolving conflicts among multiple assertions of jurisdiction. Oppenheim referred to 'the rules of politeness, convenience and goodwill observed by States in their mutual intercourse without being legally bound by them.'[196] Comity has generally been applied by US courts in cases involving competing rules of decision,[197] competing assertion of adjudicatory jurisdiction,[198] or a pre-existing foreign judgment.[199] Ronald Slye points out that some US courts have been reluctant in recent years to use the doctrine of international comity to foreclose judicial review of cases that implicate important policies of the domestic US forum.[200] Providing accountability for gross violations of human rights would arguably qualify as such an important policy.[201] Moreover, US courts have also narrowed the broad application of international comity.[202] While it is true that particular rules of comity, maintained over a long period, may develop into rules of customary law,[203] immunities in regards to proceedings for international crimes cannot be justified solely on a comity basis. Given that in *Verlinden B. V.* v. *Central Bank of Nigeria* the US Supreme Court determined that immunity is a matter of comity and

---

[196] L. Oppenheim, *International Law: A Treatise,* Vol. 1 (London: Longmans, Green and Co, 1912), at 24-25, quoted in Ian Brownlie, *Principles of Public International Law*, 4th edn. (Oxford: OUP, 1990), at 30. The classic expression of international comity by US courts is that of the US Supreme Court in *Hilton* v. *Guyot*: '"Comity," in the legal sense, is neither a matter of absolute obligation, on the one hand, nor of mere courtesy and good will, upon the other. But it is the recognition which one nation allows within its territory to the legislative, executive or judicial acts of another nation, having due regard both to international duty and convenience, and to the rights of its own citizens or of other persons who are under the protection of its laws.' *Hilton* v. *Guyot*, 159 US 113, at 163-64.

[197] E.g., *Lauritzen* v. *Larsen*, 345 US 571 (1953), at 582.

[198] E.g., *Bremen* v. *Zapata Off-shore Co.*, 47 US 1 (1972), at 8-9.

[199] E.g., *Somportex Ltd.* v. *Philadelphia Chewing Gum Corp.*, 453 F.2d 435 (3d Cir. 1971), cert. denied, 405 US 1017 (1972).

[200] Ronald C. Slye, "The Legitimacy of Amnesties under International Law and General Principles of Anglo-American Law: Is Legitimate Amnesty Possible", 43 *VJIL* 173 (2002), citing *Allied Bank* v. *Banco Credito Agricola de Cartaga*, 757 F.2d 516.

[201] Slye, "The Legitimacy of Amnesties under International Law", at 213-14.

[202] In *Hartford Fire Insurance Co.* v. *California*, the US Supreme Court narrowed the application of the doctrine to cases presenting a 'true conflict' between domestic and foreign law, i.e., where a person subject to domestic and foreign law cannot comply with both. *Hartford Fire Insurance Co.* v. *California*, 509 US 764 (1993), at 798-99. In such a case, the domestic law gives way to the foreign law.

[203] Brownlie, *Principles of Public International Law*, at 30.

grace rather than a rule of law,[204] it is certainly arguable that there is no clear legal rule mandating State immunity in cases of international crimes, suggesting that an interests-analysis approach would be an appropriate means to settle the question of jurisdiction.

On the one hand, the 'fundamental right' rationale is unpersuasive in light of the continuing development of restrictions upon State immunity in State practice. If the sovereignty argument really gave rise to a 'fundamental right' to immunity, then the restrictive approach to State immunity could never have been justified or accepted, let alone the 'torts exception' or 'treaty exception.' Clearly, notions of fairness and equity have impacted upon courts' interpretation of the scope of State immunity as well as a State's own foreign policy concerns, suggesting that the rationale is hinged upon State immunity as an exception to exclusive territorial jurisdiction influenced by considerations of comity. On the other hand, the UN State Immunity Convention adopted by the UN General Assembly in 2004 provides strong authority to support immunity as a rule of international law, not a mere privilege granted for reasons of comity by the territorial State.[205]

5.3.5 **National immunity**

National immunity is generally justified on the grounds of the need for separation of powers so that courts cannot interfere with political organs in a way that would put their independence or political action at risk.[206] Arguably, by ratifying a treaty criminalising certain behaviour, the executive and legislative branches have signalled that courts may look into such matters in spite of national immunities. Where national immunity is contained in legislation, the principle of 'last in time' would resolve any conflict between the laws. If the immunities are contained in the constitution, there may have to be some constitutional modification to ensure that the State is not in violation of its treaty obligations.[207]

5.4 Legal rationales with regard to functional and personal immunities for international crimes

As noted in the introduction, a number of legal rationales have been employed by courts and commentators to lift functional and personal immunities, not all of which are coherent or consistent with each other. Because of the close connections

---

[204] *Verlinden B. V.* v. *Central Bank of Nigeria* 461 US 480 (1983), at 486.

[205] Hazel Fox, "In Defence of State Immunity: Why the UN Convention on State Immunity is Important", 55 *ICLQ* 405 (April 2006). The preamble to the convention refers to the jurisdictional immunities of States and their property as 'generally accepted as a principle of customary international law' and affirms that 'the rules of customary international law continue to govern matters not regulated' by the Convention.

[206] Cassese, *International Criminal Law*, at 264.

[207] E.g., France modified its national immunities granted to the Head of State and parliamentarians in its Constitution after having ratified the Rome Statute.

in historical origins and rationales between the various types of immunity impediments, there is much cross-fertilisation of legal argumentation. Essentially six distinct arguments have been employed by courts and/or commentators to reject functional and personal immunity in cases dealing with international crimes. These are: (1) that treaty obligations to prosecute State officials accused of international crimes are incompatible with immunity; (2) that States have impliedly waived the immunity of their officials by signing treaties criminalising certain international offences; (3) that there is a rule of customary international law lifting functional [and personal] immunity in case of international crimes; (4) that the *jus cogens* nature of international crimes trumps immunity; (5) that international crimes fall outside of the notion of 'acts performed in a sovereign capacity'; and (6) that the fundamental rights of victims are incompatible with immunities.

5.4.1 Treaty obligations to prosecute or extradite persons accused of international crimes are incompatible with immunities

The argument that the duties laid down in certain treaties prohibiting serious misconduct to prosecute or extradite alleged offenders are incompatible with the notion of immunity has significant currency both in terms of logic and in terms of practice. As a matter of logic, it seems clear that if a State consents to an obligation to prosecute certain crimes committed by State officials, this obligation would be inconsistent with a rule of domestic law or customary law that prevented such a trial from taking place. With regard to judicial practice, in *Pinochet III*, all the Law Lords, except Lord Millett,[208] relied on the Torture Convention and interpreted it as meaning that in the specific case of torture – as the Convention's express provisions refer to the official character of torture as a constituent element of the international crime giving rise to universal jurisdiction – immunity would be incompatible with obligations to criminalise and prosecute offenders.[209] Thus, the Convention provided an exception to the general rule of immunity *ratione materiae*. This type of reasoning obviously has to be restricted to the crime of torture, and for this reason the judgment of the House of Lords has been described by one commentator as

[208] For Lord Millett, immunity was always overridden by the evidence of international crimes.

[209] Lord Saville expressed a similar view: 'So far as parties to the Convention are concerned, I cannot see how, so far as torture is concerned, this immunity can exist consistently with the terms of the Convention. Each state party has agreed that the other states parties can exercise jurisdiction over alleged official torturers within their territories ... and thus to my mind can hardly simultaneously claim an immunity from extradition or prosecution that is necessarily based on the official nature of the alleged act.' Lord Saville also found that under customary international law, a former head of State was immune from suit for acts amounting to international crimes, even where such crimes had a *jus cogens* nature, so long as the crimes were conducted in an official capacity. However, the Torture Convention modified this immunity, at least with respect to States parties. The Convention, by covering torture by a 'person acting in an official capacity,' included torture for State purposes. This meant that immunity would be inconsistent with the terms of the Torture Convention.

'rather disappointing as far as a general statement on the limits to immunities of former heads of state is concerned.'[210]

Lord Millet took a more expansive interpretation, arguing that any State is permitted under international law to assert its jurisdiction over international crimes which have attained a *jus cogens* status and thus may be regarded 'as an attack on the international legal order.'[211] Relying on *Eichmann* and *Demjanjuk*,[212] he stated that the commission of such crimes in the course of one's official duties does not bar the exercise of jurisdiction by a national court. Moreover, in the case of torture as defined under the Convention, since the offence must be committed by or at the instigation of or with the consent or acquiescence of a public official or other person acting in an official capacity, '[t]he official or governmental nature of the act, which forms the basis of the immunity, is an essential ingredient of the offence. No rational system of criminal justice can allow an immunity which is co-extensive with the offence.'[213] Although other treaties criminalising certain behaviour do not necessarily include the involvement of a State official as a constituent element in the definition of the crime as does the Torture Convention, an argument may certainly be made that the Geneva Conventions of 1949, as well as AP I, and the Genocide Convention are principally concerned with the acts of State officials. With regard to grave breaches of the 1949 Geneva Conventions, while the relevant provisions do not specify that offenders need be State officials, given that the grave breaches regime only applies to international armed conflicts, the majority of those taking part in hostilities would be acting on the instructions of a State party to the conflict, and hence be acting in an 'official' capacity.[214] In the case of genocide, it may be recalled that the Convention was drafted in the light of the mass extermination of the Jews and other groups by the German government during WW II, i.e., by State officials, and it is likely that at the time of its drafting it was assumed that only a State would have the resources and planning required to effect a genocidal policy.

The argument is bolstered by the fact that certain treaty rules on specific international crimes implicitly or expressly state that immunities – whether functional or

[210] Stern, "Immunities for Heads of State", at 101.

[211] *Pinochet III*, *per* Lord Millet, at 177d.

[212] *Eichmann*, Israel, Supreme Court, Judgment of 29 May 1962, English translation in 36 *ILR* 227-324 (hereafter, *Eichmann* Supreme Court Judgment); *Demjanjuk* v. *Petrovsky*, United States, 776 F.2d 571 (6th Cir. 1985); cert. den. 475 US 1016 (1986), 628 F. Suppl. 1370; 784 F.2d 1254 (1986) (hereafter, *Demjanjuk* case).

[213] *Pinochet III*, *per* Lord Millet, at 179a.

[214] This does not discount the fact that civilians (i.e., non-State actors), such as arms dealers, may be held to be complicit in the perpetration of grave breaches. See, e.g., *United States* v. *Krauch*, VIII Trials of War Criminals before the Nuremberg Military Tribunals under Control Council Law No. 10 at 1081(Washington D.C.: United States Government Printing Office, 1949) (the *I.G. Farben* case); *United States* v. *Krupp*, IX Trials of War Criminals Before the Nuremberg Military Tribunals under Control Council Law No. 10 at 1327 (Washington D.C.: United States Government Printing Office, 1949); *United States* v. *Flick*, VI Trials of War Criminals before the Nuremberg Military Tribunals under Control Council Law No. 10 at 1187 (Washington D.C.: United States Government Printing Office, 1949) (the *Flick* case).

personal – do not relieve officials of responsibility for the crimes prescribed. This is the case for the Genocide Convention (Art. IV)[215] and the Convention against Torture (Arts. 1 and 4).[216] While the grave breaches provisions of the Geneva Conventions do not mention the question of immunity, one may assume that official function would not relieve persons accused of such crimes otherwise no soldier or commander could ever be prosecuted for war crimes. The ILC, when adopting the Draft Code of Crimes against the Peace and Security of Mankind in 1996, explained why the removal of functional and personal immunity was necessary:

> '… crimes against the peace and security of mankind often require the involvement of persons in positions of governmental authority who are capable of formulating plans and policies involving acts of exceptional gravity and magnitude. These crimes require the power to use or to authorise the use of the essential means of destruction and to mobilize the personnel required for carrying out these crimes. A governmental official who plans, instigates, authorises or orders such crimes not only provides the means and personnel required for carrying out the crime, but also abuses the authority and power entrusted to him. He may, therefore, be considered to be even more culpable than the subordinate who actually commits the criminal act. It would be paradoxical to allow the individuals who are, in some respect, the most responsible for the crime … to invoke the sovereignty of the state.'[217]

Moreover, the ICTY and ICTR, in Articles 7(2) and 6(2) respectively, both provide that 'The official position of any accused person, whether as Head of State or Government or as responsible Government official, shall not relieve such person of criminal responsibility nor mitigate punishment.' The ICC Statute explicitly excludes the right to invoke functional and personal immunities as a bar to prosecution (Art. 27). While the ICC Statute does not oblige States parties to prosecute persons accused of international crimes, the preamble of the ICC Statute recalls 'the duty of every State to exercise its criminal jurisdiction over those responsible for international crimes,' implying that such a rule exists at international law.[218] Significantly, the Paris Court of Appeal in the *Qaddafi* case[219] cited this paragraph of the preamble of the ICC as evidence of the alleged obligation to prosecute authors of international crimes, binding on any State party as a result of 'the intent of the international community to prosecute the most serious facts, even though perpetrated by heads of State in the exercise of their functions, when-

---

215 Art. IV of the Genocide Convention provides: 'Persons committing genocide or any of the other acts enumerated in article III shall be punished, whether they are constitutionally responsible rulers, public officials or private individuals.'

216 Art. 1 of the Torture Convention defines 'torture' as an act 'inflicted by or at the instigation of or with the consent or acquiescence of a public official or other person acting in an official capacity.' Art. 4 provides that 'Each State Party shall ensure that all acts of torture are offences under its criminal law. The same shall apply to an attempt to commit torture and to an act by any person which constitutes complicity or participation in torture.'

217 Quoted in Stern, "Immunities for Heads of State", at 86.

218 On the legal merit of such an argument, see Chapter 2, *supra*.

219 *Kadhafi*, France, *Cour d'appel de Paris*, *Chambre d'accusation*, decision of 20 October 2000.

ever they amount to international crimes, contrary to the demands of universal conscience.'[220] National courts in the US and UK and the Special Court for Sierra Leone (in criminal proceedings) have denied such immunity to former heads of State[221] and the prosecutor for the ICTY has indicted and tried a sitting head of State.[222] In the face of such practice, the ICJ has been criticised for 'missing the trend' in the *Arrest Warrant* judgment, finding that a foreign minister enjoys full immunity from criminal prosecution by the courts of a foreign state while he holds that office, even for acts which constitute international crimes.[223]

Certainly, it would seem that the ICJ gave little regard to the development of international criminal law upon immunities in international law, but it is also true that State practice remains mixed. Some States have shown resistance to this way of interpreting treaty obligations. For example, in March 2000, the US State Department upheld the personal (diplomatic) immunity of a Peruvian allegedly involved in acts of torture.[224] More recently in the United States a civil case was brought against Avi Dichter, the former Director of Israel's General Security Service (GSS) for war crimes and other gross violations of human rights arising out of a bombing of an apartment building in Gaza City, in which 15 persons were killed and 150 civilians injured. The case was dismissed on 2 May 2007 by Judge Pauley of the Southern District of New York, who found that Dichter had immunity under the FSIA because, according to the Israeli government, Dichter was acting in the course of his official duties. The US government submitted a statement of interest in the case arguing that Dichter should be immune for official acts, including war

---

220 The Court appears to be referring to functional immunity, rather than personal immunity, however.

221 See, e.g., *Hilao* v. *Marcos*, 25 F.3d 1467 (9th Cir. 1994) *cert. denied*, 513 US 1126 (1995) (civil suit in US against former President of the Philippines, Ferdinand Marcos); *Paul* v. *Avril*, 812 F. Suppl. 207 (S.D. Fla. 1993) (civil suit in US against former leader of Haiti, Prosper Avril); *Ex Parte Pinochet*, 28 *ILM* 581 (1999) (UK House of Lords Decision concerning extradition of former Chilean President Augusto Pinochet to Spain for torture); *Taylor* Decision on Immunity, *supra* note 62.

222 Indictment, *Prosecutor* v. *Milošević*, ICTY, Case No. IT-99-37 (22 May 1999).

223 *Arrest Warrant* case, para. 54. See, e.g., Jonathan H. Marks, "Mending the Web: Universal Jurisdiction, Humanitarian Intervention and the Abrogation of Immunity by the Security Council", 42 *Columbia Journal of International Law* 445-490 (2004) (arguing that where public officials perpetuate serious international crimes, the arguments for upholding immunities are weak). The *ad hoc* Judge of Belgium, Judge Van den Wyngaert, in her dissenting opinion, stated that: 'The Court's conclusion is reached without regard to the general tendency towards the restriction of immunity of the State officials (including even Heads of State), not only in the field of private and commercial law where the in par parem principle has become more and more restricted and deprived of its mystique, but also in the field of criminal law, when there are allegations of serious international crimes.' Dissenting Opinion of *ad hoc* Judge Van den Wyngaert, para. 23.

224 Cassese, *International Criminal Law*, at 273. Major Tomas Ricardo Anderson Kohatsu, a retired officer of Peru's Army Intelligence Service, was accused in 1997 of having perpetrated 'horrendous crimes.' He was detained by the FBI in early March 2000 pursuant to the 1984 Convention against Torture, but was released soon after following a decision by the Under-Secretary of State, Thomas Pickering, on the basis that Anderson was entitled to diplomatic immunity because he held a G-2 visa, granted to accredited members of the staff of the Peruvian Mission to the Organisation of American States. See the case summary at <www.windos/temp/centerforconstitutional rights.htm>.

crimes.[225] It based this contention not upon the FSIA, but upon 'longstanding common law that the FSIA did not displace.'[226] However, this case concerned a civil lawsuit, not criminal proceedings, and hence does not necessarily have a bearing upon the issue of whether functional immunity may be lifted in criminal proceedings against State officials accused of international crimes. The government made this distinction clear in its statement of interest, strongly suggesting that Dichter would not enjoy functional immunity in respect of criminal proceedings.[227]

In summary, in light of the quest for coherence and consistency in the international legal order, the apparent contradiction between specific treaty obligations which criminalise certain behaviour when perpetuated by State officials and functional and personal immunity rules should be resolved in favour of the former, which represent the consenting will of the States parties to prosecute State officials who are accused of international crimes. The limit of this argument is obviously that those international crimes that are not regulated by treaty – i.e., crimes against humanity and serious violations of the laws and customs of war – could arguably still be overridden by immunity in the absence of clearly agreed rules lifting such immunity in these cases. What does seem to be clear, however, is that there is no legal rule *mandating* immunity for international crimes, suggesting that a balancing approach is the most appropriate means of resolving the inconsistency.

5.4.2 States have impliedly waived immunity of their officials by signing treaties criminalising certain international offences

The argument that by signing treaties requiring parties to criminalise certain conduct and to assert jurisdiction over all persons accused thereof, States have impliedly waived the immunity of their officials, has generated considerable academic support and some judicial support.[228] This argument differs from the previous one which simply recognises two opposing rules and favours one over the other as a matter of logical consistency. A waiver, on the other hand, pertains to the renouncing or disclaiming of a judicial benefit. By abandoning the remedy (i.e., immunity) that international law provides by accepting universal jurisdiction over the crimes committed by State officials, a State may be said to have waived its immunity over these crimes by implication.[229]

---

225 *Ra'ed Mohamed Ibrahim Matar* v. *Avraham Dichter*, 05 Civ.10270 (WHP), ECF Case, Statement of Interest of the United States of America, United States District Court, Southern District of New York, 17 November 2006, available at: <http://www.ccr-ny.org/v2/legal/human_rights/docs/Statement_of_Interest_Dichter.pdf>. In its submission, the US government reiterated its 'serious objections' to the attack, which the Bush administration had previously condemned as a 'deliberate attack against a building in which civilians were known to be located.'

226 *Ibid.*, at 2.

227 *Ibid.*, at 30.

228 See, e.g., Bianchi, "Denying State Immunity to Violators of Human Rights", at 214 (in relation to State immunity).

229 Some commentators have questioned the validity of the waiver argument, at least in regards to some types of immunity. Van Alebeek has argued that 'the concept of waiver does not agree with

It may be recalled that all domestic legislation regarding State immunity recognises that a foreign State may waive its immunity, providing such a waiver is explicit.[230] The idea that a State may impliedly waive its immunity by ratifying a human rights convention is less readily accepted. In *Von Dardel I*, the plaintiffs succeeded in convincing the District Court of an implied waiver of State immunity by reason of the USSR's ratification of the UN Charter.[231] However, on appeal, the plaintiffs changed the focus of the implied waiver to the 1973 Convention on the Prevention and Punishment of Crimes against Internationally Protected Persons, arguing that the USSR should have anticipated that US courts could assert jurisdiction over such crimes, since the Convention obliges State parties to prosecute those accused of offences. The Court rejected this argument, based on the argument that a waiver of State to its immunity could not be implied from the ratification of an instrument which 'requires jurisdiction over crimes, not civil suits and in any event not necessarily over foreign States.'[232] The implied waiver to State immunity argument was also rejected in *Princz* v. *Germany*.[233] However, one may question whether a similar argument could be brought in relation to criminal proceedings, to which the same objections cannot be raised.

Analogous to the waiver argument is the exception to immunity under US legislation which may occur in the case where the forum State has ratified a particular treaty requiring the exercise of jurisdiction. For example, sections 1303(a) and 1604 of the FSIA subjects the application of the general rule on immunity to international agreements to which the US is a party. This 'treaty exception' may be an important way to overcome the hurdle of immunity in foreign jurisdictions, particularly where conventions such as the Torture Convention or the Geneva Conventions of 1949 are relevant. However, such arguments are unlikely to fare well unless the treaty is considered to be self-executing and the crimes are well-defined. A similar exception exists with regard to the Act of State doctrine, which has been interpreted as applicable 'in the absence of a treaty or other unambiguous agreement regarding controlling legal principles.'[234]

---

the rule of functional immunity.' Van Alebeek, *The Immunity of States and their Officials*, at 135. Her reasoning is that while a State may waive its *own* immunity, it is not possible for a State to waive the immunity accruing to its own officials if they have acted in an official capacity. A State may of course argue that an official did not act under its authority or within the limits of his or her mandate. But this is not a waiver of immunity; it is a defeat of the presumption of authority. However, this is a slightly different argument. Here, van Alebeek appears to be referring to the practice of waiving immunity *ex post facto*, whereas the argument we are concerned with is whether, by ratifying an international treaty accepting that State officials may be prosecuted for certain universally condemned behaviour, a State has waived functional immunity.

[230] E.g., FSIA (US), § 1605 (a)(1).

[231] Such an argument has some support in legal literature. See R. Lillich and F. Newman, *International Human Rights: Problems of Law and Policy* (Boston: Little, Brown and Co., 1979).

[232] *Von Dardel* v. *Soviet Socialist Republics*, United States, 736 F Supp 1 (DDC 1990).

[233] *Princz* v. *Federal Republic of Germany*, United States, 26 F. 3d. 1166 (1994).

[234] *Banco Nacional de Cuba* v. *Sabbatino*, United States, 376 US 398 (1964), at 468. See also *Kalamazoo Spice Extraction Co* v. *Provisional Military Government of Socialist Ethiopia*, 729 F 2d 422 (6th Cir 1984).

In *Pinochet III*, the Law Lords disagreed with each other as to whether the Torture Convention implied a waiver of functional immunity. The one dissenting judge, Lord Goff of Chiveley, held that there was nothing in the Torture Convention to suggest an express waiver of immunity for acts of torture, nor could such a waiver be implied, noting that there was no discussion of a waiver of immunity in the *travaux préparatoires*.[235] Lord Hutton, on the other hand, found that 'there is no waiver issue as the immunity to which Pinochet is entitled as a former head of state does not arise in relation to, and does not attach to acts of torture' by reason of it having been outlawed at the time the acts were committed.[236] In his view, the mere criminalisation of torture meant that such acts were axiomatically not covered by immunity, so there was no question of 'waiving' the immunity. By contrast, Lord Hope found that torture and other crimes could be within the official functions of a head of State and would therefore have immunity. However, he construed Chile's ratification of the Torture Convention as having abrogated or waived this immunity.[237] By ratifying the Convention, Chile assented to the system of mandatory universal jurisdiction over State officials involved in acts of torture thereby abandoning the remedy that international law gives officials for wrongful acts.

The question of whether States parties of the ICC have implicitly waived the immunities of their officials remains unresolved. While some commentators have argued that ratification entails a State party's waiver of all the immunities of its officials even before the national courts of other States parties,[238] others assert that States parties to the ICC Statute have only waived immunities *vis-à-vis* cases

---

[235] *Pinochet III*, at 128-9, *per* Lord Goff.

[236] *Ibid.*, at 116e, *per* Lord Hutton. He argued that although the alleged acts were carried out by Pinochet 'under colour of his position as head of state … they cannot be regarded as functions of a head of state under international law when international law expressly prohibits torture as a crime.' *Ibid.*, at 165d.

[237] Although Lord Hope recognised that the *jus cogens* nature of a crime means that all States have to refrain from such acts and have an obligation *erga omnes* to punish such conduct, he found that a former head of State would still have immunity over *jus cogens* crimes before a foreign national court. Only international courts whose statutes specifically lift such immunity are not bound to respect such bars to prosecution. For national courts, immunity would prevail unless it was limited by an express or implied provision in an international convention to which both the State asserting immunity and the State being asked to refuse immunity were parties. The Torture Convention being silent on this issue, he found that isolated acts of torture did not remove immunity, however, systematic torture was a crime against humanity and a *jus cogens* crime by September 1988, when Chile ratified the Torture Convention, and therefore assented to the system of universal jurisdiction in the Convention, meaning that Chile could no longer assert immunity for systematic torture. Thus, immunity was lost on 30 October 1988, when Chile ratified the Torture Convention. However, Lord Hope was 'content to accept the view of … Lord Saville … that Senator Pinochet continued to have immunity until 8 December 1988, when the United Kingdom ratified the Convention.'

[238] Dapo Akande, "International Law Immunities and the International Criminal Court", 98 *AJIL* 422 (2004); Jann K. Kleffner, "The Impact of Complementarity on National Implementation of Substantive International Criminal Law", 1 *JICJ* 86 (2003), at 106; Micaela Fruilli, "The Question of Charles Taylor's Immunity – Still in Search of a Balanced Application of Personal Immunities?", 2 *JICJ* 1118 (2004), at 1129.

heard by the ICC.[239] Article 27 of the Statute, which clearly removes such obstacles from the exercise of the ICC's jurisdiction, has also been interpreted as implicitly requiring States parties to change their national legislation on immunities to allow them to institute proceedings against State officials and/or to arrest them and transfer them to The Hague.[240] This reasoning is based upon the operation of the complementarity principle, whereby the Prosecutor could find that by not prosecuting a State official based upon immunities, a State has shown that it is unable or unwilling to prosecute.[241] The problem with such an argument is that by upholding immunities of foreign officials States are not acting in bad faith – the principle underlying the rules on inadmissibility; they are merely complying with what they perceive to be their other international law obligations.[242] As previously noted, some State parties have chosen to abrogate immunities in their own national jurisdiction, while others have expressly retained immunities.[243] In the *Sharon* case, the Belgium Court of Cassation held that Article 27(2) of the ICC Statute does not affect or prevent the application of the customary rule on immunities when a court is exercising 'universal jurisdiction by default.'[244] The Rome Statute acknowledges as much in Article 98, which recognises that States may not proceed with a request for surrender or assistance which would entail acting in contravention to its obligations under international law with respect to the State or the diplomatic immunity of a person of a third State, without having first sought the co-operation of the third State for the waiver of the immunity.[245] The waiver requirement has been identified as a potentially major obstacle to the ICC ever being able to prosecute a head of State.[246] For this reason, it has been argued that States that have ratified the ICC may have also waived all immunities regarding the arrest and transfer of persons to the ICC.[247] This would mean that the reference to 'third State' in Article 98(1)

---

[239] Antonio Cassese, "The Belgium Court of Cassation v. the International Court of Justice: the *Sharon and others* Case", 1 *JICJ* (2003), at 442 ('Under another, more convincing interpretation, immunities are lifted only in proceedings before the ICC').

[240] Paola Gaeta, "Official Capacity and Immunities", in Antonio Cassese, Paola Gaeta and John R.W.D. Jones (eds.), *The Rome Statute of the International Criminal Court: A Commentary*, Vol. I (Oxford: OUP, 2002), at 999.

[241] See Art. 17 ICC Statute.

[242] See also Mark A. Summers, "Immunity or Impunity? The Potential Effect of Prosecutions of State Officials for Core International Crimes in States like the United States That Are Not Parties to the Statute of the International Criminal Court", 31 *Brooklyn Journal of International Law* 489-492 (2005-2006).

[243] Compare the International Criminal Court Bill of 26 June 2002 (South Africa), Section 2 (removing all immunities) to International Crimes Act of 19 June 2003 (The Netherlands), Section 16 (retaining all immunities).

[244] *Sharon* case. See also Cassese, "The Belgium Court of Cassation", at 437.

[245] Art. 98(1) ICC Statute.

[246] Otto Triffterer, "Article 27: Irrelevance of official capacity", in Otto Triffterer (ed.), *Commentary on the Rome Statute of the International Criminal Court: Observers' Notes, Article by Article* (Baden-Baden: Nomos Verlagsgesellschaft, 1999), at 513.

[247] See, e.g., the UK's International Criminal Court Act 2001, s23(1): 'Any state or diplomatic immunity attaching to a person by reason of a connection with a state party to the ICC Statute does

refers to non-party States only.[248] The argument finds little textual support, but it does comport with the principle of effectiveness as an interpretative device, allowing Article 27 to have some meaning.

The basic premise of the waiver argument – that States may explicitly or impliedly lift the immunities of their officials – is further evidence of the lack of a rule of international law requiring the respecting of immunities in cases of international crimes, thereby supporting an approach that looks rather to balance competing interests.

5.4.3 Customary international law lifts functional (and personal) immunity in case of international crimes

There is large support in State practice and doctrine for the argument that a customary rule of international law lifts functional immunity in case of international crimes.[249] The question of whether there is a similar customary rule lifting personal immunity remains controversial. Article 227 of the Treaty of Versailles which provided for the establishment of an allied tribunal to try the German Emperor Wilhelm II for 'a supreme offence against international morality and the sanctity of treaties' is perhaps the first example of an instrument specifically lifting personal immunities for the prosecution of a sitting Head of State for international offences. However, as the trial never took place, the first clear sign of the development of lifting personal and functional immunities was the recognition during WW II and its aftermath that State officials could not be 'shielded' from prosecution by reason of their official function, including as Head of State, for war crimes, crimes against humanity and crimes against peace.[250] Control Council Law No. 10 also rejected functional immunity as a bar to prosecution before these tribunals of the occupying forces.[251] Subsequently, a large number of national courts have proceeded to prosecute former State officials for acts committed ostensibly as part of their offi-

---

not prevent proceedings under this part in relation to that person.' Sub-paragraph (6)(c) makes it clear that State or diplomatic immunity includes 'any rule of law derived from customary international law.'

[248] Gaeta, "Official Capacity and Immunities", at 994.

[249] See, e.g., Cassese, *International Criminal Law*, at 267: 'It seems indisputable that by now an international general rule has evolved on the matter.' For a contrary view, see Torsten Stein, "Limits of International Law Immunities for Senior State Officials in Criminal Procedure", in Christian Tomuschat and Jean-Marc Thouvenin (eds.), *The Fundamental Rules of the International Legal Order.* Jus Cogens *and Obligations* Erga Omnes (Leiden/Boston: Martinus Nijhoff Publishers, 2006), at 249.

[250] Article 7 of the Statute of the IMT, annexed to the London Agreement of 8 August 1945 stated that: 'The official position of defendants, whether as Heads of State or responsible officials in Government departments, shall not be considered as freeing them from responsibility or mitigating punishment.'

[251] Art. 5 stated that: 'In any trial or prosecution for a crime herein referred to, the accused shall not be entitled to the benefits of any statute of limitation in respect to the period from 30 January 1933 to 1 July 1945, nor shall any immunity, pardon or amnesty granted under the Nazi regime be admitted as a bar to trial or punishment.'

cial functions which amount to international crimes.[252] Some authoritative national military manuals also provide that a person who has committed an international crime while under colour of authority may not use this as a defence.[253] In 1946, the UN General Assembly unanimously adopted Resolution 95, which affirmed the principles recognised by the Charter of the Nuremberg Tribunal and the judgment of the Tribunal. The ILC formulated the principle in its Principles of International Law Recognized in the Charter of the Nürnberg Tribunal and in the Judgment of the Tribunal of 1950 in Principle III.[254] The Israeli Supreme Court in *Eichmann* recognised that these principles 'have become part of the law of nations and must be regarded as having been rooted in it also in the past.'[255] Functional immunity has been consistently treated as no bar to jurisdiction in all of the constituent instruments setting up international and hybrid courts.[256] The ICTY has described Article 7(2) of its Statute rejecting functional immunity as reflecting 'a rule of customary international law.'[257] In recent practice, the Committee of Eminent African

---

[252] See, e.g., *Eichmann* Supreme Court Judgment; *Barbie*, France, *Cour de cassation*, decision of 6 October 1983, *Gaz.Pal.* 1983, 710. English translation in 78 *ILR* 126-31; *Barbie*, France, *Cour de cassation*, decision of 26 January 1984, JCP 1984, II, no. 20197. English translation in 78 *ILR* 132-6; *Kappler (Appeal),* Italy, Supreme Military Tribunal, Judgment of 25 October 1952, no. 1714, in *RDI* (1953), at 193-9; *Hass and Priebke*, Italy, Supreme Court of Cassation, Judgment of 16 November 1998, 959; *Rauter, Hans Albin*, Netherlands, Special Court of Cassation, Decision of 12 January 1949, in *NederJ* (1949), no. 87, at 144-61 (526-48); *Albecht*, The Netherlands, Special Court of Cassation, Judgment of 11 April 1949, *NederJ* (1949), at 747-51; *Bouterse, Desi*, the Netherlands, Decision of the Court of Appeal of Amsterdam, 20 November 2000, unofficial English translation by Peter Kell in 3 *YIHL* 677 (2000); *Bouterse, Desi*, the Netherlands, Supreme Court [*Hoge Raad*], Criminal Chamber, judgment of 18 September 2001, No. 00749/01 (CW 2323), summary available at: <http://www.icrc.org/ihl-nat.nsf/39a82e2ca42b52974125673e00508144/07c5ae1b4a999f1cc1256da200518c91?OpenDocument>; *Kesserling*, British Military Court sitting in Venice, verdict of 6 May 1947, *LRTWC*, Vol. 8, at 9-14; *von Lewinski*, British Military Court sitting at Hamburg, verdict of 19 December 1949, in Annual Digest 1949, 509-25; *Pinochet III*; *Yamashita*, United States, US Supreme Court, Judgment of 4 February 1946, 18 *AILC* 1-23 ; 327 US 1, 66 S.Ct.340, 90 L.Ed 499 (1946), at 1599 et seq.; *Buhler*, Poland, Supreme National Tribunal, Krakow, Judgment of 10 July 1948, in *LRTWC*, Vol. 14, 23 et seq. at 682; *Pinochet,* Spain, Central Criminal Court (*Audiencia nacional*), Order (auto) of 24 September 1999, no. 1998/28720, rec. 84/1999, at 4-8; *Scilingo, Adolfo*, Spain, Third Section of the Criminal Division (*Audiencia Nacional*), Judgment no. 16/2005 of 19 April 2005, *Sentencia por crímenes contra la humanidad en el caso Adolpho Scilingo*, available at: <http://www.derechos.org/nizkor/espana/juicioral/doc/sentencia.html>; *Cavallo Ricardo Miguel*, Mexico, order (auto) of 12 January 2001, online: <www.derechos.org/nizkor/arg/epana/mex.html>.

[253] See, e.g., US Department of the Army Field Manual, *The Law of Land Warfare* (July 1956), at paras. 498 and 510; British manual, *The Law of War on Land* (1958), para. 632.

[254] Principle III states: 'The fact that a person who committed an act which constitutes a crime under international law acted as Head of State or responsible Government official does not relieve him from responsibility under international law.' 2 *YILC* (1950), para. 97.

[255] *Eichmann* Supreme Court Judgment, at 311.

[256] See Art. 7 IMT Charter; Art. 6 IMTFE Charter; Art. 5 Allied Control Council Law No. 10; Art. 7(2) ICTY Statute; Art. 6(2) ICTR Statute; Art. 27(1) ICC Statute; Art. 29 Law on the Establishment of the Extraordinary Chambers in the Courts of Cambodia for the Prosecution of Crimes Committed during the Period of Democratic Kampuchea of 2001, as amended; Art. 6(2) SCSL Statute; and Section 15, UNTAET Regulation 2000/15.

[257] *Milošević*, ICTY, Trial Chamber, Decision on Preliminary Motions, 8 November 2001, Case No. IT-02-54-PT, paras. 26-34.

Jurists on the case of Hissene Habré considered that Habré should not be able to be shielded from prosecution from any immunity as a former head of State.[258] In Belgium, a judge held that Pinochet enjoyed no official immunity for crimes against humanity.[259] In the *Sharon* case, by distinguishing between the personal immunities of Sharon (which prevented his prosecution) and the functional immunities of Yaron, who was still a high-ranking official,[260] but who the Belgian Court of Cassation held could still be prosecuted notwithstanding his having acted in an official capacity at the time of the acts in question, the Court appeared to consider there to be an exception for functional immunities in the case of international crimes.[261] Zappalà, after examining the treaty provisions on international crimes, finds that they 'are generally considered to have confirmed the existence, under customary international law, of an exception to functional immunity for those state officials who may be responsible for international crimes.'[262]

On the other hand, commentators have not generally accepted that the ICJ's judgment in the *Arrest Warrant* case has settled the matter with regard to the personal immunities of high-ranking State officials.[263] Andrew Clapham notes that, 'the Court deduces an absolute immunity for foreign ministers in office, although the judgement fails to offer any obvious evidence of the familiar requirements of state practice or *opinio juris* to confirm evidence of such a rule in contemporary international law.'[264] Brigitte Stern has called the decision 'a step backwards.'[265] While no domestic court of a foreign State has thus far prosecuted an incumbent head of State or high-ranking State official, in the *Qaddafi* case, the French *Cour de Cassation* implicitly recognised that exceptions to head of State immunity exist by dismissing the case on the grounds that the crime of terrorism did not form part of the customary law exceptions to immunity.[266] Procedural immunity has been explicitly lifted in two instruments setting up international or hybrid courts: Article

[258] *Report of the Committee of Eminent African Jurists on the Case of Hissene Habré*, available at: <http://www.hrw.org/justice/habre/CEJA_Repor0506.pdf>, paras. 14 and 15.

[259] *Pinochet*, Belgium, Brussels Investigating Judge (*juge d'instruction*), order of 16 November 1998, in 79 *RDPC* (1999), 278-300, at 281-288.

[260] He was director general in the Israeli Ministry of Defence.

[261] *Sharon* case.

[262] Salvatore Zappalà, "Do Heads of State in Office Enjoy Immunity from Jurisdiction for International Crimes? The *Ghaddafi* Case Before the French *Cour de Cassation*", 12 *EJIL* 604 (2001).

[263] See Antonio Cassese, "When May Senior State Officials Be Tried for International Crimes? Some Comments on the *Congo* v. *Belgium* Case", 13 *EJIL* 853 (2002).

[264] Clapham, "National Action Challenged", at 316.

[265] Stern, "Immunities for Heads of State", at 73. The main source of her disappointment relates to the third 'exception' to immunity identified by the ICJ, that a court of a third State may try a former Minister of Foreign Affairs for those acts done in 'private capacity,' without specifying whether international crimes would be included in the notion of acts done in a 'private capacity' or not.

[266] *Kadhafi*, France, *Cour de Cassation*, decision of 13 March 2001, no. 1414, in Bulletin des arrêts de la Court de Cassation, Chambre criminelle, March 2001, no. 64, at 218-19 ('at this stage of development of international customary law, the crime charged [i.e. terrorism], no matter how serious, does not fall within the exceptions to the principle of immunity from jurisdiction of foreign Heads of State in office.' Transl. in Zappalà, at 601.) It is possible, however, that the Court was referring to functional immunity, not personal immunity.

27(2) of the ICC Statute and Section 15.2 of UNTAET Regulation 2000/15. In addition, Article 7 of the IMT Charter has also been interpreted as rejecting personal immunities.[267] Given that all States are bound to co-operate with the ICTY and ICTR, one could equally imply an exception to procedural immunity inherent in Articles 7(2) and 6(2) respectively. While the SCSL did not enjoy the same benefit, it has noted that '[t]he nature of the offences for which jurisdiction was vested in these various [international] tribunals is instructive as to the circumstances in which immunity is withheld.'[268] The trend of these instruments is undeniably the rejection of procedural immunity over international crimes. With regard to genocide, it is arguable that the ICJ implicitly recognised the customary law nature of the obligation to lift head of State immunity in its *Advisory Opinion on Reservations to the Convention on Genocide* by holding that 'the principles underlying the Convention are principles which are recognised by civilized nations as binding on States, even without any conventional obligation.'[269] This signals that Article IV, which provides that 'Persons committing genocide ... shall be punished, whether they are constitutionally responsible rulers, public officials or private individuals,' is a customary rule of international law.

However, at least one national court has rejected this view. Belgium's Court of Cassation, in its decision on the indictment of *Sharon, Ariel; Yaron, Amos and others*,[270] after recognising that international customary law is opposed to the idea that current heads of State and Government should be judged by foreign tribunals in the absence of treaty or customary rules that oblige the States concerned to lift immunities, has ruled that the exclusion of immunity established in Article IV of the Genocide Convention is only applicable in respect to the competent courts according to the Convention itself (i.e., the territorial State or an international penal tribunal). It also found that Article 5(3) of the 1993 Belgian law (which states that the official status of a person accused of international crimes does not preclude his prosecution) does not impose prosecution of incumbent heads of states or governments. Rather, this provision merely entails that the nature of a State organ is not a ground for exemption from criminal responsibility when international crimes are involved.[271] This case raises the question of whether States entitled to prosecute the crime of genocide under customary international law are barred from exercising jurisdiction by reason of official immunity. Addressing this question, Cassese contends that '[a]rguably, it would be contrary to the object and purpose of the Convention to make senior officials only punishable in the state where they have engaged in genocide, that is, precisely the state where they are most unlikely to be

[267] Arguably, Admiral Doenitz, who succeeded Hitler as Head of State on 1 May 1945 following the latter's suicide was tried and convicted (to 10 years imprisonment) on the basis that Art. 7 IMT Charter rejected personal immunity.

[268] *Taylor* Decision on Immunity, para. 49.

[269] *Reservations to the Convention on Genocide* (Advisory Opinion), 1951 ICJ Reports 15 (1951), para. 24.

[270] *Sharon* case.

[271] Cassese, "The Belgium Court of Cassation", at 439-440.

prosecuted and tried (unless there is a change in government).'[272] The drafters of the Genocide Convention did not adequately take this *realpolitik* consideration into account, apart from also providing for the possibility of an international criminal court to deal with genocide cases (which did not come into existence until 50 years later), and history has shown that those countries where structures of power have remained unchanged following genocidal campaigns have not attempted to prosecute those responsible.

Under customary international law therefore it would appear that there is a conflict between the right of all States to prosecute the crime of genocide on the one hand, no matter where it has been committed, and the exception to the exercise of jurisdiction in the case of immunities of incumbent high-ranking foreign officials, on the other. In order to reconcile these two rules, some have suggested that the exercise of universal jurisdiction be made conditional when a court is faced with a competing rule of immunity. These conditions could be, for example, a close link between the prosecuting State and the criminal conduct (e.g. courts having active or passive personality jurisdiction), or on the basis of links such as the residence of the accused on the territory of the prosecuting State (though this would probably only be the case for diplomatic agents). However, such conditions really amount to a rejection of reliance on the jurisdictional principle of universality where immunity is involved.

Interestingly, the issue of immunity of a sitting government official in the court of a third State did not appear be part of the German prosecutor's decision not to proceed with an investigation of Almatovich Almatov, the Interior Minister of Uzbekistan, for crimes against humanity (tied to the Andijan massacre of 13 May 2005) and systematic torture committed in Uzbekistan's prisons, though Cassese had submitted an affidavit stating that Almatov could not benefit from diplomatic immunity as a government official because he had entered Germany for private purposes. The ICJ decision in the *Arrest Warrant* case could perhaps be taken to indicate that Almatov, as an incumbent high-ranking government minister, would have complete personal immunity during his tenure, notwithstanding whether he was travelling to Germany for official or private reasons. This argument could possibly be refuted on the basis that while the functions of a minister of foreign affairs (such as Mr. Yerodia) require frequent travel abroad, the functions of an interior minister do not; hence by reason of the functionality rationale, the scope of immunity from foreign jurisdiction is reduced. Moreover, Uzbekistan, as a party to the Torture Convention as of 28 September 1995, could arguably be deemed to have waived the immunity of its officials for acts of torture under the reasoning adopted by some of the judges in *Pinochet III*. Although in the latter case the judges did not appear to accept the existence of an exception to immunity *ratione personae*, this part of the judgment was arrived at by the majority of Law Lords by reliance on the UK State Immunity Act, which clearly confers immunity upon incumbent heads of State, not upon customary international law.[273]

---

[272] *Ibid.*, at 441.

[273] Professor Christopher Greenwood, who was instructed by the Crown Prosecution Service for the Commissioner of Police and the government of Spain in the *Pinochet III* proceedings in the House

Cassese bases the rationale of a customary rule lifting functional immunity for international crimes on the idea that: 'in the present international community respect for human rights and the demand that justice be done whenever human rights have been seriously and massively put in jeopardy, override the traditional principle of respect for State sovereignty. The new thrust towards protection of human dignity has shattered the shield that traditionally protected State agents acting in their official capacity.'[274] Such arguments are supported by the interpretative theory enunciated by Andrea Bianchi that courts should endeavour to give expression to the values the legal system is intended to uphold.[275] Such rationales equally apply in the case of personal immunities. As noted, the insistence of the ICJ in the *Arrest Warrant* case to uphold the absolute immunity of an incumbent foreign minister was based less on evidence of State practice and *opinio juris* supporting such a rule and more on the functionality rationale underlying the personal immunity of ministers of foreign affairs. With this in mind, and given the equally, if not more cogent, rationales for the prosecution of the masterminds behind the mass perpetration of international crimes, the scope of the rule of absolute personal immunity in the case of international crimes before foreign national courts appears to be on shaky ground.[276]

It is perhaps worth recalling Justice Robert H. Jackson's statement that '[w]e do not accept the paradox that legal responsibility should be the least where power is the greatest. We stand on the principle of responsible government declared some three centuries ago to King James by Lord Justice Coke, who proclaimed that even a King is still "under God and the law."'[277] The ICTY in *Tadić* has also stated that '[it] would be would a travesty of law and a betrayal of the universal need for justice, should the concept of State sovereignty be allowed to be raised success-

---

of Lords, stated in this regard: 'If I can distinguish between two different points there, at the previous hearings we accepted that under the State Immunity Act, as a matter of United Kingdom law a serving head of state would be able to invoke immunity, but as a matter of international law our submission has always been that there is no immunity in respect of torture and other crimes against humanity. That is why I took your Lordships yesterday to the various passages in Sir Arthur Watts' lectures in international law.' Reed Brody and Michael Ratner (eds.), *The Pinochet Papers: The Case of Augusto Pinochet in Spain and Britain* (The Hague: Kluwer Law International, 2000), at 226.

[274] Cassese, *International Criminal Law*, at 271. Cassese cites five elements in support of this contention: (1) case law; (2) other State practice; (3) the rationale behind, and the essence of, the distinction between procedural and substantive immunities; (4) the very logic of international criminal law; and (5) new trends in the development of international law. Cassese, "The Belgium Court of Cassation", at 445-451.

[275] Bianchi, "Denying State Immunity to Violators of Human Rights", at 195-229.

[276] Bianchi argues that the 'alleged commission of international law crimes should also dispose of a claim of immunity *ratione personae*. Were it not so, one would be left with the impression that it is power more than law which protects office holders and that no matter whether they place themselves well beyond the legitimate boundaries of their official authority, they will be protected by law as long as they retain their power, whereas they will be left to their fate once that power comes to an end.' Bianchi, "Immunity versus Human Rights", at 261.

[277] Justice Robert H. Jackson, Report to the US President on 6 June 1945, in *International Conference on Military Trials*, at 47.

fully against human rights.'[278] Furthermore, the IMT's response to the challenge to its jurisdiction based upon functional immunity did not rely upon its status as an international court, but on the nature of the crimes being prosecuted. The point was that international law does not protect acts condemned as criminal by international law: 'He who violates the laws of war cannot obtain immunity while acting in pursuance of the authority of the State if the State in authorizing action moves outside its competence under international law.'[279] This general principle undermines the ICJ's *obiter* observation that (apart from his own State) only certain international criminal courts are able to exercise jurisdiction over incumbent high-ranking officials.[280] Such a conclusion may be consistent with policy considerations about the risk to inter-State relations caused by frivolous litigation against heads of States in foreign States – a risk that can be minimised through the prudent application of prosecutorial discretion. It does not, however, logically follow from the reason that immunity, whether procedural or substantive, does not apply to those accused of international crimes. This is particularly so in cases where States exercise universal jurisdiction and are thereby in theory acting as an agent of the international community much in the same way as an international court. In sum, the state of customary international law with regard to personal immunities is unclear due to a mix of State practice and *opinio juris*. Unfortunately, a recent resolution on 'International Crimes and Immunities from jurisdiction of States and their agents' adopted by the IDI does little to clarify the matter.[281] Article III(1) articulates that 'No immunity from jurisdiction other than personal immunity in accordance with international law applies with regard to international crimes.' This would appear to confirm the rejection of functional immunity for international crimes, while upholding personal immunities 'in accordance with international law.' The latter wording may imply that the scope of personal immunity under international law may be subject to varying interpretations. The use by the ICJ of the functionality rationale to justify the absolute immunity of a sitting minister of foreign affairs accused of international crimes supports the view that absent a clear rule of international law, policy considerations provide appropriate guidelines to judicial determinations on jurisdiction.

5.4.4 The *jus cogens* nature of international crimes overrides immunity

An argument to defeat immunity that has attracted much scholarly and judicial notice in recent years is that based upon the theory of 'normative hierachy.' Under this theory, a State's or State's officials' jurisdictional immunity is abrogated when the State/individual violates human rights protections that are considered peremp-

[278] *Tadić* (Decision on the defence motion for Interlocutory Appeal on Jurisdiction), ICTY, Appeals Chamber, Decision of 2 October 1995, Case No. IT-94-1-AR72, 35 *ILM* 32 (1996), at 483.

[279] IMT Judgment, quoted in The United Nations War Crimes Commission, *History of the United Nations War Crimes Commission*, at 272.

[280] *Arrest Warrant* case, para. 61.

[281] IDI Resolution on International Crimes and Immunities, *supra* note 59.

tory international law norms. The definition of a norm of *jus cogens* is a rule 'recognised by the international community as a whole as a norm from which no derogation is permitted and which can be modified only by a subsequent norm of general international law having the same character.'[282] The Vienna Convention on Treaties of 1969 lays down the principle that any treaty that conflicts with a peremptory norm of general international law is void.[283] The idea of normative hierarchy in the international legal order may help to resolve clashes between competing principles such as the rule of immunity and the right or obligation to exercise jurisdiction over international crimes. One could also argue that the denial of immunity by domestic courts could be one of the international law consequences of a serious breach of a peremptory norm. While the two particular consequences spelled out in the ILC's Articles on State Responsibility do not easily encompass this consequence (i.e., the exercise of jurisdiction)[284] – unless the upholding of immunity could be deemed as recognition of the situation caused by the breach as lawful[285]– the Articles make it clear that other consequences may arise under international law.

Christine Chinkin presented the dilemma faced by the House of Lords in *Pinochet* in deciding whether to recognise the immunity *ratione materiae* of a former head of State for official acts of torture as 'a choice between two visions of international law: a horizontal system based upon the sovereign equality of state and a vertical system that upholds norms of *jus cogens* such as those guaranteeing fundamental human rights.'[286] The notion of *jus cogens* was clearly influential in the *Pinochet* judgment. Lord Hope gave one of the clearest reasoning on this aspect:

> 'The principle of immunity *ratione materiae* protects all acts which the head of state has performed in the exercise of the functions of government. The purpose for which

[282] Art. 53 VCLT (1969).

[283] *Idem.*

[284] Art. 41 ILC Articles on State Responsibility (2001): '(1) States shall cooperate to bring an end through lawful means any serious breach within the meaning of article 40. (2) No State shall recognize as lawful a situation created by a serious breach within the meaning of article 40, nor render aid or assistance in maintaining that situation.'

[285] It would be difficult to argue along these lines given that the notion of immunity implies that an unlawful act has taken place. For commentary, see Stefan Talmon, "The Duty Not to 'Recognise as Lawful' a Situation Created by the Illegal Use of Force or Other Serious Breaches of a *Jus Cogens* Obligation: An Obligation without Real Substance?", in Christian Tomuschat and Jean-Marc Thouvenin (eds.), *The Fundamental Rules of the International Legal Order.* Jus Cogens *and Obligations* Erga Omnes (Leiden/Boston: Martinus Nijhoff Publishers, 2006), at 99. In support of this thesis, one may note that Willem Riphagen, the third Special Rapporteur on State Responsibility, cited 'immunities of foreign States and their property' under general international law as an example of a legal consequence that may be ignored if the factual situation giving rise to that immunity was created in violation of international law. 2 *YILC* (1980), at 115-116. The fourth Special Rapporteur, Gaetano Arrangio-Ruiz interpreted 'the obligation not to recognize as "legal"' in the sense of not 'producing legal effects at the international level and in the respective national systems.' UN Doc. A/CN.4/453/Add.2, 8 June 1993, 29, para. 50. Talmon finds that 'it is arguable that the general legal consequences of acts of State under international law, such as the personal and functional immunity of State officials from the jurisdiction of foreign courts or State immunity, may be denied if the acts in question constitute genocide or other breaches of *jus cogens* obligations.' *Ibid.*, at 118.

[286] Christine Chinkin, "International Decisions", 3 *AJIL* 711 (1999).

> they were performed protects these acts from any further analysis. There are only two exceptions to this approach which customary international law has recognized. The first relates to criminal acts which the head of state did under the colour of his authority as head of state but which were in reality for his own pleasure or benefit. The examples which Lord Steyn gave [1998] 3 *WLR* 1456, 1506B-C of the head of state who kills his gardener in a fit of rage or who orders victims to be tortured so that he may observe them in agony seem to me plainly to fall into this category and, for this reason, to lie outside the scope of the immunity. The second relates to acts the prohibition of which has acquired the status under international law of *jus cogens*. This compels all states to refrain from such conduct under any circumstances and imposes an obligation *erga omnes* to punish such conduct.'[287]

One commentator has observed that the judgment of the House of Lords in *Pinochet* (*I* and *III*) may indicate 'that the emerging notion of an international public order based on the primacy of certain values and common interests is making its way into the legal culture and common practice of municipal courts.'[288]

However, this analysis of the legal problem of immunities does not explain why incumbent heads of State or other high-ranking officials enjoying personal immunity still retain these immunities when they commit or order to be committed international crimes.[289] If one followed the 'normative hierarchy' theory to its logical conclusion, all rules of immunity should be superseded by the *jus cogens* consequences of international crimes. A hierarchy of norms suggests that any competing norms should be resolved by reference to the hierarchy. As expressed by Judges Rozakis and Caflisch, joined by Judges Wildhaber, Costa, Cabral Barreto and Vajic, in the dissenting opinion in *Al-Adsani* v. *United Kingdom*:

> 'the basic characteristic of a *jus cogens* norm is that, as a source of law in the now vertical international legal system, it overrides any other rule which does not have the same status. In the event of a conflict between a *jus cogens* rule and any other rule of international law, the former prevails. The consequence of such prevalence is that the conflicting rule is null and void, or, in any event, does not produce the legal effects which are in contradiction with the content of the peremptory rule.'[290]

The only way this would not occur would be if the customary rule of personal immunity was also one of *jus cogens*. Lord Hope was of this view in the *Pinochet III* case, however, the position is easy to refute given that immunities can indeed be derogated from, for example, by having the represented State waive such immu-

---

287 *Pinochet III* (*per* Lord Hope).

288 Bianchi, "Immunity v Human Rights", at 238.

289 Stern, "Immunities for Heads of State", at 103: 'If the solution is based on the *jus cogens* nature of the prohibition of a crime that overrides any other rule, it is hard to explain why is should not apply also to heads of state in office, unless their absolute immunity is also considered as a *jus cogens* rule.'

290 Dissenting Opinion of Judges Rozakis and Caflisch joined by Judges Wildhaber, Costa, Cabral Barreto and Vajić in *Al-Adsani* v. *United Kingdom*, ECHR, ECtHR 2001-XI 79 (21 November 2001), para. 1.

nity or, in the case of diplomatic and consular inviolability, by agreement between the sending and receiving State.[291] Most commentators do not find the rule of absolute personal immunity to be *jus cogens*, but nonetheless support strict adherence to the rule in view of the risk which could be posed to peaceful inter-State relations by having heads of State put on trial in third States.[292] Cassese has argued that although personal immunity is not considered as peremptory in customary law, the rule should always be respected because in such circumstances, 'the need to avoid conflicts in international relations may be held to override the demands of justice.'[293] In other words, it is a question of balancing competing interests.

There does not appear to be a *jus cogens* exception to functional immunity in civil jurisdiction. The UN Convention on Jurisdictional Immunities of States and Their Property of 2004[294] (not in force) does not contain such an exception,[295] having failed to gain sufficient support during the drafting.[296] The House of Lords also recently rejected such an exception in a case concerning alleged acts of torture.[297] With regard to State immunity, the argument that *jus cogens* norms trump other

[291] In the *Arrest Warrant* case, the Congo argued that immunity of a serving State representative could indeed be waived by the represented State: 'It is quite obvious that there is no violation of immunity from suit when the State represented agrees to waive immunity. Immunity may be waived on the occasion of a specific criminal prosecution. It may also be excluded in advance, under the express terms of a treaty.' Mr. D'Argent, CR 2001/5, 15 October 2001, at 22-23, uncorrected verbatim record. See also the dissenting opinion of Judges Rozakis and Caflisch joined by Judges Wildhaber, Costa, Cabral Barreto and Vajić in the European Court of Human Rights in the *Al-Adsani* v. *United Kingdom* judgment (21 November 2001): 'The Court's majority do not seem, on the other hand, to deny that the rules on State immunity, customary or conventional, do not belong to the category of *jus cogens*; and rightly so, because it is clear that the rules of State immunity, deriving from both customary and conventional international law, have never been considered by the international community as rules with a hierarchically higher status. It is common knowledge that, in many instances, States have, through their own initiative, waived their rights of immunity; that in many instances they have contracted out of them, or have renounced them. These instances clearly demonstrate that the rules on State immunity do not enjoy a higher status, since *jus cogens* rules, protecting as they do the "*ordre public*", ie the basic values of the international community, cannot be subject to unilateral or contractual forms of derogation from their imperative contents.' (para. 2).

[292] Stern, "Immunities for Heads of State", at 103-4 (noting the example of a Belgrade court condemning, on 21 September 2000, fourteen Western leaders, including Bill Clinton, Tony Blair and Jacques Chirac, to 20 years imprisonment for the NATO bombings).

[293] Cassese, "The Belgium Court of Cassation", at 442.

[294] UN GA Res. A/59/38 (2004), 2 December 2004.

[295] For a commentary on the considerations of *jus cogens* within the rubric of the Convention, see Lorna McGregor, "State Immunity and *Jus Cogens*", 55 *ICLQ* 437-446 (April 2006); Christopher Keith Hall, "UN Convention on State Immunity: The Need for a Human Rights Protocol", 55 *ICLQ* 411-426 (April 2006); Hazel Fox, "In Defence of State Immunity: Why the UN Convention on State Immunity is Important", 55 *ICLQ* 399-406 (April 2006).

[296] Report of the ILC to the General Assembly on the Work of Its Fifty-First Session, UN Doc. A/54/10 (1999), at 171-172. Art. 3 of the Convention states that the provisions are without prejudice to immunities of diplomatic and consular posts and heads of States *ratione personae*. Para. 2 of the GA resolution adopting the Convention accepts 'the general understanding of the ad hoc Committee that the convention does not cover criminal proceedings.'

[297] *Jones* case, para. 27: 'There is no evidence that states have recognised or given effect to an international law obligation to exercise universal jurisdiction over claims arising from alleged breaches of peremptory norms of international law, nor is there any consensus of judicial and learned opinion

rules of international law, such as State immunity, was first advanced in doctrine in the late 1980s.[298] While the theory has been advanced by plaintiffs in a number of cases in common law countries, usually on the basis that by violating a *jus cogens* norm, a State has implicitly waived its immunity before foreign courts, it has never been the basis of a decision to lift immunity, although it has been influential in judges' opinions.[299] In the *Siderman* case,[300] the US Court of Appeal considered the argument that Argentina could not benefit from immunity under international law for official acts of torture which constituted a *jus cogens* norm. The Court, accepting that torture qualified as a peremptory norm and finding that sovereign immunity was also a rule of international law, held that since *jus cogens* norms 'enjoy the highest status within international law … they prevail over and invalidate … other rules of international law.'[301] Despite this finding, the Court held in favour of State immunity on the basis of the *Amerada Hess* holding that 'immunity is granted in those cases involving alleged violations of international law that do not come within one of the FSIA's exceptions.'[302] The Court concluded that 'if violations of *jus cogens* committed outside the United States are to be exceptions to immunity, Congress must make them so.'[303]

In *Al-Adsani* v. *The United Kingdom*, the ECHR accepted the idea that the prohibition of torture has now become a rule of *jus cogens*. Nonetheless, the majority drew a distinction between immunity *ratione materiae* from criminal jurisdiction and *ratione personae* of sovereign States from civil jurisdiction for acts of torture. The ECHR considered that 'the grant of sovereign immunity to a State in civil proceedings pursues a legitimate aim of complying with international law, to promote comity and good relations between States through the respect of another State's sovereignty,'[304] even if the civil proceedings had the aim of securing reparations for acts of torture. The dissenting opinion of Judges Rozakis and Caflisch, joined by Judges Wildhaber, Costa, Cabral Barreto and Vajic, criticised this distinction:

---

that they should … But this lack of evidence is not neutral: since the rule on immunity is well-understood and established, and no relevant exception is generally accepted, the rule prevails.'

[298] Adam C. Belsky, Mark Merva and Naomi Roht-Arriaza, "Implied Waiver Under the FSIA: A Proposed Exception to Immunity for Violations of Peremptory Norms of International Law", 77 *California Law Review* 365 (1989).

[299] See, e.g., *Von Dardel* v. *Union of Soviet Socialist Republics*, 623 F. Suppl. 46, 256 (D.D.C. 1985); *Susana Siderman de Blake* v. *Republic of Argentina,* 965 F.2d 699 (9th Cir. 1992); *Princz* v. *Federal Republic of Germany*, 26 F.3d 1166 (D.C. Cir. 1994). The theory has also been used in arguments in the following cases: *Smith* v. *Socialist People's Libyan Arab Jamahiriya*, 101 F.3d 239 (2d Cir. 1996); *Boshnjaku* v. *Federal Republic of Yugoslavia*, 2002 WL 1575067 (N.D. I11. 18 July 2002); *Garb* v. *Republic of Poland*, 207 F. Suppl. 2d 16 (EDNY 2002); *Abrams* v. *Societe Nationale des Chemins de Fer Francais*, 175 F. Suppl. 2d 423 (EDNY 2001); *Joo* v. *Japan*, 172 F. Suppl. 2d 52 (D.D.C. 2001); In re *World War II Era Japanese Forced Labor Litigation*, 164 F. Suppl. 2d 1160 (N.D. Cal. 2001); *Hirsh* v. *State of Israel*, 962 F. Suppl. 377 (SDNY 1997).

[300] *Susana Siderman De Blake, et al.,* v. *The Republic of Argentina*, 965 F 2d 699 (1992) (US Court of Appeals, 9th Cir.).

[301] *Ibid.*, at 717.

[302] *Argentine Republic* v. *Amerada Hess Shipping Co*, at 436.

[303] *Siderman*, at 719.

[304] *Al Adsani* v. *United Kingdom,* ECtHR 2001-XI 79 (hereafter, *Al Adsani* case), para. 54.

> '[t]he distinction made by the majority between civil and criminal proceedings, concerning the effect of the rule of the prohibition of torture, is not consonant with the very essence of the operation of the *jus cogens* rules. It is not the nature of the proceedings which determines the effects that a *jus cogens* rule has upon another rule of international law, but the character of the rule as a peremptory norm and its interaction with a hierarchically lower rule.'[305]

On the other hand, the theory was explicitly endorsed in the Greek case of *Prefecture of Voiotia* v. *Federal Republic of Germany*.[306] On the preliminary matter of jurisdiction, the court of first instance held that Germany was not immune from suit because 'according to the prevailing contemporary theory and practice of international law opinion … the state cannot invoke immunity when the act attributed to it has been perpetrated in breach of a *ius cogens* rule.'[307] The rule of *jus cogens* that the court identified was contained in Articles 43 and 46 of the regulations annexed to the 1907 Hague Convention Respecting the Laws and Customs of War on Land (Hague Regulations).[308] The Hellenic Supreme Court, *Areios Pagos*, affirmed the lower court's holding and arguably supported its reasoning relating to the normative hierarchy theory.[309] The normative hierarchy theory was also successfully applied in the *Ferrini* case in Italy with regard to the violations of forcible deportation and forced labour.[310] The court in this case applied a 'systematic

---

305 *Ibid.*, Dissenting Opinion, para. 4.

306 *Prefecture of Voiotia* v. *Federal Republic of Germany*, No. 137/1997 (Ct. 1st Inst. Leivadia, 30 October 1997), translated in Maria Gavounei, "War Reparation Claims and State Immunity", 50 *Revue Hellénique de Droit International* 595 (1997). For an English summary, see Ilias Bantekas, "Case Report: *Prefecture of Voiotia* v. *Federal Republic of Germany*, " 92 *AJIL* 765 (1998).

307 *Ibid.*, at 599.

308 Art. 43 obligates an occupying power to respect the laws in force in the occupied territory and to ensure public order and safety. Art. 46 obliges occupying powers to protect certain rights of the occupied, especially the rights to family honour, life, private property, and religious convictions. The reasoning of the court was as follows: 'a) When a state is in breach of a peremptory rules of international law, it cannot lawfully expect to be granted the right of immunity. Consequently, it is deemed to have tacitly waived such right (constructive waiver through the operation of international law); b) Acts of the state in breach of peremptory international law cannot qualify as sovereign act of state. In such case the defendant state is not considered as acting within its capacity as sovereign; c) Acts contrary to peremptory international law are null and void and cannot give rise to lawful rights, such as immunity (in application of the general principle of law *ex iniuria ius non oritur*); d) the recognition of immunity for an act contrary to peremptory international law would amount to complicity of the national court to the promotion of an act strongly condemned by the international public order; e) the invocation of immunity for acts committed in breach of a peremptory norm of international law would constitute abuse of right; and finally f) Given that the principle of territorial sovereignty, as a fundamental rule of the international legal order, supersedes that principle of immunity, a state in breach of the former when in illegal occupation of foreign territory, cannot possibl[y] invoke the principle of immunity for acts committed during such illegal military occupation.' *Ibid.*, at 599-600.

309 *Prefecture of Voitia* v. *Federal Republic of Germany*, No. 11/2000 (Areios Pagos [Hellenic Supreme Court] 4 May 2000) (hereafter, *Prefecture of Voitia II*). For an English summary and commentary, see Maria Gavouneli and Ilias Bantekas, "Case Report: *Prefecture of Voiotia* v. *Federal Republic of Germany*", 95 *AJIL* 198 (2001).

310 *Ferrini* v. *Federal Republic of Germany*, Italy (Cass. Sez. Un. 5044/04); 87 *RDI* 539 (2004). The facts of the case concerned a civil claim for reparation before Italian courts based upon the plain-

interpretation' of the rule of State immunity that placed the rule within the system of international law as a whole to get to its conclusion.[311]

Notwithstanding whether distinctions may be made in civil or criminal jurisdictions, the normative hierarchy theory can be criticised from a theoretical point of view. Caplan has forcefully argued that the normative hierarchy theory is unpersuasive because it rests on false assumptions regarding the doctrine of State immunity:

> 'the norms that are purportedly at odds with each other under the normative hierarchy theory (i.e. state immunity and *jus cogens*) in reality never clash. There is no inherent right of state immunity. The practice of States of waiving adjudicatory jurisdiction to create immunity privileges has created binding norms through the development of international custom as to only a core body of State conduct. Such norms do not apply to State conduct that undermines the aim and purpose of the international legal order. Accordingly, the norms of State immunity and *jus cogens* do not clash at all insofar as human rights violations are concerned.'[312]

Rather than being compelled by the principle of sovereign equality, he argues that a State's entitlement to immunity instead derives from the forum State's waiver of adjudicatory jurisdiction with the aim of promoting mutually beneficial inter-State relations.[313] Caplan's theory of 'collective benefits' is based on the notion that State immunity exists only for the 'mutual benefits' of 'intercourse' between States so that only conduct that enhances inter-State relations is protected by immunity.[314] He founds this argument mostly on a reading of *The Schooner Exchange* and finds further indirect support from the *Prefecture of Voiotia*, in which the Hellenic High Court recognised that even in the field of armed conflict a State is not immune when it abuses its official power to the detriment of citizens of the forum State.[315]

---

tiff allegedly being forcibly deported from Italy to Germany by the German army during WW II for the purpose of forced labour. For commentary, see Andrea Bianchi, "Ferrini v. Federal Republic of Germany", 99 *AJIL* (2005); P. De Sena and F. De Vittor, "State Immunity and Human Rights: The Italian Supreme Court Decision in the *Ferrini* Case", 16 *EJIL* 89 (2005); Andrea Gattini, "War Crimes and State Immunity in the *Ferrini* Decision", 2 *JICJ* 224 (2005); Massimo Iovane, "The *Ferrini* Judgment of the Italian Supreme Court: Opening Up Domestic Courts to Claims of Reparation for Victims of Serious Violations of Fundamental Human Rights", 14 *Italian Yearbook of International Law* 165 (2004).

[311] Possibly partly as a result of such varying judicial outcomes, the IDI in its 2009 Resolution on International Crimes and Immunities, adopted a 'no prejudice' clause in regard to State immunity, effectively choosing not to pronounce itself upon the subject. See IDI Resolution on International Crimes and Immunities, Art. IV.

[312] Caplan, "State Immunity, Human Rights and Jus Cogens: A Critique of the Normative Hierarchy Theory", at 771.

[313] *Ibid.*, at 755. See *Verlinden* v. *Central Bank of Nigeria*, 461 US 480 (1983), at 486.

[314] *The Schooner Exchange*, 11 US 136-137. See Caplan, "State Immunity, Human Rights and Jus Cogens: A Critique of the Normative Hierarchy Theory", at 778.

[315] The Court noted that the commentary to Art. 12 of the ILC Draft Articles on State Immunity, Art. 31 of the European Convention on State Immunity, and section 16(2) of the UK State Immunity Act all indicate a rule of customary international law that entitled States to immunity in regard to military activity. The Court held, however, that this rule contained an exception 'for damages arising from crimes, such as crimes against humanity, that affect, not necessarily as a consequence of war,

Caplan contends that this holding conforms with the theory of collective benefit in the sense that a foreign State's unlawful killing of the forum State's civilians destroys bilateral relations between forum and foreign State and may even jeopardise the security and stability of the community of States. He also cites the 1996 amendment to the FSIA as an example of the application of the theory of collective benefit by creating an additional exception to the immunity of certain foreign States for a limited range of human rights violations.[316] The new exception is consistent with the theory of collective State benefit in that it stands to protect one of the most vital interests of the democratic State, the well-being of its citizenry.[317] In sum, Caplan suggested a new test to determine immune and non-immune transactions of foreign States, which 'should be not whether the state conduct is public or private, as the theory of restrictive immunity requires, but whether such conduct would substantially harm the vital interests of the forum state.'[318]

Caplan's theory is certainly a novel way of presenting the problem of State immunity. Moreover, the reductionist view of immunity has been taken up by the US Supreme Court in its recent decision *Austria* v. *Altmann*.[319] In particular, Caplan may have a point that norms of *jus cogens* and State immunity don't in reality clash. It is only the *exercise of jurisdiction* over violations of *jus cogens* norms that may be inconsistent with a rule of immunity. As argued in previous chapters,[320] the obligation or right to prosecute alleged authors of *jus cogens* crimes does not necessarily have the same *jus cogens* nature as the norm itself. The entitlement to

---

particular civilians, not civilians at large and which have no connection with the armed conflict during military occupation.' The Court concluded: '[T]here is no state immunity from criminal acts of the organ of the occupying power that take place by abusing their sovereign power as reprisals for acts of resistance movements against innocent and non-participant persons.' *Prefecture of Voitia II*, at 10. The Court continued: '[T]he torts in question (murder that also constitutes crimes against humanity) were directed against specific persons limited in number who resided in a specific place, who had nothing to do with the resistance activity resulting in the death of German soldiers taking part in a terror operation against the local population … [They were] hideous murders that objectively were not necessary in order to maintain the military operation of the area or subdue the underground action, carried out in the territory of the forum by organs of the German Third Reich in an abuse of sovereign power.' *Ibid.*, at 14-15.

316 28 U.S.C. §1605(a)(7) (2000).

317 The FSIA exception requires no territorial link to the US, but jurisdiction is predicated on the American nationality of the victim or claimant. Caplan concedes that the scope of the exception could extend to a broader class of potential foreign State defendants, not only those designated as sponsors of terrorism.

318 Caplan, "State Immunity, Human Rights and Jus Cogens: A Critique of the Normative Hierarchy Theory", at 777.

319 *Republic of Austria* v. *Altmann*, US Supreme Ct (4 July 2004) ('the principal purpose of foreign sovereign immunity has never been to permit foreign States and their instrumentalities to shape their conduct in reliance on the promise of future immunity from suit in US courts. Rather, such immunity reflects current political realities and relationships, and aims to give foreign States and their instrumentalities some present protection from the inconvenience of suit as a gesture of comity. *Dole Food C* v. *Patrickshon* 538 US 468 (2003), at 479. Throughout history, courts have resolved questions of foreign sovereign immunity by deferring to the "decisions of the political branches … on whether to take jurisdiction," a privilege granted by the forum State to foreign States. *Verlinden*, 461 US 486'.)

320 See Chapter 2, *supra*.

prosecute may indeed be *erga omnes*, but the rule of enforcement does not have the same non-derogable nature as the rule prohibiting the behaviour. Therefore, it is not completely clear that the obligation or entitlement to prosecute international crimes is a hierarchically superior rule to the customary rules of immunity. The characterisation of State immunity as an exception to the normal principle of adjudicatory jurisdiction also has merit and is well-supported in doctrine.[321]

Having said this, there are some conceptual problems to Caplan's theory of 'collective benefit.'[322] First, it is not necessarily the case that the reasoning of *The Schooner Exchange* is equally applicable when a foreign State or State official is sued in domestic proceedings for acts committed in another jurisdiction. In this scenario, there is no clash between the *acta jure imperii* and the adjudicatory jurisdiction of the forum State.[323] Second, there is little evidence that courts have assessed the validity of a claim of State immunity by reason of collective benefit. The theory also suffers from an overly American-centric viewpoint, with little heed to the fact that most States view State immunity as a rule of customary international law, often with an absolute scope.[324] Nonetheless, the general premise of the theory aligns well to an interests-analysis approach, as advocated in this book. Since the obligation or entitlement to prosecute international crimes is not hierarchically superior to the customary rules of immunity, courts, when faced with these competing principles, may decide the issue based upon the values each principle seeks to protect. In this context, the *jus cogens* nature of the crimes at issue may signal that enforcement of such violations, which offend the most fundamental values of the international legal order, is more important than the risk posed to inter-State relations.[325]

[321] For example, Lauterpacht notes that the language of *The Schooner Exchange* clearly indicates that 'the governing, the basic, principle is not the immunity of the foreign state but the full jurisdiction of the territorial state and that any immunity of the foreign state must be traced to a waiver – express or implied – of its jurisdiction on the part of the territorial state.' Hersch Lauterpacht, "The Problem of Jurisdictional Immunities of Foreign States", 28 *BYIL* 220 (1951), at 229. Ian Sinclair has described the 'true foundation' of foreign State immunity as its 'operation by way of exception to the dominating principle of territorial jurisdiction.' Ian Sinclair, *The Law of Sovereign Immunity: Recent Developments*, 167 *RdC* 113 (1980 II), at 215. See also Robert Jennings, *The Place of the Jurisdictional Immunity of States in International and Municipal Law* 19 (Vortrag vor dem Europa-Institut der Universität des Saarlandes No. 108, 1987) (positing that in regard to State immunity, 'territorial jurisdiction is the dominating principle') and Rosalyn Higgins, "Certain Unresolved Aspects of the Law of State Immunity", 29 *Netherlands International Law Review* 265 (1982), at 271.

[322] See Van Alebeek, *The Immunity of States and their Officials*, at 325 (arguing that the 'theory advanced by Caplan is hence based on a misconception of the nature and scope of the law of state immunity.')

[323] Although it could be argued that the commission of international crimes perpetuated anywhere harm the vital interests of all States, regardless of any direct link thereto.

[324] This is the case for China and for many States formerly of the USSR.

[325] As argued by Bianchi, '[i]t would be contrary to elementary logic to deem that the international legal order wants to extend the cover of such a form of protection when States act in marked contrast with the foundations of the same system.' Bianchi, "Denying State Immunity", at 200.

5.4.5 International crimes fall outside of the notion of 'acts performed in a sovereign capacity'

Another argument that has been commonly posited in order to defeat immunity is that the commission of international crimes does not fall in into the notion of 'acts performed in a sovereign capacity,' and hence does not attract immunity. As an historic example of such reasoning, one may recall that while Napoleon was never criminally indicted, the Vienna Conference declared on 13 March 1815 that by engaging in aggressive war he had placed himself outside the boundaries of law. The IMT first alluded to this view in its judgment at Nuremberg when it stated that 'the principle of international law, which under certain circumstances, protects the representatives of a state, cannot be applied to acts which are condemned as criminal by international law ... He who violates the laws of war cannot obtain immunity while acting in pursuance of the authority of the state if the state in authorizing action moves outside its competence under international law.'[326] Since Nuremberg, perhaps the clearest holding in support of this theory is the *Pinochet* case in which the House of Lords determined that the crime of torture could not be considered part of the functions of a head of State for the purposes of functional immunity of former heads of State.[327] Lord Browne-Wilkinson, in introducing the *Pinochet* judgment, stated:

> 'Although the reasoning varies in detail, the basic proposition common to all, save Lord Goff of Chively, is that torture is an international crime over which international law and the parties to the Torture Convention have given universal jurisdiction to all courts whenever the torture occurs. A former head of state cannot show that to commit an international crime is to perform a function which international law protects by giving immunity.'[328]

The implication is that international law cannot regard as official conduct something that international law prohibits and criminalises.[329] Lord Phillips had a different

[326] Judgment of the International Military Tribunal for the Trial of German Major War Criminals, Nuremberg, 30 September and 1 October, 1946, London, His Majesty's Office, Cmd. 6964, reprinted in *Trial of German Major War Criminals* (Buffalo/New York: William S. Hein & Co., Inc., 2001), at 42.

[327] *Pinochet III.*

[328] Brody and Ratner, *The Pinochet Papers*, at 253-4. Lord Browne-Wilkinson stated that he believed 'there to be strong ground for saying that the implementation of torture as defined by the Torture Convention cannot be a state function.' Lord Hutton also took the same approach: 'The alleged acts of torture by Senator Pinochet were carried out under colour of his position as head of state, but they cannot be regarded as functions of a head of state under international law when international law expressly prohibits torture as a measure which a state cannot employ in any circumstances whatsoever and has made it an international crime.'

[329] In *Pinochet III*, the presiding judge, Lord Browne-Wilkinson, argued that the prohibition of torture was a 'fully constituted international crime' by the adoption of the Torture Convention which set up a 'worldwide universal jurisdiction.' For this reason, 'the notion of continued immunity for ex-heads of state is inconsistent with the provisions of the Torture Convention' and torture, as defined in the Convention, 'cannot be a state function.' *Pinochet III*, at 114-115 a-e, *per* Lord Browne-Wilkinson.

view. While he did recognise that the UK State Immunity Act of 1978 might accord Pinochet immunity for acts committed as a head of State, such immunity could not extend to acts contrary to international law because Article 3 of the Vienna Convention on Diplomatic Relations of 1961 defines the functions of diplomatic mission as those 'within the limits permitted by international law.' If one applied this by analogy to former heads of State, their functions must also be similarly limited. While arrived at via different reasoning, the basic premise of the argument remains the same.

Some national courts have argued along the same lines. In *Von Dardel I*, the District Court found that the foreign sovereign immunity doctrine 'is inherently limited and appropriately disallowed where the foreign State defendant has acted in clear violation of international law.'[330] Distinction has also been made by national courts between official and unofficial public acts.[331] Applying this distinction, courts have refused to characterise torture and other violations of fundamental human rights as official public acts. The argument is that since the foreign State is unlikely to have enacted official legislation to compel its organs to commit human rights violations, the acts themselves cannot be regarded as official, even if they were perpetrated by State agents.

Many commentators share the view that international crimes cannot be considered as 'official' acts under international law.[332] Rosalyn Higgins defines 'acts in the exercise of sovereign authority (*acta jure imperii*) as 'those which can only be performed by states, but not by private persons.' Applying this logic, she notes that '[p]roperty deprivation might fall into this category; torture would not.'[333] The Working Group on Jurisdictional Immunities of States and their Property of the ILC expressed the following view:

> 'Although the judgement of the House of Lords in that case [*Pinochet*] only holds that a former head of State is not entitled to immunity in respect of acts of torture committed in his own State and expressly states that it does not affect the correctness of decisions upholding the plea of sovereign immunity in respect of civil claims, as it was concerned with a criminal prosecution, there can be no doubt that this case, and the widespread publicity it received, has generated support for the view that State officials

---

330 *Von Dardel* v. *Union of Soviet Socialist Republics*, United States, 623 F. Suppl. 246 (D.D.C. 1985), 63 *ILR* 378. The case concerned the kidnapping, imprisonment and alleged murder of a Swedish diplomat by agents of the USSR.

331 *Filatiga* v. *Pena-Irala,* United States, 630 F.2d 876 (1980); *Forti* v. *Suarez Mason*, United States, 672 F Supp 1531 (ND Cal 1987).

332 Andrew Clapham adds some perspective to the notion that international crimes would be protected as 'official' acts, noting the bizarre result that 'a former minister could be tried for something clearly private, such as shop-lifting during an official visit, but not tried for war crimes involving grave breaches of the Geneva Conventions.' Clapham, "National Action Challenged", at 314.

333 Rosalyn Higgins, "The Role of Domestic Courts in the Enforcement of International Human Rights: the United Kingdom", in Benedetto Conforti and Francesco Francioni (eds.), *Enforcing International Human Rights Before Domestic Courts* (The Hague/Boston: Martinus Nijhoff, 1997), at 53.

should not be entitled to plead immunity for acts of torture committed in their own territories in both civil and criminal actions.'[334]

However, the judgment of the ICJ in the *Arrest Warrant* case has cast some doubt on the validity of these arguments. In listing some 'exceptions' to the principle of absolute personal immunity of incumbent ministers of foreign affairs, it observed that:

'... after a person ceases to hold the office of Minister for Foreign Affairs, he or she will no longer enjoy all the immunities accorded by international law in other States. Provided that it has jurisdiction under international law, a court of one State may try a former Minister for Foreign Affairs of another State in respect of acts committed prior or subsequent to his or her period of office, as well as in respect of acts committed during that period of office in a *private* capacity.'[335]

Unhelpfully, the Court does not elaborate upon whether certain acts, such as international crimes, fall into the functions of a head of State, or whether these would be considered 'private acts.'[336] Cassese has severely criticised this part of the judgment, noting that international crimes

'are not as a rule "private acts" ... These crimes are seldom perpetrated in [a private] capacity ... Indeed, individuals commit such crimes by making use (or abuse) of their official status. It is primarily through the position and rank they occupy that they are in a position to order, instigate, or aid and abet or culpably tolerate or condone such crimes as genocide or crimes against humanity or grave breaches of the Geneva Conventions. In the case of torture (not as a war crimes or a crime against humanity), the "instigation or consent or acquiescence of a public official or other person acting in an official capacity" is one of the objective requirements of the crime.'[337]

Several national court decisions have upheld immunity in cases involving international crimes based on the view that the unlawfulness of the act is irrelevant to the question of whether the act was an act of the State. The argument is one of logic. The point of having immunity is to avert liability for wrongful acts. By definition, both civil and criminal proceedings will challenge the lawfulness of an official's

---

[334] Report of the work of the ILC, UN Doc. A./54/10, 1999, report of the Working Group on Jurisdictional Immunities of States and their Property, appendix to the Report of the Working Group, at para. 12.

[335] *Arrest Warrant* case, para. 61. [Emphasis added]

[336] For critical commentary on this part of the judgment, see Steffan Wirth, "Immunity for Core Crimes? The ICJ's Judgment in the *Congo* v. *Belgium* Case", 13 *EJIL* 877 (2002); Marina Spinedi, "State Responsibility for International Crimes: *Tertium Non Datur*?", 13(4) *EJIL* 895 (2002).

[337] Antonio Cassese, "When May Senior State Officials Be Tried for International Crimes? Some Comments on the *Congo* v. *Belgium* Case", 13 *EJIL* 868 (2002). With regard to the consideration of Judges Higgins, Kooijmans and Buergenthal in their separate concurring opinion that international crimes do *not* qualify as official acts, Cassese observed that this would mean that the crimes for which von Ribbentrop (Reich Minister for Foreign Affairs from 1938 to 1945) was sentenced to death by the IMT should be regarded as 'private acts.' *Ibid.*, at 870.

acts.[338] Therefore the relevant inquiry is whether the official's actions constitute State conduct.[339] In the *Nelson* case, involving a civil claim against Saudi Arabia for the alleged torture of a US national by Saudi police officers, the Supreme Court of the United States observed that 'however monstrous such an abuse may be, a foreign state's exercise of power of its police has long been understood as peculiarly sovereign in nature.'[340] Similarly, in *Pinochet I*, the two dissenting Law Lords argued that 'where a person is accused of organising the commission of crimes as the head of the government, in cooperation with other governments, and carrying out those crimes through the agency of the police and the secret service, the inevitable conclusion is that he was acting in a sovereign capacity.'[341] For these judges, the 'criminality and moral obliquity' of the act was irrelevant to the question of whether it was performed under the colour of authority or not.[342] In the *Dichter* case, the plaintiffs argued that because a *jus cogens* norm 'by definition permits of no derogation … Israel could not authorize the acts alleged.'[343] This would appear to be another version of the argument that unlawful action cannot be legitimately authorised. While derogation from a *jus cogens* norm would certainly be unlawful, it does not necessarily follow that the act cannot be attributed to Israel. In fact, the ILC Articles on State Responsibility make it clear that States are responsible for violations of peremptory norms.[344]

There would appear to be two different approaches to this theory, which vary drastically in outcome. One approach is to acknowledge that international crimes may be carried out under colour of authority, but cannot be considered as a 'State function' for the purpose of attributing immunity. The implication is that immunity should only extend to those acts permitted by international law. The other approach is to look only at the question of whether the act constitutes State conduct. In this approach, the illegality of the act does not affect the scope of the notion of State conduct. The confusion between the two approaches underscores the difficulty of continued reliance on the distinction of State conduct along private and public lines. International law sources would seem to acknowledge that States may vio-

---

[338] See *Waltier*, 189 F. Suppl. at 321; *Jones* case, para. 12: 'The fact that conduct is unlawful or objectionable is not, of itself, a ground for refusing immunity.'

[339] See *Doe I*, 400 F. Suppl. at 104: 'Suits against officers in their personal capacities must pertain to private action – that is, to actions that exceed the scope of authority vested in that official so that the official cannot be said to have acted on behalf of the State.'

[340] *Saudi Arabia* v. *Nelson*, United States, 113 Sup. Ct. 1471 (1993); case report by Leigh in 87 *AJIL* 442 (1993).

[341] *R* v. *Bow Street Metropolitan Stipendiary Magistrate,* ex parte *Pinochet Ugarte*, United Kingdom, House of Lords Judgment of 25 November 1998, 3 *WLR* 1456 (HL 1998) (referred to as *Pinochet I* in the text), *per* Lord Lloyd, at 1323.

[342] *Ibid.*, at 1309 (*per* Lord Slynn, citing the test enunciated by Sir Arthur Watts, "The Legal Position in International Law of Heads of State, Heads of Governments and Foreign Ministers", 247 *RdC* (1994), at 56: 'whether the conduct in question was engaged under the colour of or in ostensible exercise of the Head of State's public authority').

[343] Plaintiff's Brief, at 10.

[344] See Arts. 40-41 ILC Articles on State Responsibility.

late peremptory norms and do so fully in the exercise of official conduct.[345] It suffices to recall the definition of 'torture' in Article 1 of the Torture Convention which requires the involvement of a State official. Does immunity only extend to lawful official conduct? It seems a strange conclusion given that immunity would not be necessary if there was no illegal conduct to speak of. It would appear more accurate and logical to argue that there is an exception to immunity in the case of international crimes, rather than an inherent limitation to immunity to lawful official acts. Thus, while the second approach is more logically consistent, it stops a step short of the full enquiry – the subsequent question being whether any exception to such immunity is apparent in international law.

5.4.6 The fundamental rights of victims are incompatible with fundamental human rights

An argument may be made that immunity is incompatible with certain fundamental human rights pertaining to the right to fair trial, access to courts, the right to an effective remedy or the right to judicial protection. It is worth recalling that it was precisely these types of concerns that prompted courts to begin to restrict the absolute immunity of States when claims regarding their commercial dealings came to pass before them. It was the possibility of the denial of justice that led to the restrictive approach to State immunity.[346] In this respect, one may draw analogies to the arguments used by courts to invalidate amnesties that prevent investigation and prosecution of individuals accused of serious human rights violations. Similarly, where the prosecution of an individual is blocked by reason of his status or the fact that the acts were committed in an official capacity, the victim's right to access to justice, to an effective remedy, and to judicial protection may be violated.[347]

The European Court of Human Rights has been asked to consider whether State immunity violates Article 6(1) (right to a fair trial/access to court) of the ECHR on three occasions.[348] In all three cases, the Court ruled that the rule of State immunity did raise an issue under Article 6(1) of the Convention, but found the rule to have a legitimate aim and to constitute a proportionate restriction of the applicants' right of access to court.[349] The 'legitimate aim' of granting sovereign immunity to a State in civil proceedings was 'complying with international law to promote comity and good relations between States through the respect of another State's

---

[345] See ILC Articles on State Responsibility, Arts. 40-41.

[346] Van Alebeek, *The Immunity of States and their Officials*, at 1.

[347] D.C. Holland, "Diplomatic Immunity in English Law", 4 *Current Legal Problems* 81 (1951), at 106 (recognising that diplomatic immunity in English law 'clearly infringes the rule of law, in that it necessitates an exception being made to the doctrine that all men should be equal before the law and subject to the same laws administered in the same courts.')

[348] *McElhinney* v. *Ireland* (2001), 34 *EHRR* 322, 123 *ILR* 73; *Al Adsani* case; and *Fogarty* v. *United Kingdom* (2001), 34 *EHRR* 302, 123 *ILR* 53.

[349] For the arguments of the parties, see *McElhinney*, at 331 et seq., para. 27 et seq.; *Ad-Adsani*, at 287 et seq., at para. 50 et seq.; *Fogarty*, at 311, para. 29 et seq.

sovereignty.'[350] In *McElhinney*, Judge Loucaides dissented from the approach outlined by the Court, arguing that:

> 'a blanket immunity which is applied by a court in order to block completely the judicial determination of a civil right without balancing the competing interests, namely those connected with the particular immunity and those relating to the nature of the specific claim which is the subject matter of the proceedings, amounts to a disproportionate restriction on the right of access to court.'[351]

Noting that the doctrine of State immunity has been subjected to an increasing number of restrictions in view of the developments in human rights, he argued that absolute immunity from judicial proceedings appeared to be 'an anachronistic doctrine incompatible with the demands of justice and the rule of law.' While Article 6 may indeed be subject to inherent limitations, these limitations should not affect the core substance of the right. Thus, in his view, if the operation of State immunity serves to completely prevent someone 'from having his case determined by a court, without any fault on his part and regardless of the nature of the case,' Article 6(1) has been contravened.[352] As noted previously, in *Ad-Adsani* the majority found that there was no exception to the rule of State immunity when acts of torture were alleged and concluded that the grant of immunity to Kuwait had not been an unjustified restriction of the right of access to court.[353] The significant minority (seven out of 15 judges) argued that the *jus cogens* nature of the prohibition of torture meant that States could not invoke hierarchically lower rules, such as State immunity, to avoid the consequences of the violation, and that therefore the applicant's right under Article 6 had been violated. In this book, it is argued that the notion of 'inherent limitations' to fundamental rights is not compatible with the principle that exceptions to human rights conventions must reflect a proper balance of interests. Rather, the interests of the individual having access to court should be weighed against the interests protected by the rule of immunity. This entails that the rule of immunity cannot completely obfuscate the right to access to court.

With regard to the right to an effective remedy, protected under Article 2(3) of the ICCPR and Article 13 of the ECHR, which applies 'notwithstanding that the violation has been committed by persons acting in an official capacity,' it has been argued that by agreeing to such a guarantee, States have implicitly accepted that their courts may be used to assess the conduct of foreign States.[354] Moreover, when fundamental rights such as the right to life or the prohibition of torture have been

---

350 *McElhinney*, at 333, para. 35; *Al-Adsani*, at 289, para. 54; *Fogarty*, at 313, para. 34.

351 *McElhinney*, Dissenting Opinion of Judge Loucaides, 340 at 340-341. See also *Al-Adsani*, at 301; *Fogarty*, 317 at 319.

352 *Idem*.

353 *Al Adsani* case.

354 Andrea Bianchi, "Overcoming the Hurdle of State Immunity in the Domestic Enforcement of International Human Rights", in Benedetto Conforti and Francesco Francioni (eds.), *Enforcing International Human Rights in Domestic Courts* (The Hague/Boston: Martinus Nijhoff, 1997), at 424; J. Brömer, *State Immunity and Human Rights Violations* (1997), at 171-177 and 186-188 (arguing that

violated, the ECHR, as well as other treaty-monitoring bodies, has held that the notion of effective remedy entails 'a thorough and effective investigation capable of leading to the identification and punishment of those responsible and including effective access for the complainant to the investigatory procedure.'[355] However, it may be argued that the obligation to provide a remedy for human rights violations only applies to violations committed in the forum State, not to violations committed by foreign State officials abroad. Whereas in the case of amnesty laws, these operate to prevent the investigation and prosecution of crimes committed in the forum State, the question of immunity (excluding national immunity) only arises with regard to acts committed by foreign officials.[356] Thus, in *Bouzari and Others* v. *Islamic Republic of Iran* the Canadian Court accepted the opinion given by the expert Greenwood that Article 14 of the Torture Convention only requires Canada to provide a civil remedy for torture committed within its jurisdiction,[357] though notably this decision was criticised by the UN Committee Against Torture.[358] A similar conclusion was reached by the UK Court of Appeal in *Jones* v. *Saudi Arabia*.[359] In May 2007, the Swiss Supreme Court also refused to exercise jurisdiction in a civil case for reparations for torture allegedly committed in Tunisia, suggesting that absent a sufficient link to the crime there is no obligation arising under human rights law on a State to provide an effective remedy.[360] One may additionally note that the obligation to exhaust domestic remedies before applying for regional or international adjudication of human rights violations supports the view that it is only incumbent upon the territorial State to guarantee an effective remedy. Otherwise this condition might never be held to be fulfilled if victims had

when a right under the ECHR has been violated, all contracting States are obliged to provide a remedy, even when the violation has been committed by a non-party State).

355 *Zeki Aksoy* v. *Turkey*, ECtHR (judgment), 18 December 1996, No. 100/1995/606/694; *Assenov and Others* v. *Bulgaria* (1998), 28 *EHRR* 652, at 704; *Z and Others* v. *United Kingdom* (2001), 34 *EHRR* 97, at 141, para. 109; *Kaya* v. *Turkey* (1998), 28 *EHRR* 1, at 50-51, para. 107.

356 However, diplomatic agents or other State officials on private or official visits who commit international crimes within the forum State would be covered by the 'effective remedy' argument.

357 *Bouzari and Others* v. *Islamic Republic of Iran,* Canada, Ontario Court of Appeal, *OJ* No. 2800 (2004).

358 The Committee pointed to the 'absence of effective measures to provide civil compensation to victims of torture in all cases and recommended that Canada 'review its position under Article 14 of the Convention to ensure the provision of compensation through its civil jurisdiction to all victims of torture.' Committee Against Torture, *Summary Record of the Second Part (Public) of the 646th Meeting*, 6 May 2005, CAT/C/SR.646/Add.1, at paras. C(4)(g) and D(5)(f) respectively. It also observed that 'as a countermeasure permitted under international public law, a State could remove immunity from another State – a permitted action to respond to torture carried out by that State. There was no peremptory norm of general international law that prevented States from withdrawing immunity from foreign States in such cases to claim for liability for torture.' *Ibid.*, para. 67.

359 *Jones* v. *Ministry of Interior Al-Mamlaka Al-Arabiya AS Saudiya (the Kingdom of Saudi Arabia) and others,* United Kingdom, EWCA Civ 1394 (2004): 'article 14(1) is dealing with (no more than) a right of redress in the legal system of the state … by whose official … the alleged act of torture was committed.'

360 The plaintiff was a Tunisian national, Abdennacer Naït-Liman. The Swiss Supreme Court handed down its decision on 22 May 2007. See <www.trial-ch.org/fr/actions/details/year/21/article/demande-en-reparation-contre-la-tunisie.html?txttnews%5BbackPid%5D=50&cHash=d1a483710f>.

the opportunity of insisting upon their right to a remedy before the courts of every State. Furthermore, a right to a remedy does not necessarily amount to the same thing as a right to access to court,[361] though the right must of course be effective to ensure compliance with the prohibition to violate human rights, therefore it does not directly clash with the principle of immunity.

On the other hand, the argument that the right to judicial protection is incompatible with immunities is persuasive. There are two aspects to this right which merit attention. The first is that effective protection of fundamental rights is required in order that there is effective deterrence against violations. Arguably, criminal enforcement is the best-suited mechanism to impose a degree of societal deterrence.[362] Secondly, as noted in the chapter on amnesties, there are strong arguments to support the view that the right to effective protection entails an obligation on the State to bring those who violate human rights within its territorial borders to justice.[363] Rules of immunity appear to be incompatible with both aspects. There is little deterrence for a person who knows he is beyond the reach of municipal courts. Schermers in 1965 had already expressed concern that immunity from penal jurisdiction may favour the commission of unlawful acts because there is no real threat of punishment.[364] Again, the scope of this argument would be limited to where the crimes were perpetuated by foreign officials on the territory of the State party at issue. Nevertheless, analogy to arguments made in the context of invalidating amnesties resonates to significant degree to immunities, and may be further evidence of the shifting values towards the protection of human rights over matters of sovereignty.

5.5 Preliminary conclusions

Although the rules of immunity differ in operation and are grounded in somewhat different rationales, it is argued that an interests analysis approach, whereby courts weigh the competing values protected by rules of immunity on the one hand and

[361] See, e.g., ECHR, *Leander* v. *Sweden* (1987) (ser. A-116), 9 *EHRR* 433, at 457; ECHR, *Z and Others* v. *United Kingdom* (2001), 34 *EHRR* 97, at 141.

[362] See, e.g., *X and Y and Z* v. *Netherlands* 91 ECtHR (ser. A) (1985) (judgment) (holding that when 'fundamental values and essential aspects of private life are at stake … [e]ffective deterrence is indispensable … and it can be achieved only by criminal-law provisions.')

[363] Diane F. Orentlicher, "Settling Accounts: The Duty to Prosecute Human Rights Violations of a Prior Regime", 100 *Yale Law Journal* (1991), at 2568 (arguing that 'authoritative interpretations' of comprehensive human rights treaties 'makes clear … that these treaties require States Parties generally to investigate serious violations of physical integrity … and to bring to justice those who are responsible.') See, e.g., *Velàsquez Rodriguez*, IACtHR (ser. C) No. 4 (1988); Report No. 26/92 (El Salvador), 82nd Sess., OEA/ser.L/V/II/82 (September 24, 1992); General Comment No. 20 in relation to Article 7 ICCPR (1992), Report of the Human Rights Committee, UN Doc. A/47/40 (1992), Annex VI (at 193-195).

[364] H.G. Schermers, "L'immunité devant le droit pénal, en particulier en ce qui concerne les infractions aux règles de la circulation", in *Le Droit Pénal International, Recueil d'Etudes en Homage à J.M. Bemmelen* (1965), 174 at 181.

the need to prosecute those accused of international crimes on the other, serves as a legitimate framework for resolving any clashes of principle. The IDI has approached the issue of international crimes and immunities in a similar way, having adopted a resolution that refers in its premable to the 'the underlying conflict between immunity from jurisdiction of States and their agents and claims arising from international crimes' and the need to make 'progress towards a resolution of that conflict.'[365]

First, one may observe that similarities between policy justifications for immunities for heads of State and senior officials and amnesties are apparent. It is argued that if such immunity is not recognised, harmonious and peaceful inter-State relations may be jeopardised, thus increasing the possibility of international conflict and tension. The counter argument is that the effect of not holding such leaders accountable creates an incentive for human rights abusers to become senior officials so as to be immune from legal accountability. This is analogous to the pro-amnesty argument that they are necessary to secure the peace and the anti-amnesty argument that such laws foster impunity and encourage human rights violations. As may be recalled, the concluding argument in the chapter on amnesties was that a prudent use of prosecutorial discretion that sought to balance competing interests and which focused on those most responsible may achieve the appropriate balance between peace, justice and reconciliation objectives. The tension between a selective prosecution policy of targeting those 'most responsible' and the protection of senior officials from prosecution before foreign courts under customary international law puts increased pressure on courts to justify upholding immunities in cases of international crimes. In particular, the exercise of jurisdiction based upon universality would be all but nullified by an immunity rule that prevented foreign domestic courts from prosecuting those current or former State officials most responsible for the commission of international crimes.

In terms of the arguments advanced by commentators and applicants in litigation in favour of overturning immunity, the strongest in terms of supporting practice is that regarding a customary exception to functional immunity. Applying an interests-analysis approach to the scope of personal immunity could also have an impact on the recognition of an exception in the case of international crimes. In the *Arrest Warrant* case, Judges Higgins, Kooijmans and Buergenthal explained in their Joint Separate Opinion that '[t]he law of privileges and immunities … retains its importance since immunities are granted to high State officials to guarantee the proper functioning of the network of inter-State relations, which is of paramount importance for a well-ordered and harmonious international system,' but they added that 'the weights on the two scales are not set for all perpetuity.'[366] Noting that, as a technical matter, the ICJ's judgment in the *Arrest Warrant* case is only binding on and between the parties to the dispute,[367] Clapham posits the pos-

---

[365] IDI Resolution on International Crimes and Immunities, preambular para. 3.

[366] *Arrest Warrant* case, Joint Separate Opinion of Judges Higgins, Kooijmans and Buergenthal, at 85, para. 75.

[367] Art. 59 Statute of the International Court of Justice.

sibility that '[s]ome judges may feel that it is no longer appropriate to protect the dignity of a state in this way when faced with a competing good faith attempt to protect the dignity of the victims of atrocities.'[368]

Arguments based upon the notion of implied waiver make some sense in terms of logical consistency in the international legal order, but have not been readily accepted by courts. Moreover, the implied waiver argument is incoherent with the idea that immunity does not extend to behaviour outside the scope of State functions, although the latter idea also lacks logical consistency with the idea of immunity. The implied waiver argument also founders on the weakness of reliance upon implied evidence of State consent to waive important sovereign rights. The normative hierarchy theory is rejected in this book in its classic formulation (i.e., that norms of *jus cogens* trump rules of immunity), not because this would not be so, but because in reality the two do not clash. However, it is argued that the importance of the values underlying *jus cogens* prohibitions and the consequences attendant to them casts a heavy weight for courts to dispel in relation to rules of immunity. In addition, the argument that legal rules should be construed 'systematically and coherently with the goals and values of the international legal system'[369] lends further support to the view that the values underlying repression of the most serious crimes in the international legal order override the value of protecting certain aspects of State sovereignty.[370] Thus, in *Ferrini*, the Italian Court of Cassation denied Germany the protection of immunity on the basis that it 'would *hinder* the protection of values whose safeguard is to be considered … essential to the whole international community.'[371] The same outcome is reached when applying an interests-analysis approach to the question of how to resolve the incompatibility of immunities with fundamental human rights.

[368] Clapham, "National Action Challenged", at 331.

[369] Bianchi, "Denying State Immunity to Violators of Human Rights", at 219.

[370] See *ibid.*, at 220: '[g]iven the recent trend towards the steady erosion of traditional concepts of state sovereignty, a coherent interpretation of the international legal system cannot but solve the inconsistency between the rule of state immunity and the principle of protection of fundamental human rights in favour of the latter value.'

[371] *Ferrini* v. *Federal Republic of Germany*, Italy (Cass. Sez. Un. 5044/04); 87 *RDI* 539 (2004), at para. 9.2, transl. in De Sena and De Vittor, *supra* n. 310, at 98. [Emphasis in translation and original]

Chapter 6
THE PRINCIPLE OF *NE BIS IN IDEM*

The jurisdictional impediment of *ne bis in idem* is designed to protect individuals against harassment by the State by bringing multiple prosecutions for the same offence and to ensure legitimacy and certainty in the legal system. The principle that no person may be tried twice for the same crime originated in domestic law, but has since been guaranteed as an international human right, as well as being commonly included in extradition treaties (as a valid basis not to extradite) and in the principles governing jurisdiction of the constitutive statutes of international and hybrid courts. Although the general principle appears to be universally recognised at the domestic level, the exact contours of this rule vary considerably between jurisdictions and international instruments and the principle is subject to numerous exceptions and qualifications, making it difficult to pronounce as a general principle of law or to define the exact scope of the principle as a customary right.[1]

A variety of rationales to not apply *ne bis in idem* to serious crimes have arisen in practice and are often legislated or included in treaty provisions. Recent times have seen a weakening of the *ne bis in idem* protection for those acquitted of serious crimes in certain domestic jurisdictions mainly as a response to public outcry at the acquittals of persons accused of such crimes.[2] With regard to the criminal judgments of other States' courts, the majority of States do not recognise any *ne bis in idem* effect due to the dual sovereignty doctrine or the interpretation of the right

[1] See M.N. Morosin, "Double Jeopardy and International Law: Obstacles to Formulating a General Principle", 64 *Nordic Journal of International Law* 261 (1995); Alex Bailin, "Double jeopardy", in Marisa Leaf (ed.), *Cross-Border Crime. Defence rights in a new era of international judicial co-operation*, (London: Justice, 2006), at 116. But see Sure Log, "The Practical Applications of *Ne Bis in Idem* in International Criminal Law", in *International Crime and Punishment. Selected Issues, Volume 2*, Sienho Yee (ed.) (Lanham, Maryland: University Press of America, Inc., 2004), at 169-170 (describing *ne bis in idem* as a 'fundamental principle of international law' and 'a universally recognised human right').

[2] See, e.g., Nyssa Taylor, "England and Australia Relax the Double Jeopardy Privilege for Those Convicted of Serious Crimes", 19 *Temple International and Comparative Law Journal* 189 (2005). The cases that prompted the changes in legislation include the following: *Dunlop*, United Kingdom [2001] 2 *Cr App R* para. 8 (involving the 'discharge' of a person accused of murder who later admitted to having committed the crime); Sir William Macpherson of Cluny, *The Stephen Lawrence Inquiry* (1999), Cm. 4262-I, paras. 1.2-1.3 (involving the discharge of suspects in a murder case after police failed to diligently investigate); *R.* v. *Carroll*, Australia, 213 *CLR* 653 (in which the High Court of Australia dismissed the defendant's perjury conviction because the Court of Criminal Appeal had previously acquitted him of murder despite 'new' evidence of his guilt).

to double jeopardy only applying within one jurisdiction. However, the increasing tendency of national courts to exercise jurisdiction over persons accused of international crimes pursuant to the principle of universality or other jurisdictional principles has caused a number of commentators to advocate a transnational (horizontal) *ne bis in idem* protection.[3] In Europe, such a transnational right has begun to be manifested in the Schengen Convention[4] and a number of treaties regulating mutual assistance in criminal enforcement. The *ne bis in idem* provisions of the *ad hoc* ICTs and the ICC, as well as the SCSL and Special Panels for East Timor have instituted a trans-jurisdictional *ne bis in idem* effect (vertical). Nevertheless, these protections remain subject to exceptions and qualifications, in particular, that the principle of *ne bis in idem* should not prevent a second trial from taking place where the first trial was conducted with a view to shielding the defendant from responsibility, or was otherwise not conducted impartially or independently.

In the absence of a universal rule of transnational *ne bis in idem*, the test for whether a court should accept jurisdiction over a person who has been either acquitted or convicted by another State's court is predicated upon a need to balance countervailing considerations – the interest in protecting the individual from State harassment in the form of multiple prosecutions for the same crime and the need for certainty and finality in the law on the one hand and the international community interest in ensuring that those accused of international crimes are properly prosecuted and if convicted, punished, on the other. Without a consistent and coherent approach to the *ne bis in idem* principle, it is likely that the legitimacy of the international criminal system, consisting of multilevel jurisdiction, will be seriously called into question.

6.1 Definition and historical background

6.1.1 **Historical background**

While the rule that no person should be prosecuted twice for the same crime has come to be a universally recognised principle,[5] the origins of the rule remain to a

[3] See, e.g., Alexander Poels, "A Need for Transnational *Non Bis In Idem* Protection in International Human Rights Law", 23(3) *Netherlands Quarterly of Human Rights* 329 (2005); Dax Eric Lopez, "Not Twice for the Same: How the Dual Sovereignty Doctrine is Used to Circumvent *Non Bis In Idem*", 33 *Vanderbilt Journal of Transnational Law* 1263 (2000).

[4] Convention of 19 June 1990, applying the Schengen Agreement of 14 June 1985 between the Governments of the States of the Benelux Economic Union, the Federal Republic of Germany and the French Republic, on the Gradual Abolition of Checks at their Common Borders 30 *ILM* 84 (1991) (hereafter, Schengen Convention).

[5] See José Luis De La Cuesta, "Concurrent National and International Criminal Jurisdiction and the Principle '*Ne Bis In Idem*' General Report", 73 *International Review of Penal Law* (2002) (discussing a large number of State reports on national implementation of *ne bis in idem*). Many States include the rule in their constitutions. See, e.g., Art. 39 Japanese Constitution; Art. 103 German Constitution; Section 26(3) New Zealand Bill of Rights Act 1990; Arts. 10.2 and 96.1 Spanish Constitution; Fifth

large degree a matter of speculation.[6] There is no reference to the principle in the Babylonian Code of Hammurabi and Talmudic law does not describe the principle, although Hebrew Law makes brief mention of it.[7] Most writers trace the origins of the rule to Roman and Greek law.[8] According to Demosthenes, writing in 355 B.C., Greek laws 'forbid the same man to be tried twice on the same issue.'[9] The *Digest of Justinian* required that 'the governor must not allow a man to be charged with the same offense of which he has already been acquitted.'[10] This led to the development of the maxim *nemo bis in idem debet vexari*,[11] or *non bis in idem*.[12] The principle was included in canon law[13] after the fall of the Roman Empire and was mentioned in the writings of early Christian authors.[14] This arose possibly due to St. Jerome's reading of I Nahum 9 in 391 A.D. as commanding that 'there shall not rise up a double affliction.'[15] In 847 A.D. the church recognised that even God does not judge an individual twice for the same transgression.[16] However, it seems that widespread acceptance of the principle did not occur until the dispute between St. Thomas Becket and King Henry II in the 12th century.[17] Becket had objected to the King's desire to further prosecute church clerics in civil tribunals who had already been tried and convicted in the ecclesiastical courts. He argued, relying on canon law that such prosecutions would violate the maxim *nemo bis in idipsum* – 'no man ought to be punished twice for the same offence.'[18] In 1176, six years after

Amendment Constitution of the United States of America; Art. 23 Constitution of Ethiopia. Poels, "A Need for Transnational *Non Bis In Idem* Protection", at 33, fn. 4.

[6] Jay A. Sigler, "A History of Double Jeopardy", 7 *American Journal of Legal History* 283 (1963); Jill Hunter, "The Development of the Rule Against Double Jeopardy", 5 *Journal of Legal History* 3 (1984).

[7] "Note", *Indian Law Journal* (1960) 445 (citing Makkot, 136).

[8] Sigler, "A History of Double Jeopardy", at 284; Hunter, *supra* n. 6, at 4.

[9] George C. Thomas III, *Double Jeopardy: The History, The Law* (New York: New York University Press, 1998), at 73.

[10] *Digest of Justinian*, Book 48, Title 2, Note 7, translated in Francine Ward, "The Double Jeopardy Clause of the Fifth Amendment", 26 *American Criminal Law Review* 1477 (1989). The *Digest of Justinian* was published in 533 A.D. It consists of a collection of Roman law drawn from the writings of classical jurists. This principle is distinct from the civil law maxim *res judicata pro veritate accipitur* which is mentioned in the *Digest* at Book 50, Title 17, Note 207.

[11] 'No one should be troubled twice for the same matter.' In re *Extradition of Montiel Garcia*, United States, 802 F. Suppl. 773, 777 (EDNY 1992).

[12] Bryan A. Garner, *Black's Law Dictionary*, 8th edn. (St. Paul, Minn: West Group, 2004) (defining double jeopardy as '[t]he fact of being prosecuted or sentenced twice for substantially the same offense').

[13] Canon law, which developed at the close of the Roman Empire, constituted a body of laws and regulations for the government of the Christian organisation made or adopted by the ecclesiastical authority and included regulations borrowed from Roman law.

[14] *Bartkus*, United States, 359 US 152 (Black J. dissenting).

[15] Sigler, "A History of Double Jeopardy", at 284, citing the Douay version. The King James version reads: 'Affliction shall not rise up a second time.'

[16] Sir Frederic Pollock and Frederic William Maitland, *The History of English Law*, 2nd edn. (Cambridge: CUP, 1899), at 448-49.

[17] Lopez, "Not Twice for the Same", at 1268.

[18] Martin Friedland, *Double Jeopardy* (Clarendon: Oxford University Press, 1969), at 5.

Becket's murder by King Henry's knights, the King agreed that clerics convicted in the ecclesiastical courts could not be re-prosecuted before the King's courts.[19] Notably, these courts drew their powers from different sovereigns, leading one commentator to argue that this gives 'credence to the argument that the focus of prohibiting successive prosecutions is on the rights of the defendant and not of the prosecution.'[20] The principle entered the English common law by around 1250, mainly through both the canon law and the influence of Roman law scholars.[21] The concept appeared in the Spanish *Siete Partidas* of 1263.[22] By the early 14th century the pleas of *autrefois acquit* (otherwise acquitted) and *autrefois convict* (otherwise convicted) became part of criminal procedure, allowing a defendant to avoid a second prosecution by proving prior acquittal or conviction on the same charge.[23] However, the contemporary notion of the substantive principle of double jeopardy did not enter into legal literature until Blackstone in the 19th century recognized that the plea of *autrefois acquit* was a 'universal maxim of the common law of England' grounded in the idea that 'no man is to be brought into the jeopardy of his life more than once for the same offence.'[24] The Napoleonic code of 1804 also makes reference to the principle.[25]

6.1.2 *Ne bis in idem* and international and hybrid criminal courts and tribunals

A very limited *ne bis in idem* protection is guaranteed in the IMT Charter with regards to a person who had been tried for membership of a criminal organisation,[26]

---

[19] *Idem.*

[20] Lopez, "Not Twice for the Same", at 1268.

[21] M. Cherif Bassiouni, *Substantive Criminal Law* (Springfield: Thomas, 1978), at 499.

[22] Mohamed El Zeidy, "The Doctrine of Double Jeopardy in International Criminal and Human Rights Law", 6 *Mediterranean Journal of Human Rights* 186 (2002), citing Paul McDermott, *Res Judicata and Double Jeopardy* (Ireland: Butterworths, 1999), at 201.

[23] Hunter, "The Development of the Rule Against Double Jeopardy", at 4-5 (stating that 'up to the end of the sixteenth century … the protection remained a mere statement of procedure replete with exceptions and compromises which would deny it the status of being a fundamental right and a cornerstone of English justice.')

[24] William Blackstone, *Commentaries on the Laws of England*, Vol. 4 (Oxford: Clarendon Press, 1873), at 335. Neither the Magna Carta nor other legal instruments made any mention of *ne bis in idem*. However, works by Glanville and Bracton discuss the prohibition against multiple prosecutions with regard to trial by ordeal. In addition, Coke had described and clarified the principle of double jeopardy in his *Second Institutes*, largely reiterated by Blackstone in his *Commentaries*. Sigler, "A History of Double Jeopardy", at 1962-1963.

[25] El Zeidy, "The Doctrine of Double Jeopardy in International Criminal and Human Rights Law", at 186, citing Paul McDermott, *Res Judicata and Double Jeopardy* (Ireland: Butterworths, 1999), at 201.

[26] Art. 11 IMT Charter states: 'Any person convicted by the Tribunal may be charged before a national, military or occupation court, referred to in Article 10 of this Charter, *with a crime other than membership in a criminal group or organisation*, and such court may, after convicting him, impose upon him punishment independent of and additional to the punishment imposed by the Tribunal for participation in the criminal activities or such group or organisation.' [Emphasis added]

while the IMTFE Charter made no mention at all of this impediment. Control Council Law No. 10 was also silent on this particular impediment.

The *ad hoc* Tribunals for the Former Yugoslavia and Rwanda institute a trans-jurisdictional *non bis in idem* rule,[27] effectively preventing national courts from prosecuting persons for acts for which he or she has already been prosecuted by the ICTs.[28] The Tribunals are also prevented from re-prosecuting a person who has been tried for the same acts at the national level, unless the act was characterised as an 'ordinary crime'[29] or where the national proceedings were not impartial or independent, were designed to shield the accused from international criminal responsibility, or the case was not diligently prosecuted.[30] Rule 13 of the ICTY and ICTR Rules of Procedure and Evidence also provides that when the President receives reliable information to show that criminal proceedings have been instituted against a person before a court of any State for a crime for which that person has already been tried by the Tribunal, a Trial Chamber shall issue a reasoned order requesting that court permanently to discontinue its proceedings. If that court fails to do so, the President may report the matter to the Security Council.

The formulation of the principle of *ne bis in idem* in the Rome Statute was drafted bearing in mind the need to balance two countervailing considerations.[31] First, the fact that the ICC jurisdiction would be in addition to existing mechanisms of enforcement at the national level and hence the need to ensure that multiple prosecutions on the same facts was avoided and second, the general perception that the existing national mechanisms of enforcement have been under- and selectively utilised, which has led to large-scale impunity.[32] The *sui generis* context of the *ne bis in idem* provisions of the Rome Statute is also based upon the fact that the relationship between the ICC and national courts is not one of two sovereigns with competing claims.[33] For this reason, while the principle is applicable fully

[27] There are terminological differences between '*non bis in idem*' and '*ne bis in idem.*' The ICTY and ICTR Statutes adopt the former variation, while the Rome Statute adopts the latter.

[28] ICTY Statute, Art. 10(1); ICTR Statute, Art. 9(1).

[29] In the *Bagasora* case, in which the defendant challenged the ICTR's jurisdiction by invoking *ne bis in idem*, arguing that he had already been tried for the same facts in Belgium, the ICTR rejected the plea, but stated that had Bagasora been convicted for war crimes, rather than an 'ordinary' crime, he could not be retried by the ICTR on charges of genocide or crimes against humanity. *Bagasora*, Trial Chamber I, Decision on the Application by the Prosecutor for a Formal Request for Deferral of 17 May 1996, ICTR-96-7-D, at 13.

[30] Provisions in both Statutes state that: 'A person who has been tried by a national court for acts constituting serious violations of international humanitarian law may be subsequently tried by the International Tribunal … only if: (a) the act for which he or she was tried was characterized as an ordinary crime; or (b) the national court proceedings were not impartial or independent, were designed to shield the accused from international criminal responsibility, or the case was not diligently prosecuted.' ICTY Statute, Art. 10(2); ICTR Statute, Art. 9(2).

[31] See Art. 20 ICC Statute.

[32] Immi Tallgren, "Article 20: Ne bis in idem", in Otto Triffterer (ed.), *Commentary on the Rome Statute of the International Criminal Court: Observers' Notes, Article by Article* (Baden-Baden: Nomos Verlagsgesellschaft, 1999), at 420.

[33] *Idem.*

with regard to decisions of the ICC,[34] those of national courts may, in exceptional circumstances, not preclude the ICC from re-trying the person.[35] The complementarity principle of the ICC's jurisdiction does, however, mean that decisions of national courts are subject to a presumption of *ne bis in idem* in a way that such judgments do not have *vis-à-vis* the jurisdiction of the *ad hoc* international criminal tribunals, which are based upon primacy of jurisdiction.[36]

For its part, the Law on the Establishment of the Extraordinary Chambers in the Courts of Cambodia for the Prosecution of Crimes Committed during the Period of Democratic Kampuchea (as amended)[37] is silent on the principle of *ne bis in idem*. By contrast, the principle of *non bis in idem* is dealt with in Article 9 of the SCSL Statute, which broadly mirrors the rule laid down in the Statutes of the ICTY and ICTR. The *ne bis in idem* principle for the Panels with Exclusive Jurisdiction Over Serious Criminal Offences in East Timor is essentially the same as that set out in the Rome Statute. Given the widespread criticism of the Ad Hoc Human Rights Court on East Timor in Jakarta,[38] the 'sham trial' exception to the *ne bis in idem* rule may mean it could be possible for those persons who were acquitted by the Ad Hoc Human Rights Court (all 18 indicted persons but one) to be tried again before the courts in Dili,[39] although the likelihood of such an occurrence remains slim for political and logistical reasons.

6.1.3 **Definition**

Different terms are used by States to describe the doctrine encompassed by the principle of *ne bis in idem*, not all of which are exactly approximate. In the United

[34] However, a national court may try a person convicted by the ICC for crimes under *national* law for the same conduct because the *ne bis in idem* principle under the ICC Statute only applies to crimes 'referred to in article 5.' See *ibid.*, at 428.

[35] Art. 20(3) of the ICC Statute permits the ICC to proceed where the national proceedings were conducted in order to shield the person from criminal responsibility or otherwise were not conducted independently or impartially and were conducted in a manner inconsistent with an intent to bring the person to justice.

[36] For instance Art. 10 of the ICTY Statutes provides that retrial before the ICTY if the national prosecution was based on an 'ordinary' crime.

[37] See *Law on the Amendments to the Law on the Establishment of the Extraordinary Chambers in the Courts of Cambodia for the Prosecution of Crimes Committed during the Period of Democratic Kampuchea, Kram* NS/RKM/1004/006, 27 October 2004, available at: <http://www.cambodia.gov.kh/krt/pdfs/Kram%20and%20KR%20Law%20amendments%2027%20Oct%202004%20--%20Eng.pdf>.

[38] See Summary of the report to the Secretary-General of the Commission of Experts to Review the Prosecution of Serious Violations of Human Rights in Timor-Leste (then East Timor) in 1999, Annex I to the Letter dated 24 June 2005 from the Secretary-General to the President of the Security Council, UN Doc. S/2005/458, 15 July 2005, paras. 16-17.

[39] For a discussion of the possibilities for future prosecutions of serious crimes before the courts of Timor Leste, see Judicial System Monitoring Programme, *Overview of Timor Leste Justice Sector 2005*, January 2006, at 33, available at: <http://www.jsmp.minihub.org/Reports/2006/Final%20Overview%20Report%202005%20(e).pdf>.

States, the term 'double jeopardy' has been adopted, reflecting the protection set out in the Fifth Amendment of the Constitution: 'Nor shall any person be subject for the same offence to be twice put in jeopardy of life or limb …' This formulation underscores the protective function of the principle, i.e., the *substantive* effect of *ne bis in idem*. The English and Australian law pleas of *autrefois acquit* and *autrefois convict* on the other hand, focus upon the fact of a previous legal outcome by the judicial system, i.e., the *procedural* effect. The latter two pleas have slightly different purposes. While *autrefois convict* prevents double punishment, it does not necessarily bar 'the hardship of a second trial.'[40] *Autrefois acquit*, however, promotes the defendant's civil liberties by 'ending the fear of renewed prosecution after acquittal.'[41] In these jurisdictions, the double jeopardy rule also includes the abuse of process standard.[42] The abuse of process standard allows a court to exercise 'its undoubted power to prevent an abuse of its process … apart from the common law principles' to stop the prosecution.[43] The doctrine gives courts the power to stay the prosecution's case where putting the defendant on trial would be unfair.[44] In this way, it is used to 'safeguard the moral integrity of verdicts, and of the criminal process generally.'[45] However, while an *autrefois* plea gives the defendant an 'absolute right to relief,'[46] the abuse of process standard depends on a judge's assessment of fairness and due process and is therefore only a qualified right.[47]

Most European continental systems know the principle of double jeopardy by the Latin maxim *nemo debet bis vexari pro una et eadem causa* (no one should have to face more than one prosecution for the same offence).[48] In Belgium, the term *chose jugée* is used, while France uses the terms *autrefois acquité/convict de même felonie*, as well as *autorité de la chose jugée*.[49]

Perhaps the only universal definition one may identify is that right guaranteed by the International Covenant of Civil and Political Rights of 1966 (ICCPR),[50]

---

[40] Claire de Than and Edwin Shorts, "Double Jeopardy – Double Trouble", 64 *Journal of Criminal Law* 624 (2000), at 625. Thus, if no sentence was handed down in the first trial, this plea would be futile.

[41] *Ibid.*, at 627.

[42] *R.* v. *Carroll*, Australia, 213 *CLR* 640 (C.J. Gleeson and J. Hayne). See also Justices Gaudron and Grummow at 660-61.

[43] *Connolly*, United Kingdom [1964] AC 1334 (L.J. Hodson). For more on the abuse of process doctrine, see Chapter 7, *infra*.

[44] The Law Commission, *Double Jeopardy and Prosecution Appeals* (2001), Cm. 5084, at 18.

[45] Andrew L.-T. Choo, "Halting Criminal Prosecutions: The Abuse of Process Doctrine Revisited", *Criminal Law Review* 865 (1995).

[46] *Connolly*, United Kingdom [1964] AC at 1358.

[47] *Idem.*

[48] Christine van den Wyngaert and Guy Stessens, "The International *Non Bis in Idem* Principle: Resolving Some of the Unanswered Questions", 48 *ICLQ* 780 (1999).

[49] El Zeidy, "The Doctrine of Double Jeopardy in International Criminal and Human Rights Law", 198-199, citing Christian T. Campbell, *International Civil Procedures* (New York/London/Hamburg: Lloyd's of London Press Ltd, 1995), at 270.

[50] The Universal Declaration of Human Rights of 1948 does not contain a *ne bis in idem* protection. As of July 2009, there are 164 States parties to the ICCPR.

which provides that 'No one shall be liable to be tried or punished again for an offence for which he has already been finally convicted or acquitted in accordance with the law and penal procedure of each country.'[51] A more restricted version appears in the American Convention on Human Rights: 'An accused person acquitted by a nonappealable judgment shall not be subjected to a new trial for the same cause,'[52] while the European Convention on Human Rights (ECHR) and the African Charter on Human and Peoples' Rights are both silent on the issue. However, in the European context, the principle has since been incorporated in a number of instruments, all of which use slightly varying formulations. The European Commission on Human Rights has implied the right into Article 6(1)[53] and Article 4 of Protocol No. 7 adds the rule explicitly to the ECHR and makes it a non-derogable right.[54] Article 54 of the Convention implementing the Schengen Agreement provides a definition for the purposes of a transnational *ne bis in idem* principle for EU members.[55] Article 50 of the EU Charter of Fundamental Rights[56] also includes a right not to be tried twice in criminal proceedings for the same offence

[51] Art. 14(7) ICCPR.

[52] Art. 8(4) ACHR. There does not appear to be an equivalent protection for persons who have been convicted and sentenced.

[53] See *X* v. *Austria*, ECommHR No. 1519/62, 10 CD 59(27/3/63); *X* v. *Netherlands*, ECommHR No. 9433/81, 27 *D&R* 233 (11 December 81). Art. 6(1) of the ECHR provides: In the determination of his civil rights and obligations or of any criminal charge against him, everyone is entitled to a fair and public hearing within a reasonable time by an independent and impartial tribunal established by law. Judgement shall be pronounced publicly by the press and public may be excluded from all or part of the trial in the interest of morals, public order or national security in a democratic society, where the interests of juveniles or the protection of the private life of the parties so require, or the extent strictly necessary in the opinion of the court in special circumstances where publicity would prejudice the interests of justice.'

[54] Art. 4, Protocol No. 7 (22 December 1984) provides: '1. No one shall be liable to be tried or punished again in criminal proceedings under the jurisdiction of the same State for an offence for which he has already been finally acquitted or convicted in accordance with the law and penal procedure of that State. 2. The provisions of the proceeding paragraph shall not prevent the reopening of the case in accordance with the law and penal procedure of the State concerned, if there is evidence of or newly discovered facts, or if there has been a fundamental defect in the previous proceedings, which could affect the outcome of the case. 3. No derogation of this Article shall be made under Article 15 of the Convention.'

[55] [2000] *OJ* L239/19. Art. 54 provides that: 'A person whose trial has been finally disposed of in one Contracting Party may not be prosecuted in another Contracting Party for the same acts provided that, if a penalty has been imposed, it has been enforced, is actually in the process of being enforced or can no longer be enforced under the laws of the sentencing Contracting Party.' The Schengen Convention was later integrated into the framework of EU law as part of the Schengen *acquis*. Protocol integrating the Schengen *acquis* into the Framework of the European Union, annexed to the Treaty of Amsterdam [1997] *OJ* C340. The Convention's provisions on *ne bis in idem* have been incorporated into Title VI EU on police and judicial co-operation in criminal matters, the Union's 'third pillar.' The UK and Ireland have not signed the Convention, but they take part in Arts. 54-58 thereof. The provisions also apply in Norway and Iceland through their Schengen association agreements with the EU.

[56] [2000] *OJ* C354/1. The EU Charter was proclaimed in December 2000 and incorporated as Part II of the Treaty establishing a Constitution for Europe on 18 June 2004 ([2004] *OJ* C310/1).

within the Union.[57] However, the legal status of the Charter remains unclear being neither a treaty, constitutional, or legal document, but rather constituting a 'solemn proclamation' by three of the Union's most important institutions, the European Parliament, the Council of the European Union, and the European Commission.[58] This suggests that while the Charter does not represent Community law, the three institutions, as well as the European Court of Justice (ECJ), are not likely to act in an incompatible manner with its provisions.[59] In view of the desire to create an area of freedom, security and justice (AFSJ) by the extension of criminal and judicial co-operation,[60] a proposal for a framework decision on *ne bis in idem* has also been put on the table as part of the establishment of basic rights protections for defendants.[61] If adopted, this would have the effect of requiring all member States to harmonise their laws on *ne bis in idem* along the lines of the decision. Other instruments adopted in the framework of the Council of Europe have also broadened the scope of the *ne bis in idem* principle to other (contracting) States.[62] *Ne bis in idem* is also referred to in the European Arrest Warrant[63] and the EU Convention on the Protection of the European Communities' Financial Interests.[64] The European Court of Justice (ECJ) had stated that *ne bis in idem* constitutes a general principle of Community law, which is applicable regardless of any legislative provision.[65]

In as far as definitional issues are concerned two main issues of interpretation remain controversial. The first relates to what is meant by an '*idem*'; the second is at which stage of proceedings the principle may be triggered, or in other words, what constitutes a '*bis*.'

6.1.3.1 *What constitutes an* 'idem'

With regard to the first issue, an '*idem*' has either referred to the same *conduct* or the same *offence* for which a person cannot be tried twice. Obviously, these have

---

[57] Art. 50 of the EU Charter provides: 'No one shall be liable to be tried or punished again in criminal proceedings for an offence for which he or she has already been finally acquitted or convicted within the Union in accordance with the law.'

[58] See the European Commission's explanation as to the Charter's dubious legal status at: <http://ec.europa.eu/justice_home/unit/charte/en/about-status.html>.

[59] Although the Charter is not yet directly enforceable by the EU courts or national courts (until all 25 Member States ratify the Contitutional Treaty), the Charter has become an importance reference document and the European Court of Justice has referred to it on several occasions in order to identify the fundamental rights that must be respected by the Community. See, e.g., *Laval un Partneri Ltd* v. *Svenska Byggnadsarbetareförbundet and others* (C-341/05).

[60] See Arts. 2, 31 and 34 of the Treaty on European Union.

[61] *Initiative of the Hellenic Republic with a view to adopting a Council Framework Decision concerning the application of the ne bis in idem principle*, *OJ* (2003) C 100, at 24-27.

[62] E.g., Arts. 53-57 European Convention on the International Validity of Criminal Judgments [1970] *ETS* 70 and Arts. 35-37 European Convention on the Transfer of Proceedings in Criminal Matters [1972] *ETS* 73.

[63] Council Framework Decision on the European Arrest Warrant and the Surrender Procedures between Member States [2002] *OJ* L190/1, Arts. 3(2), 4(3) and 4(5).

[64] [1995] *OJ* C316/49, Art. 4.

[65] *X* v. *European Central Bank*, Case T-333/99.

vastly different outcomes. If a person may not be tried twice for the same conduct, then this provides for a very broad *ne bis in idem* protection. If, on the other hand, the principle of *ne bis in idem* refers to the same offence, then it is possible for a person to be tried again for different offences arising out of the same conduct. Generally-speaking, most continental systems tend to use the broad concept of *ne bis in idem*,[66] though there are significant variations.[67] Common law countries on the other hand, tend to refer either to the same offence[68] or to the test of whether the crime is *substantially the same* as the crime for which he or she has been previously tried.[69] The difference between the approaches has been explained by reason of the fact that common law systems ascribe the prosecutor with a significant degree of discretion in choosing which offences to prosecute, while civil law systems require the prosecution of all crimes that may arise from known facts.[70]

With regard to the possibility to re-prosecute a person for international crimes, the difference between adopting a conduct-based '*idem*' and an offence-based '*idem*' is acute. The cases against former Argentine General Jorge Videla are a compelling example. Videla was tried and convicted in Argentina in 1985 (for assassination and torture) and sentenced to life imprisonment but was pardoned in 1990 by President Carlos Menem. He was re-arrested on 9 June 1998 pursuant to an arrest warrant issued by federal judge Roberto Marquevich, who was investigating five cases of 'theft' of children of persons who were 'disappeared' by the armed forces. The former Prosecutor, Luis Moreno Ocampo, who was involved in the earlier prosecution, has stated that Videla cannot be retried for the crimes for which he has already been tried and amnestied. However, as the baby-snat-

---

[66] Van den Wyngaert and Stessens, "The International *Non Bis In Idem Principle*", at 790.

[67] The Netherlands, for example, applies a broad definition of *ne bis in idem*, using 'facts' as the relevant '*idem*.' Dutch Supreme Court [*Hoge Raad*], 13 December 1994, *Ars Aequi*, at 720. In Belgium, the broad definition applies to Belgian judgments, while the narrow *ne bis in idem* effect is given to foreign judgments. Compare Art. 360 Belgian Code of Criminal Procedure with Art. 13 of the Preliminary Title to the Criminal Procedure Code. See also Court of Appeal of Antwerp, 24 June 1982, *Rechtskundig Weekblad* (1982-83), at 1812.

[68] US courts apply the double jeopardy bar on successive prosecutions only to offences composed of the same elements of fact and law. M. Cherif Bassiouni, *Substantive Criminal Law* (1978), at 501. *Blockburger* v. *United States*, United States, 284 US 299 (1932), at 304: 'the test to be applied to determine whether there are two offenses or only one, is whether each provision requires proof of an additional fact which the other does not.' See *Elcock* v. *United States*, United States, 80 F. Suppl. 2d 70 (EDNY 2000), at 84 (holding that given there was no international consensus on the interpretation of 'offense' in extradition treaties, the court would have to defer to the Executive Branch's interpretation of the term and apply the *Blockburger* test).

[69] *Connelly* v. *DPP* [1964] AC 1254. See also the Harvard Draft Convention on Jurisdiction, *AJIL Supplement* (1935), at 613-614, which uses the phrase 'a crime requiring proof of substantially the same acts or omissions.' *Sindona* v. *Grant*, 619 F.2d, at 177-78 (holding that the test of the word 'offence' in an extradition treaty between Italy and the US should be 'a modified and more flexible test of whether the same conduct or transaction underlines the criminal charges in both transactions'). *United States* v. *Jurado-Rodriguez*, 907 F. Suppl. at 580-581 (holding that an indictment for crimes that are substantively different and have a sufficiently separate evidentiary base did not violate even the express limiting language of *non bis in idem* in an extradition treaty).

[70] M. Cherif Bassiouni, *International Extradition: United States Law and Practice* (New York: Oceana Publications, 1996), at 600-601.

ching and kidnapping charges were not part of the 1985 charges, the current case is unbarred by the rule of *ne bis in idem*. In addition, Videla was subsequently charged in 2001 with charges related to Operation Condor. Had the Buenos Aires Court of Appeal interpreted the double jeopardy protection in the Argentine Constitution as relating to the same *conduct*, Videla's claim that the recent prosecution was barred on double jeopardy grounds may have succeeded. Instead, the Court noted that the Condor-related charges included in the current indictment had not been part of his 1985 trial.[71] Moreover, the fact that these charges were not included in the accusation in 1985 (commonly referred to as Case 13) did not mean that there was an implied pardon for all the other crimes that were not chosen to be prosecuted in the case.[72]

There is no real consensus in international instruments as to which '*idem*' should be employed. The ICCPR refers to 'offence,'[73] as does Article 4 of Protocol No. 7 of the ECHR. The European Court of Human Rights has interpreted the '*idem*' in Protocol No. 7 as applying to the 'same essential elements,' which may signal a movement away from a purely technical offence-based interpretation,[74] but its jurisprudence is somewhat conflicting and inconclusive.[75] The English version of the ACHR uses the dubious term 'same cause,'[76] while Article 54 of the Schengen Convention refers to the 'same acts.'[77] The ECJ has interpreted the 'same acts' as referring to the identity of the facts or material acts and not to the identity of the legal qualification of these acts in the various Member States. In coming to this view, the Court took the perspective of the mutual recognition principle:

---

[71] *Videla, Jorge R. s/procesamiento*, Cámera Federal de Buenos Aires, Causa 33714, Sala I, 23 May 2002 (appeals court).

[72] *Videla*, CSJN [2003-F] 87 (2003), discussed in Luis Márquez Urtubey, "Non-Applicability for Statutes of Limitation for Crimes Committed in Argentina: Barrios Altos", 11 *Southwestern Journal of Law and Trade in the Americas* 114 (2005). In any case, in April 2007, a federal appeals court held that the presidential pardons were unconstitutional and reinstated the life sentence handed down in 1985. Judgment available at: <http://www.trial-ch.org/fileadmin/user_upload/documents/trialwatch/Videla_indulto_2007.doc>.

[73] See *Schweizer* v. *Uruguay*, Human Rights Committee, Communication No. 66/1980, UN Doc. Suppl. No. 40 (A/38/40) at 117 (1983) (holding that to violate Art. 14(7) ICCPR, a person must be tried again for an offence for which he has already been acquitted or convicted in a case where a military tribunal tried to re-try a person for acts that had already been investigated by an ordinary judge several years previously with an additional charge).

[74] *Franz Fischer* v. *Austria* [2001] ECHR 25; *Sailor* v. *Austria* [2002] ECHR 24.

[75] Compare, e.g., *Gradinger* v. *Austria*, Case No. 33/1994/480/562 in which the ECHR prevented a second (aggravated) charge of negligent driving that was based on the same conduct as the first charge, with *Olivera* v. *Switzerland*, Case No. 84/1997/868/1080, in which the ECHR stated that a single act (negligent driving) constituted various offences, thus allowing different charges to be brought at a later point.

[76] This would appear to be a broader scope of protection than an '*idem*' based on 'offence.' See *Loayza Tamayo* v. *Peru*, Case IACTHR (ser. C), No. 33, Judgment 17 September 1997, para. 66. See also *Ruth del Rosario Garcés Valladares* v. *Ecuador*, IAComHR, Communication No. 64/99, Case No. 11.778, 13 April 1999; *Wilson Guttiérez Soler* v. *Colombia*, IAComHR, Communication No. 76/01, Case No. 12.291, 10 October 2001.

[77] However, the Dutch, French and German versions of Art. 54, which are the authentic versions, use the word 'facts,' not 'acts.' Van den Wyngaert and Stessens, "The International *Non Bis In Idem* Principle", at 790.

> 'because there is no harmonization of national criminal law, a criterion based on the legal classification of the acts or on the protected legal interest might create as many barriers to freedom of movement within the Schengen territory as there are penal systems in the Contracting States. In those circumstances, the only relevant criterion for the application of Article 54 CISA [Schengen Convention] is the identity of material acts, understood as the existence of a set of concrete circumstances which are inextricably linked together.'[78]

This presents a fair argument for the relevant '*idem*' as the underlying conduct rather than the offence prosecuted in transnational application of *ne bis in idem*.[79] The danger of this approach is that a person may be tried on the same facts but for a lesser charge.[80] It might also represent an overly-broad application of the *ne bis in idem* principle disproportionate to the need to ensure that those accused of international crimes are properly tried and, if convicted, punished. If instead the narrower 'offence'-based *ne bis in idem* rule is adopted trans-nationally, this could be softened by application of the deduction of sentence principle, which many States use with regard to foreign sentences pertaining to the same offence.[81]

The trans-juridictional *ne bis in idem* rules have adopted a selective '*idem*' approach. The ICTY and ICTR Statutes use the term 'acts constituting serious violations of international humanitarian law' for the downwards *ne bis in idem* rule,[82] suggesting that national courts would be barred from re-prosecuting any of the underlying conduct that could be characterised as war crimes (and presumably also genocide and crimes against humanity), but leaving open the possibility that the same conduct could be prosecuted for other offences (e.g. murder).[83] The upwards *ne bis in idem* rule, which allows the *ad hoc* ICTs to prosecute a person

---

[78] Case C-436/04, *Van Esbroeck* [2006] ECR quoted in Martin Wasmeier and Nadine Thwaites, "The development of ne bis in idem into a transnational fundamental human right in EU law: comments on recent developments", 31 *European Law Review* 573 (2006).

[79] It has been argued that a transnational *ne bis in idem* principle should consider the '*idem*' in terms of the 'same act' as opposed to the 'same offence' in view of the fact that national penal provisions have vastly different characterisations of crimes, which would make it extremely difficult to decide if the offense was indeed the same. The 'same facts' test may be more objective. See, e.g., Draft Resolution, adopted in Berlin on 4 June 2003, "Concurrent and International Criminal Jurisdiction and the Principle of '*Ne Bis In Idem*'", 73 *International Review of Penal Law* 1182 (2002), Art. II, 2.1. For a contrary view, see Van den Wyngaert and Stessens, "The International *Non Bis In Idem* Principle", at 791: '... any general *non bis in idem* provision should, in principle, bar only new prosecutions for the same offence, not for the same facts.'

[80] Van den Wyngaert and Stessens, "The International *Non Bis In Idem* Principle", at 791.

[81] E.g., Art. 13 Preliminary Title to the Belgian Criminal Procedure Code, para. 66 of the Austrian Penal Code, para. 51 III of the German Criminal Code, Art. 56 of the Schengen Convention, Art. 10(3) of the 1997 EU Anti-Corruption Convention. See *S* v. *Germany*, Decision of 12 December 1983 Appl. No. 8945/80, 39 DR 43 (applying the principle of deduction to an individual who was re-prosecuted in Germany for a drug offence for which he had already been convicted and imprisoned in the Netherlands).

[82] Art. 10(1) ICTY Statute; Art. 9(1) ICTR Statute.

[83] Where a national court violates the *ne bis in idem* principle by prosecuting someone already judged by the ICTs, the Trial Chamber may issue an order to discontinue proceedings. If that court fails to do so, the Tribunal's President may issue a report to the Security Council. Rule 13 RPE.

for international crimes if they had already been prosecuted at the national level for an 'ordinary crime,' clearly shows that it is the legal characterisation of the underlying conduct that is relevant to the *ne bis in idem* protection.[84] As suggested by the ICTR in *Bagosora*, if a national court prosecuted someone for genocide, the Tribunal would not be able to re-prosecute that person.[85] However, the principle of deduction is mandatory for the ICT's if convicting a person for the second time.[86] The ICTs may prosecute a person for multiple charges, so long as the crimes fulfill the *Blockburger* test – that is, each offence contains an element not required by the other.[87] Nevertheless, the prosecutor is sometimes obliged to concentrate on just some crimes, raising the question of whether other crimes forming part of the same criminal enterprise may be prosecuted later.

The *ne bis in idem* rule binding the ICC to its own previous judgments refers to 'conduct which formed the basis of crimes,' which suggests that the same conduct is the relevant '*idem*.'[88] Thus, the prosecutor would be barred from re-trying a person for the same conduct for a different crime later on (e.g. a person acquitted of genocide cannot later be prosecuted for crimes against humanity on the basis of the same conduct). Two exceptions exist for appeal (Art. 81) and revision (Art. 84).[89] By contrast, the relevant '*idem*' for the downward *ne bis in idem* rule is 'a crime referred to in article 5,'[90] which is clearly an offence-based '*idem*,' allowing national courts to re-prosecute a person convicted or acquitted by the ICC for other crimes (including some international crimes not covered by the ICC Statute, such as torture *per se*).[91] However, the upwards *ne bis in idem* rule uses the term 'same conduct,'[92] providing for a broader *ne bis in idem* effect, with the important 'sham

[84] Art. 10(2)(a) ICTY Statute; Art. 9(2)(a) ICTR Statute. As stated in the Secretary-General's Report, the ICTY could exercise jurisdiction if '[t]he characterization of the act by the national court did not correspond to its characterization under the statute.' Report of the Secretary-General pursuant to paragraph 2 of Security Council Resolution 808 (1993), UN Doc. S/25704, 3 May 1993.

[85] *Bagosora*, ICTR, Trial Chamber I, Decision on the Application by the Prosecutor for a Formal Request for Deferral of 17 May 1996, Case No. ICTR-96-7-D, para. 13. In this case, the ICTR rejected the defendant's plea of *non bis in idem* due to his previous prosecution in Belgium because the Belgian court had tried him for murder and serious violations of the Geneva Conventions, not for crimes falling within the Statute of the ICTR (i.e., crimes against humanity and genocide).

[86] Art. 10(3) ICTY Statute; Art. 9(3) ICTR Statute ('In considering the penalty to be imposed on a person convicted of a crime under the present Statute, the International Tribunal for Rwanda shall take into account the extent to which any penalty imposed by a national court on the same person for the same act has already been served.')

[87] *Blockburger* v. *United States*, 284 US 299 (1932), at 304: 'the test to be applied to determine whether there are two offenses or only one, is whether each provision requires proof of an additional fact which the other does not.'

[88] Art. 20(1) ICC Statute.

[89] These provisions clearly reflect the civil law tradition that *ne bis in idem* does not apply until all appeals are exhausted. Unlike in common law countries, a judgment is not final in the ICC before the final appellate judgment.

[90] Art. 20(2) ICC Statute.

[91] Should a State violate the *ne bis in idem* protections in Art. 20, Art. 87(5)(b) provides for a referral to the States Parties' Assembly or to the Security Council.

[92] Art. 20(3) ICC Statute.

trial' exception.[93] Unlike the *ad hoc* ICTs, there is no exception for 'ordinary crimes' prosecuted at the national level, although arguably this could be inferred into the 'sham trial' exception. There is also no mandatory deduction of sentence principle, which could present a formidable problem for re-convicted felons.[94] Thus, if a person is prosecuted for a different offence (e.g. multiple murder) at the national level that is also proscribed by Articles 6, 7 or 8 in the ICC Statute, the same conduct cannot be used as the basis for a prosecution before the ICC, unless it can be shown that the first trial was conducted with a view to shielding the person from justice. Notably, aggression does not form part of the upwards *ne bis in idem* rule, which might indicate that domestic proceedings for the crime of aggression would never block the ICC's jurisdiction. In addition, a 'temporal *ne bis in idem*' effect is instituted in the sense that the ICC Prosecutor will not prosecute if an investigation by the State of jurisdiction is still pending.

The Regulation setting up the Special Panels for East Timor uses the exact same formulation at the ICC Statute.[95] The Statute of the SCSL instead refers to 'acts' as the '*idem*' in the downwards *ne bis in idem* rule, suggesting that the same conduct cannot be used for re-prosecution on different charges at the national level.[96] However, the upwards *ne bis in idem* rule, by referring to 'acts referred to in articles 2 to 4 of the present Statute,'[97] seems to intimate that the word 'acts' in the Statute is used to mean 'offence' rather than underying conduct, signifying a narrow *ne bis in idem* protection in either direction.

6.1.3.2 *Types of procedures to which* ne bis in idem *may attach*

In terms of the second issue – what types of procedures may trigger *ne bis in idem* – common law and civil law countries have approached the issue in two distinct ways. Both systems generally require the court of final instance to be a criminal court.[98] However, civil law systems, unlike those of the common law, allow prosecutors to appeal errors of law and questions of fact under *ne bis in*

[93] Art. 20(3)(a) and (b) ICC Statute.

[94] Art. 78(2) ICC Statute provides: 'In imposing a sentence of imprisonment, the Court shall deduct the time, if any, previously spent in detention in accordance with an order of the Court. The Court *may* deduct any time otherwise spent in detention in connection with conduct underlying the crime.' [Emphasis added]

[95] Section 11 (under General Principles of Criminal Law), UNTAET Regulation 2000/15, 6 June 2000.

[96] Art. 9(1) SCSL Statute: 'No person shall be tried before a national court of Sierra Leone for acts for which he or she has already been tried by the Special Court.'

[97] Art. 9(2) SCSL Statute: 'A person who has been tried by a national court for the acts referred to in articles 2 to 4 of the present Statute may be subsequently tried by the Special Court if: (a) The act for which he or she was tried was characterized as an ordinary crime; or (b) The national court proceedings were not impartial or independent, were designed to shield the accused from international criminal responsibility or the case was not diligently prosecuted.'

[98] José Luis De La Cuesta, "Concurrent National and International Criminal Jurisdiction and the Principle '*Ne Bis In Idem*' General Report", 73 *International Review of Penal Law* 722 (2002).

idem.[99] Thus, while in the common law system, the principle arises after a person has been acquitted or convicted of a crime,[100] civil law systems require all possible prosecutorial appeals to have been exhausted before recognising the finality of a judgment.[101]

The traditional approach was to exclude decisions of instructors and public prosecutors putting an end to proceedings from the *ne bis in idem* effect; in other words, the decision had to be on the merits of the case.[102] This approach was challenged in a decision of the ECJ of 11 February 2003, concerning the transnational application of *ne bis in idem* provisions (Art. 54 of the Schengen Convention) in the context of the AFJS introduced by the Amsterdam Treaty, which asserted the *ne bis in idem* effect of out-of-court settlements concluded in another State's jurisdiction.[103] The ECJ adopted a broad interpretation of *ne bis in idem* for the purposes of defining what constitutes a 'final decision' in view of the objective of the principle.[104] The Court reasoned that the involvement of a court judgment was not necessary as 'such matters of procedure and form do not impinge on the effects of the procedure.'[105] Thus, so long as proceedings are discontinued by 'an authority required to play a part in the administration of criminal justice in the national legal systems concerned,' the effect in terms of *ne bis in idem* should be same.[106] The Court also relied on a mutual recognition approach,[107] affirming that there is a

---

[99] Lopez, "Not Twice for the Same", at 1293. France for e.g., allows a party to appeal a conviction, an acquittal, a dismissal, and or a sentence in a criminal case, while any party may appeal errors of law and questions of fact.

[100] This approach stems from the role of juries in the Anglo-American system. It is considered unfair that a determination on the facts by a jury could be overturned by an appellate court consisting of appellate judges. Gerard Conway, "*Ne Bis In Idem* and the International Criminal Tribunals", 14 *Criminal Law Forum* 364 (2003).

[101] Some delegations to the Preparatory Committee on the Rome Statute held the view that preclusion of a prosecution appeal was a general principle of criminal law. UN Doc. A/51/22, at 86-87. The Inter-American Commission on Human Rights has interpreted 'non appealable judgment' as expressing the exercise of jurisdiction that acquires the immutability and incontestability of *res judicata*. See *Garcia* v. *Peru*, Case 11.006 (Peru) IACTHR Annual Report 1994, No. 1/95.

[102] Notably, the Harvard Draft Convention on Jurisdiction refused to regard dismissal for want of jurisdiction or a procedural technicality as an acquittal with a *ne bis in idem* effect. Harvard Draft Convention on Jurisdiction, *AJIL Supplement* (1935), at 613-614.

[103] Joined cases C-187/01 and 385/01, *Gözütok and Brügge* [2003] ECR 1-1345.

[104] *Idem*. The ECJ ruled: 'Article 54 of the CISA, the objective of which is to ensure that no one is prosecuted on the same facts in several Member States on account of his having exercised his right to freedom of movement, cannot play a useful role in bringing about the full attainment of that objective unless it also applies to decisions definitively discontinuing prosecutions in a Member State, even where such decisions are adopted without the involvement of a court and do not take the form of a judicial decision.' In *France* v. *Krombach*, a French conviction adopted *in absentia* on the same evidence that had led the highest competent German Court not to prosecute was considered as an infringement of Art. 6 of the ECHR and by Austria as a violation of *ne bis in idem* that impeded extradition. 12(1-2) *Human Rights Case Digest* (2001), at 67-71(5).

[105] *Gözütok and Brügge*, *supra* n. 103 at 31.

[106] *Ibid.*, at 28.

[107] The political guidelines set by the European Council provide that 'the principle of mutual recognition … should become the cornerstone of judicial co-operation in both civil and criminal matters within the Union' and 'apply to both judgments and to other decisions of judicial authorities,' as

'necessary implication that the Member States have mutual trust in their criminal justice systems and that each of them recognises the criminal law in force in the other Member States even when the outcome would be different if its own national law were applied.'[108] The decision also underlined the intrinsic link between *ne bis in idem* and the freedom of movement.[109]

However, in the 2005 *Miraglia* case,[110] the ECJ reverted to some degree back to the traditional approach, holding that Article 54 of the Schengen Convention did not apply when the decision of the court in the first member State to discontinue proceedings is based solely on the fact that proceedings are taking place in another case, without any *adjudication on the merits* of the case.[111] The Court considered that its interpretation was the only one that could ensure that Article 54 'has proper effect,'[112] as applying *ne bis in idem* to the case 'would … make it more difficult, indeed impossible … to penalize in the Member States concerned the unlawful conduct with which the defendant is charged.'[113] It added that in an area of freedom, security and justice, 'free movement of persons is assured in conjunction with appropriate measures with respect to … preventing and combating crime.'[114] This is an important finding in view of the fact that prosecutors often decide to exercise their discretion not to prosecute those accused of international crimes. If such a decision were taken to have a *ne bis in idem* effect, no other member State would be able to prosecute for the same offence. A pertinent example are the decisions of the German federal prosecutors to dismiss the *Almatov* case regarding tortures committed in Uzbekistan and the *Rumsfeld and others* case regarding the tortures committed in Iraq at the Abu Ghraib prison. It would seem odd in view of the need to combat crimes of such gravity that these decisions, based on a technical procedural aspect of German law,[115] should prevent other Schengen States from taking on these cases, should complaints be made in other forums.[116] Only final

---

approved by the Hague Programme in November 2004. See Presidency Conclusions of the European Council of Tampere, 15-16 October 1999, para. 33. Annex to the Presidency Conclusions of the European Council of Brussels, 4-5 November 2004, point 3.3.1.

[108] *Ibid.*, at 33.

[109] *Gözütok and Brügge, supra* n. 103, at 35.

[110] Case C-469/03 (15 March 2005, 5th Chamber). The case concerned a mutual assistance request made by Italy to the Netherlands in a drugs case, which was refused on the grounds that under Dutch law, a 'final decision' had been made pursuant to closure of the case in view of the Italian proceedings.

[111] *Ibid.*, at 35.

[112] *Ibid.*, at 31.

[113] *Ibid.*, at 33.

[114] *Ibid.*, at 34.

[115] Although presence of the offender on German territory is not a formal requirement for the exercise of jurisdiction, the public prosecutor is not *required* to prosecute if the suspect is not present on German territory and such presence is not to be anticipated. Act to Introduce the Code of Crimes against International Law of 26 June 2002, available at: <http://www.iuscomp.org/gla/statutes/VoeStGB.pdf>, Art. 3, s. 153f. The prosecutor may also dispense with prosecuting if the suspect is not a German national, the offence was not committed against a German, or the suspect is being prosecuted by an international criminal tribunal or by the State of territoriality, nationality or passive personality.

[116] In comments made by Walter Kaleck, the lead attorney for the complainants in the *Rumsfeld and others* case in Germany at the Asser Institute in The Hague on 13 June 2007, it appeared that the

decisions on the merits of the case (not because of procedural reasons) are generally taken into account in transnational *ne bis in idem*.[117] A notable exception is the Netherlands, where an out-of-court settlement in a foreign country bars re-prosecution before Dutch courts when the accused has complied with the conditions set out in the settlement.[118]

The Spanish cases dealing with the amnesty of Pinochet provide an example of whether an amnesty should be treated like a foreign conviction, acquittal or pardon. While Spanish law appears to prohibit the prosecution of an individual who is the beneficiary of certain foreign pardons, the Spanish courts interpreted the Chilean amnesty as the equivalent of a 'standard acquittal for reason of political convenience,' and thus not a bar to Spanish prosecution.[119] It may, however, be more difficult for courts to ignore plea bargains or promises of partial immunity in return for collaboration or truth-telling entered into by foreign prosecutorial authorities in efforts to apprehend the persons most responsible for perpetuating international crimes. The efficiency of the international criminal system could be seriously undermined if States do not co-operate together in a systemic effort to prosecute strategically and in a manner most likely to bring about international peace and security. Obviously, this would require a much more sophisticated and developed system of international co-operation and criminal law enforcement assistance than is currently the case. Nonetheless, one may observe that no State has attempted to try any of the persons who testified before the South African Truth and Reconciliation Commission (TRC) and who were granted an amnesty, even though the facts of their participation in international crimes were revealed. While it might be stretching legal theory to ascribe a *res judicata* aspect to the TRC-Amnesty Commission process, States do seem to have decided to respect the outcome of these procedures given the legitimate objectives underlying the mechanism.

Such respect contrasts markedly to the lack of international recognition of the blanket amnesty laws passed in Latin America, such as that in Chile. In the *Pinochet* case, the UK House of Lords did not for a moment consider that the amnesty might preclude the jurisdiction of a foreign State from trying Pinochet based on the principle of *ne bis in idem*.[120] Pardons and amnesties are excluded from having a *ne bis in idem* effect in France and French-influenced systems, in order to avoid the effect of possible mercy measures, given by political reasons and to impede prosecutions in France.[121] Egypt also does not recognise foreign judgments where

case may indeed be taken to alternative jurisdictions in Europe such as Spain or Sweden, where more favourable legislation exists.

117 De La Cuesta, "Concurrent National and International Criminal Jurisdiction", at 724.

118 Art. 68 of the Dutch Penal Code (as supplemented in 1985).

119 See Antoni Pigrau Solé, "The Pinochet Case in Spain", 6 *ILSA J. Int'l and Comp. L* 653 (2000), at 664; Derechos Human Rights, *The Criminal Procedures against Chilean and Argentinean Repressors in Spain: A Short Summary* (1998) (interpreting Spanish law not to allow recognition of Chilean and Argentinean amnesties) available at: <www.derechos.net/marga/papers/spain.html>.

120 *R* v. *Bow Street Metropolitan Stipendiary Magistrate*, ex parte *Pinochet Ugarte*, United Kingdom, House of Lords Judgment of 24 March 1999, 2 *WLR* 827 (HL 1999); [1999] 2 *All ER* 97.

121 De La Cuesta, "Concurrent National and International Criminal Jurisdiction", at 725.

the sentence cannot be enforced by reason of a statute of limitations, or in case of amnesty or pardon.[122] Coming back to the question of whether out-of-court settlements could have a *ne bis in idem* effect, it has been reasoned that 'A limited, *inter partes* international *non bis in idem* effect of out-of-court settlements can be envisaged only if these settlements have been negotiated on an international level, that is, involving the authorities of various States and taking into account the various State interests.'[123] It may be argued that the policy considerations discussed in the chapter on amnesties also provide guidelines as to when such deals could be considered as legitimate, entailing international recognition.

In addition to the general requirement that the decision be a final one by a criminal court on the merits, the conventions pertaining to a transnational *ne bis in idem* effect require that the judgments have been enforced or can no longer be enforced according to the laws of the State where the judgment was rendered.[124] Pardon and amnesty are mentioned in the Council of Europe conventions as the type of situation where a judgment can no longer be enforced. Similarly, the UN Model Convention on Extradition cites 'lapse of time or amnesty' as one of the mandatory grounds for refusal.[125] Article 54 of the Schengen Convention also seems to cover this possibility. While this might suggest that amnesty, pardon and statutes of limitation covering international crimes would bar subsequent trials in other States' courts, the legal rationales discussed in previous chapters as to why such impediments do not necessarily apply to international crimes must be borne in mind. States parties to the Schengen Convention and other relevant conventions would need to consider their other obligations under international law, such as the obligation to prosecute those accused of international crimes, when deciding whether a pardon, amnesty or statute of limitation pertaining to a foreign judgment regarding international crimes has any *ne bis in idem* effect. One may recall that both pardon and amnesty were rejected as a basis for *ne bis in idem* in the context of Article 20 of the Rome Statute, which may signal that an exception exists for international crimes in this respect.[126]

In order to block the ICTs from prosecuting, a national court's decision must be a final one on the merits of the case.[127] This means that amnesties or decisions not to prosecute based on a lack of evidence or because the prosecution would not

---

[122] El Zeidy, "The Doctrine of Double Jeopardy", at 208.

[123] Van den Wyngaert and Stessens, "The International *Non Bis In Idem* Principle", at 802.

[124] Donnedieu de Vabres argued that the *res judicata* effect of a foreign judgment should be respected only when it legal consequences have been enforced. *AIDI*, Vol. II (1950), at 261.

[125] GA Res. 45/116, 14 December 1990, Model Treaty on Extradition, Art. 3(e).

[126] Report of the Preparatory Committee on the Establishment of an International Criminal Court, Vol. 1, at 40, para. 174 (Proceedings of the Preparatory Committee during March-April and August 1996) GAOR, 51st Sess., Suppl. (No. 22), UN Doc. A/51/22); UN Doc. A/CONF./283/2/Add.1 (1998), Art. 19.

[127] *Tadić*, ICTY, Trial Chamber II, Decision of 14 November 1995 on the defence motion on the principle of *non bis in idem*, Case No. IT-94-1-T (in which the ICTY rejected the defence's claim of a violation of the *non bis in idem* principle because he had already been tried in Germany, as there had been no German decision on the merits of the case, only interlocutory decisions).

serve the interests of justice would not suffice.[128] With regard to the downwards *ne bis in idem* effect of the ICC, a ruling of inadmissibility is not sufficient to prevent a national court from exercising jurisdiction on the basis of *ne bis in idem*; there must have been a conviction or an acquittal.[129] However, the upwards *ne bis in idem* provision makes reference only to the need for a person to be 'tried' at the national level, not to any necessary legal consequence, i.e., conviction or acquittal, which raises the question as to what constitutes a '*bis*.' Would a plea bargain, out-of-court settlement, diversionary measure, parole deal, or conversion of sentence suffice to block prosecution before the ICC? The only clear guidance in the text of the Statute is that if such methods, or indeed a conviction and sentence were designed to shield the perpetrator from responsibility, or the proceedings were otherwise not prosecuted independently and impartially and were conducted in a manner inconsistent with an intent to bring the person to justice, the jurisdiction of the ICC is not barred by the rule of *ne bis in idem*.[130] The language 'tried in another court' suggests that this would cover other international courts as well, such as the *ad hoc* ICTs and hybrid courts, but would probably exclude truth commissions.[131]

In terms of the ICTY, the matter has been somewhat clarified by a decision of the Trial Chamber in the *Orić* case.[132] Orić, a Senior Commander of Bosnian Muslim forces in municipalities in eastern Bosnia and Herzegovina from 1992 to 1995, was found guilty by a Trial Chamber of murder and cruel treatment under Articles 3 and 7(3) of the Statute,[133] but had these convictions overturned on appeal[134] and he returned to Bosnia and Herzegovina. In December 2008, he submitted a motion before the ICTY arguing that the Prosecutor's Office in Bijeljina had instituted criminal proceedings against him for crimes for which he had already been tried and acquitted by the Tribunal.[135] The Trial Chamber held that since there was no evidence that Orić was actually being tried before a court in Bosnia and Herzegovina for any of the alleged crimes which are the subject of the criminal investigation being conducted against him by the Bijeljina Prosecutor's Office, there had been no breach of Article 10(1) of the Statute.[136] It further found that Rule 13 was

[128] De La Cuesta, "Concurrent National and International Criminal Jurisdiction", at 730.

[129] Art. 89(2) of the Statute provides that if a person being sought for surrender brings a challenge to a national courts based on *ne bis in idem*, the requested State must consult with the Court to determine if a decision on admissibility has been made. If a positive ruling has been made, the requested State must proceed with the execution of the surrender. If the ruling is still pending, the State may postpone the surrender until the Court makes a determination.

[130] Art. 20(3)(a) and (b) ICC Statute.

[131] But see De La Cuesta, "Concurrent National and International Criminal Jurisdiction", at 735 (arguing that truth commissions could be covered by the language in Art. 20).

[132] *Orić,* ICTY, Trial Chamber, Case No. IT-03-68-A, Decision in Orić's Motion Regarding a Breach of *Non-Bis-In-Idem*, 7 April 2009.

[133] *Orić,* ICTY, Trial Chamber, Case No. IT-03-68, Judgment, 20 June 2006, para. 782.

[134] *Orić,* ICTY, Appeals Chamber, Case No. IT-03-68-A, Judgment, 3 July 2008, at 64.

[135] *The Prosecutor* v. *Orić*, Case No. IT-03-68-A, Motion Regarding a Breach of *Non-Bis-In-Idem*, 11 December 2008.

[136] *Orić,* ICTY, Trial Chamber, Case No. IT-03-68-A, Decision on Orić's Motion Regarding a Breach of *Non-Bis-In-Idem*, 7 April 2009, at 5.

not applicable since there was no information to show that criminal proceedings had been instituted against Orić before a court in Bosnia and Herzegovina.[137] The ICTY therefore interpreted 'criminal proceedings' strictly, pertaining only to actual court proceedings, not simply investigative proceedings, even where potential charges have been laid against a suspect. Presumably, however, this would mean that if the Bijeljina Prosecutor's Office decided subsequent to its investigation to actually lay charges and bring Orić to trial, this would contravene the *non bis in idem* protections under the Statute and the Rules, and an order could be issued by a Trial Chamber to the court to discontinue proceedings in so far as these are in respect to the same crimes for which he has already been tried and acquitted before the Tribunal.

The unresolved definitional issues discussed above lend further support to the contention that *ne bis in idem* is subject to too many variants as to qualify as a general principle of law or a clear customary rule. This means that courts, when deciding whether or not to proceed with a prosecution where the defendant has already been tried for the same crime, require a methodological approach that will rationally guide the determination of the fairest and most just solution. The following section outlines the policy considerations that courts would do well to examine in such an interests-analysis approach.

6.2 Contextual and policy considerations

Two broad streams of policy rationales govern and justify the principle of *ne bis in idem*. The first stream relates to the protection of the individual. The second relates to the legitimacy of the legal system in pursuance of social peace.[138]

With regard to the first policy stream, most legal systems recognise the inherent unfairness caused to individuals by having them put twice on trial for the same crime as well as the disrespect to human dignity.[139] This rationale was famously captured by the United States Supreme Court, which recognised that 'the State with all its resources and power should not be allowed to make repeated attempts to convict an individual for an alleged offense, thereby subjecting him to embarrassment, expense and ordeal and compelling him to live in a continuing state of anxiety and insecurity.'[140] Moreover, the anxiety and stress likely affects not only the defendant, but also his or her family, witnesses on both sides of the trial and

[137] *Idem.*

[138] Log, "The Practical Applications of *Ne Bis in Idem* in International Criminal Law", at 172. See also "The '*non bis in idem*' principle in criminal law in the EEC", Report of the Legal Affairs Committee of 20 February 1984 (Doc. 1-1397/83), published in *Human Rights Law Journal* (1984), at 391.

[139] Martin Friedland, *Double Jeopardy* (Oxford: Clarendon Press, 1969), at 358.

[140] *Green* v. *U.S.*, United States, 355 US 184 (1957), at 187-88.

even the victim[141] and is likely to be exacerbated by media attention,[142] especially in cases of international crimes.[143] In addition, the *ne bis in idem* protection aims to limit the risk of wrongful conviction.[144] Multiple prosecutions may cause the defendant to lose stamina in defending him or herself.[145] As noted by the United States Supreme Court, such trials 'would present an unacceptably high risk that the Government, with its vastly superior resources, might wear down the defendant so that even though innocent he may be found guilty.'[146] Having more than one trial increases the risk of improper conviction due to erroneous jury verdicts.[147] Further, prosecutors have the advantage of having already seen the defence strategies at the first trial, making these less effective and undermining the principle of equality of arms.[148] In sum, by limiting a State's ability to prosecute, the *ne bis in idem* rule 'helps maintain a healthy balance between state interests and individual freedom.'[149] Notably, the human rights rationale is equally valid at the transnational and trans-jurisdictional level, although generally only protected as such on the latter level.

The second stream of policy rationales underlying the *ne bis in idem* protection focuses upon the systemic effects of the principle upon the legal system. This is sometimes referred to as the 'pragmatic' rationale.[150] There is the notion in some legal systems that once a 'criminal claim' (*action pénale*) has been dealt with it is extinguished.[151] German law refers to this as the rule of *Erledigungprinzip*, entailing that a first judgment has 'emptied' the 'criminal claim' with regard to a certain offence.[152] Moreover, re-prosecuting a person for the same crime is inefficient.[153] The *ne bis in idem* rule is an incentive for prosecutors to pursue an investigation with utmost diligence.[154] Finally, the principle has sometimes been characterised as

---

141 The Law Commission, Consultation Paper No 156, *Double Jeopardy: A Consultation Paper* (1999) (UK), available at: <http://www.lawcom.gov.uk/docs/Cp156.pdf> (hereafter, Law Commission, *Double Jeopardy: A Consultation Paper*), at 31, para. 4.6.

142 Taylor, "England and Australia Relax the Double Jeopardy Privilege", at 206.

143 *Aleksovski (Appeal),* ICTY, Appeals Chamber, Judgment of 24 March 2000, Case No. IT-95-14/1-A, at para. 190 (noting that account should be taken of the increased anxiety and stress to the accused as a result of having to face a second sentencing and also for having undergone a second detention following release).

144 Law Commission, *Double Jeopardy: A Consultation Paper*, at 30, para. 4.5.

145 Log, "The Practical Applications of *Ne Bis in Idem*", at 173.

146 *United States* v. *Scott*, United States, 437 US 82 (1978).

147 Law Commission, *Double Jeopardy: A Consultation Paper*, at 30, para. 4.5.

148 *Idem.*

149 Paul Roberts, "Acquitted Misconduct Evidence and Double Jeopardy Principles, from *Sambasivum* to *Z*", *Criminal Law Review* 952 (2000), at 954. Roberts argues that chipping away at *ne bis in idem* protection changes the proper balance between a State and the individual.

150 Van den Wyngaert and Stessens, "The International *Non Bis In Idem* Principle", at 780; Log, "The Practical Applications of *Ne Bis in Idem*", at 173-74.

151 Van den Wyngaert and Stessens, "The International *Non Bis In Idem* Principle", at 780, fn. 6, citing Dutch, Belgian and German law.

152 *Ibid.*, at 781.

153 Law Commission, *Double Jeopardy: A Consultation Paper*, at 32, para. 4.11.

154 Log, "The Practical Applications of *Ne Bis in Idem*", at 173-74.

a corollary of the recognition of the *res judicata* effect of other judgments, aimed at protecting the finality of judgments.[155] The idea is that once a case has been dealt with, it should not be reopened (*factum praeteritum*) as this would seriously undermine respect for judicial proceedings and the judiciary in general. Rather, courts should accept the final judgment of other courts (*res judicata pro veritate habeur*) in order to prevent conflicting judgments.[156] With regard to transposing this rationale to the transnational level, at the Bath Session (1950) of the *Institut de Droit International*, the *rapporteur général* Henri Donnedieu de Vabres held the view that *res judicata* was the bedrock of any *ne bis in idem* protection at the international level, although this view was opposed by other distinguished scholars.[157] It is also possible to argue that recognising the *res judicata* effect of other State's judgments might impede the sovereign right to prosecute.[158] However, as the enforcement of international criminal law through multilevel jurisdiction is considered more and more as a coherent *system*, the infringement of sovereignty argument starts to have less weight and the need for respect of judicial decisions and for efficiency more leverage.

With regard to the particular policy considerations in terms of the prosecution of international crimes, the *ne bis in idem* rule has only recently been considered as a legitimate bar to multiple prosecutions suggesting that the gravity of these crimes outweighs the importance of the values underlying the double jeopardy protection. In 1919 the Commission on the Responsibility of the Authors of the War and on Enforcement and Penalties took note of the rule that 'no trial or sentence by a court of the enemy country shall bar trial and sentence by the tribunal or by a national court belonging to one of the Allied or Associated States.'[159] As noted, the IMT Charter provided for an extremely limited *ne bis in idem* protection applying only to the charge of membership of a criminal organisation.[160] As a result, the three individuals acquitted at Nuremberg, Hans Fritzsche, Franz von Papen and Hjalmar Schacht, were all subjected to further penal proceedings after their release.[161] The

---

[155] See R. Theofanis, "The Doctrine of *Res Judicata* in International Criminal Law", 3 *International Criminal Law Review* 195 (2003).

[156] Van den Wyngaert and Stessens, "The International *Non Bis In Idem* Principle", at 781.

[157] E.g., Fitzmaurice. See *AIDI*, Vol. II (1950), 259-261, 278-280, 280-281.

[158] Van den Wyngaert and Stessens, "The International *Non Bis In Idem* Principle", at 782.

[159] *Violations of the Laws and Customs of War, Reports of Majority and Dissenting Reports of America and Japanese Members of the Commission on Responsibilities, Conference of Paris, 1919* (Oxford: Clarendon Press, 1919); 14 *AJIL* 95 (1920).

[160] Art. 11 of the IMT Charter provided: 'Any person convicted by the Tribunal may be charged before a national, military or occupation court, referred to in Article 10 of this Charter, with a crime other than of membership in a criminal group or organization and such court may, after convicting him, impose upon him punishment independent of and additional to the punishment imposed by the Tribunal for participation in the criminal activities of such group or organization.'

[161] The Spruchkammer in Nuremberg sentenced Fritzsche to nine years of hard labor, loss of voting, pension, and public office rights; von Pappen was sentenced by the same court to ten years in a labor camp. Similarly, Schacht was sentenced by a Stuttgart court to eight years in the Ludwigsburg labor camp; on appeal he was acquitted, but then subjected to further denazification proceedings in Lüneburg. Alfred De Zayas, "The Nuremberg Trials", Lecture at the University of Toronto, June 1996, available at: <http://alfreddezayas.com/Lectures/nuremberg_toronto.shtml>.

IMTFE was similarly silent on *ne bis in idem*, suggesting that further prosecutions were possible at the national level. Allied Control Council Law No. 10 did not refer to the principle of double jeopardy, although it did set up detailed rules of jurisdictional priority where more than one jurisdiction wanted to try a person, suggesting that multiple prosecutions were not contemplated.[162] Moreover, the rule was referred to in some of the judgments issued by the military tribunals.[163] However, one may note that the 1953 Draft Statute for an International Criminal Court stated that everyone who had been judged or acquitted by the ICC could not be tried again before a national court (Art. 50).[164] The principle was codified in the Third Geneva Convention on Prisoners of War,[165] which affirmed the protection already provided in the 1929 Geneva Convention.[166] It was also included as one of the 'Fundamental Guarantees' of Additional Protocol I of 1977,[167] largely to reflect the right contained in the 1966 ICCPR.[168]

The ICTY and then the ICTR were thus the first international criminal tribunals to institute a trans-jurisdictional *ne bis in idem* rule for international crimes. The inclusion of this rule has been associated with the need for the tribunals to manifest the principle of primacy in their jurisdiction.[169] This contrasts with the ICC's jurisdictional principle of complementarity, and explains to some degree the differences in the way that each of the Statutes deal with trans-jurisdictional *ne bis in idem*. In addition, the development of human rights in the area of fair trial and particularly the rights of defendants would likely have contributed to the decision to include *ne*

---

[162] Allied Control Council Law No. 10, Art. IV.

[163] See, e.g., *Flick* case, in which Judge Richman stated that 'the only purpose of the Charter was to bring to trial major war criminals; we conceive the only purpose of this Tribunal is to bring to trial war Criminals that have not already been tried.' *Trials of War Criminals Before the Nuremberg Military Tribunals Under Control Council Law No. 10*, Vol. VI (1952), at 1213. A cause of action in the *Justice* case was that a case that was 'again tried [was a] violation of the fundamental principles of justice that no man should be tried twice for the same offence.' *Trials of War Criminals Before the Nuremberg Military Tribunals Under Control Council Law No. 10*, Vol. III (1951), at 1147-49.

[164] Christine Van den Wyngaert and Tom Ongena, "*Ne bis in idem* Principle, Including the Issue of Amnesty", in Antonio Cassese, Paola Gaeta and John R.W.D. Jones (eds.), *The Rome Statute of the International Criminal Court: A Commentary*, Vol. I (Oxford: OUP, 2002), at 718.

[165] GC III, Art. 86: 'No prisoner of war may be punished more than once for the same act, or on the same charge.'

[166] Art. 52(3) Convention relative to the Treatment of Prisoners of War. Geneva, 27 July 1929.

[167] Art. 75(4)(h) AP I: 'no one shall be prosecuted or punished by the same Party for an offence in respect of which a final judgement acquitting or convicting that person has been previously pronounced under the same law and judicial procedure.' The rule did not make it into the penal provision of Additional Protocol II relative to non-international armed conflicts (Art. 6).

[168] ICRC, *Commentary on the Additional Protocols of 8 June 1977 to the Geneva Conventions of 12 August 1949* (Dordrecht: Martinus Nijhoff Publishers, 1987), at 884: 'The provision on *ne bis in idem* … is drawn from the United Nations Covenant on Civil and Political Rights … and is so drafted as to pose minimum difficulties to States in an area where practice varies widely.'

[169] As stated by the Report of the UN Secretary General, 'given the primacy of the International Tribunal, the principle of *non-bis-in-idem* would preclude subsequent trial before a national court.' Report of the Secretary-General pursuant to paragraph 2 of Security Council Resolution 808 (1993), UN Doc. S/25704, 3 May 1993, para. 66. See also Van den Wyngaert and Ongena, "*Ne bis in idem* Principle", at 717; Log, "The Practical Applications of *Ne Bis in Idem*", at 185.

bis in idem in the Statutes. However, the Regulation setting up the Special Panels for East Timor is the only constitutive instrument of an international or hybrid court that lists the principle within the section on 'General Principles of Criminal Law.'[170] The Statutes of the ICTY, ICTR, ICC and SCSL all make mention of the principle in the context of jurisdictional principles.[171] In this sense, *ne bis in idem* is conceived as a procedural bar to jurisdiction,[172] rather than any substantive 'right' of the defendant. The 'sham trial' exception included in the ICTY, ICTR, ICC and SCSL Statutes and in the Regulation setting up the Special Panels encapsulates the policy objection to the *ne bis in idem* principle stemming from the need to ensure that jurisdictional obstacles do not lead to impunity.

6.3 Legal rationales with regard to the principle of *ne bis in idem* and international crimes

A large number of different legal rationales to deny or restrict the application of *ne bis in idem* have arisen in practice, particularly in regard to the re-prosecution of serious crimes, including international crimes. The principal ones are: (1) legal arguments countering a transnational *ne bis in idem* principle; (2) the exception for fundamental defects/sham trial pertaining to the first trial; (3) newly discovered facts or evidence; (4) the State claim to exercise jurisdiction over offences committed on its territory; (5) exceptions for certain offences; and (6) the exception in case of additional serious offences.

6.3.1 **Legal arguments countering a transnational *ne bis in idem* principle**

Current international law does not obligate a State to recognise the *res judicata* effect of foreign penal judgments, thus allowing States to re-prosecute a person for a crime for which he has already been tried in another jurisdiction. In other words, there is no international double jeopardy rule regarding prosecutions by different sovereign States. This state of affairs has been justified on the basis that the international community lacks the unified and coherent legal system required for the recognition of *res judicata*, as conceived in the domestic context.[173] Legally, the lack of a transnational *ne bis in idem* protection is argued from two perspectives. First, the right to be protected from double jeopardy in human rights treaties has been

[170] UNTAET Regulation 2000/15, Part III, Section 11.

[171] The ICTY Statute includes Art. 10 (*non bis in idem*) after Art. 9 on concurrent jurisdiction. The ICTR Statute includes Art. 9 (*non bis in idem*) after Art. 8 on concurrent jurisdiction. The ICC Statute includes Art. 20 (*ne bis in idem*) in Part Two on Jurisdiction, Admissibility and Applicable Law, after Art. 19 on Challenges to the Jurisdiction of the Court or the admissibility of a case. The SCSL Statute includes Art. 9 (*ne bis in idem*) after Art. 8 on concurrent jurisdiction.

[172] Conway, "*Ne Bis In Idem* and the International Criminal Tribunals", at 354.

[173] Van den Wyngaert and Stessens, "The International *Non Bis In Idem* Principle", at 792.

interpreted by treaty-monitoring bodies[174] and national courts[175] as only applying to multiple prosecutions within the same sovereign State. With regard to the right in the ICCPR, the Human Rights Committee has stated that 'article 14, paragraph 7 of the Covenant does not guarantee *ne bis in idem* with regard to the national jurisdiction of two or more states ... [T]his provision prohibits double jeopardy only with regard to an offence adjudicated in a given state.'[176] Protocol No. 7 to the ECHR explicitly states that it applies only the 'jurisdiction of the same State.'[177]

The second legal argument rests on the notion that an individual's conduct violates the laws of two sovereign nations, thus constituting two separate and independent offences for the purpose of punishment.[178] In the United States, the so-called 'dual sovereignty' doctrine is based on the contention that a single act may be a violation of the laws of two governments. The violation of each law 'must be considered as separate and distinct crimes.'[179] In a number of cases, the US Supreme Court has held that the double jeopardy clause in the Fifth Amendment of the Constitution applies only at the federal level and does not prevent a state from re-prosecuting a person in its courts for an offence that has already been examined at the federal level.[180] Transposing this to the inter-State level, US courts have tended to dismiss claims of double jeopardy or *ne bis in idem vis-à-vis* foreign judgments, relying on the dual sovereignty doctrine developed under the US Constitution, unless there is a treaty provision providing for the right explicitly.[181] In other words, the principle has been limited to a defence against requests for extra-

[174] *A.P.* v. *Italy*, Communication No. 204/1986, at para. 7.3, Report of the HRC, 43d Sess., Suppl. No. 40, UN Doc. A/43/40 (1988). In this case, Italy, as a signatory to the ICCPR, was held to be not precluded from prosecuting an individual previously convicted and sentenced by Switzerland for the same offence.

[175] *United States* v. *Benitez*, 120 F. Suppl. 2d 1361 (S.D. Fla. 1988), *aff'd* 208, F.3d 1282 (11th Cir. 2000) (hereafter, *Benitez* case) (holding that Art. 14(7) ICCPR bars only successive prosecutions by the same government). The facts of the case concerned charges of assault by the defendants against two agents of the US Drug Enforcement Agency, who had already been convicted by a Colombian court for the assault.

[176] *A.P.* v. *Italy*, Communication No. 204/1986, at para. 7.3, Report of the HRC, 43rd Sess., Suppl. No. 40, UN Doc. A/43/40 (1988). This view was reiterated in *A.R.J.* v. *Australia*, HRC, Communication No. 692/1996, UN Doc. CCPR/C/60/D/692/1996, 11 August 1997, para. 6.4.

[177] Protocol No. 7 to the European Convention for the Protection of Human Rights and Fundamental Freedoms, Art. 4, 22 November 1984, ETS No. 117 (1985).

[178] Bassiouni, *International Extradition*, at 598.

[179] *People* v. *Papaccio*, United States, 251 N.Y.S. 717, at 720 (Ct. Gen. Sess. N.Y. County, 1931). In this case, Mr. Papaccio was initially prosecuted in Italy for the crime of murder committed in the United States. Thomas Franck interpreted the US prosecution of Papaccio as an indication of displeasure at the Italian assertion of jurisdiction based on nationality, rather than territory. Thomas Franck, "An International Lawyer Looks at the Bartkus Rule", 34 *N.Y.U. L. Rev.* 1096 (1959), at 1098.

[180] *US* v. *Lanza* US 227 (1922); *US* v. *Bartkus* 359 US 121 (1959).

[181] See *Benitez* case (citing the rule that absent a treaty, sovereign nations are not obliged to respect or enforce the penal judgments of another sovereign); *United States* v. *Rashed*, United States, 83 F. Suppl. 2d 96 (D.D.C. 1999); *United States* v. *Richardson*, United States, 580 F.2d 946 (9th Cir. 1978); *United States* v. *Martin*, United States, 574 F.2d 1359 (5th Cir. 1978). See also Restatement (Third) of the Foreign Relations Law of the United States, § 483, cmt. 3 (1987) (stating that unless required by treaty, no State enforces the penal judgments of other States).

dition.[182] In so holding, US courts have rejected the argument that *ne bis in idem* applies as a principle of international law or a customary right that may nullify the double sovereignty doctrine.[183]

The dual sovereignty doctrine has been justified by the greater weight attributed by courts to the principle of sovereignty than to the protection against double jeopardy.[184] One of the concerns driving the US courts to adopt the doctrine was that prosecution by one sovereign of a minor offence might bar another sovereign's court from prosecuting a much more serious offence, thereby effectively depriving the latter from the right to enforce its own laws.[185] An exception to the doctrine was formulated in the case of 'sham' trials, which entailed the rule that a prosecution by one sovereign cannot be used as a 'sham and cover' for another sovereign's re-prosecution for the same crime.[186] This would happen where a sovereign that had failed in its attempt to convict a person then encouraged and supported a second sovereign to re-prosecute the person.[187] In such a case, the two sovereigns are deemed to be acting as one hence there is no case of dual sovereignty.[188] In the *United States* v. *Rashed*,[189] this exception was considered for the first time at the international level. The defendant, indicted with charges of aircraft bombing in the United States after having been convicted and having served an eight year sentence in Greece, argued that the United States had dominated and directed the Greek proceedings so completely that there was no 'dual sovereignty' and hence double jeopardy attached.[190] The Court held that this exception was extremely narrow and that the defendant would need to show that Greek officials 'had little or no independent volition in the state proceedings' and that the United States used Greek prosecution to achieve an objective they could not otherwise achieve under the Constitution.[191] The Court found that mere co-operation by the United States did not mean that Greece did not act independently, and in any case the United States gained nothing from the prosecution except for a delay for its own proceedings.[192]

The United States is certainly not alone in not recognising the *ne bis idem* effect of foreign judgments.[193] However, the dual sovereignty doctrine has been subject-

---

[182] *Sidona* v. *Grant*, United States, 619 F.2d 167, at 177-78 (2nd Cir. 1980).

[183] *Benitez* case, at 1364. Lopez, "Not Twice for the Same", at 1281. See also *United States* v. *Martin*, 574 F.2d at 1360 (holding that the 'Constitution of the United States has not adopted the doctrine of international double jeopardy').

[184] See, e.g., *Bartkus* v. *Illinois*, 359 US 121 (1959).

[185] *Abate*, 359 US 195.

[186] *Bartkus*, 359 US 123-4.

[187] *United States* v. *Koon*, 34 F.3d 1416, at 1438 (9th Cir. 1994).

[188] *Idem.*

[189] *United States* v. *Rashed*, 83 F. Suppl. 2d 96, at 101 (D.C. 1999).

[190] *Ibid.*, at 97.

[191] *Ibid.*, at 102, quoting *United States* v. *Liddy*, 542 F.2d 76, at 79 (D.C. Cir. 1979).

[192] *Idem.*

[193] A number of States apply *ne bis in idem* only to judgments of their own courts. E.g., Art. 13 of the German Constitution provides that an individual may be prosecuted in a German court for an offence even if the individual has been previously tried for by a foreign court. Log, "The Practical Applications of *Ne Bis in Idem*", at 175-76.

ed to significant criticism on a number of bases.[194] It has been noted that it perpetuates injustice as prosecutors are virtually guaranteed a conviction on the second try (particularly where the evidence has already led to a previous conviction),[195] not to mention the fact that in some cases (such as *Rashed*), the person may have already served time in prison for the crime.[196] In the US, the Department of Justice has taken steps to limit the effect of the doctrine by voluntarily abstaining from prosecuting unless compelling federal interests are present.[197] However, the 'Petite Policy' as it is called has little if no effect at the international level.[198]

Both common law and civil law systems have recognised the legitimacy of foreign acquittals and convictions.[199] It may be noted that the United States application of the dual sovereignty doctrine is the exception rather than the rule for common law States, which often do recognise the *res judicata* effects of foreign judgments.[200] Given that the Fifth Amendment of the US Constitution was intended to conform to the 'universal practice in Great Britain,'[201] it is unlikely that the framers of the Constitution would have accepted such an exception to the double jeopardy protection.[202] Notably, the early case law of the US Supreme Court followed the English precedent by barring successive prosecutions in different sove-

---

194 See, e.g., Lopez, "Not Twice for the Same", at 1293-95; Robert Matz, "Dual Sovereignty and the Double Jeopardy Clause: If at First You Don't Convict, Try, Try Again", 24 *Fordham Urb. Law Journal* 353 (1997); Eric J. McDonald Guadalupe, "Double Jeopardy, Dual Sovereignty and Other Legal Fictions", 28 *Rev. Jur. U.I.P.R.* 201 (1994).

195 Lopez, "Not Twice for the Same", at 1294; Matz, *supra* n. 194, at 372.

196 *Idem.*

197 See, e.g., Ala. Code. § 12.20.010 (1984); Cal. Penal Code § 656 (West 1988); Ga. Code Ann. § 16-1-8 (Michie 1992); Utah Code Ann. § 76-1-404 (1990).

198 Lopez, "Not Twice for the Same", at 1294. See *Petite* v. *United States*, United States, 361 US 529 (1960).

199 Franck, at 1099-1101, citing to British, Canadian, French, and German examples of courts deferring to foreign prosecutions. See also Martin Friedland, *Double Jeopardy* (Oxford: Clarendon Press, 1969), at 358 (stating that the majority of legal systems provide some level of protection against multiple prosecutions for the same crime). The Netherlands, Peru, Canada and Senegal all fully recognise the *ne bis in idem* effect of foreign judgments. Poels, "A Need for Transnational *Non Bis In Idem* Protection", at 342. Sweden applies the protection in cases where the defendant was previously convicted, but disregards it when the defendant was previously acquitted. Lopez, "Not Twice for the Same", at 1273. Egypt also recognises the *ne bis in idem* effect of foreign judgments for crimes committed abroad. Art. 4 Criminal Penal Code, quoted in El Zeidy, "The Doctrine of Double Jeopardy", at 199.

200 This is the case for the United Kingdom and for South Africa. See, e.g., *Rex* v. *Thomas,* I *Keble* 677 (1664) (holding that an acquittal in Wales for a murder charge barred a second prosecution in England); *Rex* v. *Hutchinson*, cited in *Leach* 134 (1677) (holding that an acquittal for murder in Portugal barred a second prosecution in England); *Aughet* (1919) 13 *Cr App R* 101 (respecting a foreign acquittal); *Treacy* v. *DPP* [1971] AC 537, cited by P. Murphy (ed.), *Blackstone's Criminal Practice* (1996), at 1212; See, e.g., *Pokela* 1968 (4) SA 703 (OK).

201 Sigler, "A History of Double Jeopardy", at 32.

202 Lopez, "Not Twice for the Same", at 1296 ('… it is logical to conclude that if the framers of the Constitution had intended to allow for multiple prosecutions by separate sovereigns, they would have specified or provided an exception similar to the dual sovereignty doctrine.')

reign States for the same crime.[203] In *United States* v. *Furlong*, the Court held that for certain crimes, such as piracy, over which all States may exercise criminal jurisdiction, 'there can be no doubt that the plea of *autre fois acquit* would be good in any civilized state, though resting on a prosecution instituted in the Courts of any civilized state.'[204] Recent practice disregarding the dual sovereignty doctrine includes NATO Status of Forces Agreements, in which signatory States agreed to recognise each other's criminal judgments, except as regards breaches of military discipline.[205] It is likely that this would include judgments over war crimes. In the *Guatemala Genocide* case, the Spanish Constitutional Tribunal found that the principle of *ne bis in idem* (where the suspect had been convicted, found innocent, or pardoned abroad) was the only limitation to its exercise of universal jurisdiction over the crime of genocide according to the plain language and legislative intent of Article 23(4) of the *Ley Orgánica del Poder Judicial* (Organic Law of the Judicial Branch).[206] Thus, it would appear that where crimes may be defined under international law and attract universal jurisdiction and when States have sufficient trust in the legal systems of other States, the dual sovereignty doctrine loses much of its relevance.

Further evidence of a transnational *ne bis in idem* effect may be found in extradition treaties. Many treaties allow a State to refuse an extradition request if a court in the requested State has rendered a final judgment in respect of the same offence for which the suspect's extradition is sought.[207] The scope of the *ne bis in idem* principle would depend upon the specific provision in the co-operation treaty. The *ne bis in idem* principle in such cases creates international obligations only between the signatories (obligations *inter partes*).[208] While some of these conventions contain a mandatory *ne bis in idem* provision,[209] others provide *ne bis in idem* as an optional ground for refusal[210] or allow States to make an explicit

---

[203] See, e.g., *Rose* v. *Himley*, 8 US 241 (1808), at 276: 'if the port of St. Domingo had jurisdiction of the case, its sentence is conclusive.'

[204] *United States* v. *Furlong*, 18 US 184 (1820), at 197.

[205] Art. VII, § 5 of the Agreement provides: 'Where an accused has been tried in accordance with the provisions of this Article by the authorities of one Contracting Party and has been acquitted, or has been convicted and is serving, or has served, his sentence or has been pardoned, he may not be tried again for the same offence within the same territory by the authorities of another Contracting Party. However, nothing in this paragraph shall prevent the military authorities of the sending State from trying a member of its force for any violation of rules of discipline arising from an act or omission which constituted an offence for which he was tried by the authorities of another Contracting Party.' NATO Status of Forces Agreement, 19 June 1951, 4 U.S.T. 1792.

[206] *Ley Orgánica* 6/1985, B.O.E. 1985, at 157, available at: <http://www.juridicas.com/base_datos/Admin/lo6-1985.l1tl.html>.

[207] Van den Wyngaert and Stessens, "The International *Non Bis In Idem* Principle", at 784-785.

[208] *Idem.*

[209] E.g., European Convention on Extradition (Art. 9), 13 December 1957; European Convention on the International Validity of Criminal Judgments (Art. 53), 28 May 1970; European Convention on the Transfer of Proceedings in Criminal Matters (Art. 35), 15 May 1972.

[210] E.g., Convention on Laundering Search, Seizure and Confiscation of the Proceeds from Crime (Art. 18(1)(e)), 1990.

declaration in this respect.[211] In treaties regulating the transfer of proceedings in criminal matters, State parties are also often under an obligation to bar prosecution where a person is the subject of a pardon or amnesty in another contracting State due to the principle of *ne bis in idem*.[212] However, there does not appear to be an actual rule of international rule prohibiting a State from extraditing a person who has already been acquitted or convicted of the same crime to another country for the same offence.[213]

Member States of the ICC Statute have begun to draft legislation aimed as ensuring co-operation and judicial assistance. It has been suggested that such Acts should include a complete regulation of *ne bis in idem* implementing and developing Article 20 of the ICC Statute at the transnational horizontal level.[214] Given that the ICC is bound to a large extent by the decisions of national courts, including those of non-party States, it makes little sense that State parties should not also be so bound.

6.3.2 **Fundamental defects in the trial/Sham trial**

An important exception to the *ne bis in idem* rule is when there were fundamental defects in the first trial which could affect the outcome the case. Such an exception was included in Article 4(2) of Protocol No. 7 of the ECHR.[215] English law allows retrials in cases of mistrials or hung juries,[216] although these technically do not amount to an acquittal.[217] The ICC Statute also allows for a conviction or sentence to be revised if 'one or more of the judges who participated in the conviction or

[211] E.g., European Convention on Mutual Assistance in Criminal Matters 1959 (see, e.g., the declarations of Belgium (*Belgisch Staatsblad – Moniteur belge*, 23 October 1975)).

[212] For example, the European Convention on Transfer of Proceedings in Criminal Matters, 15 May 1972, provides in Art. 35 (Under Part V *Ne bis in idem*): '1. A person in respect of whom a final and enforceable criminal judgment has been rendered may for same act neither be prosecuted nor sentenced nor subjected to enforcement of a sanction in another Contracting State: (b) if the sanction imposed: (ii) has been wholly, or with respect to the part not enforced, the subject of a pardon or amnesty'; the UN Model Treaty on Extradition, UN Doc. A/RES/45/116 of 14 December 1990, provides that a request for extradition for a person may be refused if that person has become immune from prosecution or punishment, including by reason of amnesty (Art. 3(e)); see also Arts. 10(3), Art. 12(1), and Art. 53 (1)(b)(ii) European Convention on the International Validity of Criminal Judgments, 28 May 1970; Art. 62(2) of the Convention Applying the Schengen Agreement of 14 June 1985 between the Governments of the States of the Benelux Economic Union, the Federal Republic of Germany and the French Republic, on the Gradual Abolition of Checks at Their Common Borders.

[213] See, e.g., German Constitutional Court [*Bundesverfassungsgericht*], 31 May 1987, BVerfGE 75, 1 *Neue Juristische Wochenschrift* 2155 (1987) (holding that a person who had been convicted and sentenced for three years in Greece could be extradited to Turkey where he had been convicted and sentenced to a custodial sentence of eight years on the same facts).

[214] De La Cuesta, "Concurrent National and International Criminal Jurisdiction", at 733.

[215] Art. 4(2) of Protocol No. 7 of the ECHR: 'The provisions of the proceeding paragraph shall not prevent the reopening of the case in accordance with the law and penal procedure of the State concerned … if there has been a fundamental defect in the previous proceedings, which could affect the outcome of the case.'

[216] The Law Commission, *Double Jeopardy and Prosecution Appeals* (2001), Cm. 5048, at 30.

[217] See *Richardson* v. *United States*, United States, 468 US 317 (1984), at 325-26.

confirmation of the charges has committed … an act of serious misconduct or serious breach of duty of sufficient gravity to justify removal of that judge or those judges.'[218]

The fundamental defect exception has developed through the constitutive instruments of the *ad hoc* international criminal tribunals and the ICC and the hybrid courts to include the rule that *ne bis in idem* shall not apply if the first proceeding was for the purpose of shielding the person concerned from criminal responsibility or was otherwise not conducted independently or impartially in accordance with the norms of due process recognised by international law and was conducted in a manner which, in the circumstances, was inconsistent with an intent to bring the person concerned to justice.[219] According to the UN Secretary-General's 1993 Report, Article 10(2)(b) of the ICTY Statute allows the ICTY to prosecute an individual previously tried by a national court where 'conditions of impartiality, independence or effective means of adjudication were not guaranteed in the proceedings before national courts.'[220]

Some national laws have adopted the same approach. For example, in Canada, the Crimes Against Humanity and War Crimes Act of 2000 provides that a person may not plead *autrefois acquit* or *autrefois convict*, or pardon, if he or she was tried by a foreign court and the proceedings were for the purpose of shielding him or her from criminal liability, or were not otherwise conducted independently or impartially and were conducted in a manner that, in the circumstances, was inconsistent with an intent to bring the person to justice.[221] In a similar vein, the Constitutional Court of Colombia held in a 2003 judgment that where a human rights supervisory organ has found that Colombia breached its treaty obligations by failing to carry out an effective investigation, a case resulting in a judgment of acquittal can be reopened without violating the principles of *res judicata* and *non bis in idem*.[222] The Inter-American Court of Human Rights has held in two judgments that the *ne bis in idem* protection in Article 8(4) of the ACHR is not absolute and does not apply where: 'i) the intervention of the court that heard the case and decided to dismiss it or to acquit a person responsible for violating human rights or international law, was intended to shield the accused party from criminal responsibility; ii) the proceedings were not conducted independently or impartially in accordance with due procedural guarantees, or iii) there was no real intent to bring those responsible

[218] Art. 84(b) ICC Statute.

[219] ICTY Statute, Art. 10(2)(b); ICTR Statute, Art. 9(2)(b); ICC Statute, Art. 20(3)(a) and (b); SCSL Statute, Art. 9(2)(b), UNTAET Regulation 2000/15, Section 11.3(a) and (b), affirmed in UNTAET Regulation 2000/30 on Transitional Rules of Criminal Procedure, Section 4. The ILC also included this rule in Art. 12(2)(a)(i) and (ii) of its Draft Code of Crimes against the Peace and Security of Mankind, ILC Report 1996.

[220] Report of the Secretary-General pursuant to paragraph 2 of Security Council Resolution 808 (1993), UN Doc. S/25704, 3 May 1993, para. 66.

[221] Art. 12(2) Crimes Against Humanity and War Crimes Act, 2000, c.24, available at: <http://www.iccnow.org/documents/Canada.CrAgH.WcrEng.pdf>.

[222] Judgment C-004/03 (20 January 2003).

to justice.'[223] According to the Court, a judgment rendered in such circumstances produces an 'apparent' or 'fraudulent' *res judicata* case.[224]

International law scholars have advocated such an exception to be part of any transnational *ne bis in idem* principle.[225] The exception reflects an appropriate balance between the legitimacy of the procedural bar and the need to ensure that this does not result in impunity in cases of international crimes. However, some States may be reluctant to allow their courts to make such politically sensitive findings about the judgments of other States' courts. In the *Guatemala Genocide* case, the Spanish Supreme Court (*Tribunal Supremo*) raised the concern that asserting universal jurisdiction based upon on 'the real or apparent inactivity of local courts implies a judgment of one state's courts about the ability to administer justice of the similarly situated organs of another sovereign state (sec. II[6]).'[226] While such an 'unable or unwilling' inquiry 'might be appropriate for the International Criminal Court, national courts should not be making these kinds of judgments, which could have an important effect on foreign relations and should be left to the political branches.'[227] In this respect, a question may be raised as to whether the 'sham trial' exception is easily transposable to the transnational context.

As noted previously, the fundamental defect exception could also have been used to allow the Extraordinary Chambers in the Courts of Cambodia to avoid the bar of *ne bis in idem* in relation to re-prosecuting Ieng Sary, had he been indicted with this offence, who has previously been tried and convicted for genocide in an *in absentia* trial in 1979 and was later pardoned in 1996, for genocide. Although some significant efforts were made at the first trial to ensure the proceedings had a semblance of fairness under the circumstances prevailing at the time,[228] the fact

---

[223] *Almonacid-Arellano, et al.,* v. *Chile*, IACtHR, Preliminary Objections, Merits, Reparations and Costs. Judgment of 26 September 2006 (ser. C), No. 154, para. 154. The Court cites the Rome Statute as authority for this interpretation. See also *Case of La Cantuta* v. *Peru*, IACtHR, Merits, Reparations and Costs. Judgment of 29 November 2006 (ser. C), No. 162, at para: 130(1) and 153: 'The reopening of investigations within domestic jurisdiction would not affect in any way whatsoever the *non bis in idem* principle embodied in Article 8(4) of the American Convention, since the *res judicata* principle never applied, because the alleged perpetrators were tried by a court which, under Article 8 of the Convention, was not competent, independent and impartial and did not satisfy the requirements of a competent tribunal. This is so because the requirement of a previous acquittal is not met when said judgment lacks legal effects for standing in open contradiction to international duties. Accordingly, the Peruvian State must conduct a new trial with all the guarantees of due process in order to rectify the structural deficiencies of previous military proceedings.'

[224] *Case of Carpio-Nicolle, et al.,* Judgment of 22 November 2004 (ser. C), No. 117, para. 131. See also *Case of La Cantuta* v. *Peru*, IACtHR, Merits, Reparations and Costs. Judgment of 29 November 2006 (ser. C), No. 162, at para.153: 'A judgment issued in the circumstances described above only provides "fictitious" or "fraudulent" grounds for double jeopardy.'

[225] E.g., international law scholars approved the exception generally at the transnational level in the Draft Resolution adopted in Berlin on 4 June 2003, "Concurrent and International Criminal Jurisdiction and the Principle of '*Ne Bis In Idem*'", 73 *International Review of Penal Law* 1182 (2002), Art. II, 7.

[226] Naomi Roht-Arriaza, "Guatemala Genocide Case", 100 *AJIL* 208-209 (2006).

[227] *Idem.*

[228] Defendants were entitled to a lawyer or other representation, were given prior notice of the charges, and could cross-examine witnesses and present a defence in court. Where the accused was

remains that the Tribunal was not completely impartial or independent[229] and suffered from a paucity of resources and investigative expertise[230] leading most States to view it as a show trial staged to justify the intervention of Vietnam in Cambodia.[231]

6.3.3 Retrial in the case of newly discovered evidence or facts

Another exception that has been formulated to *ne bis in idem* is where newly discovered evidence or facts have come to light signifying that a different outcome could have been achieved in the first trial.[232] Article 4(3) of Protocol No. 7 of the ECHR explicitly allows a case to be re-opened if there is evidence of new or newly discovered facts. The ICC Statute also permits individuals convicted by the ICC to apply for revisions of their convictions or sentences if they can introduce new evidence that was not available at the time of trial that would have likely caused a different result.[233] They may also apply for such revision if it is discovered that evi-

---

absent, a lawyer would be appointed by the Tribunal and the subpoena would be posted at the office of the Phnom Penh city People's Committee or broadcast on radio (which is what happened). The trial was also to be conducted in public. In addition, a significant number of foreign lawyers were participants in the trial, 'for the evident reason of reflecting international standards of justice and thereby enhancing the legitimacy of the proceedings.' See Decree Law No. 1: Establishment of People's Revolutionary Tribunal at Phnom Penh to Try the Pol Pot-Ieng Sary Clique for the Crime of Genocide, Phnom Penh, 15 July 1979, Heng Samrin, President, People's Revolutionary Council of Kampuchea, Arts. 5-7. See also Presiding Judge, Decision on Trial Procedure at the Session on the Crime of Genocide of the Pol Pot-Ieng Sary Clique, Phnom Penh, 4 August 1979, Keo Chanda, Presiding Judge, People's Revolutionary Tribunal, Document 1.07 in Howard J. De Nike, John Quigley and Kenneth J. Robinson (eds.), *Genocide in Cambodia: Documents from the Trial of Pol Pot and Ieng Sary* (Philadelphia: University of Pennsylvania Press, 2000), at 53, paras. II, VII. See also List of Foreign Lawyers, Document 1.11b in *ibid.*, at 62.

[229] At that time, there was no strict separation of the judicial function from the executive function. The presiding judge, Mr. Keo Chanda, was the Minister of Information, Press and Culture. Two of the people's assessors were also government employees. A third member was an army official. Composition of the People's Revolutionary Tribunal at Phnom Penh to Try the Pol Pot-Ieng Sary Clique for the Crime of Genocide, Instituted by Decree Law No. 1 of July 15, 1979, of the People's Revolutionary Council of Kampuchea, Document 1.08 in De Nike, Quigley & Robinson (eds.), *Genocide in Cambodia*, at 56. Some of the others had provided incriminating evidence at the pretrial stage. One of the people's assessors had filed a statement as a victim, while another, a doctor of pediatrics, had written a report about the effects of Khmer Rouge policy on the health of children. J. Quigley, "Introduction", in De Nike, Quigley & Robinson (eds.), *Genocide in Cambodia*, at 8.

[230] Due to a scarcity of lawyers and other personnel (most intellectuals had been killed during the Khmer Rouge regime) and a paucity of resources, 'no one practiced law, and there were no regular courts.' There were few police who had knowledge of scientific methods of evidence gathering.

[231] When the trial was concluded, Vietnam's representative at the UN asked the UN Secretary-General to circulate a copy of the tribunal's judgment as a UN document, which was done. Letter dated 17 September 1979 from the Permanent Representative of Viet Nam to the United Nations addressed to the Secretary-General, UN Doc. A/34/491, 20 September 1979.

[232] This exception probably stems from the *Ball* doctrine by which a defendant may be tried twice for the same offence by successfully appealing his erroneous conviction. *United States* v. *Ball*, United States, 163 US 662 (1896), at 672.

[233] Art. 81 ICC Statute.

dence on which the conviction depended was false, forged or falsified.[234] However, not all countries accept these exceptions to *ne bis in idem*.[235]

A broadening of this exception has occurred in England and Australia in recent times in cases of *acquittals* of serious crimes, including international crimes.[236] In England, the Criminal Justice Act of 2003 (CJA)[237] abrogated the *ne bis in idem* protection of those acquitted of serious crimes, including the crimes under sections 51 or 52 of the International Criminal Court Act (2001), c.17,[238] where 'new and compelling evidence' exists[239] and it is in 'in the public interest for the application to proceed.'[240] This also applies to acquittals in foreign courts if the offence amounts to a qualifying offence under the Act.[241] 'New' evidence is defined in the Act as that which was 'not adduced in the proceedings in which the person was acquitted (nor, if those were appeal proceedings, in early proceedings to which the appeal related).'[242] 'Compelling [evidence] is reliable ... substantial ... and in the context of the outstanding issues ... highly probative of the case against the acquitted person.'[243] Given that the prosecutor may rely on evidence that was 'not adduced' in the first trial, this essentially allows him or her to use evidence that he or she had in possession and decided not to use or had previously ignored.[244]

In Australia, similar legislation has been proposed by the Model Criminal Code Officers Committee (MCCOC), Australia's national body of criminal law experts.[245] One state – New South Wales – has adopted legislation implementing the suggested amendments. The Crimes (Appeal and Review) Amendment (Double

---

[234] Art. 84(b) ICC Statute.

[235] E.g., Egypt, where Art. 455 of the Criminal Procedure Code provides that: 'The issuance of a final judgment bars the reopening of the same case, even if, new evidence of new facts have arisen or if, the criminal act may be prosecuted under a different provision of law.' Quoted in El Zeidy, "The Doctrine of Double Jeopardy", at 199. This is also the case in Italy. Bailin, "Double jeopardy", at 104.

[236] Finland allows criminal proceedings to be re-opened where an acquittal has been obtained through fraud and where fresh evidence becomes available which could have led to a conviction which is substantially more severe than that which was imposed. See Finland's reservation to the ICCPR, para. 6.

[237] Criminal Justice Act, 2003, c. 44 (England), available at: <www.hmso.gov.uk/acts/acts 2003/20030044.htm>.

[238] *Ibid.*, § 75(1).

[239] *Ibid.*, § 78(1).

[240] *Ibid.*, § 76(4)(b).

[241] *Ibid.*, § 75(4). Bailin has observed that it may be difficult to reconcile this provision with Art. 54 of the Schengen Convention which contains no similar exception for new and compelling evidence. Bailin, "Double jeopardy", at 114.

[242] Criminal Justice Act, 2003, c. 44 (England), § 78(2).

[243] *Ibid.*, § 78(3).

[244] Taylor, "England and Australia Relax the Double Jeopardy Privilege", at 191. Notably, this differs from the previous definition of 'new' and 'compelling' in the Criminal Justice Bill, which was evidence 'not known to an officer or prosecutor at or before the time of acquittal.'

[245] Model Criminal Code Officers Committee of the Standing Committee of Attorneys-General, *Discussion Paper: Chapter 2, Issue Estoppel, Double Jeopardy, and Prosecution Appeals Against Acquittals*, November 2003 (hereafter, MCCOC Discussion Paper).

Jeopardy) Act No. 69 (2006) (NSW Act)[246] allows retrial of a person acquitted of a 'life sentence offence' where there is 'fresh and compelling' evidence of guilt and it is 'in the interests of justice.'[247] 'Fresh' evidence is defined as that which was 'not adduced in the proceedings in which the person was acquitted' and 'could not have been adduced in those proceedings with the exercise of reasonable diligence.'[248] The test for 'fresh' evidence is thus more stringent than the English equivalent. The legislation adopts the same test for 'compelling' evidence as the UK Criminal Justice Act.[249] The legislation also allows for a retrial after an acquittal is 'tainted' by the commission of an administrative justice offence (e.g. perjury).[250] In both the CJA and the MCCOC Discussion Paper the section permitting retrial applies retroactively.[251]

To some extent, the new legislation in the UK and Australia departs from the so-called *Sambasivam* principle,[252] which holds that a verdict 'is binding and conclusive in all subsequent proceedings.'[253] The English House of Lords referred to this as 'cause of action estoppel.'[254] Australian courts have interpreted the principle as meaning that 'the prosecution could not, in any subsequent trial, lead evidence which called into question a previous acquittal.'[255] Thus, for example, a subsequent charge of perjury may not be brought against a person acquitted in a previous criminal trial in which they had stated they had not committed the offence.[256] English courts, by contrast, have applied a more lenient interpretation of *Sambasivam*,

---

[246] The Crimes (Appeal and Review) Amendment (Double Jeopardy) Act No. 69 (2006), available at: <http://www.legislation.nsw.gov.au/maintop/scanact/sessional/NONE/0> (hereafter, NSW Act).

[247] *Ibid.*, § 100.

[248] *Ibid.*, § 102(2).

[249] *Ibid.*, § 102(3).

[250] *Ibid.*, § 101(1).

[251] Criminal Justice Act, 2003, c. 44, § 75(6); MCCOC Discussion Paper, at 103. One can imagine that this might constitute an abuse of process in certain circumstances. Bailin, "Double jeopardy", at 111.

[252] *Sambavisum* v. *Public Prosecutor, Federation of Malaya* [1950] AC at 458.

[253] *Rogers* v. *Q.*, Australia, 181 *CLR* 251 (1994), at 259 (quoting *Sambasivam* [1950] AC at 479).

[254] MCCOC Discussion Paper, at 5. This is distinguished from 'issue estoppel,' which arises when the Crown seeks to 're-litigate a … factual issue determined in favour of the accused in a previous trial.' *Rogers* v. *Q.*, Australia, 181 *CLR* 251 (1994). Courts deal with 'issue estoppel' under the abuse of process standard by staying proceedings when 'their continuance would be unjustifiably vexatious and oppressive for the reason that it sought to litigate anew a case which had already been disposed of by earlier proceedings.' *Rogers* v. *Q.*, Australia, 181 *CLR* 256 (1994).

[255] MCCOC Discussion Paper, at 5. *R.* v. *Storey*, 140 *CLR* 364 (1978); *Garrett* v. *The Queen*, Australia 139 *CLR* 437 (1977), at 445 (*per* C.J. Barwick); *R.* v. *Kemp*, Australia, 83 *CLR* 341. See also the Canadian case *R.* v. *Arp*, Canada [1998] 3 SCR 339.

[256] *Carroll*, 213 *CLR* 648 (citing *Rogers*, at 273). In this case, the defendant had denied killing a seventeen-month-old baby under oath at trial in 1985. His conviction was quashed by the Court of Criminal Appeal of Queensland on the basis that the jury had not been properly instructed as to the prosecution's burden of proving the case beyond a reasonable doubt. 15 years later, a perjury charge was brought against Carroll after 'new' evidence showed the bruise marks on the deceased's thigh to match the defendant's teeth. The High Court dismissed the perjury verdict as an abuse of process, stating that the perjury trial was an attempt to 'try again the issue which was central to his trial for murder.'

which permits evidence in a subsequent trial for a different offence, which if true, would prove a defendant's guilt in an earlier case.[257] So long as the purpose of leading the evidence is to prove that the defendant is guilty in the subsequent offence, not to punish the defendant for the offence of which he has been acquitted, it may be admitted.[258] The NSW Act, by allowing a retrial after an acquittal is 'tainted' by the commission of an administrative justice offence, moves closer to the English interpretation. The New Zealand Court of Appeal has also recently followed the English approach.[259]

With regard to international crimes, such 'chipping away' at the *ne bis in idem* protection where 'fresh and compelling evidence' has come to light might be warranted in view of the gravity of such crimes, the overwhelming need for justice for the victims, and the dangers of impunity to continued social stability.[260] Applying a type of value-based test, the Inter-American Court of Human Rights has similarly held that 'if there appear new facts or evidence that make it possible to ascertain the identity of those responsible for human rights violations or for crimes against humanity, investigations can be reopened, even if the case ended in an acquittal with the authority of a final judgment, since the dictates of justice, the rights of the victims, and the spirit and the wording of the American Convention supersedes the protection of the *ne bis in idem* principle.'[261]

In its General Comment on Article 14(7), the Human Rights Committee has expressed the view that the reopening of criminal proceedings 'justified by exceptional circumstances' did not violate the principle of *ne bis in idem* by drawing a distinction between the 'resumption' of criminal proceedings, which was allowed under Article 14(7) and 'retrial' which was not.[262] Thus, Article 14(7) 'permits a state's prosecuting authorities to apply to "re-open" an acquittal, in exceptional circumstances, after it has the quality of *res judicata*; but it prevents the prosecuting authorities from bringing fresh criminal proceedings on their own initiative.'[263] From this perspective a proceedings based on 'new evidence' is more properly characterised as continuation of the first case rather than a new trial for the same crime, hence the *ne bis in idem* rule does not arise.

---

[257] *R.* v. *Z.* [2000] 2 AC 483 (2000).

[258] *Idem.* In this case, the defendant charged with rape alleged that his victim consented to intercourse or in the alternative that he believed she consented. The prosecution wished to introduce the testimony of four other women from earlier trials in which the defendant had used the same argument. Applying this interpretation of *Sambasivum*, the House of Lords permitted the prosecution to introduce the testimony.

[259] *R.* v. *Degnan*, New Zealand [2001] 1 *NZLR* 280.

[260] See El Zeidy, "The Doctrine of Double Jeopardy", at 214, noting that 'the reopening of cases in circumstances of acquittals guarantees the rights of victims and society.'

[261] *Almonacid-Arellano, et al.,* v. *Chile*, IACtHR, Preliminary Objections, Merits, Reparations and Costs. Judgment of 26 September 2006 (ser. C), No. 154, para. 154.

[262] HRC General Comment No. 13: 'Equality before the courts and the right to a fair and public hearing by an independent court established by law' (Art. 14), 13 April 1984, at para. 19.

[263] Bailin, "Double jeopardy", at 110.

6.3.4 The State claim to exercise jurisdiction over offences committed on its territory

The enforcement of the principle of *ne bis in idem* is extremely sensitive to the 'hierarchy' of jurisdictional principles in the sense that those States with a stronger jurisdictional claim (i.e., territoriality) are less likely to recognise the *res judicata* effects of other States' judgments, while those States with the weaker jurisdictional claim (i.e., universality) are more likely to recognise the *res judicata* effect of foreign judgments.[264] Many continental jurisdictions have consistently refused to recognise the *res judicata* effect of foreign judgments in cases where the crime was committed in its territory.[265] Thus in Belgium courts have allowed new prosecutions for crimes despite a foreign acquittal or conviction of the same persons.[266] This is also the position in Austria,[267] France,[268] and Germany.[269] The notable exception to the trend is the Netherlands, which recognizes the *res judicata* effects of foreign judgments regardless of where the crime took place.[270] In addition, almost every international *ne bis in idem* protection system, such as the Schengen Convention, includes an exception for acts that took place in the territory of the State that wants to initiate fresh proceedings against a person previously tried.[271] In the case of the Schengen Convention, this does not apply where the facts also took place on the territory of the State where the first trial took place, however this still supports the tendency to give more weight to the territorial State.

Conversely, where States are exercising extra-territorial jurisdiction, they tend to consider that primacy should be given to the judgment of the court in the State where the offence took place. This is the case for Belgium, which recognises foreign judgments with regard to crimes committed outside Belgium provided that the defendant must have been tried abroad for the same offence and must have either been acquitted or have served his sentence, if convicted.[272] This remains the case where the sentence could not be enforced due to a statute of limitations, amnesty or pardon.[273] In France, the *ne bis in idem* principle does not apply in

---

[264] El Zeidy, "The Doctrine of Double Jeopardy", at 206-210.

[265] Van den Wyngaert and Stessens, "The International *Non Bis In Idem* Principle", at 783.

[266] See, e.g., Belgian Supreme Court, 15 December 1952 (1953) I Pasicrisie 262 and 20 February 1991, *Rechtskundig Weekblad* (1991-92), at 131.

[267] See Art. 65 Austrian Code of Criminal Procedure.

[268] See M. Pralus, "Etude en droit pénal international et en droit communautaire d'un aspect du principe non bis in idem: non bis", *Revue des Sciences Criminelles* (1996), at 559-564.

[269] See W. Schomburg, "Das Schengener Durchführungsübereinkommen. Anmerkungen und Bewertungen zu Titel III (Polizei und Sicherheit) aus einer deutschen justitiellen Sicht", *J.Bl.* 556-557 (1997).

[270] Art. 68 Dutch Penal Code. See P. Blaaw, "*Non Bis In Idem*", in Bert Swart and André Klip (eds.), *International Criminal Law in The Netherlands* (Edition iuscrim, 1997), at 75-84.

[271] Art. 54(1)(a) Schengen Convention; Art. 53(3) European Convention on the International Validity of Criminal Judgments; Art. 35(3) European Convention on the Transfer of Proceedings in Criminal Matters.

[272] Art. 13 of the Preliminary Title to the Criminal Procedure Code (Belgium).

[273] *Idem.*

the case of extraterritorial jurisdiction on the basis of the protective principle.[274] However, in Germany and Italy, no such *ne bis in idem* principle extends to extraterritorial offences.[275]

6.3.5 Exception for certain offences

States often include an exception to the *ne bis in idem* rule for a number of specific offences. These are invariably tied to the public interests of the State, such as State security, and for this reason, often mirror the offences over which a State exercises the protective principle. Such exceptions have been linked to the right of every State to prosecute political offences.[276] A further exception is made for the territorial State where the act was committed by a public servant of that State in breach of his or her official duties.[277] The treaties providing for *ne bis in idem* also contain such exceptions. Such provisions grant the States parties a wide margin of discretion to refuse the foreign judgments of other States based upon national interests.

One could argue that since all States have an interest in the repression of international crimes, these should also form an exception to the *ne bis in idem* rule. This proposition is rejected in this book. Any exception to the principle of *ne bis in idem* should be narrowly construed in view of the need to protect individuals from the unfairness of being tried and perhaps punished twice for the same crime. The exceptions to the rule for certain offences, while giving States a fairly wide margin of discretion, are still limited to those crimes which specially affect a particular State's national interests. Opening this up to all international crimes would counter the rationale behind the exception and be a disproportionate response to the need to fight impunity in relation to the need to ensure the universal rights of defendants.

6.3.6 Additional serious offences

Some commentators have argued that where an additional serious offence is possible that was not prosecuted at the first trial then a second trial may be justified, providing that the principle of deduction is applied.[278] As noted, one of the concerns driving the dual sovereignty doctrine was that a State might be prevented from prosecuting a person for a more serious charge when already acquitted or convicted in another State's courts for a minor offence. A contrary position was taken by the UK House of Lords in the seminal case of *Connelly* v. *D.P.P.*,[279] in which the Court found that the *autrefois* plea prohibited retrials for both lesser and

274 M. Pralus, "Etude en droit pénal international et en droit communautaire d'un aspect du principe non bis in idem: non bis", *Revue des Sciences Criminelles* (1996), at 561-562.

275 Van den Wyngaert and Stessens, "The International *Non Bis In Idem* Principle", at 748.

276 Donnedieu de Vabres, *AIDI*, Vol. II (1950), at 259-261.

277 Draft Resolution, adopted in Berlin on 4 June 2003, "Concurrent and International Criminal Jurisdiction and the Principle of '*Ne Bis In Idem*'", 73 *International Review of Penal Law* 1182 (2002), Art. II, 2.3.

278 See, e.g., *ibid.*, Art. II, 2.2.

279 *Connelly* v. *D.P.P.*, United Kingdom [1964] AC at 1254.

greater offences: 'a party accused of a minor offence ... shall not be charged again on the same facts in a more aggravated form.'[280] An exception to this is for murder 'if the death occurs after the acquittal or conviction on the lesser charge.'[281]

The exception to the *ne bis in idem* rule in the Statutes of the ICTY and ICTR which allows the tribunals to re-prosecute a person who has been acquitted or convicted at the national level for 'an ordinary crime' would seem to be a variation of this rationale. Relying on this practice, the argument has been put forward that such a rule is transposable to the national and inter-State level, so that a hybrid or domestic court could re-try a person for an international crime who had been previously tried on the same facts by another court for an ordinary crime. For example, David Boyle has argued that there would be no double jeopardy bar to Ieng Sary being tried by the Extraordinary Chambers of Cambodia for genocide despite the fact that Sary was found guilty of 'genocide' in the 1979 *in absentia* trial (and later pardoned in 1996) because the definition of the crime prosecuted at the first trial, 'adjusted in language to ensure a conviction,'[282] differed from the 1948 Genocide Convention to such as degree that it may be seen as an application of purely internal law.[283] The strength of this argument is debatable. Notwithstanding any doubts about the independence or impartiality of the 1979 trial (which might be used to argue that the first trial was fundamentally defective), it would seem that the offence prosecuted in the 1979 trial was substantially the same as the definition of genocide contained in the 2001 Law Establishing the Extraordinary Chambers. Even if the language of the definition of genocide in the Decree setting up the tribunal varied slightly from the definition in the 2001 Law, during the proceedings John Quigley, an international lawyer from the United States, was asked to provide a statement on whether he thought that genocide as defined in the 1948 Genocide Convention had been committed in Cambodia during the 1979 trial, and concluded that it had.[284] This indicates that the Decree intended to reflect the definition in the Genocide Convention, as does the 2001 Law. Therefore it would be difficult to argue that Ieng Sary was convicted in 1979 for 'an ordinary crime' and may now be re-tried for 'an international crime.'

It would seem that rather than relying on the 'more serious charge' rationale, courts would do better to strictly apply the offence-based '*idem*' test, so that if the first trial prosecuted a person for a crime that varied substantially in its constituent elements from the international crime for which he has subsequently been indicted, the second court is not barred from re-trying the person. This might also resolve the

---

[280] *Ibid.*, at 1332 (*per* L.J. Hodson).

[281] *Idem.* See also *R.* v. *Kerry Young*, United Kingdom, Court of Appeal, 24 October 2005 (unreported) Case No. 0405955 D2 – extempore judgment.

[282] This definition, established by Decree-Law No. 1 of the PRK, is reproduced in UN Doc. A/C3/34/1, 30 July 1979, para. C1.

[283] David Boyle, "Trying Ieng Sary", *Phnom Penh Post*, Issue 9/21, 13-16 October 2000, available at: <http://www.phnompenhpost.com/TXT/letters/L921-4.htm>. On this point, see *Polyukhovich* v. *The Commonwealth*, High Court of Australia, 65 *CLR* 521 (1991), *per* Brennan J, at 545.

[284] Quigley, "Introduction", in *Genocide in Cambodia*, at 2.

question of whether the more aggravated form of international crime is sufficiently distinct from the lesser offence to warrant a further proceeding.

6.4 Preliminary conclusions

The move towards a transnational *ne bis in idem* principle may be another manifestation of the changing face of sovereignty in international relations, which puts increased emphasis on the protection of individual rights rather than the protection of sovereign interests.[285] Many commentators have advocated a 'transnational application of the classical *non bis in idem* rule balancing the interests of the individual not to undergo double jeopardy and the interests of States to exercise their international *erga omnes* obligations under the often conventional or customary rule of *aut dedere aut iudicare* relative to most international crimes.'[286] The problem with a transnational *ne bis in idem* protection is said to lay in the diversity of judicial systems and legal characterisations of proscribed acts, as well as the limited mutual confidence between States. While the Schengen Convention and budding European *ne bis in idem* transnational right provide a model for how a transnational double jeopardy rule could work, it may be many years before the international community will feel the same level of mutual trust in the legal systems of every State as do the members of the EC or the EU.

Having said this, the corollary effects of the trans-jurisdictional ICC *ne bis in idem* procedural bar might hasten this development at least as between States parties to the ICC Statute.[287] Moreover, the clarification of the definitions of genocide, crimes against humanity and war crimes in the Rome Statute will have helped to harmonise to a large extent the elements of those offences in domestic legislation, thereby removing one of the main sources of difficulty courts face when trying to implement *ne bis in idem* at the international level, i.e., identifying what counts as the '*idem*.' In this book, it is advocated that any transnational *ne bis in idem* principle as applied to international crimes be based on an offence-based '*idem*' in view of the gravity and distinct characteristics of international crimes, which have specific consequences under international law. A conduct-based '*idem*' would provide too broad a protection disproportionate to and perhaps even inconsistent with the distinct obligation to prosecute international crimes. The narrowness of this protection could be offset by application of the deduction of sentence principle in any subsequent conviction.

---

[285] Kofi Annan, "Two Concepts of Sovereignty", *The Economist*, 18 September 1999, at 49. See also El Zeidy, "The Doctrine of Double Jeopardy", at 200: 'the traditional view of the doctrine of dual sovereignties or separate sovereignties is rapidly changing with the development of international and regional human rights norms.'

[286] Poels, "A Need for Transnational *Non Bis In Idem* Protection", at 343.

[287] For a discussion on how it might affect third States, see Giuseppe Palmisano, "ICC and Third States", in Flavia Lattanzi and William A. Schabas (eds.), *Essays on the Rome Statute of the International Criminal Court*, Vol. I (Il Sirente, 1999), at 415.

With regard to the question of whether out-of-court settlements (including 'use immunity,' truth-for-amnesty deals and plea bargains) should be given a *ne bis in idem* effect trans-nationally in cases of international crimes, international law does not seem to proscribe a set answer, though the weight of State practice suggests that only final criminal judgments have a *res judicata* character. Nonetheless, courts might be influenced by the underlying principles underlying the international criminal system, such as the right to the truth, the need for justice, and reparations for victims, as well as the concern for social stability and international peace and security. Where such deals appear to respect such principles and particularly where they have been brokered with the participation of international actors, it may be prudent for the courts of other States to extend a *ne bis in idem* effect to these types of out of court settlements, particularly in view of the need for coherency and legitimacy in the international criminal law enforcement system.

In those countries that do not recognise a *ne bis in idem* blocking effect to foreign decisions,[288] there is usually a statutory obligation to deduct, mitigate or remit the sentence in order to give 'a certain effect' to the foreign sentence already fully or partially enforced.[289] Most commentators advocate the view that courts adopt the *ne bis poena in idem* principle – a corollary principle to *ne bis in idem* – which entails that any sentencing or penalties already served or paid by an accused for the same offence or set of facts should be deducted from any subsequent penalty imposed for the same offence or facts. This, it is argued, is less of a restriction upon a State's sovereignty than full *ne bis in idem* protection, and hence more likely to be accepted.[290] The basic fairness of the principle of deduction would seem to be apparent and the rule is an important safety net for those falling between the significant cracks of the *ne bis in idem* protection.

In sum, an interests-analysis approach that balances the policy and value-based rationales underlying the *ne bis in idem* principle and the interests of States to prosecute those accused of international crimes provides an appropriate framework for resolving the question of whether a transnational *ne bis in idem* principle should be recognised.[291] For example, the ECJ in interpreting the scope of the transnational *ne bis in idem* principle contained in Article 54 of the Schengen Convention has attempted to 'to strike a delicate and appropriate balance between two central interests enshrined in the Treaties: on the one hand, ensuring a high level of security for citizens, which includes to eliminate "save havens" for criminals; and on the other hand, to avoid double prosecutions/convictions for the same acts in the light of the individual's freedom of movement.'[292] One group of commentators has

[288] E.g., Japan, the People's Republic of China and Poland.

[289] De La Cuesta, "Concurrent National and International Criminal Jurisdiction", at 724.

[290] Conway, "*Ne Bis In Idem* and the International Criminal Tribunals", at 357.

[291] El Zeidy, "The Doctrine of Double Jeopardy", at 232: 'Two conflicting interests need to be saved: on the one hand, the fundamental right of the individual not to face multiple harassment, and on the other hand, the right of the international community in reprisal and guaranteeing the imposition of adequate sentences on those who committed such grave crimes.'

[292] Martin Wasmeier and Nadine Thwaites, "The development of *ne bis in idem* into a transnational fundamental human right in EU law: comments on recent developments", 31 *European Law Review* 578 (2006).

argued that *ne bis in idem* should be treated as a matter public policy rather than a fundamental principle of international law. In this sense, the principle is conceived not as a rule of law, but rather as 'a declaration of an ancient and well-established public policy, which may be disregarded when some other overriding policy consideration intervenes.'[293] This somewhat extreme position is rejected in this book. If international criminal law is to be conceived as a system, encompassing both national and international levels of enforcement jurisdiction, then a transnational and trans-jurisdictional *ne bis in idem* protection is vital to ensuring the integrity of that system and the fairness of proceedings for defendants. The 'sham trial' exception, as defined in the ICC Statute and other instruments, provides a useful measuring tool to decide if a subsequent prosecution is required in order to achieve justice or is merely a case of sovereign harassment of the individual contrary to the universal right of *ne bis in idem*.

---

[293] El Zeidy, "The Doctrine of Double Jeopardy", at 241, citing Paul A. McDermott, *Res Judicata and Double Jeopardy* (Ireland: Butterworths, 1999), at 207.

Chapter 7
ABUSE OF PROCESS

As noted in previous chapters, the doctrine of abuse of process is often raised in the context of prosecutions for international crimes where procedural irregularities in the way that accused persons have been brought before the court are alleged. This chapter concentrates on the abuse of process doctrine as a means to stay proceedings when used in the context of trials for international crimes. Commentators have noted that such issues go 'to the very legality of the criminal trial of an individual and highlights the separation of function between judiciary and executive.'[1]

The question in cases of abuse of process is not whether courts are automatically deprived of jurisdiction, but whether in the specific circumstances of a case, a court *should* exercise jurisdiction.[2] Thus, for instance the Appeals Chamber of the ICTY has held that a Trial Chamber's failure to dismiss the charges against an accused as an abuse of process do not fall within the purview of Rule 72(D) of the Rules of Procedure and Evidence, which deals exclusively with challenges to jurisdiction, i.e., challenges that an indictment on the ground that it does not relate to: (i) any of the persons indicated in Articles 1, 6, 7 and 9 of the Statute; (ii) the territories indicated in Articles 1, 8 and 9 of the Statute; (iii) the period indicated in Articles 1, 8 and 9 of the Statute; or (iv) any of the violations indicated in Articles 2, 3, 4, 5 and 7 of the Statute.[3]

Given that it is a question of discretion, it is perhaps not surprising that case law on the subject tends to be conflicting, depending on the specific facts of each case.[4] Nonetheless, although the results may differ, it is possible to discern a trend

[1] Robert J. Currie, "Abducted Fugitives Before the International Criminal Court: Problems and Prospects", 18 *Criminal Law Forum* 350 (2007).

[2] F.A. Mann, "Reflections on the Prosecution of Persons Abducted in Breach of International Law", Yoram Dinstein (ed.), *International Law at a Time of Perplexity: Essays in Honour of Shabtai Rosenne* (Dordrecht: Nijhoff, 1989), 407 at 414. See also *Situation in the Democratic Republic of the Congo in the Case of The Prosecutor* v. *Thomas Lubanga Dyilo*, ICC, Judgment on the Appeal of Mr. Thomas Lubanga Dyilo against the Decision on the Defence Challenge to the Jurisdiction of the Court pursuant to article 19(2) of the Statute of 3 October 2006, Case No. ICC-01/04-01/06 (OA4), 14 December 2006 (hereafter, *Lubanga* Appeals Judgment of 14 December 2006), para. 24.

[3] *Boškoski and Tarčulovski,* ICTY, Appeals Chamber, Case No. IT-04-82-AR72.2, Decision on Ljube Boškoski's Appeal on Jurisdiction, 9 January 2007, para. 5.

[4] The English Court of Appeal in *R.* v. *S. (SP)* noted that the discretion was 'an exercise of judicial assessment dependent on judgment rather than on any conclusion as to fact based on evidence.' [2006] 2 *Cr App R* 23, at 341, at H7.

in the balancing test that is applied by courts deciding on whether to apply the abuse of process doctrine in cases involving the most serious of crimes. To date, no court has ruled that the abuse of process doctrine cannot *per se* be applied to cases involving international crimes, although the most recent cases on the international level evidence a heavy presumption in favour of exercising jurisdiction in spite of prejudice to the defendant where they are accused of international crimes.

7.1 DEFINITION AND HISTORICAL BACKGROUND

The doctrine of abuse of process is often described as a *sui generis* procedural mechanism.[5] Abuse of process has been defined as something so unfair or wrong with the prosecution that the court should not allow a prosecutor to proceed with what is, in all other respects, a perfectly supportable case.[6] The doctrine is used to prevent miscarriages of justice which may occur in the event of prosecutorial behaviour that seriously circumvents basic defence rights of the accused, which may result in prejudice to the accused, and lead to a wrongful conviction.[7]

The doctrine has its roots in common law judicial practice and has been applied in a variety of situations. Most commonly, it has been applied as a way to stay proceedings in which the admission of evidence would have an adverse effect on the fairness of proceedings;[8] or where law enforcement officials are implicated in serious misconduct. With regard to the latter event, one of the situations in which this doctrine has been applied is where an accused has been kidnapped abroad. In addition to being a breach of the accused's rights to a lawful arrest, this may entail a breach of the sovereignty of the country where the kidnap occurred, and also may be a violation of existing extradition obligations.[9]

The jurisdiction to exercise the powers of staying proceedings is 'inherent' in the sense that such jurisdiction does not derive from any statute or rule of law,

---

[5] Geert-Jan Alexander Knoops, *Redressing Miscarriages of Justice: Practice and Procedure in National and International Criminal Law Cases* (Ardsley, NY: Transnational Publishers, Inc., 2006), at 175. See also *Lubanga* Appeals Judgment of 14 December 2006, para. 24.

[6] *Hui-Chi Ming* v. *R.* [1992] 1 AC 34, PC. *Black's Law Dictionary* defines it as 'the improper and tortuous use of a legitimately issued court process to obtain a result that is either unlawful or beyond the process's scope.' Bryan A. Garner, *Black's Law Dictionary,* 8th edn. (St. Paul, Minn: West Group, 2004), at 11.

[7] See *Brđanin and Talić*, ICTY, Trial Chamber II, Decision on Second Motion by Brđanin to Dismiss the Indictment, Case No. IT-99-36-PT, 16 May 2001, para. 5 (finding that if a 'Trial Chamber is satisfied that the absence of such resources will result in a miscarriage of justice, it has the inherent power and the obligation to stay the proceedings until the necessary resources are provided, in order to prevent the abuse of process involved in such a trial.'

[8] See *R* v. *Loosely and Attorney General's Reference (No 3 of 2000)* (2001) 4 *All ER* 897 *per* Lord Hofman; *R.* v. *Shannon* [2001] *WLR* 51, at 68.

[9] See *R.* v. *Horseferry Road Magistrates' Court*, Ex Parte *Bennett* [1994] 1 AC 42 (hereafter, *Bennett*); see also *State* v. *Ebrahim*, 1991 (2) SA 553, translated in 95 *ILR* 417, at 442 (hereafter, *Ebrahim*), on which see John Dugard, "No Jurisdiction over Abducted Persons in Roman-Dutch Law: *Male Captus, Male Detentus*", 7 *South African Journal of Human Rights* 199 (1991).

but 'from the very nature of the court as a superior court of law.'[10] Warbrick describes abuse of process as 'a power inherent to the criminal courts to avoid trials or processes oppressive to the accused.'[11] The ICC Appeals Chamber has stated in a similar vein that '[t]he power to stay proceedings is par excellence a power assumed by the guardians of the judicial process, the judges, to see that the stream of justice flows unpolluted.'[12]

The origins of the discretion to stay proceedings on the basis of abuse of process may be traced to its use in civil litigation, which goes back at least over 100 years.[13] Lord Blackburn noted in an 1885 civil case that:

> '... from early times ... the Court had inherently in its power the right to see that its process was not abused by a proceeding without reasonable grounds, so as to be vexatious and harassing – the Court had the right to protect itself against such abuse; but that was not done upon demurrer, or upon the record, or upon the verdict of a jury or evidence taken in that way, but it was done by the Court informing its conscience upon affidavits, and by a summary order to stay the action which was brought under such circumstances as to be an abuse of process of the Court; and in a proper case did stay the action.'[14]

Early examples of the application of the abuse of process doctrine in civil litigation include cases which were stayed on account of the action brought being 'absolutely groundless.'[15] Order 25, rule 4 of the Supreme Court Rules of 1883 (United Kingdom) explicitly authorised the stay of an action which was shown by the pleadings to be 'frivolous or vexatious,' although the term 'abuse of process' was not used until the Rules were revised in 1962.[16]

Although the abuse of process doctrine was commonly applied in civil litigation for over a century, it did not figure prominently in criminal proceedings until it attracted attention in the 1964 House of Lords decision in *Connelly* v. *DPP*.[17] The issue in this case was whether the Crown could properly prosecute a count of robbery following the appellant's acquittal of murder, whether the appellant could rely on a plea of *autrefois acquit*, and whether prosecution of the robbery count could be characterised as an abuse of the process of the court. The House of Lords found that double jeopardy protection in English law is afforded not only by the pleas in bar (*autrefois acquit* and *autrefois convict*), but also by the judicial discretion to stay proceedings as an abuse of process. In deciding to stay the proceeding, Lord

---

[10] Andrew L.-T. Choo, *Abuse of process and judicial stays of criminal proceedings* (Oxford: OUP, 1993), 2, quoting I.H. Jacob, "The Inherent Jurisdiction of the Court", 23 *Current Legal Problems* 23 (1970). See also *R.* v. *Forbes, ex p. Bevan*, 127 *CLR* 1 (1972), at 7, *per* Menzies J.

[11] Colin Warbrick, "Judicial Jurisdiction and Abuse of Process", 49 *ICLQ* 490 (2000).

[12] *Lubanga* Appeals Judgment of 14 December 2006, para. 28.

[13] Choo, *Abuse of process and judicial stays of criminal proceedings*, at 4.

[14] *Metropolitan Bank* v. *Pooley* (1885) LR 10 AC 210, 220-1.

[15] *Castro* v. *Murray* (1875) LR 10 Ex. 213.

[16] Choo, *Abuse of process and judicial stays of criminal proceedings*, at 3.

[17] [1964] AC 1254.

Devlin observed that the court had the 'inescapable duty to secure fair treatment for those who come or are brought before them.'[18]

The development of this doctrine, therefore, has principally occurred in the last four decades; starting from its unsuccessful application in *Eichmann*,[19] its use in international criminal cases is even more recent.

7.2 Contextual and policy considerations

The contextual and policy considerations that domestic and international courts have taken into account in deciding whether or not to apply the abuse of process doctrine have encompassed a number of rationales, including: the rule of law; the integrity of the executive branch (which should not be rewarded for its illegal behaviour); the integrity of the judicial branch; the fairness of the legal process; and respect for State sovereignty.[20] However, there are in essence two main justifications for applying the abuse of process doctrine. These are the need to ensure the right to fair trial and the need to preserve the integrity of the judicial system. Thus the stay a criminal proceeding is justified 'if there is a sufficient danger either that the accused will be convicted even if innocent, or that the continuation of the proceedings will undermine the moral integrity of the criminal process.'[21] Each of the other rationales may be seen as a subset of one of these two main considerations.[22] Choo notes that having in mind the two basic rationales for the abuse of process doctrine – the need to protect the innocent from conviction, and the need to ensure the moral integrity of the criminal justice system – is 'unlikely to give much practical guidance' but nonetheless 'remains a useful benchmark by which to assess the merits of individual decisions as well as the merits of any guidelines which may have evolved to govern consideration of the discretion in particular contexts.'[23] As will be seen in the discussion below, both rationales have had a profound impact on the way that courts have interpreted the scope of the abuse of process doctrine when applied to proceedings dealing with international crimes.

7.2.1 **The need to ensure a fair trial**

The abuse of process doctrine is said to be a derivative of the general principle of the right to fair trial and due process.[24] A fair trial is 'in essence … one which ade-

[18] *Ibid.*, at 401.

[19] See discussion *infra* notes 52-56 and accompnanying text.

[20] James Sloan, "*Prosecutor v. Dragan Nikolić*, Decision on Defence Motion on Illegal Capture", 16 *LJIL* 541 (2003), at 546-47.

[21] Andrew L.-T. Choo, "Halting Criminal Prosecutions: The Abuse of Process Doctrine Revisited", *Criminal Law Review* 865 (1995).

[22] The violation of sovereignty, which is particular to the issue of illegal apprehension, may also be related to the integrity of the judicial function, which should be not be seen to be complicit in violations by the executive of international or national law, including extradition obligations.

[23] Choo, "Halting Criminal Prosecutions", at 874. Footnotes omitted.

[24] Knoops, *Redressing Miscarriages of Justice*, at 181.

quately protects the right – described by Ronald Dworkin as a "profound right"[25] – not to be convicted of offences of which one is innocent.'[26] The concept of a fair trial involves fairness to the prosecution and to the public as well as to the defendant.[27] It has been argued that the doctrine is able to prevent wrongful convictions in that it helps to avoid errors of fact.[28]

For instance, in *Teixeira* v. *Portugal*, law enforcement agencies provoked the accused to commit a crime he otherwise would not have committed. The European Commission on Human Rights held that it would be impossible to hold a fair trial in the circumstances and that Portugal had irremediably violated Article 6(1) of the European Convention on Human Rights.[29] Similarly, in *R* v. *Loosely; Attorney General's Reference (No 3 of 2000)*,[30] the House of Lords held that it is not acceptable for the state to lure its citizens into committing illegal acts and then to seek to prosecute them for doing so. In this respect, it has been argued that 'improper entrapment should lead automatically to a stay of the proceedings, rather than merely being a factor to be considered in deciding whether to exclude evidence in the exercise of discretion.'[31]

In cases dealing with international crimes, the right to a fair trial has been deemed an essential pre-requisite to the exercise of jurisdiction, so that any breach thereof would irredeemably lead to a stay of proceedings, at least until the fair trial issues are resolved. Indeed for the ICC Appeals Chamber, the fair trial rationale has come to govern its application of abuse of process principles.[32]

7.2.2 **The need to preserve the integrity of the judicial system**

In addition to the need to protect the innocent from wrongful conviction, 'there is also a need to safeguard the moral integrity of verdicts, and of the criminal process generally.'[33] United States Supreme Court Justice Brandeis summed up this consideration in his famous statement that:

> 'Decency, security and liberty alike demand that government officials shall be subjected to the same rules of conduct that are commands to the citizen. In a government of laws, existence of the government will be imperilled if it fails to observe the law scrupulously. Our Government is the potent, the omnipresent teacher. For good or for ill, it teaches the whole people by its example. Crime is contagious. If the Government becomes a lawbreaker, it breeds contempt for law; it invites every man to become a law unto himself: it invites anarchy. To declare that in the administration of the criminal

---

25 Ronald Dworkin, *A Matter of Principle* (Oxford: OUP, 1986), at 72.
26 Choo, "Halting Criminal Prosecutions", at 865.
27 *DPP* v. *Meakin* [2006] EWHC 1067.
28 Knoops, *Redressing Miscarriages of Justice*, at 177.
29 Judgment, 9 June 1998, Appl. No. 25829/94.
30 [2002] 1 *Cr App R* 29.
31 Choo, "Halting Criminal Prosecutions", at 871.
32 See *infra* notes 192-198 and accompanying text.
33 Choo, "Halting Criminal Prosecutions", at 865.

law the end justifies the means—to declare that the Government may commit crimes in order to secure the conviction of a private criminal—would bring terrible retribution. Against that pernicious doctrine this Court should resolutely set its face.'[34]

In fact, the two main rationales for the abuse of process doctrine are intimately related. Thus, the Supreme Court of Canada has expressed the rationale for staying proceedings in the following way:

'A stay should be granted where "compelling an accused to stand trial would violate those fundamental principles of justice which underlie the community's sense of fair play and decency" ... or where the proceedings are "oppressive or vexatious" ...[35] The doctrine is one of the safeguards designed to ensure "that the repression of crime through the conviction of the guilty is done in a way which reflects our fundamental values as a society" ... It acknowledges that courts must have the respect and support of the community in order that the administration of criminal justice may properly fulfil its function. Consequently, where the affront to fair play and decency is disproportionate to the societal interest in the effective prosecution of criminal cases, then the administration of justice is best served by staying the proceedings.'[36]

Similarly, in *Barayagwiza*, the rationale of the doctrine was held by the ICTR Appeals Chamber to be twofold: the need to ensure the public interest in the integrity of criminal proceedings and the safeguard of the fundamental rights of the accused.[37] The Appeals Chamber concluded that:

'The Tribunal – an institution whose primary purpose is to ensure that justice is done – must not place its imprimatur on such violations. To allow the Appellant to be tried on the charges for which he was belatedly indicted would be a travesty of justice. Nothing less than the integrity of the Tribunal is at stake in this case. Loss of public confidence in the Tribunal, as a court valuing human rights of all individuals – including those charged with unthinkable crimes – would be among the most serious consequences of allowing the Appellant to stand trial in the face of such violations of his rights. As difficult as this conclusion may be for some to accept, it is the proper role of an independent judiciary to halt this prosecution, so that no further injustice results.'[38]

In the *Hartley* case in New Zealand concerning a covert extradition, Judge Woodhouse stated 'this must never become an area where it will be sufficient to consider that the end has justified the means. The issues raised by this affair are basic to the whole concept of freedom in society.'[39] In another New Zealand case, *Moevao* v. *Dept. of Labour*, the court focused on 'the misuse of the court process by those

---

[34] *Olmstead, et al.*, v. *United States*, 277 US 438 (1928), at 485.

[35] *Keyowski* v. *R.* (1988) 62 CR (3d) 349, at 350 *per* Wilson J.

[36] *R.* v. *Conway* (1989) 70 CR (3d) 209, at 222-223 *per* L'Heureux-Dubé J.

[37] *Barayagwiza*, ICTR, Appeals Chamber Decision, Case No. ICTR-97-19-AR72, 3 November 1999 (hereafter, *Barayagwiza*), paras. 74-77.

[38] *Ibid.*, para. 112.

[39] *Reg.* v. *Hartley* [1978] 2 *NZLR* 199, at 216-217, *per* Woodhouse J.

responsible for law enforcement. It is whether the continuation of the prosecution is inconsistent with the recognised purposes of the administration of criminal justice …'[40] In Canada, the Supreme Court in *States* v. *Shulman* found that in allowing threats to be made by the United States judge who sentenced the accused's co-conspirators and by the United States prosecutor if Shulman wished to contest the extradition to Canada, the requesting State had abused the process in the Canadian Court.[41] This entitled the accused to dismissal, both as a common law remedy for abuse of process and because the abuse of process violated his rights under Section 7 of the Charter of Rights and Freedoms (Canada). The Court found that it would be inconsistent with the principles of fundamental justice to allow the process to proceed.[42] Australian courts have upheld the abuse of process doctrine on similar grounds.[43] In Cyprus, the Supreme Court has referred to the inherent power of the court to stay proceedings in cases of abuse of process, in particular where the judicial process has been used in an oppressive manner to the rights of the counter party.[44]

The Zimbabwean Court in the *Mlambo* case emphasised the importance of staying a criminal proceeding brought in abuse of process even where the crimes alleged are serious:

> 'The charges against the applicant are far from trivial and there can be no doubt that it would be in the best interests of society to proceed with the trial of those who are charged with the commission of serious crimes. Yet, that trial can only be undertaken if the guarantee under … the Constitution has not been infringed. In this case it has been grievously infringed and the unfortunate result is that a hearing cannot be allowed to take place. To find otherwise would render meaningless a right enshrined in the Constitution as the supreme law of the land.'[45]

Although the dismissal of a case would amount to a sanction against the prosecutorial authorities, this is not usually cited as a reason to uphold the doctrine.[46] For instance in *Bennett,* Lord Lowry acknowledged that a stay of proceedings might have the effect of discouraging police from engaging in similar conduct in the future, but he and Lord Griffiths emphasised that the primary purpose of staying proceedings is not to discipline the police.[47]

---

[40] [1980] 1 *NZLR* 464.

[41] [2001] SCC 21, Judgment of 24 March 2001. See also *Glorian Keyowski* v. *Her Majesty The Queen*, Judgment, 28 April 1988 [1988] 1 SCR 657, at 658-59.

[42] *Ibid.*, para. 2 (*per* Arbour J).

[43] See, e.g., *William* v. *Spautz* [1992] HCA 34; 174 *CLR* 509 (1992) (27 July 1992); *Jago* v. *District Court of NSW* [1989] HCA 46; 168 *CLR* 23 (1989) (12 October 1989); *Levinge* v. *Director of Custodial Services* 9 NSWR 546 (Ct App 1987); *Barton* v. *The Queen* [1980] HCA 48; 147 *CLR* 75 (1980), at 96, 107, 116; *Clyne* v. *N.S.W. Bar Association* [1960] HCA 40; 104 *CLR* 186 (1960), at 201.

[44] *Director of Prisons* v. *Djenaro Perella* [1995] 1 *CLR* 217.

[45] In re *Mlambo* (1993) 2 LRC 28, quoted in *Barayagwiza*, para. 111.

[46] *R.* v. *Crown Court at Norwich ex parte Belsham*, 94 *Cr App R* 382 (1992), QBD, at 395 *per* Watkins LJ.

[47] *Bennett*, 74-75, *per* Lord Lowry; 62, *per* Lord Griffiths.

Courts have found that the discretion to remedy an abuse of process should only be exercised in the 'clearest of cases,'[48] that is, where there is 'conduct which shocks the conscience of the community and is so detrimental to the proper administration of justice that it warrants judicial intervention.'[49]

7.3 Legal rationales with regard to the doctrine of abuse of process and international crimes

The abuse of process doctrine has been invoked in a variety of situations which are probably impossible to catalogue definitively. However, in the context of international crimes, it has been invoked principally in the following areas: (1) abduction/disguised extradition; (2) violation of procedural rights; (3) delay; (4) withholding of exculpatory evidence; (5) double jeopardy; (6) promises of non-prosecution; and (7) misuse of the criminal process.[50]

7.3.1 **Abduction/Disguised extradition**

7.3.1.1 *National level*

The illegal rendition of criminal defendants has been raised as a bar to court proceedings since at least the 19th century.[51] In terms of international criminal law, the first example of where abduction was raised as a bar to prosecution was *Israel* v. *Eichmann*.[52] Eichmann, who was the head of the Jewish Office of the German Gestapo during WW II, was abducted from his home in Argentina by Israeli agents and taken to Israel for trial. Argentina protested the violation of its sovereignty, and was supported in this regard by the UN Security Council.[53] Argentina and Israel eventually issued a joint declaration in which Israel appeared to acknowledge the illegality of the abduction at international law, and both declared that they considered the matter as closed.[54]

---

[48] See, e.g., *Jones* v. *Whalley*, Judgment, House of Lords, 26 July 2006 [2006] 4 *All ER* 113; *Attorney General's Reference (No 1 of 1990)* [1992] QB 630, CA; *Attorney General's Reference (No 2 of 2001)* [2004] 2 AC 72, HL.

[49] *R.* v. *Power* [1994] 1 SCR 601 ('Where there is conspicuous evidence of improper motives or bad faith or of an act so wrong that it violates the conscience of the community such that it would genuinely be unfair and indecent to proceed, then, and only then, should courts intervene to prevent an abuse of process which could bring the administration of justice into disrepute.')

[50] For a discussion of abuse of process in the context of statutes of limitation, see Chapter 4, *supra*.

[51] E.g., *Lawler*, cited in Lord McNair, *International Law Opinions: Selected and Annotated*, Vol. I (Cambridge: CUP: 1956), at 78; *Ker* v. *Illinois*, 119 US 436 (1886) (Sup. Ct.). For a comprehensive survey of case-law, see Geoff Gilbert, *Transnational Fugitive Offenders in International Law* (The Hague: Nijhoff, 1998), at 337-377.

[52] *Eichmann*, Israel, District Court of Jerusalem, Judgment of 12 December 1961, English translation in 36 *ILR* 5-276; *Eichmann* Supreme Court Judgment.

[53] UN Doc. S/4349 (1960), S/RES/138, 1960, para. 2.

[54] *Eichmann*, Israel, District Court of Jerusalem, at 59.

During his trial and on appeal, Eichmann argued that the illegality of his apprehension deprived the Israeli courts of jurisdiction. The District Court, having reviewed State practice, found that as 'an established rule of law' it was not open to a criminal accused to challenge the legality of the criminal proceedings on the basis of how he was brought into the jurisdiction of the State.[55] This rule is expressed in the Latin maxim *mala captus bene detentus*, which entails that because the illegality involved in the accused's rendition arises from an international *delict*, the domestic court 'will assert *in personam* jurisdiction without inquiring into the means by which the presence of the defendant was secured.'[56] The Supreme Court upheld the District Court's view.

The *Eichmann* case suggests that while abductions in the sense of the exercise of police or criminal enforcement powers on the territory of another State without its permission do amount to a violation of state sovereignty, this in and of itself does not provide standing to the captured individual to request a remedy for the violation.[57] Instead, individuals must rely on the violation of human rights norms, in particular, the right to due process and fair trial. However, arguably these would only come into play where the domestic State's law enforcement authorities were directly involved in the abduction.[58]

In re *Argoud*, the French Court of Cassation in 1964 similarly opined that the conditions in which a suspect is apprehended and delivered to justice '*... ne sont pas de nature, si déplorables qu'elles puissant appiraître, à entraîner par elles-mêmes la nullité de la poursuite ...*'[59] In the *Barbie* case, the Court in 1983 applied the same reasoning, asserting its jurisdiction over the accused despite the claim that he was a victim of a disguised extradition based, *inter alia*, on the special nature of the crimes of which he was accused, namely, crimes against humanity.[60]

The *mala captus bene detentus* principle rules that the domestic judicial forum should not consider issues related to the issue of capture.[61] The principle rose to prominence in the US Supreme Court's decision in *Alvarez-Machain*.[62] In that case, the US Drug Enforcement Agency (DEA) abducted a Mexican accused from his office and brought him to Texas where he was arrested by DEA authorities. The lower courts upheld his motion to dismiss the indictment on the basis that the Executive had violated the extradition between the US and Mexico, and Mexico's

---

[55] *Idem.*

[56] M. Cherif Bassiouni, *International Extradition: United States Law and Practice*, 4th edn. (Dobbs Ferry, New York: Oceana Publications, 2002), at 250.

[57] Currie, "Abducted Fugitives Before the International Criminal Court", at 354.

[58] *Idem.*

[59] Cass. Crim. 4 June 1964, Bull. 192, JCP 1964, II No. 13806 Rapport Compte; 45 *ILR* 90. But compare In re *Jollis*, Tribunal Correctionnel d'Aversnes, 22 July 1933, 7 Ann Dig (1933-1934), at 191.

[60] Cass. Crim. 6 October 1983, Bull. JCP 1983, II, No. 20107 Rapport Le Gunehec, Conc. Dontenwille.

[61] See, e.g., *Ex parte Susanna Scott* (1829) 9 B. & C. 446, 109 E.R. 106; *Sinclair* v. *HM Advocate* (1890) 17 R.(J.) 38; *R* v. *Officer Commanding Depot Battalion, RASC Colchester, ex parte Elliot* [1949] 1 *All ER* 138; *R* v. *Plymouth Justices, ex parte Driver* [1985] 2 *All ER* 681.

[62] *United States* v. *Alvarez-Machain*, 112 S.Ct. 2188 (1992).

formal protests about the abduction at the international level. The Supreme Court, however, applying the *mala captus bene detentus* rule – also known in the US as the *Ker-Frisbie* Doctrine named after two formative precedents,[63] found that while the government's actions may have violated international law, the forcible extra-territorial abduction did not prevent the courts from exercising criminal jurisdiction over Alvarez-Machain.

However, State practice in cases dealing with illegal capture of criminal suspects also reveals a countering trend to the *mala captus bene detentus* principle; this is based on the Latin maxim *ex injuria ius non ortiur* ('certain violations of law [should] not ripen into lawful results')[64] and has been described as 'a specific application of the doctrine of abuse process.'[65] The State 'must come to court "with clean hands" as it were.'[66] In the *Ebrahim* case, which concerned a South African citizen who was a member of the military wing of the African National Congress (ANC) who was abducted in Swaziland by persons posing as South African police agents and taken to South Africa where he was tried for treason, the South African Court of Appeals applying principles of 'Roman-Dutch law,' reasoned that the individual has to be protected against unlawful detention and against abduction and that the limits of territorial jurisdiction and the sovereignty of states has to be respected, the fairness of the legal process guaranteed and the abuse thereof prevented so as to preserve the dignity and integrity of the judicial system.[67] The participation of State agents in violations of international law is seen as tainting the dignity, legitimacy and legality of the judicial process to the extent that a court should decline to exercise jurisdiction over an individual.[68] In a much earlier case, *Jacob-Salomon*, an ex-German citizen abducted on Swiss territory and taken to Germany for trial on a charge of treason, was eventually returned to the Swiss Government following vigorous protest on the latter's part.[69]

In the seminal case of *Ex Parte Bennett*, the House of Lords declined to exercise jurisdiction in exercise of the abuse of process doctrine where the accused, Bennett, a New Zealand national, sought by Britain for alleged criminal offences, was irregularly deported from South Africa and unofficially delivered to the United Kingdom in disregard of the existing extradition procedures between the United

[63] *Ker* v. *Illinois* 119 US 436 (1886) (finding that forcible abduction of a US national kidnapped from Peru and brought back to the US was not a sufficient reason for the court not to try him); *Frisbie* v. *Collins* 342 US 519 (1952) (finding that the fact that a person was forcibly abducted and taken from one state to another to be tried for a crime does not invalidate his conviction in a court of the latter state under the Due Process Clause of the Fourteenth Amendment).

[64] Bassiouni, *International Extradition*, at 287.

[65] Currie, "Abducted Fugitives Before the International Criminal Court", at 356.

[66] *Ebrahim*, at 442.

[67] *Idem.*

[68] Subsequent case law on the issue in South Africa has been inconsistent. Some cases, such as *S* v. *Mahala* [1994] 1 SACR 510 and *S* v. *Buys* [1994] 1 SACR 539, have followed *male captus bene detentus* (distinguishing *Ebrahim* by reason of good faith on the part of the arresting officers) and other cases have followed *Ebrahim*, such as *S* v. *Wellen* [1993] 2 SACR 19 E Cap Div.

[69] See Preuss Lawrence, "Settlement of the *Jacob* Kidnapping Case (Switzerland-Germany)", 30(1) *AJIL* 123-124 (1936).

Kingdom and South Africa.[70] The Law Lords found that courts may enquire into the manner in which an accused was brought before them and may stay the prosecution if justified by the circumstances. The House of Lords was of the view that the judiciary should not 'countenance behaviour that threatens either basic human rights or the rule of law' and therefore, that 'if it comes to the attention of the court that there has been a serious abuse of power it should … express its disapproval by refusing to act upon it.'[71] While the Law Lords were clearly concerned about the subverting of the extradition procedures, it was the respect for the rule of law which lay at the basis of their decision:

> 'when it is shown that the law enforcement agency responsible for bringing a prosecution has only been enabled to do so by participation in violations of international law and the laws of another state in order to secure the presence of the accused … I think that respect for the rule of law demands that the court take cognisance of that circumstance.'[72]

Moreover, for a court to take the view that it 'may turn a blind eye to executive lawlessness beyond the frontiers of its own jurisdiction' is 'insular and unacceptable.'[73] The decision acknowledges that pre-trial police or prosecutorial improprieties may lead to a stay not only if the accused's right to a fair trial is compromised, but also if the continuation of the proceedings would undermine the moral integrity of the criminal process.[74] Lord Bridge made the triggering condition for a stay the participation of the prosecuting authorities 'in violations of international law and of the laws of another state' to obtain custody over a defendant.[75] He noted that '[s]ince the prosecution could never have been brought if the defendant had not been illegally abducted, the whole proceeding is tainted. … To hold that in these circumstances the court may decline to exercise its jurisdiction on the ground that its process has been abused may be an extension of the abuse of process but is, in my view, a wholly proper and necessary one.'[76]

The *Bennett* principle was further refined in *Latif*,[77] where Lord Steyn said that the court considering an abuse of process case had to weigh the 'affront to the public conscience' against the public interest 'in ensuring that those who are

---

[70] *Bennett*, at 62-64. In an earlier case, *Mackeson*, an English court refused to hear a case against a defendant who had been brought to England by a collusive process between the English and Zimbabwean authorities, which arguably breached the laws of both countries, if not international law. See *R* v. *Bow Street Magistrates, ex parte Mackeson* 1 *All ER* 138.

[71] *Bennett*, at 62, *per* Lord Griffiths.

[72] *Ibid.*, at 67, *per* Lord Bridge of Harwich. In the end Bennett was tried in Scotland on different charges and a full inquiry into the facts of his deportation from South Africa concluded that the police conduct had not been sufficiently 'abusive' to warrant declining jurisdiction. See *Bennett* v. *H.M. Advocate* 1995 S.L.T. 510.

[73] *Bennett*, at 62, *per* Lord Bridge of Harwich.

[74] *Ibid.*, at 74, *per* Lord Lowry.

[75] *Ibid.*, at 155, *per* Lord Bridge of Harwich.

[76] *Ibid.*, at 68, *per* Lord Bridge of Harwich.

[77] *R* v. *Latif* [1996] 1 *All ER* 353.

charged with grave crimes should be tried.'[78] Such a balancing test was applied in *Mullen*,[79] which concerned an accused who was returned from Zimbabwe to England to face terrorist charges as a result of collusion between English and Zimbabwean officials, in disregard of existing extradition procedures. The Court of Appeal acknowledged the seriousness of the crimes for which Mullen was convicted, but found that there had been 'a blatant and extremely serious failure to adhere to the rule of law' and that there was a need to discourage such behaviour.[80] It thus held that 'the discretionary balance comes down decisively against the prosecution of this offence.'[81] Warbrick notes that, in applying this test, 'the Court emphasised the discretionary nature of the remedy – the seriousness of the (alleged) crime had to be weighed against the gravity of the prosecution misdemeanour: sometimes, as in *Latif*, the balance would come out the other way.'[82]

In the *Toscanino* case,[83] the United States 2nd Circuit Court declined to exercise jurisdiction on the basis of the physical torture inflicted on the accused during an irregular trans-border transfer by US authorities from Uruguay, through Brazil (where the interrogation and physical mistreatment took place), to the US. The Court reasoned that due process required 'a court to divest itself of jurisdiction over the person of a defendant where it has been acquired as the result of the government's deliberate, unnecessary and unreasonable invasion of the accused's constitutional rights' and that any other decision in such a situation would 'reward police brutality and lawlessness.'[84] Evidence that an accused had been tortured by police or other investigating authorities prior to the trial, to force a confession or for other reasons, has been consistently held to amount to sufficiently serious and egregious conduct to stay the proceedings under the abuse of process doctrine. The rationales include the fact that the gravity of the conduct itself is a breach of fundamental rights and that secondly, particularly where a confession has been procured by torture, the potential conviction may be held to be 'unsafe.'[85]

---

[78] *Ibid.*, at 361.

[79] *R.* v. *Mullen* [1999] 3 *WLR* 777.

[80] *Ibid.*, at 790, [2000] QB 520, at 535.

[81] *Idem.*

[82] Warbrick, "Judicial Jurisdiction and Abuse of Process", at 494.

[83] *United States* v. *Toscanino*, 500 F.2d 267 (Ct. App. 2nd Circ., 1974), at 274.

[84] *Ibid.*, at 275.

[85] See *R.* v. *Criminal Cases Review Commission*, ex *Twitchell*, 26 October 1999, Case No. 9800326/S2. In this case, the accused was initially convicted of manslaughter and armed robbery, mainly on the basis of his confessions. He had tried prior to the trial to withdraw his confessions claiming that they had been obtained through torture by police officers. An inquiry failed to support his claim. However, a few years later, another accused, Treadaway, proved in a civil suit against the UK Government that he had been tortured during an interview with the West Midlands Serious Crime Squad, which was the same police squad that had interviewed Twitchell. The CCRC referred the *Twitchell* case to the Court of Appeal for a new trial on the basis that 'subsequent findings against police officers involved in the appellant's case, coupled with the similarity of misconduct, demonstrates a system of corrupt and dishonest conduct by officers of the West Midlands Crime Squad such as to render the convictions unsafe.' The Court of Appeals subsequently quashed Twitchell's conviction.

Commentators have noted that the tension between the two approaches – *mala captus bene detentus* and abuse of process – and the inconsistent State practice perpetuating the tension, would suggest that neither may be said to have the status of a rule of customary international law.[86] The case law at the international level reviewed below attests to this conclusion.

7.3.1.2 *International level*

On the international level, human rights bodies have generally taken an approach closer to that of abuse of process, determining that the threshold question is whether a State should exercise jurisdiction in view of violations of rights or illegal transfer.[87] For instance, in *Lopez Burgos*, the UN Human Rights Committee found a violation of Article 9(1) of the ICCPR (right to liberty and security of person) in a case where a Uruguayan refugee was forcibly abducted from Argentina.[88] The European Court of Human Rights found a violation of Article 5(1) of the ECHR (right to liberty and security of person) in a case where the petitioner had been seized in France and deported to Switzerland, and then extradited to Italy, which amounted to a disguised extradition.[89] It has been observed that while the Human Rights Committee tends to view the attitude of the State whose territorial sovereignty as irrelevant, the European Court of Human Rights seems more inclined to consider that the forcible abduction of a fugitive is only a violation where the authorities of the territorial State do not consent to the abduction and where the existing extradition procedures have not been followed.[90]

This observation seems to have been confirmed by the ECHR Grand Chamber's *Öcalan* judgment.[91] In this case, the petitioner, a prominent Kurdish leader indicted by a Turkish arrest warrant for terrorism charges, sought refuge in Kenya which did not have an extradition treaty with Turkey. However, Kenyan governmental officials co-operated with Turkey by surreptitiously delivering Öcalan to a Turkish aircraft in the international zone of the Nairobi airport, where he was arrested. Öcalan argued that his right to liberty and security had been violated by this 'abduction' or disguised extradition. The Court held that the arrest was lawful. In coming to its decision, it considered that Turkey had validly issued several arrest warrants for Öcalan, and that the formal arrest complied with Turkish domestic law. It also took into account that it had no power of review over Kenyan law so any viola-

[86] Currie, "Abducted Fugitives Before the International Criminal Court", at 359.

[87] See, e.g., *Stocké* v. *Federal Republic of Germany* (European Commission of Human Rights, 12 October 1989), 95 *ILR* 328, at 332-33; *Garcia* v. *Ecuador* (Human Rights Committee), Comm. No. 319/1988, UN Doc. A/47/40 (1994), at 287-90; *Celiberti de Casariego* v. *Uruguay* (Human Rights Committee), Comm. No. 56/1979, UN Doc. A/36/40 (1981), at 185.

[88] UN Doc. A/36/40 (1981), reprinted in 68 *ILR* 29.

[89] *Bozano* v. *France* (1986) ECHR (ser. A), No. 111; *European Human Rights Report* 297 (1987).

[90] Silvia Borelli, "Terrorism and Human Rights: Treatment of Terrorist Suspects and Limits on International Co-operation", 16 *LJIL* 802 (2003), at 807.

[91] *Öcalan* v. *Turkey*, Appl. No. 00046221/99, Merits, Judgment of 12 May 2005 (hereafter, *Öcalan*).

tions of that law were non-justiciable. Finally, it noted that Kenyan officials had co-operated with Turkish officials in his apprehension[92] and found that the 'fact that a fugitive has been handed over as a result of cooperation between States does not in itself make the arrest unlawful or, therefore, give rise to any problem under Article 5.'[93]

At the ICTY, the first case to deal with the issue of illegal transfer was *Dokmanović*.[94] Slavko Dokmanović had been indicted for his role in the massacre at Vukovar, Croatia, in 1991. He was a resident in the Federal Republic of Yugoslavia (FRY) when he was lured by an official of the Office of the Prosecutor (OTP) into Eastern Slavonia under false pretences, whereupon he was arrested and transferred to The Hague. Dokmanović challenged the jurisdiction of the Tribunal on the basis that he had been illegally arrested and that the 'kidnapping' had violated the sovereignty of the FRY.[95] The Trial Chamber dismissed the application, finding that 'luring' did not violate international law and that there had been 'no actual physical violation of FRY territory.'[96] It recognised, however, that abduction did violate international rules and could possibly ground a dismissal in appropriate cases. Commentators have noted that the 'distinction made by the Trial Chamber between luring and abduction seems strained, founded as it was on the controversial view that luring is not a sovereignty violation.'[97] It has been suggested that it is the Security Council's Chapter VII powers through which the ICTY functions that overrides any sovereignty issues.[98]

The second case to raise the issue of illegal transfer was *Todorović*, which concerned the accused's claim that he had been kidnapped from his home in Zlatibor, Western Serbia, that he had been blindfolded, gagged and beaten with a baseball bat, and then transferred by helicopter to the NATO-led stabilisation force (SFOR), and that SFOR and the OTP had some involvement in the capture. He applied through a series of motions for the Chamber to require SFOR and the OTP to disclose relevant information. The Trial Chamber issued a decision in which it ordered SFOR to provide such information, including the identification of the individuals involved in the capture, as well as a subpoena for the testimony of the Commanding General of SFOR.[99] The illegal capture issue was never ruled on by the Tribunal since Todorović ended up entering into a plea agreement with the OTP

---

[92] This was despite the fact that the Kenyan Minister of Foreign Affairs had stated that there had been no official involvement in the arrest of transfer of Öcalan. *Ibid.*, para. 98.

[93] *Ibid.*, paras. 86-87.

[94] *Mrkšić, Radić, Sljivančanin and Dokmanović*, Decision on the Motion for Release by the Accused Slavko Dokmanović, Case No. IT-95-13a-PT, 22 October 1997.

[95] *Ibid.*, paras. 16-18.

[96] *Ibid.*, para. 77.

[97] Currie, "Abducted Fugitives Before the International Criminal Court", at 363.

[98] Michael Scharf, "*The Prosecutor v. Slavko Dokmanović*: Irregular Rendition and the ICTY", 11 *LJIL* 369 (1998), at 373-373; Currie, "Abducted Fugitives Before the International Criminal Court", at 364;

[99] *Simić, Simić, Tadić, Todorović and Zarić*, ICTY, Trial Chamber, Decision on Motion for Judicial Assistance to be Provided by SFOR and Others, Case No. IT-95-9-PT, 18 October 2000.

and was sentenced to 10 years' imprisonment.[100] However, it is significant that the Tribunal was willing to compel SFOR to provide information about the circumstances of his arrest, suggesting that they considered it appropriate to look into the way that he was arrested as a threshold issue.

Slobodan Milošević also asserted that his transfer to the ICTY was an abuse of process in that procedures of the FRY were bypassed and he was unlawfully transferred to the International Tribunal.[101] The problem lay in the fact that the ICTY sent the arrest warrants to the authorities of the FRY but it was the government of the Republic of Serbia that transferred the accused to the Tribunal. The Trial Chamber decided to treat the motion as the proceedings by which the accused was challenging the legality of his detention.[102] The Trial Chamber found that although the arrest warrants were directed to the authorities of the FRY, not the Republic of Serbia, Rule 58 of the Rules of Procedure and Evidence – which provides that obligations under Article 29 of the Statute shall prevail over any legal impediment to the surrender or transfer of a witness to the Tribunal under national law or extradition treaties – should be given an interpretation that 'takes full account of its purpose,' and that therefore the transfer was effected in accordance with the provisions of the Statute.[103] It further noted that under Article 27 of the Vienna Convention on the Law of Treaties (which it found, without discussion, could be applied to interpret the Statute), the FRY could not invoke its internal law as justification to fail to abide by treaty obligations.[104] With regard to the doctrine of abuse of process, the Chamber noted that if there is such an abuse, 'it does not lead to a lack of jurisdiction on the part of the International Tribunal; what it raises is the question whether, assuming jurisdiction, the International Tribunal should exercise its discretion to refuse to try the accused.'[105] It secondly noted that 'the International Tribunal will exercise its discretion to refuse to try the accused if there has been an egregious breach of the rights of the accused.'[106] Ultimately, the Trial Chamber held that the doctrine of abuse of process was inapplicable on the basis that 'the circumstances in which the accused was arrested and transferred – by the government of the Republic of Serbia, to whom no request was made, but which is a constituent part of the Federal Republic of Yugoslavia, to whom the request for transfer and transfer was made – are not such as to constitute an egregious violation of the accused's rights.'[107] In other words, the violation in the manner apprehension was not serious enough to warrant the dismissal of the case.

---

[100] *Todorović*, ICTY, Trial Chamber, Case No. IT-95-9-1-S, Sentencing Judgment, 31 July 2001.

[101] *Milošević*, ICTY, Trial Chamber, Case No. IT-02-54-PT, Decision on Preliminary Motions, 8 November 2001, para. 35.

[102] *Ibid.*, para. 40.

[103] *Ibid.*, para. 46.

[104] *Ibid.*, para. 47.

[105] *Ibid.*, para. 48.

[106] *Idem.*

[107] *Ibid.*, para. 51.

In *Nikolić*,[108] the accused – who was indicted for war crimes committed during his time as a commander of the *Susica* camp, a Bosnian-Serb detention camp in eastern Bosnia – was forcibly taken by unknown persons, put into the trunk of a car, and smuggled from the FRY to Bosnia and Herzegovina, where he was handed over to SFOR, which arrested him and subsequently transferred him to the ICTY. According to an agreed statement of facts, there was no connection between SFOR, the OTP and the abductors. Nikolić argued that his arrest had both violated the sovereignty of the FRY and his human rights and constituted an abuse of process, justifying dismissal of the case.[109]

Although both the Trial and Appeals Chamber upheld the doctrine of abuse of process, they held that it did not apply in this particular case. Interestingly, the Appeals Chamber took the following as the threshold question: assuming there had been either a breach of sovereignty or human rights, in what circumstances should the Tribunal decline to exercise jurisdiction?[110] The framing of the inquiry in this way implicitly accepted the contention that the breach of sovereignty or of human rights was not, by itself, sufficient to justify dismissal as a remedy.[111]

On the claim of a violation of sovereignty, the Trial Chamber held that there were no factual links to justify attribution to either SFOR or the OTP, and emphasised the 'vertical context' of the relationship between the ICTY and UN member States, which meant that because of the ICTY's status 'as an enforcement measure under Chapter VII,' 'sovereignty by definition cannot play the same role.'[112] The Appeals Chamber, having reviewed national case law on the matter, determined that 'it is difficult to identify a clear pattern.'[113] However, it noted that in 'cases concerning the same kinds of crimes as those falling within the [ICTY's] jurisdiction' such as *Eichmann* and *Barbie*, State practice shows that courts found 'a good reason for not setting aside jurisdiction.'[114] It also observed that 'absent a complaint by the State whose sovereignty has been breached or in the event of a diplomatic resolution of the breach,' courts were more willing to exercise jurisdiction.[115] The Appeals Chamber set out what commentators have described as a 'decisive policy declaration' on the significance of exercising jurisdiction over 'universally condemned offences':

> '… the damage caused to international justice by not apprehending fugitives accused of serious violations of international humanitarian law is comparatively higher than the

---

[108] *Nikolić*, Case No. IT-94-2-PT, Decision on Defence Motion Challenging the Exercise of Jurisdiction by the Tribunal, 9 October 2002 (hereafter, *Nikolić* Trial Chamber Decision); *Prosecutor* v. *Dragan Nikolić*, Case No. IT-94-2-AR73, Decision on Interlocutory Appeal Concerning Legality of Arrest, 5 June 2003 (hereafter, *Nikolić* Appeals Chamber Decision).

[109] *Nikolić* Trial Chamber Decision, paras. 17, 25.

[110] *Nikolić* Appeals Chamber Decision, para. 19.

[111] Currie, "Abducted Fugitives Before the International Criminal Court", at 368.

[112] *Nikolić* Trial Chamber Decision, para. 100.

[113] *Nikolić* Appeals Chamber Decision, para. 24.

[114] *Idem.*

[115] *Idem.*

> injury, if any, caused to the sovereignty of a State by a limited intrusion in its territory, particularly when the intrusion occurs in default of the State's cooperation. Therefore, the Appeals Chamber does not consider that in cases of universally condemned offences, jurisdiction should be set aside on the ground that there was a violation of the sovereignty of the State, when the violation is brought about by the apprehension of fugitives from international justice, whatever the consequences for the international responsibility of the State or organisation involved.'[116]

On the question of human rights violations, the Trial Chamber held that in order to apply the doctrine of abuse of process, 'it needs to be clear that the rights of the accused have been egregiously violated.'[117] In this case, it found that this standard was not met, particularly when considered in proportion to the serious war crimes charges. The Appeals Chamber agreed, finding that

> '[a]lthough the assessment of the seriousness of the human rights violations depends on the circumstances of each case and cannot be made *in abstracto*, certain human rights violations are of such a serious nature that they require that the exercise of jurisdiction be declined. It would be inappropriate for a court of law to try the victims of these abuses.'[118]

In this case, the accused's illegal capture and transfer was held not to have passed the threshold of seriousness required to justify a stay of proceedings. It noted that this approach was consistent with *Toscanino*, although it opined that the remedy of dismissal would 'usually be disproportionate.' In essence, it found that the 'correct balance must therefore be maintained between the fundamental rights of the accused and the essential interests of the international community in the prosecution of persons charged with serious violations of international humanitarian law.'[119]

Although the Appeals Chamber in *Nikolić* invoked *Eichmann* to support the proposition that State practice is more accepting of the *mala captus bene detentus* rule where the accused is being prosecuted for 'universally condemned crimes,' the Israeli Supreme Court did not rely on the nature of the crimes for which Eichmann was indicted to support the *mala captus* principle; instead the nature of the crimes merely grounded the jurisdiction of the court substantively.[120] Commentators have thus observed that the *Nikolić* Appeals Decision 'truly breaks new ground' in its 'remarkable expression of the weight behind the goals of international criminal justice.'[121] In fact, the effect of the decision has been said to be that '*mala captus bene detentus* is elevated from its former status as a declining principle of domestic

[116] *Ibid.*, para. 26.

[117] *Nikolić* Trial Chamber Decision, para. 111.

[118] *Nikolić* Appeals Chamber Decision, para. 30.

[119] *Idem.*

[120] Sloan, "*Prosecutor v. Dragan Nikolić*, Decision on Defence Motion on Illegal Capture", at 330, fn. 75.

[121] Currie, "Abducted Fugitives Before the International Criminal Court", at 370.

jurisdiction to being the new sword of the international criminal legal order, cutting through virtually all of the substantive and procedural concerns that might impair an international court's ability to try an individual before it.'[122]

The ICTR has held on a number of occasions that it is not responsible for the illegal arrest and detention of a defendant if the act was not the result of its order.[123] In *Rwamakuba*, it found that it was not empowered to rule upon the conditions of a defendant's detention period which occurred prior to any Tribunal request and that any relief in this respect must be directed toward the court that authorised such detention.[124]

The difficulty of the trend towards embracing the *mala captus bene detentus* principle is that it reveals a paradox in the goals of international criminal law. From one perspective, international criminal justice is about the enforcement of basic human rights and deterring mass atrocities in the future. From another, the process of such enforcement must itself uphold and protect human rights. As said by Judge Mansfield in *Toscanino*, '[s]ociety is the ultimate loser when, in order to convict the guilty, it uses methods that lead to decreased respect for the law.'[125] The *Nikolić* case therefore is a clear case of balancing interests, with a heavy presumption working on the side of exercising jurisdiction. Indeed the only circumstance which seems to be contemplated by the ICTY Appeals Chamber as a possibly countervailing consideration is where the fugitive was subject to physical abuse amounting to torture or inhuman, cruel or degrading treatment.

Commentators have pointed out that the ICC is likely to be faced with this type of issue in the future in view of its unique characteristics which make the likelihood of consensual and legal transfers of accused persons slim.[126] Article 59(1) of the ICC Statute provides that fugitives whose arrest has been requested should be apprehended 'in accordance with the law of that state,' and Article 59(2) obliges the 'competent judicial authority' of the arresting state to determine 'in accordance with the law of that State, that … (b) The person has been arrested in accordance with the proper process; and (c) The persons rights have been respected.' Article 55(1) further provides that any individual being investigated 'shall not be subjected to arbitrary arrest or detention.' Finally, the Court must apply and interpret the law in a manner 'consistent with internationally recognized human rights.'[127] The obligation to surrender fugitives to the Court would seem to indicate that it is the Court that should deal with any arrest irregularities. Indeed Article 85(1) provides that

---

[122] *Ibid.*, at 371.

[123] See, e.g., *Semanza*, ICTR, Appeals Chamber, Decision, Case No. ICTR-97-20-A, 31 May 2000, paras. 79, 91-104; *Kajelijeli*, ICTR, Trial Chamber II, Decision on the Defence Motion Concerning the Arbitrary Arrest and Illegal Detention of the Accused and on the Defence Notice of Urgent Motion to Expand and Supplement the Record of 8 December 1999 Hearing, Case No. ICTR-98-44-1, 8 May 2000, para. 35.

[124] *Rwamakuba*, ICTR, Trial Chamber II, Decision on the Defence Motion Concerning the Illegal Arrest and Illegal Detention of the Accused, Case No. ICTR-98-44-T, para. 30.

[125] *Toscanino*, at 274.

[126] Currie, "Abducted Fugitives Before the International Criminal Court", at 352.

[127] Art. 23(1) ICC Statute.

'Anyone who has been the victim of an unlawful arrest or detention shall have an enforceable right to compensation.' Therefore the proposition that 'the ICC must at least make an inquiry (probably under 21(3) into whether the circumstances of an accused's arrest and detention can and should have an effect on its exercise of jurisdiction'[128] is quite well supported.

Given that the ICC system is based on mutual support between the Court and member States, Currie has expressed concern about the *Nikolić* precedent being applied.[129] In his view, the destructive effect on inter-State relations caused by international abductions has the potential to itself post a threat to international peace and security.[130] While the ICTY was able to rely on its Security Council Chapter VII credentials to override concerns about violations to sovereignty, this is not the case for the ICC. Moreover, the situation for non-State parties is even less clear. Certainly a full embrace of the *mala captus bene detentus* rule would seem to be an unwise path for the ICC, as well as running counter to the rules enunciated above. Rather the answer lies in 'an exercise of flexible balancing, driven equally by the interests of criminal justice, international security and international human rights norms.'[131] In other words, there should be some proportionality between the remedy and the seriousness of the crime for which the accused has been indicted. Currie has suggested a 'multi-factored balancing test' that comes very close to a balance of interests test advocated in this book. In his view, the Court should take into consideration any inter-State international law violations, any human rights violations (including those perpetrated by 'unknown persons'), the seriousness of the crimes for which the person is be prosecuted, bearing in mind the presumption of innocence, as well as whether the Court's integrity has been undermined.[132] It is in balancing these factors together that the Court may reasonably and coherently decide if it should continue to exercise jurisdiction. Where the circumstances are such that dismissal is considered too extreme a remedy, the accused may still benefit from another lesser remedy such as compensation as foreseen in Article 85 of the Statute, or a reduction in prison sentence.

7.3.2 **Procedural rights**

Courts at both the national and international level have evinced a willingness to stay proceedings for serious violations of procedural rights of the accused. In cases

---

[128] Currie, "Abducted Fugitives Before the International Criminal Court", at 375.

[129] *Ibid.*, at 387: 'Adopting a *Nikolić*-type stance that will see virtually all abducted or illegally arrested fugitives face process, however, has the strong potential to defeat the Court's mission by: (1) tilting the uncertain balancing which is inherent in international criminal justice too far towards substantive justice at the expense of a process which requires adherence to human rights standards; and (2) undermining the very foundations, as well as the work, of the ICC by fanning the flames of disagreement about its existence and jurisdiction.'

[130] *Ibid.*, at 384.

[131] *Ibid.*, at 388.

[132] *Ibid.*, at 389.

dealing with international crimes, the violations must be egregious so that the remedy of dismissal is proportionate to the interest in prosecuting the person.

7.3.2.1 *National level*

On the national level, courts have focused on the deliberate misuse of authority as a determining factor in abuse of process cases for procedural irregularities. Thus, for instance, in the Australian case of *Truong* v. *The Queen*, which concerned the prosecution of an accused charged with a number of serious crimes, including murder and kidnapping, who had been extradited from the United Kingdom for a number of crimes excluding the specific crimes of murder and kidnapping, constituting a breach of the double criminality requirement in extradition law, High Court judges Gummow, Callinan and Kirby found that the breach did not amount to an abuse of process, chiefly because 'the element of deliberate misuse of authority is missing.'[133]

7.3.2.2 *International level*

In the ICTR case of *Barayagwiza*, the accused was legally arrested, but was detained for an extremely long period and had his right to prompt information as to the charges against him and to *habeas corpus* violated. It is worth briefly recalling the facts. Barayagwiza had been arrested on 15 April 1996 together with other suspects in Cameroon on suspicion of having committed genocide and crimes against humanity in Rwanda in 1994. Two months later the Prosecutor informed the Cameroonian authorities that she did not intend to pursue a prosecution against Barayagwiza, but the Cameroonian authorities continued to detain him. In October 1996, the Prosecutor informed Barayagwiza that his detention was not at the behest of the Tribunal. On 21 February 1997, the Court of Appeal of Cameroon ordered the release of the suspects following the rejection of Rwandan and Belgian extradition requests. Upon their release, the Prosecutor made a request pursuant to Rule 40 of the Rules of Procedure and Evidence for the provisional detention of Barayagwiza, and he was subsequently re-arrested. The Prosecutor requested an 'Order for Arrest and Transfer' on 24 February and 3 March 1997, but this was not executed until 19 March 1997. His first appearance did not occur until 23 February 1998.

The Appeals Chamber found that the 96-day delay between Barayagwiza's transfer to the Tribunal's detention unit and his initial detention constituted a violation of his fundamental rights as expressed in Articles 19 and 20 of the Statute, internationally recognised human rights standards, and Rule 62 of the Rules.[134] It also noted that he was detained for a total of 11 months before he was informed of the general nature of the charges against him, which violated the right to be

[133] *Truong* v. *The Queen*, 223 *CLR* 122 (2004); 205 *ALR* 72 (2004).

[134] *Barayagwiza*, para. 71.

promptly informed of the charges against him following arrest.[135] Therefore, 'in light of serious and egregious violations of the accused's rights [that] would prove detrimental to the court's integrity,' it would exercise its power of dismissal.[136] The Appeals Chamber took due account of the fact that '[t]he crimes for which the Appellant is charged are very serious.' However, it found that:

> 'in this case the fundamental rights of the Appellant were repeatedly violated. What may be worse, it appears that the Prosecutor's failure to prosecute this case was tantamount to negligence. We find this conduct to be egregious and, in light of the numerous violations, conclude that the only remedy available for such prosecutorial inaction and the resultant denial of his rights is to release the Appellant and dismiss the charges against him.'[137]

Notably, the Appeals Chamber was of the view that '[e]ven if fault is shared between the three organs of the Tribunal – or is the result of a third party, such as Cameroon – it would undermine the integrity of the judicial process to proceed … Thus, under the abuse of process doctrine, it is irrelevant which entity or entities were responsible for the alleged violations of the Appellant's rights.'[138]

The Appeals Chamber recognised that its disposition may be 'troubling' to some,[139] but was of the view that '[l]oss of public confidence in the Tribunal, as a court valuing human rights of all individuals – including those charged with unthinkable crimes – would be among the most serious consequences of allowing the Appellant to stand trial in the face of such violations of his rights. As difficult as this conclusion may be for some to accept, it is the proper role of an independent judiciary to halt this prosecution, so that no further injustice results.'[140] Although the remedy of dismissal was altered in a subsequent review requested by the Prosecutor,[141] it has been pointed out that '"*Barayagwiza II*" did not in any way affect the guiding principles established in "*Barayagwiza I*."'[142]

Similar issues were raised by Thomas Lubanga Dyilo before the International Criminal Court, who argued before a Pre-Trial Chamber that he had been mistreated while incarcerated in the Democratic Republic of the Congo prior to his surrender to the Court, that the Prosecutor was complicit in such treatment, and consequently, that the Court should relinquish jurisdiction under Article 19(2) and release him on the basis of the abuse of process doctrine. The Pre-Trial Chamber found that such a remedy could theoretically be granted for abuse of process and

---

135 *Ibid.*, para. 85.

136 *Ibid.*, para. 74.

137 *Ibid.*, para. 106.

138 *Idem.*

139 *Ibid.*, para. 108.

140 *Ibid.*, para. 112.

141 *Barayagwiza*, Appeals Chamber, Decision (Prosecutor's Request for Review or Reconsideration), Case No. ICTR-97-19-A, 31 March 2000.

142 Göran Sluiter, "International Criminal Proceedings and the Protection of Human Rights" 37 *New England Law Review* 935 (2003), at 945.

by reason of the fundamental rights of the accused in Article 21(3), but dismissed the application for lack of evidence. The Appeals Chamber upheld the Pre-Trial Chamber's decision, although it found that the issue was not one of 'jurisdiction' under Article 19, but rather a *sui generis* motion, 'a procedural step not envisaged by the Rules of Procedure and Evidence or the Regulations of the Court invoking a power possessed by the Court to remedy breaches of the process in the interests of justice.'[143] It examined the abuse of process doctrine and found that because the doctrine is not really known to civil law systems, it 'is not generally recognised as an indispensable power of a court of law, an inseverable attribute of judicial power,' and therefore was not one of the inherent powers of the Court.[144]

Nevertheless, the Appeals Chamber held that because Article 21(3) imposed on the Court the obligation to abide by human rights standards, this gave the Court the power to stay proceedings where the treatment of an accused violates 'first and foremost, in the context of the Statute, the right to a fair trial.'[145] In particular, it held that where 'the breaches of the accused are such as to make it impossible for him/her to make his/her defence within the framework of his rights, no fair trial can take place and the proceedings can be stayed.'[146] Interestingly, the Appeals Chamber also applied a balance of interests test, finding that '[i]n those circumstances, the interest of the world community to put persons accused of the most heinous crimes against humanity on trial, great as it is, is outweighed by the need to sustain the efficacy of the judicial process as the potent agent of justice.'[147]

Before the ICTY, the accused Radovan Karadžić brought an abuse of process motion, arguing that two raids – one on his wife's home in Pale, Bosnia and Herzegovina on 2 December 2008 by NATO troops and one on the home of his sister-in-law in Pale on 27 March 2009 pursuant to a search warrant of a Bosnian court in Sarajevo – were an abuse of process, thereby justifying a stay of proceedings.[148] Specifically, he submitted that the purpose of the searches was to frustrate his efforts to mount an effective defence and have a fair trial and that the searches were designed to intimidate and discourage his potential witnesses in Bosnia.[149] The Trial Chamber dismissed the Motion on the basis that there was no 'egregious violation of the Accused's rights such that the abuse of process doctrine could be invoked to dismissed the Indictment ...'[150] It also took into account the fact that there was no Prosecution involvement in the NATO raid,[151] although it noted the Appeals Chamber's holding in *Nikolić* that jurisdiction would not have been set

[143] *Lubanga* Appeals Judgment of 14 December 2006, para. 24.

[144] *Ibid.*, para. 35.

[145] *Ibid.*, para. 37.

[146] *Ibid.*, para. 39.

[147] *Idem.*

[148] *Prosecutor* v. *Radovan Karadžić*, Case No. IT-95-5/18-PT, Motion to Dismiss for Abuse of Process, 14 April 2009.

[149] *Ibid.*, paras. 1, 10-13.

[150] *Karadžić*, ICTY, Trial Chamber, Case No. IT-95-5/18-PT, Decision on Motion to Dismiss for Abuse of Process, 12 May 2009, para. 13.

[151] *Idem.*

aside in that case even if the conduct of Nikolić's captors had been attributed to SFOR and, by extension, to the Prosecution.[152] This suggests that even if the Prosecution had been involved in the December raid, the Trial Chamber would probably still have dismissed the motion.

In regard to the March search, the Trial Chamber observed that it was conducted legally in accordance with a duly certified search warrant and that Karadžić had made no allegations of impropriety or serious misconduct on the part of the authorities which conducted the search.[153] The Trial Chamber found that the purpose of the search was to obtain documentation relevant to his case and that there were no legal grounds for the assertion that any search of his family's properties would be an egregious violation of his rights.[154] The Trial Chamber also invoked the principle of proportionality in the remedy sought, finding that '[e]ven if the search in question was deemed to be unreasonable or in breach of the Accused's rights, the remedy would not be to dismiss the proceedings, but a more proportionate measure, such as excluding the evidence obtained.'[155] Moreover, since the Prosecution was under an obligation of disclosure, and had made representations that it would comply with this obligation as soon as they were in possession of the documents, Karadžić had shown no real prejudice to his fair trial rights.[156]

In the contempt proceedings against Florence Hartmann before the ICTY, the defence argued that 'serious violations' in the course of the investigation were attributable to the *Amicus Curiae* Investigator and individually or cumulatively amounted to an abuse of process.[157] In particular, the Defence argued that there was a complete failure to investigate *à décharge*; the Investigator had violated United Nations immunities and the ICTY Statute; there was a failure to abide by basic standards of investigative diligence in the process of collecting information; there was a failure to provide the Chamber with a reliable factual basis on which to decide to initiate contempt proceedings; and there had been a refusal to answer legitimate questions by the Defence.[158] The Specially Appointed Chamber adopted the view of the Trial Chamber in *Nikolić* that in order to invoke abuse of process, 'it needs to be clear that the rights of the Accused have been egregiously violated.'[159] Having assessed each alleged violation by the Investigator, the Chamber found no violations to have occurred and thus concluded that the arguments of the Defence individually or cumulatively did not amount to abuse of process.[160]

---

[152] *Ibid.*, para. 11.

[153] *Ibid.*, para. 14.

[154] *Ibid.*, para. 15.

[155] *Idem.*

[156] *Idem.*

[157] *Hartmann*, ICTY, Trial Chamber, Case No. IT-02-54-R77.5, Reasons for Decision on the Defence Motion for a Stay of Proceedings for Abuse of Process, 3 February 2009, para. 1.

[158] *Idem.*

[159] *Ibid.*, para. 4.

[160] *Ibid.*, para. 13.

7.3.3 **Delay**

It is a recognised human right to have a fair trial within a reasonable time.[161] On the national level, delay has been used to justify a stay of proceedings where this results in prejudice to the defence. To date, international courts have shown less willingness to accord the problem of delay the measure of seriousness justifying a stay of proceedings, even where the delay has amounted to years of incarceration prior to trial.

7.3.3.1 *National level*

While '[t]he passage of time is, of itself, no impediment to the fairness of a re-trial,'[162] courts have shown a tendency to stay proceedings where the effect of that delay can be said to have had on the ability of the defendant to mount an effective case.[163] In *Attorney-General's Reference (No. 1 of 1990)*,[164] the UK Court of Appeal held that a stay should be the exception rather than the rule, even in cases where the delay could be considered unjustifiable; it would be even more rare to grant a stay where the delay was not caused by the fault of the prosecution. It also held that a stay should never be ordered if the delay was due merely to the complexity of the case or the accused contributed to it. Finally, the accused must be able to show on the balance of probabilities that he or she would suffer serious prejudice to the extent that no fair trial could take place.[165] This case would appear to be treated as the leading English authority on the extent to which proceedings can be stayed on account of prejudicial delay.[166]

In *Attorney General's Reference (No 2 of 2001)*, Lord Bingham stated that 'Criminal proceedings may be stayed on the ground that there has been a violation of the reasonable time requirement in Article 6(1) of the Convention only if (a) a fair hearing is no longer possible or (b) it is for any compelling reason unfair to try the defendant.' In *R.* v. *Grays Justices* ex parte *Graham*, the Queen's Bench stated in *obiter dicta* that: 'prolonged delay in starting or conducting criminal proceedings may be an abuse of process when the substantial delay was caused by the improper use of procedure or inefficiency on the part of the prosecution and the

---

[161] Art. 14(3)(c) ICCPR (guarantees the right to be tried without undue delay); Art. 6(1) ECHR (guarantees the right to a fair trial within a reasonable time); Art. 8(1) ACHR (guarantees the right to a hearing within a reasonable time); Art. 7(1)(d) African Charter on Human and Peoples Rights (guarantees the right to be tried within a reasonable time). See also *Lubanga* Appeals Judgment of 21 October 2008, para. 30.

[162] *R* v. *Dunlop* [2006] EWCA Crim. 1354 [2007] 1 *Cr App R* 8.

[163] *R* v. *Gateshead Justices ex parte Smith* (1985) 149 J.P. 681 (finding that a stay would only be appropriate if (a) there had been inordinate or unconscionable delay due to the prosecution's inefficiency; and (b) prejudice to the defence could either be proved or inferred).

[164] [1992] QB 630.

[165] *Ibid.*, at 643-644.

[166] See *Attorney-General of Hong Kong* v. *Cheung* [1994] 1 AC 1; *R* [1994] *CrimLR* 948.

accused has neither caused nor contributed to the delay.'[167] Choo adds the point that 'even if there is no danger of wrongful conviction, the delay may, by causing the accused to suffer oppression, anxiety and concern, have compromised the moral integrity of the criminal process to such an extent that a stay of the proceedings is appropriate.'[168]

7.3.3.2 *International level*

The issue of delay in the context of abuse of process arose in the Extraordinary Chambers in the Courts of Cambodia (ECCC) in an order for the provisional detention of Kaing Guek Eav, alias Duch, who has been charged with crimes against humanity and grave breaches of the Geneva Conventions of 1949 allegedly committed in Cambodia between 1975 and 1979.[169] Duch had been charged with murder, torture, and membership of an outlawed group and placed in provisional detention since 1999 by the order of the Military Court of Phnomh Penh and had therefore been in provisional detention for some eight years prior to the ECCC order for provisional detention. He argued that the length of this detention violated his rights and that he should be released in application of the abuse of process doctrine.

The ECCC co-investigating judges found that '[h]is continued provisional detention is problematic in light of international standards, and more specifically, articles 9(3) and 14(3)(c) of the International Covenant on Civil and Political Rights (ICCPR), which states that any individual arrested or detained for a criminal offence shall be entitled to a trial within a reasonable time period or be released.'[170] However, since his eight year provisional detention was not at the behest of the ECCC itself, the co-investigating judges had to decide whether this detention as a result of separate proceedings before a different jurisdiction so tainted the ECCC's proceedings as to justify a stay and warrant his release.[171] The ECCC co-investigating judges reviewed both the *male captus bene detentus* principle and the abuse of process doctrine. With regard to *male captus bene detentus*, they observed that there were many examples in domestic as well as in international law which apply this 'maxim'[172] and that there was therefore 'a solid tradition supporting the strict separation of, on the one hand, a legal procedure before one jurisdiction and, on the other hand, the prior illegal arrest and detention ordered by a different authority.'[173]

---

[167] *R* v. *Grays Justices ex parte Graham* (1982) QB 1239.

[168] Choo, "Halting Criminal Prosecutions", at 869.

[169] Extraordinary Chambers in the Courts of Cambodia, Office of the Co-Investigating Judges, Criminal Case File No: 002/14-08-2006, Investigation No: 001/18-07-2007-ECCC-OCIJ, Closing order indicting Kaing Guek Eav alias Duch, Public redacted version, 8 August 2008.

[170] Extraordinary Chambers in the Courts of Cambodia, Office of the Co-Investigating Judges, Criminal Case File No: 002/14-08-2006, Investigation No: 001/18-07-2007-ECCC-OCIJ, Order of Provisional Detention, 31 July 2007 (hereafter, Order of Provisional Detention), para. 2.

[171] *Ibid.*, para. 3.

[172] *Ibid.*, para. 5.

[173] *Ibid.*, para. 11.

However, the ECCC also found that 'this tradition is limited by the doctrine of "*abuse of process*."'[174] Having reviewed a number of cases on abuse of process, the Co-investigating Judges concluded that they did not have jurisdiction to determine the legality of Duch's prior detention on the basis that (1) the ECCC did not act in concert with the military court, and therefore can only be held responsible for the time lapse between the lodging of the Introductory Submission and the arrest warrant (12 days), which cannot be deemed to be excessive;[175] (2) the abuse of process doctrine did not apply because 'in a case of crimes against humanity, the proceedings should be stayed only where the rights of the accused have been seriously affected, at least, for example, to the degree in *Toscanino*.'[176] In other words, it found that the doctrine could only be applied if Duch had been subjected to torture or serious mistreatment, which was not the case.[177] Applying a proportionality test, it determined that 'prolonged detention under the Military Court, in comparison with the crimes against humanity alleged against the Accused, cannot be considered a sufficiently grave violation of the rights of the Accused.'[178] It added that an eventual remedy for the prejudice caused by the prior detention in the form of a reduction of sentence or other means might be possible, but was not at issue during the investigative stage.[179]

The decision was appealed to the Pre-Trial Chamber, which upheld the Co-investigating Judges order.[180] The Pre-Trial Chamber confined itself to observing that there was no relationship between the ECCC and the Military Court or any evidence of concerted action between them; it did not pronounce itself on the abuse of process doctrine or the *mala captus bene detentus* principle.[181] It is unclear if this amounts to a rejection of the application of these principles by the ECCC, although since the appeal was grounded on a claim that the ECCC acted in concert with the Cambodian Military Court, this could explain why the Pre-Trial Chamber approached the decision in this way without explicitly considering abuse of process *per se*.[182]

Some commentators, such as Ryngaert, have supported the Co-investigating Judges' decision, arguing that firstly, 'from a policy perspective, a high standard of applying abuse of process in international criminal law – resulting in less protection for the defendant's rights – is appropriate, in the light of the grave crimes for

[174] *Idem*.

[175] *Ibid.*, para. 20.

[176] *Ibid.*, para. 21.

[177] *Idem*.

[178] *Idem*.

[179] *Idem*.

[180] Extraordinary Chambers in the Courts of Cambodia, Pre-Trial Chamber, Criminal Case File No: 002/18-07-2007-ECCC-OCIJ (PTC01), Decision on Appeal against Provisional Detention Order of Kaing Guek Eav alias 'Duch,' 3 December 2007.

[181] *Ibid.*, at para. 15: 'The Pre-Trial Chamber is of the view that it can only take a violation of this Article [9 ICCPR] into account when the organ responsible for the violation was connected to an organ of the ECCC, or had been acting on behalf of any organ of the ECCC or in concert with organs of the ECCC.'

[182] *Ibid.*, para. 13.

which the defendants are prosecuted before international criminal tribunals' and secondly, 'from a consistency perspective, the ECCC abuse of process standard is in line with applications of the doctrine by the (other) international criminal tribunals.'[183] However, Ryngaert also notes the basic problem of this approach in relation to the presumption of innocence that applies to any accused, even those accused of the most serious crimes, that it would appear 'unfair to rely on a presumption of his having committed grave crimes, a presumption that may tip in the balance in favour of not staying the proceedings.'[184] He alleviates his concern, however, by arguing that 'the societal return of not staying the proceedings initiated against those who committed heinous crimes, in terms of deterrence and political reconciliation, may outweigh the societal value associated with strict protection of non-fundamental human rights standards, such as the right to a trial within a reasonable time.'[185]

7.3.4 **Withholding of exculpatory evidence**

Other prosecutorial malpractice has been deemed sufficient to amount to an abuse of process where they are so serious and so detrimental to the rights of the accused that a subsequent trial would be severely tainted, and in fact result in a miscarriage of justice. In such cases, 'the likelihood of a serious contamination of the criminal proceedings should be excluded by a prospective remedy to anticipate a wrongful conviction.'[186] An example of this is when the court finds that the investigating or prosecuting authorities have deliberately or negligently withheld exculpatory evidence to the detriment of the accused.[187] The prosecution's failure to disclose materials led the court to stay proceedings on grounds of abuse of process in *R.* v. *Birmingham and Others*.[188] The defence's inability to question prosecution witnesses can also result in a successful stay of proceedings on the grounds of abuse of process.[189]

At the international level, in *Blaškić*, the ICTY Appeals Chamber had to decide whether the prosecution's failure to disclose three exhibits which were exculpatory to the accused justified a stay of proceedings.[190] The Appeals Chamber found that the defence had not suffered any material prejudice as a result and declined to sanction the prosecution.[191]

---

[183] Cedric Ryngaert, "The Doctrine of Abuse of Process: A Comment on the Cambodia Tribunal's Decisions in the Case against Duch (2007)", 21 *LJIL* 720 (2008).

[184] *Ibid.*, at 731.

[185] *Ibid.*, at 732.

[186] Knoops, *Redressing Miscarriages of Justice*, at 179.

[187] See, e.g., *R.* v. *Kamara*, Court of Appeal, Case No. 9902769X4, Criminal Division on Appeal from Liverpool Crown Court, 9 May 2000 (concerning a case in which a re-trial was ordered on the basis, *inter alia*, of an unsafe conviction due to deficiencies in the identification procedure).

[188] [1992] *CrimLR* 117.

[189] *R.* v. *J.A.K.* (1992) *CrimLR* 30.

[190] *Blaškić*, ICTY, Appeals Chamber, Judgment, Case No. IT-95-14-T-A, 29 July 2004.

[191] *Ibid.*, para. 299.

The ICC had occasion to consider the abuse of process doctrine within the context of the Prosecution withholding exculpatory evidence from the defendant Lubanga consisting of some 200 documents that were subject to a confidentiality agreement with third parties (mainly the United Nations) under Article 54(3)(e) of the Statute, which had not agreed to lift confidentiality.[192] The Appeals Chamber reiterated its view expressed in the 2006 judgment that the doctrine of abuse of process, as practised in common law jurisdictions, finds no application as such under the Statute, but held that 'to the extent it aims to stem breaches of fundamental principles of justice, it is endorsed by the Statute as a means of protecting the individual from violations of his/her fundamental rights and in order to ensure a fair trial that earmarks the parameters of the administration of justice.'[193] The Appeals Chamber ultimately ruled that the failure on the part of the Prosecutor to discharge the duty of obtaining exonerating evidence known to exist and eventual inability to disclose exonerating evidential material in his possession constituted a breach of the right of the accused under Article 67(2) of the Statute, which was fundamental for the preparation of his defence and of direct relevance to the main issue of the trial, his guilt or innocence. This was fatal to the exercise of jurisdiction: 'The finding of impossibility to hold a fair trial seals the end of the proceedings.'[194] However, in a separate judgment issued the same day, the Appeals Chamber found that this did not necessarily signify the need to release the defendant.[195] Because the stay of proceedings was conditional, this did not render the release of the accused 'inevitable.'[196] Hence, it determined that 'a conditional stay is neither an acquittal nor a final termination of the proceedings, but may be lifted in appropriate circumstances' which meant that 'the Court is not necessarily permanently barred from exercising jurisdiction in respect of the person concerned.'[197] The stay of proceedings was eventually lifted by Trial Chamber I on 18 November 2008 once the issues had been resolved, and Lubanga's trial commenced on 26 January 2009.[198]

---

192 *Situation in the Democratic Republic of the Congo in the Case of The Prosecutor* v. *Thomas Lubanga Dyilo*, Case No. ICC-01/04-01/06 (OA13), Judgment on the appeal of the Prosecutor against the decision of Trial Chamber I entitled "Decision on the consequences of non-disclosure of exculpatory materials covered by Article 54(3)(e) agreements and the application to stay the prosecution of the accused, together with certain other issues raised at the Status Conference on 10 June 2008", 21 October 2008 (hereafter, *Lubanga* Appeals Judgment of 21 October 2008).

193 *Ibid.*, para. 29.

194 *Ibid.*, para. 51.

195 *Situation in the Democratic Republic of the Congo in the Case of The Prosecutor* v. *Thomas Lubanga Dyilo*, Case No. ICC-01/04-01/06 (OA12), Judgment on the appeal of the Prosecutor against the decision of Trial Chamber I entitled "Decision on the release of Thomas Lubanga Dyilo", 21 October 2008, para. 1.

196 *Ibid.*, para. 31. The Appeals Chamber explained that 'in the ordinary course of events, if a permanent and irreversible stay of the proceedings is imposed the accused person will have to be released because continued detention would not be in connection with the exercise of criminal jurisdiction by the Court.' *Ibid.*, para. 36.

197 *Ibid.*, para. 37.

198 Transcript of hearing on 18 November 2008, ICC-01/04-01/06-T-98-ENG, page 3, lines 22-25, page 4, line 1.

7.3.5 Double jeopardy

As noted in chapter 6, in certain common law jurisdictions, the abuse of process doctrine has been used to stay proceedings in cases which place the accused in double jeopardy even though the pleas in bar (*autrefois aquit* and *autrefois convict*) are unavailable.[199] The House of Lords in *DPP* v. *Humphrys*[200] recognised the close relationship between the pleas of *autrefois acquit* and *autrefois convict* and which operate as bars to subsequent trials and stays based on abuse of process. As opposed to the absolute right of relief that a defendant is entitled to pursuant to a plea in bar, the abuse of process doctrine gives only a qualified right.[201]

Choo has observed that in the context of double jeopardy, 'the abuse of process doctrine may be viewed as compensation for the narrow scope of the pleas in bar, and for the unavailability in English criminal law of the doctrine of issue estoppel.'[202] As for the operation of *ne bis in idem*, courts have tended to exercise their discretion to stay proceedings under abuse of process only where the initial proceedings were the same type of proceedings as the second proceedings. Where pleas of autrefois acquit or *convict* has been rejected by the court, it is open to the defendant to still argue that to allow the prosecution to continue in the circumstances of the case would amount to an abuse of process. The court would still retain the discretion to stay the proceedings if persuaded by the defence's argument notwithstanding the fact that it rejected the plea in bar.[203]

7.3.6 Breach of promises of non-prosecution (amnesty)

7.3.6.1 *National level*

It has been held that the 'prosecution of a person who has received a promise, undertaking or representation from the police that they will not be prosecuted is capable of being an abuse of process.'[204] The Divisional Court in the United Kingdom in *R.* v. *Croydon JJ.,* ex parte *Dean* took the view that the prosecution should be stayed on account of such a promise even though the police had no authority to make such a promise and even though the police did not act in bad faith.[205] Gene-

---

[199] *Connolly* v. *DPP*, United Kingdom [1964] AC 1254, at 1334 (L.J. Hodson).

[200] *DPP* v. *Humphrys* [1977] AC 1.

[201] *Ibid.*, at 1358 (*per* L. Devlin)

[202] Choo, "Halting Criminal Prosecutions", at 865, citing *DPP* v. *Humphrys*, United Kingdom [1977] AC 1 and *Rogers*, Australia, 68 *A.L.J.R.* 688 (1994).

[203] *R.* v. *Horsham Justices ex parte Reeves*, 75 *Cr App R* 236; *R.* v. *Beedie* (1997), 2 *Cr App R* 167; but see *R.* v. *Willesden Justices ex parte Clemmings*, 87 *Cr App R* 280.

[204] *R.* v. *Croydon JJ.,* ex parte *Dean*, United Kingdom [1993] QB 769, at 778.

[205] *Idem*. Choo notes that this case concerned a 17 year old, and suggests that the Court was influenced by this fact in deciding to stay the prosecution. Choo, "Halting Criminal Prosecutions", at 867, citing *ibid.*, at 776-779. See also *R.* v. *Bloomfield* [1997] 1 *Cr App R* 135 (in which it was held to have been an abuse of process where, at a previous plea and directions hearing, prosecuting counsel had indicated informally to defence counsel that the prosecutor proposed to offer no evidence against the

rally, there will be no abuse of process where there is no suggestion of bad faith or substantial prejudice to the defendant.[206]

The Privy Council in *Attorney-General of Trinidad and Tobago* v. *Phillip*[207] held that the re-prosecution of offenders after a pardon had been granted and an order of *habeas corpus* made would constitute an abuse of process even if the pardon was in fact invalid. Choo observes that 'both considerations underlying the abuse of process doctrine (protection of the innocent from conviction and protection of the moral integrity of the criminal process) may be at play in this area.'[208] This is because a person who does not think that he or she will be prosecuted might not bother to preserve evidence, leaving the possibility that this person might be convicted even if they are innocent.[209] It is also said to be 'morally questionable for the prosecution to launch proceedings which the accused has been led, either expressly or impliedly, to believe would not be brought.'[210]

7.3.6.2 *International level*

Such views have considerable ramifications at the level of international criminal trials, where promises of non-prosecution or *de facto* amnesties have often been traded for participation of alleged perpetrators in peace talks. In fact, this argument has been brought by Radovan Karadžić before the ICTY, who has argued that he was promised on 18-19 July 1996 by United States diplomat Richard Holbrooke that he would not face prosecution in The Hague if he agreed to withdraw completely from public life and that this promise is attributable to the ICTY,[211] and applied for the inspection and disclosure of numerous documents pertaining to this claim.[212]

In its Decision dealing with this Application, the Trial Chamber granted the motion in part, ordering the Prosecution to disclose 'any written agreement made at the alleged meeting in Belgrade on 18-19 July 1996' and any notes thereof.[213] However, the Trial Chamber held that such documents were only material with

---

defendant, which was repeated before the judge in his chambers, and the matter was been adjourned, at the prosecutor's request, to another day for no evidence to be offered).

206 *R.* v. *Jobe* [2004] EWCA Crim. 3155; *R* v. *Mulla* [2004] 1 *Cr App R* 6.

207 [1994] 3 *WLR* 1134.

208 Choo, "Halting Criminal Prosecutions", at 867.

209 *Idem.*

210 *Idem.*

211 According to Charles W. Ingrao and Thomas A. Emmert (eds.), *Confronting the Yugoslav Controversies: A Scholar's Initiative* (Indiana: Purdue University Press, 2009), three senior State Department officials have said that Mr. Holbrooke told them about such an agreement. Holbrooke has emphatically denied the existence of the deal. See Marlise Simons, "U.S. diplomats back Karadžić's claim of immunity deal", *International Herald Tribune*, 22 March 2009.

212 *Prosecutor* v. *Radovan Karadžić*, Case No. IT-95-5/18-PT, Motion for Inspection and Disclosure: Holbrooke Agreement, 6 November 2008, para. 3.

213 *Karadžić*, ICTY, Trial Chamber, Case No. IT-95-5/18-PT, Decision on Accused's Second Motion for Inspection and Disclosure: Immunity Issue, 17 December 2008.

respect to their potential relevance in sentencing,[214] not with regard to any defence argument with some prospect of success, since the Trial Chamber considered that it is 'well established that any immunity agreement in respect of an accused indicted for genocide, war crimes and/or crimes against humanity before an international tribunal would be invalid under international law.'[215] It further considered that 'pursuant to the Statute and the Rules of the Tribunal, neither its own mandate nor that of the Prosecutor is affected by an alleged undertaking made by Mr. Holbrooke.'[216]

In appealing this decision, Karadžić argued that even if the Trial Chamber was correct in finding that the alleged Holbrooke Agreement was invalid under international law, this agreement may potentially constitute an abuse of process on the basis of which the Tribunal may choose to decline to exercise jurisdiction and stay the case.[217] The Appeals Chamber did not make any findings on this point since it found the issues moot by reason of the fact that the Prosecution had been ordered to disclose all materials in relation to the so-called Holbrooke Agreement.[218]

However, Karadžić then filed a further motion requesting the Trial Chamber to dismiss the Indictment against him on the ground that, as a result of the alleged Agreement, the Tribunal lacks jurisdiction, or alternatively, that the Trial Chamber exercise its discretion and decline to exercise jurisdiciton under the abuse of process doctrine.[219] The Trial Chamber rejected the motion, finding the Agreement could not be attributed to the ICTY Prosecutor nor the UN Security Council and that Karadžić had failed to show that any abuse of process had occurred, since 'even in light of the Agreement', proceeding with the case would not affect his right to a fair trial.[220] It also found that the doctrine of abuse of process could not be triggered by a promise allegedly made by a third party, unconnected with the Tribunal, granting immunity to a person years before his transfer to the Tribunal.[221]

Although the Appeals Chamber was critical of the Trial Chamber's decision since it had made certain factual findings when it had stated at the outset of its decision that it would accept Karadžić's factual allegations as if they were true (*pro veritae*),[222] it essentially agreed with the Trial Chamber that absent a Security Council resolution amending the jurisdiction of the Tribunal, the alleged Agree-

---

214 *Ibid.*, para. 23.

215 *Ibid.*, para. 25.

216 *Idem.*

217 *Prosecutor* v. *Radovan Karadžić*, Case No. IT-95-5/18-AR73.1, Appeal of Decision Concerning Holbrooke Agreement Disclosure, 28 January 2009, para. 99.

218 *Karadžić*, ICTY, Appeals Chamber, Case No. IT-95-5/18-AR73.1, Decision on Appellant Radovan Karadžić's Appeal Concerning Holbrooke Agreement Disclosure, 6 April 2009, para. 17.

219 *Prosecutor* v. *Radovan Karadžić*, Case No. IT-95-5/18-PT, Holbrooke Agreement Motion, 25 May 2009, with Annexes, paras. 1, 3. He also asked for an evidentiary hearing so that the Trial Chamber could make findings of fact on the existence of the Agreement.

220 *Karadžić*, ICTY, Trial Chamber, Case No. IT-95-5/18-PT, Decision on The Accused's Holbrooke Agreement Motion, 8 July 2009, paras. 51-56, 57-78, 84.

221 *Ibid.*, paras 84-85, 88.

222 *Karadžić*, ICTY, Appeals Chamber, Case No. IT-95-5/18-AR73.4, Decision on Karadžić's Appeal of Trial Chamber's Decision on Alleged Holbrooke Agreement, 12 October 2009 (hereafter, *Karadžić* Appeals Chamber Decision), para. 27.

ment could not in and of itself limit the jurisdiction of the Tribunal by excluding its reach to certain individuals,[223] underscoring that '[j]urisdiction of criminal courts is not a negotiable matter.'[224] It also found that even if the Agreement could be attributed to the Prosecutor, the Prosecution would have been unable to withdraw the indictment against Karadžić without leave of a Judge of the Tribunal, so the Agreement could not have been binding on the Tribunal.[225]

On the question of abuse of process, the Appeals Chamber notably found that its decisions in *Barayagwiza* and *Nikolić* did not create a dual standard for the abuse of process doctrine depending on the nature of the entity which carried out the alleged misconduct.[226] It held that the abuse of process doctrine, as set out in the Appeals Chamber's jurisprudence, applies in respect of 'serious and egregious violations of the accused's rights', irrespective of the author of the alleged misconduct.[227] The Appeals Chamber compared the legitimate interest of the international community in the prosecution of Karadžić against his expectation that he would not be prosecuted by the Tribunal by reason of the Agreement and the fact that he had resigned from all his positions in the Republika Srpska government in July 1996 and completely withdrew from public life in exchange for this promise.[228] On the basis of its previous legal findings, the Appeals Chamber considered that 'any alleged expectation of the Appellant not to be tried before the Tribunal would be grounded on a flawed reading of the applicable law.'[229] Since none of Karadžić's allegations could 'qualify as a situation making a fair trial impossible,' the real question for the Appeals Chamber was whether proceeding with the trial would contravene the Tribunal's sense of justice or be detrimental to its integrity.[230] In this respect, it underlined the fundamental aim of international criminal courts and tribunals 'to end impunity and to ensure that serious violations of international humanitarian law are prosecuted and punished,' which entailed that persons accused of such crimes 'can have no legitimate expectations of immunity from prosecution.'[231] Therefore, it concluded, even if Karadžić's allegations about the Agreement were proved, they 'would not trigger the doctrine of abuse of process justifying a stay of the proceedings agianst the Appellant.'[232]

Notwithstanding the force of the Appeals Chamber's decision, the national precedents cited above give some reason to give credence to Karadžić's argument. At the same time, it may be recalled that when the Lomé amnesty was raised as a potential bar to prosecution by reason of the abuse of process doctrine before the Special Court for Sierra Leone, the Court found that due to the Special Court's

[223] *Ibid.*, para. 37.
[224] *Ibid.*, para. 38.
[225] *Ibid.*, para. 41.
[226] *Ibid.*, para. 47.
[227] *Idem.*
[228] *Ibid.*, para. 49.
[229] *Ibid.*, para. 50.
[230] *Ibid.*, para. 51.
[231] *Ibid.*, para. 52.
[232] *Ibid.*, para. 53.

independent and autonomous nature, it was 'not tainted' by whatever undertaking any accused claiming the benefit of the amnesty may have believed he had from the Government of Sierra Leone.[233] In any case, the Court argued, the 'crystallising norm' in customary international law that amnesties for international crimes are unlawful reduced the potency of the abuse of process argument.[234] This holding would seem to suggest again a type of balancing in the considerations of a court in deciding whether a promise of non-prosecution should have any effect on the decision to exercise jurisdiction. Since it is commonly accepted that so-called 'immunity agreements,' or 'amnesties' or promises of non-prosecution do not have any impact on the jurisdiction of international tribunals, this would be one factor that a court would need to weigh in consideration of applying the abuse of process doctrine. At the same time, the moral integrity of the tribunals would be jeopardised where they operated in flagrant rejection of the sensitive political negotiating tactics that are used to end wars and make peace deals. Therefore, an outright rejection of such arguments would not be a wise path for the ICC or the international tribunals to follow. Rather a reasonable balancing of these interests in the specific circumstances of the particular case would best resolve the dilemma of whether to prosecute in such situations.

7.3.7 **Misuse of the criminal process**

Courts have regarded the misuse of the criminal process, or evidence that the prosecution has been launched for an improper purpose, as a basis for staying proceedings.[235] Even if there is no suggestion that a fair trial will be impossible, *mala fides* on the part of the prosecution may impair the moral integrity of the criminal process and thus justify a stay of proceedings. At the same time, courts have cited the lack of *mala fides* as a reason for not applying the abuse of process doctrine.[236]

Since one of the criticisms of the ICC of non-member States such as the United States has been the danger of having the Prosecutor initiate *proprio motu* politically-motivated investigations into crimes allegedly committed by nationals of certain countries,[237] an inherent power of the Court to stay proceedings on the basis of *mala fides* pursuant to the abuse of process doctrine might remove one cause of consternation. Of course, the concern over this power of the Prosecutor is hardly supported since in any case the Prosecutor is obliged in such situations to submit to the Pre-Trial Chamber a request for authorisation of the investigation,[238] and the Pre-Trial Chamber must itself make a determination that there is a reasonable basis

[233] *Kallon and Kamara* Decision on Amnesty case, para. 88.

[234] *Ibid.*, at para. 84.

[235] Choo, "Halting Criminal Prosecutions", at 866.

[236] *R.* v. *Milton Keynes Magistrates' Court,* ex parte *Roberts*, United Kingdom [1995] *CrimLR* 224; *R.* v. *Old Street Magistrates' Court,* ex parte *Davies,* United Kingdom [1995] *CrimLR* 629.

[237] Art. 15(1) ICC Statute: 'The Prosecutor may initiate investigations *proprio motu* on the basis of information on crimes within the jurisdiction of the Court.'

[238] Art. 15(3) ICC Statute.

to proceed with an investigation before any such investigation can take place.[239] Nevertheless, it would arguably be open to the Pre-Trial Chamber, in deciding on the *reasonableness* of the basis to investigate, to take into account the *intention* of the Prosecutor in deciding to investigate.

7.4 Preliminary conclusions

None of the constitutive statutes or rules of procedure and evidence of the international criminal courts and tribunals contain any mention of the abuse of process doctrine, the issue of abduction, or for that matter, the *mala captus bene detentus* rule. As seen above, this has not stopped the courts from applying such principles as part of their inherent judicial function, except for the ICC, which has preferred to rely on its power to enforce the guarantees of fair trial to consider stays of proceedings based on prosecutorial misconduct. The rejection of the abuse of process doctrine may be a limiting move by the ICC in its ability to deal with a range of problems that are likely to arise in the course of its life, including the difficult issue of abduction, which also raise violations of sovereignty as well as human rights abuses. The approach of the ICC as focusing on human rights guarantees under the Statute would seem to suggest that the *mala captus bene detentus* rule would have difficulty in being applied by the Court.

Warbrick has cautioned that by taking solely the viewpoint of human rights violations, 'the discretionary power which characterises the abuse of process determination may be overridden by a mandatory obligation to give relief to a defendant.'[240] At the same time, the conditional application of principles underlying abuse of process by the ICC Appeals Chamber signals that it may be able to accommodate the concerns underlying the abuse of process doctrine through its interpretation of the fair trial standard, and might also be able to assess the appropriate remedy using principles of proportionality, which is broadly in line with the application of the abuse of process doctrine in other jurisdictions.

In spite of the important rationales underlying the abuse of process doctrine relating to the basic rights of the accused and the integrity of the judicial branch, there has undoubtedly emerged from recent judicial practice a heavy presumption in favour of exercising jurisdiction even where prejudice has arisen to the defendant in cases which involve the allegation of international crimes.

In the context of abduction or disguised extradition, it has rightly been observed that the tension between the two approaches – *mala captus bene detentus* and abuse of process – and the inconsistent State practice perpetuating the tension, suggests that neither may be said to have the status of a rule of customary international law.[241] This means that a balancing of interests test remains the most reasonable

[239] Art. 15(4) ICC Statute.

[240] Warbrick, "Judicial Jurisdiction and Abuse of Process", at 495.

[241] Currie, "Abducted Fugitives Before the International Criminal Court", at 359.

and coherent way of resolving the dilemma of whether to continue to exercise jurisdiction in the face of an illegal abduction.

In this regard, courts must pay due regard to the seriousness of the violations of the accused's rights and in particular to the extent to which these violations have undermined the integrity of the process. Ryngaert points out that the most liberal interpretation of the abuse of process doctrine in the context of international criminal law by the ICTR Appeals Chamber in *Barayagwiza* concerned a case in which the violations lay with organs of the Tribunal.[242] Similarly, the ECCC Pre-Trial Chamber was only willing to consider a stay of proceedings where the violation of human rights had occurred at the behest of the Chambers itself or where it acted in concert with the Military Court. Ryngaert thus argues that 'in the absence of concerted action by the tribunals and the entity responsible for the violations … only torture or serious mistreatment by that entity will lead to a stay of proceedings on the basis of abuse of process.'[243] His position is also supported in part by *Nikolić*, in which the Appeals Chamber found that

> '*A fortiori*, and leaving aside for the moment human rights considerations, the exercise of jurisdiction should not be declined in cases of abductions carried out by private individuals whose actions, unless instigated, acknowledged or condoned by a State, or an international organisation, or other entity, do not necessarily in themselves violate State sovereignty.'[244]

However, this rather strict reading of the precedents seems to be countered by the ICTR Appeals Chamber in *Barayagwiza*, which held that

> 'even if fault is shared between the three organs of the Tribunal – *or is the result of the actions of a third party*, such as Cameroon – it would undermine the integrity of the judicial process to proceed. Furthermore, it would be unfair for the Appellant to stand trial on these charges if his rights were egregiously violated. Thus, under the abuse of process doctrine, *it is irrelevant which entity or entities were responsible for the alleged violations of the Appellant's rights*.'[245]

This interpretation of the abuse of process standard comports more readily with common law standards. While the involvement of the government's or the court's organs in the violations might be a factor for a court to take into account in assessing the gravity of the violations and the extent to which these violations undermined the integrity of the judicial proceedings, it is not the determinative factor. To hold that only violations amounting to torture or cruel, inhuman or degrading treatment would justify a stay of proceedings in the absence of governmental or prosecutorial involvement in the violations is inconsistent with the need for a court to enter into the appropriate balancing test for application of the abuse of process

242 Ryngaert, "The Doctrine of Abuse of Process", at 735.
243 *Ibid.*, at 736.
244 *Nikolić* Appeals Chamber Decision, para. 26.
245 *Barayagwiza,* para. 70. [Emphasis added]

doctrine. As the discussion above demonstrates, there are a number of grounds justifying a stay in proceedings that do not require evidence of such extreme violations as torture and inhuman treatment, but which nonetheless have the potential effect of undermining the integrity of the judicial process.

Having said this, the second most important factor for courts to take into account in deciding whether to apply the abuse of process doctrine is surely the community interest in prosecuting persons accused of the most serious crimes of concern. The difficult part of factoring this into account is the need to also bear in mind the presumption of innocence that attaches to all accused, even those accused of international crimes. Nonetheless, as explained elsewhere in this book, the myriad of rationales that support exercising jurisdiction over persons accused of such crimes must weigh heavy on a court's deliberation when considering if violations of the accused's rights (and possibly sovereignty violations) are so serious as to justify a stay of proceedings.

This relates to the final major consideration that a court would need to bear in mind, which is that the remedy provided must be proportional to the seriousness of the misconduct. In *Nikolić*, the Appeals Chamber acknowledged that there might be 'exceptional' situations which justified the stay of proceedings, but it opined that

> '... the remedy of setting aside jurisdiction will, in the Appeals Chamber's view *usually be disproportionate*. The correct balance must therefore be maintained between the fundamental rights of the accused and the essential interests of the international community in the prosecution of the persons charged.'[246]

Some commentators have contended that 'in the most serious instances of prosecutorial misconduct, courts are legally bound to resort to the most drastic remedy, that is, dismissal of the indictment.'[247] However, as seen in the lifting of the stay of proceedings in the *Lubanga* case, a remedy need not always be so drastic as to require the unconditional release of the accused. It may be that the violations of the accused's rights require some remedy to be provided, such as a reduction of sentence, or simply that the alleged defect in prosecutorial conduct is amended. Obviously, the more serious the violation, the more damage to the court's integrity and the more justification to dismiss the case altogether. A balancing of interests test may help to guide decision-makers in deciding where the tipping point lies.

---

[246] *Nikolić,* ICTY, Appeals Chamber, Case No. IT-94-2-AR73, Decision on Interlocutory Appeal Concerning Legality of Arrest, 5 June 2003.

[247] Knoops, *Redressing Miscarriages of Justice*, at 182, citing Antonio Cassese, *Effective Remedies for Abuse of Process in General International Law, Treaty Law and the Russian Legal System*, unpublished paper (2004), at 2.

Part Three
General Conclusion

Chapter 8
GENERAL CONCLUSION

The clash of rules which occur when a court is faced with an impediment to adjudicatory jurisdiction over international crimes requires a workable theoretical framework for resolving the question of whether to continue with a prosecution. The evolution of international criminal law has led to the expectation that prosecutions are generally required every time a rule prohibiting international crimes is breached. This development largely resulted from two phenomena. First, the adoption and ratification of a number of conventions requiring States parties to prosecute persons accused of certain crimes or to extradite that person to a State that will do so. Second, the impact of the development of human rights law on the imperative to prosecute and in particular the rights of victims of serious human rights violations to justice, truth and reparation.[1] This development was aided by the human rights advocacy movement in response to the perceived 'culture of impunity' for State-sponsored crimes, which was sometimes formalised by the institution of amnesty laws or a cynical use by courts of other barriers to prosecution.

As a result, legal impediments to the exercise of adjudicatory jurisdiction over international crimes came to be viewed as *ipso facto* contributing to the culture of impunity, even where other legal, practical or policy considerations might suggest that exercise of jurisdiction should be stayed. This reflex response to the question of barriers to prosecution is an incomplete, inaccurate and simplistic answer to the issue of their legality under international law for a number of reasons. It is incomplete because this conclusion does not take into account the legitimate objectives of the legal impediments themselves, and looks only to their result – the non-prosecution of the person concerned. It is inaccurate because a positive duty to prosecute only arises in limited cases under conventional law: grave breaches, torture and genocide (and probably only for the territorial State or the State where the alleged offender is present). Otherwise a customary entitlement to prosecute (crimes against humanity, other serious violations of IHL) means that States are not precluded from staying prosecutions, so long as the State does not by its actions condone the acts or absolve the perpetrators from all responsibility and does not violate its obligations to guarantee fundamental human rights to victims, which

[1] Orentlicher argues that the impact of the international human rights movement on international criminal law processes has been to transform it from victor's justice to victim's justice. Diane Orentlicher, "The Future of Universal Jurisdiction in the New Architecture of Transnational Justice", in Stephen Macedo (ed.), *Universal Jurisdiction: National Courts and the Prosecution of Serious Crimes Under International Law* (Philadelphia, PA: University of Pennsylvania, 2004), at 231.

does not necessarily require prosecution in every case. Even where a positive duty to prosecute is present, State practice has indicated that this does not entail that every instance of violation must be prosecuted, but such a duty may be fulfilled by the use of exemplary trials instituted by way of strategic prosecutorial discretion, notably of leaders who orchestrated the international crimes and those who may be considered 'most responsible' for the perpetration of crimes. Moreover, much of the argumentation supporting the rejection of jurisdictional barriers to prosecution of international crimes rests on implied duties or waivers of sovereign rights stemming from obligations to guarantee certain rights or to prosecute crimes in international treaties. However, limitations on State sovereignty should generally not be presumed but should be expressly stated in international law. In this light, the relative silence in international instruments as to the legality of these measures should arguably be regarded as leaving each State free to decide to adopt any law or policy it deems to be equitable in the matter.

Finally, such an assumption is simplistic because it fails to take into account other legitimate competing interests, such as the need to secure peace deals, or to create conditions leading to lasting peace by offering incentives to warring parties for demobilisation and reintegration, and the differing ways that societies and cultures reckon with reconciliation in the aftermath of conflict.[2] Even those commentators arguing that 'states confronted with challenges to accountability should treat them as presumptively invalid' have advocated a rebuttal of this presumption 'if the state granting the immunity in question does so pursuant to a process that does not undermine the quest for accountability.'[3]

It is suggested that when courts are confronted with these sorts of impediments when dealing with international crimes, such impediments should not be either categorically accepted or rejected but that an interests-analysis approach would allow the court to assess the legitimacy of such impediments in a way that furthers the underlying goals of international criminal law, in particular, the securing and maintenance of peace, the establishment of truth, contributing to reconciliation, and reparations to victims. Such an approach should help to ensure coherence, consistency and legitimacy in the way that courts reckon with impediments to jurisdiction. The theoretical foundation of this approach is grounded in a policy-oriented approach to international law that views law not as merely the application of 'neutral rules' but as a process of authoritative and controlling decision which is sensitive to community expectations, responsive to the circumstances of each context, and expressly mindful of competing principles and policies that may help

---

[2] Leila Nadya Sadat, "Universal Jurisdiction, National Amnesties, and Truth Commissions: Reconciling the Irreconcilable", in Macedo, *supra* n. 1, at 194: 'Realists would argue … that this "legalistic" approach to the problem of atrocities is either hopelessly naïve or simply wrong, that in the anarchy existent in the international law, law and legal aspirations have little place, and may even be counterproductive.' In such situations, it is argued, a bystander court should defer to national policies of reconciliation which 'satisfy generally-accepted indicia of legitimacy.' Orentlicher, "The Future of Universal Jurisdiction", at 238.

[3] Sadat, "Universal Jurisdiction, National Amnesties", at 194.

guide a decision on jurisdiction, but which ultimately strives towards a world order based on human dignity.

The first part of this book explained that impediments are relevant factors that courts should take into account when assessing the propriety of exercising adjudicatory jurisdiction. Proper consideration of these helps to ensure that international criminal processes are fair, equitable and justified and remain in keeping with the overall objective of international law to maintain friendly international relations. Given that the principles of fairness, justice and convenience – all of which require the balancing of countervailing interests – are increasingly regarded as the foundation of jurisdiction, an interests-analysis approach aligns neatly with the process of considering the question of adjudicatory jurisdiction. An analysis of the various jurisdictional principles justifying adjudicatory jurisdiction reveals an intrinsic relationship between these and barriers to jurisdiction. State interest in prosecution or non-prosecution remains pertinent to the manner in which courts treat various impediments. This is perhaps best displayed in the examination of how courts act when exercising universal jurisdiction.

National courts are subject to two conflicting set of pressures when considering whether to exercise jurisdiction over international crimes based on the universality principle. On the one hand, there is the pressure to prosecute emanating from the notion that the court is acting as an agent of the international community to enforce the most fundamental rules of the international legal system. By exercising jurisdiction, the court is ensuring that alleged offenders of such norms are given no safe haven, thereby guaranteeing the rights of victims who may otherwise receive no redress, and strengthening the international legal order by so acting. Courts may also be bound to exercise universal jurisdiction where treaties, such as the Geneva Conventions of 1949 or the Torture Convention so require. On the other hand, the exercise of criminal jurisdiction over a non-national for crimes committed extra-territorially with no connection to the forum State puts national courts in the mostly unfamiliar and somewhat uncomfortable position of having to rule on the legality of the conduct of foreign State officials in their own country or in other countries.[4] This decision may be made even more sensitive if the State in question has already made decisions about how to deal with its past human rights violations, e.g., by issuing amnesties in conjunction with establishing a truth commission. Naomi Roht-Arriaza has aptly described the increased domestic exercise of jurisdiction under universality as 'the judicialization of interstate relations in the area of grave human rights violations.'[5]

Unsurprisingly, therefore, courts have responded to these pressures in a variety of ways: those wishing to embrace the possibilities of universal jurisdiction taking a liberal stance on rules such as the principle of legality, relying heavily

[4] Michael Kirby, "Universal Jurisdiction and Judicial Reluctance: A New 'Fourteen Points,'" in Macedo, *supra* n. 1, at 240.

[5] Naomi Roht-Arriaza, *The Pinochet Effect: Transnational Justice in the Age of Human Rights* (Philadelphia: University of Pennsylvania Press, 2005), at 138.

on customary law to justify their decisions,[6] others, possibly concerned about the potential negative effects of unchecked universal jurisdiction, taking a narrow interpretation of such rules, and insisting upon clear and explicit domestic authorisation for exercising jurisdiction on this basis.[7] In this context, the consideration of legal impediments to jurisdiction takes on an even greater significance, not only at the legal and procedural level, but also at the symbolic level. Those courts which are inclined to prosecute emphasise the greater moral values invested in criminal prosecution of serious human rights offenders *vis-à-vis* legal bars because of the gravity of the crimes at issue. Here, universal jurisdiction is used as evidence of the seriousness of such crimes and the absolute necessity of prosecution, in spite of legal obstacles at the procedural level. Indeed, the very fact of universal jurisdiction over such crimes is used in a sense as a 'sword' to invalidate any barriers to prosecution. Thus, amnesties have been dismissed as having no effect upon a court exercising universal jurisdiction.[8] Similarly, functional immunity has been viewed as inconsistent with the principle of universal jurisdiction established by treaty to ensure the prosecution of State officials engaged in torture.[9] By contrast, those courts more cautious about operating under universality are able to justify non-prosecution on the basis that their hands are tied at the procedural level due

---

[6] E.g., in the *Scilingo* case in Spain, the Court relied on the customary prohibition of crimes against humanity in international law in order to assert that the principle of legality, enshrined in the Spanish Constitution, was not violated by the conviction of Scilingo pursuant to a legal provision which entered into force in 2004 for acts committed in 1977. The Court determined that in cases dealing with serious international crimes, a more flexible interpretation to the *nullum crimen, nulla poena sine praevia lege* principle could be adopted. *Scilingo, Adolfo*, Spain, Third Section of the Criminal Division (*Audiencia Nacional*), Judgment no. 16/2005 of 19 April 2005, *Sentencia por crímenes contra la humanidad en el caso Adolpho Scilingo*, available at: <http://www.derechos.org/nizkor/espana/juicioral/doc/sentencia.html>.

[7] E.g., *Nulyarimma and others* v. *Thompson*, Australia, Federal Court of Australia, Full Court, 1 September 1999, 39 *ILM* 29 (2000); *Bouterse, Desi*, the Netherlands, Decision of the Court of Appeal of Amsterdam, 20 November 2000, unofficial English translation by Peter Kell in 3 *YIHL* 677 (2000); *Bouterse, Desi*, the Netherlands, Supreme Court [*Hoge Raad*], Criminal Chamber, judgment of 18 September 2001, No. 00749/01 (CW 2323), summary available at: <http://www.icrc.org/ihl-nat.nsf/39a82e2ca42b52974125673e00508144/07c5ae1b4a999f1cc1256da200518c91?OpenDocument>.

[8] E.g., *Ely Ould Dah*, France, Court of Cassation, Criminal division, decision of 23 October 2002, *Bulletin criminel* 2002 no. 195 at 725 (finding that universal jurisdiction could not be impinged upon by a foreign amnesty law); *Kallon, Morris and Kamara, Brima Bazzy*, SCSL, Appeals Chamber Decision on Challenge to Jurisdiction: Lomé Accord Amnesty, 13 March 2004, Case No. SCSL-2004-15-AR72(E), para. 67 (finding that '[w]here jurisdiction is universal, a State cannot deprive another State of its jurisdiction to prosecute the offender by the grant of amnesty,' based on the reasoning that '[a] State cannot bring into oblivion and forgetfulness a crime, such as a crime against international law, which other States are entitled to keep alive and remember'); *Simon, Julio, Del Cerro, Juan Antonio s/sustracción de menores de 10 años,* Juzgado Nacional en lo Criminal y Correccional Federal No. 4, Dr. Gabriel Cavallo, 6 March 2001, available at: <www.derechos.org/nizkor/arg/ley/juezcavallo03mar.htm> (holding that customary universal jurisdiction over crimes against humanity and other serious human rights violations supports the decision declaring the *punto final* and due obedience laws in Argentina null and void because 'by judging and condemning those responsible for these acts, the state acts in the interests of the whole of the international community').

[9] *R* v. *Bow Street Metropolitan Stipendiary Magistrate*, ex parte *Pinochet Ugarte*, United Kingdom, House of Lords Judgment of 24 March 1999, 2 *WLR* 827 (HL 1999); [1999] 2 *All ER* 97.

to the existence of such an impediment.[10] Jurisdiction by reason of universality is viewed as a doubtful justification for prosecution in the absence of some definite link to the forum State that would provide a special reason to exercise jurisdiction in the case at issue. From this viewpoint, legal impediments may be given greater leverage as a way to limit this kind of judicial 'activism.'[11]

The first part also revealed that international crimes are of a particular character because they violate universal values. This has significant implications for the basis of jurisdiction in that all States are entitled to exercise jurisdiction and signifies a moral imperative to prosecute. Nonetheless, the only impediment that has been explicitly rejected by all the international and hybrid tribunals and may be said to be lifted as a matter of customary international law is the defence of official position (functional immunity). By contrast, personal immunity has only been rejected explicitly in two instruments – the ICC Statute and the Regulation setting up the Special Panels for East Timor.[12] However, most commentators and courts have interpreted the rejection of official position in the other instruments as also implying the rejection of personal immunities of incumbent State officials. Whether such an interpretation is warranted is not completely convincing and the clarification in Article 27 of the Rome Statute will be helpful to future prosecutions in this regard, providing States will agree to waive the immunity of their incumbent officials in order to have them transferred them to the ICC.

With regard to the remaining impediments under study, amnesties have been explicitly dealt with (and rejected) in three instruments – Allied Control Council Law No. 10, the Extraordinary Chambers for Cambodia, and the Statute of the Special Court for Sierra Leone.[13] The silence in the other instruments regarding amnesties has generally been interpreted to mean that any amnesty would be contrary to the object and purpose of the relevant statute, although the Rome Statute may provide slightly more flexibility under some interpretations. Pardons are rejected in two of the instruments (Allied Control Council Law No. 10 and (partially in) the Extraordinary Chambers of Cambodia) and are regulated in three others (the ICTY, ICTR and the SCSL), indicating some ambiguity as to the legality of issuing a pardon to a person convicted of an international crime. The principle of *ne bis in idem* is specifically upheld in five statutes (ICTY, ICTR, ICC, SCSL and Spe-

---

[10] E.g., the decisions of the German Federal Prosecutors not to open investigations in the *Almatov* case (concerning torture and crimes against humanity in Uzbekistan), and the *Rumsfeld and others* case (concerning war crimes in Iraq) due to the discretion in the German 2002 law.

[11] See, e.g., *Sharon Ariel and others*, Belgium, Court of Cassation, Judgment of 12 February 2003, available at: <www.cass.be/cgi-juris/juris-cass-a1.pl> (refusing to exercise universal jurisdiction over a sitting head of State accused of genocide due to the principle of personal immunity).

[12] Allied Control Council Law No. 10 does reject 'immunities ... granted by the Nazi regime' but it is unclear if this refers to immunities under international law or merely under German law at the time.

[13] Notably, amnesties were in existence in the territorial jurisdiction of these courts. In Germany, there were: the Decree of Reichspräsident (21 March 1933), laws of 7 August 1934 (after Hindenburg's death), of 28 February 1935 (after the return of the 'Saarland'), 23 April 1936 and 30 April 1938 (after reunion of Austria with Germany). Glueck, *War Criminals*, at 84. In Sierra Leone, the Lomé Peace Agreement amnesty and for Cambodia the general amnesty of 1994 and the 1996 Royal pardon.

cial Panels for East Timor). In all of these provisions, there is the possibility for re-trial before the courts where there has been a 'sham' trial at the national level. Statutes of limitation were rejected for international crimes in four instruments (Allied Control Council Law No. 10, ICC, Extraordinary Chambers for Cambodia and the Special Panels for East Timor). The silence in regard to such time bars in the remaining instruments probably indicates that this particular impediment was not seen as problematic for the tribunals in question because of the temporary nature of the courts themselves (IMT, IMTFE, ICTY, ICTR, SCSL), although the work of the ICTY and ICTR has undoubtedly gone on many years longer than the Security Council originally anticipated.[14] In contrast with the other impediments, the abuse of process doctrine has not figured in any of the constitutive instruments of the international or hybrid tribunals, which is not suprising in view of the fact that is generally consdered an 'inherent' part of the judicial function. However, its absence in the ICC Statute proved fatal for its application in proceedings in that jurisdiction, leading the judges to only apply the fair trial part of its rationale.

A comparative analysis of the six impediments under study reveals some similarities in the way that courts and commentators have striven to overcome jurisdictional barriers, but also highlights various inconsistencies, which might be remedied using a different approach. With regard to their definitions, the impediments vary considerably. While amnesties constitute a kind of politically expedient exception to the normal rules of prosecution, pardons emanate from a sovereign right to forego punishment while retaining legal liability. Both may have a basis in international law if contained in a peace treaty, as has often been the case, but are generally considered as exercises of sovereign authority. Statutes of limitation on the other hand represent domestic law principles (mainly of civil law countries) and probably do not have a basis in international law, though the underlying rationale of preventing unfair trials based on stale evidence is universally recognised. Immunities – both personal and functional – meanwhile derive from international law, and generally strive to regulate the relations between sovereign nations. The principle of *ne bis in idem* has both domestic and international law roots and stands alone as the one impediment that constitutes a right of the defendant for the stay of proceedings. It is also notable for being the only impediment that commentators have actually argued should be broadened in scope and reach when applied to international crimes and particularly when courts are operating under the principle of universality. Abuse of process on the other hand is defined as an inherent part of the judicial function with common law origins, but has been increasingly strictly construed in cases involving international crimes in view of the community interest in repressing such crimes.

---

[14] Although the Statute of the SCSL does not specify an end date for when its jurisdiction over 'serious violations of international humanitarian law and Sierra Leonean law committed in the territory of Sierra Leone since 30 November 1996' terminates, it is commonly understood that the Court is only competent to try cases committed during the war in Sierra Leone and is not open-ended. See Art. 1, SCSL Statute.

In as far as historical background is concerned the six impediments came about in totally different ways. The oldest impediment under study is probably the use of pardon (dating back to the Code of Hammurabi, 18th century B.C.), followed by amnesty (as used in peace treaties, possibly as early as 1286 B.C. in the Battle of Kadesh), and *ne bis in idem* (as noted in Greek and Roman law, around 300 B.C.). Comparatively speaking, abuse of process and statutes of limitation (recognised in the common law by the 17th century), and the functional and State immunities (given judicial recognition in the 19th century) are rather recent phenomena, although diplomatic immunity and head of State immunity date back to ancient times.

The rationales or contextual and policy considerations underlying each of the six impediments demonstrate that all barriers seek to protect important values which should not be discounted lightly by a court exercising adjudicatory jurisdiction, even when confronted with allegations of international crimes. In the case of amnesties, such a stay of prosecution has been justified by reason of the need to secure and/or maintain the peace, as an incentive for perpetrators to divulge the truth about the circumstances in which offences were committed, and to foster efforts at reconciliation between divided societies. Other considerations, however, militate against blanket amnesties with no conditions attached, such as the risk of impunity leading to an unstable peace, the desire for a historical record as created by a criminal trial, the need to strengthen and uphold the law in fragile democracies, and the possible deterrent effect of prosecution. Pardons have been justified on similar grounds of contributing to social stability or the 'public good,' but differ by also carrying a sense of forgiveness while still recognising the liability of perpetrators. As opposed to most amnesties, pardons are more attuned to the individual circumstances of a particular potential beneficiary, such as whether he or she has displayed rehabilitative characteristics indicating that they no longer present a social threat, or whether the person has shown sincere remorse, or has co-operated in a significant way with prosecutorial authorities that is likely to bring about more accountability, truth and reparations for victims.

By contrast, statutes of limitation, *ne bis in idem* and the abuse of process doctrine focus upon the fairness of proceedings for those accused of international crimes, in the first case by preventing a trial from taking place where a person would be at risk of being convicted on stale or insufficient evidence, in the second case by protecting individuals from State harassment in the form of multiple prosecutions for the same crime and in the third case by protecting indviduals from oppressive prosecutorial misconduct. However, neither of the first two sets of rationales are an exact fit for when these impediments are used to stay proceedings for international crimes. For statutes of limitation, traditional rationales such as 'quieting title' and reduced public clamour for retribution do not seem to transcribe to trials involving international crimes. Moreover, the myriad difficulties in bringing prompt prosecutions in the aftermath of serious violence militate against a time bar. In the case of *ne bis in idem*, the *res judicata* effect of judgments involving international crimes would seem to be contingent upon whether the trial was conducted independently and impartially and with a genuine intent to bring the person to justice. Whether a pardon or amnesty could also have a *ne bis in idem* effect would also appear to be a question based upon a similar 'impunity test.' It is argued in this book that where an amnesty or pardon satisfies commonly accepted 'legitimating indicia,' a *ne bis in idem* effect at the domestic, transnational and trans-jurisdictional levels would ensure coherency and consistency in the international legal system. While the rationales behind the abuse of process doctrine equally hold in cases dealing with international crimes, in practice, courts in recent times have given increasingly short thrift to the importance of these rationales in the face of the community interest in prosecuting a person accused of such crimes.

The rationales underlying the various types of immunity contrast quite markedly from the latter three impediments in that the stay of prosecution is not justified by some right of the defendant. Rather, these types of impediments prevent State officials from being prosecuted as a means to safeguard inter-State relations, and in this sense resonate to some degree with those pragmatic rationales upholding amnesties and pardons. However, inconsistency arises between immunities and 'accountable amnesties' in that the proper use of prosecutorial discretion that may delineate an acceptable amnesty from an unacceptable amnesty is likely to focus prosecution efforts on those 'most responsible' for the commission of international crimes. Yet those considered 'most responsible' are usually those political and military leaders benefiting from functional and/or personal immunity. It is argued that the basic rationale lifting functional immunity for international crimes is also pertinent to the lifting of personal immunity. Such recognition would serve to close this significant gap in the strategic enforcement of international criminal law. However, given the risk that could be posed to international relations in the event that domestic courts start prosecuting visiting Heads of State and other high-ranking government officials on official visits, it might be prudent that only international criminal courts exercise jurisdiction over such persons.

The host of legal rationales used to deny or restrict the scope of impediments to jurisdiction over international crimes vary to a considerable extent due to the differing operations of the impediments. However, three common legal arguments are used to reject all impediments except two (*ne bis in idem* and abuse of process) when used to stay prosecutions for international crimes. The first relates to the scope of the obligation to prosecute and punish those accused of international crimes in treaty and/or custom, which has been argued to be incompatible with amnesties, pardons, statutes of limitation and immunities. This argument has been sometimes formulated in the sense that if a treaty provides for a system of universal jurisdiction over a particular crime, States may have implicitly waived their sovereign prerogative to issue amnesties or pardons, bar prosecutions after a set time limit, or protect its officials from prosecution. This argumentation is limited to those international crimes contained in treaties, which makes it difficult to relate to other international crimes such as crimes against humanity and other violations of the laws and customs of war, despite the fact that such crimes are of equal or similar gravity. State practice does not yet support a customary duty to prosecute all international crimes. The 'obligation to prosecute' argument also suffers from the weakness of having to rely on the implied rejection of impediments as a corollary – something many States would be reticent to accept.

The second argument that has been commonly used is that the fundamental rights of victims to an effective remedy, to the truth and to reparation vitiates the validity of impediments that prevent these from being guaranteed. Such arguments have been particularly successful in relation to amnesties covering serious human rights violations, but less so in relation to immunities because immunity has been held to be a 'proportionate restriction' to these rights in view of the importance of the values it seeks to uphold. Conversely, pardons or reduced sentences that allow for the rights of victims to be respected appear to be contemplated by international instruments, signalling a balancing of interests in this respect.

Thirdly, courts have relied on the *jus cogens* nature of international crimes to deny the effect of impediments to jurisdiction. Because *jus cogens* norms are hierarchically superior to other rules in the international legal order, it has been argued that rules which prevent such crimes from being enforced would be void and have no legal effect. This argument has been particularly prevalent in relation to amnesties, statutes of limitation and immunities. However, it is argued in this book that the consequence of a *jus cogens* crime (i.e., an entitlement to prosecute) does not have the same character as the norm itself and hence there is no 'clash of principles' between the impediment and a *jus cogens* norm. On the other hand, where the effect of an impediment serves to condone, authorise or absolve a person from responsibility from a *jus cogens* crime, this would violate a State's obligations under the law of State Responsibility. Neither statutes of limitations nor personal immunities are likely to fulfil this test given that both inherently recognise the criminality of the underlying offence and merely avert the possibility of trial and do not pronounce upon the question of liability. Certain amnesties and pardons, however, which fail to satisfy legitimating indicia tied to alternative forms of accountability and the rights of victims, would probably not be recognised on this basis.

This book has attempted to demonstrate that an alternative approach to the problem of how courts should decide whether or not to exercise adjudicatory jurisdiction over international crimes when faced with these six impediments is to enter into an analysis of competing interests, and to attempt to balance these in a manner that best suits the overall goals of the international legal system.

With regard to amnesties, a court deciding on whether to exercise jurisdiction should have in mind whether the impediment satisfies the range of legitimating indicia which seek to balance the interests of victims to truth, reparation and participation, with the objective of the amnesty, and any obligations or entitlements to prosecute. It is argued that a strategic use of prosecutorial discretion, which takes into account the public interest and balances the concerns of victims with societal expectations, and which is subject to review at the judicial level, may be an important way of accommodating the needs of transitional societies without violating the general obligation to prosecute international crimes. When deciding whether a pardon should be given international legitimacy, including a *ne bis in idem* effect, a court should have in mind the need to balance between the obligation to punish offenders of international crimes (taking into account the main purposes of punishment – deterrence, stigmatisation, rehabilitation and reparation) and the objectives that may be achieved by pardon or reduced sentence, including contributing to reconciliation, truth-telling by way of guilty pleas, and increased co-operation from prisoners to ensure that victims' rights (in particular, to reparation) are satisfied.

The legality of statutes of limitation over international crimes is increasingly doubtful given the number of States with legislation removing such barriers and the difficulty of applying the traditional rationales to cases involving international crimes. Nonetheless, courts contemplating such a law should be mindful of the need to balance the need to ensure a fair trial and to create certainty and stability in the legal system with the need of victims to have their perpetrators brought to justice. It is argued that the abuse of process doctrine that allows a common law judge to stay proceedings where the delay in bringing proceedings renders a trial inherently unfair provides a good example of how judges may balance these competing interests. Applying an interests-analysis approach to the question of immunities may also provide an appropriate framework for resolving disputes. In this regard, the 'proper functioning of the network of inter-State relations'[15] needs to be balanced against the need to protect the dignity and rights of victims of human rights atrocities. The *jus cogens* nature of international crimes lends considerable weight to the latter interest and suggests that the overall goals of the international legal system should be resolved in favour of prosecution, with proper safeguards to ensure that the 'harmonious international system'[16] stays that way. With regard to abuse of process, there are two main interests which courts should bear in mind when deciding whether or not to exercise jurisdiction or to stay proceedings: these are the seriousness of the violations of the defendant's rights and the effect these violations have had on integrity of the judicial system and the community interest in prosecuting crimes of such gravity. Courts applying the abuse of process doctrine have long entered into a balancing exercise, but the special circumstances attendant to international criminal trials has no doubt an important effect upon the application of this test. It may also be that proportionality may be applied to the remedy decided upon. Where staying a proceeding would appear disproportionate, it may be possible for courts to institute a less severe remedy that still upholds the integrity of the process and comports with the fair trial rights of the accused.

A further common strand of argumentation that has supported this tipping of the balancing point is the changing notion of sovereignty, which arguably has increasingly emphasised the protection of individual rights over sovereign interests.[17] One clear manifestation of this trend is the increased calls for a transnatio-

---

[15] *Arrest Warrant of April 11th 2000 (Democratic Republic of the Congo* v. *Belgium*), Judgment, Merits, 41 *ILM* 536 (2002), Joint Separate Opinion of Judges Higgins, Kooijmans and Buergenthal, at 85, para. 75.

[16] *Idem.*

[17] Kofi Annan, "Two Concepts of Sovereignty", *The Economist*, 18 September 1999, at 49.

nal *ne bis in idem* protection, which would put the individual right not to be tried twice for the same crime in different jurisdictions ahead of the sovereign right to prosecute a person who has breached the international legal order. The trans-jurisdictional *ne bis in idem* rule inscribed in the instruments of international criminal courts demonstrates that States have already accepted the abdication of a part of their sovereign right in this regard. An interests-analysis approach has arguably been incorporated into the statutes of the international criminal courts in the sense that the upwards 'sham prosecution' exception to *ne bis in idem* ensures a balance between the interest in protecting persons from multiple prosecutions in different jurisdictions and the interest in ensuring that *ne bis in idem* is not used as a shield from criminal responsibility. Similar considerations could inform courts in their examination of whether out-of-court settlements, diversionary measures, pardons or plea bargains could have a similar *res judicata* effect where international crimes are involved.

The final point to be emphasised from the comparative analysis of the legal rationales relating to the impediments under study is that international law remains disputed, unclear or in a state of development in all areas. Courts adjudicating such cases are thus presented with various views and interests which may all have some merit and 'it is the task of the judge to decide the distribution as between them of values at stake, taking into account not only the interests of the parties, but the interests of the world community as a whole.'[18] This has long been accepted as falling within the proper functions of the lawyer and judge.[19] Judge Lauterpacht underlined that this is not a choice between claims that are fully justified but between claims that have varying degrees of legal merit.[20] When making the choice, courts must have consideration of the humanitarian, moral and social purposes of the law[21] – hence policy considerations are integral elements of the decision-making process of international law. This observation supports the view propounded by Judge Higgins that international law is the whole process of competent persons making authoritative decisions in response to claims which various parties are pressing upon them, in respect of various views and interests.[22] This approach is not an approach mandated by an *ad hoc* international law rule, but is an inherent part of the judicial process. This theory posits that legal decision-making occurs when decisions are made by authorised persons or organs, in appropriate forums,

---

[18] Rosalyn Higgins, "Policy Decisions and the International Judicial Process", 17(1) *ICLQ* 59 (1968).

[19] Thus, US Judge Oliver Wendell Holmes in 1899 noted that 'Where there is doubt the simple tool of logic does not suffice, and even if it is disguised and unconscious, the judges are called on to exercise the sovereign prerogative of choice.' "Law in Science and Science in Law", *Collected Legal Papers* (1920), at 239.

[20] Hersch Lauterpacht, *The Development of International Law by the International Court* (New York: Praeger, 1958), at 398.

[21] Higgins, "Policy Decisions and the International Judicial Process", at 62.

[22] *Ibid.*, at 58-84.

within the framework of certain established practices and norms.[23] The notion that international law is the entire decision-making process 'applies especially where the trend of past decisions is not overwhelmingly clear, and with a mind to policy alternatives for the future.'[24] This is most definitely the case with regard to the impediments under study in this book.

While the uttermost limit for such judicial interpretation is where there is an express rule of international law, a wide scope for such interpretation remains where there are inadequacies in the international legal system as is arguably the case in regard to these issues.[25] Judge Sir Gerald Fitzmaurice similarly felt that while judges could not of course legislate, it was also true that a constant process of development of the law goes on through the courts and this involves a certain amount of innovation.[26] In answer to the claim that this would lead to subjectivity, fragmentation and arbitrariness, Lauterpacht wrote that when regard is had to the entirety of social and legal relationships within the community, then the judge is fulfilling what the legislator would have intended if he could have foreseen the changes occurring in the life of the community.[27] Thus, a judge's appreciation of choice must be guided by the interests of the world community which international law serves. In this sense, the fact that international crimes have a *jus cogens* character must surely serve as an important factor in determining the fundamental interests of the world community and the relative weight to be attributed to prosecution of such crimes.

Given that courts are not the only agencies which apply legal principles, other institutions such as international organisations and governments also participate in this particular decision-making process, and hence would be covered by the same methodology. Thus domestic legislation and international treaties may also contain elements of a balancing of interests approach. The *ne bis in idem* provision and review of sentence rules of the ICC Statute may well evince examples of this. One could argue that the rejection of procedural immunity in the ICC Statute satisfies the balancing of interests test because there would be less risk to inter-State relations in proceedings before the ICC. Similarly, the rejection of statutes of limitation makes sense because it allows the Prosecutor to stay prosecutions for a period of time when it might not be appropriate to bring proceedings without losing the opportunity to prosecute. In any case, the strict fair trial rights and rules of evidence applicable to proceedings before the ICC would preclude a conviction on unreliable evidence.

---

[23] See Myres S. McDougal, "Some Basic Theoretical Concepts about International Law: A Policy-oriented framework of enquiry", 4 *Journal of Conflict Resolution* 337-354 (1960).

[24] Higgins, "Policy Decisions and the International Judicial Process", at 59.

[25] Hersch Lauterpacht, *The Function of Law in the International Community* (Oxford: Clarendon Press, 1933) at 75.

[26] Gerald Fitzmaurice, "Judicial Innovation – It's Uses and its Perils", in D.W. Bowett, et al. (eds.), *Cambridge Essays in International Law: Essays in Honour of Lord McNair* (London: Stevens & Sons. 1965), at 24-25.

[27] Lauterpacht, *The Development of International Law by the International Court,* at 80.

This legal methodology is one that is well-versed at the national level especially and does not apply solely to international courts. Judge Lauterpacht was of the view that the role of the judge at both levels was not merely finding the appropriate rule, but the necessity of choice between conflicting legal claims – this was the essence of the judicial function.[28] Moreover, the impediments under review in this book arise before both national and international courts. Thus, the Special Court for Sierra Leone used the reasoning employed by the Supreme Court of Israel in *Eichmann* and the US Supreme Court in *Demjanjak* to support its claim to universal jurisdiction and hence its treatment of amnesties for international crimes.[29] This was despite the fact that it had a specific provision in its Statute which stated that the amnesty would have no effect on the SCSL. The UK House of Lords made much of the ICTY Trial Chamber's *obiter dictum* in *Furundžija* to support the claim that torture was an international crime and had the status of *jus cogens*.[30] The ICTY, ICTR and Extraordinary Chambers in the Courts of Cambodia made liberal use of national case law in deciphering the scope of the abuse of process doctrine. This cross-referencing across levels of jurisdiction suggests that an interests-analysis approach would work both at the national and international level and is not constrained by some principle to only apply one level of jurisdiction.

In sum, the question of exercising adjudicatory jurisdiction, whether by an international or national court, is one generally founded upon a sense of fairness, justice and convenience which necessitates courts recognising the elements of validity of competing principles which together form a rationale guide that is at once contextually-specific and consistent with the basic values underlying the international legal order. The approach advocated in this book may help the international criminal law system, consisting of multi-level jurisdiction, to apply principles to the question of the legality of impediments to jurisdiction over international crimes in a transparent, considered, consistent and coherent way, rather than relying on simply an assumption of the invalidity of barriers to prosecution to international crimes or entering into a purely positivist analysis of neutral rules in a manner that obfuscates the policy interests impacting upon the interpretation of relevant norms and practice. This applies both at the national level (in both monist and dualist systems) and the international level. One would hope that international criminal law's legitimacy would be thereby enhanced, providing for a stronger system of enforcement within the context of real world complexity.

---

[28] Lauterpacht, *The Development of International Law by the International Court*, at 399: '... the necessity of choice between conflicting legal claims is of the very essence of the judicial function, whether within the State or in the international sphere.'

[29] *Kallon, Morris and Kamara, Brima Bazzy*, SCSL, Appeals Chamber Decision on Challenge to Jurisdiction: Lomé Accord Amnesty, 13 March 2004, Case No. SCSL-2004-15-AR72(E).

[30] *R* v. *Bow Street Metropolitan Stipendiary Magistrate*, ex parte *Pinochet Ugarte*, United Kingdom, House of Lords Judgment of 24 March 1999, 2 *WLR* 827 (HL 1999); [1999] 2 *All ER* 97.

BIBLIOGRAPHY

Afghan Independent Human Rights Commission, *A Call for Justice: A National Consultation on Past Human Rights Violations in Afghanistan*, January 2005. Available at: <http://www.aihrc.org.af/Rep_29_Eng/rep29_1_05call4justice.pdf>.

Akande, Dapo, "International Law Immunities and the International Criminal Court", 98 *AJIL* (2004): 407.

Akehurst, Michael, "Jurisdiction in International Law", *BYIL* (1972-1973): 145.

Akhavan, Payam, "Beyond Impunity: Can International Criminal Justice Prevent Future Atrocities?", 95(1) *AJIL* (2001): 7.

Amar, Akhil Reid, "Double Jeopardy Law Made Simple", 106 *Yale Law Journal* (1997): 1807.

Ambos, Kai, "Individual Criminal Responsibility in International Criminal Law: A Jurisprudential Analysis – From Nuremberg to The Hague", in Gabrielle Kirk McDonald & Olivia Swaak-Goldman (eds.), *Substantive and Procedural Aspects of International Criminal Law: The Experience of International and National Courts* (The Hague: Kluwer Law International, 2000): 3.

Amnesty International, *Universal Jurisdiction: The duty of states to enact and implement legislation* (London: AI International Secretariat, 2001).

Arendt, Hannah, *Eichmann in Jerusalem: A Report on the Banality of Evil* (New York: Penguin Books, 1994) (first published by Viking Press in 1963).

Bailin, Alex, "Double jeopardy", in Marisa Leaf (ed.), *Cross-Border Crime. Defence rights in a new era of international judicial co-operation* (London: Justice, 2006): 103.

Bakker, Christine A.E., "A Full Stop to Amnesty in Argentina: The *Simón* Case", 3(5) *JICJ* (2005): 1106.

Bantekas, Ilias & Nash, Susan, *International Criminal Law* (London: Cavendish Publishing, 2003).

Barboza, Julio, "International Criminal Law", 278 *RdC* (The Hague) (1999): 21.

Bassiouni, M. Cherif, "The History of Universal Jurisdiction and Its Place in International Law", in Stephen Macedo (ed.), *Universal Jurisdiction: National Courts and the Prosecution of Serious Crimes under International Law* (Philadelphia: University of Pennsylvania Press, 2004): 39.

Bassiouni, M. Cherif, *International Extradition: United States Law and Practice*, 4th edn. (Dobbs Ferry, New York: Oceana Publications, 2002).

Bassiouni, M. Cherif, *International Criminal Law Conventions and Their Penal Provisions* (Ardsley Park, NY: Transnational Publishers, 1997).

Bassiouni, M. Cherif, "International Crimes: *Jus Cogens* and *Obligatio Erga Omnes*", 59 *Law and Contemporary Problems* (1996): 63.

Bassiouni, M. Cherif (ed.), *International Criminal Law* (Dobbs Ferry, New York: Transnational, 1986).

Belsky, Adam C., Mark Merva and Naomi Roht-Arriaza, "Implied Waiver Under the FSIA: A Proposed Exception to Immunity for Violations of Peremptory Norms of International Law", 77 *California Law Review* (1989): 365.

Bianchi, Andrea, "*Ferrini v. Federal Republic of Germany*", 99 *AJIL* (2005): 242.

Bianchi, Andrea, "Serious Violations of Human Rights and Foreign States' Accountability before Municipal Courts", in Lal Chand Vohrah, et al. (eds.), *Man's Inhumanity to Man. Essays on International Law in Honour of Antonio Cassese* (The Hague: Kluwer Law International, 2003): 149.

Bianchi, Andrea, "Immunity v Human Rights: The *Pinochet* Case", 2 *EJIL* (1999): 238.

Bianchi, Andrea, "Individual Accountability for Crimes against Humanity: Reckoning with the Past, Thinking of the Future", 19 *SAIS Review* (1999): 97.

Bianchi, Andrea, "Overcoming the Hurdle of State Immunity in the Domestic Enforcement of International Human Rights" in Benedetto Conforti and Francesco Francioni (eds.), *Enforcing International Human Rights in Domestic Courts* (The Hague/Boston: Martinus Nijhoff, 1997): 405.

Bianchi, Andrea, "Denying State Immunity to Violators of Human Rights", 46 *Austrian Journal of Public and International Law* (1994): 195.

Black, Forrest Revere, "Statutes of Limitation and the Ex-Post Facto Clauses", 26 *Kentucky Law Journal* (1937-1938): 41.

Blakesley, Christopher L., "Atrocity and its Prosecution: The Ad Hoc Tribunals for Former Yugoslavia and Rwanda" in Timothy L.H. McCormack & Gerry J. Simpson (eds.), *The Law of War Crimes: National and International Approaches* (The Hague: Kluwer Law International, 1997): 189.

Boed, Roman, "The Effect of a Domestic Amnesty on the Ability of Foreign States to Prosecute Alleged Perpetrators of Serious Human Rights Violations", 33(3) *Cornell International Law Journal* (2000): 297.

Boisson de Chazournes, Laurence, and Luigi Condorelli, "Common Article 1 of the Geneva Conventions Revisited: Protecting Collective Interests", 82(837) *IRRC* (March 2000): 67.

Borelli, Silvia, "Terrorism and Human Rights: Treatment of Terrorist Suspects and Limits on International Co-operation", 16 *LJIL* (2003): 802, 807.

Brierly, James L., "The Lotus Case", 44 *Law Quarterly Review* (1928): 154.

Bringa, Tone, "Reconciliation in Bosnia-Herzegovina", in Elin Skaar, Siri Gloppen and Astri Suhrke (eds.), *Roads to Reconciliation* (Maryland: Lexington Books, 2005): 187.

Brody, Reed, and Michael Ratner (eds.), *The Pinochet Papers: The Case of Augusto Pinochet in Spain and Britain* (The Hague: Kluwer Law International, 2000).

Brownlie, Ian, *Principles of Public International Law*, 6th edn. (Oxford: OUP, 2003).

Brownlie, Ian, *Principles of Public International Law*, 4th edn. (Oxford: OUP, 1990).

Brubacher, Matthew R., "The development of prosecutorial discretion in international criminal courts", in Edel Hughes, William A. Schabas and Ramesh Thakur (eds.), *Atrocities and International Accountability: Beyond Transitional Justice* (Tokyo/New York/Paris: United Nations University Press, 2007): 142.

Brubacher, Matthew R., "Prosecutorial Discretion within the International Criminal Court", 2 *JICJ* (2004): 71.

Burke-White, William W., "Reframing Impunity: Applying Liberal International Law Theory to an Analysis of Amnesty Legislation", 42(2) *Harvard Int'l Law J* (2001): 468.

Buscher, Frank M., *The U.S. War Crimes Trial Program in Germany, 1946-1955* (New York: Greenwood Press, 1989).

Campbell, Colm, "Peace and the laws of war: the role of international humanitarian law in the post-conflict environment", 839 *IRRC* (2000): 630.

Caplan, Lee M., "State Immunity, Human Rights and Jus Cogens: A Critique of the Normative Hierarchy Theory", 97 *AJIL* (2003): 741.

Cass, Deborah Z., "Navigating the Newstream: Recent Critical Scholarship in International Law", 65 *Nordic Journal of International Law* (1996): 341.

Cassese, Antonio, *International Law*, 2nd edn. (Oxford: OUP, 2005).

Cassese, Antonio, *International Criminal Law* (Oxford: OUP, 2003).

Cassese, Antonio, "Terrorism as an International Crime", in Andrea Bianchi (ed.), *Enforcing International Law Norms Against Terrorism* (Oxford: Hart Publishing, 2003): 213.

Cassese, Antonio, "The Belgium Court of Cassation v. the International Court of Justice: the *Sharon and others* Case", 1 *JICJ* (2003): 437.

Cassese, Antonio, "Is the Bell Tolling for Universality? A Plea for a Sensible Notion of Universal Jurisdiction", 1 *JICJ* (2003): 589.

Cassese, Antonio, "When May Senior State Officials Be Tried for International Crimes? Some Comments on the *Congo* v. *Belgium* Case", 13 *EJIL* (2002): 853.

Cassin, Barbara, "'Removing the perpetuity of hatred': on South Africa as a role model", 862 *IRRC* (Cambridge) (June 2006): 235.

Castillo, Pablo, "Rethinking Deterrence: The International Criminal Court in Sudan", *UNISCI Discussion Papers* 13 (January 2007): 167.

ChavezTafur, Gabriel, "Using International Law to By-pass Domestic Legal Hurdles: On the Applicability of the Statute of Limitations in the *Menéndez et al.* Case", 6 *JICJ* (2008): 1061.

Chigara, Ben, *Amnesty in International Law: The Legality under International Law of National Amnesty Laws* (Essex: Pearson Education Limited, 2002).

Chinkin, Christine, "International Decisions", 3 *AJIL* (1999): 703.

Choo, Andrew L.-T., "Halting Criminal Prosecutions: The Abuse of Process Doctrine Revisited", *Criminal Law Review* (1995): 865.

Choo, Andrew L.-T., *Abuse of process and judicial stays of criminal proceedings* (Oxford: OUP, 1993).

Clapham, Andrew, *Human Rights Obligations of Non-State Actors* (Oxford: OUP, 2006).

Clapham, Andrew, "National Action Challenged: Sovereignty, Immunity and Universal Jurisdiction before the International Court of Justice", in Mark Lattimer and Philippe Sands QC (eds.), *Justice for Crimes Against Humanity* (Oxford and Portland, Oregon: Hart Publishing, 2003): 303.

Clapham, Andrew, "Revisiting Human Rights in the Private Sphere: Using the European Convention on Human Rights to Protect the Right of Access to the Civil Courts", in C. Scott (ed.), *Torture as Tort: Comparative Perspectives on the Development of Transnational Human Rights Litigation* (Oxford: Hart Publishing, 2001): 513.

Clark, Roger S., "Nuremberg and Tokyo in Contemporary Perspective", in Timothy L.H. McCormack & Gerry J. Simpson (eds.), *The Law of War Crimes: National and International Approaches* (The Hague: Kluwer Law International, 1997): 171.

Cohen, Stanley, *States of Denial: Knowing about Atrocities and Suffering* (London: Polity Press, 2001).

"Commission on the Responsibility of the Authors of the War and on Enforcement of Penalties", 14 *AJIL* (1920): 95.

Conway, Gerard, "*Ne Bis In Idem* and the International Criminal Tribunals", 14 *Criminal Law Forum* (2003): 351.

Cowles, Willard B., "Universal Jurisdiction over War Crimes", 33 *California Law Review* (1945): 177.

Currie, Robert J., "Abducted Fugitives Before the International Criminal Court: Problems and Prospects", 18 *Criminal Law Forum* 350 (2007): 350.

Crawford, James, "The ILC's Draft Statute for an International Criminal Tribunal", 88 *AJIL* (1994): 140.

Crawford, James, *The International Law Commission's Articles on State Responsibility: Introduction, Text and Commentaries* (Cambridge: CUP, 2002).

Cryer, Robert, *Prosecuting International Crimes: Selectivity and the International Criminal Law Regime* (Cambridge: CUP, 2005).

Damaška, Mirjan, "Negotiated Justice in International Criminal Courts", 2 *JICJ* (2004): 1018.

D'Amato, Anthony, "Law and War: A Doctrine of Deterrence", *UN Chronicle* 35, Code A982 (1998): 52-53.

De Greiff, Pablo, "Comment: Universal Jurisdiction and Transitions to Democracy", in Stephen Macedo (ed.), *Universal Jurisdiction: National Courts and the Prosecution of Serious Crimes under International Law* (Philadelphia: University of Pennsylvania, 2004): 121.

De La Cuesta, José Luis, "Concurrent National and International Criminal Jurisdiction and the Principle '*Ne Bis In Idem*' General Report", 73 *International Review of Penal Law* (2002): 707.

De Nike, Howard J., Quiqley, John & Robinson, Kenneth J. (eds.), *Genocide in Cambodia: Documents from the Trial of Pol Pot and leng Sary* (Philadelphia: University of Pennsylvania Press, 2000).

Dean Moore, Kathleen, *Pardons: Justice, Mercy, and the Public Interest* (Oxford: OUP, 1989).

Del Ponte, Carla, "Prosecuting the Individuals Bearing the Highest Level of Responsibility", 2 *JICJ* (2004): 516.

Delmas-Marty, Mireille, "La responsibilité pénale en échec (prescription, amnistie, immunités)" in Antonio Cassese & Mireille Delmas-Marty (eds.), *Jurisdictions nationales et crimes internationaux* (Paris: PUF, 2002): 613.

Derby, Daniel H., "Torture", in M. Cherif Bassiouni (ed.), *International Criminal Law*, 2nd edn. (Ardsley, New York: Transnational Publishers, Inc., 1999): 705.

Dickinson, Laura, "The Promise of Hybrid Courts", 97 *AJIL* (2003): 295.

Dinstein, Yoram, "Defences", in Gabrielle Kirk MacDonald & Olivia Swaak-Goldman (eds.), *Substantive and Procedural Aspects of International Criminal Law: The Experience of National and International Courts*, Vol. I, *Commentary* (The Hague: Kluwer Law International, 2000): 371.

Dinstein, Yoram, "The Universality Principle and War Crimes", in Michael N. Schmitt & Leslie C. Green (eds.), *The Law of Armed Conflict: Into the Next Millennium* (Newport: Naval War College, 1998): 27.

Dinstein, Yoram, "International Criminal Law", 20 *Israel Law Review* (1985): 206.

Doria, José, "Angola: A Case Study in the Challenges of Achieving Peace and the Question of Amnesty or Prosecuting of War Crimes in Mixed Armed Conflicts", 5 *YIHL* (2002): 3.

Dugard, John, "Possible Conflicts of Jurisdiction with Truth Commissions", in Antonio Cassese, Paola Gaeta and John R.W.D. Jones (eds.), *The Rome Statute of the International Criminal Court: A Commentary* (Oxford: OUP, 2002): 693.

Dugard, John, "Dealing with Crimes of a Past Regime: Is Amnesty Still an Option?" 12(4) *LJIL* (1999): 1001.

Dugard, John, "No Jurisdiction over Abducted Persons in Roman-Dutch Law: *Male Captus, Male Detentus*", 7 *South African Journal of Human Rights* (1991): 199.

Dworkin, Ronald, *A Matter of Principle* (Oxford: OUP, 1986).

Edelenbos, Carla, "Human Rights Violations: A Duty to Prosecute?", 7(5) *LJIL* (1994): 14.

El Zeidy, Mohamed, "The Doctrine of Double Jeopardy in International Criminal and Human Rights Law", 6 *Mediterranean Journal of Human Rights* (2002): 183.

Etcheberry, Alfred, "The Principles of Legality and *Non Bin in Idem*", in *International Criminal Law: Quo Vadis?*, Proceedings of the International Conference held in Siracusa, Italy, 28 November-3 December 2002 (Ramonville Saint-Agne: Editions Eres, 2004): 337.

Falk, Richard, "Casting the Spell: The New Haven School of International Law", 104 *Yale Law Journal* (1995): 1991.

Farer, Tom J., "Restraining the Barbarians: Can International Criminal Law Help?", 22(1) *Human Rights Quarterly* (2000): 90.

Ferdinandusse, Ward N., *Direct Application of International Criminal Law in National Courts* (The Hague: T.M.C. Asser Press, 2006).

Fitzmaurice, Gerald, "Judicial Innovation – It's Uses and its Perils", in D.W. Bowett, et al. (eds.), *Cambridge Essays in International Law: Essays in Honour of Lord McNair* (London: Stevens & Sons, 1965): 24.

Fox, Hazel, "In Defence of State Immunity: Why the UN Convention on State Immunity is Important", 55 *ICLQ* (April 2006): 399.

Frulli, Micaela, "Le droit international et les obstacles à la mise en oevre de la responsibilité pénale pour crimes internationaux", in Antonio Cassese & Mireille Delmas-Marty (eds.), *Crimes internationaux et jurisdictions internationales* (Paris: PUF, 2002): 215.

Gaeta, Paola, "Official Capacity and Immunities", in Antonio Cassese, Paola Gaeta and John R.W.D. Jones (eds.), *The Rome Statute of the International Criminal Court: A Commentary*, Vol. I (Oxford: OUP, 2002): 975.

Garapon, Antoine, "Three Challenges for International Criminal Justice", 2 *JICJ* (2004): 716.

Garner, Bryan A., *Black's Law Dictionary*, 8th edn. (St. Paul, Minn: West Group, 2004).

Gavron, Jessica, "Amnesties in the light of developments in international law and the establishment of the International Criminal Court", 51(1) *ICLQ* (2002): 91.

George Jn., B.J., "Immunities and Exceptions", in M. Cherif Bassiouni (ed.), *International and Criminal Law*, 2nd edn., Vol. II (Ardsley, New York: Transnational Publishers, Inc., 1999): 107.

Gilbert, Geoff, *Transnational Fugitive Offenders in International Law* (The Hague: Nijhoff, 1998).

Gil Gil, Alicia, "The Flaws of the Scilingo Judgment", 3(5) *JICJ* (2005): 1082.

Glueck, Sheldon, *War Criminals: Their Prosecution and Punishment* (New York: Alfred A. Knopf, 1944).

Gowlland-Debbas, Vera, "The role of the Security Council in the new International Criminal Court from a systemic perspective", in Laurence Boisson de Chazournes & Vera Gowlland-Debbas (eds.), *The International Legal System in Quest of Equity and Universality, Liber-Americorum Georges Abi-Saab* (The Hague: Kluwer Law International, 2001): 629.

Greenwood, Christopher, "The Development of International Humanitarian Law by the International Criminal Tribunal for the Former Yugoslavia", 2 *Max Planck UNYB* (1998): 97.

Gregory, Charles Noble, "The Effect of War on the Operation of Statutes of Limitation", 28 *Harvard Law Review* (1914-1915): 673.

Grotius, Hugo, *The Rights of War and Peace (De jure belli ac pacis)*, Knud Haakonssen (Gen. ed.); Richard Tuck (ed.) (Indianapolis: Liberty Fund, 2005).

Hafner, Gerhard, Kristen Boon, Anne Rübesame, & Jonathan Huston, "A Response to the American View as Presented by Ruth Wedgwood", 10 *EJIL* (1999): 108.

Hall, Christopher Keith, "UN Convention on State Immunity: The Need for a Human Rights Protocol", 55 *ICLQ* (April 2006): 411.

Hart, Herbert L.A., *The Concept of Law*, 2nd edn. (Oxford: Clarendon, 1994).

"Harvard Research Draft Convention on Jurisdiction With Respect to Crime", 29 *AJIL Supplement* (1935): 443.

Hayner, Priscilla B., "Truth Commissions: A schematic overview", 862 *IRRC* (Cambridge) (June 2006): 295.

Hayner, Priscilla B., *Unspeakable Truths: Confronting State Terror and Atrocity* (London: Routledge, 2001).

Hayner, Priscilla B., "Fifteen truth commissions – 1974 to 1994: A comparative study", 15 *Human Rights Quarterly* (1994): 597.

Hays Butler, A., "The Growing Support for Universal Jurisdiction in National Legislation", in Stephen Macedo (ed.), *Universal Jurisdiction: National Courts and the Prosecution of Serious Crimes under International Law* (Philadelphia: University of Pennsylvania Press, 2004): 67.

Heder, Stephen, and Brian D. Tittemore, *Seven Candidates for Prosecution: Accountability for the Crimes of the Khmer Rouge*, available at: <http://www.wcl.american.edu/war-crimes/khmerrouge.cfm> (War Crimes Research Office, Washington College of Law, July 2001).

Heise, Michael, "Mercy by the Numbers: An Empirical Analysis of Clemency and its Structure", 89(2) *Virginia Law Review* (April 2003): 239.

Henckearts, Jean-Marie, and Louise Doswald-Beck, *Customary International Humanitarian Law*, Vols. I and II (Cambridge: CUP, 2005).

Higgins, Rosalyn, *Problems and Process: International Law and How We Use It* (Oxford: Oxford Clarendon Press, 1994).

Higgins, Rosalyn, "Policy Decisions and the International Judicial Process", 17(1) *ICLQ* (1968): 58.

Honwana, Alcinda, "Healing and Social Reintegration in Mozambique and Angola", in E. Skaar, S. Gloppen & A. Suhrke (eds.), *Roads to Reconciliation* (Oxford: Lexington Books, 2005): 83.

Human Rights Watch, *The Pinochet Precedent: How Victims Can Pursue Human Rights Criminals Abroad* (New York: Human Rights Watch, September 2000).

International Law Association, Committee on International Human Rights Law and Practice, *Final Report on the Exercise of Universal Jurisdiction in Respect of Gross Human Rights Offences*, London Conference (ILA, 2000).

Iovane, Massimo, "The *Ferrini* Judgment of the Italian Supreme Court: Opening Up Domestic Courts to Claims of Reparation for Victims of Serious Violations of Fundamental Human Rights", 14 *Italian Yearbook of International Law* (2004): 165.

Jennings, Robert Y., "The *Caroline* and *McLeod* cases", 32 *AJIL* (1938): 82.

Kadelbach, Stefan, "*Jus Cogens*, Obligations *Erga Omnes* and other Rules – The Identification of Fundamental Norms", in Christian Tomuschat and Jean-Marc Thouvenin (eds.), *The Fundamental Rules of the International Legal Order. Jus Cogens and Obligations Erga Omnes* (Leiden/Boston: Martinus Nijhoff Publishers, 2006): 21.

Kamatali, Jean Marie, "The Challenge of Linking International Criminal Justice and National Reconciliation: the Case of the ICTR", 16(1) *LJIL* (March 2003): 115.

Kamminga, Menno T., "Lessons Learned from the Exercise of Universal Jurisdiction in Respect of Gross Human Rights Offenses", 23(4) *Human Rights Quarterly* (2001): 940.

Kaul, Hans-Peter, "Preconditions to the Exercise of Jurisdiction", in Antonio Cassese, Paola Gaeta and John R.W.D. Jones (eds.), *The Rome Statute of the International Criminal Court: A Commentary* (Oxford: OUP, 2002): 583.

Kelly, Michael J., *Nowhere to Hide: Defeat of the Sovereign Immunity Defense for Crimes of Genocide and the Trials of Slobodan Milosevic and Saddam Hussein* (New York: Peter Lang, Inc., 2005).

Kelsen, Hans, *Principles of International Law*, 2nd edn. (New York: Holt, Rinehart & Winston, 1966).

Kiernan, Ben, "The Demography of Genocide in Southeast Asia: The Death Tolls in Cambodia, 1975-79, and East Timor, 1975-80", 34(4) *Critical Asian Studies* (2003): 585.

Kirby, Michael, "Universal Jurisdiction and Judicial Reluctance: A New 'Fourteen Points'", in Stephen Macedo (ed.), *Universal Jurisdiction: National Courts and the Prosecution of Serious Crimes under International Law* (Philadelphia: University of Pennsylvania Press, 2004): 240.

Kirk McDonald, and Olivia Swaak-Goldman, *Substantive and Procedural Aspects of International Criminal Law: The Experience of International and National Courts*, Vol. II. Part 2, *Documents and Cases* (The Hague: Kluwer Law International, 2000).

Kirsch, Philippe, "The Rome Conference on the International Criminal Court: A Comment", *ASIL Newsletter* (Washington, D.C., American Society of International Law, November-December 1998): 1.

Kittichaisaree, Kriangsak, *International Criminal Law* (Oxford: OUP, 2001).

Knoops, Geert-Jan Alexander, *Redressing Miscarriages of Justice: Practice and Procedure in National and International Criminal Law Cases* (Ardsley, NY: Transnational Publishers, Inc., 2006).

Kok, Ruth A., *Statutory Limitations in International Criminal Law* (The Hague: TMC Asser Press, 2007).

Koskenniemi, Martti, "Between impunity and show trials", 6 *Max Planck UNYB* (2002): 1.

Koskenniemi, Martti, *The Gentle Civilizer of Nations. The Rise and Fall of International Law 1870-1960* (Cambridge: CUP, 2002).

Kritz, Neil J. (ed.), *Transitional Justice: How Emerging Democracies Reckon with Former Regimes*. Vol. III, *Laws, Rulings and Reports* (Washington, D.C.: United States Instiute of Peace Press, 1995).

Lafontaine, Fannie, "No Amnesty or Statute of Limitation for Enforced Disappearances: The *Sandoval* Case before the Supreme Court of Chile", 3 *JICJ* (2005): 469.

Lasswell, Harold D. and Myres S. McDougal, *Jurisprudence for a Free Society: Studies in Law, Science and Policy* (New Haven, Conn.: New Haven Press/Martinus Nijhoff Publishers, 1992).

Lawrence, Preuss, "Settlement of the *Jacob* Kidnapping Case (Switzerland-Germany)", 30(1) *AJIL* (1936): 123.

Lauterpacht, Hersch, *The Development of International Law by the International Court* (New York: Praeger, 1958).

Lauterpacht, Hersch, "The Problems of Jurisdictional Immunities of Foreign States", 28 *BYIL* (1951): 220.

Lauterpacht, Hersch, *The Function of Law in the International Community* (Oxford: Clarendon Press, 1933).

Legarre, Santiago, "Crimes against Humanity, Reasonableness and the Law: the *Simon* case in the Supreme Court of Argentina", 5(3) *Chinese JIL* (2006): 723.

Lelieur-Fischer, Juliette, "Prosecuting the Crimes against Humanity Committed during the Algerian War: an Impossible Endeavour? The 2003 Decision of the French Court of Cassation in *Aussaresses*", 2 *JICJ* (2004): 231.

Lemkin, Raphael, *Axis Rule in Occupied Europe: Law of Occupation, Analysis of Government, Proposal for Redress* (Washington, D.C.: Carnegie Endowment for International Peace, 1944).

Linton, Suzannah, "Rising from the Ashes: The Creation of a Viable Justice System in East Timor", 25(1) *Melbourne University Law Review* (2001): 122.

Linton, Suzannah, and Caitlin Reiger, "The Evolving Jurisprudence and Practice of East Timor's Special Panels for Serious Crimes on Admissions of Guilt, Duress and Superior Orders", 4 *YIHL* (2001): 167.

Log, Sure, "The Practical Applications of *Ne Bis in Idem* in International Criminal Law", in Sienho Yee (ed.), *International Crime and Punishment*, Selected Issues, Vol. 2 (Lanham, Maryland: University Press of America, Inc., 2004): 169.

Lopez, Dax Eric, "Not Twice for the Same: How the Dual Sovereignty Doctrine is Used to Circumvent *Non Bis In Idem*", 33 *Vanderbilt Journal of Transnational Law* (2000): 1263.

Mani, Rama, "Does power trump morality? Reconciliation or transitional justice?", in Edel Hughes, William A. Schabas and Ramesh Thakur (eds.), *Atrocities and International Accountability: Beyond Transitional Justice* (Tokyo/New York/Paris: United Nations University Press, 2007): 23.

Mann, Frederick A., "The Doctrine of Jurisdiction in International Law", 111 *RdC* (1964-1): 9.

Mann, Frederick A., "Reflections on the Prosecution of Persons Abducted in Breach of International Law", in Yoram Dinstein (ed.), *International Law at a Time of Perplexity: Essays in Honour of Shabtai Rosenne* (Dordrecht: Nijhoff, 1989): 407.

Marks, Susan, and Andrew Clapham, *International Human Rights Lexicon* (Oxford: OUP, 2005).

Marks, Susan, *The Riddle of All Constitutions: International Law, Democracy and the Critique of Ideology* (Oxford: OUP, 2000).

Mattarollo, Rodolfo, "Recent Argentine Jurisprudence in the Matter of Crimes Against Humanity", 62-63 *The Review: International Commission of Jurists* (September 2001): 11.

McCormack, Timothy L.H., "Their Atrocities and Our Misdemeanours: The Reticence of States to Try Their 'Own Nationals' for International Crimes", in Mark Lattimer and Philippe Sands QC (eds.), *Justice for Crimes Against Humanity* (Oxford and Portland, Oregon: Hart Publishing, 2003): 107.

McCormack, Timothy L.H., "From Sun Tzu to the Sixth Committee: The Evolution of an International Criminal Law Regime", in Timothy L.H. McCormack and Gerry J. Simpson (eds.), *The Law of War Crimes: National and International Approaches* (The Hague: Kluwer Law International, 1997): 31.

McDonald, Avril, "Sierra Leone's Uneasy Peace: The Amnesties Granted in the Lomé Peace Agreement and the United Nations' Dilemma", 13(1) *Humanitares Volkerrecht* (2000): 11.

McDougal, Myres S., "Some Basic Theoretical Concepts about International Law: A policy-oriented framework of enquiry", 4 *Journal of Conflict Resolution* (1960): 337.

McDougal, Myres S., Harold D. Lasswell and Lung-Chu Chen, *Human Rights and World Public Order* (New Haven, New Haven Press, 1980).

McDougal, Myres S. and Siegfried Wiessner, "Law and Minimum World Public Order, Introduction to the Reissue", in Myres S. McDougal and Florentino P. Feliciano, *The International Law of War: Transnational Coercion and World Public Order* (New Haven: New Haven Press, 1994).

McGregor, Lorna, "State Immunity and *Jus Cogens*", 55 *ICLQ* (April 2006): 437.

McLachlan, Campbell and Peter Nygh, *Transnational Tort Litigation: Jurisdictional Principles* (Oxford: Clarendon Press, 1996).

McKay, Fiona, *Universal Jurisdiction in Europe: Criminal Prosecutions in Europe Since 1990 for War Crimes, Crimes Against Humanity, Torture and Genocide* (Redress, 1999).

McNair, Lord Arnold Duncan, *International Law Opinions: Selected and Annotated*, Vol. I (Cambridge: CUP: 1956).

Meron, Theodor, "International criminalization of internal atrocities", 89 *AJIL* (1995): 554.

Meron, Theodor, *Human Rights and Humanitarian Law as Customary Law* (Oxford: Clarendon Press, 1989).

Mettraux, Guénaël, "Dutch Courts' Universal Jurisdiction over Violations of Common Article 3 *qua* War Crimes", 4(2) *JICJ* (2006): 362.

Miller, Robert H., "The Convention on the Non-Applicability of Statutory Limitations to War Crimes and Crimes against Humanity", 65 *AJIL* (1971): 476.

Moreno Ocampo, Luis, "Beyond Punishment: Justice in the Wake of Massive Crimes in Argentina", 52(2) *Journal of International Affairs* (Spring 1999): 599.

Morris, Madeleine, "High Crimes and Misconceptions: The ICC and Non Party States", 64 *Law and Contemporary Problems* (2001): 26.

Muñoz-Rojas, Daniel, and Jean-Jacques Frésard, ICRC, *The Roots of Behaviour in War: Understanding and Preventing IHL Violations* (Geneva: ICRC, October 2004).

Naqvi, Yasmin, "The right to the truth in international law: Fact or fiction?", 88(862) *IRRC* (June 2006): 245.

Naqvi, Yasmin, "Amnesty for war crimes: Defining the limits of international recognition", 85(851) *IRRC* (September 2003): 583.

Neier, Aryeh, *War Crimes: Brutality, Genocide, Terror and the Struggle for Justice* (London: Times Books, Random House, 1998).

Ntanda Nsereko, Daniel D., "Prosecutorial Discretion before National Courts and International Tribunals", 3 *JICJ* (2005): 124.

Orentlicher, Diane, "The Future of Universal Jurisdiction in the New Architecture of Transnational Justice", In Stephen Macedo (ed.), *Universal Jurisdiction: National Courts and the Prosecution of Serious Crimes Under International Law* (Philadelphia, PA: University of Pennsylvania, 2004): 214.

Orentlicher, Diane F., "Setting Accounts: The Duty to Prosecute Human Rights Violations of a Prior Regime", 100 *Yale Law Journal* (1991): 2537.

O'Shea, Andrea, *Amnesty for Crime in International Law and Practice* (The Hague: Kluwer Law International, 2002).

Paust, Jordan, "My Lai and Vietnam: Norms, Myths and Leader Responsibility", 57 *Military Law Review* (1972): 118.

Pictet, Jean S., *Commentary to IV Geneva Convention Relative to the Protection of Civilian Persons in Time of War* (Geneva: ICRC, 1958).

Pinzauti, Giulia, "An Instance of Reasonable Universality: The *Scilingo* Case", 3(5) *JICJ* (2005): 1092.

Poels, Alexander, "A Need for Transnational *Non Bis In Idem* Protection in International Human Rights Law", 23(3) *Netherlands Quarterly of Human Rights* (2005): 329.

Quigley, John, "Introduction", in Howard J. De Nike, John Quigley and Kenneth J. Robinson (eds.), *Genocide in Cambodia: Documents from the Trial of Pol Pot and Ieng Sary* (Philadelphia: University of Pennsylvania Press, 2000): 1.

Randall, Kenneth C., "Universal Jurisdiction under International Law", 66 *Texas Law Review* (1988): 785.

Ratner, Steven R. & Jason S. Abrams, *Accountability for Human Rights Atrocities: Beyond the Nuremberg Legacy*, 2nd edn. (Oxford: OUP, 2001).

Ratner, Michael, "The Lords' Decision in *Pinochet III*", in Reed Brody and Michael Ratner (eds.), *The Pinochet Papers: The Case of Augusto Pinochet in Spain and Britain* (The Hague: Kluwer Law International, 2000): 33.

Redress, *Universal Jurisdiction: Fourteen Principles on the Effective Exercise of Universal Jurisdiction* (Redress, June 1999).

"Report of the Subcommittee on the Trial and Punishment of War Criminals", 37 *AJIL* (1943): 663.

Reydams, Luc, *Universal Jurisdiction* (Oxford: OUP, 2003).

Reydams, Luc, "Belgium Reneges on Universality: The 5 August 2003 Act on Grave Breaches of International Humanitarian Law", 1 *JICJ* (2003): 679.

Reydam, Luc, "Belgium's First Application of Universal Jurisdiction: The Butare Four Case," 1 *JICJ* (2002): 428.

Reydams, Luc, "Case note: Belgian Tribunal of First Instance of Brussels (investigating magistrate), 8 November 1998", 93 *AJIL* (1999): 700.

Rigby, Andrew, *Justice and Reconciliation: After the Violence* (Boulder, C.O.: Lynne Rienner, 2001).

Rodley, Nigel S., *The Treatment of Prisoners under International Law*, 2nd edn. (Oxford: OUP, 1999).

Roht-Arriaza, Naomi, "Guatemala Genocide Case", 100 *AJIL* (2006): 207.

Roht-Arriaza, Naomi, *The Pinochet Effect: Transnational Justice in the Age of Human Rights* (Philadelphia: University of Pennsylvania Press, 2005).

Roht-Arriaza, Naomi, and Lauren Gibson, "The Developing Jurisprudence on Amnesty", 20 *Human Rights Quarterly* (1998): 843.

Roht-Arriaza, Naomi, "Sources in International Treaties of an Obligation to Investigate, Prosecute, and Provide Redress", in Naomi Roht-Arriaza (ed.), *Impunity and Human Rights in International Law and Practice* (Oxford: OUP, 1995): 26.

Roht-Arriaza, Naomi, "State Responsibility to Investigate and Prosecute Grave Violations of Human Rights in International Law", 78 *California Law Review* (1990): 451.

Ryngaert, Cedric, "The Doctrine of Abuse of Process: A Comment on the Cambodia Tribunal's Decisions in the Case against Duch (2007)", 21 *LJIL* (2008): 719.

Ryngaert, Cedric, *Jurisdiction in International Law* (Oxford: OUP, 2008).

Sadat, Leila Nadya, "Universal Jurisdiction, National Amnesties, and Truth Commissions: Reconciling the Irreconcilable", in Stephen Macedo (ed.), *Universal Jurisdiction: National Courts and the Prosecution of Serious Crimes under International Law* (Philadelphia: University of Pennsylvania Press, 2004): 193.

Sadat, Leila Nadya, and S. Richard Carden, "The New International Criminal Court: An Uneasy Revolution", 88 *Georgetown Law Journal* (2000): 407.

Sarooshi, Dan, "Prosecutorial Policy and the ICC: Prosecutor's *Proprio Motu* or Self-Denial?", 2 *JICJ* (2004): 940.

Schabas, William A., *The UN International Criminal Tribunals: The Former Yugoslavia, Rwanda and Sierra Leone* (Cambridge: CUP, 2006).

Schabas, William A., "The Crime of Torture and the International Criminal Tribunals", 37(2&3) *Case Western Reserve Journal of International Law* (2006): 349.

Schabas, William A., "A Synergistic Relationship: The Sierra Leone Truth and Reconciliation Commission and the Special Court for Sierra Leone", in William A. Schabas & Shane Darcy (eds.), *Truth Commission and Courts: The Tension between Criminal Justice and the Search for Truth* (Dordrecht: Kluwer Academic Publishers, 2004): 3.

Schabas, William A., *Genocide in International Law* (Cambridge: CUP, 2000).

Schabas, William A., "Article 29: Non-applicability of statute of limitations", in Otto Triffterer (ed.), *Commentary on the Rome Statute of the International Criminal Court: Observers' Notes, Article by Article* (Baden-Baden: Nomos Verlagsgesellschaft, 1999): 523.

Scharf, Michael P., "From the eXile Files: An Essay on Trading Justice for Peace", 63(1) *Washington and Lee Law Review* (2006): 339.

Scharf, Michael P., "Trading Justice for Efficiency", 2 *JICJ* (2004): 1070.

Scharf, Michael P. & Melanie K. Corrin, "On Dangerous Ground: Passive Personality Jurisdiction and the Prohibition of Internet Gambling", 8(1) *New England Journal of International and Comparative Law* (2002): 19.

Scharf, Michael P., "Application of Treaty-Based Jurisdiction to Nationals of Non-Party States", 35 *NELR* (2001): 363.

Scharf, Michael P., "The Amnesty Exception to the Jurisdiction of the International Criminal Court", 32 *Cornell International Law Journal* (1999): 507.

Scharf, Michael P., "*The Prosecutor* v. *Slavko Dokmanović*: Irregular Rendition and the ICTY" 11 *LJIL* (1998): 369.

Scharf, Michael P., "Swapping Amnesty for Peace: Was there a duty to prosecute international crimes in Haiti?", 31(1) *Texas International Law Journal* (1996): 1.

Schmidt, Michael L., "The International Criminal Court: An Effective Means of Deterrence?", 167 *Military Law Review* (2001): 156.

Schwarzenberger, G., "The Problem of an International Criminal Law", 3 *CLP* (1950): 263.

Scully, Laura, "Neither Justice, Nor Oasis: Algeria's Amnesty Law", 33 *Brooklyn Journal of International Law* (2007-2008): 975.

Sebastian Elias, Jose, "Constitutional Changes, Transitional Justice, and Legitimacy: The Life and Death of Argentina's 'Amnesty Laws'", 31 *Hastings International and Comparative Law Review* (2008): 628.

Sigler, Jay A., "A History of Double Jeopardy", 7 *American Journal of Legal History* (1963): 283.

Simbeye, Yitiha, *Immunity and International Criminal Law* (Aldershot: Ashgate Publishing Limited, 2004).

"Symposium on Method in International Law", 93(2) *AJIL* (1999): 291.

Simpson, Gerry J., "War Crimes: A Critical Introduction", in Timothy L.H. McCormack & Gerry J. Simpson (eds.), *The Law of War Crimes: National and International Approaches* (The Hague: Kluwer Law International, 1997): 1.

Skaar, Elin, "Argentina: Truth, Justice, and Reconciliation", in E. Skaar, S. Gloppen and A. Suhrke (eds.), *Roads to Reconciliation* (Lanham: Lexington Books, 2005): 157.

Slaughter, Anne-Marie, "International Law in a World of Liberal States", 6 *EJIL* (1995): 503.

Sloan, James, "*Prosecutor* v. *Dragan Nikolić*, Decision on Defence Motion on Illegal Capture", 16 *LJIL* (2003): 541.

Sluiter, Göran, "International Criminal Proceedings and the Protection of Human Rights" 37 *New England Law Review* (2003): 935.

Slye, Ronald C., "The Cambodian Amnesties: Beneficiaries and the Temporal Reach of Amnesties for Gross Violations of Human Rights", *ExpressO Preprint Service – Working Paper* 33, available at : <http://law.bepress.com/cgi/viewcontent.cgi?article=1063&context=expresso> (2003).

Slye, Ronald C., "The Legitimacy of Amnesties under International Law and General Principles of Anglo-American Law: Is Legitimate Amnesty Possible", 43 *VJIL* (2002): 173.

Solé, Antoni Pigrau, "The Pinochet Case in Spain", 6 *ILSA J. Int'l and Comp. Law* (2000): 653.

Spinedi, Marina, "State Responsibility for International Crimes: *Tertium Non Datur*?", 13(4) *EJIL* (2002): 894.

Sriram, Chandra Lekha, *Globalizing Justice for Mass Atrocities: A Revolution in Accountability* (London: Routledge, 2005).

Stahn, Carsten, "Complementarity, Amnesties and Alternative Forms of Justice: Some Interpretative Guidelines for the International Criminal Court", 3 *JICJ* (2005): 695.

Stahn, Carsten, "United Nations peace-building, amnesties and alternative forms of justice: A change in practice?", 84(845) *IRRC* (March, 2002): 191.

Stein, Torsten, "Limits of International Law Immunities for Senior State Officials in Criminal Procedure", in Christian Tomuschat and Jean-Marc Thouvenin (eds.), *The Fundamental Rules of the International Legal Order.* Jus Cogens *and Obligations* Erga Omnes (Leiden/Boston: Martinus Nijhoff Publishers, 2006): 249.

Stern, Brigitte, "Immunities for Heads of State: Where Do We Stand?", in Mark Lattimer and Philippe Sands QC (eds.), *Justice for Crimes Against Humanity* (Oxford and Portland, Oregon: Hart Publishing, 2003): 73.

Stern, Brigitte, "Better Interpretation and Enforcement of Universal Jurisdiction", in Christopher C. Joyner (ed.), *Reining in Impunity for International Crimes and Serious Violations of Fundamental Human Rights: Proceedings of the Siracusa Conference 17-21 September 1998* (St Agnes: Erès, 1998): 175.

Strohmeyer, Hansjörg, "Collapse and Reconstruction of a Judicial System: The United Nations Missions in Kosovo and East Timor", 95 *AJIL* (2001): 50.

Summers, Mark A., "Immunity or Impunity? The Potential Effect of Prosecutions of State Officials for Core International Crimes in States like the United States That Are Not Parties to the Statute of the International Criminal Court", 31 *Brooklyn Journal of International Law* (2005-2006): 463.

Tallgren, Immi, "Article 20: *Ne bis in idem*", in Otto Triffterer (ed.), *Commentary on the Rome Statute of the International Criminal Court: Observers' Notes, Article by Article* (Baden-Baden: Nomos Verlagsgesellschaft, 1999): 419.

Talmon, Stefan, "The Duty Not to 'Recognise as Lawful' a Situation Created by the Illegal Use of Force or Other Serious Breaches of a *Jus Cogens* Obligation: An Obligation without Real Substance?", in Christian Tomuschat and Jean-Marc Thouvenin (eds.), *The Fundamental Rules of the International Legal Order.* Jus Cogens *and Obligations* Erga Omnes (Leiden/Boston: Martinus Nijhoff Publishers, 2006): 99.

Tarzi, Amin, "Afghanistan: Amnesty Deal Places Karzai in Dilemma", *Radio Free Europe/ Radio Liberty*, 23 February 2007.

Taylor, Nyssa, "England and Australia Relax the Double Jeopardy Privilege for Those Convicted of Serious Crimes", 19 *Temple International and Comparative Law Journal* (2005): 189.

Teitel, Ruti, "Transitional Jurisprudence: The Role of Law in Political Transformation", 106(7) *Yale Law Journal* (1997): 2009.

The Trial of German Major War Criminals. Opening Speeches of the Chief Prosecutors (London: His Majesty's Stationary Office, 1946).

The United Nations War Crimes Commission, *History of the United Nations War Crimes Commission and the Development of the Laws of War* (London: H.M. Stationary Office, 1948).

Tomuschat, Christian, "Universal Criminal Jurisdiction With Respect to the Crime of Genocide, Crimes Against Humanity and War Crimes", in *Institute of International Law Yearbook* (Paris: Pedone, 2005): 215.

Tomuschat, Christian, "Issues of Universal Jurisdiction in the *Scilingo* Case", 3(5) *JICJ* (2005): 1074.

Trainin, A.N., and A.Y. Vishinski (eds.), in *Hitlerite Responsibility under Criminal Law* (Rothstein, Andrew. London: Hutchinson & co., 1946); Institute of Law, Academy of Sciences of the U.S.S.R.

Triffterer, Otto, "Preamble: Legal and political importance", in Otto Triffterer (ed.), *Commentary on the Rome Statute of the International Criminal Court: Observers' Notes, Article by Article* (Baden-Baden: Nomos Verlagsgesellschaft, 1999): 4.

Triffterer, Otto, "Preamble – Paragraph 6: Recalling to States their duties", in Otto Triffterer (ed.), *Commentary on the Rome Statate of the International Criminal Court: Observers' Notes Article by Article* (Baden Baden: Nomos Verlagsgesellschaft, 1999): 12.

Triffterer, Otto, "Article 27: Irrelevance of official capacity", in Otto Triffterer (ed.), *Commentary on the Rome Statute of the International Criminal Court: Observers' Notes, Article by Article* (Baden-Baden: Nomos Verlagsgesellschaft, 1999): 501.

Triggs, Gillian, "Australia's War Crimes Trials: All Pity Choked", in Timothy L.H. McCormack & Gerry J. Simpson (eds.), *The Law of War Crimes: National and International Approaches* (The Hague: Kluwer Law International, 1997): 123.

U.S. Delegation Draft, "State Practice Regarding Amnesties and Pardons", 1 August 1997. Available at: <http://www.iccnow.org/documents/USDraftonAmnestiesPardons.pdf>.

Urtubey, Luis Márquez, "Non-Applicability for Statutes of Limitation for Crimes Committed in Argentina: Barrios Altos", 11 *Southwestern Journal of Law and Trade in the Americas* (2005): 111.

Van Alebeek, Rosanne, *The Immunity of States and their Officials in the Light of International Criminal Law and International Human Rights Law* (Oxford: OUP, 2008).

Van den Wyngaert, Christine, and John Dugard, "Non-Applicability of Statute of Limitations", in Antonio Cassese, Paola Gaeta and John R.W.D. Jones (eds.), *The Rome Statute of the International Criminal Court: A Commentary*, Vol. I (Oxford: OUP, 2002): 873.

Van den Wyngaert, Christine, and Tom Ongena, "*Ne bis in idem* Principle, Including the Issue of Amnesty", in Antonio Cassese, Paola Gaeta and John R.W.D. Jones (eds.), *The Rome Statute of the International Criminal Court: A Commentary*, Vol. I (Oxford: OUP, 2002): 705.

Van den Wyngaert, Christine, and Guy Stessens, "The International *Non Bis In Idem* Principle: Resolving Some of the Unanswered Questions", 48 *ICLQ* (1999): 77.

von Hebel, Herman, and Darryl Robinson, "Crimes within the jurisdiction of the Court", in Roy S. Lee (ed.), *The International Criminal Court, The Making of the Rome Statute: Issues, Negotiations, Results* (The Hague: Kluwer Law International, 1999): 122.

von Mehren, Arthur Taylor, "Adjudicatory Jurisdiction: General Theories Compared and Evaluated", 63(2) *Boston University Law Review* (1983): 279.

Warbrick, Colin, "Judicial Jurisdiction and Abuse of Process", 49 *ICLQ* (2000): 489.

Wasmeier, Martin, and Nadine Thwaites, "The development of *ne bis in idem* into a transnational fundamental human right in EU law: comments on recent developments", 31 *European Law Review* (2006): 565.

Watts, Sir Arthur, "The Legal Position in International Law of Heads of States, Heads of Governments and Foreign Ministers", 247 *RdC-III* (1994): 13.

Wedgwood, Ruth, "The International Criminal Court: An American View", 10 *EJIL* (1999): 93.

Wiessner, Siegfried and Andrew R. Willard, "Policy-Oriented Jurisprudence and Human Rights Abuses in Internal Armed Conflict: Toward a World Public Order of Human Dignity", 93 *AJIL* (1999): 320.

Wenig, Jonathan M., "Enforcing the Lessons of History: Israel Judges the Holocaust", in Timothy L.H. McCormack & Gerry J. Simpson (eds.), *The Law of War Crimes: National and International Approaches* (The Hague: Kluwer Law International, 1997): 103.

Williams, Paul R., and Michael P. Scharf, *Peace with Justice? War Crimes and Accountability in the Former Yugoslavia* (Lanham: Rowman & Littleman Publishers, Inc., 2002).

Williams, Sharon A., "Article 17: Issues of admissibility", in Otto Triffterer (ed.), *Commentary on the Rome Statute of the International Criminal Court: Observers' Notes, Article by Article* (Baden-Baden: Nomos Verlagsgesellschaft, 1999): 383.

Wilmshurst, Elizabeth, "Jurisdiction of the Court", in Roy S. Lee (ed.), *The International Criminal Court: The Making of the Rome Statute – Issues, Negotiations, Results* (The Hague: Kluwer Law International, 1999): 132.

Wippman, David, "Atrocities, Deterrence, and the Limits of International Justice", 23 *Fordham International Law Journal* (1999): 473.

Wirth, Steffan, "Immunity for Core Crimes? The ICJ's Judgment in the *Congo* v. *Belgium* Case", 13 *EJIL* (2002): 877.

Witness to Truth: Report of the Sierra Leone Truth and Reconciliation Commission, 5 October 2004. Available at: <http://www.trcsierraleone.org/drwebsite/publish/index.shtml>.

Zappalà, Salvatore, "The German Federal Prosecutor's Decision not to Prosecute a Former Uzbek Minister: Missed Opportunity or Prosecutorial Wisdom?", 4(3) *JICJ* (2006): 602.

Zappalà, Salvatore, "Do Heads of State in Office Enjoy Immunity from Jurisdiction for International Crimes? The *Ghaddafi* Case Before the French Cour de Cassation", 12(3) *EJIL* (2001): 595.

TABLE OF CASES

Permanent Court of International Justice and International Court of Justice

Application of the Convention on the Prevention and Punishment of the Crime of Genocide (Bosnia and Herzegovina v. *Serbia and Montenegro),* Judgment, 26 February 2007 — 29, 54, 111

Application of the Convention on the Prevention and Punishment of the Crime of Genocide (Bosnia and Herzegovina v. *Serbia and Montenegro),* Preliminary Objections, Judgment of 11 July 1996 — 28, 53

Armed Activities on the Territory of the Congo (Democratic Republic of the Congo v. *Rwanda)*, Jurisdiction of the Court and Admissibility of the Application, Judgment, 3 January 2006 — 29

Arrest Warrant of April 11th 2000 (Democratic Republic of the Congo v. *Belgium*), Judgment, Merits, 41 *ILM* 536 (2002) — 65, 119, 222, 376

Barcelona Traction case (Second Phase), ICJ Reports 1970, 3 — 27, 28, 140

Certain Criminal Proceedings in France (Republic of the Congo v. *France),*Request for the Indication of a Provisional Measure, Order, 17 June 2003 — 47

East Timor (Portugal v. *Australia)*, ICJ Reports 1995, 90 — 140

Legal Consequences for States in the Continuing Presence of South Africa in Namibia (South West Africa) notwithstanding Security Council Resolution 276 (1970), ICJ Reports, 1971, at 16 — 143

Legal Consequences of the Construction of a Wall in Occupied Palestinian Territory, Advisory Opinion of 9 July 2004, ICJ Reports 2004 — 143

Legality of the Threat or Use of Nuclear Weapons, Advisory Opinion of 8 July 1996, ICJ Reports 1996 — 27, 117, 120, 140

Military and Paramilitary Activities in and against Nicaragua (Nicaragua v. *United States)*, 1986, ICJ Reports 14 (1986) — 27, 36, 114, 120

North Sea Continental Shelf (West Germany v. *Denmark; West Germany* v. *the Netherlands)*, 1969, ICJ Reports 3 (20 February 1969) — 114

Reservations to the Convention on Genocide (Advisory Opinion), 1951, ICJ Reports 15 (1951) — 24, 53, 111, 265

United States Diplomatic and Consular Staff in Tehran, ICJ Reports 1980, 3 — 141, 229

Arbitral Tribunals

In re *Janes* (*US* v. *Mexico*), 4 *RIAA* 32 (1926) — 141

In re *Neer* (*US* v. *Mexico*), 4 *RIAA* 60 (1926) — 141

International Criminal Tribunals

Aleksovski (Appeal), ICTY, Appeals Chamber, Judgment of 24 March 2000, Case No. IT-95-14/1-A — 167, 307

Akayesu, ICTR, Trial Chamber I, Judgment of 2 September 1998, Case No. ICTR-96-4-T — 61, 62, 107

Bagilishema, ICTR, Trial Chamber, Judgment of 7 June 2001, Case No. ICTR-95-1A-T — 43

Bagosora, ICTR, Trial Chamber I, Decision on the Application by the Prosecutor for a Formal Request for Deferral of 17 May 1996, Case No. ICTR-96-7-D — 291, 299

Barayagwiza, ICTR, Appeals Chamber, Decision, Case No. ICTR-97-19-AR72, 3 November 1999 334, 335, 348-349, 360, 363

Barayagwiza, Appeals Chamber, Decision (Prosecutor's Request for Review or Reconsideration), Case No. ICTR-97-19-A, 31 March 2000 — 349

Blaškić, ICTY Appeals Chamber, Judgment, Case No. IT-95-14-T-A, 29 July 2004 — 355

Blaškić, ICTY, Trial Chamber I, Judgment of 3 March 2000, Case No. IT-95-14-T — 167

Blaškić (judgment on the request of Croatia), ICTY, Appeals Chamber, Judgment of 29 October 1997, Case No. IT-95-14-AR108*bis* — 223, 247

Boškoski and Tarčulovski, ICTY, Appeals Chamber, Case No. IT-04-82-AR72.2, Decision on Ljube Boškoski's Appeal on Jurisdiction, 9 January 2007 — 329

Brđanin and Talić, ICTY, Trial Chamber II, Decision on Second Motion by Brđanin to Dismiss the Indictment, Case No. IT-99-36-PT, 16 May 2001 — 330

Delalić and others (*Celebici* case), ICTY Trial Chamber II, Judgment of 16 November 1998, Case No. IT-96-21.T — 62

Delalić and others (*Celebici* case) *(appeal)*, ICTY Appeals Chamber, Judgment of 20 February 2001, Case No. IT-96-21-A — 25, 27, 36, 144, 145, 167

Erdemović (sentencing judgment), ICTY, Trial Chamber I, Judgment of 29 November 1996, Case No. IT-96-22-T — 167

Furundžija, ICTY, Trial Chamber II, Judgment of 10 December 1998, Case No. IT-95-17/1-T; 39 *ILM* (1999) — 27, 30, 61, 62, 112, 140, 167, 174, 199, 200, 205

Hartmann, ICTY, Trial Chamber, Case No. IT-02-54-R77.5, Reasons for Decision on the Defence Motion for a Stay of Proceedings for Abuse of Process, 3 February 2009 — 351

Kajelijeli, ICTR, Trial Chamber II, Decision on the Defence Motion Concerning the Arbitrary Arrest and Illegal Detention of the Accused and on the Defence Notice of Urgent Motion to Expand and Supplement the Record of 8 December 1999 Hearing, Case No. ICTR-98-44-1, 8 May 2000 — 346

Karadžić, Appeals Chamber, Case No. IT-95-5/18-AR73.4, Decision on Karadžić's Appeal of Trial Chamber's Decision on Alleged Holbrooke Agreement, 12 October 2009 — 359-360

Karadžić, ICTY, Trial Chamber, Case No. IT-95-5/18-PT, Decision on Motion to Dismiss for Abuse of Process, 12 May 2009 — 350-351

Karadžić, ICTY, Appeals Chamber, Case No. IT-95-5/18-AR73.1, Decision on Appellant Radovan Karadžić's Appeal Concerning Holbrooke Agreement Disclosure, 6 April 2009 — 360

Karadžić, ICTY, Trial Chamber, Case No. IT-95-5/18-PT, Decision on Accused's Second Motion for Inspection and Disclosure: Immunity Issue, 17 December 2008 — 358-359

Kambanda, ICTR, Judgment of 4 September 1998, Case No. ICTR-97-23-S — 176

Kunarac and others, ICTY, Appeals Chamber, Judgment of 12 June 2002, Case No. IT-96-23 and IT-96-23/1-A — 65

Kvočka, ICTY, Trial Chamber, Judgment of 2 November 2001, Case No. IT-98-30/1-T — 62

Milošević, ICTY, Decision on Preliminary Motions, 8 November 2001, Case No. IT-02-54-PT — 231, 243, 244, 263, 343

Mrškić, ICTY, Appeals Chamber, Case No. IT-95-13/1-A, Judgment of 5 May 2009 — 37

Mrkšić, Radić, Sljivančanin and Dokmanović, ICTY, Trial Chamber, Decision on the Motion for Release by the Accused Slavko Dokmanović, Case No. IT-95-13a-PT, 22 October 1997 — 342

Nikolić, ICTY, Appeals Chamber, Case No. IT-94-2-AR73, Decision on Interlocutory Appeal Concerning Legality of Arrest, 5 June 2003 — 344, 364

Nikolić, ICTY, Trial Chamber, Case No. IT-94-2-PT, Decision on Defence Motion Challenging the Exercise of Jurisdiction by the Tribunal, 9 October 2002 — 344

Orić, ICTY, Trial Chamber, Case No. IT-03-68-A, Decision in Orić's Motion Regarding a Breach of *Non-Bis-In-Idem*, 7 April 2009 — 305

Plavsic, ICTY, Trial Chamber, Sentencing Judgment of 27 February 2003, Case Nos. IT-00-39 and 40/1-S — 175

Rwamakuba, ICTR, Trial Chamber II, Decision on the Defence Motion Concerning the Illegal Arrest and Illegal Detention of the Accused, Case No. ICTR-98-44-T — 346

Semanza, ICTR, Appeals Chamber, Decision, Case No. ICTR-97-20-A, 31 May 2000 — 346

Simić, Simić, Tadić, Todorović and Zarić, ICTY, Trial Chamber, Decision on Motion for Judicial Assistance to be Provided by SFOR and Others, Case No. IT-95-9-PT, 18 October 2000 — 342

Situation in the Democratic Republic of the Congo in the Case of The Prosecutor v. *Thomas Lubanga Dyilo*, ICC, Judgment on the Appeal of Mr. Thomas Lubanga Dyilo against the Decision on the Defence Challenge to the Jurisdiction of the Court pursuant to Article 19(2) of the Statute of 3 October 2006, Case No. ICC-01/04-01/06 (OA4), 14 December 2006 — 329, 330, 331, 350

Situation in the Democratic Republic of the Congo in the Case of The Prosecutor v. *Thomas Lubanga Dyilo*, Case No. ICC-01/04-01/06 (OA13), Judgment on the appeal of the Prosecutor against the Decision of Trial Chamber I entitled "Decision on the consequences of non-disclosure of exculpatory materials covered by Article 54(3)(e) agreements and the application to stay the prosecution of the accused, together with certain other issues raised at the Status Conference on 10 June 2008", 21 October 2008 — 352, 356

Situation in the Democratic Republic of the Congo in the Case of The Prosecutor v. *Thomas Lubanga Dyilo*, Case No. ICC-01/04-01/06 (OA12), Judgment on the appeal of the Prosecutor against the Decision of Trial Chamber I entitled "Decision on the release of Thomas Lubanga Dyilo", 21 October 2008 — 356

Tadić (Appeal), ICTY, Appeals Chamber, Judgment of 15 July 1999, Case No. IT-94-1-A — 173

Tadić (Decision on the defence motion for Interlocutory Appeal on Jurisdiction), ICTY, Appeals Chamber, Decision of 2 October 1995, Case No. IT-94-1-AR72, 35 *ILM* 32 (1996) — 62, 113, 268, 346

Tadić, ICTY, Trial Chamber II, Decision of 14 November 1995 on the defence motion on the principle of *non bis in idem*, Case No. IT-94-1-T — 304

Todorović, ICTY, Trial Chamber, Case No. IT-95-9-1-S, Sentencing Judgment, 31 July 2001 — 343

Hybrid tribunals

Extraordinary Chambers in the Courts of Cambodia, Office of the Co-Investigating Judges, Criminal Case File No: 002/14-08-2006, Investigation No: 002/14-08-2006, Instruction No. 002/19-09-2007-ECCC/OJIC, Provisional Detention Order, 14 November 2007 — 159

Extraordinary Chambers in the Courts of Cambodia, Office of the Co-Investigating Judges, Criminal Case File No: 002/14-08-2006, Investigation No: 001/18-07-2007-ECCC-OCIJ, Closing order indicting Kaing Guek Eav alias Duch, Public redacted version, 8 August 2008 — 353

Extraordinary Chambers in the Courts of Cambodia, Office of the Co-Investigating Judges, Criminal Case File No: 002/14-08-2006, Investigation No: 001/18-07-2007-ECCC-OCIJ, Order of Provisional Detention, 31 July 2007 — 353

Extraordinary Chambers in the Courts of Cambodia, Pre-Trial Chamber, Criminal Case File No: 002/18-07-2007-ECCC-OCIJ (PTC01), Decision on Appeal against Provisional Detention Order of Kaing Guek Eav alias 'Duch,' 3 December 2007 — 354

Kallon and Kamara, SCSL, Appeals Chamber Decision on Challenge to Jurisdiction: Lomé Accord Amnesty, 13 March 2004, Case No. SCSL-2004-15-AR72(E) — 31, 83, 92, 113, 119, 124, 139, 170, 171, 361

Norman, SCSL, Case No. SCSL-2003-08-PT, *Decision on Appeal by the Truth and Reconciliation Commission of Sierra Leone ('TRC' or 'The Commission' and Chief Samuel Hinga Norman JP against the Decision of His Lordship, Mr. Justice Bankole Thompson, delivered on 20 October 2003, to Deny the TRC's Request to Hold a Public Hearing with Chief Hinga Norman JP* (SCSL-2003-08-PT), 28 November 2003 — 100

Norman, SCSL, Case No. SCSL-2003-08-PT, *Decision on the Request by the Truth and Reconciliation Commission of Sierra Leone to Conduct a Public Hearing with Samuel Hinga Norman*, 29 October 2003 — 100

Norman, SCSL, Case No. SCSL-2003-14-AR72(E), Decision on Preliminary Motion based on Lack of Jurisdiction (Child Recruitment), 31 May 2004 — 37

Taylor, SCSL, Indictment, Case No. SCSL-03-I, 3 March 2003 — 245

Taylor, SCSL, Case No. SCSL-2003-01-I, Decision on Immunity from Jurisdiction, 31 May 2004 — 231, 245, 247, 256

Inter American Court of Human Rights

Almonacid-Arellano, et al., v. *Chile*, IACtHR, Preliminary Objections, Merits, Reparations and Costs. Judgment of 26 September 2006 (ser. C) No. 154 — 80, 129, 205, 317, 321

Barrios Altos (Chumbipuma Aguirre and others. v. *Peru)*, IACtHR (ser. C) (2001) — 30, 31, 80, 90, 124, 129, 135, 139, 142, 144, 146, 205, 209

Blake, Preliminary Exceptions, IACtHR (ser. C) No. 27 (1996) — 80, 128

Caballero Delgado and Santana, IACtHR (ser. C) No. 22 (1995) — 80, 125

Case 10.150, Informe 3/90 (Suriname), OEA/ser.L./V/II.77, doc. 23, at 14 (1990) — 130

Case 1870, IACtHR 52, OEA/ser.L./V/II.43, doc. 21 (1978) — 130

Case 2088, IACtHR 38, OEA/ser.L./V/II.0. doc. 13, rev. 1 (1980) — 130

Case of La Cantuta v. *Peru*, IACtHR, Merits, Reparations and Costs. Judgment of 29 November 2006 (ser. C), No. 162 — 80, 129, 317

Castillo Paez and others v. *Peru*, IACtHR (ser. C) No. 34 (1997) — 80, 128

Castillo Petruzzi and others v. *Peru*, IACtHR (ser. C) (1999) — 1, 35

IACtHR OEA/ser.L./V/II.68.doc. 8 rev.1 (1986) — 130

Loayza Tamayo v. *Peru*, Case IACTHR (ser. C), No. 33, Judgment 17 September 1997 — 297

Neira Alegra and others, IACtHR (ser. C), No. 20 (1995) — 80, 128

Velàsquez Rodriguez, Compensation Judgment of 21 July 1989, IACtHR (ser. C), No. 7 (1989) — 128

Velàsquez Rodriguez, IACtHR (ser. C), No. 4 (1988) — 80, 128, 135, 168, 284

American Commission of Human Rights

Speech by Ambassador Oliver H. Jackman before the First Committee of the XIX Regular Meeting of the General Assembly to Present the Annual Report of the IACTHR, November 1989 — 130

Report No. 26/92 (El Salvador), 82nd Sess., OEA/ser. L/V/II/82 (24 September 1992) — 80, 130

Hugo Leonardo de los Santos Mendoza, et al., Case No. 10-029, Annual Report of the Inter-American Commission on Human Rights (1992-3), at 121 — 80, 125

Report No. 29/92 (Uruguay), 82nd Sess. OEA/ser. L/V/II.82, Doc. 25 (1 October 1992) — 80, 130

Report No. 28/92 (Argentina), Cases 10.147, 10.181, 10.240, 10.262, 10.309, 10.311, 82nd Sess., OEA/ser. L/V/II.82, Doc. 24 (2 October 1992) — 162, 168

Report No. 36/96, (Chile) Case 10,843, 15 October 1996 — 130

Report No. 199, (El Salvador), Case 10,480, *Lucio Parada Cea and others* 27 January 1999 — 122

Report No. 133/99, (Chile) Case 11,725 *Carmelo Soria Espinoza*, 19 November 1999 — 146

Ruth del Rosario Garcés Valladares v. *Ecuador*, IAComHR, Communication No. 64/99, Case No. 11.778, 13 April 1999 — 297

Wilson Guttiérez Soler v. *Colombia*, IACommHR, Communication No. 76/01, Case No. 12.291, 10 October 2001 — 297

European Court and Commission of Human Rights

Al Adsani v. *United Kingdom,* ECtHR 2001-XI 79 — 239, 270, 271, 272, 281, 282

Banković v. *Belgium*, ECtHR, Appl. No. 52207/99, Admissibility Decision of 12 December 2001 — 138

Bozano v. *France* (1986) ECHR (ser. A), No. 111; *European Human Rights Report* 297 (1987) — 341

Case of Klass and others (F.R.G.), 28 ECtHR (ser. A) (1978) — 131

Dujardin and Others v. *France*, ECommHR, Admissibility Decision, 2 September 1991, Appl. No. 16734/90, 72 D&R 236 (1992), at 243-244 — 140, 241

Fogarty v. *United Kingdom* (2001), 34 *EHRR* 302, 123 *ILR* 53 — 281, 282

Franz Fischer v. *Austria* [2001] ECHR 25 — 297

Gradinger v. *Austria*, ECtHR, Case No. 33/1994/480/562 — 297

Ireland v. *U.K.*, 25 ECtHR (ser. A) (1978) — 131

Kiss v. *United Kingdom*, 7 *Decisions and Reports* 55 (1976), at 64 — 131

Kurt v. *Turkey*, ECtHR, Case No.15/1997/799/1002, 25 May 1998 — 134

McElhinney v. *Ireland* (2001), 34 *EHRR* 322, 123 *ILR* 73 — 281, 282

Mrs. W. v. *United Kingdom*, 32 *Collection of Decisions* 190 (28 February 1983), at 200 — 131

Olivera v. *Switzerland*, ECtHR Case No. 84/1997/868/1080 — 297

Öcalan v. *Turkey*, Appl. No. 00046221/99, Merits, Judgment of 12 May 2005 — 341-342

Ould Dah v. *France*, ECtHR, Appl. No. 13113/03, Admissibililty Decision of 17 March 2009 — 113

Priebke v. *Italy*, 12 *Human Rights Case Digest* 413 (2001) — 203

Sailor v. *Austria* [2002] ECHR 24 — 297

Stocké v. *Federal Republic of Germany*, European Commission of Human Rights, 12 October 1989, 95 *ILR* 328 — 341

Teixeira v. *Portugal*, ECtHR, Appl. No. 25829/94, Judgment, 9 June 1998 — 333

The Greek Case, *Y.B. ECHR* 196 (1969) (Eur. Comm'n of Hum. Rts.) — 132

X and Y and Z v. *Netherlands*, 91 ECtHR (ser. A) (1985) (judgment) — 131, 132, 284

Zeki Aksoy v. *Turkey*, ECtHR (judgment),18 December 1996, No. 100/1995/606/694 — 63, 131, 283

X v. *Netherlands*, ECommHR No. 9433/81, 27 *D&R* 233 (11 December 1981) — 294

European Court of Justice

Joined cases C-187/01 and 385/01, *Gözütok and Brügge* [2003] ECR — 301

Case C-469/03, *Miraglia* [2005] ECR — 302

Case C-436/04, *Van Esbroeck* [2006] ECR — 298

X v. *European Central Bank*, Case T-333/99 — 295

National cases

Alphonse Higaniro, Vincent Ntezimana, Consolata Mukangango and Julienne Mukabutera ('The Butare 4'), Belgium, Cour d'assise of Brussels, 8 June 2001, available at: <http://www.asf.be/AssisesRwanda2/fr/fr_VERDICT_verdict.htm> — 37

Altstötter and others (*Justice* case), US Military Tribunal sitting at Nuremberg, Judgment of 4 December 1947, in *TWC*, Vol. 3, at 954-1201 — 41, 309

Arancibia Clavel, Enrique Lautaro y otros, Argentina, Corte Suprema de Justicia [CSJN], 24/08/2004, Colección Oficial de Fallos de la Corte Suprema de Justicia de la Naćion [Fallos] (2004-327-3294) — 115, 206

Argentine Republic v. *Amerada Hess Shipping Co.,* 488 US 428, 109 S Ct 683, 102 L Ed 2d 818 (1989) — 272

Attorney-General of Hong Kong v. *Cheung,* United Kingdom [1994] 1 AC 1 — 352

Attorney General's Reference (No 1 of 1990), United Kingdom [1992] QB 630, CA — 185, 336, 352

Attorney General's Reference (No 2 of 2001), United Kingdom [2004] 2 AC 72, HL — 336, 352

Attorney-General of Trinidad and Tobago v. *Phillip,* Privy Council [1994] 3 *WLR* 1134 — 358

Aussaresses, France, Criminal Chamber of the Court of Cassation, Judgment of 17 June 2003, *Bull. crim.* (2003) 122, at 465-469 — 78, 192, 206, 207

Azanian People's Organisation and Others v. *The President of the Republic of South Africa and Others*, South Africa, 1996 (4) SA 671 (CC) 1996 (8) BCLR 1015 (CC) — 21, 83, 96, 97, 99, 109, 112, 121

Baker v. *Carr*, United States, 369 US 186 (1962) — 242

Banco Nacional de Cuba v. *Sabbatino*, United States, 376 US 398 (1964) — 248, 249, 259

Barbie, France, *Cour de cassation*, Decision of 6 October 1983, *Gaz.Pal.* 1983, at 710. English translation in 78 *ILR* 126-31 — 263, 337

Barbie, France, *Cour de cassation*, Decision of 26 January 1984, JCP 1984, II, no. 20197. English translation in 78 *ILR* 132-6 — 263

Barbie, France, *Cour de cassation*, Decision of 20 December 1985, JCP 1986, II, no. 20655; *Bull. crim.* 1985, 1038-55. English translation in 78 *ILR* 136-47 — 45, 191, 195, 203, 207, 242

Barton v. *The Queen*, Australia, [1980] HCA 48; 147 *CLR* 75 (1980) — 335

Bennett v. *H.M. Advocate* 1995 S.L.T. 510 — 339

Blockburger v. *United States*, United States, 284 US 299 (1932) — 296, 299

Bouterse, Desi, the Netherlands, Decision of the Court of Appeal of Amsterdam, 20 November 2000, unofficial English translation by Peter Kell in 3 *YIHL* 677 (2000) — 370

Bouterse, Desi, the Netherlands, Supreme Court [*Hoge Raad*], Criminal Chamber, judgment of 18 September 2001, No. 00749/01 (CW 2323), summary available at: <http://www.icrc.org/ihl-nat.nsf/39a82e2ca42b52974125673e00508144/07c5ae1b4a999f1cc1256da200518c91?OpenDocument> — 263, 370

Bouzari and Others v. *Islamic Republic of Iran,* Canada, Ontario Court of Appeal, *OJ* No. 2800 (2004) — 283

Butare Four case, see *Alphonse Hiyaniro et al.*

Buttes Gas v. *Hammer (Nos. 2 &3)*, United Kingdom [1981] 3 *All ER* 616, at 628; *(no. 3)* [1982] AC 888 — 227

Camps, Argentina, Supreme Court, 310:1162, 1301-3 (22 June 1987) — 83

Castro, Fidel, Spain (*Audiencia nacional*), Order (auto) of 4 March 1999, no. 1999/2723, in CD Rom, EL DERECHO, 2002, Criminal case law — 45, 231, 250

Castro v. *Murray* (1875) LR 10 Ex. 213 — 331

Cavallo Ricardo Miguel, Spain (*Audiencia nacional*), Order (auto) of 20 December 2006, no. 139/1997, available at: <http://www.trial-ch.org/fileadmin/user_upload/documents/trialwatch/Decision_AN_incompetencia_caso_Cavallo.doc> — 57, 58

Cavallo, Ricardo Miguel, Mexico, Extradición Ricardo Miguel Cavallo, Suprema Corte de Justicia de la Nación, Amparo en Revisión 140/2002, 10 June 2003, <http://www.scjn.gob.mx/Asuntos/2003/CAVALLOENGROSE(X)2.pdf> — 57, 206

Cavallo Ricardo Miguel, Mexico, order (auto) of 12 January 2001, on line: <www.derechos.org/nizkor/arg/epana/mex.html> — 263

Clyne v. *N.S.W. Bar Association* [1960] HCA 40; 104 *CLR* 186 (1960) — 335

Connolly v. *D.P.P*, United Kingdom [1964] AC1254 — 293, 357

Contreras Sepúlveda, Juan y otros (crimen) cascación fondo y forma, Chile, Corte Suprema, 517/2004, Resolución 22267, available at: <www.derechos.org/nizkor/chile/doc/krassnoff.html> — 120, 209, 214

Cvjetković Duško, Austria, Supreme Court [*Oberster Gerichtshof*], Decision of 13 July 1994, unreported — 54

Demjanjuk v. *Petrovsky*, United States, 776 F.2d 571 (6th Cir. 1985); cert. den. 475 US 1016 (1986), 628 F. Suppl. 1370; 784 F.2d 1254 (1986) — 44, 255

Director of Prisons v. *Djenaro Perella*, Cyprus [1995] 1 *CLR* 217 — 335

Djajić, Novislav, Germany, *Bayerisches Oberstes Landesgericht*, Judgment of 23 May 1997, 3 *Strafrecht* 20/96;19 *Neue Juristische Wochenschrift* 392 (1998) — 58

DPP v. *Humphrys*, United Kingdom [1977] AC 1 — 357

DPP v. *Meakin*, United Kingdom [2006] EWHC 1067 — 333

Duke of Brunswick v. *King of Hanover*, United Kingdom (1848) 2 HL Cas. 1 — 227

Dunlop, United Kingdom [2001] 2 *Cr App R*, para. 8 — 287, 352

Eichmann, Israel, District Court of Jerusalem, Judgment of 12 December 1961, English translation in 36 *ILR* 18 — 227, 336

Eichmann, Israel, Supreme Court, Judgment of 29 May 1962, English translation in 36 *ILR* 227 — 23, 44, 255, 263, 336

Elcock v. *United States*, United States, 80 F. Suppl. 2d 70 (EDNY 2000) — 296

Ely Ould Dah, France, Court of Cassation, Criminal division, Decision of 23 October 2002, *Bulletin criminel* 2002 No. 195, at 725 — 66, 83, 112, 370

Fallos de la Corte Suprema de Justicia de la Nación, Argentina, Supreme Court, Buenos Aires, no. 310, 1984 — 158

Ferrini v. *Federal Republic of Germany*, Italy (Cass. Sez. Un. 5044/04) 87 *RDI* (2004) 539 — 273, 286

Filatiga v. *Pena-Irala,* United States, 630 F.2d 876 (1980) — 68, 114, 278

Flick and others, United States Military Tribunal sitting at Nuremberg, Judgment of 22 December 1947, *TWC*, Vol. 6, at 1187-223 — 41

Forti v. *Suarez Mason*, United States, 672 F Suppl. 1531 (ND Cal 1987) — 227, 278

Fortunato Galtieri case, Argentina, Judgment of March 1997, available at: <http://www.derechos.org/nizkor/arg/espana/authgalt.html> — 83

Frisbie v. *Collins,* United States, 342 US 519 (1952) — 338

Glorian Keyowski v. *Her Majesty The Queen*, Judgment, Canada, 28 April 1988 [1988] 1 SCR 657 — 334, 335

Green v. *U.S.*, United States, 355 US 184 (1957), at 187-88 — 306

Greifelt and others, United States Military Tribunal sitting at Nuremberg, Judgment of 10 March 1948, in *TWC*, Vol. 5, at 88-169 — 50

Guevara Portillo case, El Salvador, Salade lo Penal de la Corte Suprema de Justicia, San Salvador, Judgment of 16 August 1995 — 121

Habré, Hissène, Senegal, Supreme Court, Judgment of 20 March 2001, available at: <www.icrc.og/ihl-nat-nsf> — 69

Hass and Priebke (Appeal), Italy, Military Court of Appeal of Rome, Judgment of 7 March 1998, in *L'Indice Penale* (1998), at 959-1000 — 45, 203

Hass and Priebke, Italy, Supreme Court of Cassation, Judgment of 16 November 1998 — 200, 203, 263

Hoess Rudolf Ferdinand, Poland, Supreme National Tribunal, March 1947, in *LRTWC*, Vol. 7, at 11 — 50, 61

Hui-Chi Ming v. *R*, United Kingdom [1992] 1 AC 34 — 330

In re *Extradition of Montiel Garcia*, United States, 802 F. Suppl. 773, 777 (EDNY 1992) — 289

Jago v. *District Court of NSW*, Australia [1989] HCA 46; 168 *CLR* 23 (1989) (12 October 1989) — 185, 335

Javor and others, France, Paris Court of Appeal, *Quatrième Chambre d'accusation*, Decision of 24 November 1994, no. A 94/02071, unreported — 66

Javor and others, France, Cour de Cassation, 26 March 1996, in *Bull. crim.*, no. 132 1996 — 42, 66, 115

Jean v. *Dorélien*, United States, Judgment of the 11th Circuit of the Court of Appeals, 1 December 2005 — 216, 217

Jorgić, Germany, Federal Constitutional Court [*Bundesgerichtshof*], Judgment of 30 April 1999, printed in 8 *Neue Zeitschrift für Strafrecht* 396-404 (1999) — 58

Jorgić, Germany, Higher State Court [*Oberlandsgericht*] of Düsseldorf, Judgment of 26 September 1997, 3 *Strafrecht* 215/98 — 58

Jones v. *Ministry of Interior Al-Mamlaka Al-Arabiya AS Saudiya (the Kingdom of Saudi Arabia) and others*, United Kingdom [2006] UKHL 26; [2007] 1 AC 270 — 239, 240, 271, 280

Jones v. *Ministry of Interior Al-Mamlaka Al-Arabiya AS Saudiya (the Kingdom of Saudi Arabia) and others*, United Kingdom, EWCA Civ. 1394 (2004) — 283

Jones v. *Whalley*, Judgment, United Kingdom, House of Lords, 26 July 2006 [2006] 4 *All ER* 113 — 336

Kadhafi, France, *Cour d'appel de Paris*, *Chambre d'accusation*, Decision of 20 October 2000 — 256

Kadhafi, France, *Cour de Cassation*, Decision of 13 March 2001, no. 1414, in Bulletin des arrêts de la Court de Cassation, Chambre criminelle, March 2001, no. 64, at 218-19 — 232, 264

Kadic v. *Karadzic*, United States, 70 F. 3d 232 (2nd Cir. 1995); case report by Posner in the *AJIL* (1996), at 658 — 61, 227

Kappler (Appeal), Italy, Supreme Military Tribunal, Judgment of 25 October 1952, no. 1714, in *RDI* (1953), at 193-9 — 263

Ker v. *Illinois*, United States, 119 US 436 (1886) — 336, 338

Krupp and others, United States, US Military Tribunal sitting at Nuremberg, judgment of 30 July 1948, in *TWC*, Vol. 9, at 1327-484 — 255

Levinge v. *Director of Custodial Services*, Australia, 9 *NSWR* 546 (Ct App 1987) — 335

Linder v. *Carrero-Portocarrero*, United States, 963 F.2d 332 (11th Cir. 1992), reprinted in 99 *ILR* 55 — 242, 248

List and others (*Hostages* case), United States, US Military Tribunal sitting at Nuremberg, Judgment of 19 February 1948, *TWC*, Vol. 11, at 1230-319 — 22

McDonald v. *Mabee*, United States, 243 US 90 (1917), at 91 — 15

Menéndez Luciano Benjamín, et al., p.ss.a autores de privación ilegítima de la libertad, imposición de tormentos agravado y homicidio agravado, Oral Tribunal for Federal Crimes No.1, File 40/M/2008, 24 July 2008 — 205

Medina, Ernest L., United States, US Court of Military Appeals, Decision of 9 March 1971, 20 *USCMA* 430; 43 CMR 243 — 161

Metropolitan Bank v. *Pooley*, United Kingdom (1885) LR 10 AC 210 — 331

Ministries case (*Weizaecker*), United States, US Military Tribunal sitting at Nuremberg, Decision of 12 December 1949, in *TWC*, Vol. 14, at 308-942 — 41

Miranda v. *Arizona*, United States, 384 US 436 (1966) — 60

Moevao v. *Dept. of Labour,* New Zealand [1980] 1 *NZLR* 464 — 334

Niyonteze, Switzerland, *Tribunal Militaire d'Appel* 1A, Judgment of 26 May 2000, available at: <www.icrc.org/ihl-nat-nsf> — 51

Niyonteze, Switzerland, *Tribunal Militaire de Cassation*, Judgment of 27 April 2001, available at: <www.icrc.org/ihl-nat-nsf> — 51

Niyonteze, Switzerland, *Tribunal Militaire de Division* 2, Lausanne, Judgment of 30 April 1999 — 37, 51

Nulyarimma and others v. *Thompson*, Australia, Federal Court of Australia, Full Court, 1 September 1999, 39 *ILM* 29 (2000) — 51, 370

Ohlendorf and others (*Einsatzgruppen* case), United States, US Military Tribunal sitting at Nuremberg, Judgment of 10 April 1948, in *TWC*, Vol. 4, at 3-596, 1 Official Documents 223 (1947), reprinted in 41 *AJIL* (1947) — 41

Olmstead, et al., v. *United States*, United States, 277 US 438 (1928) — 334

Papon, France, Court de Cassation, Decision of 23 January 1997, no. 502, at 15 — 45, 207

People v. *Papaccio*, United States, 251 N.Y.S. 717 (Ct. Gen. Sess. N.Y. County, 1931), at 720 — 311

Petite v. *United States*, United States, 361 US 529 (1960) — 313

Pinochet, Chile, Santiago Court of Appeal, Decision of 5 June 2000, available at: <www.tercera.cl/casos/pinochet/documentos/desafuero/fallo1.html> — 241

Pinochet, Chile, Supreme Court of Chile, Decision of August 2004, available at: <www.emol.com/noticiaas/documentos/desafuero_pinochet.asp> — 241

Pinochet, Belgium, Brussels Investigating Judge (*juge d'instruction*), order of 16 November 1998, in 79 *RDPC* 281-8 (1999) — 46, 264

Pinochet, Spain, Central Criminal Court (*Audiencia nacional*), Order (auto) of 24 September 1999, no. 1998/28720, rec. 84/1999 — 66, 263

Polyukhovich v. *Commonwealth*, Australia, 172 *CLR* 501 (Austl. 1991) — 185, 324

Prefecture of Voiotia v. *Federal Republic of Germany*, Greece, No. 11/2000 (*Areios Pagos* [Hellenic Supreme Court] 4 May 2000). For an English summary and commentary, see Maria Gavouneli and Ilias Bantekas, "Case Report: *Prefecture of Voiotia* v. *Federal Republic of Germany*", 95 *AJIL* 198 (2001) — 273, 275

Prefecture of Voiotia v. *Federal Republic of Germany*, Greece, No. 137/1997 (Ct. 1st Inst. Leivadia, 30 October 1997), translated in Maria Gavounei, "War Reparation Claims and State Immunity", 50 *Revue Hellénique de Droit International* 595 (1997). For an English summary, see Ilias Bantekas, "Case Report: *Prefecture of Voiotia* v. *Federal Republic of Germany*", 92 *AJIL* 765 (1998) — 273

Priebke, Erich (extradition), Argentina, Supreme Court of Argentina, Decision of 2 November 1995, in Fallos de la Corte Supreme de Justicia. Tomo 318/3 at 2148-228. English translation in *YIHL* 1998 (Priebke, Erich's extradition request, Case 16.063/94, 2 November 1995) — 203

Princz v. *Federal Republic of Germany*, United States, 26 F. 3d. 1166 (1994) — 259, 272

R. v. *Carroll*, Australia, 213 *CLR* 640 — 287, 293, 320

R. v. *Conway,* Canada (1989) 70 CR (3d) 209 — 334

R. v. *Horseferry Magistrates' Court:* Ex Parte *Bennett*, United Kingdom [1994] 1 AC — 330, 335, 338, 339

R. v. *Anthony Sawoniuk*, United Kingdom, Decision of 10 February 2000 [2000] 2 *Cr App R* 220 — 186

Resolución del Cavallo, Argentina, Decision of 6 March 2001 Case 8686/2000, *Juzgado Nacional en lo Criminal y Correccional Federal*, No. 4 (6 March 2001), available at: <http://www.derechos.org/nizkor/arg/ley/juezcavallo03mar.html> — 83, 112, 192, 205, 370

Augusto Pinochet Ugarte, United Kingdom, Judgment of 28 October 1998, Divisional Court Judgment of the Queen's Bench Division, 38 *ILM* 68 (1999) (QB Div'l Ct. 1998) (referred to as *Divisional Court* in the text) — 239

In re *Argoud,* France, Cass. Crim. 4 June 1964, Bull. 192, JCP 1964, II, No. 13806 Rapport Compte; 45 *ILR* 90 — 337

In re *Jollis,* France, Tribunal Correctionnel d'Aversnes, 22 July 1933, 7 *Ann Dig* 191 (1933-1934) — 337

In re *Mlambo*, Zimbabwe (1993) 2 *LRC* 28 — 335

R. v. *Birmingham and Others*, United Kingdom [1992] *CrimLR* 117 — 355

R v. *Bow Street Metropolitan Stipendiary Magistrate,* ex parte *Pinochet Ugarte*, United Kingdom, House of Lords Judgment of 25 November 1998, 3 *WLR* 1456 (HL 1998) (referred to as *Pinochet I* in the text) — 57, 227, 239, 280

R v. *Bow Street Metropolitan Stipendiary Magistrate, ex parte Pinochet Ugarte*, United Kingdom, House of Lords Judgment of 24 March 1999, 2 *WLR* 827 (HL 1999); [1999] 2 *All ER* 97 (referred to as *Pinochet III* in the text) — 30, 57, 67, 69, 222, 227, 230, 232, 239, 247, 250, 254, 255, 260, 263, 266, 267, 270, 277

R v. *Bow Street Magistrates,* ex parte *Mackeson,* United Kingdom, 1 *All ER* 138 — 339

R. v. *Criminal Cases Review Commission*, ex *Twitchell*, United Kingdom, 26 October 1999, Case No. 9800326/S2 — 340

R. v. *Crown Court at Norwich* ex parte *Belsham*, United Kingdom (1992) 94 *Cr App R* 382, QBD — 335

R. v. *Croydon JJ.,* ex parte *Dean*, United Kingdom [1993] QB 769 — 357

R. v. *Degnan*, New Zealand [2001] 1 *NZLR* 280 — 321

R. v. *Forbes, ex p. Bevan*, Australia, 127 *CLR* 1 (1972) — 331

R. v. *Grays Justices* ex parte *Graham* (1982) QB 1239 — 352, 353

Reg. v. *Hartley*, New Zealand [1978] 2 *NZLR* 199 — 334

R. v. *Horseferry Road Magistrates' Court*, ex parte *Bennett*, United Kingdom, 1 AC 42 (1994) — 330, 335, 338, 339

R. v. *Kamara*, Court of Appeal, United Kingdom, Case No. 9902769X4, Criminal Division on Appeal from Liverpool Crown Court, 9 May 2000 — 355

R v. *Latif*, United Kingdom [1996] 1 *All ER* 353 — 339, 340

R v. *Loosely and Attorney General's Reference (No 3 of 2000)*, United Kingdom 4 *All ER* 897 (2001) — 330, 333

R. v. *Milton Keynes Magistrates' Court,* ex parte *Roberts*, United Kingdom [1995] *CrimLR* 224 — 361

R. v. *Mullen*, United Kingdom [1999] 3 *WLR* 777 — 340

R. v. *Old Street Magistrates' Court,* ex parte *Davies,* United Kingdom [1995] *CrimLR* 629 — 362

R. v. *Power* [1994] United Kingdom, 1 SCR 601 — 336

R. v. *S. (SP)*, United Kingdom [2006] 2 *Cr App R* 23, at 341 — 329

R. v. *Shannon*, United Kingdom [2001] *WLR* 51, 68 — 330

R. v. *Z*. United Kingdom [2000] 2 AC 483 (2000) — 321

R v. *Zardad*, United Kingdom, Judgment of 18 July 2005 — 71

Regina v. *Finta*, Canada [1994] 1 SCR 701, Supreme Court of Canada, 24 March 1994; case note by Cotler in the 90 *AJIL* 460 (1996) — 12, 44, 45, 178

Rogers v. *Q.*, Australia, 181 *CLR* 251 (1994) — 320

Romo Mena case, Chile, Corte Surprema de Chile, Judgment of 26 October 1995 — 121

Sambavisum v. *Public Prosecutor, Federation of Malaya* [1950] AC at 458 — 320

Saudi Arabia v. *Nelson*, United States, 113 Sup. Ct. 1471 (1993); case report by Leigh in the 87 *AJIL* 442 (1993) — 280

Schooner Exchange, v. *M'Faddon*, United States, 11 US 116 (1812) — 232, 237, 246, 251, 274, 276

Scilingo, Adolfo, Spain, Central Criminal Court (*Audiencia Nacional*), Order (auto) of 5 November 1998, no. 1998/22605, rec. 173/1998, Case 19/97, in EL DERECHO, 8 — 12, 112, 178

Scilingo, Adolfo, Spain, Third Section of the Criminal Division (*Audiencia Nacional*), Judgment no. 16/2005 of 19 April 2005, *Sentencia por crímenes contra la humanidad en el caso Adolpho Scilingo*, available at: <http://www.derechos.org/nizkor/espana/juicioral/doc/sentencia.html> — 20, 31, 47, 58, 263, 370

Sharon Ariel and others, Belgium, Appeals Court of Brussels, Decision of 26 June 2002, available at: <www.sabra-shatila.be/documents/arrest020226.pdf> — 46

Sharon Ariel and others, Belgium, Court of Cassation, Judgment of 12 February 2003, available at: <www.cass.be/cgi-juris/juris-cass-a1.pl> — 46, 59, 231, 261, 264, 265, 371

Sidona v. *Grant*, United States, 619 F.2d 167, at 177-78 (2nd Cir. 1980) — 312

Simon, Julio, Del Cerro, Juan Antonio s/sustracción de menores de 10 años, Argentina, Juzgado Nacional en lo Criminal y Correccional Federal No. 4, Dr. Gabriel Cavallo, 6 March 2001, available at: <www.derechos.org/nizkor/arg/ley/juezcavallo03mar.htm> — 205

Simón, Julio Héctor y otros s/privación ilegítima de la libertad, Argentina, case S. 1767. XXXVIII (14 June 2005) — 115, 169

Smith v. *Socialist People's Libyan Arab Jamahiriya*, 886 F. Suppl. 306 (EDNY 1996), aff'd 101 F. 3d 239 (2d Cir. 1996) — 238, 272

State v. *Ebrahim*, South Africa, Judgment (Appellate Division) 11 February 1991 (2) SA 553, translated in 95 *ILR* 417, reprinted in 31 *ILM* 896 (1992) — 330, 338

States v. *Shulman,* Canada [2001] SCC 21 — 335

Susana Siderman De Blake, et al., v. *The Republic of Argentina*, United States, 965 F 2d 699 (1992) (US Court of Appeals, 9th Cir.) — 248, 272

S. v. *Basson*, South Africa, Constitutional Court, 10 March 2004, Published in 2004 (6) BCLR 620 (CC) — 112

S v. *Buys*, South Africa [1994] 1 SACR 539 — 338

S v. *Mahala,* South Africa [1994] 1 SACR 510 — 338

S v. *Wellen*, South Africa [1993] 2 SACR 19 E Cap Div — 338

Touvier, France, *Cour de cassation*, Decision of 21 October 1993, *Bull. crim.* 1993, at 770-4 — 207

Touvier, France, *Cour de cassation*, Decision of 1 June 1995, *Bull. crim.* 1995, at 547-58 — 45

Truong v. *The Queen*, Australia, 223 *CLR* 122 (2004); 205 *ALR* 72 (2004) — 348

Underhill v. *Hernandez*, United States, 168 US 250 (1897) — 226, 248

United States v. *Alvarez-Machain*, 112 S.Ct. 2188 (1992) — 337, 338

United States v. *Ball*, United States, 163 US 662 (1896), at 672 — 318

United States v. *Bartkus* United States, 359 US 121 (1959) — 311, 312

United States v. *Benitez*, United States, 120 F. Suppl. 2d 1361 (S.D. Fla. 1988), *aff'd* 208, F.3d 1282 (11th Cir. 2000) — 311, 312

United States v. *Furlong*, United States, 18 US 184 (1820), at 197 — 314

United States v. *Lanza,* United States (1922) US 227 — 311

United States v. *Rashed*, United States, 83 F. Suppl. 2d 96 (D.D.C. 1999) — 311, 312, 313

United States v. *Scott*, United States, 437 US 82 (1978) — 307

United States v. *Toscanino*, United States, 500 F.2d 267 (Ct. App. 2nd Cir., 1974) — 340, 345, 346, 354

Videla, Jorge Rafael, s/recursos de apelacíon y nulidad, Argentina, Resolution of the Cámera Federal de Apelaciones en lo Criminal y Correccional, Sala I, 9 September 1999 — 215

Videla, Chile, Appeal Court of Santiago (Third Criminal Chamber), Judgment, 26 September 1994 — 112, 208

Von Dardel v. *Union of Soviet Socialist Republics*, United States, 623 F. Suppl. 246 (D.D.C. 1985); 63 *ILR* 378 — 259, 272, 278

Von Leeb and others (*High Command* case), US Military Tribunal sitting at Nuremberg, Judgment of 28 October 1948, in *TWC*, Vol. 11, at 462-697 — 24

Williams v. *Spautz*, Australia [1992] HCA 34; 174 *CLR* 509 (1992) (27 July 1992) — 335

Yamashita, United States, US Supreme Court, Judgment of 4 February 1946, 18 *AILC* 1-23 ; 327 US 1, 66 S.Ct.340, 90 L.Ed 499 (1946) — 263

INDEX

A

abuse of process, 27, 131, 170, 171, 185-186, 218, 293, 329-364
- amnesties and pardons, 171, 357-361
- 'clean hands' principle, 338
- delay, 352
- disguised extradition, 336-351
- double jeopardy, 293, 320, 357
- *Duch* case, 353
- forcible abduction, 336-351
- historical origins, 330-332
- inherent power, 331
- integrity of the judicial system, 333-336
- right to fair trial, 332-333
- statutes of limitation, 185-186, 218
- withholding of exculpatory evidence, 355-356

Act of State doctrine, 28, 221, 223, 225-227, 241, 248-249, 259, 273

adjudicatory jurisdiction, 3, 4, 5, 9, 11, 12, 13-21, 42, 57, 183, 221, 251, 252, 274, 276, 367, 369, 373, 375, 379

Afghanistan, 37, 71, 97, 239

African Charter on Human and Peoples' Rights, 24, 63, 124, 294, 352

African Commission on Human and Peoples' Rights, 134

Almatov case, 71-72, 266, 302, 371

American Convention on Human Rights, 24, 663, 80, 115, 124, 127, 129, 134, 135, 162, 168, 169, 294, 297, 316, 352

American Declaration of the Rights and Duties of Man, 129, 162, 168

amnesties, 75-147
- Africa, 79, 82, 96, 97, 106, 108-109
- Algeria, 78, 82, 84, 102, 133, 139
- Angola, 78, 82, 84, 97-98, 108, 109, *see also Luena Memorandum*
- Argentina, 78, 83, 96, 97, 99, 102, 112, 115, 118, 130, 133, 136, 137
- armistice agreements, 77, 196
- Article 6(5) of Additional Protocol II, 121-123
- Bangladesh war of 1971, 78
- Burundi, 78, 84, 103, 135

amnesties, cont.
- civil wars, 78-80
- contextual and policy considerations, 93-95
- difference from pardon, 75-76, 149, 150
- Evian Accord of 1962, 78, 104
- Former Yugoslav Republic of Macedonia, 86
- Haiti, 79, 80, 82, 95, 126, 135
- history, 75-85
- interests of justice, 87-90
- Japan, 77-78, 146-147
- Latin America, 80-81
- legal rationales, 110-143
- liberalist approach, 94, 95, 97, 100, 102, 106
- Nazis, 75, 77, 86, 105, 139
- peace treaties, 76-79
- probationary amnesty periods, 102
- realist approach, 94, 95, 96, 101, 106, 368
- Rome Statute, 86-91
- rule of law and principle of legality, 102-103
- Security Council power of deferral under Rome Statute, 90
- shielding, 88, 120, 316
- Sierra Leone, 79, 82, 83, 84, 92, 98, 99, 100, 116, 139, *see also Lomé Peace Agreement of 1999*
- South Africa, 79, 82, 83, 84, 85, 91, 95, 96, 97, 98, 99, 101, 108, 109, 112, 118, 136, 143, 153, 156, *see also Amnesty Commission (South Africa)* and *Truth and Reconciliation Commission of South Africa*
- Treaty of Lausanne of 1923, 38, 77, 103
- Treaty of Sèvres, 38, 77
- Unit 731, 77-78, 147

Amnesty Commission (South Africa), 7, 98, 156, 303

Argentina, 20, 48, 56, 57, 58, 66, 78, 83, 96, 97, 99, 102, 112, 115, 118, 130, 133, 136, 137, 156, 157-158, 162, 167, 168, 169, 175, 178, 179, 191, 192, 193, 194, 196, 203, 205, 206, 212, 215, 272, 296, 297, 336, 341, 370

Aristotle, 59, 75

Armenians, 38, 49, 77, 103

Arrest Warrant case, 55, 56, 119, 222, 228, 231, 233-236, 243, 244, 245, 250, 251, 257, 264, 266, 267, 268, 271, 279, 285, 376, *see also immunities*

B

Barrios Altos case, 30, 31, 80, 90, 124, 129, 135, 139, 142, 144, 146, 205, 209

C

Cambodia, 43, 44, 51, 52, 62, 78, 91-92, 98, 101, 151, 155, 157-159, 170-171, 175, 178, 189, 191, 213, 245, 263, 292, 317-318, 324, 353-355, 371, 372, 379
charge bargaining, 175-177
Chile, 56, 66, 78, 79, 80, 81, 96, 97, 99, 102, 112, 116, 118, 120, 121, 124, 126, 129, 130, 131, 133, 135, 136, 137, 144, 146, 162, 179, 198, 204, 205, 206, 208, 209, 210, 214, 222, 231, 240, 257, 260, 303, 317, 321
civil law systems, 15, 17, 18, 186, 187, 218, 226, 296, 299, 300, 301, 313, 350
clemency, 12, 150, 152, 153, 154, 160-161, 171, 175-177
collective guilt, 97, 161
Colombia, 84, 149, 150, 169, 180, 187, 200, 297, 311, 316
Commission of Truth and Friendship established by Indonesia and Timor-Leste, 85, 177
common Article 3 to the Geneva Conventions, 35-37, 61, 113, 210, 242
common law, 15, 16, 184, 185, 193, 218, 226, 227, 232, 272, 293, 296, 299, 300, 301, 313, 330, 335, 356, 357, 363, 372, 373, 376
Constitutional Court of South Africa, 97, 112
Control Council Law No. 10, 22, 40, 49, 60-62, 67, 86, 151, 154, 171, 188, 197, 243, 262, 291, 309, 371, 372
Convention against Torture and Other Cruel, Inhuman or Degrading Treatment or Punishment, *see Torture Convention*
Convention on Special Missions, 233, 234
Convention on the Non-Applicability of Statutory Limitations to War Crimes and Crimes against Humanity, 41, 42, 115, 164, 165, 183, 196, 197, 203, 206
Convention on the Prevention and Punishment of Crimes against Internationally Protected Persons, including Diplomats, 233, 259
Convention on the Prevention and Punishment of the Crime of Genocide, *see Genocide Convention*
crimes against humanity, 37-49
  Belgium, 37, 41, 45, 46
  Demjanjuk case, 41, 190, 191, 212, 255
  Eichmann case, 44, 47, 52
  Finta case, 44, 45, 177, 178
  France, 42, 45, 46-47
  Scilingo case, 45, 47-48
  Spain, 45, 47-48
  UN GA resolution 3(1), 40
culture of impunity, 3, 81, 367
customary rule, 4, 27, 34, 47, 53, 59, 67, 113, 114, 142, 192, 200, 201, 202, 208-210, 217, 228, 229, 244, 261, 262, 265, 267, 270, 276, 306, 325

D

Darfur, Sudan, 105, 135
deterrence, 89, 103-105, 132, 163, 164, 167, 174, 181, 191, 213, 284, 355, 376
diplomatic immunity, 229-230, 249, 257, 261, 262, 266, 281, 373
Draft Code of Crimes against the Peace and Security of Mankind, 43, 117, 144, 165, 256, 316
duty to investigate, 30, 80, 81, 126, 127, 129, 138, 168, 205
duty to prosecute, 4, 35, 42, 43, 67, 81, 84, 85, 110-124, 163-171, 209-211, 254-258, 367, 368, 374

E

effective remedy, 63, 80, 90, 124, 125, 126, 131-135, 138, 162, 201, 281-283, 375
Eichmann case, 20, 23, 44, 47, 52, 75, 101, 111, 225, 255, 263, 332, 336, 337, 344, 345, 379
El Salvador, 21, 79, 80, 81, 83, 96, 97, 99, 116, 118, 122, 124, 126, 130, 134, 135, 136, 137, 144, 162, 241, 284
erga omnes obligations, 26-31, 48, 53, 139-140, 143, 171, 208, 260, 269, 270, 276, 325
European Commission of Human Rights, 140, 241, 341
European Convention on Human Rights, 24, 63, 124, 131, 132, 134, 138, 270, 272, 281, 282, 283, 284, 294, 297, 301, 311, 315, 318, 333, 341, 352

European Court of Human Rights, 66, 112, 113, 131, 134, 203, 212, 271, 281, 297, 341

F

forgiveness, 12, 75, 89, 109, 149, 153, 156, 162, 176, 373

forum non conveniens, 10, 16, 18

G

GA Principles on International Cooperation in the Detection, Arrest, Extradition and Punishment of Persons guilty of War Crimes and Crimes against Humanity, 42, 43, 116, 165

genocide, 49-59
  Argentina, 49, 56-58
  Austria, 54
  Belgium, 59
  Germany, 49, 58-59
  Guatemala, 51, 54-56
  International Court of Justice, 53-54
  Mexico, 57-58
  Spain, 58
  universal jurisdiction, 59

Genocide Convention, 24, 28, 29, 49, 50-58, 92, 111, 112, 155, 163, 169, 171, 178, 197, 255, 256, 265, 266, 324

grave breaches, 31, 32-34, 35, 61, 111, 112, 116, 117, 123, 159, 164, 189, 193-194, 198, 209, 210, 255, 256, 278, 279, 253, 367, *see also war crimes*

Grotius, 165-166

guilty plea, 12, 175-177, 376

H

Hitler, 101, 103, 265

Human Rights Chamber for Bosnia and Herzegovina, 134

Human Rights Committee, 80, 102, 122, 124, 125, 126, 127, 133, 142, 284, 297, 311, 321, 341

I

ICRC, *see International Committee of the Red Cross*

ICRC Customary Law Study, 123, 195

ICTR, *see International Tribunal for Rwanda*

ICTY, *see International Tribunal for the former Yugoslavia*

Ieng Sary, 51, 91, 155, 157, 158, 170, 171, 178, 213, 317, 324

ILC, *see International Law Commission*

Immunities, 221-286
  acts performed in a sovereign capacity, 277-281
  collective benefits theory, 274-276
  comity, 234, 238, 246, 248, 252, 253, 272, 275, 281
  compatibility with fundamental human rights, 281-284
  customary rule, 262-268
  functional immunity, 21, 30, 221, 223-226, 228, 229, 236-248, 257, 258, 259, 260, 262, 263, 277, 285, 370, 371, 374
  head of State immunity, 45, 46, 47, 57, 61, 69, 228-229, 231, 232, 233, 234, 235, 236, 240, 243, 244, 245, 246, 249-250, 256, 260, 261, 262, 264, 265, 267, 269-270, 277, 278, 279, 371, 373
  implied waiver, 258-262
  national immunity, 240-243, 253
  normative hierarchy, 268-277
  parliamentary immunities of Pinochet, 231
  personal immunity, 45, 46, 47, 57, 61, 69, 228-229, 231, 232, 233, 234, 235, 236, 240, 243, 244, 245, 246, 249-250, 256, 260, 261, 262, 264, 265, 267, 269-270, 277, 278, 279, 371, 373
  State immunity, 30, 221, 225, 232, 236-240, 251-253, 259, 271-272, 274, 275, 276, 281, 282, 286, 273
  treaty obligations, 254-258
  UK State Immunity Act, 232, 238, 266, 267, 274, 278
  UN Convention on Jurisdictional Immunities of States and Their Property, 234, 271
  US Anti-Terrorism and Effective Death Penalty Act, 238
  US Foreign Sovereign Immunities Act, 232, 238, 240, 257, 258, 259, 272, 275

impediments, 3, 4, 5, 7, 9, 10, 11-13, 18, 19, 21, 31, 54, 139, 178, 189, 217, 221, 222, 226, 243, 251, 287, 291, 304, 343, 367, 368, 369, 370-379

IMT, *see International Military Tribunal at Nuremberg*

IMTFE, *see International Military Tribunal for the Far East*

Inter-American Commission on Human Rights, 80, 122, 124, 129, 133, 134, 146, 168, 301

Inter-American Convention on the Forced Disappearances of Persons, 198, 199

Inter-American Court of Human Rights, 80, 128, 134, 135, 139, 144, 146, 168, 205, 316, 321
interests-analysis approach, 5-9, 18, 19, 72, 75, 150, 162, 177, 218, 221, 222, 242, 246, 253, 276, 284, 285, 286, 306, 326, 368, 369, 376, 377, 379
International Committee of the Red Cross, 33, 112, 121, 122, 123, 164, 195, 196, 309
International Convention for the Protection of All Persons from Enforced Disappearances, 32, 116, 187, 202, 214, 215
International Court of Justice, 27, 28, 29, 36, 47, 53, 55, 59, 70, 78, 92, 111, 114, 117, 118, 119, 120, 140, 209, 222, 231, 233, 234, 235, 243, 244, 245, 250, 251, 257, 261, 264-268, 279, 285
International Covenant on Civil and Political Rights, 24, 63, 80, 115, 124, 125, 127, 133, 134, 138, 142, 169, 178, 214, 282, 284, 293, 294, 297, 309, 311, 319, 341, 352, 353, 354
international crimes, 21-72
  customary law basis, 22-23
  fundamental character, 22-23
  moral values, 24
  need to maintain international peace and security, 23-24
  universal jurisdiction, 25-26
international criminal justice, 3, 9, 75, 84, 94, 104, 105, 177, 345, 346, 347
international criminal law, 4, 5, 11, 15, 19, 22, 23, 24, 25, 26, 49, 84, 94, 101, 104, 105, 114, 137, 145, 151, 181, 200, 204, 257, 308, 326, 327, 336, 346, 354, 363, 367, 368, 374, 379
  jurisdictional principles, 18-21
International Law Commission, 22, 26, 27, 28, 30, 40, 43, 117, 140, 142, 143, 165, 197, 199, 234, 256, 263, 269, 278, 280
International Military Tribunal at Nuremberg, 23, 34, 35, 39, 40, 41, 49, 50, 60, 78, 86, 154, 188, 196, 207, 243, 262, 263, 265, 268, 277, 279, 290, 308, 372
International Military Tribunal for the Far East, 49, 50, 86, 154, 188, 228, 243, 244, 263, 291, 309, 372
International Tribunal for Rwanda, 23, 36, 43, 44, 61, 62, 106-107, 149, 151, 154, 155, 171, 172, 173, 174, 176, 177, 182, 188, 189, 199, 242, 243, 244, 245, 246, 256, 291, 292, 298, 299, 299, 309, 310, 324, 334, 346, 348, 363, 371, 372, 379
International Tribunal for the former Yugoslavia, 23, 26, 30, 35, 36, 41, 43, 61, 62, 65, 67, 86, 103, 112, 122, 139, 142, 144, 154, 155, 167, 171, 172, 173, 174, 175, 176, 182, 188, 189, 199, 204, 208, 242, 243, 244, 245, 246, 256, 257, 267, 291, 292, 298, 305, 306, 309, 310, 316, 324, 329, 342, 343, 344, 346, 347, 350, 351, 355, 358, 359, 371, 372, 379
International Truth and Reconciliation Commission for Sierra Leone, 84

J

Joinet Report, 3, 81, 89, 126, 135, 138
jurisdiction, 13-21
  fairness, 17
  reasonableness, 17
jus cogens, 26, 27-31, 48, 67, 68, 69, 81, 138-143, 162, 200, 203, 205, 208, 209, 254, 255, 268-276, 280, 282, 286, 375, 376, 378, 379

K

Kallon and Kamara case, 31, 84, 92, 113, 119, 124, 139, 170, 171, 361
Khmer Rouge, 44, 91, 155, 157, 158, 159, 175, 213, 318

L

Law on the Establishment of the Extraordinary Chambers in the Courts of Cambodia for the Prosecution of Crimes Committed in the Period of Democratic Kampuchea, 43, 44, 91, 155, 171, 189, 263, 292
Lomé Peace Agreement of 1999 (Sierra Leone), 31, 82, 83, 84, 92, 98, 113, 124, 153, 157, 170, 360, 370, 371, 379
Luena Memorandum (Angola), 82, 98

M

male captus bene detentus, 337-338, 353
methodology, 4-9

N

ne bis in idem, 287-328
  autrefois acquit and *autrefois convict*, 290, 293, 316, 331, 357
  double jeopardy, 293
  dual sovereignty doctrine, 287, 311-314, 323
  European context, 293-295, 296, 297, 300, 301-303, 325

ne bis in idem, cont.
extradition treaties, 314-315
fundamental defect exception, 315-318
legal rationales, 310-325
origins of the rule, 288-290
policy streams, 306-310
res judicata, 301, 303, 304, 308, 310, 313, 316, 317, 321, 322, 326, 373, 377
Rome Statute, 291-292
Sambasivam principle, 320
'sham trial' exception, 315-318
transnational *ne bis in idem*, 288, 289, 294, 298, 301, 303, 304, 307, 308, 310, 314, 315, 317, 325, 326
non-justiciability, 10, 226, 227, 249
Nuremberg Tribunal, *see International Military Tribunal at Nuremberg*

O

obligation to prosecute international crimes, 33, 42, 54, 69, 110-124, 138, 144, 145, 162, 163, 208, 210, 254, 256, 304, 325, 374, 375

P

pardon, 149-182
Argentina, 156, 157-158, 162, 167, 168, 169, 175, 178, 179
Cambodia, 151, 155, 157, 158, 159, 170, 171, 175, 178
distinction from amnesty, 75-76, 149, 150
history, 288-290
Rome Statute, 172-173
peremptory norms, see *jus cogens*
Pinochet case, 30, 46, 56, 57, 66-70, 140, 179, 204, 215, 221, 222, 227, 230, 231, 232, 239, 247, 250, 254, 255, 257, 260, 263, 264, 266, 269, 270, 277, 278, 280, 303, 370, 379
policy-oriented approach, 5-9, 378
positivism, 4, 5, 8, 379
Principles of International Cooperation in the Detection, Arrest, Extradition, and Punishment of Persons Guilty of War Crimes and Crimes Against Humanity, 42, 43, 116

R

reconciliation, 19, 20, 23, 24, 55, 77, 82, 84, 85, 87, 88, 89, 91, 92, 93, 94, 97, 99, 101, 106-110, 114, 118, 121, 136, 137, 146, 158, 175, 176, 177, 181, 192, 213, 285, 303, 355, 368, 373, 376
Rwanda, 106-107
Restatement (Third) of the Foreign Relations Law of the United States, 14, 15, 20, 32, 52, 54, 111, 141, 142, 227, 311
restorative justice, 7, 85, 108, 146, 180
retribution, 89, 104, 121, 167, 174, 181, 191, 212, 213, 334, 373
right to judicial protection, 80, 129, 130, 168, 281, 284
right to the truth, 98-101, 132, 133-138, 146, 176, 177, 326
Rome Statute, 12, 19, 28, 34, 36, 37, 51, 55, 62, 371
abuse of process, 346, 347, 356, 361, 362
amnesties, 83, 86-91, 105, 119, 120,
complementarity, 36, 51, 55, 83, 105, 119, 120, 189, 200, 261, 292, 309
immunities, 241, 244, 245, 253, 261-262
ne bis in idem, 291-292, 301, 304, 309, 317, 325
pardons, 172, 180, 181
statutes of limitation, 188, 200-201, 209

S

Scilingo case, 12, 20, 31, 47-48, 56, 58, 178, 263, 370
SCSL, *see Special Court for Sierra Leone*
sentence bargaining, 175-175
serious violations of the laws and customs of war, 31, 34-37, 258 *see also war crimes*
sham prosecution, 12, 180, 292, 299, 300, 310, 315-318, 327, 372, 377
Sierra Leone, 31, 37, 43, 79, 82, 83, 84, 92, 98, 99, 100, 101, 116, 139, 153, 155, 157, 170, 171, 189, 231, 245, 257, 360, 361, 371, 372, 379
sovereignty, 13, 128, 143, 155, 179, 197, 210, 223, 224, 225, 236, 247, 250, 252, 253, 256, 267, 272, 273, 282, 284, 286, 308, 312, 325, 326, 330, 332, 336, 337, 338, 341, 342, 344, 245, 347, 362, 363, 364, 368, 376
Special Court for Sierra Leone, 31, 37, 43, 83, 92, 96, 100, 113, 119, 124, 139, 151, 155, 170, 171, 189, 231, 245, 257, 263, 265, 288, 292, 300, 310, 316, 360, 370, 371, 372, 379
Special Panels for East Timor, 43, 62, 93, 155, 189, 199, 245, 288, 300, 310, 371, 372
statutes of limitation, 183-219
Australia, 185, 186, 194, 200, 218
customary rule, 192-209
eye witness evidence, 190

statutes of limitation, cont.
historical origins, 184-188
imprescriptible nature, 196, 204, 207
prescription, 184, 186, 187, 188, 193, 198, 199, 202, 203, 204, 205, 209, 210, 214, 215, 217, 218
retroactivity, 197, 206, 219
Rome Statute, 188, 200-201, 209
United States, 184, 190, 191, 195, 216, 217

T

Toyko Tribunal, *see International Military Tribunal for the Far East*
torture, 59-72
France, 59, 65, 66, 71
Germany, 60, 71-72
Habré case, 69-70
historical development, 59-65
laws of war, 60-61
Netherlands, 70
official capacity, 65
Pinochet case, 68-69
Statutes of international criminal tribunals, 62
territorial requirement, 65-67
United Kingdom, 68, 70, 71
universal jurisdiction, 65-72
transitional justice, 7, 19, 83, 85, 90, 118
Truth and Reconciliation Commission of South Africa, 7, 85, 91, 101, 108, 109, 156, 303

U

UN Commission on Human Rights, 81, 116, 117, 118, 125, 135
UN Human Rights Committee, 80, 102, 122, 124, 125, 126, 127, 133, 142, 284, 297, 311, 321, 341
United Nations, 3, 31, 40, 41, 52, 55, 69, 82, 83, 85, 92, 95, 106, 110, 118, 197, 318, 351, 356

V

Velásquez Rodriguez case, 80, 128, 130, 135, 168, 284
victims' fundamental human rights, 19, 75, 94, 98, 124-138, 150, 162, 188, 254, 281-284, 324, 367, 369, 375, 376
Vienna Convention on Diplomatic and Consular Relations, 189, 223, 229, 230, 232, 234, 278

W

war crimes, 32-37, *see also grave breaches* and *serious violations of the laws and customs of war*